Intellectual Property and Human Development

This book examines the social impact of intellectual property laws. It addresses issues and trends relating to health, food security, education, new technologies, preservation of bio-cultural heritage and contemporary challenges in promoting the arts. It explores how intellectual property frameworks could be better calibrated to meet socio-economic needs in countries at different stages of development, with local contexts and culture in mind. Options and scenarios for the future are discussed. A resource for policymakers, stakeholders, non-profit organizations and students, this volume furthermore highlights alternative modes of innovation that are emerging to address such diverse challenges as neglected or resurgent diseases in developing countries and the harnessing of creative possibilities on the Internet. The collected essays emphasize not only fair access by individuals and communities to intellectual property–protected material – whether a cure, a crop variety, clean technology, a textbook or a tune – but also the enhancement of their own capabilities in cultural participation and innovation.

Tzen Wong is a researcher and writer on topics including intellectual property, innovation and development. She has a background in law and social sciences. After obtaining her Masters degree in law from the University of Cambridge, UK, she has been active in the non-profit sector and is managing editor for the Intellectual Property and Human Development research project at Public Interest Intellectual Property Advisors, funded by the Ford Foundation. She has also written for the *European Intellectual Property Review* and the *Encyclopedia of International Development.*

Graham Dutfield is Professor of International Governance at the School of Law, University of Leeds. He is also an Adjunct Professor at the Centre for Studies of Intellectual Property Rights, Zhongnan University of Economics and Law, Wuhan, China, and a Research Affiliate at the Intellectual Property Law and Technology Program at Osgoode Hall Law School, York University, Toronto. He has a Doctorate in geography from Oxford University. He has authored several books, the most recent being an expanded second edition of *Intellectual Property Rights and the Life Science Industries,* now subtitled *Past, Present and Future.*

Public Interest Intellectual Property Advisors (PIIPA) is a leading global network and non-profit resource for developing countries and public interest organizations seeking expertise in intellectual property matters to promote health, agriculture, science, education, culture, biodiversity and the environment.

Through our IP Corps network of over 400 pro bono attorneys, academics and practitioners in 49 countries, we have coordinated pro bono IP support for 100 projects in developing countries and emerging economies. Examples of PIIPA's work include:

- Negotiated use of maize varieties for small, resource-poor farmers in Sub-Saharan Africa affecting the welfare and livelihoods of over 100 million people;
- Successfully challenged the validity of patents filed by two US companies on the medicinal properties of *maca*, a plant used by indigenous peoples in the Andes for medicinal and other purposes for centuries; and
- Published a seminal landscape analysis for the World Intellectual Property Organization and the World Health Organization on patent issues related to avian flu viruses and their genes, which is helping to remove obstacles to avian flu research and protect the ability of developing countries to share in the benefits of innovation.

Support for PIIPA

PIIPA provides professional services and capacity-building programmes to organizations worldwide. With a global network of volunteers we are able to keep our administrative costs low ensuring a high impact for all grants, contracts and donated funds. PIIPA has received generous support for the publication of this book from the Ford Foundation. For more information visit www.piipa.org.

Intellectual Property and Human Development

Current Trends and Future Scenarios

Edited by
Tzen Wong
Public Interest Intellectual Property Advisors
Graham Dutfield
School of Law, University of Leeds

CAMBRIDGE
UNIVERSITY PRESS

CAMBRIDGE UNIVERSITY PRESS
Cambridge, New York, Melbourne, Madrid, Cape Town, Singapore,
São Paulo, Delhi, Dubai, Tokyo, Mexico City

Cambridge University Press
32 Avenue of the Americas, New York, NY 10013-2473, USA

www.cambridge.org
Information on this title: www.cambridge.org/9780521138284

First published 2011

Printed in the United States of America

A catalog record for this publication is available from the British Library.

Library of Congress Cataloging in Publication data

Intellectual property and human development : current trends and future scenarios / edited by Tzen Wong, Graham Dutfield.
p. cm.
Includes bibliographical references and index.
ISBN 978-0-521-19093-0 (hardback) – ISBN 978-0-521-13828-4 (pbk.)
1. Intellectual property (International law) 2. Sociological jurisprudence.
I. Wong, Tzen. II. Dutfield, Graham. III. Title.
K1401.I5533 2010
346.04′8 – dc22 2009039186

ISBN 978-0-521-19093-0 Hardback
ISBN 978-0-521-13828-4 Paperback

Contents

Appendices

Boxes

Contributors

Claudia Chamas is a researcher at the Oswaldo Cruz Foundation (FIOCRUZ), Ministry of Health in Brazil. She is also a professor in the Masters and PhD Programs on Public Policies, Strategies and Development at the Institute of Economics of the Federal University of Rio de Janeiro (in association with FIOCRUZ). She works on intellectual property issues and is the author of several journal articles on biotechnology and pharmaceuticals. She received a bachelor's degree in chemical engineering and an MSc and DSc in production engineering at the Federal University of Rio de Janeiro. In 2000 and 2002, she was visiting researcher at the Max-Planck-Institut für Geistiges Eigentum, Wettbewerbs- und Steuerrecht in Munich. She has organized seminars and coordinated research projects funded by Brazilian funding agencies (including CNPq and Faperj). She is a member of the Brazilian Association of Intellectual Property and the Brazilian Ministry of Health's Intellectual Property Committee.

Margaret Chon is the Associate Dean for Research and the Donald & Lynda Horowitz Professor for the Pursuit of Justice at Seattle University School of Law. The author of more than forty articles, book chapters and essays, including recent pieces on global intellectual property and development, she characterizes her scholarship genre as global intellectual property equality. Professor Chon is a graduate of Cornell University College of Arts and Science, University of Michigan School of Public Health and the University of Michigan Law School. Throughout her legal career, Professor Chon has been active in many community and professional organizations. Her recent publications include 'A Rough Guide to Global Intellectual Property Pluralism' in *Working Within the Boundaries of Intellectual Property* (R. Dreyfuss, H. First & D. Zimmerman, eds., Oxford University Press, 2010) and 'Intellectual Property and the Development Divide', 27 Cardozo Law Review 2821 (2006).

Claudia Fernandini is Director General of Clarke, Modet & C° Peru and founder of Fernandini Abogados. Her responsibilities include general company administration, strategy and prosecution of intellectual property, litigation, unfair competition, licensing, Internet, advertising and consumer defence, among other areas related to management of intellectual property in Peru and abroad. She is an attorney at law admitted to the Lima Bar Association since 1992, and has a masters degree in business administration. She has conducted many (national and international) presentations and seminars, published numerous articles and is frequently interviewed in local media on issues related to intellectual property. She has been ranked among the top IP lawyers in Latin America by *Latin Lawyer* magazine.

Sakiko Fukuda-Parr is Professor of International Affairs at the New School. She is a development economist working on human development and human rights perspectives on international development policy, including access to global technology. From 1995 to 2004, she was director of the United Nations Development Programme (UNDP) *Human Development Reports*. She has written widely on issues of poverty, inequality, gender, human rights, technology and development aid. Her most recent publications include *The Gene Revolution: GM Crops and Unequal Development* (2007, main contributor and editor) and *Readings in Human Development* (2003, edited with A.K. Shiva Kumar).

Michael A. Gollin is a patent attorney at Venable LLP in Washington, DC, where he chairs the life sciences group. He is Adjunct Professor at Georgetown University's McDonough School of Business and at the Franklin Pierce Law Center. He is the chair of Public Interest Intellectual Property Advisors (PIIPA), which he launched in 2002. Mr. Gollin is the author of *Driving Innovation: Intellectual Property Strategies for a Dynamic World* (Cambridge University Press, 2008) and many other works. He holds a JD from Boston University School of Law (1984), a *Diplom* (MS) in zoology and molecular biology from the University of Zurich (1981), and a BS in biochemical sciences from Princeton University (1978).

Hans Morten Haugen is Associate Professor at Diakonhjemmet University College in Oslo. He has a PhD in law from the University of Oslo, awarded for his dissertation on 'The Right to Food and the TRIPS Agreement: With a Particular Emphasis on Developing Countries' Measures for Food Production and Distribution' (Martinus Nijhoff Publishers, 2007). He writes on human rights, intellectual property rights and environment and resource rights. He is a member of the International Project on the Right to Food in Development (IPRFD) at the Norwegian Centre for Human Rights, University of Oslo. Before embarking on his academic career, he worked on international affairs and human rights for the Church of Norway Council on Ecumenical and International Relations.

Gwen Hinze is the Director of International Policy at the Electronic Frontier Foundation (EFF), an international civil liberties legal service and public interest advocacy organization based in San Francisco, California. She directs legal and policy analysis for EFF's international programme which aims to educate global policymakers about the need for balanced intellectual property regimes that protect creators, preserve access to knowledge, foster technological innovation and empower digital consumers. Ms. Hinze previously litigated in California, practised commercial and finance law at Australian law firm Allens Arthur Robinson and worked for the Australian government in public policy and litigation. Ms. Hinze is a member of the State Bar of California and is admitted to practise as a Barrister and Solicitor in Victoria, Australia.

Charles McManis is the Thomas and Karole Green Professor of Law and Director of the Intellectual Property and Technology Law Program at Washington University in St. Louis, Missouri. He received his BA degree from Birmingham-Southern College in 1964, and both his MA (in philosophy) and JD degrees from Duke University in 1972. During 1993 and 1994, he was Fulbright Fellow in Korea, where he lectured and did research at the International Intellectual Property Training Institute in Taejon. He has served as a consultant for the World Intellectual Property Organization (WIPO) in India, Korea and Oman. His book, *Intellectual Property and Unfair Competition in a Nutshell,* is now in its sixth edition. He is also co-author of *Licensing Intellectual Property in the Information Age,* the second edition of which was published in 2005 by Carolina Academic Press, and editor of a multi-authored volume *Biodiversity and the Law: Intellectual Property, Biotechnology and Traditional Knowledge* (Earthscan, 2007).

Manuel Ruiz Muller is a lawyer from the Catholic University in Lima, Peru, with a masters degree in intellectual property and competition law. Since 1991 he has been working and doing research on biodiversity and related issues, such as biotechnology, traditional knowledge, biosafety and agrobiodiversity. He has published extensively on these issues and has been a consultant for FAO, UNDP, UNEP, IUCN, ICTSD, WIPO, the World Bank, Bioversity International and other national, regional and international organizations. He is currently the Director of the International Affairs and Biodiversity Program of the Peruvian Society for Environmental Law.

Savita Mullapudi Narasimhan is a consultant on intellectual property, trade and development with a focus on the importance of balanced rights to achieve human development goals. Her specialized areas of work include intellectual property and access to medicines and genetic resources. Towards this end, she has worked with various intergovernmental organizations including WIPO, the World Bank and UNDP providing advice to governments from more than twenty developing countries. At UNDP, she conceptualized the IP, Trade and Biodiversity project. Her educational qualifications include a BA (economics), LLB from University of Bombay, India, and an LLM from George Washington University. She teaches as an adjunct faculty member at several universities in India and the United States including the Indian Institute of Technology, Bombay, and New York University.

Ben Prickril is an International Programs Officer within the National Cancer Institute's (NCI) Office of International Affairs (OIA). In this role he helps coordinate international research on the detection, prevention, treatment and palliation of cancers. He is also active in international scientific exchange, coordination of cancer activities under collaborative international agreements and coordination with other federal organizations involved in international activities, including the National Institutes of Health's Fogarty International Center, the Office of Global Health Affairs, the State Department and other federal offices. Before joining NCI's Office of International Affairs, Dr. Prickril served as an international biotechnology consultant and was the Chief Scientific Officer (2004–2006) of the World Life Sciences Forum, BioVision in Lyon, France. He received his PhD in bioinorganic chemistry from the University of Georgia (US) in 1992.

Joshua D. Sarnoff is Associate Professor at DePaul University College of Law, Chicago. He is a registered patent attorney and a member of the Board of Directors of the Federal Circuit Bar Association and has been involved in a wide range of intellectual property legal and policy disputes. He has submitted testimony to the United States Congress on patent law reform bills, has filed numerous amicus briefs in the United States Supreme Court and the Court of Appeals for the Federal Circuit on important patent law issues, and has been a pro bono mediator for the Federal Circuit as well as a consultant to the United Nations Conference on Trade and Development (UNCTAD) on intellectual property, trade and environmental issues. Mr. Sarnoff was formerly in private practice in intellectual property, environmental and food and drug law. He previously taught at the Washington College of Law, American University, and at the University of Arizona College of Law.

Dalindyebo Shabalala is a University Lecturer in International Economic Law (Intellectual Property) at Maastricht University and Academic Coordinator for Project Acquisition at the Institute for Globalisation and International Regulation (IGIR). Previously, he was the managing attorney of the Center for International Environmental Law (CIEL) Geneva office, and Director of CIEL's Intellectual Property and Sustainable Development Project which focused on issues at the intersection of intellectual property and climate change, human health, biodiversity and food security, as well as addressing systemic reform of the international intellectual property system. Mr. Shabalala was a Research Fellow in the Innovation, Access to Knowledge, and Intellectual Property Programme at the South Centre (2005–2006). He received his BA degree in political science and cognitive science from Vassar College in 1998, where he was a Ford Foundation Scholar in the Political Science Department. Mr. Shabalala received his Juris Doctor, cum laude, from the University of Minnesota Law School in 2004, where he worked with Professor David Weissbrodt on researching the human rights responsibilities of transnational corporations.

Yolanda Terán is a member of the Kichwa people, from Ecuador, and a museologist, educator and researcher. She has degrees in museum studies from the University of Leicester and the Universidade do Rio de Janeiro. She has served as special adviser to the Minister of External Affairs of Ecuador on indigenous issues. She has also taught as a Fulbright Scholar at Sisseton Wahpeton Community College in South Dakota on 'Contemporary Issues for Indian Life' and at the University of New Mexico, where she is a doctoral candidate on indigenous languages. She was a consultant and interpreter for the National Museum of the American Indian, New York. She is a member of the Indigenous Women Network on Biodiversity from Latin America and the Caribbean (RIMB). She is also the education coordinator of Andes Chinchasuyo Indigenous Organization from Ecuador. In 2006 she was the regional coordinator for Latin America and the Caribbean for the Traditional Knowledge Indicators Working Group of the Convention on Biological Diversity (CBD).

Molly Torsen has been the Vice President of the International Intellectual Property Institute (IIPI) in Washington, DC, since early 2006. Overlapping with her work at IIPI, she completed a consultancy at WIPO and wrote a legal compendium for WIPO's Creative Heritage Project. The focus of this project was to look at practical applications and uses of current intellectual property laws with regard to traditional cultural expressions. Prior to her work at IIPI and WIPO, Ms. Torsen completed a legal fellowship at the Arts and Humanities Research Council (AHRC) Research Centre in Edinburgh where she focused her research and publication on the nexus between intellectual property law and contemporary art. She is a graduate of the University of Washington School of Law.

Tzen Wong is a researcher and writer on topics including intellectual property, innovation and development. She has a background in law and social sciences (economics and sociology). After obtaining her masters degree in law in 1999 from the University of Cambridge, UK, she worked on health and governance issues at the Monitoring and Evaluation Division of the International Federation of Red Cross and Red Crescent National Societies in Geneva. In 2005, she co-drafted the 'Practice Note on Traditional Knowledge, Access to Genetic Resources, and Benefit-sharing' with members of a Taskforce at the United Nations Development Programme (UNDP). She is Managing Editor at PIIPA for its Intellectual Property and Human Development research project, funded by the Ford Foundation. She is also working with the creative sectors to link copyright law to cultural policy and development. She has worked in Singapore and Budapest and is currently based in New York.

Foreword

Sakiko Fukuda-Parr

One of the major challenges of the twenty-first century is to make globalization more inclusive and equitable, to better serve the purpose of human development. In this endeavour, managing intellectual property (IP) is a key issue. Few issues were as contentious in the negotiations over multilateral trade rules. Negotiations over the Agreement on Trade-Related Aspects of Intellectual Property Rights (TRIPS Agreement) were pivotal in finalizing the 1994 Marrakesh Agreement which created the World Trade Organization (WTO), and in adopting the 2001 Doha Declaration which launched the WTO's Doha 'Development Round'.

A core purpose of intellectual property rights (IPRs) including patents and copyrights is to achieve a balance between two potentially conflicting social objectives: encouraging innovation by recognizing private rights in intangible creations and ensuring the diffusion of new technologies and cultural works to a broad range of stakeholders. Superficially, the controversies that arise can be understood as a conflict of economic interests. The different interpretations and potentially competing objectives of IP can lead to tensions between the interests of inventors or authors and those of the public, between the technologically advanced countries and those with weaker capacities, between corporations that seek to maximize profit and the public that seeks access at least cost. But, as this book argues, much more is at stake than conflicts over material gains and losses: IP laws and policies must take on a much broader set of human development goals and concerns. The social function of IP is not only about providing incentives and rewards for creativity; it is also about ensuring that innovations, including new technologies, ultimately help to improve capabilities, sustain livelihoods and support people's fundamental rights.

While bargaining between governments defending their perceived economic interests has done much to shape the international IP and trade agendas, pressure from social and political movements to consider the human consequences of IPRs has been influential since the 1990s. Civil society concerns, for example, about the rights of indigenous peoples, farmers and the plight of persons living with HIV/AIDS, was part of a larger critique about the social impacts of 'Washington Consensus' policy-led international development agendas, liberalization policies and economic globalization.

By the late 1990s, as country after country liberalized trade and capital flows, and many began to dismantle post-war social welfare systems, controversies over globalization began to dominate debates about development policy. As Joseph Stiglitz put it, globalization was a force – '*like a giant wave, that can either capsize nations or carry them forward*'.[1] Much of the controversy was growth and income oriented, concerned with whether globalization (or liberalization policies) is good or bad for growth, income, income distribution and poverty reduction. From the human development perspective, however, the questions are broader. The UNDP Human Development Reports, which I led between 1995 and 2004, explored policy agendas for promoting integration for human development, focusing on distributional impacts within and between countries and on the potential of harnessing globalization for the empowerment of people. We argued for stronger national policies to protect human priorities, as well as more appropriate global governance in which both the multilateral rules and the process for their formulation would be inclusive and equitable. One major question relating to IP was the nexus between technology, globalization and human development. Breakthrough science in information communications and biotechnology was a key driver of globalization; the computer and the Internet have made possible the mass dissemination of information, and high-yielding varieties of rice and maize have turned food-deficit countries into major food exporters. History has shown, however, that breakthrough technologies can be a source not only of opportunities for improving human well-being, but also of new inequalities. Although the social function of IP is not only about incentivizing technological innovations, it is important to design appropriate IP policies and laws to ensure that new technologies ultimately enlarge genuine choices and foster human development.

As stated earlier, the analysis of IPRs and their broad range of social ramifications go beyond economic considerations. Economic analysis framed in the utilitarian perspective of providing incentives for more material production is particularly limiting in this context. The utilitarian perspective is at best neglectful of, and at worst blind to, the effects on distribution of benefits and costs, the far-reaching social consequences of technological innovation, the social priority in technological innovation and diffusion that can solve enduring problems of poverty, and the claims that human beings have basic rights to participate in and benefit from innovations and creative expressions.

Intellectual property rights are intended to promote innovation, but research has shown that this is not always the case and that IPRs can also put obstacles in front of research and innovation. They are intended

[1] World Bank 2000, 'World Bank Sees "Localization" as Major New Trend in 21st Century', World Development Report 1999/2000 press release, available at http://web.worldbank.org/WBSITE/EXTERNAL/NEWS/0, contentMDK:20014638~menuPK:34463~pagePK:34370~piPK:34424~theSitePK:4607,00.html (accessed 28 October 2009).

to reward creators, but in certain contexts fail to recognize the creativity and innovation of local communities and other social networks. They are intended to fulfil a social purpose, but that purpose can be too narrowly defined and miss out on some essential human challenges.

As the chapters in this volume show, the range of legal rights within the umbrella of IP impact human capabilities and endeavours in complex ways. The human development and capabilities approach provides a broad and useful framework for analysing the social impact of IPRs because the approach defines the purpose of development as enlarging the choices and capabilities that people have to lead a life they value. This framework focuses on a wide range of actual and potential human consequences that are of concern to diverse peoples in the world. The wide range of challenges that different individuals and communities face, and the diversity of their priorities, is precisely what makes a single policy approach to IPRs inappropriate and impossible. How IP frameworks might be reformed to meet these diverse challenges requires greater exploration. It is also the shades of grey that make the topic fascinating to study. This is a unique volume that brings together scholarly papers on all the key issues of human development and intellectual property rights. I expect that this book will provide an enjoyable and informative read, and it will become a much valued resource for individuals at all levels of knowledge and involvement in the IP and international development spheres.

Preface

Michael A. Gollin

We all share the desire to live healthy and meaningful lives, in communities that keep us safe, provide us and our children with educational and employment opportunities and leave us the freedom to choose our own paths. Economist Amartya Sen challenged societies to pursue these ends – referred to as human development – rather than only narrower objectives like increasing gross domestic product. That is, we should measure individual endeavour and national wealth in terms of how well each of us can live rich rewarding lives, not just how much financial output we produce per capita. Moreover, we should organize our social institutions to help us in this broader effort.

This book brings a human development perspective to the complex institutions, laws and practices referred to collectively as intellectual property, or 'IP'. What is the role of IP in human development? The answers to be found in the following chapters provide a fresh look at IP and how it affects the ability of people in developing countries to benefit from advances in medicine, agriculture, education, the arts and cultural traditions. The authors go further by looking at how trends and future changes in IP laws might impact people in developing countries, for better or worse.

Innovation has played a central role in human development through history, leading to advances in culture, knowledge, agriculture, health and technology, but also to imbalances in access to and control over these fruits of creativity. The roots of intellectual property may be found in ancient practices for controlling access to innovation, such as guild secrecy and the use of trade names. Intellectual property laws in the modern sense first emerged 500 years ago and have expanded to become a principal force channelling and shaping innovation and commerce around the world. Yet the extensive research, debate, reform and training about IP in recent years show no signs of leading to a global consensus on the impact of current IP systems on human welfare, much less how potential reforms would help, or hurt, larger society.

The increasing social importance of IP is easily gauged by the rising intensity of arguments for stronger or weaker rights. Many of these arguments are laid out among the diverse views summarized in the chapters. For example, some stakeholders argue that patents on AIDS medicines are too strong to permit fair access to existing drugs, while others counter that weaker patents are destroying the incentive to discover new drugs. Some groups argue that copyright law blocks public access to educational and artistic works and hampers collaboration. Others point out that weak copyright protection undercuts the creative work of artists and authors. There is debate over where IP rights support – or thwart – traditional practices. Ultimately, there is no simple answer except the need to strike a productive balance between the many interests involved – a balance that serves the public interest in human development.

Several years ago, in writing *Driving Innovation,* I realized that IP, often viewed as a tool of human capital, can be seen instead as an instrument by which innovators express individual and collective choices regarding their creations. In this light, IP can contribute not just to economic development, but also to the development of freedom – of personal choice, individual responsibility and free expression. IP can be a tool for human development.

Of course 'development' has different meanings in different countries, and the dynamics differ among the sectors considered here (medicine, agriculture, education, cultural heritage, contemporary arts and communication technology). In each sector, different predictions about the future of IP have been made. The future scenario planning exercises explored in this book are a fascinating tool for guiding action away from destructive paths towards balanced outcomes.

This book began with the effort by Public Interest Intellectual Property Advisors (PIIPA) to find practical ways for IP to help serve the public interest in developing countries. Since 2002, PIIPA has assembled teams of experienced IP practitioners and made matches with developing country clients seeking help in accessing technology via licensing, protecting their cultural expressions, preventing expropriation of traditional knowledge and in reforming national IP legislation to meet international requirements and local needs.

In 2007, the Ford Foundation commissioned PIIPA to assemble an expert team, drawn from PIIPA and partner institutions, to survey the literature on IP trends and future scenarios and how different outcomes might impact neglected groups. An aim of the Ford initiative was to contribute to the development of more balanced IP regimes which highlight the importance of the public interest, strengthen the public domain, respect the right to development and support the voices of frequently neglected stakeholders. With continued support from Ford until mid-2010, the research team compiled a unique body of literature on issues, trends and future scenarios relating to IP and human development. That shared resource was invaluable to the authors of these individual chapters, and the resulting bibliography will facilitate further research. The research team, under Tzen Wong's direction, expanded and revised the initial study to address further dimensions of IP and human development, and this book is the result of that effort. The contributing authors span the globe and include a diverse group of legal practitioners, professors and development activists. They bring a breadth of perspective and experience with the practical implications of IP policy debates. The editors worked deftly with the authors to weave the various chapters and perspectives into a comprehensive work that addresses the crucial questions of how IP impacts human welfare and how changes in IP laws, and new approaches, might make it easier or harder for disadvantaged individuals and communities to improve their lives. These questions, and the answers that follow, should be of great interest to policymakers and activists, businesses and consumers, researchers and students, artists and engineers, IP professionals and lay people alike. On behalf of PIIPA and the many volunteers who contributed to the completion of this work, we welcome your interest and participation in promoting the goals of human development.

Acknowledgements

We are grateful to the Ford Foundation for supporting the independent research that produced this volume, as well as for their support for its distribution. With the Foundation's generous support, copies of the book have been directly mailed through Cambridge University Press to a cross section of stakeholders around the world. Guidance from the Ford International Intellectual Property Initiative (IIPI) Committee in 2007–2008 was invaluable in the genesis of this research project, and we are especially appreciative to Ana Toni, Alan Divack and Kyle Reis for their wonderful support and insights towards the broadening of the research in 2009–2010 to cover important areas of human development.

Project funding has been leveraged manyfold by in-kind pro bono help from members of PIIPA's extensive international network, including IP Corps members who provide pro bono support to developing country organizations, and other individuals working on the public interest dimensions of IP. Significant support has also been received from partner institutions around the world. We are particularly indebted to the following individuals and their host organizations for their excellent support towards the outreach and literature review in various regions: Jorge Garcia and Alfredo Schwarz (formerly) of the Ibero-American Science and Technology Education Consortium; Dalindyebo Shabalala (formerly) of the Center for International Environmental Law (now with the University of Maastricht); Shauna Eisenberg, Sarah Huisentruit, Teresita Ramos and Michael Ryan of the Creative and Innovative Economy Center at the George Washington University Law School; Beatrice Chaytor and Roselynn Lewis (former intern) of the Policy Planning and Research Division, Ministry of Trade and Industry, Sierra Leone; and Paul Asiimwe of Sipi Law Associates in Uganda.

We are most grateful to Sakiko Fukuda-Parr of the New School (Director, 1995–2004, UNDP Human Development Reports) for her encouragement and Foreword. We also wish to thank the contributors and participants from different regions for their commitment to a multidisciplinary approach in tackling the new and complex issues in IP and human development. We hope that the process has been an enriching one for all who shared time and thoughts.

Along with the chapter authors, we wish to thank various individuals for their contribution of case studies or extracts, especially David

Clark (Brooks World Poverty Institute), Gwen Hinze (Electronic Frontier Foundation), Jakkrit Kuanpoth (University of Wollongong), Gary Martin and Hattie Wells (Global Diversity Foundation), Geoff Tansey (Joseph Rowntree Visionary for a Just and Peaceful World), Emily Taylor (International Development Research Centre), Brendan Tobin (National University of Ireland) and Uma Suthersanen (Queen Mary, University of London). We are also grateful to Matt Spannagle (UNDP Environment and Energy Group) for his salient contribution on climate change issues and to Fred von Lohmann (Electronic Frontier Foundation) for his interesting updates on Internet law.

We are especially grateful to Margaret Chon at Seattle University School of Law for her many inspiring ideas and to her (former) research assistants, Therese Norton and Nancy Yamashiro, for their meticulous help. Our further thanks go to the reference librarian, Kerry Fitz-Gerald, at Seattle University School of Law. We also wish to thank Charles McManis at the School of Law, Washington University in St. Louis, and his (former) research assistant Mackenzie Dewerff.

We are grateful to many individuals who contributed to the peer review or provided relevant literature and comments. We wish to thank the following individuals: Samuel Adewusi, Keith Aoki, Jane Anderson, Christopher Antons, Paul Asiimwe, Edson Beas, Jeremy de Beer, Joshua Bell, Kathy Bowrey, Molly Beutz Land, Ronaldo Lemos, Beatrice Dove-Edwin, Beatriz Fernandez, Brian Fitzgerald, Sean Flynn, Brett Frischmann, Roya Ghafele, Haidy Geismar, Hala Essalmawi, Honor Keeler, Debora Halbert, Marjorie Heins, Victoria Henson-Apollonio, John Howkins, Stanley Kowalski, Tina Kuklenski-Miller, Maria Mendoza, Richard Owens, Ruchi Pant, Pedro Roffe, Sisule Musungu, Richard Ponzio, Laura Quilter, Rakhi Rashmi, Ilko Rogovich, Madhavi Sunder, Yeswanth Shenoy, Benny Spiewak, Antony Taubman, Isabel Triana, David Vivas, Martin Watson and Daphne Zografos.

We are indebted to PIIPA chair Michael Gollin for his invaluable guidance. We are also most grateful to PIIPA's President and CEO, Mark Davis and to PIIPA board members and advisors, especially Rita Khanna, Joshua Sarnoff, Charles McManis, Manuel Ruiz and Roy Widdus. Our thanks also go to Ben Prickril for his early outreach efforts.

We have been fortunate to have the support of a resourceful research team at PIIPA who worked in different parts of the world and time zones to put this book together. They come from a variety of disciplines. We are especially grateful to our assistant editor (law), Claire Comfort, for her meticulous help in legal editing from PIIPA's offices in Washington. We are also appreciative of the professional teamwork from our assistant editor (social science), Robyn Tan, now pursuing a masters degree in development studies in Mumbai, India; public health researchers Sharon Low and Claudia Trezza, both with masters degrees in public health, now based in Liberia and New York respectively; and law researchers (based in the US) Sarah Coleman, Marybeth Gunster and Sarah Gurfein, along with Dhruv Paul, in legal practice in New Delhi.

Our further thanks go to Tasmin Rajotte at the Quaker International Affairs Programme (QIAP) for her support and indispensable publication advice. We are also grateful to Tim Scott at the UNDP Human Development Report Office for his invaluable insights. Review and proofreading of manuscripts was the task of many helpful individuals. We thank especially Rosemary Wolson, David Wong and Terence Hay-Edie.

We are most grateful to Cambridge University Press for taking on the publication of this monograph and in particular to the Press's senior editor, John Berger, for his keen and open-minded guidance throughout the process. We learnt a lot from the excellent work of their production team, especially project manager Barbara Walthall and copy editor Marjorie Ballentine, and we also wish to thank the anonymous Cambridge University Press reviewers whose comments and suggestions were most helpful in fine-tuning the study.

Finally, our heartfelt thanks extend to our families and friends whose encouragement and active support made this research endeavour possible.

Acronyms and abbreviations

A2K	Access to knowledge
AAP	Association of American Publishers
ABS	Access and benefit-sharing
ACTA	Anti-Counterfeiting Trade Agreement
AIATSIS	Australian Institute of Aboriginal and Torres Strait Islander Studies
AIDS	Acquired immune deficiency syndrome
ALACDE	Latin American and Caribbean Law and Economics Association
AMC	Advanced market commitments
ANDES	Association for Nature and Sustainable Development
AOC	Apellation d'origine contrôlée
API	Active pharmaceutical ingredient
ARIPO	African Regional Intellectual Property Organization
ARV	Antiretroviral
ASEAN	Association of Southeast Asian Nations
ASSINSEL	International Association of Plant Breeders
ATRIP	Advancement of Teaching and Research in Intellectual Property
CAFTA	Central American Free Trade Agreement
CAN	Andean Community of Nations
CARICOM	Caribbean Community
CBD	Convention on Biological Diversity
CESCR	Committee on Economic, Social and Cultural Rights
CFS	Committee on World Food Security
CGIAR	Consultative Group on International Agricultural Research
CI	Consumers International
CIEL	Center for International Environmental Law
CIFOR	Center for International Forestry Research
CIP	International Potato Center
CIPIH	Commission on Intellectual Property Rights, Innovation and Public Health
CIPR	Commission on Intellectual Property Rights
COP (CBD)	Conference of the Parties (to the Convention on Biological Diversity)
CP TECH	Consumer Project on Technology
CRC	Convention on the Rights of the Child
CSIR	Council for Scientific and Industrial Research (South Africa)
CSO	Civil society organization

CTEA	Copyright Term Extension Act
DIGERPI	General Office for the Registry of the Industrial Property of the Ministry of Commerce and Industry (Panama)
DMCA	Digital Millennium Copyright Act
DNDI	Drugs for Neglected Diseases Initiative
DRM	Digital rights management
ECHR	European Court of Human Rights
EDV	Essentially derived variety
EFF	Electronic Frontier Foundation
eIFL	Electronic Information for Libraries
EPO	European Patent Office
EU	European Union
FAO	Food and Agriculture Organization of the United Nations
FDA	Food and Drug Administration (United States)
FDI	Foreign direct investment
FHSST	Free High School Science Texts
FIS	International Seed Trade Federation
FOEI	Friends of the Earth International
FPIC	Free, prior and informed consent
FTA	Free trade agreement
GATT	General Agreement on Tariffs and Trade
GDI	Gender-related Development Index
GDP	Gross Domestic Product
GEM	Gender Empowerment Measure
GI	Geographical indication
GMO	Genetically modified organism
GPL	General Public License
GRAIN	Genetic Resources Action International
HDI	Human Development Index
HIV	Human immunodeficiency virus
HRBA	Human rights-based approach
IAASTD	International Assessment of Agricultural Knowledge, Science and Technology for Development
IAVI	AIDS Vaccine Initiative
ICBG	International Cooperative Biodiversity Group
ICCPR	International Covenant on Civil and Political Rights
ICESCR	International Covenant on Economic, Social and Cultural Rights
ICOM	International Council of Museums
ICTs	Information and communication technologies
ICTSD	International Centre for Trade and Sustainable Development
IDRC	International Development Research Centre
IEGBIIP	International Expert Group on Biotechnology, Innovation and Intellectual Property
IELRC	International Environmental Law Research Centre
IESA	Institut d'Etudes Supérieures des Arts
IFLA	International Federation of Library Associations and Institutions

IFPMA	International Federation of Pharmaceuticals Manufacturers & Associations
IGF	Internet Governance Forum
IGNCA	Indira Gandhi National Centre for the Arts
IGWG	Intergovernmental Working Group on Public Health, Innovation and Intellectual Property
IIED	International Institute for Environment and Development
IITF	International Indigenous Information and Communication Technologies Task Force
ILO	International Labour Organization
IMPACT	International Medical Products Anti-Counterfeiting Taskforce
INTECH	Institute for New Technologies
IP	Intellectual property
IPRs	Intellectual property rights
ISE	International Society of Ethnobiology
ISF	International Seed Federation
ISTEC	Ibero-American Science and Technology Education Consortium
ITPGRFA	International Treaty for Plant Genetic Resources for Food and Agriculture
IUCN	International Union for Conservation of Nature
KEI	Knowledge Ecology International
LCA	Library Copyright Alliance
LDC	Least developed country
MDGs	Millennium Development Goals
MERIT	Maastricht Economic Research Institute on Innovation and Technology
MIHR	Centre for the Management of Intellectual Property in Health Research and Development
MIT	Massachusetts Institute of Technology
MMV	Medicines for Malaria Venture
MTA	Material transfer agreement
NEA	National Education Association (United States)
NGO	Non-governmental organization
NIAAA	National Indigenous Arts Advocacy Association (Australia)
OAPI	African Intellectual Property Organization
OECD	Organisation for Economic Co-operation and Development
OSDD	Open Source Drug Discovery
OTOP	One Tambon One Product
OVOP	One Village One Product
P2P	Peer to peer (file sharing system)
PAHO	Pan American Health Organization
PCT	Patent Cooperation Treaty
PDP	Product development partnership
PGR	Plant genetic resources
PGRFA	Plant genetic resources for food and agriculture

PIC	Prior informed consent
PIIPA	Public Interest Intellectual Property Advisors
PIPRA	Public Intellectual Property Resource for Agriculture
PPP	Public-private partnership
PVP	Plant variety protection
QALY	Quality-adjusted life year
QMRD	Qualified Medical Research and Development
QUNO	Quaker United Nations Office
R&D	Research and development
SAARC	South Asian Association for Regional Cooperation
SADC	Southern Africa Development Community
SCCR	Standing Committee on Copyright and Related Rights
SIDS	Small island developing states
SME	Small and medium enterprise
SMTA	Standard Material Transfer Agreement
SPDA	Peruvian Society for Environmental Law
SPLT	Substantive Patent Law Treaty
TAK	Traditional agricultural knowledge
TBA	Tuberculosis Alliance
TCE	Traditional cultural expression
TEBTEBBA	Indigenous Peoples' International Centre for Policy Research and Education
TK	Traditional knowledge
TMK	Traditional medicinal knowledge
TPMs	Technology protection measures
TRALAC	Trade Law Centre for Southern Africa
TRIPS	Trade-Related Aspects of Intellectual Property Rights
TTAB	Trademark Trial and Appeal Board (United States)
TWN	Third World Network
UDHR	Universal Declaration of Human Rights
UN	United Nations
UNAIDS	Joint United Nations Programme on HIV/AIDS
UNCTAD	United Nations Conference on Trade and Development
UNDP	United Nations Development Programme
UNDRIP	United Nations Declaration on the Rights of Indigenous Peoples
UNEP	United Nations Environment Programme
UNESCO	United Nations Educational, Scientific and Cultural Organization
UNFCCC	United Nations Framework Convention on Climate Change
UNICEF	United Nations Children's Fund
UNPFII	United Nations Permanent Forum on Indigenous Issues
UNU	United Nations University
UNU-IAS	United Nations University Institute of Advanced Studies
UPOV	International Union for the Protection of New Varieties of Plants
USPTO	United States Patent and Trademark Office
WBU	World Blind Union
WCO	World Customs Organization

WCT	WIPO Copyright Treaty
WHA	World Health Assembly
WHO	World Health Organization
WIPO	World Intellectual Property Organization
WPPT	WIPO Performances and Phonograms Treaty
WTO	World Trade Organization
WWF	World Wide Fund for Nature

Overview

Scope and aims

This book examines the social impact of intellectual property (IP) policies and laws. Addressing both current trends and future scenarios relating to IP and human development, it is aimed at the calibration of IP frameworks to better meet social needs in countries at different stages of economic development, according to local contexts and culture. While the priorities for human development may evolve with time and vary between communities, this volume addresses topics that are of concern to all: health, food security, access to education, opportunities and risks from new technologies, the protection of the environment and the preservation of bio-cultural heritage, as well as the promotion of contemporary expression in the arts. As highlighted in the various contributions to this volume, IP laws interact with all these areas of human endeavour in palpable ways, and a multidisciplinary approach is needed to assess their impact on human well-being. In particular, this study introduces and engages the concept of 'capabilities' (developed by Sen, Nussbaum, Fukuda-Parr and many others) in evaluating human welfare and links these ideas to the existing literature on IP and innovation. Since the choices and capabilities of individuals and communities relating to particular areas, such as health and education, inevitably affect other important capabilities – for example, free expression and political participation – the diverse areas of human development cannot be approached in isolation. It is hoped that their treatment side by side in one book may draw out inter-connections not only between areas or sectors, but also in the responses contemplated by policymakers and civil society towards more balanced solutions for the future. Concerns of human rights and social justice cut across all topics in this volume and are given particular emphasis. Other cross-cutting or related themes, such as gender equality and climate change, are addressed in particular sections within chapters.

This book begins by revisiting some of the basics in IP law including long-held assumptions in patent and copyright laws on the dynamics of innovation. In doing so, it considers whether these assumptions adequately account for the different cultural values and attitudes towards creativity, as well as the essential role of social networks in fuelling innovation. The chapters of this book look beyond the kind of innovation commonly associated with scientific laboratories or the R&D divisions of companies to consider, for example, the innovative practices of farmers, indigenous and other traditional communities bound by customary practices and the virtual or 'imagined communities' of cyberspace (Strathern 2005). Are the same assumptions on income incentives for innovation in high-tech laboratories and large-scale operations of equal meaning and relevance to innovators in other contexts and cultures? Going beyond Anglo-American analyses of IP (particularly copyright and patents) as mainly providing economic incentives for innovation, or the natural rights arguments for protecting IP as an extension of the 'personality' of creators (Fisher 2001), this book explores how different cultural values and contexts shape the motivations and capabilities of individuals and communities in their innovative endeavours.

The UNESCO Convention on the Protection and Promotion of the Diversity of Cultural Expressions of 2005 highlights in its Preamble that 'cultural diversity creates a rich and varied world, which increases the range of choices and nurtures human capacities and values, and therefore is a mainspring for sustainable development for communities, peoples and nations'.[1] One question explored in this book is how IP protection, cultural diversity and human development link up in practice. Some answers may be found, for example, in the unfolding literature on the IP protection of traditional knowledge (TK). Indigenous peoples and local communities guided by customary practices have emphasized the pursuit of 'development with culture and identity' as central to their human rights and human development,[2] and the inter-generational transmission of their TK is part of this endeavour. Discussions on the IP protection of TK have taken place internationally at the World Intellectual Property Organization (WIPO), UNESCO and also within the context of the 1992 Convention on Biological Diversity, especially for TK relevant to the conservation of biodiversity. There is increasing awareness, however, that biodiversity is intrinsically linked to cultural diversity. For example, the TK of indigenous peoples weaves together elements of both, and there is a tendency now to speak of the protection of their bio-cultural heritage. How exactly does IP intersect with the protection of bio-cultural diversity? Do IP frameworks have a 'homogenizing' effect on agricultural practices and cultural products as some discern from trends of globalization (Tansey 2008, p. 216), or can they be adapted to strengthen the diversity of innovation systems and cultural expressions in the world? Some suggest that the notions of Western private property central to IP laws are simply incompatible with the social relations underpinning 'communal' forms of innovation (Leach 2005; Anderson 2009); others see hope for

1 UNESCO Convention on the Protection and Promotion of the Diversity of Cultural Expressions (Paris, 20 October 2005), 45 I.L.M. 269 (2006), available at: http://unesdoc.unesco.org/images/0014/001429/142919e.pdf (accessed 3 February 2010).

2 This has been identified as a special theme at the Permanent Forum on Indigenous Issues, Ninth Session, 19–30 April 2010. See http://www.un.org/esa/socdev/unpfii/en/session_ninth.html (accessed 10 January 2010).

solutions within the diverse legal forms and regimes making up IP (e.g. trademarks and geographical indications serve different functions from patents and copyright). Yet others would emphasize the agency of individuals and communities in shaping public policies and coming up with unique, *sui generis* solutions. The aim of this book is to reflect these contrasting perspectives in nuanced ways, drawing literature from different regions and disciplines.

The United Nations Declaration on the Right to Development recognizes in its Preamble that 'development is *a comprehensive economic, social, cultural and political process*, which aims at the constant improvement of the well-being of the entire population and all individuals on the basis of their *active, free and meaningful participation* in development and in the *fair distribution of benefits* resulting therefrom' (emphasis added).[3] In relation to developing countries and economies in transition, the United Nations Millennium Declaration further calls for 'policies and measures, at the global level, which correspond to the needs of developing countries and economies in transition and are formulated and implemented with their effective participation' (para. I.5).[4] Do global and national IP rules adequately address the differentiated needs of developing countries, and those of marginalized stakeholders in all countries? Various chapters of this book examine whether patents and copyright currently incentivize the kind of innovations most needed by stakeholders in developing countries and elsewhere, whether in relation to health, food security, education or cultural participation. The chapters also examine whether IP frameworks enable *access* by stakeholders to those innovations and knowledge products most relevant to their needs, in ways that help to build their capabilities in these areas. As Sunder (2007, p. 122) notes: 'The traditional utilitarian understanding of intellectual property focuses on incentivizing the creation of more knowledge goods . . . But utilitarianism does not ask who makes the goods or whether the goods are fairly distributed to all who need them'.

There is certainly room for fine-tuning where and how IP laws currently draw the lines between protection of private rights and public access to 'knowledge, knowledge-creating tools and knowledge-embedded goods' (Balkin 2008, p. 2). Although theoretically protecting the 'intangible creations of the mind', IP laws in effect calibrate the flow of innumerable goods and resources relevant to advancing capabilities in all societies, including medicines, books, computers, seeds, radios and clean-energy turbines, just to name a few. While most policymakers would be familiar with the challenges in balancing public and private interests at the domestic level, ideas of a 'global public' or 'publics'

[3] United Nations Declaration on the Right to Development (4 December 1986), G.A. Res. 41/128, UN Doc. A/RES/41/128 (1986), available at: http://www.un.org/documents/ga/res/41/a41r128.htm (accessed 10 January 2010).

[4] United Nations Millennium Declaration (8 September 2000), G.A. Res. 55/2, UN Doc. A/RES/55/2 (2000) [hereinafter 'UN Millennium Declaration'], available at: http://www.un.org/millennium/ (accessed 22 June 2009).

inevitably would demand different ways of drawing those lines. Such a change in mindset does not occur overnight, but is nevertheless crucial to deal with many pressing global and local challenges, such as the high incidence of neglected or resurgent diseases in the developing world, the persistent lack of textbooks and access to information and communication technologies (ICTs) in poor regions or sectors within rich countries and the plight of many farmers in accessing appropriate agricultural technology while maintaining local crop diversity. Many challenges, such as access to clean energy technology, affect stakeholders in all societies. In discussing fair access by individuals and communities to material potentially protected by IP, this book emphasizes the enhancement of their capabilities in cultural participation and innovation as in itself a goal for human development. As Sen (1999, p. 11) underlines, the human development approach regards the individual as an agent rather than a 'patient' or passive recipient of the benefits of development programmes.

Looking beyond current ways of organizing social relations around IP, this book furthermore highlights alternative modes of innovation and collaboration that are emerging to address diverse challenges for human development. Many hybrid innovation models and partnerships that have emerged to meet challenges in global health equity or food security involve combining traditional know-how and Western scientific approaches to research. An example is the research into HIV/AIDS and cancer cures derived from TK on the mamala plant in Samoa. 'Cooperation not compulsion' is needed to find the middle ground in these and other challenges such as climate change adaptation and mitigation (Shabalala 2009). Finding equitable arrangements that recognize the contributions of different participants in these endeavours – whether a national research institute, a local community, a private firm or a civil society group – is an ongoing challenge in which laws, codes of ethics, goodwill and creativity all have a place. Geller (1998) suggests that innovation depends on the 'feedback' into 'communication networks' of 'new' creations, many of which are based on prior works. Open source production, prize funds, patent pools and public-private partnerships all demonstrate the importance of social networks in finding creative solutions. These innovation models have been applied in an increasing number of fields including medical, agricultural and climate change–related R&D. While some of these 'alternatives' are licensing arrangements premised on the existence of IP, they represent a changing ethos on the role of IP in human development, and may inspire altogether new ways of approaching innovation.

Background and methodology

In 2007, the Ford Foundation commissioned a literature review by PIIPA of published trends and future scenarios relating to IP with a focus on implications for human development. An aim of the Ford International Intellectual Property Initiative (IIPI) was to contribute to the development of more balanced IP regimes which highlight the importance of the public interest, respect the right to development and support the voices of frequently neglected stakeholders. The remit of the commissioned study was to prepare a synthesis and review of gathered literature towards building 'an overall understanding on the future trends, challenges and opportunities in this field'. The commissioned study focused on the overlapping areas of medicine, traditional knowledge, education, as well as culture and the arts. Following this remit, PIIPA formed a team of researchers, including both members of its pro bono network and the participation of partner institutions, to conduct a systematic search for literature relevant to this study by regions, substantive areas and a mapping of key organizations working in spheres relating to IP and public interest. The literature review covered the work of international and regional inter-governmental organizations, as well as academic institutions and other civil society organizations (CSOs) around the world. PIIPA issued a public call for literature, alongside direct invitations to more than 6000 individuals and entities working in IP-related areas around the world to share relevant literature towards the study. Several partner organizations, duly listed in the Acknowledgements, helped actively to extend the call for literature in particular regions through their networks.

The literature review uncovered a wealth of materials relating to IP and human development. The Ford Foundation provided further support from 2008 to mid-2010 towards the updating and extension of this study to cover other important areas of human development and to explore modes of dissemination to bring the results of the study readily to the public. As part of that dissemination process, this book features a series of articles by the research team and further participants covering key areas and concerns of IP and human development. While the chapters present ideas and options for reforms in the various areas, the intention is less on prescription – given that policy choices will need to cater to local contexts and culture – and more on encouraging new perspectives and fruitful exchange on these topics among policymakers, stakeholders, CSOs and academics from different disciplines. Further knowledge resources and options for civil society action are available on the PIIPA website for this research project (http://www.piipa.org/IP_and_Human_Development/).

In discussing options for the future, this book also explores literature relating to 'future scenarios' on IP and human development. Unlike forecasts or projections of the future, scenarios are 'stories designed to stimulate new ways of thinking about the future' (McNeely 2005, p. 62). Participants in 'scenario planning' explore the trends, driving forces and uncertainties of today to develop and describe a set of plausible, alternative future outcomes relating to a theme (ibid.). The idea is not to accurately predict a single outcome but to highlight a variety of plausible futures (Evans et al. 2006). In the process, stakeholders are invited to think beyond their existing stand-points or institutional agendas, in search of alternative solutions for the future. In engaging the device of 'stories' to broach the future, this book hopes to illustrate the variety of narrative forms that can be creatively engaged to enrich discussions relating to IP and human development. Stories will likely speak to different cultures, including those with oral traditions. Narrative methodologies can also add new information and perspectives to economic and legal writing and have inspired a whole genre of legal scholarship (see Brooks & Gewirtz 1996).

The remit of the Ford-commissioned study extends to a literature review of scenario plans relating to IP, as published by international and regional entities. The results of this literature review should not be confused with a full-scale scenario planning exercise with its particular methodologies. Examples of the latter can be seen in the Millennium Ecosystem Assessment and the 'AIDS in Africa' scenario planning spearheaded by the Joint United Nations Programme on HIV/AIDS (UNAIDS). An extensive process directly relating to IP was completed by the European Patent Office (EPO) in 2007, and the resultant scenario plan is analysed in detail in Chapters 2 and 9 of this book. Scenario planning is not widespread in the IP field. To spur discussion and creative exchange on topics yet to be covered by institutional scenario plans, some alternative future options or scenarios in relation to particular sectors and themes are broached in chapters of this book. These are not meant to be exhaustive; they suggest, rather, some considerations and potential directions for future scenario thinking in these areas.

A recurring topic in the book relates to how ICTs have transformed options for producing and disseminating creative works. Modern publishing is on the move with such developments and increasingly multimedia in nature. The design of this study likewise engages both 'traditional' and electronic methods of making materials as accessible as possible to the public. Through Ford Foundation support, copies of this book have been sent directly to policymaking institutions and a cross-section of stakeholders, particularly in developing countries. Copies will also be made available to public interest organizations, including libraries, and disseminated at public events hosted by PIIPA and partner institutions on themes relating to IP and human development. To promote open access, an electronic version of this study will also be placed on various online repositories in addition to dissemination through PIIPA's website (http://www.piipa.org). The content of the e-version will be shared with the public under a Creative Commons licence.

Structure of the book

Participants from different fields and regions have contributed ideas and literature to the various topics addressed in this volume. While those directly involved in writing or co-authoring the chapters are acknowledged within our list of contributors, many other individuals have contributed comments and case studies to fine-tune and illustrate the material (see Acknowledgements). This section provides a synopsis of each chapter, as well as some commentary on how the different chapters connect together.

Chapter 1 introduces basic notions in IP law, along with some tools of analysis for approaching IP from a human development perspective. It first highlights the expanding range of intangible creations and legal regimes that fall within the umbrella term 'intellectual property'. The chapter explores common justifications and assumptions behind IPRs such as copyright and patents. Along with natural law arguments, it discusses the utilitarian arguments that shape current economic approaches to these forms of IPRs. Within a utilitarian framework, IP is basically seen as providing an income incentive for innovation, which in turn is meant to contribute towards overall welfare through the maximization of incentivized works. This approach is said to obscure concerns of distribution (Sunder 2007). It also does not guarantee that IP frameworks (combined with market dynamics) ultimately incentivize the kind of innovation needed by a broad range of stakeholders, including those with less purchasing power, for human development. Exploring alternative paradigms for development which could enrich the current discussions on IP, the chapter looks particularly at the capability approach to human development pioneered by Nobel Laureate Amartya Sen and others. The capability approach suggests that the ends of development should be conceptualized 'in terms of people's capabilities to function, that is, their effective opportunities to undertake the actions and activities that they want to engage in, and be whom they want to be' (Robeyns 2005, p. 95; see further Appendix A). The chapter explores how this capability approach might be applied to the context of IP and innovation and suggests areas for future research. It also considers how further studies on the dynamics of IP and innovation might equally enrich future work on the capability approach. For example, studies on social networks as drivers of innovation highlight the relevance of understanding 'group' and 'collective' capabilities alongside 'individual' capabilities for human development. The chapter then addresses other important approaches to social justice and human development, especially the implications of human rights for IP law. It concludes by posing some questions for the reader, for example on how the usual 'trade-offs' in IP and public interest might be re-visualized to address the interests of a global public.

Chapter 2 traces the complex overlap between IP and medicine, drawing from the joint perspectives of a researcher with the Brazilian Ministry of Health, a programme officer with the National Cancer Institute (US) and an associate professor at DePaul University College of Law, Chicago. Since the TRIPS Agreement requires WTO members to extend patentability to all technological fields, member states that formerly did not grant patents for pharmaceutical products or processes had to alter their legislation within implementation deadlines provided by the Agreement. While least developed countries (LDCs) received time extensions for implementation (see the Doha Declaration on the TRIPS Agreement and Public Health), many countries have not made full use of their grace period in customizing legal reforms according to their local needs. As discussed in the chapter, the TRIPS Agreement and TRIPS-plus provisions in free trade agreements (FTAs) significantly impact on global R&D, as well as on the distribution and pricing of both innovative and generic medicines. The chapter examines, among other things, flexibilities within the TRIPS regime for patent exemptions, compulsory licences, parallel imports and price controls to facilitate access to essential medicines in developing countries. The experiences of generic drug producing countries such as Brazil and India are highlighted. The chapter also looks at trends in pharmaceutical innovation in developed countries, including changes to the test of 'obviousness' under patent regimes, the discernible emphasis on life-style drugs in wealthier countries and the proliferation of secondary inventions in patent applications. It then explores recent initiatives at the World Health Organization (WHO) to address the well-documented innovation gap for neglected and resurgent diseases in developing countries. Appendix B provides a summary of alternative, collaborative models of medical innovation that have emerged to address this gap, including public-private partnerships, advanced market commitments, prizes, open source solutions and patent pools. In the last section of the chapter, some future scenarios published by international and regional entities in relation to IP and health are described and analysed. The chapter ends by highlighting the need not only for legal reforms on IP and capacity building in developing countries, but also for improved corporate governance and social responsibility of pharmaceutical companies.

Chapter 3 addresses the intersection between IP, biodiversity and food security. It combines the inputs of a Norwegian specialist on IP and human rights, a Peruvian director of research on IP and biodiversity, and a South Asian consultant on IP and trade with the United Nations Development Programme (UNDP). The affluence and over-consumption in some parts and by some populations of the world contrast with the glaring incidence of hunger elsewhere: The Food and Agriculture Organization of the United Nations (FAO) estimated in June 2009 that 1.02 billion persons suffered from hunger, an increase of more than 150 million people in just two years.[5] Chapter 3 first addresses the nature of the right to food under international human rights instruments and how IP laws may affect that right. It then discusses the interface between IPRs and

[5] See World Food Programme, '1.02 Billion People Hungry', available at: http://www.wfp.org/news/news-release/102-billion-people-hungry (accessed 18 March 2010).

recent agricultural trends, focusing on how the increasing reliance on the private sector for agricultural research in many contexts – and on IPRs such as patents and plant variety protection (PVP) to incentivize such research – affects farming communities in developing countries. Exploring the social and environmental effects of IPRs in transgenic technology and biological resources, the chapter contrasts the highly mechanized agriculture system in most developed countries with the traditional farming practices still found in many parts of the world. These traditional practices (which usually include seed saving, reuse and exchange) are increasingly being displaced by industrial farming models based, for example, on a reliance on patented transgenic seeds. This is despite the fact that local agro-biodiversity is essential for food security. Of course, higher yields are likely, at least in the short term. But this does not always mean farmers will be better off. If farmers become dependent on a few dominant global firms holding patents on most of the seeds they sow, the increased cost of seed and, in some cases, of other inputs like pesticides, may actually make them more vulnerable. The chapter suggests that developing countries should make full use of the flexibilities under the TRIPS Agreement in customizing their PVP according to local contexts and needs. Some examples are drawn from recent legislation in Thailand, Malaysia and India. The chapter then looks at other trends of 'enclosure' on the genetic commons, including the affirmation of sovereign rights over genetic resources under the CBD,[6] and some countervailing implications of the FAO International Treaty for Plant Genetic Resources for Food and Agriculture (ITPGRFA). The chapter ends by emphasizing R&D strategies in developing countries which prioritize the development of national and community-based seed banks, the stimulation of collective participatory breeding, the implementation of farmers' rights (under ITPGRFA) and the appropriate protection of the TK of indigenous communities. Open source or cross-licensing structures that may create a defined technological commons to address food security are also explored, along with R&D strategies which combine new research techniques and the inputs of local farmer-innovators.

Chapter 4 discusses present trends and future options in the legal protection of traditional knowledge (TK). It brings together perspectives from an IP law professor at the Washington University in St. Louis and a post-graduate researcher in ethno-museology who is herself a representative from the Kichwa Indigenous People in Ecuador. The chapter suggests the need not only for multidisciplinary research in this area, but also for the direct involvement of local community members as co-researchers and scholars in their own right. The protection of TK is integral to the cultural and physical survival of indigenous peoples, as well as to other non-indigenous communities guided by customary practices including many local farming communities. Barsh (1999, pp. 74–75)

6 Access and benefit-sharing provisions under the CBD are addressed in Chapter 4.

observes that: '[W]hat is "traditional" about traditional knowledge is not its antiquity, but *the way it is acquired and used*. In other words, the social process of learning and sharing knowledge, which is unique to each indigenous culture, lies at the very heart of its "traditionality"'. Māori representative Aroha Te Pareake Mead has said that: 'Traditional knowledge defines who we are, what makes us unique, what breathes integrity into our existence and relationship with our natural and cultural landscapes' (Mead 2005, p. 18). Exploring concepts of TK, Chapter 4 qualifies that 'contrary to popular belief, TK is not static and unchanging, but rather develops and changes over time, albeit by means of traditional or customary practices'. Issues concerning the IP protection of TK have come to the fore in international frameworks especially in cases of misappropriation of TK (or plant genetic materials which embody TK) by third parties. The chapter highlights existing means of legal protection for TK, the development of *sui generis* means for protecting TK within countries and regions, as well as the evolution of internationally harmonized approaches to the protection of TK. Appendix C discusses some international and regional strategies in relation to the promotion of traditional medicinal knowledge, and includes a case study of the *sui generis* law in Thailand to promote such knowledge. Under the CBD, significant work is taking place towards the elaboration of an international regime for access and benefit-sharing of genetic resources, with implications for the protection of associated TK. Chapter 4 highlights some priorities for capacity building and legal support to enable indigenous peoples' full participation in such forums to define the future contours of their TK protection and resource rights. The chapter calls for a holistic (rather than piecemeal) approach to preserving bio-cultural heritage which recognizes the intrinsic links of TK to the cultural identity, land rights and customary laws of indigenous peoples and local communities.

Chapter 5 addresses challenges faced by indigenous peoples and non-indigenous local communities in the legal protection of their traditional cultural expressions (TCEs). It highlights considerations for governments, public institutions and non-profit organizations in promoting TCEs to support these peoples and communities in their cultural, economic and social development. Written by a Peruvian IP lawyer and a contributing editor, it incorporates comments from indigenous representatives, anthropologists and legal scholars. Surveying relevant literature from different disciplines, it poses questions relating to the 'commodification' of TCEs, a process that can transform the social relations underpinning creative processes in indigenous communities. At the same time, the making and marketing of some forms of TCEs present potential sources of livelihoods to many indigenous communities currently marginalized in the socio-economic order. Given a global environment where the TCEs of indigenous peoples are increasingly copied and commercially mass-produced by third parties, some potentials and limitations in relation to IP protection of TCEs are discussed. The chapter draws a distinction, especially, between forms of IP such as patents and copyright, which historically emphasize the protection of individual creators, and those forms of IPRs which support to some extent concepts of 'communal' innovation and 'authenticity' relevant to TCE custodians. It notes how labelling devices such as geographical indications, trademarks, collective marks and certification marks can potentially be used by local communities to distinguish their TCEs from mass-produced copies. The chapter then explores developments in *sui generis* protection at the national, regional and international levels for TCEs. It questions the extent to which the 'unique' or hybrid measures being developed really depart from conventional IP concepts and embrace principles of relevance to TCE custodians. Some of these principles and customs are reflected in indigenous protocols and standards being developed to govern third-party access to and use of TCEs, including within the context of the Internet. Exploring some future scenarios, the chapter reiterates the need for the legal protection of TCEs to be approached within integrated solutions to protect bio-cultural heritage. The legal protection of TCEs also needs to be understood in relation to human rights and other international norms relevant to promoting cultural rights and cultural diversity.

A note may be helpful here on how various chapters connect in the book. The discussion on IP and human rights in Chapter 1, for example, is taken up further in different chapters. The right to health discussed in Chapter 2 is connected to the right to food addressed in Chapter 3. Cultural rights as human rights are discussed further in Chapter 8 on cultural diversity and the arts (see synopsis below); these rights are also relevant to the discussions on traditional knowledge and cultural expressions in Chapters 4 and 5. The latter chapters are closely connected. Although TCEs are embraced within the broad, holistic definition of TK adopted in Chapter 4, the particular legal developments in relation to TCEs called for a separate chapter on the topic. Chapter 5 on TCEs also complements Chapter 8, and these two chapters were conceived as part of a larger inquiry on the relation between IPRs and cultural diversity. While Chapter 8 explores themes including the intersection between copyright protection and the contemporary arts, clean-cut lines cannot always be drawn between 'traditional' and 'contemporary' expressions, and innovation occurs in all realms. In discussing traditional livelihoods, it is also important to account for the multiple priorities and aspirations of human development among individuals within communities. The right to education, for example, is integral to human development in all societies. Two chapters (Chapters 6 and 7) in this book address the important nexus between copyright laws and access to knowledge and education. As seen in the rest of the summary, they approach the topic from different angles.

Chapter 6 examines the implications of global IP regimes and national copyright policies on capabilities for education, particularly in developing countries. Contributed by a law professor from the Seattle University School of Law, it describes the top-down bias in global IP regulation and its particular impact on education as a global public good. To tackle this bias, the author proposes an 'IP from below' approach linking IP to human development and distributive justice. The chapter explores how such an approach might be applied towards building capabilities for basic education in countries lacking adequate access to textbooks and other educational materials. It poses the question whether access to hard copies for educational purposes could be re-imagined, just as the digitizing of books is allowing us to re-imagine our global digital informational universe. For many countries, both developed and developing, books remain an appropriate and useful 'technology', especially for primary and secondary education. The chapter focuses on Article 10(2) of the Berne Convention for the Protection of Literary and Artistic Works[7] – the so-called illustration for teaching exception – as a potential policy space for signatory nations of either the Berne Convention or the TRIPS Agreement to mandate access to educational materials for development needs. Article 10(2) endorses national exceptions to copyright for purposes of access to education. Emphasizing the need for a substantive equality principle in global IP norm setting and interpretation, the author explores how this principle might be applied to educational exceptions to copyright so as to justify an increase in national policy space. Appendix D provides a comparison of educational use exceptions in different jurisdictions, including developing countries (or economies in transition) such as Argentina, China, Czech Republic, India, Jordan and Nigeria; it also surveys the relevant exceptions in developed countries including France, Japan, the United States and the UK. Importantly, Chapter 6 situates the challenge of access to educational materials within a larger problem of fragmented policymaking for global public goods including education. It argues that an approach to IP 'from below' can help to link IP, beyond the dynamics of trade, to human development.

Chapter 7 explores the impact of copyright on public access to information products, focusing on issues and recent developments relating to information and communication technologies (ICTs). The chapter is contributed by a lecturer in International Economic Law at the University of Maastricht, Netherlands, formerly a project director at the Center for International Environmental Law (CIEL). The chapter considers, in particular, how ICTs have significantly altered the power relations between creators, intermediaries and users of information

[7] Berne Convention for the Protection of Literary and Artistic Works (Berne, 9 September 1886), *revised at* Paris, 24 July 1971, *and amended* 28 September 1979, 1161 U.N.T.S. 30 [hereinafter 'Berne Convention'], available at: http://www.wipo.int/treaties/en/ip/berne/trtdocs_wo001.html (accessed 3 February 2010).

products. It surveys the potentials unleashed by the Internet and digitization for the creation and dissemination of a wide range of information resources, noting the encouraging trends towards open source production, e-journals and open access repositories. These technology-led trends empower both creators and users of information in many ways. The chapter highlights, at the same time, the current tendency towards a strengthening of IP protection internationally, as reflected in trade-related instruments and the WIPO Internet Treaties. It calls for a closer examination of the impact of IP enforcement policies and techniques on human development concerns including access to educational materials in developing countries, looking especially at the increasing availability and use of criminal sanctions to enforce copyright. The on-going negotiation led by developed countries (including the United States, Canada, Japan and the EU) of an Anti-Counterfeiting Trade Agreement (ACTA), outside of WIPO, has also emerged as an area for further scrutiny. The chapter suggests some developing country options and civil society actions towards achieving an effective balance between copyright protection and access to information products for human development. Some reforms being discussed in this much-debated area include the elaboration of an international instrument to govern copyright exceptions and limitations, whether through mandatory provisions or soft law. Noting that the legal boundaries and exceptions to copyright are ambiguous, especially in the context of the digitization of works, the chapter highlights some useful resources for policymakers, civil society actors, educators (including media educators) and librarians to broach these issues.

Chapter 8 explores the relationship between cultural diversity and copyright protection. It combines perspectives from a researcher in IP and contemporary arts, a Peruvian lawyer and a contributing editor. Exploring different interpretations of culture and cultural diversity, the chapter poses a basic question: Does copyright in its current forms incentivize a wide range of cultural endeavours? To address this question, it highlights not only the activities of professionals in the cultural sector (e.g. writers, musicians, visual artists, performers and filmmakers) but also the creative efforts of other individuals and communities. Looking first at the situation of professional creators, the chapter discusses some discernible trends in the corporate ownership of copyright, especially in the music and film industries. Among other things, it notes how statutory provisions on 'works for hire' and contractual arrangements such as copyright assignment and licensing contour the rights of creators, especially in common law jurisdictions. Making further comparisons between sectors within the arts as well as among some world regions, the chapter shows how the incentive function of copyright may be relevant only to a subset of creative sectors and communities. More studies are needed on the pecuniary factors and non-pecuniary motivations driving creativity in other sectors. As a case study, the chapter examines the position of contemporary artists ('contemporary art' defined here as post–World War II visual or multimedia art) in relation to copyright (see Appendix E). Whether in terms of their potential claims to copyright as creators or as avid users of copyright-protected works, contemporary artists have an ambiguous position under copyright laws. The examples of 'appropriation art' or parodies illustrate that the line between creators and users – or between free expression and copying – may be a fine one. The chapter further explores how concepts of authorship and originality are changing rapidly, not least with the advent of digital technology and new forms of 'remixing' or 'retelling'. It argues that our understanding of 'public access' to cultural works needs to be broadened to consider not only access to cultural goods, but also the promotion of cultural participation. Where copyright law draws the boundaries for defences or exceptions to infringement, such as fair use or fair dealing, influences the capabilities of individuals and communities to use and transform copyright-protected works as a form of creative expression.

Chapter 9 casts the spotlight on the future of IP and human development. Combining inputs from PIIPA's chair, the Director of International Policy at the Electronic Frontier Foundation, and a contributing editor, it first reviews scenario plans published by international organizations and CSOs on the future of IP. The chapter explores the results of the three-year scenario planning process at the European Patent Office (EPO) on how IP regimes might evolve by the year 2025 (see EPO 2007). It also looks at scenario planning conducted elsewhere on particular themes relating to IP, such as the future of the public domain or the future of digital media (scenarios on IP and public health are explored in detail in Chapter 2). Scenario planning remains a relatively new approach for exploring IP-related reforms. The authors suggest that further attention might be placed on scenario planning in areas of particular relevance to developing countries, such as food security, the protection of TK, access to textbooks and ICTs, as well as the impact of IP enforcement on informal sectors and livelihoods. The implications of IPRs for clean technology innovation and transfer present another emergent area where scenario planning might be useful. Many of these themes (explored in the various chapters of this book) are collected and woven together within the evolving Development Agenda at WIPO. Describing the background as well as recent initiatives concerning the Development Agenda, the chapter explores whether scenario planning might be a helpful option in advancing a human development agenda. Given both the politicized and multifaceted nature of the WIPO Development Agenda, scenario planning may help to clarify alternative models and measurements of development (beyond economic indicators) to emphasize the social and cultural priorities of development. Scenario planning can also highlight solutions developed in one sector (such as open source production in information technology or public-private partnerships in health research) as potential lessons for other sectors (such as education, agriculture or climate change adaptation and mitigation). The chapter further reminds us that WIPO is not the only forum in which priorities for IP and development are being elaborated. Pointing to the CBD framework and the increasing involvement of many other UN organizations, governments and CSOs in formulating international and national strategies relevant to IP and human development, the chapter argues that the Development Agenda at WIPO needs to link constructively with these other initiatives.

As seen from this summary, the chapters in this book cover the full gamut of IP and development-related issues. Despite their thematic differences, all of these chapters emphasize that policy reform on IP, whether at international, regional or local levels, must transcend economic cost-benefit analysis so as to give appropriate weight to the social and cultural aspects of development. But this is not all. Reform must also give attention to the ways that IP can, or cannot, promote innovation, and this requires evidence derived from sound analysis and experience. The challenge ahead lies in integrating the many dimensions and concerns of human development not only into IP-related policies, but also into the very assumptions about incentives and innovation in IP law.

REFERENCES

Anderson, J. 2009, *Law, Knowledge, Culture: The Production of Indigenous Knowledge in Intellectual Property Law*, Edward Elgar, Cheltenham, UK.

Balkin, J. 2008, 'Foreword', in L. Shaver (ed.), *Access to Knowledge in Brazil: New Research on Intellectual Property, Innovation and Development*, Information Society Project, Yale Law School, available at: http://www.law.yale.edu/documents/pdf/ISP/A2KBrazil_bkmk.pdf (accessed 27 October 2009).

Barsh, R.L. 1999, 'Indigenous Knowledge and Biodiversity', in D.A. Posey (ed.), *Cultural and Spiritual Values of Biodiversity*, Intermediate Technology Publications, London.

Brooks, P. & Gewirtz, P. (eds.) 1996, *Law's Stories: Narrative and Rhetoric in the Law*, Yale University Press, New Haven, CT, and London.

European Patent Office (EPO) 2007, *Scenarios for the Future: How Might IP Regimes Evolve by 2025? What Global Legitimacy Might Such Regimes Have?*, EPO, Munich, available at: http://documents.epo.org/projects/babylon/eponet.nsf/0/63a726d28b589b5bc12572db00597683/$file/epo_scenarios_bookmarked.pdf (accessed 26 October 2009).

Evans, K., Velarde, S.J., Prieto, R.P., Rao, S.N., Sertzen, S., Dávila, K., Cronkleton, P. & de Jong, W. 2006, *Field Guide to the Future: Four Ways for Communities to Think Ahead*, E. Bennett & M. Zurek (eds.), Center for International Forestry Research (CIFOR), ASB-Partnership for the Tropical Forest Margins and the World Agroforestry Centre, available at: http://www.asb.cgiar.org/ma/scenarios/field-guide.asp (accessed 30 October 2009).

Fisher, W. 2001, 'Theories of Intellectual Property', in S.R. Munzer (ed.), *New Essays in the Legal and Political Theory of Property*, Cambridge

University Press, New York, pp. 168–200, available at: http://www.law.harvard.edu/faculty/tfisher/iptheory.html. (accessed 12 May 2009).

Geller, P.E. 1998, 'Hiroshige v. Van Gogh: Resolving the Dilemma of Copyright Scope in Remedying Infringement', *Journal of the Copyright Society of the USA*, vol. 46, pp. 39–72, available at: http://papers.ssrn.com/sol3/papers.cfm?abstract_id=186931 (accessed 27 October 2009).

Leach, J. 2005, 'Modes of Creativity and the Register of Ownership', in R.A. Ghosh (ed.), *CODE: Collaborative Ownership and the Digital Economy*, pp. 29–45, Massachusetts Institute of Technology Press, Cambridge, MA.

McNeely, J.A. 2005, 'Protected Areas in 2023: Scenarios for an Uncertain Future', *Conservation Practice at the Landscape Scale*, vol. 22, no. 1 , pp. 61–74, available at: http://www.georgewright.org/221mcneely.pdf (accessed 15 February 2010).

Mead, A. 2005, 'Emerging Issues in Māori Traditional Knowledge – Can These be Addressed by United Nations Agencies?', *Technical Report for the International Workshop on Traditional Knowledge*, 21–23 September 2005, Panama City, Department of Economic and Social Affairs, United Nations, available at: http://www.un.org/esa/socdev/unpfii/documents/workshop_TK_mead.pdf (accessed 18 November 2009).

Robeyns, I. 2005, 'Capability Approach, a Theoretical Survey', *Journal of Human Development*, vol. 6, no. 1, pp. 93–114.

Sen, A.K. 1999, *Development as Freedom*, Oxford University Press, Oxford and New York.

Shabalala, D. 2009, 'Cooperation Not Compulsion on Clean Technology Transfer', *Science and Development Network*, 3 June 2009, available at: http://www.scidev.net/en/climate-change-and-energy/opinions/cooperation-not-compulsion-on-clean-technology-tra.html (accessed 27 October 2009).

Strathern, M. 2005, 'Imagined Collectivities and Multiple Authorship', in R.A. Ghosh (ed.), *CODE: Collaborative Ownership and the Digital Economy*, pp. 13–29, Massachusetts Institute of Technology Press, Cambridge, MA.

Sunder, M. 2007, 'The Invention of Traditional Knowledge', *Law and Contemporary Problems*, vol. 70, no. 2, pp. 97–124.

Tansey, G. 2008, 'Global Rules, Local Needs', in G. Tansey & T. Rajotte (eds.), *The Future Control of Food: A Guide to International Negotiations and Rules on Intellectual Property, Biodiversity and Food Security*, Earthscan Publications Ltd., London and Sterling, VA, available at: http://www.idrc.ca/openebooks/397-3/ (accessed 27 October 2009).

1

Intellectual property through the lens of human development

Tzen Wong[1]

> *[T]he legal regime of intellectual property has insinuated itself more deeply into our lives and more deeply into the framework of international law, affecting everything from the recreational home user's ability to share music, to the farmer's ability to replant seed, to the production and distribution of life-saving drugs. Indeed, with full compliance to the Trade-Related Aspects of Intellectual Property Rights (TRIPS) Agreement now required (as of January 1, 2005) in all but the world's very least developed countries, intellectual property law becomes literally a question of life or death. Despite these real world changes, intellectual property scholars increasingly explain their field through the lens of economics.* (Sunder 2006, p. 261)

Introduction

Intellectual property rights (IPRs) intersect with many vital areas of human well-being and development. From access to medicines, food, education and the arts, through to the preservation of cultural heritage, there are few human endeavours untouched by intellectual property (IP). As knowledge-based economies rapidly expand in our information age, the need for balance between private rights and the public interest over intangible creations becomes ever more pertinent. There are divided views, meanwhile, on how and if IP can advance the public interest. Sir Hugh Laddie (2002) wrote in his foreword to the seminal report of the Commission on Intellectual Property Rights (CIPR) on *Integrating Intellectual Property Rights and Development Policy*:

> On the one side, the developed world side, there exists a powerful lobby of those who believe that all IPRs are good for business, benefit the public at large and act as catalysts for technical progress. They believe and argue that, if IPRs are good, more IPRs must be better. On the other side, the developing world side, there exists a vociferous lobby of those who believe that IPRs are likely to cripple the development of local industry and technology, will harm the local population and benefit none but the developed world. They believe and argue that, if IPRs are bad, the fewer the better. The process of implementing TRIPS has not resulted in a shrinking of the gap that divides these two sides, rather it has helped to reinforce the views already held . . . So firmly and sincerely held are these views that at times it has appeared that neither side has been prepared to listen to the other. Persuasion is out, compulsion is in. (Ibid., p. iii)

[1] This chapter is dedicated to the memory of Sir Hugh Laddie (1946–2008). I am grateful to many for their review and invaluable comments on earlier drafts of this chapter, especially Margaret Chon, David Clark, Claire Comfort, Graham Dutfield, Brett Frischmann, Sakiko Fukuda-Parr, Michael Gollin, Hans Haugen Morten, Richard Ponzio, Tim Scott and David Wong.

Fervent debate continues over the socio-economic impacts of IP, generating increased public awareness of these issues and at least some notable legal reforms. Increasingly drawn into the debate are a spectrum of individuals and communities who grapple with IP in many different ways. Some are uncertain about their rights whether as IP holders or as users of material which might be under IP protection. Others seek to inform themselves further on the social dimensions of IP – in a field marked by the lack of reliable empirical evidence on the economic impacts of IP, the social dimensions are even more opaque and harder to gauge. Yet others are only beginning to explore how IPRs have come to pervade and circumscribe their daily lives in palpable ways.[2] In addressing these social and legal dimensions, this study explores how the social impact of IP might be approached and evaluated more systematically.

What developments have there been in the law, along with calls for reforms, since the publication of the CIPR report almost a decade ago? The various chapters in this book try to trace some of those developments. Notably, at the behest of developing countries and civil society organizations, a 'Development Agenda' has emerged at the World Intellectual Property Organization (WIPO).[3] This agenda brings to focus many continuing socio-economic concerns that developing countries have in relation to IP, and is intended to mainstream development into WIPO's work. That the path of adopting and evolving such an agenda has been jagged reveals, however, many challenges ahead in reconciling the socio-economic agendas and cultural interpretations that diverse stakeholders bring to a discussion on IP and development. While a 2008 report by the International Expert Group on Biotechnology, Innovation and Intellectual Property (IEGBIIP) heralds a 'new era of IP collaboration' – in contrast to the 'Old IP' era, said to be waning and 'out of sync with the level and types of innovation' socially needed – many challenges lie ahead in finding the right social equilibrium for IP.[4]

Importantly, new – though some might say 'old' – questions have been raised on the very models of development that continue to inform IP policies. Chon (2007, p. 476) observes that 'recent debates within international intellectual property law reveal a development divide – not only a divide between developed and developing countries according to their material well-being, but also a divide in understanding development as growth contrasted with development as freedom'. In other

[2] This is framed positively on WIPO's virtual tour of 'IP in Everyday Life' at http://www.wipo.int/about-ip/en/athome.htm (accessed 1 May 2009).

[3] WIPO member states finally adopted in September 2007 a Development Agenda, consisting of a series of recommendations to enhance the development dimension of the Organization's activities. For background on the Development Agenda and related proposals, see http://www.wipo.int/ip-development/en/agenda/ (accessed 15 January 2010); for some history and implications of WIPO's work on the Development Agenda, see Halbert 2007; de Beer 2009; New 2009. See also Chapter 9 of this book.

[4] See International Expert Group on Biotechnology, Innovation and Intellectual Property (IEGBIIP) 2008, 'Toward a new era of intellectual property: From confrontation to negotiation', Montreal, Canada, September 2008 ('IEGBIIP Report 2008'), p. 13. See p. 2 of the report for the composition of the expert group, led by principal investigator Richard Gold from the Faculty of Law, McGill University, Canada.

words, the debate surrounds the very understanding of development itself. Within an 'economic growth' model for development, IPRs are often assumed to play a crucial role as an engine of growth and innovation in a country as well as a conduit for foreign investment and technology transfer (see CIPR 2002, pp. 20–26; Straus 2008). It is not uncommon to encounter descriptions of IP or forms of IP (e.g. patents or copyright) as the 'engine of growth' (Idris 2003) or the 'engine of development' (Oman 2000).[5] Such literature suggests IP protection as an essential driver or even pre-condition of economic growth and development in a country. These viewpoints remain powerful in shaping IP policies at many national and international forums, even though the empirical evidence connecting IP protection and economic development is mixed and inadequate (CIPR 2002; Chon 2006; IEGBIIP 2008). Economic studies have yielded ambivalent results on these connections, not least because it is often difficult to separate out the impact of IP from other intertwined factors relating to an economy. Economists themselves differ in their views on the linkages between IP and economic development. Surveying the existing economics literature on IP, Maskus (2008, p. 500) observes that:

> There are multiple relationships in principle between intellectual property protection and economic development, most of them complex and difficult to measure. Despite extensive literature on the subject, much of the available evidence is anecdotal and may be interpreted in various ways.[6]

What seems less debatable is that similar levels of IP protection will have differential socio-economic impact, depending on the stage of development and cultural contexts of countries (United Nations Development Programme [UNDP] 2001; Ostergard 2007; Maskus 2008).[7] Thus, the evolving Development Agenda at WIPO is an opportunity for countries to nuance their engagement with IP according to many more considerations, including meeting basic needs in food and health, increasing capabilities for education, attaining human rights, protecting cultural heritage and sustaining the environment for future generations. In exploring these and other dimensions of development, this book highlights 'human development' as a particularly useful framework for broaching social and legal reforms around IP.[8] Central to the human development paradigm is the work of economist and Nobel laureate Amartya Sen since the 1980s on the 'capability approach' to development (Sen 1987, 1999). The human development paradigm views the expansion of 'human

[5] For further examples, see IPcentral Weblog, 'IP as the Engine of Economic Growth' (7 November 2005), available at: http://weblog.ipcentral.info/archives/2005/11/ip_as_the_engin_1.html (accessed 20 March 2010).

[6] While noting that some of the earlier empirical studies (e.g. Gould & Gruben 1996) on positive correlation between strong IPRs and economic growth may hold true for advanced, industrialized countries, Ostergard (2007) attempts to show through economic modelling that this relationship may actually prove negative for those developing countries which lack strong capacity for domestic R&D. For a recent review of literature in this area, see Chatterjee, S., David, J. Deng, F., Dippon, C. & Lopez, M. 2008, 'Worldwide: Intellectual Property Rights in Developing Countries', available at: http://www.mondaq.com/article.asp?articleid=57856 (accessed 5 July 2009).

[7] On differential impacts of IPRs on developed and developing countries, see further Park & Ginarte 1997.

[8] See the discussion in Dutfield & Suthersanen 2007, pp. 3–12.

capabilities' (discussed in Section 3) and genuine choices as an important goal of development policies. It draws attention, for example, to questions of social justice and empowerment that may present blind spots in pure income measures of development. Although its application to innovation and IP is more recent, the human development perspective is not new to policymakers. National human development reports have been produced by more than 140 countries, and particular themes have been tackled in the regional and global reports of the United Nations Development Programme (UNDP).[9] Along with Sen's capability approach, some aspects of the 'basic needs' approach to development from the 1970s have also been influential in the human development literature and policies (Haq & Jolly 2008). Some of the essential elements of the human development paradigm are reflected in the following passage from the UNDP *Human Development Report 2001:*

> Human development is about much more than the rise or fall of national incomes. It is about creating an environment in which people can develop their full potential and lead productive, creative lives in accord with their needs and interests. People are the real wealth of nations. Development is thus about expanding the choices people have to lead lives that they value. And it is thus about much more than economic growth, which is only a means – if a very important one – of enlarging people's choices... Fundamental to enlarging these choices is building human capabilities – the range of things that people can do or be in life. The most basic capabilities for human development are to lead long and healthy lives, to be knowledgeable, to have access to the resources needed for a decent standard of living and to be able to participate in the life of the community. Without these, many choices are simply not available, and many opportunities in life remain inaccessible. (UNDP 2001, p. 9)

It has been suggested that 'there can be as many human development dimensions as there are ways of enlarging people's choices', and that key parameters of human development can evolve over time and vary both across and within countries.[10] The concept of human development itself is also subject to revision and rethinking to meet new challenges.[11] While it is impossible to embrace the entire spectrum of subject areas pertaining to human development and IP in one book, the following chapters address in detail the main topics of health, food security, access to education, implications of new technologies, protecting bio-cultural heritage and promoting cultural diversity and the arts. Some cross-cutting themes, such as gender equality and climate change, are addressed in sections within chapters.

9 See UNDP webpage, 'Human Development Reports', available at: http://hdr.undp.org/en/reports/ (accessed 15 March 2010). See the discussion in Ponzio 2008; Fukuda-Parr 2008.

10 UNDP, 'Origins of the human development approach', available at: http://hdr.undp.org/en/humandev/origins/ (accessed 15 January 2010). The succession of Human Development Reports (HDR) produced by UNDP since the 1990s – with topics as diverse as 'new technologies' (UNDP 2001), 'cultural liberty' (UNDP 2004), 'climate change' (UNDP 2007) and 'human mobility' (UNDP 2009) – testify to the broad range of potential subject matter within the umbrella of human development. See also Fukuda-Parr 2003a, 2003b.

11 This is an important topic explored in the (forthcoming) UNDP *Human Development Report 2010*, 'Twentieth Anniversary Edition: Rethinking Human Development', see http://hdr.undp.org/en/reports/global/hdr2010/ (accessed 1 February 2010).

This introductory chapter aims to provide some background on IP, while highlighting key human development concerns. Section 1 touches on the nature of IPRs and explores the increasing breadth of subject matter coming under the various forms of IP protection. Section 2 discusses common rationales for protection of IPRs such as copyright and patents, along with some historical trends. Section 3 then sketches some of the basic ideas in the capability approach to human development and explores their potential relevance within the IP context. The capability approach is only one aspect of the human development paradigm and does not exclude other ways of viewing development. Section 4 highlights some important perspectives intertwined with human development, bringing to the fore human rights considerations that increasingly overlap with IP debates. Some questions are then posed in the conclusion for further thought as the reader ventures into other chapters of this book.

1. The expanding matrix of intellectual property rights

Intellectual property refers to a class of legal rights which typically protect intangible creations of the mind. It was only in the twentieth century that the term 'intellectual property' became used generically to refer to a 'group of legal regimes which began their existence independently of each other and at different times in different places' (Drahos 1996, p. 14; see also Tansey 2008, p. 11). While many think of patents, copyrights and trademarks when discussing IP, there are various other regimes governing IPRs such as trade secrets, geographical indications, plant variety protection (PVP), industrial designs and utility models. Though working quite independently of one another, albeit with increasing subject-matter overlap, these property regimes together encompass all kinds of intangible elements, including 'inventions' in almost any field imaginable, expressions on any topic in any medium, databases, reputations and, indeed, ideas.

A non-exhaustive description of various forms of IPRs is found in Box 1.1. There is significant variation in the kinds of subject matter covered by the many forms of IPRs, the nature of the rights granted, the conditions for exercise of the rights (or how the rights are infringed), and the exemptions or privileges retained for the public in terms of access to the intangible elements protected and their physical embodiments (such as drugs, books and branded goods). Although it is impossible to touch on all of these aspects in this introduction, a few points will be highlighted here about the nature of IPRs and the expanding subject matter of IP protection. Various chapters in this book delve with more detail into particular forms of IPRs. This introductory chapter focuses mainly on patents and copyright.

It has been said that information is by nature non-rivalrous and non-excludable. By treating certain embodiments or applications of information as private property, IP laws effectively 'parcel' information and enable the rights owners to prevent others from handling and commercially exploiting the information in certain ways without their permission. As Cornish and Llewelyn note, 'the right-owner does not need the right in order to exploit a market for its goods and services: a patent is not a pre-condition to exploiting one's own invention' (2003, p. 6). Since IPRs are 'rights to stop others doing certain things', it is said that they are essentially

BOX 1.1. Some types of intellectual property rights[12]

Copyright: Copyright protection covers a broad range of literary and artistic works such as novels, poems, plays, mimes, dance, songs, films, drawings, paintings, photographs, sculptures, architectural designs and multimedia productions. Computer programs now fall within copyright protection under the category of 'literary works' (TRIPS Agreement, Article 10(1)). It has been said that copyright 'prevents unauthorised reproduction, public performance, recording, broadcasting, translation, or adaptation, and allows the collection of royalties for authorised use' of protected works (CIPR 2002, p. 13). Copyright 'only prevents copying, not independent derivation' (ibid.). The general rule is that copyright protects 'expressions of ideas' but not the ideas themselves. The expression involved has to pass a test of 'originality', which is not defined in the Berne Convention on Literary and Artistic Works ('Berne Convention') and which is interpreted differently in different jurisdictions. There are no formalities for copyright subsistence in countries which are signatories to the Berne Convention. Articles 9 to 14 of the current 1971 version of the Berne Convention leave some discretion as to what acts may be defined as infringement under national laws. National statutes usually lay down a list of acts which would infringe copyright, along with provisions dealing with exceptions or defences to infringement. The Berne Convention provides for a *minimum* copyright term of author's life plus 50 years (Article 7(1); Article 7(6)). Different rules apply for pseudonymous and anonymous works (Article 7(3)), works of joint authorship (Article 7 *bis*), cinematographic works (Article 7(2)), photographic works and works of applied art (Article 7(4)). Copyright can be assigned and licensed in most jurisdictions. Along with copyright, most countries also recognize moral rights, although to varying extents (see definitions in Chapter 5 and 8).

(Source: CIPR 2002, p. 13; Berne Convention (Paris Act, 1971); see further Chapters 5–8)

Related Rights: The purpose of related rights is 'to protect the legal interests of certain persons and legal entities who contribute to making works available to the public; or who produce subject matter which, while not qualifying as works under the copyright systems of all countries, contain sufficient creativity or technical and organizational skill to justify a copyright-like property right' (WIPO 2005a, p. 18). Related rights are known as 'neighbouring rights' in some jurisdictions. The law of related rights 'deems that the productions which result from the activities of such persons and entities merit legal protection in themselves, as they are *related* to [or neighbouring on] the protection of works of authorship under copyright' (ibid. pp. 18–19). As generally understood, there are three kinds of related rights: the rights of performing artists in their performances, the rights of producers of phonograms in their phonograms, and the rights of broadcasting organizations in their radio and television programmes (WIPO 2004, p. 46). Some laws make clear, however, that 'the exercise of related rights should leave intact, and in no way affect, the protection of copyright' (WIPO 2005a, p. 19).

(Source: WIPO 2004, p. 46; WIPO 2005a, pp. 18–22; see further Chapters 7 and 8)

Trade Secrets: Trade secrets are one of the oldest forms of IP around. Gollin (2008, p. 67) notes that in IP law, 'a trade secret is any information used in the operation of a business that is sufficiently valuable and secret to give an actual or potential economic advantage over others'. Trade secrets usually consist of commercially valuable information about production methods, business plans and clientele (CIPR 2002, p. 13). They are protected as long as they remain secret, by laws which prevent acquisition by commercially unfair means and unauthorized disclosure (ibid.). Examples include customer lists, financial information and secret formulas like the recipe for Coca-Cola (Gollin 2008, p. 67). To benefit from legal protection, the owner

[12] This compilation incorporates text from the listed sources and comments from Claire Comfort and Joshua Sarnoff.

must usually take reasonable measures to keep the information secret, such as through confidentiality agreements (ibid.). Such requirements vary with jurisdictions.

(Source: CIPR 2002, p. 13; Gollin 2008, pp. 67–69)

Patents: A patent may be granted for a product or process which constitutes an 'invention' and meets specific requirements under national laws. Article 27 of the TRIPS Agreement provides that 'patents shall be available for any inventions, whether products or processes, in all fields of technology, provided that they are new, involve an inventive step and are capable of industrial application' (Article 27(1)). A patent confers exclusive rights on the owner to prevent others from making, using, offering for sale, selling or importing for these purposes the product under patent, without the owner's consent (Article 28(1)(a)). Normally, a process patent extends such control also to the use, offer for sale, sale or importation of the products directly obtained by that process (see Article 28(1)(b)). The patent is granted for a fixed period of time (Article 33 of the TRIPS Agreement stipulates 20 years minimum from filing date). In return, society requires that the patent applicant disclose the invention in a manner that enables others to put it into practice. Along with sufficient disclosure of the invention, there are typically three basic requirements (although details differ from country to country) that determine the patentability of an invention: novelty (new elements or features that are not in the 'prior art'), non-obviousness (a sufficient inventive step for one skilled in the field), and utility (as used in the US) or industrial applicability (as used in most other countries). Unlike infringement of copyright, imitation is not always necessary for there to be a patent infringement. There are, however, usually exemptions from infringement for certain uses of patented products and processes, for example, in the case of experimental use.

(Source: CIPR 2002, p. 12; TRIPS Agreement; see further Chapters 2–4)

Utility Models: While not as widespread as patents, utility models (known as petty patents, innovation patents or utility innovations in some jurisdictions) are also used to protect inventions.[13] Utility models are similar to patents, but tend to confer rights of shorter duration to certain kinds of small or incremental innovations. They are usually sought for technically less complex inventions (e.g. in the mechanical field) or for inventions that have a short commercial life. The substantive requirements for acquiring protection for a utility model are [usually] less stringent than for patents, and vary with countries. While the 'novelty' requirement must always be met, the requirements of 'inventive step' or 'non-obviousness' may be much less stringent than for patents or absent altogether. In practice, protection for utility models is often sought for innovations of a rather incremental nature, which may not meet the patentability criteria. The procedure for obtaining protection for a utility model is often shorter and simpler than for a patent, with generally lower fees for obtaining and maintaining the right.

(Source: WIPO 2005b, pp. 8–9; see further Suthersanen, Dutfield & Chow 2007).

Industrial Designs: An industrial design, in general terms, is the ornamental or aesthetic aspect of a useful article. This aspect may depend on the shape, pattern or colour of the article. In a legal sense, industrial design refers to the right granted in many countries, pursuant to a registration system, to protect the original, ornamental and non-functional features of a product that result from design activity. Industrial designs can generally be protected if they

(*continued*)

[13] Utility models are found in the laws of more than thirty countries, as well as in the regional agreements of the African Regional Intellectual Property Organization (ARIPO) and the Organisation Africaine de la Propriété Intellectuelle (OAPI). In addition, some countries, such as Australia and Malaysia, provide for titles of protection called innovation patents or utility innovations, which are similar to utility models (WIPO 2005b, p. 8). Other countries, like Ireland and Slovenia, have a short-term patent that is equivalent to the utility model (ibid.).

Box 1.1 (*continued*)

are new and original, but in contrast to copyright, the article must be useful and able to be reproduced by industrial means. In most industrial design laws, designs that are dictated solely by the article's function are excluded from protection (e.g. a screw). Industrial design registration protects against unauthorized exploitation of the design in industrial articles. It typically grants the owner of the design the exclusive right to make, import, sell, hire or offer for sale articles to which the design is applied or in which the design is embodied. The term for an industrial design right varies from country to country.

(Source: WIPO 2005b, pp. 9–10)

Trademarks: Trademarks provide exclusive rights to use distinctive signs, such as symbols, colours, letters, shapes, sounds or names to identify the producer of a product, and protect its associated reputation (CIPR 2002, p. 13). Trademarks operate as indicators of the trade source, and can also symbolize qualities associated by consumers with certain goods and services (Cornish & Llewelyn 2003, p. 587). They can provide a guarantee that the goods and services measure up to expectations (ibid.). In order to be eligible for protection a mark must be distinctive of the proprietor so as to identify the proprietor's goods or services (CIPR 2002, p. 13). The main purpose of a trademark is to prevent customers from being misled or deceived. The period of protection varies, but a trademark can be renewed indefinitely (usually on payment of fees). In addition many countries provide protection against acts of unfair competition (see Article 10*bis* of the Paris Convention for the Protection of Industrial Property), for example in preventing misrepresentations as to trade origin, regardless of whether a trademark has been registered and infringed (CIPR, p. 13). There is special protection for 'well known' marks, which typically includes protection against diminution of the value of the mark even without consumer confusion. IP protection can also extend to trade names, service marks, collective marks and certification marks.

(Source: CIPR 2002, pp. 13; see further Chapter 5)

Geographical Indications: Geographical indications (GIs) identify the specific geographical origin of a product, and the associated qualities, reputation or other characteristics. They usually consist of the name of the place of origin. For example, food products sometimes have qualities that derive from their place of production and local environmental factors. Appellations of origin are an example of GIs. Under the Lisbon Agreement,[14] 'appellation of origin' means the 'geographical name of a country, region, or locality, which serves to designate a product originating therein, the quality and characteristics of which are due exclusively or essentially to the geographical environment, including natural and human factors' (Article 2). GIs are now protected against misrepresentation under Article 22 of the TRIPS Agreement, with stronger protection given to wines and spirits (Article 23). While GIs have been used mainly in relation to agricultural products, their use has been increasingly explored for other products including crafts. Apart from local factors such as climate and soil, GIs may also 'highlight particular qualities of a product, which are due to *human factors* found in the place of origin of the products, such as specific manufacturing skills and traditions' (WIPO 2005b, p. 14).

(Source: CIPR 2002, p. 13; WIPO 2005b, pp. 14–15; see further Chapter 5)

[14] Lisbon Agreement for the Protection of Appellations of Origin and their International Registration (Lisbon, 31 October 1958) *as revised at* Stockholm, 14 July 1967, *and amended* 28 September 1979, 923 U.N.T.S. 205 (*entered into force with current regulations* 1 April 2002), available at: http://www.wipo.int/export/sites/www/lisbon/en/docs/lisbonagreement.pdf (accessed 3 February 2010).

'negative' rights (ibid., p. 6; see also Laddie et al. 2000, p. 1).[15] Thus, copyright is not so much a right for the owner to 'copy' her own work (which the owner can do anyway), but rather a right to prevent others from reproducing and handling the work in certain ways.[16] Going further in granting exclusive rights than copyright (though for shorter periods), patents in fact enable the rights owners to prevent others from making a protected invention, even where this is done through independent research efforts.[17] In this sense, patents have been described as giving rise to 'monopoly' rights (see Cornish & Llewelyn 2003, pp. 35–41). Moreover, patents may protect not only new products but even newly discovered uses of already known ones.

The terms of protection for patents and copyright have been expanding over the centuries (and particularly in the last decades). Under the TRIPS Agreement,[18] patent rights are now granted for a minimum term of twenty years from the filing of application (Article 33), though this tends to require the periodic payment of renewal fees; otherwise patents will prematurely lapse. The term of copyright protection has expanded historically from fourteen years under the English Statute of Anne of 1710,[19] to author's life plus a minimum of fifty years under Article 7 of the Berne Convention for the protection of Literary and Artistic Works (1971).[20] The latter is a 'minimum' standard only – members are free to provide longer terms under their national systems and often do.[21] Special rules may also apply to particular types of works (see Box 1.1). To give some examples, the term of protection in the US is the life of the author plus seventy years, and ninety-five years from first publication for works made for hire.[22] The term of protection for copyright is also the

[15] While some aspects of IP confer positive entitlements, such as the right to be granted a patent or to register a trademark upon fulfilling the requisite conditions, Cornish and Llewelyn (2003, p. 6) qualify that these are 'essentially ancillary'.

[16] If someone owns the copyright in a film he can stop others from showing it in public but it does not follow that he has the positive right to show it himself (Laddie et al. 2000, p. 1).

[17] As Cornish and Llewelyn (2003, p. 6) note, IPRs comprise rights to stop not only so-called 'pirates, counterfeiters, imitators' but also 'in some cases third parties who have independently reached the same ideas from exploiting them without the licence of the right-owner'.

[18] Agreement on Trade-Related Aspects of Intellectual Property Rights (Marrakesh, 15 April 1994), Marrakesh Agreement Establishing the World Trade Organization, Annex 1C, 1869 U.N.T.S. 299, 33 I.L.M. 1197 (1994) (*entered into force* 1 January 1995) [hereinafter 'TRIPS Agreement'], available at: http://www.wto.org/english/tratop_e/trips_e/t_agm0_e.htm (accessed 3 February 2010).

[19] Statute of Anne, 1710, 8 Ann., c. 19 (Eng.), available at: http://www.copyrighthistory.com/anne.html (accessed 27 March 2010).

[20] Berne Convention for the Protection of Literary and Artistic Works (Berne, 9 September 1886), *as revised at* Paris, 24 July 1971, *and amended* 28 September 1979, 1161 U.N.T.S 30 (Paris Act *entered into force* 15 December 1972) [hereinafter 'Berne Convention'], available at http://www.wipo.int/treaties/en/ip/berne/trtdocs_wo001.html (accessed 3 February 2010).

[21] Coupled with the relatively low threshold for copyright protection, an increasingly long term of protection does not have trivial results. Sir Hugh Laddie (1996, p. 256) noted in the UK context: 'As is now familiar in copyright law, the process was one of levelling up the protection rather than levelling down . . . Indeed if a modern day architect were to design a new Albert Memorial, he would have the satisfaction of knowing that his copyright is likely to be sprightly and in the prime of life long after the concrete and steel of his architectural creation have started to crumble. The question to be asked: what justification is there for a period of monopoly of such proportions? It surely cannot be based on the principle of encouraging artistic creativity by increasing the size of the carrot. No one is going to be more inclined to write programs or speeches, compose music or design buildings because 50, 60, or 70 years after his death a distant relative . . . might still be getting royalties'.

[22] See Copyright Term Extension Act of 1998, P.L. 105-298, § 102(b) (amending 17 U.S.C. § 302).

author's life plus seventy years in European Union (EU) countries.[23] While related rights typically enjoy a shorter term of protection, there are developments at the European Parliament and Commission to extend the term for those rights.[24] Meanwhile, trademarks, geographical indications and trade secret protections are potentially perpetual provided certain conditions are continually met.

While there are regional and international efforts to harmonize IP laws, the protection of IPRs still varies significantly amongst countries and is generally restricted to the geographic area of the state in question. In this sense, IPRs are territorial. In the case of some IPRs such as patents and trademarks, protection is obtained through meeting formalities in each country where it is sought. A product that is patented in country A might be reproduced legitimately (under IP laws) in another country where the same product is not patented. An applicant may, however, be able to obtain patents for the same invention in multiple countries, through filing applications in individual countries or through multiple and simultaneous patent applications under the Patent Cooperation Treaty (PCT).[25] Through provisions of reciprocity in international conventions (including the Berne Convention) and regional or bilateral agreements, some forms of IPRs such as copyright have been effectively extended to other territories without formalities. The TRIPS Agreement incorporates many provisions from other IP instruments including the Berne Convention and the Paris Convention for the Protection of Industrial Property of 1883.[26]

Conventional forms of IP such as copyright and patents emphasize what is new, rather than pre-existing, in extending protection to particular works or inventions. Though most jurisdictions have preconditions such as 'originality' for copyright, or 'novelty' and 'inventive step' for patents, interpretations vary significantly amongst countries' national courts and patent offices on the thresholds for protection, and may not coincide with a layperson's concept of these terms. The differences are especially apparent when new technology challenges both existing legal rules and ethical standards – for example, in patent claims in relation to the isolation of gene

[23] Council Directive 93/98/EEC of 29 October 1993 harmonizing the term of protection of copyright and certain related rights, OJ No. L 290 (1993), *replaced by* Council Directive 2006/116/EC of 12 December 2006 on the term of protection of copyright and certain related rights (codified version), OJ No. L 372 (2006).

[24] On 23 April 2009, the European Parliament approved a legislative proposal extending the term of copyright protection for sound recordings from fifty years to seventy years after first release. The European Parliament has also requested that the European Commission (EC) evaluate the possibility of a similar copyright term extension for performers and producers in the audiovisual sector. See European Parliament legislative resolution on the proposal for a directive of the European Parliament and the Council amending Directive 2006/116/EC of the European Parliament and the Council on the term of protection of copyright and related rights, 23 April 2009, P6_TA9(2009)0282, available at: http://www.europarl.europa.eu/sides/getDoc.do?pubRef=-//EP//NONSGML+TA+P6-TA-2009-0282+0+DOC+PDF+V0//EN (accessed 3 March 2010).

[25] Patent Cooperation Treaty (Washington,19 June 1970), 1160 U.N.T.S 231, 9 I.L.M 978 (1970), *as amended* 3 October 2001 (*entered into force as amended* 1 April 2002), available at http://www.wipo.int/pct/en/texts/articles/atoc.htm (accessed 3 February 2010).

[26] Paris Convention for the Protection of Industrial Property (1883), *as revised at* Stockholm, 14 July 1967, *and amended* 28 September 1979, 828 U.N.T.S. 303, 21 U.S.T. 1583 (*entered into force* 7 July 1884) [hereinafter 'Paris Convention'], available at: http://www.wipo.int/export/sites/www/treaties/en/ip/paris/pdf/trtdocs_wo020.pdf (accessed 3 February 2010).

sequences,[27] embryonic stem cells, or over genetically modified organisms (GMOs) such as the cancer-prone Harvard 'oncomouse'. Digital technology is further blurring the lines between what is traditionally protectable and non-protectable under copyright laws (see Chapters 7 and 8). Information and communication technologies (ICTs) are expanding the scope of knowledge creation and exchange, with the Internet making way for new 'participatory' forms of creation in terms of remixing and re-contextualizing works. Legal developments are at pains to catch up with these technological and social changes, and may over-compensate when they do through increased standards and enforcement of IPRs to control the flow of creations over these evolving networks.[28] Laws relating to technology protection measures (TPMs) have attracted significant scrutiny. For example, legally prohibiting the circumvention of technology used by IP right owners to 'lock-down' material has been criticized for allowing owners in some cases to block fair use of such material (Hinze 2008; see Chapter 7).

Along with term extension, the overall subject matter covered by IPRs has expanded tremendously over the last century, both within established categories of rights and in relation to new *'sui generis'* rights (i.e. 'of their own kind' or 'unique'). Discussing patent law in the *Diamond v. Chakrabarty* case, the United States Supreme Court held that the scope of patentable subject matter includes 'anything under the sun that is made by man' with the presumption that even a bacterium can be man-made.[29] Some might point out, though, that patents and some other forms of IPRs now border on the protection of the 'natural', covering such material as microorganisms, germplasm, a colour[30] or a scent.[31] 'Novelty' is also increasingly questioned in cases where patents are obtained, for example, for secondary uses of existing drugs (see Chapter 2).

[27] In 1997, the United States Patent and Trademarks Office (USPTO) clarified, controversially, that patent applicants could claim DNA fragments of the kind known as expressed sequence tags (ESTs). However, in 2001, the Office published new rules for DNA-related patent examinations. Patent applications disclosing DNA sequences were required to provide convincing evidence that their utility was specific, substantial and credible. This effectively closed the door on EST claims, and this was confirmed in a 2005 decision at the Court of Appeals for the Federal Circuit. See *In re Fisher*, 421 F.3d 1365 (Fed. Cir. 2005). See Dutfield 2009, p. 222.

[28] Strathern (1996, p. 531) asserts that 'where technology might enlarge networks, proprietorship can be guaranteed to cut them down to size'.

[29] *Diamond v. Chakrabarty*, 447 U.S. 303, 309 (1980).

[30] An example is Klein's patent on an ultramarine (beyond the sea) blue which he called the International Klein Blue (French Patent No. 63471, filed 19 May 1960); Klein apparently 'chose an available pigment but used in its raw form as opposed to having it mixed and compounded chemically' (Kuivski, M. 2006, 'Yves Klein: Killed by his own Immaterial Quest?', unpublished manuscript on art history, available at: http://www.scribd.com/doc/7521564/Yves-Klein-Killed-by-his-own-Immaterial-Quest). See also the discussion of the 'purple pill' in Charlafti 2008.

[31] A sense of the broad range of disparate material which may be affected by IP protection within the bracket of 'industrial property' can be drawn from Article 1(3) of the Paris Convention for the Protection of Industrial Property which notes that: 'Industrial property shall be understood in the broadest sense and shall apply not only to industry and commerce proper, but likewise to agricultural and extractive industries and to all manufactured or natural products, for example, wines, grain, tobacco leaf, fruit, cattle, minerals, mineral waters, beer, flowers, and flour'. In the case of natural products, the line is especially blurred between what is a man-made invention (and thus potentially patentable) and what is merely a discovery of something pre-existing in nature.

Meanwhile, copyright protection has expanded well beyond books, music, plays and sculptures to cover non-aesthetic material such as computer software (now protected within the category of 'literary' works despite their functional nature) and databases. While the legal axiom is that copyright protects 'expressions of ideas' and not the ideas themselves, the line is an especially fine one in the case of databases. The frontiers in the protection of databases are pushed further by *sui generis* laws which are in place in the EU[32] and under consideration in the US (see Ruiz 2004; Box 1.2).[33] These developments signal the endeavour of legislators in some developed countries to protect not only 'original' creations but also the investments in information products and recompilations of existing material (some would say 'facts'). That a lot of 'original' works might be said to be 'recombinations' of other works is a topic explored later in Section 2.

Indeed, the concept of 'originality' has been stretched in some jurisdictions to cover quite mundane subject matter. While courts have alluded to protecting the 'genius' of inventors and creators through IP,[34] Sir Hugh Laddie (1996, pp. 11–12) observed within the UK context that 'one of the problems with copyright law is that, unlike inventions protected by patent or designs protected by registration, the requirements for qualification are so low as to be virtually non-existent'. Noting that a label of instructions placed at the side of a barrel of herbicide was considered a copyright-protected literary work in the case of *Elanco v. Mandops*,[35] he added that:

> No doubt depending on the youth of the literary genius who wrote it, the label will be protected for more than a century and perhaps for as long as a century and half – certainly well beyond the date when for safety or commercial reasons the product has been removed from the market. So one of the troubles with copyright, then, is that it springs up to protect nearly every creation of the human mind, be it ever so trivial.[36] As another member of the judiciary put it, the fact that our system of communication, teaching and entertainment does not grind to a standstill is in large part due to the fact that in most cases infringement of copyright has, historically, been ignored. (Ibid.)

[32] Council Directive 96/9/EC of 11 March 1996 on the legal protection of databases, OJ No. L 077 (1996).

[33] See Collections of Information Antipiracy Act, H.R. 354, 106th Cong. (1999), http://thomas.loc.gov/cgi-bin/query/z?c106:H.R.354: (accessed 15 February 2010). This bill was introduced in the House, marked up and reported by the House Committee on the Judiciary, discharged by the House Committee on Commerce, and placed on the Union Calendar.

[34] Justice Stevens alluded to this concept in the *Eldred v. Ashcroft* case: 'Thus, with regard to copyrights on motion pictures, we have clearly identified the overriding interest in the "release to the public of the products of [the author's] creative genius." And, as with patents, we have emphasized that the overriding purpose of providing a reward for authors' creative activity is to motivate that activity and "to allow the public access to the products of their genius after the limited period of exclusive control has expired."' *Eldred v. Ashcroft*, 537 U.S. 186, 227 (2003) (Stevens, J., dissenting) (quoting *United States v. Paramount Pictures, Inc.*, 334 U.S. 131, 158 (1948) and *Sony Corp. of America v. Universal City Studios, Inc.*, 464 U.S. 417, 429 (1984)).

[35] *Elanco Products Ltd. v. Mandops (Agrochemical Specialists) Ltd.* [1980] R.P.C. 213, [1979] F.S.R. 46 (partially reported) (UK Court of Appeal).

[36] In the UK, the extension of copyright protection to prevent third-party production of three-dimensional objects based on two-dimensional plans also had significant impact on competition for industrially made, non-aesthetic objects (including spare parts of industrial objects, as per *British Leyland Motor Corp. v. Armstrong Patents Co.* [1986] A.C. 577). This was redressed to some extent by the 1988 Copyright, Designs and Patent Act (Laddie 1996, p. 6; see discussion in Cornish & Llewelyn 2003, pp. 557–558).

A song common to persons of all ages – the 'Happy Birthday' song – comes to mind. If the song is still under copyright protection as some claim (see Justice Breyer in the *Eldred* case),[37] then 'copycats' are surely ignored most of the time. Others query whether the song may already have entered the public domain, even though some royalties are still being paid to the alleged rights owners (Brauneis 2008, p. 68).

The story of IP is intertwined with the story of the public domain. Many view the public domain as a critical public resource that free expression and creativity draw from and depend upon (Litman 1990; Cohen 2006). Challenging notions of authorship and 'originality' in IP law, Litman (1990, p. 966) asserts: '[T]he very act of authorship in any medium is more akin to translation and recombination than it is to creating Aphrodite from the foam of the sea . . . in the absence of a vigorous public domain, much of it would be illegal'. Thus, commentators have often focused on the need to 'safeguard' the public domain from the encroachment of IP. In his article 'The Second Enclosure Movement and the Construction of the Public Domain', Boyle (2003, pp. 37–38) argues that there is an 'enclosure of the intangible commons of the mind', comparable to the historical 'first enclosure' of fencing off common land and converting it into private property. He sees evidence of such a second enclosure movement in the expanding scope of IPRs and the steady withering away of limits posed by old restrictions on subject matter, copyright term and exceptions.[38] He says that the 'the old limits to intellectual property rights – the anti-erosion walls around the public domain – are also under attack' (ibid., p. 38).

While the public domain has been articulated in many different ways (see definitions in Samuelson 2006; Suthersanen 2008, p. 4), IP law conventionally treats what is not covered by IP protection as part of the 'public domain'. Belder notes that 'we see the public domain as the reverse image of property, in danger of being overwhelmed by an international policy focusing on world markets and competition' (2007, pp. 51–52; see also Chapter 5). Following one definition: 'The term public domain refers to creative materials that are not protected by intellectual property laws such as copyright, trademark or patent laws. The public owns these works, not an individual author or artist. Anyone can use a public domain work without obtaining permission, but no one can ever own it.'[39] It is also possible to think of aspects of an IP-protected work (e.g. elements subject to fair use) as belonging to the public domain. Boyle (p. 69) suggests, for example, that: 'To the "bundle of rights" conception of property . . . can be counterposed the "bundle of privileges" vision of

[37] *Eldred v. Ashcroft*, 537 U.S. 186, 262 (2003) (Breyer, J., dissenting). The song (originally 'Good morning to you') is said to have been composed in the late nineteenth century by a school teacher and her sister, with the 'Happy Birthday' lyrics appearing in songbooks nearly two decades later (see Brauneis 2008, p. 15). On how a subsidiary of the Warner Music Group came to claim the copyright over the song, and other pieces of the puzzle, see Brauneis 2008.

[38] He cites, as examples, developments in relation to patenting of the human genome, business method patents, the Digital Millennium Copyright Act in the US, trademark anti-dilution rulings, and the European Database Protection Directive (ibid., pp. 37–38). The US Court of Appeals for the Federal Circuit's *In re Bilski* decision in late 2008 was thought to make it far harder to acquire and enforce patents claiming business methods. However, the recent Supreme Court decision on the case does not entirely rule out the grant of process patents over business methods. See *In re Bilski*, 545 F.3d 943 (Fed. Cir. 2008); *Bilski v. Kappos*, No. 08-964, slip opinion at p. 12 (U.S. 28 June 2010) (Kennedy, J.).

[39] Suthersanen (2008, p. 4) quoting 'Copyright and Fair Use, Stanford University Library and Academic Information Resources', available at http://fairuse.stanford.edu/Copyright_and_Fair_Use_Overview/chapter8/8-a.html (accessed 15 February 2010).

the public domain, where we assume, for example, that fair use over a copyrighted work is part of the public domain' (ibid.).

Along with exceptions and limitations to IPRs, the temporal limits for copyright protection are intended to ensure that a copyright-protected work joins the 'public domain' after a period of exclusive rights reserved to the copyright owner. Applying the relatively long copyright term of protection for books to other works such as software calls to question, however, the value of what is ultimately 'returned' to the public domain when protection finally expires.[40] A young computer programmer who writes a new piece of software may generate 'a monopoly which will normally last for over 100 years' (Laddie 1996, p. 10).

Copyright duration and its extension was a huge issue in the US in the *Eldred v. Ashcroft* case, where petitioners unsuccessfully challenged at the Supreme Court the constitutionality of the US Congress's extension of copyright term for all works by twenty years (including existing works, retroactively) through the Sonny Bono Copyright Term Extension Act (CTEA) of 1998.[41] It is notable that in his dissenting statement, Justice Stevens suggested there might be a 'functional equivalent' to 'perpetual copyrights':

> The express grant of a perpetual copyright would unquestionably violate the textual requirement that the authors' exclusive rights be only "for limited Times." Whether the extraordinary length of the grants authorized by the 1998 Act are invalid because they are the functional equivalent of perpetual copyrights is a question that need not be answered in this case because the question presented by the certiorari petition merely challenges Congress' power to extend retroactively the terms of existing copyrights.[42]

The retroactive nature of the CTEA – extending the copyright term not only for new works but also for existing works – was the subject of much controversy.[43] On the question of retroactivity, Justice Stevens observed that 'neither the purpose of encouraging new inventions nor the overriding interest in advancing progress by adding knowledge to the public domain is served by retroactively increasing the inventor's compensation . . . '.[44]

Whether we in fact need to rethink the public domain concept in itself is an important subject examined in Chapter 9. Some point out, for example, that what is in the public domain is not necessarily accessible (Chon 2006; Dinwoodie & Dreyfuss 2006; Gollin 2008). Noting that the 'public domain is more than a place

[40] Quite distinct from literary works such as books, for example, the product cycle for software tends to be short and the copyright term could be said to be 'functionally' perpetual.

[41] As Darnton (2009) notes, this is 'also known as "the Mickey Mouse Protection Act", because Mickey was about to fall into the public domain'. See further 'Free Mickey Mouse', *The Economist*, October 2002, p. 73.

[42] *Eldred*, 537 U.S. at 241 (Stevens, J., dissenting).

[43] It is notable that in their *amici curiae* brief in support of petitioners, fifty-three IP law professors at American universities argued not only that the CTEA's extension of copyright in existing works is a violation of the First Amendment but also that the CTEA's extension of future copyrights is invalid. See *Brief of Intellectual Property Law Professors as Amici Curiae Supporting Petitioners, Eldred v. Aschroft*, 537 U.S. 186 (2003) (No. 01-618), pp. 29–30, available at: http://cyber.law.harvard.edu/openlaw/eldredvashcroft/supct/amici/ip-lawprofs.pdf (accessed 10 March 2010).

[44] *Eldred*, 537 U.S. at 226 (Stevens, J., dissenting).

where the old intellectual property goes to die', Dinwoodie and Dreyfuss (2006, p. 194) suggest that: 'What matters is whether the information a second comer needs is available for use – whether it is in a domain that might be called "the domain of accessible knowledge"'. Discussing this concept, Gollin (2008, pp. 48–51) tries to map 'the accessible domain' in terms of different degrees of accessibility, from the fully accessible to the least accessible (see also Samuelson 2006). Mapping the public domain is no straightforward exercise, and there are significant discussions at WIPO in this direction within the context of implementing the Development Agenda (see Suthersanen 2008).

There is, moreover, a need to rethink public domain concepts in terms of different systems of ownership or a plurality of domains (Boyle 2003; Dutfield 2006; Chander & Sunder 2004; Samuelson 2006; see Chapter 9). It has been said, for example, that definitions of the public domain which assume a dichotomy between public domain and private property rights cannot easily accommodate systems of 'ownership' or rights over intangible material beyond Western property regimes (Dutfield 2006; Belder 2007; see Chapter 5). Thus, some representatives of indigenous peoples have argued that their traditional knowledge (TK) does not fall within the 'public domain' simply because they are not typically subject to 'private rights' (see Deer 2009).[45] These debates reveal differences in approaches not only towards property but also towards innovation. As is seen in various chapters of this book, a challenge for the existing IP systems lies in their interactions with different modes of innovation and ways of viewing creativity.[46] Do IP regimes foment certain modes of innovation but not necessarily other modes (see Chapters 3–5)? It has been argued, for example, that IP regimes such as patents were designed around particular notions of science and innovation, and may not be relevant to all innovative communities.[47]

Meanwhile, concerns over commercialization of their TK and cultural heritage by third parties, whether in terms of pharmaceutical companies scouting traditional medicinal knowledge (TMK) as a resource towards patentable inventions or the copying of indigenous arts and crafts by mass producers, have led custodians of such heritage (including indigenous peoples and local communities guided by customary practices) to grapple with IP. The United Nations (UN) Declaration on the Rights of Indigenous Peoples, adopted by the UN General Assembly in September 2007, refers in its Article 31(1) to the rights of indigenous peoples to 'maintain, control, protect and develop their intellectual property over such cultural heritage, traditional knowledge, and traditional cultural expressions'.[48] At the same time, there are those who are concerned that the application of property concepts to TK and traditional cultural expressions (TCEs), in the course of 'protecting' such material

45 See also the Saami Council arguments in UNDP 2004, p. 93.

46 Innovation does not take place only in universities or the R&D departments of companies but is a way of life for many local communities around the world, including farming communities (see Chapter 3). Technology existed in many forms and within many cultures long before so-called high technology (see Ingold 2000; see also Weber 1992).

47 Boateng (2005, pp. 68–69) notes the cultural bias of scientific perspectives which claim to be value-neutral and universal. See also Biagioli 1999; Bowrey 2006.

48 United Nations Declaration on the Rights of Indigenous Peoples (13 September 2007) 46 I.L.M. 1013 (2007), G.A. Res. 61/295, UN Doc. A/RES/61/295 (2007) [hereinafter 'UNDRIP'], available at: http://www.un.org/esa/socdev/unpfii/documents/DRIPS_en.pdf (accessed 5 February 2010).

from third-party exploitation, may transform the very social relations and processes underpinning the creation of such knowledge and expressions (Leach 2005).[49]

There are now efforts at the international and national levels to devise *sui generis* protection for TK and TCEs (see Chapters 4 and 5). Other 'unique' or *sui generis* forms of protection have already emerged over the years (see Box 1.2). Apart from database rights (discussed earlier), these include rights over integrated computer circuits and plant varieties. Each has a birth story very much shaped by the relative positions and power of stakeholders in the IP matrix (see Chapter 3, on the evolution of plant breeders' rights; see also Dutfield & Suthersanen 2008). As illustrated in various chapters of this book, with new technologies usually comes some re-alignment of the power axis (see Suthersanen 2007). However, the calibration of IP may not always correspond to considerations of social justice and often reflects who has access to the decision-making process and tools (including knowledge about IP) at the international and national levels.

2. Rationales, checks and balances

Natural rights arguments for IP tend to focus on protection of the 'personality' of creators or the idea that a creator has a natural property right in the fruits of his or her intellectual labour (Fisher 2001).[50] The personality-based arguments are most visible in the German and French systems for protecting authors' rights, especially their moral rights (see Chapters 5 and 8). Understanding how particular IP regimes have evolved within different legal traditions and historical contexts is important for a nuanced approach towards IP policy reforms. It is often said that civil law systems protect the natural rights of authors, while common law systems emphasize economic reward and incentives for innovation (cf. Mossoff 2007). In practice, cross-pollination of laws through historical circumstances, regionalism (e.g. under EU harmonization) and multilateral frameworks including TRIPS have blurred many of these distinctions.[51]

While both natural rights and economic rationales for IPRs such as patents and copyright can co-exist in a jurisdiction, the economic rationales tend to prevail in IP-related policy discussions in many countries, as well as in norm-setting activities at the international level. This section first introduces the utilitarian approach to justifying IP, as articulated in seminal literature on IP and economics (notably in Landes & Posner 1989, 2003). This approach focuses on IP as an economic incentive to creators. The overarching idea is that the 'public interest' would be advanced through the accumulation of inventions and other creative endeavours thus incentivized. Utilitarian arguments are said to underpin the US constitutional approach to IP (see Fisher 2001; Sunder 2006; Declaye 2008).

[49] Not only does the extension of IP protection to the traditional realm pose far-reaching challenges for the preservation and innovation of such heritage, but it also raises fundamental questions on the nature of IP and may have transformative effects on how IP is viewed and approached in the future. This issue is explored further in subsequent chapters of this book.

[50] This idea, influenced by John Locke's labour theory of property, can be seen in case law in some common law jurisdictions including the UK and the US (see Locke 1690; Fisher 2001; Guibault 2002). Ginsburg (2007, p. 136) suggests that early copyright law in the UK has some underpinnings in natural rights.

[51] The protection of moral rights, however, remains highly dependent on jurisdictions (see Chapters 5 and 8; see especially Appendix E).

BOX 1.2. ***Sui generis*** **systems**[52]

Integrated Computer Circuits: Layout designs of integrated circuits are not considered to be industrial designs under the laws providing for the registration of industrial designs. This is because they do not determine the external appearance of integrated circuits, but rather the physical location, within the integrated circuit, of each element with an electronic function. Moreover, layout designs of integrated circuits are not normally patentable inventions, because their creation usually does not involve an inventive step. Uncertainty surrounding the protection of layout designs led to the adoption of the *Treaty on Intellectual Property in Respect of Integrated Circuits* under WIPO's auspices on 26 May 1989.[53] While the Treaty has not entered into force, a number of its substantive provisions have been incorporated by reference in the TRIPS Agreement (Article 35). The minimum period of protection for lay-out designs under the TRIPS Agreement is ten years, and is counted from date of filing an application for registration or from 'first commercial exploitation wherever in the world it occurs' depending on national laws (see Articles 38(1) and 38(2)).

(Source: WIPO 2005b, pp. 11–12)

Plant Variety Protection (PVP): Commonly referred to as plant breeders' rights (PBRs), PVP is granted to breeders of new, distinct, uniform and stable plant varieties. Most national laws are based on the International Convention for the Protection of New Varieties of Plants ('the UPOV Convention'),[54] of which almost seventy countries are now parties. Countries' obligations vary with the particular Act of the UPOV Convention they have signed up to (see Chapter 3 on some differences between the 1978 and 1991 Acts). PVP rights normally offer protection for at least fifteen years (counted from granting), although the term is often longer for vines and trees than for annual food crops and ornamental plants. In most respects, the exclusive rights enjoyed by the owner are weaker than for patents. Under Article 27(3)(b) of the TRIPS Agreement, World Trade Organization (WTO) members must grant some form of protection towards plant varieties 'either by patents or by an effective *sui generis* system or by any combination thereof'. Countries thus have significant flexibility to design their own *sui generis* protection for plant varieties (see Chapter 3; see also the discussion on farmers' rights in Chapter 4). Most countries provide for exceptions. These include the freedom to use protected material for further breeding, and the 'privilege' for farmers to save and replant seeds, but not to sell them. In some cases replanting may require remuneration to the right owner, but in many countries no payment is necessary.

Database Protection: EU legislation[55] now provides for *sui generis* protection of databases, preventing unauthorized use of data compilations, even if non-original (CIPR 2002,

(*continued*)

[52] This compilation incorporates text from the listed sources and comments from Graham Dutfield and Joshua Sarnoff.

[53] Treaty on Intellectual Property in Respect of Integrated Circuits (Washington, DC, 26 May 1989), 28 I.L.M. 1477 (1989) (*treaty not entered into force*), available at: http://www.wipo.int/export/sites/www/treaties/en/ip/washington/pdf/trtdocs_wo011.pdf (accessed 24 February 2010).

[54] International Convention for the Protection of New Varieties of Plants (Paris, 2 December 1961), 815 U.N.T.S. 89 (*entered into force* 10 August 1968), *as revised at* Geneva, 10 November 1972, 23 October 1978 and 19 March 1991 [hereinafter 'UPOV Convention'], available at: http://www.upov.int/en/publications/conventions/index.html (accessed 24 February 2010).

[55] Council Directive 96/9/EC of 11 March 1996 on the legal protection of databases, OJ No. L 077 (1996), available at: http://eur-lex.europa.eu/LexUriServ/LexUriServ.do?uri=CELEX:31996L0009:EN:HTML (accessed 9 March 2010).

Box 1.2 (*continued*)

p. 13). This is in addition to any copyright protection for databases which meet the requirement of 'originality' in a country. For the purposes of Council Directive 96/9/EC of 11 March 1996 on the legal protection of databases, 'database' refers to 'a collection of independent works, data or other materials arranged in a systematic or methodical way and individually accessible by electronic or other means' (Article 1(2)). The *sui generis* protection is given to the 'maker of a database which shows that there has been qualitatively and/or quantitatively a substantial investment in either the obtaining, verification or presentation of the contents' (Article 7(1)). It grants the right to 'to prevent extraction and/or re-utilization of the whole or of a substantial part, evaluated qualitatively and/or quantitatively, of the contents of that database' (ibid.). There are also restrictions on 'the repeated and systematic extraction and/or re-utilization of insubstantial parts of the contents of the database' (see Article 7(5)).

Protection for Traditional Knowledge (TK) and Traditional Cultural Expressions (TCEs): A number of countries now have *sui generis* regimes for the protection of TK and/or TCEs (see the definitions and discussion in Chapters 4 and 5). Some countries have *sui generis* laws protecting particular aspects of TK, such as medicinal knowledge (e.g. in the case of Thailand; see Appendix C). In other countries, TK protection is bound up with *sui generis* laws to promote biodiversity (e.g. in Peru), recognizing that such knowledge is often embodied in the plant genetic resources managed by TK custodians (see Chapter 4; see the Convention on Biological Diversity of 1992, Art. 8(j)).[56] TCEs may comprise such expressions as symbols, stories, songs, handicrafts, costumes and even architectural forms. Countries may opt to protect TCEs as part of a holistic protection of TK, or address them through separate legislation. Most countries do not as yet have *sui generis* laws for protecting TK and/or TCEs and have sought to provide such protection through existing IP regimes. Existing forms of IPRs have varying relevance and limitations for the defensive or affirmative protection of such knowledge and cultural heritage (see Chapters 4 and 5). Along with some regional initiatives (e.g. in the Andean Community), there are discussions at international forums including WIPO to elaborate appropriate principles and frameworks for the protection of TK and TCEs.

[56] Convention on Biological Diversity (Rio de Janeiro, 5 June 1992), 1760 U.N.T.S. 79, 31 I.L.M. 818 (1992) (*entered into force* 29 December 1993) [hereinafter 'CBD'], available at: http://www.cbd.int/doc/legal/cbd-un-en.pdf (accessed 3 February 2010).

Addressing the IP clause of the US Constitution,[57] the Court in *Mazer v. Stein* (1954) noted that:

> The economic philosophy behind the clause empowering Congress to grant patents and copyrights is the conviction that encouragement of individual effort by personal gain is the best way to advance public welfare through the talents of authors and inventors in 'Science and useful Arts'.[58]

Within the utilitarian theory, IP is seen as preventing 'free riding' by third parties on the works of individual creators. Landes and Posner (1989, p. 326) suggest that a 'distinguishing characteristic' of IP is its 'public good' aspect:

[57] U.S. Const. Art. I, § 8, cl. 8.
[58] *Mazer v. Stein*, 347 U.S. 201, 219 (1954).

> While the cost of creating a work subject to copyright protection – for example, a book, movie, song, ballet, lithograph, map, business directory, or computer software program – is often high, the cost of reproducing the work, whether by the creator or by those to whom he has made it available, is often low. And once copies are available to others, it is often inexpensive for these users to make additional copies. If the copies made by the creator of the work are priced at or close to marginal cost, others may be discouraged from making copies, but the creator's total revenues may not be sufficient to cover the cost of creating the work. Copyright protection – the right of the copyright's owner to prevent others from making copies – trades off the costs of limiting access to a work against the benefits of providing incentives to create the work in the first place.

Such economic arguments for IP posit that the non-rival and non-excludable nature of information makes IP protection necessary to remedy what would otherwise be 'market failure' in the provision of information as public goods. It is said that, without property rights in the intangible, free riding would drive away the incentives for creators to produce goods embodying information.[59] This would in turn diminish the works available to the public at large and therefore their 'utility' (i.e. happiness or desire fulfilment). Utilitarian arguments have also been explored for trademarks (see Landes & Posner 2003; Scott, Oliver & Ley-Pineda 2008). Scott et al. (2008, pp. 295–296) suggest that:

> From the consumer's perspective, trade marks help reduce the risk and uncertainty of making a purchase... In most manufacturing processes, there is an enormous gap between consumer and the source of the product, making the role of the trade mark all the more important. Consequently, it is not surprising that the traditional purpose of the law has been to stop traders misrepresenting the origin of their goods. Without such legal protection, there would be few incentives for traders to build up goodwill by making good-quality products; and, from the consumer side, the very function of trade marks would be undermined.

Scott et al. argue that 'the justification is straightforwardly utilitarian' in the context of preventing confusion (ibid., pp. 296–297, 305). They qualify, however, that the utilitarian argument is less convincing with respect to the extension of trademark law to prevent dilution of a trademark, and the protection of brand value.[60]

In the case of patents, the utilitarian argument usually put forward is that patents provide economic incentives for technological innovation, while facilitating the disclosure of technical information from inventions (Landes & Posner 2003, pp. 295–333). The idea is that, in the absence of legal protection for an invention, the inventor 'will try to keep the invention secret, thus reducing the stock of knowledge

[59] See Guibault 2002, pp. 12–13, for a summary of the related economic theory, particularly from the Chicago School of Economics. See also Cornish and Llewelyn 2003, pp. 35–41.

[60] On one hand, it could be argued that extended trademark protection is needed to incentivize businesses to build up strong brands, and that 'allowing others to damage these brands, or capitalize on them, would be to lower such incentives' (ibid., p. 296). Scott et al. question, however, 'why it is better to allow them [the brand-owners] to have the exclusive right to sell the associated merchandise and hence to exploit the surplus value of the trade mark... what is the social benefit of allowing only one company to capture this surplus value, especially when doing so may drive up prices and lower quality? By allowing free competition in the exploitation of this surplus value we benefit the consumer' (ibid., p. 297).

available to society as a whole' (ibid., p. 294). Landes and Posner explain that 'the conventional rationale for granting legal protection to inventions . . . is the difficulty that a producer may encounter in trying to recover his fixed costs of research and development when the product or process that embodies a new invention is readily copiable' (ibid.). According to them, a new product may require the developer to incur heavy costs before any commercial application can be implemented, so that a competitor able to copy the product without incurring those costs will have a cost advantage that may lead to a fall in the market price to a point at which the developer cannot recover his fixed costs (ibid.).

An important part of the social bargain in granting the inventor exclusive rights to exploit the invention for a period of time is the disclosure of 'patent information' to the public. The utility of this information to the public, however, is not guaranteed by mere disclosure. Information scientists would be quick to distinguish mere information from knowledge. Bates (2005) defines knowledge as 'information given meaning and integrated with other contents of understanding'.[61] According to her, so-called knowledge in inanimate objects, such as books, is really only information: 'Some or all of that information may ultimately be integrated more or less permanently into the pre-existing knowledge stores' of a person through the act of reading. True 'access to knowledge' thus requires the acquisition or nurturing of tools of interpretation and appropriate contexts to transform mere information into knowledge. In this sense, the utility of patent information to the public is not only determined by such factors as the availability and accessibility of databases and the language in which the information is published; expert know-how, local insights or other tacit knowledge are often needed to decipher the long (and often dry) patent specifications, in order to turn the information into applicable knowledge.

Emphasizing that 'inventors do not need to capture the full social value of their inventions in order to have sufficient incentive to create', Frischmann and Lemley (2006, p. 119) warn, moreover, against excessive compensation to inventors: 'Society needs merely to give them [the inventors] enough incentive to cover the fixed costs of creation that their imitators will not face. Any greater return is at best a mere wealth transfer and at worst wasteful – it does not encourage any more innovation in the field, and it may actually interfere with downstream innovation and distort behavior in the market.' They suggest that 'with changed circumstances and over time, more and more' of the social value attendant on an invention 'will accrue to outsiders who tinker with or repurpose that invention' (ibid., p. 134).[62] In their opinion, it is important to consider the 'spillover' benefits of innovations (i.e. 'uncompensated benefits that one person's activity provides to another') that are often invisible to the market mechanism (ibid., pp. 102, 134).

An overly broad patent claim may end up stifling innovation and competition from non-patent owners, and impede downstream research by 'follow-on' inventors

[61] Bates 2005 (electronic journal article; page numbers not available).

[62] According to Frischmann and Lemley (2006, p. 102), 'spillovers are a "ubiquitous boon for society" because we share a common environment, live in communities, and interact with one another'.

(see OECD 2004; see scientists' open letter to WHO 2006).[63] The impact of 'patent thickets' and patent trolls furthermore demands scrutiny (WIPO 2009, pp. 74–76, paras. 281–282).[64] In calibrating IP policy and provisions, legislators and the courts in a country have to consider and juggle the interests of multiple stakeholders, including other inventors and so-called user innovators. For legislators, basic system design questions present themselves in terms of what subject matter to include in (or exclude from) the system, what qualification criteria to impose (if any) before granting rights, what rights to confer to owners, what rights or privileges to retain for the public, what remedies to allow, what duration to assign rights and how to channel subject matter to one system or another.[65]

There may also be material over which patent grants would be ethically inappropriate or innovations for which access is needed by particular stakeholders (e.g. innovations in health and agriculture; see Chapters 2 and 3). Specific provisions may exist in national patent laws for the exclusion of certain subject matter from patenting (e.g. diagnostic, therapeutic and surgical methods). TRIPS member states may also take into account the protection of '*ordre public* or morality' (TRIPS Agreement, Article 27(2)) in excluding subject matter from patentability (although enactment and interpretations vary between jurisdictions). There are furthermore provisions on what acts would not constitute infringement of a patent, or would provide a defence. For example, there are usually provisions for 'experimental use' or 'research exemptions' in national laws (see Ducor 2001) and compulsory licensing or price controls may be adopted for patented products in specific circumstances (see especially Chapter 2).

These 'built-in' checks and balances for patents and other areas of IP are discussed and evaluated in various chapters of this book. Copyright subject matter is limited, as seen earlier, by the 'idea/expression' distinction and 'originality' requirements. Exceptions or defences to infringement in the form of 'fair use' and 'fair dealing' also provide a filter (though not foolproof: see Chapters 6 and 8) to ensure that certain elements of copyright protected works are available for particular uses by the public without need for authorization from the copyright owners. The contours of such exceptions or defences impact on free expression and creative endeavours by third parties. Exemptions for library and educational use are also crucial to ensure sufficient public access to works, although these flexibilities have not been exploited fully in many countries (see Chapters 6 and 7). Whether formalities

[63] Open letter to WHO Executive Board (signed by 240 scientists from 47 countries) in support of the 'Global Framework on essential health research and development (Draft resolution proposed by Brazil and Kenya)', 25 January 2006, available at: http://www.whoscientistsletter.org/ (accessed 15 January 2010).

[64] As noted in a document prepared for the WIPO Standing Committee on the Law of Patents: 'In general the term "patent thicket" describes a situation where a product involves a web of patents that are owned by a number of different patentees so that a company which wants to commercialize the product is required to "clear" all the patents involved' (WIPO 2009, pp. 74–76). For an explanation on 'patent trolls', see Crain 2009. As he observes: 'Patent trolls are firms that aggregate patents for technology that they usually did not create themselves and do not themselves use, but for which they seek to exact royalty payments from commercial users' (ibid., p. 286). See also Subramanian 2008.

[65] Comment from Brett Frischmann.

are needed for a particular form of IP to subsist in a work also affects the balance between what is protected and what is in the public domain.[66]

With an artillery of levers and bolts, it is perhaps tempting to continually tweak the IP machinery for balancing and fine-tuning the rights of different stakeholders. One inherent difficulty for policymakers in finding the appropriate calibration of IP is that the nature of creative processes is more complex than, and may not in fact be in sync with, some of the assumptions under IP laws about information and innovation. While IP frameworks have tended to emphasize 'authors' and 'inventors' as individual producers of creative works and innovations, many commentators and studies now suggest that innovation is more incremental and collaborative in nature (see Box 1.3; Weber 1992; Ghosh & Soete 2006; IEGBIIP 2008). Increasingly, attention is drawn to the social relations and networks driving innovation.

The valves and controls are, moreover, not found in IP legislation and interpretation alone. The outcome of IP policies also depends on the many interactions between IP laws and other bodies of law as, for example, contract law (see Chapter 8). Copyright assignment by authors to third parties is commonplace. Indeed, many IPRs are in reality held by companies, including multinational corporations, and public or private research institutions such as universities. Contractual agreements may alter the 'bargain' between rights holders and end users as envisaged by IP legislation (Guibault 2002). Other important areas of law interact with IP laws to define the legal boundaries of protection for intangible property. These include such areas as competition, human rights, criminal, torts and privacy law. By way of example, concerns have been raised over the compatibility of patent pools – a possible solution to patent thickets – with competition law (see WIPO 2009, p. 77).[67] The interaction between IP law and human rights law is introduced in Section 4 and further examined in various chapters of this book.

Meanwhile, the internal controls and flexibilities within national IP laws are increasingly circumscribed by the harmonization of IP-related laws (including trade laws) whether at the regional or international level. For example, legal traditions and provisions on IP within member states of the EU are continually being reshaped by regional regulations and decisions, and a mixture of common law and civil law concepts may coexist in a country through this confluence. Internationally, the TRIPS Agreement welds IP protection to the world trade regime, and binds member states of the WTO to a range of minimum standards in IP protection – embracing while adding force to provisions in pre-existing instruments such as the Berne Convention and the Paris Convention. The linkage of IP to trade (and thus trade sanctions) has been deepened through other multilateral instruments and bilateral or regional free trade agreements (FTAs), including those with so-called TRIPS-plus provisions (see Chapters 2, 3 and 7).

[66] In the US, copyright owners had to comply with certain formalities, like notice, registration, renewal and deposit. This meant that the vast majority of works ended up in the public domain quite early on in their lives, and only a small minority of works (typically, those of high commercial value) remained subject to copyright. With the elimination of formalities when the US joined the Berne Convention in 1989, the default flipped such that virtually all works end up presumptively protected by copyright. Comment from Brett Frischmann.

[67] See also Chapter IV(a) of WIPO 2009.

BOX 1.3 Revisiting some assumptions on IPRs, information and innovation

A central idea in utilitarian arguments for IP is the non-excludable and non-rivalrous nature of information. Unlike physical objects, it has been said that information can be used by an infinite number of persons without diminishing the amount of use available to each person. This vision is conveyed in the oft-cited 'candle' metaphor employed by Jefferson to describe 'ideas':

> If nature has made any one thing less susceptible than all others of exclusive property, it is the action of the thinking power called an idea . . . He who receives an idea from me, receives instruction himself without lessening mine; as he who lights his taper at mine, receives light without darkening me. That ideas should freely spread from one to another over the globe, for the moral and mutual instruction of man, and improvement of his condition, seems to have been peculiarly and benevolently designed by nature, when she made them, like fire, expansible over all space, without lessening their density in any point . . . (Thomas Jefferson 1813)

Jefferson also likened ideas to 'the air in which we breathe . . . incapable of confinement or exclusive appropriation' (ibid.). While he thought that 'inventions then cannot, in nature, be a subject of property' (ibid.), IP laws in effect put invisible fences around certain ideas and enable some parties to exclude others from applying or expressing those ideas in certain ways. The utilitarian argument promoted by Jefferson and others in support of patents and copyrights is that the public will ultimately benefit from the new ideas and innovations which are incentivized by these IPRs. It is said that creators lose their economic incentive to create when others 'free ride' on the non-excludable and non-rivalrous nature of ideas and information (Landes & Posner 1989, p. 294).

However, since Jefferson's time, information and other theorists have challenged some of the preconceptions on the nature of ideas and information within IP frameworks. In 'Deconstructing Jefferson's Candle', Opderbeck (2008, p. 35) argues that 'contemporary intellectual property theory has been impoverished by its failure to recognize the stratified nature of reality and the tacit and social dimensions of knowing'.[68] He asserts that:

> From a critical realist perspective, information is not merely an input, a commodity, and/or a code word for a power play. It can be all of those things, but at some level, information also is the skeleton of all human communities. It is in this sense that information is 'infrastructure': we create information that creates communities. (Ibid., p. 49)

An approach to information as not only the creation of individuals but also a fabric of communities and identities may help refocus discussions on IP towards the role of 'social relations' (Sunder 2006, pp. 315–319) and networks in information and knowledge creation as well as diffusion (Benkler 2006; Fitzgerald 2008; Moenius & Trindade 2008). The role of communities in knowledge creation and sharing has long been recognized. Scientific research and technological development, for example, have historically been a matter of confluence and circulation of ideas and their applications (Nuvolari 2005; Ghosh & Soete 2006). Challenging the concept of 'originality', Litman (1990, pp. 966–967) asserts that:

(*continued*)

[68] Opderbeck notes (2008, p. 36): 'The idea that information has a tacit, social dimension suggests a communitarian ethical framework. A robust information policy must consider broadly the ways in which granting or restricting access to information will encourage the extension of communities that promote human flourishing.'

Box 1.3. *(continued)*

> Composers recombine sounds they have heard before; playwrights base their characters on bits and pieces drawn from real human beings and other playwrights' characters; novelists draw their plots from lives and other plots within their experience; software writers use the logic they find in other software; lawyers transform old arguments to fit new facts; cinematographers, actors, choreographers, architects, and sculptors all engage in the process of adapting, transforming, and recombining what is already 'out there' in some other form.

Is there also art in the recombination of existing elements? In 'The Wright Brothers and the Heuristics of Invention', for example, Weber argues that: 'Invention places a much heavier emphasis on synthesis than does normal analytic science. Said in another way: Science prospers by taking apart things that are normally stuck together, and invention prospers by putting together things that are normally apart. To be sure, the development of the airplane involved both modes of thought and action, but there was a great deal of putting together, combining parts in completely new ways. Flight, as with much of invention, is an emergent capability not enjoyed by its parts in isolation'.[69] He suggests, at the same time, that 'invention that is significant takes place on a time scale of months, years, lifetimes, and generations' (ibid.). This makes it 'quite difficult to validate any particular heuristic' or mental step in discovery (ibid.).

While innovation is often boxed as either 'discrete' or 'cumulative', Suthersanen (2008, p. 5) notes that 'in reality . . . a vast majority of scientific and cultural creations, if not all, are built on pre-existing creations and discoveries, and do not represent giant leaps beyond what we already know'. The concept of 'prior art' in patent law does address these concerns to some extent, and is integral in determining whether the requirements of 'novelty' and 'inventive step' or 'non-obviousness' have been met.[70] What is considered as 'prior art' and 'obvious' varies significantly under domestic laws,[71] however, and may not always coincide with the viewpoints of scientists. Polanyi (1983, p. 80) observes that 'the most daring innovations of science spring from a vast range of information which the scientist accepts unchallenged as a background to his problem'. Dinwoodie and Dreyfuss (2006, pp. 195–196) add that:

> The crucial importance of access to prior knowledge is also readily admitted by scientists. Thus, Newton famously wrote to Robert Hooke 'If I have seen further [than certain other men] it is by standing upon the shoulders of giants.' Scientists' own understanding can also be perceived in the Mertonian norms of communalism, universalism, disinterestedness, originality, and skepticism, which create an environment of open science where new work is shared and refined – and, indeed, regarded by scientists as refined because it is shared through, for example, funding and publication processes dependent on peer review.

---

[69] Weber, R. 'The Wright Brothers and the Heuristics of Invention', p. 11 of manuscript on file with author. This is an expanded version of a paper presented at the Conference on Expertise in Context, Humboldt University, Berlin, 21 July 2006.

[70] Dinwoodie and Dreyfuss (2006, p. 196) note that the test of 'inventiveness (non-obviousness) for patent grants is measured by comparing an invention to the knowledge that preceded it'. Along with the 'novelty' requirement which bars patents on material that is already known, used or described in the literature, this test is said to 'force inventors to consult the prior art' (ibid.).

[71] Dinwoodie and Dreyfuss query, for example, the dilution of the 'non-obviousness' test in a number of US court decisions (ibid., p. 202; see also Burk & Lemley 2002, 2003). However, recent US caselaw seen as raising the bar for 'non-obviousness' might suggest a shift in the opposite direction. See, for example, *KSR Int'l. Co. v. Teleflex, Inc.*, 550 U.S. 398 (2007).

The role of social networks and communities (whether real or 'imagined') not only in creating, circulating but also validating information is further exemplified by the Internet (Strathern 2005; Benkler 2006). Scholars in anthropology remind us that comparisons can also be made to social relations, including 'kinship', which underpin creative processes in traditional societies (Strathern 1996, 2005; Leach 2005). Intellectual property law has yet to fully catch up with these ideas, even though its borders are steadily expanding to engulf both new technological and so-called traditional areas.

Looking towards history, several commentators have already pointed out how the powerful industrialized countries of today have been adopting IP policies quite fluidly for centuries in advancing their industrial policies and trade interests (Drahos 1996, 2003; Chang 2002; Drahos & Braithwaite 2002; Chon 2007; Tansey 2008). The UNDP Human Development Report 2001 notes:

> [M]any of today's advanced economies refused to grant patents throughout the 19th and early 20th centuries, or found legal and illegal ways of circumventing them – as illustrated by the many strategies used by European countries during the industrial revolution... They formalized and enforced intellectual property rights gradually as they shifted from being net users of intellectual property to being net producers; several European countries... completed what is now standard protection only in the 1960s and 1970s. (UNDP 2001, p. 102; see further Chang 2002)

Similarly, the US pursued IP policies quite flexibly in the nineteenth century, for example, in providing copyright protection only for its citizens and residents. Rampancy of low-priced copies of British works in the US markets led authors such as Charles Dickens to seek international legal reforms in copyright.[72] With knowledge and cultural products now forming the mainstay of exports from first world countries to the rest of the world in the information age, it is unsurprising that IP protection has become a top agenda in international trade and investment negotiations. In such contexts, IP protection is often framed as a pre-requisite for foreign investment and technology transfer to a developing country or least developed countries (LDCs) (see CIPR 2002, pp. 23–24).

The increasing standardization of IP rules will likely have differential impact for industrialized and developing countries, with further differentiation between the more economically advanced developing countries (such as China, India and Brazil) and those of LDCs or small island developing states (SIDS). As the UNDP Human Development Report 2001 notes of the TRIPS provisions:

> A single set of minimum rules may seem to create a level playing field, since one set of rules applies to all. But the game is hardly fair when the players are of such unequal strength, economically and institutionally. For low-income countries, implementing and enforcing the intellectual property rights regime put stress on

[72] See Lohr, S. 2002, 'New Economy; The Intellectual Property Debate Takes a Page from 19th-Century America', *New York Times*, 14 October 2002. He notes that Charles Dickens – whose 'Christmas Carol' work apparently sold for 6 cents a copy in America versus the equivalent of $2.50 a copy in England – toured the US in 1842 promoting the adoption of international copyright protection. See also Yu 2003, arguing that 'piracy' is not a thing of the past with developed countries.

> already scarce resources and administrative skills. Without good advice on creating national legislation that makes the most of what TRIPS allows, and under intense pressure from some leading countries to introduce legislation beyond that required by TRIPS, many countries have legislated themselves into a disadvantageous position. Moreover, the high costs of disputes with the world's leading nations are daunting, discouraging countries from asserting their rights – hence the importance of ensuring adequate legal aid is provided through the World Trade Organization. (UNDP 2001, p. 105)

Legal commentators have distinguished 'formal' equality in the TRIPS context from 'substantive' equality (Dinwoodie & Dreyfuss 1994; Chon 2007; see Chapter 6). Under the current rubric of trade and IP laws at the international and regional levels, developing countries and LDCs have a lot less flexibility in designing IP laws to suit their local contexts, including the absence (or low levels) of IP protection for certain sectors or activities. Whereas the home-grown IP policies and laws in many now-industrialized countries are continually fine-tuned (Gold & Morin 2009) and reflect one form of rationale or another towards IP protection (see Fisher 2001), many developing countries and LDCs are not necessarily tailoring IP protection to their local contexts and needs. In some cases, laws have been 'imported' from other jurisdictions without the necessary safeguards and 'balances' existent in those jurisdictions (see Gold & Morin 2009).

More scrutiny is needed of the impacts of IP enforcement on human development, including the increasing resort to criminal sanctions to resolve civil disputes (Laddie 1996; Tapper 2004; see Chapter 7).[73] Rens et al. (2006, p. 30) furthermore caution about the indiscriminate usage of the term 'piracy' to refer to unauthorized reproduction of copyrighted material. The term is often heard in the media and foreign trade bodies in relation to projected losses of first-world countries from mass copies of information goods (or developing countries on misappropriation of genetic resources).[74] Exploring the label of 'piracy' as a 'rhetorical tool of persuasion used to change perceptions and thinking' about IP, Drahos and Braithwaite (2002, pp. 29–38) suggest that:

> Piracy remains a powerful evaluative word. To be called an intellectual property pirate is to be condemned. In a world where the attention spans are divided by the media into ten-second sound bites it is the perfect word to use on TV, videocassettes, newspaper headlines and the radio. The received folk memory of 'pyrates and rovers' on the sea does the rest. (Ibid., p. 29)

Drahos and Braithwaite suggest, at the same time, that there is no universally accepted legal definition of 'piracy', and that most jurisdictions in the world do not use the term 'piracy' in connection with IP as a term of legal art (ibid., pp. 27–28).[75] Rens et al. (2006, p. 30) note, moreover, that the boundaries between legitimate and

[73] For recent developments in various jurisdictions including the US, China and Australia, as well as European Parliament initiatives to harmonize the provision of criminal remedies in Europe, see Sugden 2009.

[74] Demonstrating that the figures (e.g. on recording industry losses from piracy) do not withstand economic analysis, Watt (2004, p. 160) notes that 'the types of numbers that have been bandied about recently are clear evidence that scant attention has been paid to the economist's word'.

[75] For a distinction between 'pirating', 'counterfeiting' and bootlegging' see *Regina v. Johnstone* [2003] UKHL 28 (Lord Nicholls), para. 1.

illegitimate copying are not always clear. Examining case studies of access to educational materials in parts of Africa, they add that 'the monopolies granted by the copyright system (and access gaps created as a result) pose a moral challenge for the blanket treatment' of unauthorized reproduction as an 'illegitimate practice'(ibid.).

Is there a systematic approach to consider and evaluate the social impact of IP, in order to better calibrate national policies and laws according to local contexts and needs? Searching for frameworks to evaluate existing policies and arguments for IP in terms of their underlying assumptions on human welfare, the legal literature has turned increasingly to the human development approach (see e.g. Sunder 2006; Chon 2006; Aoki 2007; Dutfield & Suthersanen 2007; Sunder 2008; Gollin 2008; de Beer 2009). A key component of the human development approach is that of viewing well-being in terms of enhancing capabilities, in lieu of other concepts of well-being such as utility (happiness, desire fulfillment) or opulence (income, commodity command) [see Appendix A for these distinctions]. This 'capability approach' developed by Sen, Nussbaum and others over the past two decades is introduced in the next section along with some ideas for application within the context of IP and innovation. It is qualified, at the same time, that the capability approach is only one aspect of the human development paradigm. The latter also reflects some elements from the 'basic needs' approach to development which emerged in the 1970s (see Haq 1995; Stewart 1996; Qizilbash 2006) and has evolved to embrace concepts of fundamental freedoms and human rights (see Section 4; UNDP 2000).

3. Capabilities and innovation

As highlighted by Robeyns (2005, p. 93), 'the capability approach is a broad normative framework for the evaluation and assessment of individual well-being and social arrangements, the design of policies, and proposals about social change in society' (see also Comim, Qizilbash & Alkire [eds.] 2008; Chiappero-Martinetti [ed.] 2009). According to Robeyns, the main characteristics of the capability approach are its highly interdisciplinary character, and the focus on plural or multidimensional aspects of well-being (ibid., p. 93). This approach highlights the difference between means and ends, and between substantive freedoms ('capabilities') and outcomes ('achieved functionings') (ibid.). These concepts are briefly introduced here. While the capability approach has been applied in many different fields (most notably, development),[76] little literature to date deals with its application to innovation and IP. This section aims to bridge some of the gaps, while highlighting further areas for research.

A common thread between the capability approach and the basic needs approach to development is the critique that income measures alone cannot capture the multidimensional nature of human well-being. Such limitations were recognized early in the inception of national income accounting (McGillivray 2007, p. 6; Hicks and Streeten 1979, p. 568). Sen (1999, pp. 69–70) observes that:

> At the practical level, perhaps the biggest difficulty in the real-income approach to well-being lies in the diversity of human beings. Differences in age, gender, special talents, disability, proneness to illness, and so on can make two different persons

[76] See literature review in Clark 2006. See also the bibliography of new work on the capability approach in the *Journal of Human Development and Capabilities* (published annually in issues since 2005).

> have quite divergent opportunities of quality life even when they share exactly the same commodity bundle. Human diversity is among the difficulties that limit the usefulness of real-income comparisons for judging different persons' respective advantages.

The basic needs approach placed emphasis on the fact that 'the poor require access to certain basic goods and services, and that income may not be a necessary or sufficient condition for their provision' (Harkness 2006, pp. 88–89). Sen's capability approach looks beyond income measures and access to commodities to focus on how human beings are able to 'function'.[77] As Sen (1999, pp. 74–75) explains:

> The concept of 'functionings', which has distinctly Aristotelian roots, reflects the various things a person may value doing or being...A person's 'capability' refers to the alternative combinations of functionings that are feasible for her to achieve. Capability is thus a kind of freedom: the substantive freedom to achieve alternative functioning combinations (or, less formally put, the freedom to achieve various lifestyles).

The distinctions between capabilities and other measures of well-being such as income, commodity command or utility are helpfully summarized by Clark (2006, pp. 33–35; see extract in Appendix A). Sen's own articulation of the human development approach in recent years has emphasized the concept of 'development as freedom'.[78] While Sen has given examples of 'essential capabilities' and 'freedoms' in his writings, he has avoided endorsing a unique list of capabilities as objectively valid (see Sen 1993, p. 47; Clark 2006, p. 35).[79] Nussbaum, in contrast, sets out to list 'core' capabilities, the lack of which makes it difficult for an individual to be functioning in a 'truly human way' (Nussbaum 2000, p. 72; see Chapter 6). The idea of this list is not to enclose the broad and evolving range of human capabilities within strait-jackets nor to provide weights to each item, but to offer a framework for constitutional reforms within a country to facilitate human development.[80] In Gasper's (2007, p. 55) words, Nussbaum's list 'consciously builds a basis for core rights, as parts of a legal constitution, to give a set of entrenched priorities without which we would leave too much open to domination by the powerful'.

[77] As Sen (1985, p. 19) clarifies, 'Commodity command is a *means* to the end of well-being, but can scarcely be the end itself'. He adds that to think otherwise is to 'regard goods as valuable in themselves and not for (and to the extent that) they help the person' (ibid.). In discussing public access to IP-protected goods, for example, this approach would draw attention to whether those goods are relevant to building capabilities and, if so, whether the public is able to access those goods on reasonable terms and use them in ways that improve their capabilities (this is explored later).

[78] Given that the term 'freedom' is open to many broad interpretations, it is important to understand how Sen nuances the 'perspective of freedom' in different contexts (see Sen 1999, pp. 13–34), in particular his treatment of 'capability as a kind of freedom' (ibid., p. 75). Sen's capability approach focuses on 'positive freedom' to achieve valuable capabilities; he also discusses the significance of 'negative freedom' for his approach (see Sen 1985b, pp. 216–220).

[79] An oft-heard critique of Sen's capability approach is that it does not have a built-in set of values with which to determine and measure capabilities (see Nussbaum 1988, p. 176; Qizilbash 1998, p. 54; Clark 2006). According to Sen, on the contrary, value selection and discrimination are an intrinsic part of the capability approach, so that *a priori* specifications of capabilities should be avoided. Rather than endorse a universal list of essential capabilities, Sen has argued that societies should develop their own lists based on a process of public reasoning and debate (Sen 2004 and 2005; Robeyns 2005; Fukuda-Parr 2008, p. 238).

[80] Nussbaum (2000, p. 97) sees a close relationship between her notion of core capabilities and human rights as understood in contemporary international discussions (see Section 4 of this chapter).

The capability approach makes an analytical distinction between the means and the ends of well-being and development. Only the ends have intrinsic importance, whereas means are 'instrumental to reach the goal of increased well-being, justice and development' (Robeyns 2005, p. 95). According to the capability approach, these ends should be conceptualized 'in terms of people's capabilities to function, that is, their effective opportunities to undertake the actions and activities that they want to engage in, and be whom they want to be' (ibid.). However, as Robeyns (2005, p. 95) points out, in concrete situations these distinctions between means and ends often blur, since some ends are simultaneously also means to other ends (see also Clark 2002, 2005). She provides the example of the capability of 'being in good health', which is not only an end in itself, but also a means to other capabilities such as the capability to work. Another commonly cited example of a capability key to the attainment of other capabilities is the capability of being literate or educated. The different capabilities considered in chapters within this book are thus interlinked.

The means and ends analysis is a familiar one in IP-related contexts. Those who take a consequentialist view of IP would argue that IP should be viewed as a means towards achieving larger social goals, although they may articulate these goals differently.[81] For example, the IEGBIIP Report envisages a 'New IP' era where IP is viewed as a 'servant to, and not master of, values such as equity and fairness' (IEGBIIP 2008, p. 14).[82] Notably, one of the principles set out in the Adelphi Charter on Creativity, Innovation and Intellectual Property,[83] is that 'laws regulating intellectual property must serve as means of achieving creative, social and economic ends and not as ends in themselves'. The Charter thus emphasizes an evidence-based approach to IP policy and law-making.[84] This is echoed by commentators who clarify that the success of IP regimes is to be measured by their impact on human development (i.e. the achievement of the ends) and not by economic growth figures alone or often-used indicators of 'innovation' such as the number of patents filed in a country (i.e. measuring at most the means; see Chon 2006; IEGBIIP 2008). Discussing the implementation of the WIPO Development Agenda, de Beer (2009, p. 5) argues that: 'Economic growth remains an essential indicator of development; however, it is no longer accepted as the only relevant metric for measuring progress'.

[81] At the same time, the ends and means analysis of IP may perhaps obscure 'authorial moral rights' and other claims based on natural rights which are 'quite irrespective of whether conceding such rights advances wider socio-economic goals' (pers. comm. Graham Dutfield, 22 June 2009). Some 'natural rights' proponents may well place the protection of IP as an end in itself. Yet other legal commentators have suggested that IP could be treated as both a means and ends to human development (Sunder 2007, p. 122).

[82] The report notes that the 'increased appetite for protection' under that 'Old IP' era greatly expanded the pool of what was protected under IP, but 'did not necessarily raise levels of innovation, creativity, or the new products that go along with it' (IEGBIIP 2008, p. 13).

[83] The Charter has been written by an international group of artists, scientists, lawyers, politicians, economists, academics and business experts. This Charter sets out new principles for copyrights and patents, calling on governments to apply a new 'public interest' test to ensure that everyone has access to ideas and knowledge, and that intellectual property laws do not become too restrictive. It is a project of the Royal Society for the Encouragement of Arts, Manufactures and Commerce (RSA). See their website at http://www.adelphicharter.org/default.asp (accessed 15 January 2010).

[84] The onus, according to the Charter, is on those advocating an expansion of IP rights to clearly demonstrate through 'a rigorous analysis' that such change will promote people's basic rights and economic well-being.

Within a utilitarian approach to IP, societal goals are typically articulated in terms of the maximization of 'utility', understood usually as happiness or pleasure, and in some cases as the fulfilment of desires (see Sen 1999, p. 67). This interpretation of utilitarianism underlines much legal thinking (Sunder 2006). Chon (2006, p. 2832) notes, on the other hand, that 'in the parallel universe of development economics things have moved on in past decades'. In development studies, for example, the capability approach as 'an alternative to raw utilitarianism in the measurement of social welfare' has gained important ground (ibid.).[85] Clark (2006, p. 32) observes that 'over the last decade Amartya Sen's "capability approach" has emerged as the leading alternative to standard economic frameworks for thinking about poverty, inequality and human development generally'. Distinguishing the capability approach from utility-based approaches to measuring welfare, Sen (1993, p. 48) explains:

> In fact, the more challenging part of the claim in favour of the capability approach lies in what it denies. It differs from the standard utility-based approaches in not insisting that we must value *only happiness* (and sees, instead, the state of being happy as one among several objects of value), or *only desire fulfilment* (and takes, instead, desire as useful but imperfect evidence – frequently distorted – of what the person herself values). (Original emphasis)

In regarding the 'capability set' as the primary space for evaluating human well-being,[86] the capability approach is also distinct from other, non-utilitarian, approaches to well-being which emphasize resources or primary goods as value-objects (Sen 1993, pp. 38, 48). The capability approach views resources as relevant 'only in terms of the impact [they have] on functionings and capabilities' (ibid.).[87] Likewise, variables relating to primary goods are considered 'only derivatively and instrumentally' within the capability approach and 'only to the extent that these goods promote capabilities' (ibid.).

While the utilitarian theory for copyright, as discussed earlier, assumes that the public 'benefits' or gains 'utility' by the sheer expansion of works incentivized by copyright, a human development perspective would go further in examining the types of works incentivized by market dynamics and how they impact human

85 Both mainstream and development economists have also sought to redefine utility-based approaches to measuring well-being (see Kingdon and Knight 2006). Surveying the increasing inter-disciplinary research involving, for example, social psychology in defining 'happiness' and 'subjective well-being', Frey & Stutzer (2006, p. 18) observe: 'The big progress in the measurement of individual welfare makes it tempting to pursue the old dream of maximizing aggregate happiness as a social welfare function…However, we postulate that the appropriate approach is not to maximize aggregate happiness directly in seeking to improve outcomes by direct interventions. We rather see the role of happiness research in seeking to improve the nature of the processes'.

86 This set represents the 'various alternative combinations of beings and doings any one (combination) of which the person can choose' (Sen 1993, p. 38). While Sen provides a mathematical rendition of the capability set in terms of '*n*-tuples of functioning', it has been said that most discussions and applications of the capability approach dispense with mathematical formalization, which is not strictly necessary for most purposes (Clark 2006, p. 35).

87 For example, within the IP-related context of access to genetic resources and 'benefit-sharing' under the Convention on Biological Diversity, a capability approach would emphasize the sharing of benefits in ways that ultimately improve local capabilities. This goes beyond considerations of monetary benefits to embrace arrangements for local communities, for example, to participate directly in research efforts and for the research results to be shared with them. See Chapters 3 and 4.

capabilities. As Sen (1999, pp. 60–63) acknowledges, utilitarian arguments have the merit of drawing attention to the '*well-being* of the people involved when judging social arrangements and their results' even if utility-centred approaches may be inadequate in evaluating these social arrangements. At the same time, according to Sen, utilitarian arguments are limited by their 'distributional indifference' and the 'neglect of rights, freedoms and other non-utility concerns' (ibid., p. 62).[88] Within the IP context, Sunder (2007, p. 122) observes that:

> The traditional utilitarian understanding of intellectual property focuses on incentivizing the creation of more knowledge goods... But utilitarianism does not ask who makes the goods or whether the goods are fairly distributed to all who need them. A broader understanding of intellectual property, as both an end and means of development, recognizes the importance of not just producing more knowledge goods, but also of participating in the process of knowledge creation.

Since it is the market which ultimately determines demand and incentivizes supply of many IP-protected goods, it may be argued moreover that the nature of what is incentivized by this system may be significantly skewed by disparities in purchasing power. This is evidenced, for example, by trends relating to so-called 'neglected or resurgent diseases' prevalent in developing countries (or poor sectors of developed countries) that have presented a lacuna in private pharmaceutical investment – a gap increasingly filled through philanthropic initiatives, intergovernmental programmes and public-private partnerships (see Chapter 2). Arguing for the provision of public goods beyond what the private markets can foster, Sen (1999, p. 128) has observed that: 'The rationale of the market mechanism is geared to private goods (like apples and shirts), rather than to public goods (like the malaria-free environment)'. While innovations can improve human well-being, the argument for IP as an incentive for innovation begs the question of whether the products or works incentivized under the IP system are ultimately relevant to building the capabilities of individuals and communities around the world. Is there some mismatch between goods currently incentivized by IP and the needs and priorities of developing countries (and LDCs) for human development? This is explored in detail in the various chapters of this book dealing with health, agriculture, education and the protection of cultural endeavour and heritage. Chapter 3 suggests, for example, that the agricultural technology and food products currently supported by IP regimes including patents and PVP may in certain contexts unhinge traditional agricultural systems and farming practices more suited to local environments (see also Tansey 2008). Discussing implications of IP for education and other capabilities in developing countries, Chon (2007, p. 476) observes that:

> The model of development of freedom centres human capability through the provision of basic needs in the areas of education, health, and nutrition, because these lead to the 'enhancement of human freedom, which is both the main object and the primary means of development' (Sen 1999)... Simply put, the growth model of development prioritizes the innovation mandate of intellectual property, while

[88] He notes (1999, p. 62) that the 'utilitarian calculus tends to ignore inequalities in the distribution of happiness (only the sum total matters – no matter how unequally distributed)'; furthermore, 'the utilitarian approach attaches no intrinsic importance to claims of rights and freedoms (they are valued only indirectly and only to the extent they influence utilities)' (ibid.).

the freedom model of development emphasizes its multi-dimensional aspects. In the latter paradigm, intellectual property not only stimulates innovation but also protects knowledge goods that enhance human capabilities, which in turn build national capacity for innovation.[89]

Other legal commentators are increasingly engaging the language of capabilities and freedoms in their analysis of IP. Gollin (2008, p. 343) suggests that 'the IP system, in driving the innovation cycle, serves at least in part as an instrument of individual freedom and choice'. In his opinion:

> Creators choose whether to give their innovations away or to restrict access with IP rights. For example, the individual freedom inherent in the IP system gave rise to open access communities in software, science, and entertainment, which are expressions of choice by many individuals. The owner of IP rights can trade these assets with others, and acquire more in the process of pushing an innovation out into society. On the other hand, the exclusivity of IP rights restricts the freedom of choice of those who seek access to an innovation. A creator or competitor who lacks access to an innovation lacks the freedom to use it as she chooses... The freedom of an IP owner to exclude others has limits. (Ibid.)

The challenge for policymakers is in drawing the limits to these exclusive rights. In a working paper, *Capabilities, Spillovers, and Intellectual Progress: A New IP Consequentialism?*, Frischmann explores how the capability approach might intersect with the spillovers theory.[90] He argues that IP can be and is used to *leverage* the non-rival nature of information and promote capabilities (ibid.). Importantly, his approach makes a distinction between the first-party and third-party effects of capabilities and suggests that the latter are unappreciated in the literature (ibid.).[91] He observes that '[l]aw-supported or facilitated spillovers can be seen, at least in an important subset of cases, as social investments in the capabilities of others'. As he explains:

> Some social investments in capabilities are, or may be or should be, made through legal structures that allocate freedoms to access and use resources that are necessary to participation in certain types of activities. These 'investments' may constitute spillovers in themselves because the legally allocated freedoms constitute benefits (either real value or option value) for resource users that are external to resource production and exchange. The participatory capabilities may include basic capabilities essential to survival and a good life but perhaps also more advanced capabilities essential to a productive and/or engaged life.[92] (Ibid.)

89 Chon comments: 'Focusing on capabilities helps us think about goals for the system as a whole. Should IP take into account health measures? Education measures?... in addition to or instead of pure innovation measures?' (pers. comm. Margaret Chon, 21 December 2008).

90 Frischmann, B. '*Capabilities, Spillovers, and Intellectual Progress: A New IP Consequentialism?*' (manuscript on file with author).

91 Frischmann claims that capabilities are socially valuable or meaningful not only because of what they mean for individuals but also because of what they mean for the well-being of others in the community. This is an important observation in the context of IP where the shared resources are said to be non-rivalrous and often inputs into socially relevant activities.

92 Frischmann adds that: 'When individuals choose to exercise their participatory capabilities, participation may yield spillovers vis-à-vis the impacts of such participation on interdependent social activities or systems. The enabled capabilities are thus (i) privately valuable in the sense that people have reason to value participation, even if they do not necessarily or always exercise the capability to participate, and (ii) socially valuable in the sense that when exercised, participation generates societal benefits' (ibid.).

Thinking in terms of 'social investments in capabilities' may provide policymakers with additional parameters, for example, in determining the boundaries of exceptions or defences such as 'fair use' in copyright (or exemptions under patent law). While conventional IP policies tend to approach IP-protected intangible works in terms of markets and commodities to which public access needs to be balanced with private proprietary rights, what matters for human development is whether such access is provided in a way that enhances human capabilities. Frischmann suggests that:

> As fair use illustrates rather well, some IP-supported or facilitated spillovers can be seen as direct social investments in the capabilities of others. Fair use allows for some unlicensed use and thus enhances the capabilities of users to participate in activities like criticism, commentary, news reporting, teaching, scholarship, and research. In essence, fair use reflects a social investment in public capabilities that is accomplished *by* spillovers – third party (user) benefits external from the initial production decision or subsequent transactions . . . Arguably, the social investment made via fair use is not only accomplished *by* spillovers but also to some degree, *for* spillovers – social benefits from being part of a more capable community as well as social benefits associated with the user-generated public good outputs (e.g. more ideas and expression). (Ibid.; original emphasis)

The capabilities facilitated by fair use include those for self-expression. In discussing her list of capabilities essential to human well-being, Nussbaum (2000, p. 78) mentions capabilities relating to 'senses, imagination and thought', and whether one is ultimately 'able to use imagination and thought in connection with experiencing and producing self-expressive works and events of one's own choice, religious, literary, musical, and so forth'. Apart from the more-often discussed capabilities (e.g. in relation to health, food security or education), we thus need to take into consideration the enhancement of other related capabilities including those for creative and free expression. Where the line is drawn, for example, within copyright exceptions or defences (including fair use or fair dealing) for parodies, satires and other arguably transformative uses of copyright-protected works, will have a palpable impact on the expressive capabilities of third parties (see further Chapter 8).

That IP consists of rights over intangible creations of the mind[93] means that it can never quite be divorced from considerations of cultural liberty and free expression. Arguably, as human development advances over time in any society, the exceptions to IP ought to evolve to meet the more and more sophisticated needs for self-expression of its populace. This would require a continual re-evaluation of IP as a mechanism for individuals not only to access the fruits of innovation of others, but also towards their own engagement in (not so visible and thus less quantifiable) creative processes and knowledge building (see further Sunder 2008; Netanel 2008). This approach ties in with a regard of individuals not simply as passive 'beneficiaries' of economic and social processes – 'patients' as Sen has put it[94] – but also as

[93] At the same time, IP controls the flow of many tangibles including medicines, books, computers, etc.

[94] Sen, A.K. 2008, Keynote Address at book launch of *Pioneering the Human Development Revolution: An Intellectual Biography of Mahbub ul Haq* (edited by K. Haq & R. Ponzio), 17 October 2008, Hank Shannon Conference Room, One United Nations Plaza, New York.

'agents' of change (Alkire 2002; Clark 2006; Fukuda-Parr 2008). A strong case may be made, for example, for so-called user innovators as active and important contributors towards improvements in inventions attributed to others (see Strandburg 2008, 2009; Frischmann & Lemley 2006, pp. 116–117; OECD 2007) as, for example, a doctor who adapts and improves medical technology in daily work with patients, and farmers who help to improve seeds (see Chapter 3). But the examples need not stop there. As discussed earlier in Section 2, the divide between creators and 'consumers' of IP-protected works are not clear-cut in many fields,[95] and the literature is increasingly pointing towards the role of social relations and networks in driving innovation. Within the context of the Internet, for example, a great deal of attention is being turned to 'user participants' as contributors to the creative economy (Howkins 2001; OECD 2007; United Nations 2008).

Cornish and Llewelyn (2003, p. 6) note that IPRs 'protect applications of ideas and information of commercial value'. IP ownership enables some protagonists to exclude certain actions by other participants. In doing so, it arguably creates or upholds 'value' and the opportunity to trade certain information goods (see Gollin 2008, p. 39). Given that no 'author' and 'inventor' in fact starts from a blank sheet, but rather builds on collective knowledge, is there ultimately an element of arbitrariness (or pragmatism) where the law currently reserves to some participants 'ownership' of IPRs while rendering others in the chain of creation mere 'users' and members of the public?

Can thinking in terms of capabilities help to reorient IP policies towards a better recognition of social networks as drivers of innovation? Some of the 'individualist' orientation of the capability approach has itself come under significant scrutiny and questioning (see Evans 2002; Robeyns 2005; Stewart 2005; Ibrahim 2006; Deneulin 2008, p. 48; Alkire, Qizlbash & Comin 2008, pp. 6–7; Alkire 2008, pp. 34–41). Robeyns (2005, pp. 109–110) observes that:

> ...contemporary mainstream economics is structurally unable to account for group membership on people's well-being, and does not acknowledge the limits of individual rational agency. But is this also the case for the capability approach? While some capability theorists, like Sen (1999, 2002), have a great belief in people's abilities to be rational and to resist social and moral pressure stemming from groups, other writers on the capability approach pay much more attention to the influence of social norms and other group-based processes on our choices and, ultimately, on our well-being (for example, Alkire 2002; Nussbaum 2000; Iversen 2003; Robeyns 2003). There is thus no reason why the capability approach would not be able to take the normative and constitutive importance of groups fully into account.[96]

[95] This is observed not only in the sciences but also in the arts. In literary theory, for example, there is an increasing tendency to view readers not only as the passive recipient or audience of a cultural work, but also as an active agent in interpreting, contextualizing and, in a sense, 'completing' or 'continuing' the work (see Chapter 8).

[96] She adds that: 'To fully understand the importance of groups, the capability approach should engage more intensively in a dialogue with disciplines such as sociology, anthropology, history, and gender and cultural studies. Disciplinary boundaries and structures make this kind of dialogue difficult, but there is no inherent reason why this cannot be done' (Robeyns 2005, pp. 109–110).

While Sen (2002, pp. 84–85) concedes the 'social dependence of individual capabilities', Deneulin (2008, p. 110) suggests that 'there remains a strong rationale for including irreducibly social goods in the informational basis of development for reasons that go beyond their intrinsic value to the lives of individuals' (see Gore 1997). She focuses her discussion on the relevance to the capability approach of 'structures of living together', that is, 'structures which belong to a particular historical community, which provide the conditions for individual lives to flourish, and which are irreducible to interpersonal relations and yet bound up with these' (Deneulin 2008, p. 111). Exploring how social structures and social capital influence human capabilities,[97] Ibrahim (2006, p. 409) calls for 'shifting the focus of the analysis from the individual to the collectivity'. Asserting that 'all human capabilities are in fact socially dependent', she emphasizes the need to integrate the concept of 'collective capabilities' into the analysis of capabilities (ibid., pp. 404, 409). She defines 'collective capabilities' as 'newly generated capabilities attained by virtue of [the] engagement [of individuals] in a collective action or their membership in a social network that helps them achieve the lives they value' (ibid., p. 404).[98]

Cross-disciplinary work adapting the capability approach to focus on 'group' and 'collective' capabilities[99] are relevant to our discussion of IP, not least if we are to take on board the role of communities (including those guided by customary practices) and other social networks in innovation. Discussing the concept of 'group' capabilities, Stewart (2005, p. 188) notes: '[I]n addition to the more individualistic capabilities a person may possess, their (often many) group affiliations affect their well-being... since people are essentially social their social networks form an important part of their total wellbeing'.[100] She suggests that groups are important to individual well-being and to enlargement of valuable capabilities in three ways: firstly, group membership and group achievements affect people's sense of well-being; secondly, groups are important instrumentally in determining efficiency and resource shares; and thirdly, groups influence values and choices and hence the extent to which individuals choose to pursue valuable capabilities for themselves and for others (ibid.).

While the capability approach offers some interesting avenues for considering the social impact of IP, further studies on the role of social networks and group

97 Social capital has been defined as the 'norms and networks that enable people to act collectively' (Woolcock & Narayan 2000, p. 226) or 'the glue that holds societies together' (Serageldin 1996, p. 196, quoted in Ibrahim 2006, p. 409).

98 Ibrahim (2006, p. 404) argues that collective capabilities 'are not simply the sum (or average) of individual capabilities, but rather new capabilities that the individual alone would neither have nor be able to achieve, if he/she did not join a collectivity' (see also Comim & Carey 2001, p. 17; cf. Stewart 2005, p. 192).

99 Scholars differ in their definitions of 'group' and 'collective' capabilities (see Ibrahim 2006, p. 403). Stewart (2005, p. 192), for example, explains that group capabilities are 'made up of individual capabilities – indeed they are the average of the capabilities (and sources of capabilities) of all the individuals in the selected groups – but the focus here is on the group achievements and inequalities (or horizontal inequalities) because it is these that constitute powerful group grievances, which in turn can lead to group mobilization' (cf. Ibrahim 2006, p. 404). It is important to note that Stewart defines 'groups' quite broadly as 'ways of categorising people in ways that represent common affiliations or identities' (2005, p. 186).

100 Stewart qualifies that: 'We should note that there can be a direct negative impact – the constricting effects of families or communities – as well as the positive consequences. The point is not that all effects are positive, but that they are important, for good or ill...' (ibid. p. 188).

dynamics in innovation may also help to illustrate the relevance of studying 'group' and 'collective' capabilities in discussing human well-being and development.

4. Multiple ways of viewing development

The human development approach is intertwined with various perspectives on development, many of which can contribute to a rethinking of welfare assumptions under IP law. Indeed, Sen (1993, p. 48) emphasizes the deliberate 'incompleteness' of the capability approach, which renders it 'consistent and combinable with several different substantive theories' and, arguably, value systems.[101] This qualification is particularly relevant in the context of IP and human development, where cultural perceptions not only of IP but also of property in general may vary (Alford 1995), and the priorities of stakeholders are differentiated both amongst and within countries. Indeed, differences in interpretation and selection of values (and thus what capabilities to give weight to in an evaluation of existing IP-related policies and structures) mark many ongoing debates surrounding IP. This renders the pluralist and multidisciplinary nature of the capability approach all the more relevant in IP-related contexts.

While the capability approach is a starting point for the present study, the different chapters attempt to combine ideas and frameworks from different disciplines on specific subjects relating to IP, in a commensurable and accessible way. The human development paradigm embraces many social theories and perspectives beyond the capability approach. Notably, several authors of this volume have equally looked to human rights to inform IP reforms (see especially Chapters 3, 4, 7 and 8).

4.1. Rights-based and other approaches to development

A human rights-based approach (HRBA) serves an important normative role in development policy, and has gradually been mainstreamed over the past decades into the programmes of international development organizations. Before discussing what this 'rights-based' approach to development implies in the IP context, it is helpful to explore the linkages between human rights and human development goals.

Theorists approach the relationship between human development and human rights in different ways. Nussbaum (1997a; 2000, pp. 96–101; 2003), for example, holds the view that human rights might be seen in terms of the attainment of 'combined capabilities'. Capabilities, as she sees them, extend over 'the same terrain covered by both the so-called first-generation rights (political and civil liberties) and the so-called second-generation rights (economic and social rights)' (2000, p. 97;

[101] Importantly, Sen (1993, p. 49) notes that: '[I]t may be a mistake to move on relentlessly until one gets to exactly one mechanism for determining relative weights, or – to turn to a different aspect of the 'incompleteness' – until one arrives at exactly one interpretation of the metaphysics of value. There are substantive differences between different ethical theories at different levels, from the meta-ethical (involving such issues as objectivity) to the motivational, and it is not obvious that for substantive political and social philosophy it is sensible to insist that all these general issues be resolved *before* an agreement is reached on the choice of an evaluative space'.

see also 1997a). She adds that 'all rights, understood as entitlements to capabilities, have material and social preconditions, and all require government action' (1997b, p. 21). As Nussbaum (2000, p. 97) points out, 'because the language of rights is well established, the defender of capabilities needs to show what is added by this new language'.[102] According to Sen, the two concepts – human rights and capabilities – go well together, 'so long as we do not try to subsume either concept entirely within the territory of the other' (2005, p. 163; 2004).[103]

Fukuda-Parr (2009, p. 80) observes that the fields of human rights and human development 'have developed complementary sets of analytical tools and action approaches that can be deployed to meet the common goal of securing human dignity and freedom'. Drawing from Nussbaum's comparison of capabilities with human rights, Fukuda-Parr explains that:

> ...we need the concept of capabilities and functionings to evaluate how societies are faring, to be able to make comparisons between the past and the present, between countries, and so on. The role of human rights on the other hand has a different focus, to help develop ethical norms that guide designs on institutional arrangements.[104] (Ibid., p. 96)

Significantly, the UNDP Human Development Reports treat human rights and human development as conceptually distinct but sharing a common vision and purpose – to secure the freedom, well-being and dignity of all people everywhere (see UNDP 2000, p. 1). Under this approach, the two frameworks are viewed as 'mutually reinforcing' (ibid.). Meanwhile, it has been observed that human rights and IP as bodies of law developed in 'virtual isolation' of each other (Helfer 2008; 2003, p. 48),[105] even though many ethical concerns relating to IP are closely connected to human rights and ideas of 'natural rights' have arguably influenced both bodies of law (see Afori 2004). Some commentaries emphasize the potential role for human rights to influence IP policy, legislation and interpretation (Afori 2004; Ovett 2006a; Haugen 2007b; Sun 2007). While an exhaustive description of human rights provisions relevant to IP is beyond the scope of this chapter, one might highlight the right to health (see Chapter 2),[106] the right to food (see Chapter 3),[107] the right

[102] This book explores, among other things, how a human development perspective could complement or add to the language of human rights within the context of IP reforms.

[103] Sen has qualified, for example, that the capability approach can help to deal with the 'opportunities' aspects of human rights, but not the procedural aspects (Sen 2004, 2005).

[104] Fukuda-Parr (2009, p. 88) asserts that since human rights are subject to binding legal obligations and accountability processes in international treaty bodies, they have 'a unique instrumental power'. She suggests a need to draw on Sen's work on capabilities in addressing current issues in the implementation of HRBA (ibid., p. 77).

[105] Encouraging IP students to train in human rights law, and vice versa, may help to reduce some of the perceived gaps between the two areas of law.

[106] The right to health is enshrined in Article 12 of the International Covenant on Economic, Social and Cultural Rights (New York, 16 December 1966), 993 U.N.T.S. 3, 6 I.L.M. 360 (1967), G.A. Res. 2200A (XXI), UN Doc. A/6316 (1966) (*entered into force* 3 January 1976) [hereinafter 'ICESCR'], available at: http://www2.ohchr.org/english/law/cescr.htm (accessed 3 February 2010). For other instruments and documents of relevance to the right to health, see Chapter 2; see also Ovett 2006b.

[107] See Article 11 of the ICESCR, as interpreted by Committee on Economic, Social and Cultural Rights (CESCR) 1999, *General Comment No. 12: The right to adequate food*, UN Doc. E/C.12/1999/5 (12 May 1999), available at: http://www.unhchr.ch/tbs/doc.nsf/0/3d02758c707031d58025677f003b73b9 (accessed 3 February 2010). See discussion in Chapter 3; Rajotte 2008.

to education (see Chapters 6 and 7)[108] and the right to freedom of expression (see Chapter 8). The latter right extends to the freedom to seek, receive and impart information and ideas of all kinds.[109] Equally relevant are human rights provisions and instruments dealing with so-called cultural rights, minority rights and indigenous peoples' rights (see Chapters 4, 5 and 8).

Overlapping with these and other human rights is the right to development.[110] In its Declaration on the Right to Development, the UN General Assembly affirmed: 'The right to development is an inalienable human right by virtue of which every human person and all peoples are entitled to participate in, contribute to, and enjoy economic, social, cultural and political development, in which all human rights and fundamental freedoms can be fully realized' (Article 1).[111] States have the 'primary responsibility for the creation of national and international conditions favourable to the realization of the right to development' (Article 3).

The 'cultural rights' under human rights instruments are highly pertinent to IP, and some aspects are introduced here (see discussion in Chapter 8; Prott 1998; Donders 2007). Article 27(1) of the Universal Declaration of Human Rights of 1948 (UDHR)[112] states that: 'Everyone has the right freely to participate in the cultural life of the community, to enjoy the arts and to share in scientific advancement and its benefits'. The 'right of everyone to take part in cultural life' is reflected in Article 15(1)(a) of the International Covenant on Economic, Social and Cultural Rights of 1966 (ICESCR). The Committee on Economic, Social and Cultural Rights (CESCR) has recently published its General Comment No. 21[113] aimed at clarifying the nature of this right.[114] While the General Comment does not explicitly mention IPRs, some of its implications for IP-related topics are addressed in Chapters 5 and 8 of this

108 See Article 13 of the ICESCR; see also Article 28 of the Convention on the Rights of the Child (New York, 20 November 1989), 1577 U.N.T.S. 3, 28 I.L.M. 1456 (1989), G.A. Res. 44/25, UN Doc. A/44/49 (1989) (*entered into force* 2 September 1990) [hereinafter 'CRC']. See Chapters 6 and 7.

109 See Article 19 of the International Covenant on Civil and Political Rights (New York, 16 December 1966) 999 U.N.T.S. 171 and 1057 U.N.T.S. 407, 6 I.L.M. 368 (1967), G.A. Res. 2200A (XXI), UN Doc. A/6316 (1966), (*entered into force* 23 March 1976) [hereinafter 'ICCPR'], available at: http://www2.ohchr.org/english/law/ccpr.htm (accessed 3 February 2010). See also Articles 13 and 17 of the CRC.

110 See Office of the High Commissioner on Human Rights (OHCHR), 'Background on the Right to Development', http://www2.ohchr.org/english/issues/development/right/index.htm (accessed 1 May 2010).

111 United Nations Declaration on the Right to Development (4 December 1986), G.A. Res. 41/128, UN Doc. A/RES/41/128 (1986), available at: http://www.un.org/documents/ga/res/41/a41r128.htm (accessed 10 January 2010).

112 Universal Declaration of Human Rights (Paris, 10 December 1948), G.A. Res. 217A (III), UN Doc. A/810 (1948) [hereinafter 'UDHR'], http://www.un.org/en/documents/udhr (accessed 29 March 2010).

113 Committee on Economic, Social and Cultural Rights (CESCR) 2009, *General Comment No. 21: Right of everyone to take part in cultural life (art. 15, para. 1 (a), of the International Covenant on Economic, Social and Cultural Rights)*, UN Doc. E/C.12/GC/21 (21 December 2009), available at: http://www2.ohchr.org/english/bodies/cescr/comments.htm (accessed 1 February 2010).

114 Each of the six UN human rights treaty-monitoring bodies, including the Committee on Economic, Social and Cultural Rights, periodically publishes documents known as General Comments or General Recommendations, which provide guidelines for States Parties on the interpretation of specific aspects of the human rights treaty of concern to the particular committee. General Comments clarify the content of Covenant rights in more detail, may outline potential violations of those rights and offer advice to states parties on how best to comply with their obligations under the treaties. All General Comments are accessible through the website of the Office of the High Commissioner for Human Rights. See http://www.ohchr.org/EN/HRBodies/Pages/HumanRightsBodies.aspx (accessed 15 January 2010).

book. The right to the enjoyment of the benefits of scientific progress and its applications is enshrined in Article 15(1)(b) of the ICESCR and is also the subject of significant scrutiny (Chapman 2002).

Whether IPRs can be viewed and justified as human rights in themselves has been a matter of keen debate (Idris 2004; Chapman 2002; Haugen 2005a, 2007a, 2007b; Helfer 2007; Gollin 2008). Much attention has focused on a number of provisions in human rights instruments protecting the 'material and moral interests' of authors. Article 27(2) of the UDHR provides that: 'Everyone has the right to the protection of the moral and material interests resulting from any scientific, literary or artistic production of which he is the author'. This right is reiterated in Article 15(1)(c) of the ICESCR which refers to 'the right of everyone... to benefit from the protection of the moral and material interests resulting from any scientific, literary and artistic production of which he is the author'. The latter is a human right according to Resolution 2000/7 of the Sub-Commission on the Promotion and Protection of Human Rights:

> The right to protection of the moral and material interests resulting from any scientific, literary or artistic production of which one is the author is, in accordance with article 27, paragraph 2, of the Universal Declaration of Human Rights and article 15, paragraph 1 (c), of the International Covenant on Economic, Social and Cultural Rights, *a human right, subject to limitations in the public interest.*[115] (Emphasis added)

While Article 27(2) of the UDHR and Article 15(1)(c) of the ICESCR have often been cited as justifications for IPRs such as copyright as a species of human rights (Idris 2003, p. 241; Hugenholtz & Okediji 2008), such a view has been challenged by General Comment No. 17 of the CESCR on Article 15(1)(c) of the ICESCR.[116] Emphatically distinguishing IPRs from the human right to the protection of moral and material interests of authors under Article 15(1)(c), the CESCR notes that:

> The right of everyone to benefit from the protection of the moral and material interests resulting from any scientific, literary or artistic production of which he or she is the author is a human right, which derives from the inherent dignity and worth of all persons. This fact distinguishes article 15, paragraph 1 (c), and other human rights from *most legal entitlements recognized in intellectual property systems.* Human rights are fundamental, inalienable and universal entitlements belonging to individuals and, under certain circumstances, groups of individuals and communities. Human rights are fundamental as they are inherent to the human person as such, whereas intellectual property rights are first and foremost means by which States seek to provide incentives for inventiveness and creativity,

115 Sub-Commission on the Promotion and Protection of Human Rights, Intellectual Property Rights and Human Rights, Sub-Comm. Human Rights Res. 2000/7, UN Doc. E/CN.4/Sub.2/RES/2000/7 (17 August 2000), available at: http://www.unhchr.ch/Huridocda/Huridoca.nsf/0/c462b62cf8a07b13c12569700046704e?Opendocument (accessed 5 February 2010).

116 Committee on Economic, Social and Cultural Rights (CESCR) 2005, General Comment No. 17: *The right of everyone to benefit from the protection of the moral and material interests resulting from any scientific, literary or artistic production of which he or she is the author* (article 15, paragraph 1 (c), of the Covenant), UN Doc. E/C.12/GC/17 (12 January 2006), available at: http://www.unhchr.ch/tbs/doc.nsf/7cec89369c43a6dfc1256a2a0027ba2a/03902145edbbe797c125711500584ea8/$FILE/G0640060.pdf (accessed 3 February 2010).

> encourage the dissemination of creative and innovative productions, as well as the development of cultural identities, and preserve the integrity. (CESCR 2005, para. 1; emphasis added; see also para. 2)

General Comment No. 17 stresses (in para. 3) that 'it is therefore important not to equate intellectual property rights with the human right recognized in article 15, paragraph 1 (c)'. Exploring the judicial nature of general comments by human rights committees such as the CESCR, Haugen (2007a, p. 55) notes that a general comment can never be an authoritative interpretation in accordance with Article 31 (para. 3) of the Vienna Convention on the Law of Treaties 1969, 'simply as it does not involve the state parties'. At the same time, he points out that 'a general comment must be considered to be the best effort to outline the content of specific provisions, carried out by an international body comprised of internationally recognized experts'. In his view, a general comment can be said to be the most authoritative clarification of a human rights provision (ibid.).

In referring to 'entitlements' belonging also to 'groups of individuals and communities', General Comment No. 17 leaves the door ajar for an interpretation of the protection of TK and cultural heritage as a matter of human rights (para. 3). Article 31(1) of the UN Declaration on the Rights of Indigenous Peoples (UNDRIP), adopted by the UN General Assembly in September 2007,[117] seems to go further in recognizing explicitly the right of indigenous peoples to protect their 'intellectual property' over their 'cultural heritage, traditional knowledge and traditional cultural expressions'. Is the IP protection of TK and TCEs increasingly being framed as a part of human rights? While the UN Declaration is not, strictly speaking, legally binding on State Parties, it has significant normative value, and has already been incorporated into some national laws.[118] Wiessner (2009, p. 5) adds that some of the rights stated in the Declaration may already form part of customary international law (which is binding), and 'others may become the *fons et origo* of later-emerging customary international law' (see also Anaya & Wiessner 2007).

Meanwhile, it is interesting to note that companies are also availing themselves of human rights recourse in some jurisdictions in relation to IP disputes. Exploring whether human rights law might be the 'new innovation frontier', Helfer (2008) discusses three recent cases[119] before the European Court of Human Rights (ECHR) confirming that IP falls within the scope of 'possessions' protectable under Article 1

[117] United Nations Declaration on the Rights of Indigenous Peoples (13 September 2007), 46 I.L.M. 1013 (2007), G.A. Res. 61/295, UN Doc. A/RES/61/295 (2007) [hereinafter 'UNDRIP'], available at: http://www.un.org/esa/socdev/unpfii/documents/DRIPS_en.pdf (accessed 3 February 2010).

[118] For example, Act No. 3760 of 7 November 2007 granted legal status in Bolivia to the UNDRIP. See Information from the government of Bolivia to the Permanent Forum on Indigenous Issues, fourth session, New York, 21 April – 2 May 2008, UN Doc. E/C.19/2008/5/Add.3. The document notes within the Bolivian context that 'accordingly, the Declaration no longer has solely moral and political force but also legal force, in view of its binding nature' (ibid, p. 11). In Belize, a Supreme Court decision in November 2007 cited the UNDRIP directly in recognizing the customary land rights of two Mayan villages. See *Aurelio Cal. v. Attorney General of Belize*, Supreme Court of Belize, Claim No. 171/172, paras. 131–134 (2007). See further Campbell and Anaya 2008.

[119] See *Dima v. Romania*, no. 58472/00, § 87, 16 November 2006; *Melnychuk v. Ukraine* (dec.), no. 28743/03, § 8, ECHR 2005-IX; *Anheuser-Busch Inc. v. Portugal* [GC], no. 73049/01, ECHR 2007-I; see also *Anheuser-Busch Inc. v. Portugal*, no. 73049/01, 11 October 2005. These case decisions can be found on the ECHR's online caselaw database, available at http://www.echr.coe.int/ECHR/EN/Header/Case-Law/HUDOC/HUDOC+database/. They are discussed in detail in Helfer 2008.

of Protocol No. 1 to the European Convention on Human Rights 1950.[120] This provision has been likened to a 'right to property', though the latter remains controversial under international law (see Robertson & Merrills 1996, pp. 37, 125; Council of Europe 2007, p. 1).[121] Since the entitlement under this Article extends to 'every natural or legal person', companies can claim protection under this human rights provision. The latter was the case in *Anheuser-Busch Inc. v. Portugal*, for example, where the North American brewing company of 'Budweiser' beer claimed before the ECHR that the Portuguese government's refusal to allow registration of 'Budweiser' as its trademark in Portugal was an interference with the company's entitlement to 'peaceful enjoyment of possessions' under Article 1 of Protocol No. 1. While the ECHR found in that case that there was no interference with the applicant company's right to peaceful enjoyment of its possessions under Article 1 of Protocol No. 1, it nevertheless confirmed that the Article is 'applicable to intellectual property'.[122]

As Emberland (2006, p. 5) notes, 'there is a recurrent and highly contentious discussion on the appropriateness of opening up human rights law to corporate persons and the business community'.[123] This is a trend requiring more scrutiny. In

120 European Convention for the Protection of Human Rights and Fundamental Freedoms (Rome, 4 November 1950), 213 U.N.T.S. 221, 312 E.T.S. 5 (*entered into force* 3 September 1953), *as last amended by* Protocol 11, E.T.S. 155 (Protocol 11 *entered into force* 1 November 1998) [hereinafter 'European Convention of Human Rights'], available at: http://conventions.coe.int/Treaty/EN/Treaties/html/005.htm (accessed 3 February 2010). Article 1 of Protocol No. 1 (1952) to the European Convention on Human Rights explicitly provides that 'every natural or legal person is entitled to the peaceful enjoyment of his possessions'. Helfer (2008, p. 8) comments that 'disagreement among European governments over the inclusion of a property rights clause in the treaty as well as the scope and extent of protection it provides' is reflected in the placement of the relevant Article on 'peaceful enjoyment of possessions' in Protocol No. 1 rather than in the Convention itself, along with the absence of any mention of the word 'rights' in Article 1.

121 Article 17(1) of the non-binding UDHR provides that 'everyone has the right to own property alone as well as in association with others', while Article 17 (2) provides that 'no one shall be arbitrarily deprived of his property'. This language was notably not incorporated, however, in the binding ICESCR and ICCPR subsequently adopted by nation states as it proved impossible to reach agreement between countries on a definition of this right (see Robertson & Merrills 1996, p. 37; Council of Europe 2007, p. 1). There are regional human rights instruments which incorporate what is akin to a right to property (see Robertson & Merrills 1996, pp. 125, 203, 250).

122 *Anheuser-Busch Inc. v. Portugal* [GC], no. 73049/01, §§ 72, 78 and 87, ECHR 2007-I. The question before the Court was whether 'this conclusion also applies to mere applications for the registration of a trade mark' (ibid., §72). Anheuser-Busch Inc. argued before the Court that it enjoyed the protection under Article 1 upon application to register the trademark in Portugal. The Grand Chamber held that: 'It is true that the registration of the mark – and the greater protection it afforded – would only become final if the mark did not infringe legitimate third-party rights, so that, in that sense, the rights attached to an application for registration were conditional. Nevertheless, when it filed its application for registration, the applicant company was entitled to expect that it would be examined under the applicable legislation if it satisfied the other relevant substantive and procedural conditions. The applicant company therefore owned a set of proprietary rights – linked to its application for the registration of a trade mark – that were recognised under Portuguese law, even though they could be revoked under certain conditions. This suffices to make Article 1 of Protocol No. 1 applicable in the instant case . . . '. See *Anheuser-Busch Inc. v. Portugal* [GC], no. 73049/01, § 78, ECHR 2007-I.

123 He emphasizes (2006, p. 3) that in this respect, the European Convention of Human Rights differs from regional and global arrangements such as the closely related ICCPR and the American Convention on Human Rights 1969 given that it offers wide-ranging protection for business entities such as companies in addition to not-for-profit organizations and natural persons. See ICCPR and American Convention on Human Rights (Costa Rica, 21 November 1969), 1144 U.N.T.S. 123, 9 I.L.M. 99 (1970) (*entered into force* 18 July 1978), available at: http://www1.umn.edu/humanrts/oasinstr/zoas3con.htm (accessed 3 February 2010).

discussing who might benefit from authors' rights as human rights, General Comment No. 17 (para. 17) explicitly excludes corporations and other legal entities from the scope of protection within Article 15(1)(c) of the ICESCR. Helfer (2007, p. 993) suggests that this 'represents a profound departure from Anglo American copyright laws, which have long recognized that legal entities can enjoy the status of authors of intellectual property products'. Despite other important clarifications intended in General Comment No. 17, debate also seems to linger over the relationship between human rights and IPRs.[124] While some commentators see limitations in a human rights approach to reforms surrounding IP (Hugenholtz & Okediji 2008), others have suggested ways forward (Ovett 2006a; Helfer 2007; Beutz Land 2009). The following remark by Okediji (2007, pp. 372–373) is pertinent in terms of future directions:

> [T]he human rights narrative must seriously re-engage the content of specific human rights guarantees and determine whether intellectual property rights *as they exist and in light of the conditions that produced them* can ever truly be reconciled with the core principles of international human rights law, which requires state and global attention to local conditions affecting the realization of improved social conditions. (Original emphasis)

Meanwhile, there is room for more in-depth studies on how principles in human rights law to balance and reconcile different human rights really intersect with IP-related concerns. The Vienna Declaration and Programme of Action unanimously adopted by states at the (second) World Conference on Human Rights reiterates the principle that 'all human rights are universal, indivisible, interdependent and interrelated' (para. 5).[125] Some elements involved in approaching and balancing these elements are explored in Chapter 3 of this book focusing on the right to food. Among other things, the chapter discusses parameters and mechanisms for the implementation of human rights obligations by States (see also Donders 2007).

How potential conflicts between treaties (e.g. the ICESCR and the TRIPS Agreement) are resolved in international law is also relevant in apprehending the relationship between IP and human rights (see Haugen 2007b). Recognizing potential conflicts between human rights instruments and the TRIPS Agreement,[126] the Sub-Commission on the Promotion and Protection of Human Rights has

[124] General Comment No. 17 leaves some ambiguities (see Ovett 2006b; Haugen 2007a, p. 60; Helfer 2007, pp. 992–994). Helfer (2007, p, 992) suggests, for example, that: 'The Committee's "core obligations" approach to authors' rights leaves many issues unresolved. Most notably, it does not define the content of the "moral and material interests" which states are required to "respect, protect, and fulfill"'. He adds that the General Comment does not 'specify whether – and, if so, how – a human rights framework for authors' rights differs from the legal rules contained in intellectual property treaties and domestic legislation' (ibid.).

[125] World Conference on Human Rights, Vienna Declaration and Programme of Action (25 June 1993), UN Doc. A/CONF.157/23 (1993), available at: http://www.unhchr.ch/huridocda/huridoca.nsf/(symbol)/a.conf.157.23.en (accessed 15 January 2010). On the interdependence and indivisibility of human rights, see especially Eide 2007, pp. 13–14.

[126] The Sub-Commission noted that actual or potential conflicts exist between the implementation of the TRIPS Agreement and the realization of economic, social and cultural rights in relation to, inter alia: 'impediments to the transfer of technology to developing countries, the consequences for the enjoyment of the right to food of plant variety rights and the patenting of genetically modified organisms, "bio-piracy" and the reduction of communities' (especially indigenous communities') control over their own genetic and natural resources and cultural values, and restrictions on access to patented pharmaceuticals and the implications for the enjoyment of the right to health'.

emphasized (in its Resolution 2000/7) the 'primacy of human rights obligations over economic policies and agreements' (para. 3), requesting governments to 'integrate into their national and local legislations and policies, provisions, in accordance with international human rights obligations and principles, that protect the *social function* of intellectual property' (para. 5; emphasis added). Significantly, the Sub-Commission also requested intergovernmental organizations to integrate such provisions into their policies, practices and operations (para. 6).[127] By drawing attention to the 'social function' of IP, the Sub-Commission invites further exploration of what that social function might entail in particular contexts. Linking this social function to the enhancement of specific human capabilities – such as the capabilities relating to education, health or free expression – may present a palpable approach towards IP policy and law reforms. It has also been argued that the concept of capabilities could help to shift the debate away from the apparent deadlock between those who currently support access to knowledge (A2K) as a human right and those who defend the moral and material interests of authors as human rights.[128]

As a Development Agenda is being elaborated, interpreted and implemented in WIPO in relation to IP, there is much that human rights and human development perspectives could do to enrich the discussion (see Ovett 2006a). This includes the ongoing work of human rights bodies on the right to development.[129] While promoting the 'protection of IP throughout the world' is within the mandate and objectives of WIPO,[130] the very purpose of a Development Agenda evolving at WIPO would be towards broadening the prevalent understanding of 'IP and development' to embrace further considerations of ethics and social justice, particularly in assessing the differential development needs and cultural contexts of countries and stakeholders. The Agreement between the UN and WIPO of 17 December 1974 refers to WIPO as 'being responsible for taking appropriate action in accordance with its basic instrument, treaties and agreements administered by it, *inter alia*, for promoting creative intellectual activity and for the transfer of technology related to industrial property to the developing countries *in order to accelerate economic, social and cultural development*' (Article 1; emphasis added). The Development Agenda is discussed further in Chapter 9. The human development perspective presents an

127 Specifically, it requested the WTO and the Council of TRIPS 'during its ongoing review of the TRIPS Agreement, in particular, to take fully into account the existing State obligations under international human rights instruments' (ibid., para. 8).

128 Chon has remarked that 'the capabilities approach gets us past "rights talk" and into a more pragmatic, instrumental policy space that is consistent with the prevailing IP paradigm'. She adds that 'the capabilities approach helps us to understand that the discourse is not about duelling rights but about what the goals (e.g. the Millennium Development Goals [MDGs]) can be for global public goods production facilitated by IP' (pers. comm. Margaret Chon, 21 December 08).

129 See Office of the High Commissioner on Human Rights (OHCHR), 'Background on the Right to Development', http://www2.ohchr.org/english/issues/development/right/index.htm (accessed 1 May 2010).

130 See Convention establishing the World Intellectual Property Organization (Stockholm, 14 July 1967), 828 U.N.T.S. 3, 21 U.S.T. 1749 (*entered into force* 26 April 1970), *as amended on* 28 September 1979, available at: http://www.wipo.int/export/sites/www/treaties/en/convention/pdf/trtdocs_wo029.pdf (accessed 3 February 2010). According to Article 3(i) of the Convention, the objectives of the Organization are 'to promote the protection of intellectual property throughout the world through cooperation among States and, where appropriate, in collaboration with any other international organization'.

important reminder that the term 'development' should not be equated simply with 'economic development' or 'IP development'.[131]

At the same time, it is important to recognize that recent development thinking has moved on from a polarity between the 'economic growth school' and the so-called 'people-centred' school and has become more complex and nuanced (Fukuda-Parr 2008). It has been said that development strategies today combine elements from various discourses including those that emphasize economic growth and market efficiency as priority policy objectives, the basic needs approach and the human rights approach, as well as a 'local first' approach 'committed to the communit[ies] and their livelihoods and priorities' (Fukuda-Parr 2008, p. 251).[132] Noting how policy controversies tend to 'coalesce around the tensions and contradictions between these discourses', Fukuda-Parr suggests that:

> Some of the most contentious issues in trade liberalization concern TRIPS and access to medicines, or child labour where there are contradictions among impacts on growth, basic needs of the poor, human rights such as decent work, and local livelihoods. Similarly, an issue like the new technology of genetically modified seeds is controversial because it can promote growth, but its impact on the basic needs of the poor is unclear, and it can disrupt local livelihood systems. (Ibid.)

While the different 'development' terminologies may seem a matter of semantics to some, they do frame and translate into development policies and programmes at the international and national levels with far-reaching impacts on lives and livelihoods. In UNDP's recent report on *Indigenizing development*, Ramos, Guerreiro Osorio and Pimenta (2009, p. 4) emphasize how ideas of 'development with identity' have sprung up as a reaction to perceived negative effects of some large-scale development efforts on particular segments of society, including in some contexts, indigenous peoples. A lot more work is needed to put these ideas into action (ibid.).[133] As Ramos et al. observe:

> There are no easy ways to bring acceptable development to indigenous peoples. Besides the central issue of land rights, two other key problems must be tackled: information and participation. Development makes wide use of statistics and socioeconomic indicators ... access to information is still the Achilles heel of indigenous development. The traditional indicators of development are mute about spheres of life that are important for indigenous peoples.[134] (Ibid., p. 5)

[131] See, for example, the full-fledged 'IP Development Plan' signed in 2008 by the Republic of Ghana with WIPO.

[132] Summarizing Copestake, J. 2007, 'How Relevant is Well Being to International Development Policy and Practice'? paper presented at the *International Conference of Well-Being in Developing Countries*, University of Bath, UK, 28–30 June 2007, available at: http://www.welldev.org.uk/conference2007/final-papers/plenary/JGC-WeD-plenary-d2-paper.pdf (accessed 21 December 2008).

[133] Note the special theme of 'Indigenous Peoples: Development with Culture and Identity' at the Permanent Forum on Indigenous Issues, Ninth Session, 19–30 April 2010. See http://www.un.org/esa/socdev/unpfii/en/session_ninth.html (accessed 10 January 2010).

[134] Note the ongoing work by indigenous peoples' organizations and partner institutions in identifying indicators relevant to measuring the well-being of indigenous peoples (see especially Indigenous Peoples' International Centre for Policy Research and Education [TEBTEBBA] 2008).

These concerns come alive in many areas overlapping with IP, for example, in the intersection between IP and the preservation or legal protection of bio-cultural heritage, including the TK and TCEs of indigenous peoples and local communities; the clarification of farmers' rights in agriculture (see Chapter 3); the access of poor sectors in both developed and developing countries to medicines (see Chapter 2); or the encouragement of local artists and creative endeavours to promote cultural diversity (see Chapters 5 and 8). To promote social justice, policies in IP and development must take on the concerns of both formal and informal sectors within nation states, and address the interests of marginalized groups. The protection of TK, for example, is a concern not only central to the sustainable livelihoods, cultural identity and survival of indigenous peoples, but also pertinent to other local communities such as farming communities (see Chapters 3 and 4). How community-based approaches to development can be further supported by concepts of capability expansion also remains an area to be fully explored. Indigenous peoples' representatives have argued, for example, that human development definitions should extend to address the capabilities not only of 'individuals and groups', but also of 'communities and peoples'.[135] They call for new concepts and disaggregated data on human development to reflect the well-being of indigenous peoples within national boundaries.[136]

Tracing the evolving concepts of development since the 1950s, Clark (2002, p. 19) further notes the increasing emphasis in international and national policies on 'sustainability' of development. The latter has been defined as 'development that meets the needs of the present without compromising the ability of future generations to meet their own needs' (UN 1987, para. 1). Such models of development take into account inter-generational equity. The UNDP *Human Development Report 2007/2008*, by addressing issues relating to 'climate change', also explicitly recognizes that 'development cannot be divorced from ecological and environmental concerns' (UNDP 2007, p. 28). Thinking in terms of these various nuances in development strategies is particularly helpful in IP-related arenas, where examples of the different development approaches mentioned earlier are at work simultaneously in reshaping the IP landscape.[137] Significantly, these various ways of viewing development have all played a part in informing the Millennium Development Goals (MDGs) (see Chapter 6, Box 6.1).[138]

[135] Remarks by Victoria Tauli-Corpus at 'Human Development and Indigenous Peoples', Focus Group Discussion between Representatives of Indigenous Peoples' Expert Group and UNDP, 11 January 2010, New York.

[136] See the Summary on the Focus Group Discussion between Representatives of Indigenous Peoples' Expert Group and UNDP, 11 January 2010, New York, available at: http://hdr.undp.org/en/media/IP_Experts_Meeting_HDR_2010_Jan2010.pdf (accessed 1 March 2010); see also UN 2009.

[137] For example, the protection of TK may be seen not only in terms of human rights attenuation (see UN Declaration on the Rights of Indigenous Peoples 2007, Article 31), but also in terms of a 'local first' approach to development where the perspectives of indigenous peoples and other local communities are increasingly brought to the fore – not least through their own advocacy – in defining the contours of social and legal policies, including IP policy.

[138] United Nations Millennium Declaration (8 September 2000), G.A. Res. 55/2, UN Doc. A/RES/55/2 (2000) [hereinafter 'UN Millennium Declaration'], available at: http://www.un.org/millennium/ (accessed 22 June 2009). See UNDP 2003.

5. Conclusion: Re-posing the questions

In a world increasingly connected by trade, investments and ICTs, the social impact of IP is global. While recent decades have seen the linking of IP to the international trade regime through the TRIPS Agreement and FTAs, will the coming decades see clearer linkages between IP and human development?[139] The socio-economic implications of IPRs remain unclear in many contexts, and some organizations have used scenario planning as a tool to explore the future (see Chapter 9). These 'future scenarios' may perhaps help us to rethink current options relating to IP and human development. As is discussed throughout this book, technological changes and social processes are already challenging some of the preconceptions in IP law, perhaps altering the landscape for IP irrevocably. Ethical and other social issues are continually brought to the fore in IP-related policy and structural reforms.

While it is common for legislators and law courts in a country to speak of the 'public' and 'public interest' in IP legislation, how can these concepts be understood and applied in the global order?[140] Would viewing the 'public' as a 'global public' lead policymakers in developed countries, for example, to consider more directly the access issues facing the 'public' in developing countries while weighing the 'private vs. public interest' trade-offs in IP? Such policy rethinking on IP and innovation is needed, for example, to meet many of the challenges encapsulated in the MDGs (see Chapters 2 and 6). Noting that the global IP framework poses distributive choices with different inputs for decision-making than on the domestic level, Chon explores how one might construct a conceptual frame that ties IP law and policymaking together across national boundaries (see Chapter 6).

Reviewing IP from a human development perspective requires us to pose many more questions than those often heard within utilitarian arguments for IP protection. It invites us to explore, for example, who ultimately benefits from IP protection and who are the stakeholders marginalized in this system. What are the options in designing more equitable social arrangements? How do other areas of law (e.g. contract, competition or human rights law) interact with IP laws to affect authors' rights and public access to IP-protected works? Is the incentive system for innovation presented by IP frameworks channelling funds and research attention to the areas needed by poorer sectors within both developing and developed countries (see Chapters 2–3)? Does the IP system recognize and encourage diversity in cultural traditions and endeavours (see Chapter 4–5)? This requires a closer look at the drivers of creativity, both pecuniary or non-pecuniary, in different sectors and contexts. It also means looking at the effects of poverty on access to 'all spheres of cultural life' (CESCR 2009, para. 38).

As economic welfare cannot ultimately be dismissed, but is part and parcel of human development, how should the differential socio-economic positions of stakeholders be addressed in designing IP policies to benefit a broad range of

[139] This helpful articulation is owed to an anonymous reviewer from Cambridge University Press whose comments, along with those of other reviewers, have been invaluable towards fine-tuning this book.

[140] For a discussion of how the term 'public interest' has been interpreted by the law courts in a number of countries (including UK, France, Germany and the US), see Davies 2002.

stakeholders? A nuanced approach – going beyond the 'developed vs. developing country' dichotomy – is needed to recognize not only the significant differences in innovation capabilities among developing countries but also the challenges common to marginalized stakeholders in different contexts. As Chon cogently queries in discussing user access to educational materials: 'Do poor users in rich states have more in common with poor users in poor states than with the rich users in their own states?' (see Chapter 6). While human rights and concepts of social justice present some parameters for IP reforms, what other values should help shape IP norms in a world which is resiliently diverse and colourful?[141]

As discussed in this chapter, a human development approach provides some tools for evaluating the social impact of IP. Importantly, it also emphasizes the role of human agency in shaping social reforms and development (Sen 2003; Fukuda-Parr 2008, p. 237). Within IP-related contexts, the role of collective 'agency' can already be seen in the increasing presence of civil society debate and mobilization addressing the assumptions and distributional implications of IP laws. The evolving access to knowledge (A2K) movement is but one manifestation of these steady efforts for reform.[142] A multidisciplinary approach is especially needed for policy reforms relating to IP, given that property rights in the intangible can have both positive and negative impacts on nearly all aspects of human development.

REFERENCES

Afori, O.F. 2004, 'Human Rights and Copyright: The Introduction of Natural Law Considerations into American Copyright Law', *Fordham Intellectual Property, Media & Entertainment Law Journal*, vol. 14, no. 2, pp. 497–565, available at: http://law.fordham.edu/publications/articles/200flspub6402.pdf (accessed 31 January 2009).

Alford, W.P. 1995, *To Steal a Book Is an Elegant Offense: Intellectual Property Law in Chinese Civilization*, Stanford University Press, CA.

Alkire, S. 2002, *Valuing Freedoms: Sen's Capability Approach and Poverty Reduction*, Oxford University Press, Oxford.

Alkire, S. 2008, 'Using the Capability Approach: Prospective and Evaluative Analyses', in F. Comim, M. Qizilbash & S. Alkire (eds.), *The Capability Approach: Concepts, Measures and Application*, Cambridge University Press, Cambridge.

Alkire, S., Qizilbash, M. & Comim, F. 2008, 'Introduction', in F. Comim, M. Qizilbash & S. Alkire (eds.), *The Capability Approach: Concepts, Measures and Application*, Cambridge University Press, Cambridge.

Anaya, J. & Wiessner, S. 2007, 'The UN Declaration on the Rights of Indigenous Peoples: Towards Re-empowerment', *JURIST Legal News and Research*, 3 October 2007, University of Pittsburgh, available at: http://jurist.law.pitt.edu/forumy/2007/10/un-declaration-on-rights-of-indigenous.php (accessed 10 January 2010).

141 It has often been argued that there is also 'intrinsic value' in bio-cultural diversity. Remarks from Eleanor Sterling at the North American Launch of the International Year of Biodiversity, The American Museum of Natural History, New York, 10 February 2010. See Maffi (ed.) 2001.

142 Much thinking and work remain to be carried out, not least in defining what is meant by such access, going well beyond often heard concepts of North-South 'technology transfer' to encourage balanced exchanges among knowledge holders from different cultures. Remarks from Alan Story at A2K3 Conference, Geneva, 8–10 September 2008.

Aoki, K. 2007, 'Distributive and Syncretic Motives in Intellectual Property Law (with Special Reference to Coercion, Agency, and Development)', *UC Davis Law Review*, vol. 40, no. 3, pp. 719–801, available at: http://lawreview.law.ucdavis.edu/issues/Vol40/Issue3/DavisVol40No3_Aoki.pdf (accessed 21 December 2008).

Bates, M.J. 2005, 'Information and Knowledge: An Evolutionary Framework for Information Science', *Information Research*, vol. 10, no. 4, July 2005, available at: http://informationr.net/ir/10-4/paper239.html (accessed 15 March 2010).

Belder, L. 2007, 'Cultural Expressions: From Common Source to Public Domain', in F. Macmillan (ed.), *New Directions in Copyright Law*, vol. 4, Edward Elgar, Cheltenham, UK, Northampton, MA.

Benkler, Y. 2006, *The Wealth of Networks: How Social Production Transforms Markets and Freedom*, Yale University Press, New Haven and London, available at: http://www.benkler.org/Benkler_Wealth_Of_Networks.pdf (accessed 21 December 2008).

Beutz Land, M. 2009, 'Protecting Rights Online', *Yale Journal of International Law*, vol. 34, no. 1, Winter 2009, available at: http://papers.ssrn.com/sol3/papers.cfm?abstract_id=1295448 (accessed 31 January 2010).

Biagioli, M. 1999, 'Aporias of Scientific Authorship: Credit and Responsibility in Contemporary Biomedicine', in M. Biagioli (ed.), *The Science Studies Reader*, Routledge, New York and London.

Boateng, B. 2005, 'Square Pegs in Round Holes? Cultural Production, Intellectual Property Frameworks, and Discourses of Power', in R.A. Ghosh (ed.), *CODE: Collaborative Ownership and the Digital Economy*, pp. 61–74, Massachusetts Institute of Technology Press, Cambridge, MA.

Borges Barbosa, D., Chon, M. & Moncayo von Hase, A. 2008, 'Slouching Towards Development in International Intellectual Property', *Michigan State Law Review*, vol. 2007, no. 1, available at: SSRN: http://ssrn.com/abstract=108 1366 (accessed 01 August 2009).

Bowrey, K. 2006, 'Alternative Intellectual Property? Indigenous Protocols, Copyleft and New Juridifications of Customary Practices', *Macquarie Law Journal*, vol. 6, pp. 65–95, available at: http://www.austlii.edu.au/au/journals/MqLJ/2006/6.html (accessed 21 December 2008).

Boyle, J. 2003, 'The Second Enclosure Movement and the Construction of the Public Domain', *Law and Contemporary Problems*, vol. 66, no. 33, pp. 33–75.

Brauneis, R. 2008, 'Copyright and the World's Most Popular Song', George Washington University Legal Studies Research Paper No. 1111624, available at: http://ssrn.com/abstract=1111624 (accessed 15 March 2010).

Bullard, A. 2005, 'Reinvindicando a los Piratas. ¿Es La Propiedad Intelectual un Robo?', *Latin American and Caribbean Law and Economics Association (ALACDE) Annual Papers*, Paper 7, University of California, Berkeley, available at: http://repositories.cdlib.org/bple/alacde/7 (accessed 21 December 2008).

Burk, D.L. & Lemley, M.A. 2002, 'Is Patent-Law Technology-Specific?', *Berkeley Technology Law Journal*, vol. 12, pp. 1155–1206, available at: http://papers.ssrn.com/sol3/papers.cfm?abstract_id=349761# (accessed 21 December 2008).

Burk, D.L. & Lemley, M.A. 2003, 'Policy Levers in Patent Law', *Virginia Law Review*, vol. 89, no. 7, pp. 1575–1696.

Campbell, M.S. & Anaya, J. 2008, 'The Case of the Maya Villages of Belize: Reversing the Trend of Government Neglect to Secure Indigenous Land Rights', *Human Rights Law Review*, vol. 8, pp. 377–399.

Chander, A. & Sunder, M. 2004, 'The Romance of the Public Domain', *California Law Review*, vol. 92, pp. 1331–1373, available at: http://ssrn.com/abstract=562301 (accessed 21 December 2008).

Chang, H.J. 2002, *Kicking Away the Ladder – Development Strategy in Historical Perspective*, Anthem Press, London.

Chapman, A.R. 2002, 'The Human Rights Implications of Intellectual Property Protection', *Journal of International Economic Law*, vol. 5, no. 4, pp. 861–882.

Charlafti, I. 2008, 'Managing Patent Expiration in the Pharmaceutical Industry: The Story of the Purple Pill', *MAS-IP Diploma Papers & Research Report*, Paper 11, available at: http://www.bepress.com/ndsip/reports/art11 (accessed 20 July 2009).

Chiappero-Martinetti, E. (ed.) 2009, *Debating Global Society – Reach and Limits of the Capability Approach*, Fondazione Giangiacomo Feltrinelli.

Chon, M. 2006, 'Intellectual Property and the Development Divide', *Cardozo Law Review*, vol. 27, pp. 2821–2912.

Chon, M. 2007, 'Substantive Equality in International Intellectual Property Norm Setting and Interpretation', in D. Gervais (ed.), *Intellectual Property, Trade and Development: Strategies to Optimize Economic Development in a TRIPS-Plus Era*, Oxford University Press, New York.

Clark, D.A. 2002, *Visions of Development: A Study of Human Values*, Edward Elgar, Cheltenham, UK.

Clark, D.A. 2005, 'Sen's Capability Approach and the Many Spaces of Human Well-Being', *Journal of Development Studies*, vol. 41, no. 8, pp. 1339–1368.

Clark, D.A. 2006, 'Capability Approach', D.A. Clark (ed.), in *The Elgar Companion to Development Studies*, Edward Elgar, Cheltenham, UK, pp. 32–45; earlier version published as Clark, D.A. 2006, 'The Capability Approach: Its Development, Critiques and Recent Advances', *Global Poverty Research Group Working Paper Series*, Paper 32, available at: http://www.gprg.org/pubs/workingpapers/pdfs/gprg-wps-032.pdf (accessed 21 December 2008).

Comim, F., Qizilbash, M. & Alkire, S. (eds.) 2010, *The Capability Approach: Concepts, Measures and Application*, Cambridge University Press, Cambridge.

Commission on Intellectual Property Rights (CIPR) 2002, *Integrating Intellectual Property Rights and Development Policy*, CIPR, London, available at: http://www.iprcommission.org/papers/pdfs/final_report/CIPRfullfinal.pdf (accessed 19 October 2008).

Committee on Economic, Social and Cultural Rights (CESCR) 1999, *General Comment No. 12: The right to adequate food*, UN Doc. E/C.12/1999/5 (12 May 1999), available at: http://www.unhchr.ch/tbs/doc.nsf/0/3d0 2758c707031d58025677f003b73b9 (accessed 3 February 2010).

CESCR 2005, *General Comment No. 17: The right of everyone to benefit from the protection of the moral and material interests resulting from any scientific, literary or artistic production of which he or she is the author* (art. 15, para. 1 (c)), UN Doc. E/C.12/GC/17 (12 January 2006), available at: http://www.unhchr.ch/tbs/doc.nsf/7cec89369c43a6dfc1256a2a0027ba2a/03902145edbbe797c125711500584ea8/$FILE/G0640060.pdf (accessed 3 February 2010).

CESCR 2009, *General Comment No. 21: Right of everyone to take part in cultural life* (art. 15, para. 1 (a)), UN Doc. E/C.12/GC/21 (21 December 2009), available at: http://www2.ohchr.org/english/bodies/cescr/comments.htm (accessed 1 February 2010).

Cornish, W.C. & Llewelyn, D. 2003, *Intellectual Property: Patents, Copyright, Trade Marks and Allied Rights*, 5th Edition, Sweet and Maxwell, London.

Council of Europe 2007, 'The Right to Property under the European Convention on Human Rights: A Guide to the Implementation of the European Convention on Human Rights and Its Protocols', authored by A. Grgić, Z. Mataga, M. Longar & A. Vilfan, *Human Rights Handbooks No. 10*, Council of Europe, Strasbourg, available at: http://echr.coe.int/NR/rdonlyres/97564258-437D-4FFD-A54D-2766DE255CCA/0/DG2ENHRHAND102007.pdf (accessed 15 March 2010).

Cullet, P. 2004, 'Intellectual Property Rights and Food Security in the South', *The Journal of World Intellectual Property*, vol. 7, no. 3, pp. 261–286.

Darnton, R. 2009, 'Google and the Future of Books', *The New York Review of Books*, vol. 56, no. 2, available at: http://www.nybooks.com/articles/22281 (accessed 1 June 2009).

Davies, G. 2002, *Copyright and the Public Interest*, 2nd Edition, Sweet and Maxwell, London.

de Beer, J. 2009, 'Defining WIPO's Development Agenda', in J. de Beer (ed.), *Implementing the WIPO Development Agenda*, Wilfrid Laurier University Press and International Research Development Centre, Ottawa, Canada.

Deer, K. 2009, 'Indigenous ICT Taskforce,' in U. Popova-Gosart (ed.), *Traditional Knowledge & Indigenous Peoples*, LIENIP and WIPO, Geneva, pp. 94–106, available at: http://indigenouspeoplesissues.com/images/stories/TEK IP WIPO.pdf (accessed 6 March 2010).

Deneulin, S. 2008, 'Beyond Individual Freedom and Agency: Structures of Living Together in Sen's Capability Approach', in F. Comim, M. Qizilbash & S. Alkire (eds.), *The Capability Approach: Concepts, Measures and Application*, Cambridge University Press, Cambridge, pp. 105–124.

Derclaye, E. 2008, *The Legal Protection of Databases*, Edward Elgar, Cheltenham, UK.

Dinwoodie, G.B. & Dreyfuss, R. 2004, 'TRIPS and the Dynamics of Intellectual Property Lawmaking', *Case Western Reserve Journal of International Law*, vol. 36, pp. 95–122, available at: http://papers.ssrn.com/sol3/papers.cfm?abstract_id=616664 (accessed 21 December 2008).

Dinwoodie, G.B. & Dreyfuss R.C. 2006, 'Patenting Science: Protecting the Domain of Accessible Knowledge', in L. Guibault & P.B. Hugenholtz (eds.), *The Future of the Public Domain in Intellectual Property: Identifying the Commons in Information Law* 191, Klumer Law International BV, The Netherlands, available at: http://works.bepress.com/graeme_dinwoodie/26/ (accessed 10 July 2009).

Donders, Y. 2007, 'The Legal Framework of the Right to Take Part in Cultural Life', in Y. Donders & V. Volodin (eds.), *Human Rights in Education, Science and Culture: Legal Developments and Challenges*, United Nations Educational, Scientific and Cultural Organization (UNESCO) and Ashgate Publishing, Paris.

Donders, Y. & Volodin, V. (eds.) 2007, *Human Rights in Education, Science and Culture: Legal Developments and Challenges*, UNESCO and Ashgate Publishing, Paris.

Drahos, P. 1996, *A Philosophy of Intellectual Property*, Aldershot, Dartmouth, UK.

Drahos, P. & Braithwaite, J. 2002, *Information Feudalism – Who Owns the Knowledge Economy?*, Earthscan, London.

Ducor, P. 1999, 'Research Tools Patents and Experimental Use Exemption: A No-Win?', *Nature Biotechnology*, vol. 17, pp. 1027–1028.

Dutfield, G. 2003, *Intellectual Property Rights and the Life Science Industries: A Twentieth Century History*, Ashgate, Aldershot, UK.

Dutfield, G. 2006, 'Protecting Traditional Knowledge: Pathways to the Future', *ICTSD Issue Paper No. 16*, International Centre for Trade and Sustainable Development (ICTSD), available at: http://www.iprsonline.org/unctadictsd/docs/Graham%20final.pdf (accessed 15 March 2010).

Dutfield, G. 2009, *Intellectual Property Rights and the Life Science Industries: Past, Present and Future*, World Scientific Publishing, Singapore.

Dutfield, G. & Suthersanen, U. 2007, 'Innovation and Development', in U. Suthersanen, G. Dutfield & K.B. Chow (eds.), *Innovation without Patents: Harnessing the Creative Spirit in a Diverse World*, Edward Elgar, Cheltenham, UK.

Dutfield, G. & Suthersanen, U. 2008, *Global Intellectual Property Law*, Edward Elgar, Cheltenham, UK.

Eide, A. 2007, 'Interdependence and Indivisibility of Human Rights', in Y. Donders & V. Volodin (eds.), *Human Rights in Education, Science and Culture: Legal Developments and Challenges*, UNESCO and Ashgate Publishing, Paris.

Emberland, M. 2006, *The Human Rights of Companies: Exploring the Structure of ECHR Protection*, Oxford University Press, New York.

Evans, P. 2002, 'Collective Capabilities, Culture and Amartya Sen's Development as Freedom', *Studies in Comparative International Development*, vol. 37, no. 2, pp. 54–60.

Fisher, W. 2001, 'Theories of Intellectual Property', in S.R. Munzer (ed.), *New Essays in the Legal and Political Theory of Property*, Cambridge University Press, New York, pp. 168–200, available at: http://www.law.harvard.edu/faculty/tfisher/iptheory.html (accessed 12 May 2009).

Frey, B.S. & Stutzer, A. 2006, 'Should We Maximize National Happiness?', *Institute for Empirical Research in Economics, Working Paper No. 306*, University of Zurich, Zurich, Switzerland.

Fitzgerald, B.F. 2008, 'Copyright 2010: The Future of Copyright', *European Intellectual Property Review*, vol. 30, no. 43, available at: http://eprints.qut.edu.au/13305/1/13305.pdf (accessed 27 December 2008).

Frischmann, B.M. & Lemley, M.A. 2006, 'Spillovers', *Columbia Law Review*, vol. 100, no. 2, available at: http://ssrn.com/abstract=898881 (accessed 27 December 2008).

Fukuda-Parr, S. 2003a, 'The Human Development Paradigm: Operationalizing Sen's Ideas on Capabilities, *Feminist Economics*, vol. 9, nos. 2–3, pp. 301–317.

Fukuda-Parr, S. 2003b, 'Rescuing the Human Development Concept from the Human Development Index: Reflections on a New Agenda', in S. Fukuda-Parr & A.K. Shiva Kumar (eds.), *Readings in Human Development*, Oxford University Press, New Delhi.

Fukuda-Parr, S. 2008, 'The Intellectual Journey Continues: Today's Global Agenda and the New Frontiers', in K. Haq & R. Ponzio (eds.), *Pioneering the Human Development Revolution: An Intellectual Biography of Mahbub ul Haq*, Oxford University Press, New Delhi.

Fukuda-Parr, S. 2009, 'Human Rights and Human Development', in K. Basu & R. Kanbur (eds.), *Arguments for a Better World: Essays in Honour of Amartya Sen's Seventy Fifth Birthday*, vol. 2, Oxford University Press, New York.

Ghosh, R.A. & Soete, L. 2006, 'Information and Intellectual Property: The Global Challenges', *United Nations University – Maastricht Economic and Social Research and Training Centre on Innovation and Technology (UNU-MERIT) Working Paper Series #2006–029*, available at: http://www.merit.unu.edu/publications/wppdf/2006/wp2006–029.pdf (accessed 27 December 2008).

Ginsburg, J. 2007, '"Une Chose Publique"? The Author's Domain and the Public Domain in Early British, French and US Copyright Law', in P. Torremans (ed.), *Copyright Law: A Handbook of Contemporary Research*, Edward Elgar, Cheltenham, UK.

Gold, E.R. & Morin, J.F. 2009, 'From Agenda to Implementation: Working Outside the WIPO Box', in J. de Beer (ed.), *Implementing the WIPO Development Agenda*, Wilfrid Laurier University Press and International Development Research Centre (IDRC), Ottawa.

Gollin, M.A. 2008, *Driving Innovation: Intellectual Property Strategies for a Dynamic World*, Cambridge University Press, New York.

Gore, C. 1997, 'Irreducible Social Goods and the Informational Basis of Amartya Sen's Capability Approach', *Journal of International Development*, vol. 9, no. 2, pp. 235–250.

Gould, D.M. & Gruben, W.C. 1996. 'The Role of Intellectual Property Rights in Economic Growth', *Journal of Development Economics*, vol. 48, no. 2, March 1996, pp. 323–350.

Guibault, L. 2002, *Copyright Limitations and Contracts: An Analysis of the Contractual Overridability of Limitations on Copyright*, Information Law Series, vol. 9, Kluwer Law International, London, The Hague and Boston.

Guibault, L. & Hugenholtz, P.B. 2003, 'The Nature and Scope of Limitations and Exceptions to Copyright and Neighbouring Rights with regard to General Interest Missions for the Transmission of Knowledge: Prospects for their Adaptation to the Digital Environment', *Copyright Bulletin*, December 2003, UNESCO.

Haq, M. 1995, *Reflections on Human Development*, Oxford University Press, New York.

Haq, K. & Jolly, R. 2008, 'Global Development Policy, Poverty Alleviation, and North-South Relations', in K. Haq & R. Ponzio (eds.), *Pioneering the Human Development Revolution: An Intellectual Biography of Mahbub ul Haq*, Oxford University Press, New Delhi.

Haq, K. & Ponzio, R. (eds.) 2008, *Pioneering the Human Development Revolution: An Intellectual Biography of Mahbub ul Haq*, Oxford University Press, New Delhi.

Harkness, S. 2007, 'Social and Political Indicators of Human Well-being', in M. McGillivray (ed.), *Human Well-being: Concept and Measurement*, Studies in Development Economics and Policy, United Nations University – World Institute for Development Economics Research (UNU-WIDER), Palgrave Macmillan, London.

Harlow, C. 1999, 'Access to Justice as a Human Right: The European Convention and the European Union', in P. Alston (ed.), *The EU and Human Rights*, Oxford University Press, New York, pp. 195–197.

Haugen, H.M. 2005a, 'Intellectual Property – Rights or Privileges?', *Journal of World Intellectual Property*, vol. 8, no. 4, pp. 445–458.

Haugen, H.M. 2005b, 'Traditional Knowledge and Human Rights', *Journal of World Intellectual Property*, vol. 8, no. 5, pp. 663–677.

Haugen, H.M. 2007a, 'General Comment No. 17 on Authors' Rights', *Journal of World Intellectual Property*, vol. 10, no. 1, pp. 53–69.

Haugen, H.M. 2007b, 'Patent Rights and Human Rights: Exploring Their Relationships', *Journal of World Intellectual Property*, vol. 10, no. 2, pp. 97–124.

Helfer, L.R. 2003, 'Human Rights and Intellectual Property: Conflict or Coexistence?', *Minnesota Intellectual Property Review*, vol. 5, pp. 47–61.

Helfer, L.R. 2007, 'Toward a Human Rights Framework for Intellectual Property', U.C. *Davis Law Review*, vol. 40, pp. 971–1020, available at: http://papers.ssrn.com/sol3/papers.cfm?abstract_id=891303 (accessed 27 October 2009).

Helfer, L.R. 2008, 'The New Innovation Frontier? Intellectual Property and the European Court of Human Rights', *Harvard International Law Journal*, vol. 49, no. 1, pp. 1–52, available at: http://www.harvardilj.org/attach.php?id=137 (accessed 27 December 2008).

Hicks, N. & Streeten, P. 1979, 'Indicators of Development: The Search for a Basic Needs Yardstick', *World Development*, vol. 7, no. 6, pp. 567–580.

Hinze, G. 2008, 'Making Knowledge Accessible Across Borders: The Case for Mandatory Minimum International Copyright Exceptions and Limitations for Education, Capacity Building and Development', *Electronic Frontier Foundation*, available at: http://www.eff.org/files/eff-making-knowledge-accessible-whitepaper.pdf (accessed 18 January 2009).

Howkins, J. 2001, *The Creative Economy: How People Make Money from Ideas*, Penguin, London.

Hugenholtz, P.B. & Okediji, R.L. 2008, *Conceiving an International Instrument on Exceptions and Limitations to Copyright*, Institute for Information Law University at Amsterdam and University of Minnesota Law School, available at: http://www.ivir.nl/publicaties/hugenholtz/finalreport2008.pdf (accessed 18 January 2009).

Ibrahim, S.S. 2006, 'From Individual to Collective Capabilities: The Capability Approach as a Conceptual Framework for Self-help', *Journal of Human Development and Capabilities*, vol. 7, no. 3, pp. 397–416.

Idris, K. 2003, '*Intellectual Property: A Power Tool for Economic Growth*', World Intellectual Property Organization (WIPO), Publication, No. 888.

Indigenous Peoples' International Centre for Policy Research and Education (TEBTEBBA) 2008, *Indicators Relevant for Indigenous Peoples: A Resource Book*, TEBTEBBA, Baguio, Philippines.

Ingold, T. 2000, *The Perception of the Environment: Essays in Livelihood, Dwelling and Skill*, Routledge, London and New York.

International Centre for Trade and Sustainable Development (ICTSD) 2007, 'WIPO Members Agree on Development Agenda', *Bridges*, no. 4, p. 19, available at: http://www.iprsonline.org/ictsd/news/bridges11–4.pg19.pdf (accessed 27 December 2008).

International Expert Group on Biotechnology, Innovation and Intellectual Property (IEGBIIP) 2008, *Towards a New Era of Intellectual Property: From Confrontation to Negotiation*, available at: http://www.theinnovationpartnership.org/data/ieg/documents/report/TIP_Report_E.pdf (accessed 27 December 2008).

Iversen, V. 2003, 'Intra-household Inequality: A Challenge for the Capability Approach?', *Feminist Economics*, vol. 9, no. 2–3, pp. 93–115.

Jefferson, T. 1813, 'Thomas Jefferson to Isaac MacPherson, August 13, 1813', *The Founder's Constitution Web Edition*, vol. 3, article 1, section 8, clause 8, document 12, available at: http://press-pubs.uchicago.edu/founders/documents/a1_8_8s12.html (accessed 27 December 2008).

Kingdon, G.G. & Knight, J. 2006, J. 'Subjective Well-Being Poverty vs. Income Poverty and Capabilities Poverty?', *Journal of Development Studies*, vol. 42, no. 7, pp. 119–1224.

Laddie, H. 1996, 'Copyright: Over-strength, Over-regulated, Over-rated?', *European Intellectual Property Review*, vol. 18, no. 5, pp. 253–260.

Laddie, H., Prescott, P., Vitoria, M., Speck, A. & Lane, L. 2000, *The Modern Law of Copyright and Designs*, 3rd Edition, Butterworths: London, Edinburgh and Dublin.

Laddie, H. 2002, 'Foreword', *Integrating Intellectual Property Rights and Development Policy*, CIPR, London, available at: http://www.iprcommission.org/papers/pdfs/final_report/CIPRfullfinal.pdf (accessed 19 October 2008).

Landes, W.M. & Posner R.A. 1989, 'An Economic Analysis of Copyright Law', *Journal of Legal Studies*, vol. 18, no. 2, pp. 325–363, available at: http://cyber.law.harvard.edu/IPCoop/89land1.html (accessed 27 December 2008).

Landes, W.M. & Posner, R.A. 2003, *The Economic Structure of Intellectual Property Law*, Harvard University Press, Cambridge, MA.

Leach, J. 2005, 'Modes of Creativity and the Register of Ownership', in R. A. Ghosh (ed.) *CODE: Collaborative Ownership and the Digital Economy*, Massachusetts Institute of Technology Press, Cambridge, MA.

Litman, J. 1990, 'The Public Domain', *Emory Law Journal*, vol. 39, pp. 965–989.

Locke, J. 1690, *Second Treatise of Civil Government*, available at: http://www.constitution.org/jl/2ndtreat.htm (accessed 12 April 2010).

Maffi, L. (ed.) 2001, *On Biocultural Diversity: Linking Language, Knowledge and the Environment*, Smithsonian Institution Press, Washington, DC.

Mankiw, N.G. 2004, *Principles of Economics*, Harcourt Brace College Publishers, New York.

Maskus, E. 2008, 'Incorporating a Globalized Intellectual Property Rights Regime into an Economic Development Strategy', in K.E. Maskus (ed.), *Intellectual Property, Growth and Trade*, H. Beladi & E.K. Choi (eds.), *Frontiers of Economics and Globalization*, vol. 2, Elsevier.

McGillivray, M. 2007, 'Human Well-being: Concepts and Conceptualizations', in M. McGillivray (ed.), *Human Well-being: Concept and Measurement*, Studies in Development Economics and Policy, United Nations University – World Institute for Development Economics Research (UNU-WIDER), Palgrave Macmillan, London.

Moenius, J. & Trindade, V. 2008, 'Networks, Standards and Intellectual Property Rights', in K.E. Maskus (ed.), *Intellectual Property, Growth and Trade*, H. Beladi & E.K. Choi (eds.), *Frontiers of Economics and Globalization*, vol. 2, Elsevier.

Moohr, G.S. 2003, 'The Crime of Copyright Infringement: An Inquiry Based on Morality, Harm, and Criminal Theory', *Boston University Law Review*, vol. 83, no. 4, pp. 731–741, available at: www.law.uh.edu/faculty/gmoohr/Criminal.pdf (accessed 28 December 2008).

Mossoff, A. 2007, 'Who Cares What Thomas Jefferson Thought About Patents? Reevaluating the Patent Privilege in Historical Context', *Cornell Law Review*, vol. 92, pp. 953–1012, available at: http://www.lawschool.cornell.edu/research/cornell-law-review/upload/CRN502Mossoff.pdf (accessed 28 December 2008).

Netanel, N.W. 2008, 'Introduction: The WIPO Development Agenda and Its Development Policy Context', in N.W. Netanel (ed.), *The Development Agenda: Global Intellectual Property and Developing Countries*, Oxford University Press, New York, available at: http://ssrn.com/abstract=1310388 (accessed 7 November 2009).

New, W. 2009, 'Access to Influence in WIPO's Development Agenda', in H. Essalmawi (ed.), *Bibliotheca Alexandria Access to Knowledge Toolkit II: The Access to Knowledge Movement – Opportunities, Challenges and the Road Ahead*, Bibliotheca Alexandrina, Egypt, pp. 28–36, available at: http://www.bibalex.org/a2k/attachments/references/reffileu24bkg55ykqwgc55zysxzq45.pdf (accessed 15 November 2009).

Nussbaum, M.C. 1988, 'Nature, Function and Capability: Aristotle on Political Distribution', *Oxford Studies in Ancient Philosophy*, supl. vol. 6, pp. 113–137.

Nussbaum, M.C. 1997a, 'Capabilities and Human Rights', *Fordham Law Review*, vol. 66, pp. 273–300.

Nussbaum, M.C. 1997b, 'Human Rights and Human Capabilities', *Harvard Human Rights Journal*, vol. 20, available at: http://www.law.harvard.edu/students/orgs/hrj/iss20/ (accessed 15 March 2010).

Nussbaum, M.C. 2000, *Women and Human Development: The Capabilities Approach*, Cambridge University Press, New York.

Nussbaum, M.C. 2003, 'Capabilities as Fundamental Entitlement: Sen and Social Justice', *Feminist Economics*, vol. 9, no. 2–3, pp. 33–59.

Nuvolari, A. 2005, 'Open Source Software Development: Some Historical Perspectives', *First Monday*, vol. 10, no. 10.

Okediji, R.L. 2007, 'The Limits of Development Strategies at the Intersection of Intellectual Property and Human Rights', in D. Gervais (ed.), *Intellectual Property, Trade and Development: Strategies to Optimize Economic Development in a TRIPS-Plus Era'*, Oxford University Press, New York, pp. 355–384.

Oman, R. 2000, *Copyright – Engine of Development: An Analysis of the Role of Copyright in Economic Development and Cultural Vitality*, UNESCO.

Opderbeck, D.W. 2008, 'Deconstructing Jefferson's Candle: Towards a Critical Realist Approach to Cultural Environmentalism and Information Policy', *Seton Hall Public Law Research Paper No. 1091024*, available at: http://ssrn.com/abstract=1091024 (accessed 15 March 2010).

Organisation for Economic Cooperation and Development (OECD) 2004, *Patents and Innovation: Trends and Policy Challenges*, OECD, Paris, available at: http://www.oecd.org/dataoecd/48/12/24508541.pdf (accessed 25 January 2009).

OECD 2007, *Participative Web and User-Created Content*, OECD, Paris, available at: http://www.oecd.org/dataoecd/57/14/38393115.pdf (accessed 14 May 2009).

Ostergard, R.L. 2007, 'Economic Growth and Intellectual Property Rights Protection: A Reassessment of the Conventional Wisdom', in D. Gervais (ed.), *Intellectual Property, Trade and Development: Strategies to Optimize Economic Development in a TRIPS-Plus Era*, Oxford University Press, New York.

Ovett, D. 2006a, 'Policy Brief on Intellectual Property, Development and Human Rights: How Human Rights Can Support Proposals for a World Intellectual Property Organization (WIPO) Development Agenda', *3D Policy Brief 2*, available at: http://www.3dthree.org/pdf_3D/3DPolBrief-WIPO-eng.pdf#search=%22%2BOvett%20%2B%22Policy%20Brief%20on (accessed 2 January 2009).

Ovett, D. 2006b, 'Intellectual Property and Human Rights: Is the Distinction Clear Now?: An Assessment of the Committee on Economic, Social and Cultural Rights' General Comment No. 17 (2005)', *3D Policy Brief 3*, available at: http://www.3dthree.org/pdf_3D/3D_GC17_IPHR.pdf (accessed 2 January 2009).

Park, W.G. & Ginarte, J.C. 1997, 'Intellectual Property Rights and Economic Growth', *Contemporary Economic Policy*, vol. 15, no. 3, July 1997, pp. 51–61, available at: http://www1.american.edu/cas/econ/faculty/park/park%20ginarte%20cep.pdf (accessed 15 January 2010).

Polanyi, M. 1983, *The Tacit Dimension*, Peter Smith, Gloucester, MA (reprint).

Ponzio, R. 2008, 'The Advent of the *Human Development Report*', in K. Haq & R. Ponzio (eds.), *Pioneering the Human Development Revolution: An Intellectual Biography of Mahbub ul Haq*, Oxford University Press, New Delhi.

Prott, L.V. 1998, 'Understanding One Another on Cultural Rights', in H. Niec (ed.), *Cultural Rights and Wrongs: A Collection of Essays in Commemoration of the 50th*

Anniversary of the University Declaration of Human Rights, Institute of Art & Law, UNESCO, pp. 161–175.

Qizilbash, M. 1998, 'The Concept of Well-Being', *Economics and Philosophy*, vol. 14, pp. 51–73.

Qizilbash, M. 2006, 'Human Development', in D.A. Clark (ed.), *The Elgar Companion to Development Studies*, Edward Elgar, Cheltenham, UK, pp. 245–250.

Rajotte, T. 2008, 'The Negotiations Web: Complex Connections', in G. Tansey & T. Rajotte (eds.), *The Future Control of Food: A Guide to International Negotiations and Rules on Intellectual Property, Biodiversity and Food Security*, Quaker International Affairs Programme (QIAP) and International Development Research Centre (IDRC), Earthscan, London and Sterling, VA.

Ramos, A.R., Osório, R. G. & Pimenta, J. 2009, 'Indigenising Development', *Poverty in Focus*, no. 17, International Policy Centre for Inclusive Growth (IPC-IG), Poverty Practice, Bureau for Development Policy, United Nations Development Programme (UNDP), available at: http://www.undp.org/partners/civil_society/publications/indigenous/Indigenising_Development_IPC_May_2009.pdf (accessed 3 November 2009).

Rawls, J. 1971, *A Theory of Justice*, Clarendon, Oxford.

Rens, A., Prabhala, A. & Kawooya, D. 2006, 'Intellectual Property, Education and Access to Knowledge in Southern Africa', *ICTSD Regional Research Paper Southern and Eastern Africa*, ICTSD, Geneva, available at: http://www.iprsonline.org/unctadictsd/docs/06%2005%2031%20tralac%20amended-pdf.pdf (accessed 18 January 2009).

Robertson, A.H. & Merrills, J.G. 1996, *Human Rights in the World*, Manchester University Press, Manchester and New York.

Robeyns, I. 2003, 'Sen's Capability Approach and Gender Inequality: Selecting Relevant Capabilities', *Feminist Economics*, vol. 9, no. 2-3, pp. 61–92.

Robeyns, I. 2005, 'Capability Approach, a Theoretical Survey', *Journal of Human Development*, vol. 6, no. 1, pp. 93–114.

Ruiz, M. 2004, 'An Analysis of the Implications of Intellectual Property Rights (IPR) on the Global Biodiversity Information Facility (GBIF) and Databases in General', document prepared for the GBIF Secretariat, Lima, Peru, February 2004.

Saith, R. 2001, 'Capabilities: The Concept and its Operationalisation', *QEH Working Paper Series 66*, Queen Elizabeth House, University of Oxford, Oxford, available at: http://www3.qeh.ox.ac.uk/pdf/qehwp/qehwps66.pdf (accessed 15 March 2010).

Samuelson, P. 2006, 'Enriching Discourse on Public Domains', *Duke Law Journal*, vol. 55, available at: http://ssrn.com/abstract=925052 (accessed 15 May 2010).

Scott, D., Oliver, A. & Ley-Pineda, M. 2008, 'Trade Marks as Property', in L. Bently, J. Davis & J.C. Ginsburg (eds.), *Trade Marks and Brands: An Interdisciplinary Critique*, Cambridge University Press, Cambridge, pp. 285–305.

Sen, A.K. 1983, 'Development: Which Way Now?', *Economic Journal*, vol. 93, pp. 745–762.

Sen, A.K. 1984, *Resources, Values and Development*, Basil Blackwell, Oxford.

Sen, A.K.1985a, *Commodities and Capabilities*, Elsevier Science Publishers, Oxford.

Sen, A.K. 1985b, 'Well-being, Agency and Freedom: The Dewey Lectures', *Journal of Philosophy*, vol. 82, no. 4, pp. 169–221.

Sen, A.K. 1987, *The Standard of Living: The Tanner Lectures*, Cambridge University Press, Cambridge.

Sen, A.K. 1988, 'The Concept of Development', in H. Chenery & T.N. Srinivasan (eds.), *Handbook of Development Economics*, vol. 1, pp. 10–26, Elsevier Science Publishers, Amsterdam.

Sen, A.K. 1990, 'Development as Capability Expansion', in K. Griffin & J. Knight (eds.), *Human Development and the International Development Strategy for the 1990s*, Macmillan, London, pp. 41–58.

Sen, A.K. 1992, *Inequality Re-examined*, Clarendon Press, Oxford.

Sen, A.K. 1993, 'Capability and Well-being', in M.C. Nussbaum & A.K. Sen (eds.), *The Quality of Life*, Clarendon Press, Oxford, pp. 30–53.

Sen, A.K. 1999, *Development As Freedom*, Oxford University Press, Oxford.

Sen, A.K. 2002, 'Response to Commentaries', *Studies in Comparative International Development*, vol. 37, no. 2, pp. 78–86.

Sen, A.K. 2003, 'Foreword', in S. Fukuda-Parr & K.S. Shiva Kumar, *Readings in Human Development, Concepts, Measures and Policies for a Development Paradigm*, Oxford University Press, New Delhi.

Sen, A.K. 2004, 'Capabilities, Lists and Public Reason: Continuing the Conversation', *Feminist Economics*, vol. 10, no. 3, pp. 77–80.

Sen, A.K. 2005, 'Human Rights and Capabilities', *Journal of Human Development*, vol. 6, no. 2, pp. 151–166.

Serageldin, I. 1996, 'Sustainability as Opportunity and the Problem of Social Capital', *Brown Journal of World Affairs*, vol. 3, no. 2, pp. 187–203.

Shabas, W.A. 2007, 'Study of the Right to Enjoy the Benefits of Scientific and Technological Progress and Its Applications', in Y. Donders & V. Volodin (eds.), *Human Rights in Education, Science and Culture: Legal Developments and Challenges*, UNESCO and Ashgate Publishing, Paris.

South Centre 2007, *Development & Intellectual Property under the EPA Negotiations*, South Centre, Geneva.

Stewart, F. 1996. 'Basic Needs, Capabilities and Human Development', in A. Offer (ed.), *In Pursuit of the Quality of Life*, Oxford University Press, New York, pp. 46–65.

Stewart, F. 2005, 'Groups and Capabilities', *Journal of Human Development*, vol. 6, no. 2, pp. 185–204.

Strandburg, K.J. 2008, 'Users as Innovators: Implications for Patent Doctrine', *University of Colorado Law Review*, vol. 79, no. 46, available at: http://ssrn.com/abstract=1141386 (accessed 15 June 2009).

Strandburg, K.J. 2009, 'Evolving Innovation Paradigms and the Global Intellectual Property Regime', *Connecticut Law Review*, vol. 41, pp. 861–920, available at: http://ssrn.com/abstract=1229543 (accessed 15 March 2010).

Strathern, M. 1996, 'Cutting the Network', *The Journal of the Royal Anthropological Institute*, vol. 2, no. 3, pp. 517–535.

Strathern, M. 2005, 'Imagined Collectivities and Multiple Authorship', in R.A. Ghosh (ed.), *CODE: Collaborative Ownership and the Digital Economy*, Massachusetts Institute of Technology Press, Cambridge, MA.

Straus, J. 2008, 'Is There a Global Warming of Patents?' *The Journal of World Intellectual Property*, vol. 11, no. 1, pp. 58–62.

Subramanian, S. 2008, 'Patent Trolls in Thickets: Who is Fishing Under the Bridge?' *European Intellectual Property Review*, vol. 30, no. 5, pp. 182–188.

Sugden, P. 2009, 'How Long is a Piece of String? The Meaning of "Commercial Scale" in Copyright Piracy', *European Intellectual Property Review*, vol. 31, no. 4, pp. 202–212.

Sun, H.C. 2007, 'Overcoming the Achilles Heel of Copyright Law', *Northwestern Journal of Technology and Intellectual Property*, vol. 5, pp. 265–331, available at: http://ssrn.com/abstract=1021027 (accessed 1 June 2009).

Sunder, M. 2006, 'IP^3', *Stanford Law Review*, vol. 59, no. 2, pp. 257–332.

Sunder, M. 2007, 'The Invention of Traditional Knowledge', *Law and Contemporary Problems*, vol. 70, no. 2, pp. 97–124.

Sunder, M. 2008, 'Intellectual Property and Development as Freedom', in N.W. Netanel (ed.), *The Development Agenda: Global Intellectual Property and Developing Countries*, Oxford University Press, New York.

Suthersanen, U. 2007, 'Copyright Law: A Stakeholder's Palimpsest', in F. Macmillan (ed.), *New Directions in Copyright Law*, vol. 5, Edward Elgar, Cheltenham, UK.

Suthersanen, U. 2008, 'A2K and the WIPO Development Agenda: Time to List the "Public Domain"', UNCTAD-ICTSD Project on IPRs and Sustainable Development, Policy Brief No. 1, available at: http://ictsd.net/downloads/2009/02/uma_final2.pdf (accessed 15 June 2009).

Suthersanen, U., Dutfield, D. & Chow, K.B. (eds.) 2007, *Innovation without Patents: Harnessing the Creative Spirit in a Diverse World*, Edward Elgar, Cheltenham, UK.

Tansey, G. 2008, 'Food, Farming and Global Rules', in G. Tansey & T. Rajotte (eds.), *The Future Control of Food: A Guide to International Negotiations and Rules on Intellectual Property, Biodiversity and Food Security*, QIAP and IDRC, Earthscan, London and Sterling, VA.

Tapper, C.B. 2004, 'Criminality and Copyright', in D. Vaver & L. Bently (eds.), *Intellectual Property in the New Millennium: Essays in Honour of William R. Cornish*, Cambridge University Press.

United Nations (UN) 1987, *Report of the World Commission on Environment and Development: Our Common Future*, UN Doc. A/42/427, Annex, available at: http://www.un-documents.net/wced-ocf.htm (accessed 13 February 2010).

UN 2008, *Creative Economy Report – The Challenge of Assessing the Creative Economy: Towards Informed Policy-Making*, available at: http://www.unctad.org/en/docs/ditc20082cer_en.pdf (accessed 31 January 2009).

UN 2009, State of the World's Indigenous Peoples, Department of Economic and Social Affairs, ST/ESA/328, New York.

United Nations Development Programme (UNDP) 1996, *Human Development Report 1996: Human Development and Economic Growth*, UNDP, available at: http://hdr.undp.org/en/reports/global/hdr1996/chapters/ (accessed 2 January 2009).

UNDP 2000, *Human Development Report 2000: Human Rights and Human Development*, UNDP, available at: http://hdr.undp.org/en/media/HDR_2000_EN.pdf (accessed 2 January 2009).

UNDP 2001, *Human Development Report 2001: Making New Technologies Work for Human Development*, UNDP, available at: http://hdr.undp.org/en/media/completenew1.pdf (accessed 2 January 2009).

UNDP 2003, *Human Development Report 2003: The Millennium Development Goals: A Compact among Nations to end Human Poverty*, UNDP, available at: http://hdr.undp.org/en/media/hdr03_complete.pdf (accessed 2 January 2009).

UNDP 2004, *Human Development Report 2004: Cultural Liberty in Today's Diverse World*, UNDP, available at: http://hdr.undp.org/en/media/hdr04_complete.pdf (accessed 2 January 2009).

UNDP 2007, *Human Development Report 2007/2008: Fighting Climate Change: Human Solidarity in a Divided World*, UNDP, available at: http://hdr.undp.org/en/media/HDR_20072008_EN_Complete.pdf (accessed 2 January 2009).

UNDP 2009, *Human Development Report 2009: Overcoming barriers: Human Mobility and Development,* UNDP, available at: http://hdr.undp.org/en/reports/global/hdr2009/ (accessed 15 March 2010).

Watt, R. 2004, 'The Past and the Future of the Economics of Copyright', *Review of Economic Research on Copyright Issues,* vol. 1, no. 1, pp. 151–171, available at: http://ssrn.com/abstract=1143022 (accessed 15 June 2009).

Weber, R.J. 1992, *Forks, Phonographs, and Hot Air Balloons: A Field Guide to Inventive Thinking,* Oxford University Press, New York.

Wiessner, S. 2009, 'United Nations Declaration On The Rights Of Indigenous Peoples', *United Nations Audiovisual Library of International Law,* pp. 1–7, available at: http://untreaty.un.org/cod/avl/pdf/ha/ga_61-295/ga_61-295_e.pdf (accessed 10 January 2010).

Woolcock, M. & Narayan, D. 2000, 'Social Capital: Implications for Development Theory, Research and Policy', *The World Bank Research Observer,* vol. 15, no. 2, pp. 225–249.

World Intellectual Property Organization (WIPO) 2004, 'WIPO Intellectual Property Handbook: Policy, Law and Use', WIPO Publication No. 489(E), WIPO, Geneva.

WIPO 2005a, Understanding Copyright, WIPO Publication No. 909(E), WIPO, Geneva.

WIPO 2005b, Understanding Industrial Property, WIPO Publication No. 895(E), WIPO, Geneva.

WIPO 2009, *Report on the International Patent System,* (prepared by the Secretariat) Standing Committee on the Law of Patents, Doc. SCP/12/3 REV.2, WIPO, Geneva.

Worsley, P. 1997, *Knowledges: What Different Peoples Make of the World,* Profile Books, London.

Yu, P.K. 2003, 'Four Common Misconceptions about Copyright Piracy', *Loyola Los Angeles International & Comparative Law Review,* vol. 26, pp. 127–150.

2

Intellectual property and medicine: Towards global health equity

Claudia Chamas, Ben Prickril and Joshua D. Sarnoff[1]

Introduction

The past thirty years have witnessed an explosion in the development of new biomedical and genomics technologies and other health innovations, advances in medical imaging, an evolution in information technologies and connectivity, as well as significant progress towards technological convergence between the North and some areas of the Global South. Countries such as Brazil, China and India have developed innovation capabilities in many areas including medicine. These developments bring considerable hope for long-term improvements in human well-being. However, this progress has not been realized to any great extent in many developing countries, and access to quality health care and related products and services is still lacking.

In poverty dynamics, limited access to health care and relevant technological progress stems from a combination of factors. These include the lack of public financing for health care infrastructure, along with the lack of economic incentives for the private sector to invest in such infrastructure and to provide medicines (particularly for diseases that are not endemic in higher-income countries), inadequate or inappropriate regulatory frameworks, and lack of awareness of legal options relating to intellectual property (IP). These factors are coupled in many developing countries with insufficient scientific, technological and industrial capabilities, including the inability to fully exploit technologies towards meeting users' needs. Many studies reveal, moreover, the strong relationship between poverty and disease burden (McCarthy, Wolf & Wu 2000; Marmot 2005, pp. 1099–1104; Mathers & Loncar 2006; Roffe, Tansey & Vivas-Eugui 2006).[2]

This chapter first provides an overview of issues and trends where IP intersects with access to health care and health-related products. In discussing the latter, it is necessary to point out the broad range of therapeutic drugs, diagnostics and medical devices which may be considered as health-related products and services. These include, for example, therapeutic and prophylactic vaccines, drugs and diagnostics derived from a range of biological materials (e.g. peptides, genetic materials, carbohydrates and cells), other synthetic or natural chemicals, and numerous methods of assessment or treatment. It should be noted, furthermore, that the overlap between IP and medicine is complex, going beyond issues of access to medicines and other

[1] The authors are grateful to Claire Comfort, Graham Dutfield, Sean Flynn, Michael Gollin, Stan Kowalski, Roy Widdus, Claudia Trezza and Tzen Wong for their invaluable comments towards this chapter.

[2] See also Commission on Macroeconomics and Health 2001; World Health Organization (WHO) 2008.

health-related products to cover the impact of IP on medical research and exchange of related knowledge.

Although it is impossible within the scope of one chapter to discuss all these areas in detail, some issues and trends of key relevance to developing countries are highlighted in Section 1. This is followed by a discussion of important initiatives at the international and local levels to deal with the severe problem of resurgent and 'neglected' diseases (so called for the lack of research investment targeted at them) in developing countries and least developed countries (LDCs). Strategies adopted at the international level, particularly at the World Health Organization (WHO), are discussed in Section 2, along with alternative innovation models developed largely through public-private partnerships for research and development (R&D) of new vaccines and medicines for HIV/AIDS and other diseases (see further Appendix B).[3] In Section 3, some future scenarios published by international and regional entities in relation to IP and health are described, along with analysis of their implications for human development.

1. Overview of intellectal property issues and trends relating to health

Several recent studies analyse IP through the lens of human rights, raising relevant questions and perspectives about the balance between the rights of inventors and creators and the public interest (Petersmann 2000, pp. 119–125; Chapman 2002, pp. 861–882; Anderson & Wager 2006, pp. 707–747; Barbosa, Chon & Von Hase 2007, pp. 114–123; Helfer 2007, p. 971). Human rights perspectives are becoming more and more important in reforms of IP policies and laws, especially in balancing the grant of exclusive intellectual property rights (IPRs) over innovations with rights of access to the benefits of science and technology.[4]

International human rights law imposes on States an obligation to respect, protect and fulfil the right to health. The latter is enshrined in Article 12 of the International Covenant on Economic, Social and Cultural Rights (ICESCR), adopted by the UN General Assembly in 1966.[5] General Comment No. 14 (2000) of the Committee on Economic, Social and Cultural Rights (CESCR) regarding this Article clarifies that the right to health embraces, among other things, the right to 'health facilities, goods and services' (including 'essential drugs, as defined by the WHO Action Programme on Essential Drugs').[6] The right to health is also emphasized

[3] According to a WHO definition: 'Human Immunodeficiency Virus (HIV) is the retrovirus that weakens the immune system, particularly by causing the death of many CD4+T cells, which coordinate the human immune system's response to intruders. This weakening of the immune system leaves the body open to attack from opportunistic infections, eventually leading to the development of Acquired Immune Deficiency Syndrome (AIDS)'. WHO 'Glossary of globalization, trade and health terms', available at: http://www.who.int/trade/glossary/story051/en/index.html (accessed 11 March 2010).

[4] See further Sub-Commission on the Promotion and Protection of Human Rights, Intellectual Property Rights and Human Rights (17 August 2000), Sub-Comm. Human Rights Res. 2000/7, UN Doc. E/CN.4/Sub.2/RES/2000/7 (2000), available at: http://www.unhchr.ch/Huridocda/Huridoca.nsf/0/c462b62cf8a07b13c12569700046704e?Opendocument (accessed 5 February 2010).

[5] International Covenant on Economic, Social and Cultural Rights (New York, 16 December 1966) 993 U.N.T.S. 3, 6 I.L.M. 360 (1967), G.A. Res. 2200A (XXI), UN Doc. A/6316 (1966) (*entered into force* 3 January 1976), available at: http://www2.ohchr.org/english/law/pdf/cescr.pdf (accessed 11 March 2010).

[6] Committee on Economic, Social and Cultural Rights (CESCR) 2000, *General Comment No. 14: The right to the highest attainable standard of health* (art. 12), UN Doc.E/C.12/2000/4 (11 August 2000), available at: http://www.unhchr.ch/tbs/doc.nsf/0/40d009901358b0e2c1256915005090be?Opendocument

in Article 24 of the Convention on the Rights of the Child (CRC),[7] interpreted by the Committee on the Rights of the Child in its General Comments No. 3 (2003) on 'HIV/AIDS and the Rights of the Child' and No. 4 (2003) on 'Adolescent Health' (Ovett 2006).[8]

Health and development promotion are also central components of the United Nations Millennium Project, expressed by the eight Millennium Development Goals (MDGs)[9] – a series of time-bound targets set out at the Millennium Summit in September 2000 – to be achieved by 2015 (Millennium Project 2005; see Chapter 6, Box 6.1). Several of these goals are directly or indirectly related to improving health; this includes, for example, the MDGs aiming to 'eradicate extreme poverty and hunger' (MDG1), to 'reduce child mortality' (MDG4) and to 'improve maternal health' (MDG5). The sixth goal under the MDGs explicitly addresses combating 'HIV/AIDS, malaria and other diseases'. The Target for 2015 under this goal is to 'halt and begin to reverse the spread of HIV/AIDS and the incidence of malaria and other major diseases' (MDG6). Under MDG8, which is to 'develop a global partnership for development', one of the stated targets is to provide access to essential drugs in developing countries in cooperation with pharmaceutical companies.[10]

The linkage of intellectual property rights (IPRs) to the world trade regime through the Agreement on Trade-Related Aspects of Intellectual Property Rights ('TRIPS Agreement'),[11] signed in 1994 by members of the newly established World Trade Organization (WTO), effectively introduced new minimum standards of IP protection for WTO members. Significantly, the Agreement required WTO members to extend patentability to inventions in all technological fields. Although the TRIPS Agreement does not define what constitutes an 'invention' or a 'technological field', leaving these terms open to interpretation, countries that formerly did not grant patents to pharmaceutical products or processes have been under pressure to alter their legislation within the implementation deadlines provided by the

(accessed 15 March 2010). See also WHO Model List of Essential Medicines, 16th edition (revised March 2009), available at: http://www.who.int/medicines/publications/essentialmedicines/en/ (accessed 15 March 2010).

7 Convention on the Rights of the Child (New York, 20 November 1989), 1577 U.N.T.S. 3, 28 I.L.M. 1456 (1989), G.A. Res. 44/25, annex, UN Doc. A/44/49 (1989) (*entered into force* 2 September 1990), available at: http://www2.ohchr.org/english/law/crc.htm (accessed 3 February 2010).

8 See Committee on the Rights of the Child 2003, *General Comment No. 3: HIV/AIDS and the rights of the child*, UN Doc. CRC/GC/2003/3 (17 March 2003), available at: http://www.unhchr.ch/tbs/doc.nsf/(symbol)/CRC.GC.2003.3.En?OpenDocument (accessed 3 February 2010); Committee on the Rights of the Child 2003, *General Comment No. 4: Adolescent health and development in the context of the Convention on the Rights of the Child*, UN Doc. CRC/GC/2003/4 (1 July 2003), available at: http://www.unhchr.ch/tbs/doc.nsf/(symbol)/CRC.GC.2003.4.En?OpenDocument (accessed 3 February 2010).

9 See United Nations Millennium Declaration (8 September 2000), G.A. Res. 55/2, UN Doc. A/RES/55/2 (2000) [hereinafter 'UN Millennium Declaration'], available at: http://www.un.org/millennium/ (accessed 22 June 2009).

10 For annual assessments on progress towards the Millennium Developement Goals (MDGs), see 'Millennium Development Goals Reports' (published by the Statistics Division of the United Nations Department of Economic and Social Affairs), available at: http://www.un.org/millenniumgoals/reports.shtml (accessed 11 March 2010).

11 Agreement on Trade-Related Aspects of Intellectual Property Rights (Marrakesh, 15 April 1994), Marrakesh Agreement Establishing the World Trade Organization, Annex 1C, 1869 U.N.T.S. 299, 33 I.L.M. 1197 (1994) [hereinafter 'TRIPS Agreement'], available at: http://www.wto.org/english/tratop_e/trips_e/t_agm0_e.htm (accessed 3 February 2010).

Agreement.[12] Such implementation has had a worldwide impact on the entire structure of the generic and innovative medicines industries as well as on pricing strategies.

The impact of the TRIPS Agreement on health access in developing countries and LDCs has been a source of tremendous controversy. On one hand, there are proponents who argue that effective patent protection is necessary to encourage innovation and investment in pharmaceutical and related medical technology research; on the other hand, there are voices that emphasize alternative public-private models for R&D, and the promotion of the public interest through appropriate TRIPS revisions and/or the use of existing TRIPS flexibilities (including those with the potential to refuse to grant or enforce patents, or to otherwise weaken patent protection). The latter strategies include creating policies and/or structures that guarantee the use of all TRIPS exceptions and limitations without the threat of penalties or sanctions from WTO members.

A significant development in relation to TRIPS and public health was the adoption of the Declaration on the TRIPS Agreement and Public Health at the WTO's Fourth Ministerial Conference in Doha, Qatar, on 14 November 2001 (the 'Doha Declaration').[13] The latter Declaration followed much public scrutiny, activism by civil society, and demands by developing countries especially over the impact of TRIPS on issues such as access to essential medicines in developing countries. Confrontation on access to medicine and competition issues between the South African government and pharmaceutical companies (over legislative reforms in South Africa aimed at facilitating parallel importation of patented drugs and generic substitution of off-patent drugs) was partly responsible for catalysing the international mobilization that resulted in the Doha Declaration.[14] Intended to ensure that TRIPS provisions would not prevent countries from protecting public health, the Doha Declaration clarifies that the TRIPS Agreement should be interpreted and implemented in favor of WTO members' right to public health protection. Significantly, its provisions restate and reinforce some of the flexibilities contained in the TRIPS Agreement, such as freedom to grant compulsory licences for any reason (although under specified procedures) and freedom to establish parallel importation regimes. It emphasizes that practices related to the use of such flexibilities cannot be the subject of dispute settlement at the WTO. The Doha Declaration further provides that LDCs have the option to delay implementation until 2016, a time

[12] While developing countries had to implement the relevant provisions in the TRIPS Agreement by 1 January 2000, those developing countries that had not granted product patents for an area of technology by that date were allowed to delay the introduction of such legislation until 1 January 2005. Under the TRIPS agreement, the least developed countries (LDCs) had to implement the relevant provisions by 2006. However, the Doha Ministerial Declaration (of 14 November 2001) subsquently extended the implementation deadline for LDCs to 2016 for pharmaceutical products.

[13] World Trade Organization (WTO), Ministerial Declaration (Doha, 14 November 2001), 41 I.L.M. 746 (2002), Doc. No. WT/MIN(01)/DEC/W/1 [hereinafter 'Doha Declaration'], available at: http://www.wto.org/English/thewto_e/minist_e/min01_e/mindecl_e.htm (accessed 1 March 2010).

[14] In 1997, the Republic of South Africa passed the Medicines and Related Substances Control Amendment Act, 90 of 1997, allowing parallel importation of patented drugs and generic substitution of off-patented drugs. In 1998, thirty-nine pharmaceutical companies filed a lawsuit against the South African government to block the new regulation. See *Pharmaceutical Manufacturers' Association of South Africa v. President of the Republic of South Africa*, Case No. 4,183/98 (filed 18 February 1998).

flexibility which these countries should make full use of. Other decisions at the WTO since the Doha Declaration have sought to clarify aspects of TRIPS flexibilities relating to public health and the implementation of the Doha Declaration.[15]

It is important for developing countries to be able to take full advantage of the exclusions from patent eligibility or patentability provided under the TRIPS Agreement. The law in this area is in flux. A number of court and administrative decisions (some pending) in the United States (US) and Europe concerning the scope of patent eligibility and the required level of inventive creativity could preclude or restrict patents on at least some drugs, genetic sequences and diagnostic methods even in developed countries.[16]

Some other areas that will receive increasing scrutiny include the potential for developing countries to make better use of compulsory licensing or refusals to enjoin infringement of health care-related patents (providing only compensatory remedies), and appropriate laws in relation to parallel imports in ensuring public health targets. These and other key issues and trends relating to IP and health, both within and beyond the TRIPS context, are briefly highlighted in the following sections, along with some projections on areas of growing significance.

1.1. Trends in pharmaceutical patenting and their implications for new innovations and generic production

It has been argued that IP protection (particularly patent protection) is essential to maintaining drug development efforts, especially in light of the rising costs and complexities in the development of new drugs. However, higher standards in patent protection do not necessarily induce the development of new pharmaceutical inventions. In recent years, there has been increasing emphasis in the R&D policies of many pharmaceutical companies on new therapeutic uses for known drugs and minor modifications to them. Firms now strive to obtain patents in the largest world markets to protect these new uses and modifications. For example, the United States Food and Drug Administration (FDA) has reported that new drug applications have increasingly been submitted for variations of existing drugs,

[15] World Trade Organization (WTO), Decision of the General Counsel of 30 August 2003, Implementation of Paragraph 6 of the Doha Declaration on the TRIPS Agreement and Public Health, Doc. WT/L/540 (1 September 2003), available at: http://www.wto.org/english/tratop_E/TRIPS_e/implem_para6_e.htm (accessed 7 March 2010); World Trade Organization (WTO), Decision of the General Counsel of 6 December 2005, Amendment of the TRIPS Agreement, Doc. WT/L/641 (8 December 2005), available at: http://www.wto.org/english/tratop_E/trips_e/wtl641_e.htm (accessed 7 March 2010). See also World Trade Organization (WTO), 'TRIPS and Public Health' (briefings on TRIPS, patents and pharmaceuticals and public health), available at: http://www.wto.org/english/tratop_e/trips_e/pharmpatent_e.htm (accessed 12 March 2010); see Abbott 2005 for detailed analysis and critique.

[16] See, e.g. *Classen Immunotherapies, Inc. v. Biogen Idec*, 304 Fed. Appx. 866 (Fed. Cir. 2008), *cert. granted, vacated, remanded*, 2010 WL 2571877 (U.S. 29 June 2010) (No. 08-1509) for reconsideration in view of *Bilski v. Kappos*, No. 08-964, 2010 WL 2555192 (U.S. 28 June 2010); *Association for Molecular Pathology v. U.S. Patent and Trademark Office*, No. 09-CV-4515, slip opinion (S.D.N.Y. 29 March 2010, amended 5 April 2010) (Sweet, J.), appeal docketed, No. 2010-1406 (Fed. Cir. 22 June 2010) *Pfizer, Inc. v. Apotex, Inc.*, 488 F.3d 1377 (Fed. Cir. 2007). USPTO: 'Utility Examination Guidelines', 66 Fed. Reg. 1092, 1092–1099 (2001); *ICOSCorp/Novel/V28 Seven Transmembrane Receptor* [2002] 6 OJ EPO 293; *Aeomica, Inc.* [2005] BL O/286/05. See Thambisethy 2008.

rather than for more innovative molecules (FDA 2003, 2004; Taylor 2003, pp. 408–409). According to the FDA, increases in these so-called 'me-too' drugs have been paralleled by decreases in the development of new drugs more likely to be truly innovative (FDA 2003).

Some studies focus on the effectiveness of the patent as a means of appropriability (i.e. the ability to capture returns accruing as a result of innovation) for the pharmaceutical industry (Mansfield 1986, pp. 174–175; Levin et al. 1987, pp. 795–796; Cohen, Nelson & Walsh 2000). Appropriation regimes vary from industry to industry due to differing motivations, and few other industrial sectors place such a high strategic value on patents as the pharmaceutical sector. In practice, 'appropriation' in the pharmaceutical sector is sometimes achieved through the 'evergreening' of patents, where manufacturers extend the life of their patent monopolies by filing new applications on minor modifications to the invention disclosed in the original patent, and also by adopting aggressive marketing strategies to get doctors to switch their patients over from an original drug going off patent to a new 'upgraded' version sold under a different name that may offer little if any therapeutic advantage over the first drug.[17]

In 2006, the Canadian Supreme Court set a precedent against the practice of 'evergreening' in a ruling in favor of a Canadian generics manufacturer,[18] but the issue is nonetheless highly case specific. India has also passed legislation that seeks to prevent this practice. The relevant provisions in this legislation were challenged by Novartis in the Indian courts on the basis that they were in conflict with India's obligations under the TRIPS Agreement and in breach of the Indian Constitution.[19] Novartis's challenge failed. However, there was no decision on whether these legislative provisions are consistent with the TRIPS Agreement, because the Indian court held there was lack of jurisdiction.[20] The Brazilian Government has also taken an aggressive stance towards ending abuses related to 'evergreening'. However, the Brazilian Government's 2008 decision to ban the patentability of new uses for known drugs and other trivial inventions is still under criticism from part of the pharmaceutical industry and the Brazilian Association of Intellectual Property.

With patents increasingly being used to protect new uses for old drugs (particularly for diseases for which reasonably effective treatments already exist) and small changes to existing compounds such as new drug dosages or forms, questions have been raised as to whether patents are doing enough to encourage the development

[17] For examples of the latter practice, see Angell 2004, p. 79; Goozner 2004, p. 222; Law 2006, pp. 76–78.

[18] On 3 October 2006, the Supreme Court of Canada ruled that Health Canada's regulatory regime, which allowed for the practice of 'evergreening', should not have been allowed. The case involved AstraZeneca's omeprazole drug whose patent had expired in 1999. After expiration, the company obtained a new patent for the drug despite not having incorporated new technology. *AstraZeneca Canada Inc. v. Canada (Minister of Health)*, [2006] 2 S.C.R. 560, 2006 SCC 49, available at: http://csc.lexum.umontreal.ca/en/2006/2006scc49/2006scc49.pdf (accessed 12 March 2010).

[19] See Affidavit Filed on Behalf of the Petitioner, *Novartis AG v. Union of India*, 2007) 4 MLJ 1153 (Mad) (W.P. No. 24759 of 2006), available at: http://www.cptech.org/ip/health/c/india/novartis-v-india.doc (accessed 12 March 2010).

[20] *Novartis AG v. Union of India*, (2007) 4 MLJ 1153 (Mad), available at: http://www.mljlibrary.com/nominal-index/C1MF4PD2NH6RB0L.htm (accessed 12 March 2010).

of new chemical entities that are significant improvements on existing medicines.[21] Perhaps the most significant factors contributing to the proliferation of 'me-too' drugs or new uses of existing drugs in the US are the elasticity of the novelty rules and the existing threshold for the test of 'non-obviousness' for patent grants. 'Non-obviousness' (or 'inventive step' in other jurisdictions including in Europe) is one of four traditional and internationally accepted requirements for the grant of a patent. The other three requirements are 'novelty' (i.e. that the invention be new), 'utility' (i.e. that it be useful or have 'industrial applicability'), and that the 'invention' is adequately described in the proposed patent and thus 'enabled' (Barton 2003, p. 475). Barton explains that:

> The novelty and non-obviousness principles are designed to work together to ensure that the patent monopoly is available only for genuinely new inventions. The novelty standard asks whether the invention has been previously described or practised; thus, it seeks to determine whether the invention is already within the existing state of the art. The non-obviousness principle asks whether the invention is an adequate distance beyond or above the state of the art; it clearly and unavoidably, therefore, involves an exercise of judgment. (Ibid., pp. 475–476)

Barton argues that 'contemporary patent law has weakened [the] non-obviousness requirement, leading to the grant of many patents on trivial inventions' which he considers to be 'economically wasteful' (ibid., p. 475). Examining the non-obviousness standard, he explores ways to set the standard at a level that rewards significant inventions and avoids a proliferation of economically undesirable patents (ibid.). While the TRIPS Agreement does not harmonize the level of creativity required to obtain a patent, economic theory suggests that a heightened non-obviousness requirement creates incentives for investment in more innovative – as opposed to 'me-too' – drugs and other relevant technologies. Since 2007, a significant US Supreme Court decision[22] has been thought to raise the bar in regard to showing non-obviousness (particularly in regard to new combinations that do not have new functions or significantly improved efficacy), with implications for pharmaceutical patents.

The effects of patent grants for second and subsequent uses of drugs[23] have been observed to result in delaying entry of new generic medicines in local markets (Correa 2007).[24] By generic drugs we mean drugs that are produced and distributed without patent protection but with the same dosage, safety, quality and efficacy as the branded drug. Box 2.1 presents some recent trends in relation to world generics production and patent protection of pharmaceuticals.

21 See US Government Accountability Office 2006.

22 *KSR Int'l. Co. v. Teleflex, Inc.*, 550 U.S. 398 (2007).

23 Second and subsequent medical uses of drugs may be expressed in different manners: (1) the composition of a known drug or drug formulation may be altered in order to acquire a new therapeutic effect; (2) a known composition may present new therapeutic effects when administered to patients in a different manner.

24 See Pharmaceutical Sector Inquiry – Preliminary Report 2008, DG Competition Staff Working Paper, November 2008.

BOX 2.1. Generics and the price of medicines[25]

The TRIPS Agreement requires WTO members to provide patent protection for inventions in all technological fields (Article 27).[26] The implementation deadline for developed countries was 1996. The Agreement provides additional time for developing countries and LDCs to put in place patent regimes for certain technologies and products, including pharmaceuticals. Developing countries that had already granted patents for pharmaceutical products had to implement the relevant provisions in TRIPS by 1 January 2000 (Article 65(2)). Developing countries that had not granted products patents for an area of technology could further delay the introduction of such legislation until 1 January 2005 (Article 65(4)). The Doha Declaration (para.7) has extended this deadline to 2016 for LDCs.

India has been one of the world's largest producers of generic medicines. It has a strong pharmaceutical industry, primarily in the production of generics, and it has taken significant advantage of its ten-year transition period under the TRIPS Agreement to consolidate this industry further. Bulk drug production in India increased by nearly 20% every year in the period between 1993 and 2003 (Joshi 2003). The country has been producing generic versions of essential medicines not just for its population but for patients in other developing countries and LDCs. Countries in Sub-Saharan Africa, for example, lacking their own pharmaceutical production capabilities, rely on imports of medicines and active pharmaceutical ingredients[27] from countries that produce them at low cost, including India and China. In 2001, an antiretroviral (ARV) therapy using branded medicines typically cost US$10,000 or more in the developed world (Fleshman 2005). That same year, Cipla – one of the largest Indian generic pharmaceutical companies – offered the therapy to humanitarian groups for use in Africa at the much lower price of US$350 per patient per year (ibid.). One estimate suggests that the price for first line generic ARV drugs procured for countries in Sub-Saharan Africa further decreased to US$114 per patient per year by 2006 (Chien 2007).

China and Thailand are among other countries which have taken advantage of the TRIPS extension period to produce low-cost generic medicines. Now that the extension period for TRIPS compliance has expired for these developing countries, this freedom will be affected. The full impact of TRIPS compliance on the structure of global generic production remains to be evaluated. While a number of years have passed since India issued its presidential decree[28] to conform to the 2005 deadline, a study by Janodia et al. (2008) suggests that it is still too early to examine its full effect.[29] The Indian decree will affect the prices of first line medicines

(*continued*)

---

[25] This section was contributed by Claudia Trezza.

[26] Since the Agreement does not define what constitutes an 'invention' or a 'technological field', these terms are open to interpretation.

[27] There are companies in Sub-Saharan Africa with the facilities to manufacture drugs, but almost all of them must import the active pharmaceutical ingredients (APIs). For example, Danadams, a Ghanaian company, imports APIs for some AIDS drugs, which are then produced in its own laboratory.

[28] The Patents (Amendment) Ordinance, Ord. No. 7 of 2004 (Republic of India), available at: http://lawmin.nic.in/Patents%20Amendment%20Ordinance%202004.pdf (accessed 12 March 2010).

[29] Janodia et al. (2008) suggest that one of the reasons why it is difficult to tell what impact this will have relates to the so-called 'mailbox' system in India. The 'mailbox'system was established to receive and register patent applications in 1995, directly following the implementation of the TRIPS Agreement. Since then, approximately 9,000 applications have been filed and are pending approval (ibid.). For these applications, the twenty-year patent life begins on the date of the application, and the protection will be effective on the date that any patent is ultimately granted. On the WTO dispute settlement history regarding the India 'mail-box' system, see World Trade Organization (WTO), Appellate Body Report on *India – Patent Protection for Pharmaceutical and Agricultural Chemical Products*, Doc. WT/DS50/AB/R, adopted 16 January 1998.

Box 2.1 (*continued*)

for patients. Of further concern to public health advocates, it will drive up the prices of second and third line drugs.[30]

Some commentators suggest that compulsory licensing provisions in the TRIPS Agreement should be invoked by countries manufacturing generics in order to continue exporting to other countries (Kuanpoth 2007, p. 214; see Section 1.2). While the TRIPS Agreement requires that a compulsory licence be granted 'predominantly' for the supply of the domestic market, there is still some room for exports under Article 31(f) of the Agreement (ibid.). Moreover, in cases where a compulsory licence has been granted to remedy anti-competitive practices, there is no export restriction (ibid.). Kuanpoth (2007, p. 214) highlights that the Doha Declaration, along with the WTO Decisions of August 2003 and December 2005,[31] permits the export of medicines to a country with insufficient or no manufacturing capacities in the pharmaceutical sector.

Developing countries and LDCs, especially those lacking these manufacturing capabilities, should explore flexibilities under the TRIPS Agreement to import generics from countries which produce them. Kuanpoth (2007, pp. 203–204) points out, for example, that the price of ARVs in Vietnam is generally 'much higher than current international best prices'; he adds that 'the production and importation of several generic ARV drugs, needed in order to provide treatment in line with international and WHO standards at affordable prices, is not feasible without infringing patents' in Vietnam. He suggests that countries like Vietnam may need to avail themselves of the available legal options under the TRIPS Agreement and national laws to ensure the availability of these medicines, including through parallel imports and imports of drugs sold by other countries under compulsory licensing (ibid., pp. 213–215; see Section 1.2).

Many countries that until now have benefited from imports of inexpensive generic drugs are also increasingly dependent on international regulatory bodies to create other sources of inexpensive medicine. Further developments in this area will significantly impact IP regulations, the pharmaceutical market and public health decisions in all countries. Given competition from generics and the fact that many 'blockbuster' drugs under patents since the early 1990s are going off patent (e.g. the 'cholesterol-reducing' drug Lipitor® is going off patent in 2011), brand-name pharmaceutical companies are also under pressure to adjust their pricing policies,[32] and are entering increasingly into generic production. In February 2009, the world's second largest pharmaceutical company, GlaxoSmithKline, allegedly announced that it would cut its prices for all drugs in the fifty LDCs to no more than 25% of the levels in the UK and US, while also taking steps such as placing any chemicals or processes over which it has IPRs that are relevant to finding drugs for neglected diseases into a 'patent pool'.[33] Some health campaigners are concerned, at the same time, that such moves may undermine the generics industry currently supplying the cheapest drugs in poor countries; Oxfam and Medecins Sans Frontières have suggested that any patent pools created should include the HIV/AIDS drugs (see Appendix B for an update on such patent pools).[34]

---

[30] It is important to make a distinction between first- and second-generation pharmaceuticals. The number of AIDS patients that now receive ARV therapy has grown since prices have dropped. Unfortunately, due to the highly mutative character of the virus, patients in many cases develop resistances to first-line drugs. Resistances are most complicated when patients do not adhere to the regimen of the therapy. Second-line drugs are necessary to prevent such resistances.

[31] The relevant WTO decisions are cited in footnote 15; see the discussion in Abbott 2005.

[32] 'Big Pharma Besieged', *The Guardian*, 5 September 2008.

[33] 'World's Poor and Ailing Promised Cheap Drugs', *The Guardian Weekly*, 20–26 February 2009.

[34] Ibid.

Generics have to be contrasted with counterfeit medicine, as emphasized at the World Health Assembly (WHA) in May 2008. The WHO defines counterfeit medicines as 'deliberately and fraudulently mislabeled [medicines] with respect to identity and/or source'.[35] According to this definition: 'Counterfeiting can apply to both branded and generic products. Counterfeit products may include products with the correct ingredients or with the wrong ingredients, without active ingredients, with insufficient active ingredients, or with fake packaging'.[36] The use of counterfeit drugs can have negative consequences on the health of patients taking the drugs. Often the drugs contain no active ingredients and can therefore exacerbate the disease and cause resistances among wider sections of the population (Geneva Pharma Forum 2004).[37]

The WHO has developed international guidelines and recommended national strategies and measures to put a stop to the growing problem of counterfeit drugs.[38] Recognizing that international collaboration against counterfeits is an issue affecting both developed and developing countries, WHO organized a conference 'Combating Counterfeit Drugs: Building Effective International Collaboration' in 2006. The meeting was concluded with the 'Rome Declaration',[39] in which countries agreed that: 'Counterfeiting medicines ... is a vile and serious criminal offence that puts human lives at risk and undermines the credibility of health systems ... Because of its direct impact on health ... [it] should be combated and punished accordingly' (Articles 1–2). The Declaration called for a concerted action from all relevant private and public stakeholders. It also called for the creation of the International Medical Products Anti-Counterfeiting Taskforce (IMPACT) to raise awareness, coordinate efforts, and exchange information between countries to combat counterfeit medicines globally (Article 6 of the Declaration). The IMPACT approach has been heavily criticized, however, by many developing countries. There is also disagreement on the very use of the term 'counterfeit drugs', an issue which was discussed amongst others at the 124th Session of the WHO Executive

[35] World Health Organization (WHO), 'General Information on Counterfeit Medicines' (fact sheet), available at: http://www.who.int/medicines/services/counterfeit/overview/en/index.html (accessed 1 June 2009).

[36] Ibid.

[37] Counterfeit drugs may not only cause harm to patients, but may also cause mistrust in the public towards health services and medicine; they can also lead to a waste of resources on the part of organizations or government(s) purchasing counterfeit medicines inadvertently. See Commonwealth Secretariat 2007.

[38] Department of Essential Drugs and Other Medicines, 'Counterfeit Drugs, Guidelines for the Development of Measures to Combat Counterfeit Medicines' (World Health Organization, Geneva, 1999), available at: http://whqlibdoc.who.int/hq/1999/WHO_EDM_QSM_99.1.pdf (accessed 1 June 2009). The proliferation of unregulated pharmaceutical industries and products is expected to continue into the future. Among the causes of counterfeit medicines are weak drug regulation, clandestine manufacturing, lack of sanctions and high levels of corruption, as well as high prices of medicines which force patients to look for cheaper substitutes. See WHO, 'Counterfeit Medicines', available at: http://www.who.int/medicines/services/counterfeit/en/ (accessed 1 June 2009); see also Royal Pharmaceutical Society of Great Britain 2008.

[39] Declaration of Rome, Conclusions and Recommendations of the WHO International Conference on Combating Counterfeit Medicines (18 February 2006), available at: http://www.who.int/medicines/services/counterfeit/RomeDeclaration.pdf (accessed 1 June 2009).

Board, in Geneva, on 19–27 January 2009.[40] It is relevant to highlight a recent seizure by the Netherlands authorities of losartan potassium (a drug used primarily to treat high blood pressure) in transit from India to Brazil on grounds that IPRs might be violated due to the existence of a patent right in the Netherlands. This seizure was considered a violation of WTO rules by the Brazilian government, as losartan was not patented in India or Brazil, among other reasons.

Indeed, there is a very real danger that anti-counterfeiting measures based upon unduly broad or vague definitions of 'counterfeit' medicines could inhibit the trade, supply and sale of perfectly legitimate generic drugs.[41] According to legislation recently passed in Kenya (the Anti-Counterfeit Act 2008),[42] counterfeiting refers to a range of actions which are done 'without the authority of the owner of any intellectual property right subsisting in Kenya or elsewhere in respect of protected goods' (Article 2).[43] This appears to go too far, blurring the meaning of the term and potentially enabling owners of patents not necessarily held in Kenya to have the importation, domestic manufacture and supply of otherwise perfectly legitimate generic drugs suppressed. It also reduces Kenya's abilities to take advantage of the flexibilities of TRIPS, fails to address the possible problems of originator firms selling poor quality versions of their own drugs, and may possibly exclude those fakes that do *not* infringe on any IPRs.[44] Uganda has reportedly drafted similar legislation.

Issues have also been raised over the extent to which generic manufacturers are able to import, manufacture and test a patented product prior to the expiration of the patent in order that they may fulfil the regulatory requirements imposed by particular countries for marketing the drug as a generic. Such acts are now made legal in the US by the Drug Price Competition and Patent Term Restoration Act of 1984 (commonly known as the 'Hatch-Waxman Act'), which overturned a landmark court decision (*Roche v. Bolar*, 1984)[45] by introducing what is now known as the 'Bolar Exception' or 'early working exception' to patent infringement. The WTO legality of a similar exception was confirmed in 2000 in a dispute settlement case brought by

[40] In the report on *Counterfeit Medical Products* (see WHO 2008), presented to the Executive Board by the Secretariat during the session, a revised IMPACT definition for counterfeit drugs was introduced. For an analysis on how the new definition might potentially extend the ambit of 'counterfeits', see South Centre and CIEL 2009, pp. 2–5.

[41] This paragraph was contributed by Graham Dutfield, drawing on von Braun, J. 2009, 'New Enforcement Mechanisms Challenge the Legality of Generics in the Name of Public Health', a paper prepared for the WHO, United Nations Development Programme (UNDP) and University of Capetown (UCT) *Training Course on Intellectual Property Rights & Public Health: Towards an Intellectual Property Regime that Protects Public Health: A Course Directed at Policy Makers in the WHO African Region*, Cape Town, South Africa, 22–26 June 2009.

[42] The official text of the Act is available at: http://www.kenyalaw.org/kenyalaw/klr_app/frames.php (accessed 15 February 2010). The Act is currently being challenged in Kenya's Constitutional Court. See Anyangu-Amu, S. 2009, 'Kenya: Anti-Counterfeit Law "Violates Right to Life and Health"', *Inter Press Service*, 21 December 2009, available at: http://ipsnews.net/news.asp?idnews=49764 (accessed 1 February 2010).

[43] The actions that amount to counterfeiting are described in Article 2.

[44] To the extent a fake drug does not contain any patented active ingredients, it is unlikely to infringe a patented invention. It may, however, infringe a trademark in given cases.

[45] *Roche Products, Inc. v. Bolar Pharmaceutical Co.*, 733 F.2d. 858 (Fed. Cir. 1984).

the European Union (EU) against Canada.[46] The Commission on Intellectual Property Rights (CIPR) notes these developments in its seminal 2002 report on *Integrating Intellectual Property Rights and Development Policy* (hereinafter 'CIPR Report'). The report recommends that: 'Developing countries should include an appropriate exception for "early working" to patent rights in their legislation, which will accelerate the introduction of generic substitutes on patent expiry' (CIPR 2002, p. 50). Of the sixty-three developing countries whose legislation was examined by the CIPR study, only eight specifically included a Bolar exception (ibid.). Nevertheless, many countries have experimental use exceptions that may extend to experimentation for generating test data required to obtain regulatory marketing approval.

1.2. Compulsory licensing and government use

Given that a major purpose of the TRIPS Agreement was to require the extension of patents to pharmaceutical products and processes for their manufacture,[47] the generic production of drugs will be increasingly restricted as countries implement the Agreement. A substantial amount of focus has shifted to the authorization for exceptions to the exclusive rights that must be provided under the TRIPS Agreement, especially in relation to compulsory licensing and government use which may have an important role to play in maintaining a 'pro-competitive IPR policy in the new environment' (CIPR 2002, p. 42). TRIPS Article 31 does not prohibit the issuance of compulsory licences or governmental uses on any grounds, but rather imposes procedures (including compensation) in the event of such licences or use. In cases of national emergency, extreme urgency and public non-commercial uses (under Article 31(b)), no prior efforts to obtain patent holder authorization are required. Although Article 31(f) required that such compulsory licences or government use be primarily for domestic markets, the Doha Declaration waived Article 31(f) in the case of countries seeking to export medicines to developing countries where production capacity does not exist.

Developing countries have yet to make full use of their retained compulsory licensing authorities, even though this is allowed under the TRIPS Agreement as clarified by the Doha Declaration. Concern by developing countries over reprisals from investors might be one reason. The CIPR Report notes that 'ironically, it is the developed countries that have been the most active users of compulsory licensing (not only in the pharmaceutical field) for a number of purposes, including importantly in antitrust cases in the U.S.' (CIPR 2002, p. 42). According to the report, Canada used compulsory licensing extensively in the pharmaceutical field from

[46] WTO Panel Report on *Canada – Patent Protection of Pharmaceutical Products*, Doc. WT/DS114/R, adopted 7 April 2000, available at: http://www.wto.org/english/tratop_e/dispu_e/cases_e/ds114_e.htm (accessed 9 April 2010).

[47] See Gervais 2008. The TRIPS Agreement does not on its face require pharmaceutical patents, and it remains an open question whether a country seeking to refuse such protection could treat some pharmaceuticals as not inventions or could discriminate by field of technology in a way that would also be valid under Article 30 (which authorizes national exceptions to patent rights meeting specified criteria). Thus, the Indian example is relevant – not all pharmaceuticals may be required to be potentially patentable. However, it is likely that a categorical exclusion of *all* pharmaceuticals would be found to violate these provisions, given the explicit major purpose to impose such requirements.

1969 until the late 1980s, with the result of prices of licensed drugs being 47% lower than in the US in 1982 (ibid.).

More recently, two countries – Brazil and Thailand – announced compulsory licences for pharmaceuticals. Thailand issued compulsory licences on 26 January 2007 for the heart disease drug clopidogrel (Sanofi-Aventis's Plavix®) and the HIV/AIDS drug lopinavir/ritonavir (Abbott's Kaletra®) and on 29 November 2006 for the HIV/AIDS medicine efavirenz (Merck Sharp & Dohme's Stocrin®) (Gerhardsen 2007). After declaring efavirenz a medicine of public interest, Brazil issued a compulsory licence for this patented AIDS drug on 4 May 2007, as price negotiations failed.[48] As expected, pharmaceutical multinationals strongly criticized these decisions. Since May 2007, efavirenz has been imported from India into Brazil through the United Nation's Children's Fund (UNICEF) and the Pan American Health Organization (PAHO). In September 2008, the Brazilian Minister of Health Jose Gomes Temporao announced that the 'bioavailability' tests were positive. The generic version of efavirenz is now being produced in Brazil. This generic version is expected to reach a final production cost close to the price that is paid for the Indian generic. Further analysis is required on the implications of these decisions for access to drugs in developing countries.

The approaches of Brazil and Thailand to ensure access to key ARV drugs had been different until recently. Ford et al. (2007, p. S24) note in the case of Brazil that 'price negotiations, backed by the threat of complusory licensing and local generic production, have been the main strategy used by the government to lower the price of patented antiretroviral drugs'. In contrast, direct negotiations with pharmaceutical companies have had mixed success in Thailand, where strategies to reduce the cost of antiretroviral drugs have focused on 'patent challenges and compulsory licensing' (ibid., p. S26).

The use of compulsory licences under the TRIPS Agreement is related to a larger trend towards wider use of alternative licensing techniques. Companies in South Africa and Brazil, for example, have obtained voluntary licences for AIDS drugs, sometimes with their government's assistance. Patent pooling, in which patent holders agree not to assert certain patents against each other (usually by entering into cross-licensing agreements relating to a particular technology), is also used to reduce barriers to drug development (see Appendix B). This route is also being explored for AIDS drugs by UNITAID, a WHO-hosted drug purchasing facility. These innovative mechanisms can help to improve access to needed medicines and are likely to be used increasingly by developing countries, especially when associated with incentives for local production.

Similarly, significant potential exists for governments to make greater public, non-commercial uses of patented pharmaceutical technologies, as authorized under Article 31(b) of the TRIPS Agreement. Even without government-directed production actually resulting, the potential for such production may dramatically

[48] Brazilian industrial property law recognizes compulsory licensing in cases of public interest. The Brazilian Government's Ministerial Ordinance No. 886, of 24 April 2007, declared the patent rights relating to efavirenz to be of public interest, for the purposes of granting compulsory licensing for non-commercial public use.

affect licensing behaviours or prices. For example, the US government has statutory authority to use any patented technology, subject to a potential lawsuit for the patent holder to obtain reasonable compensation.[49] In late 2005, in response to concerns about a possible avian influenza pandemic, the US government considered exercising this authority to authorize generic production of avian flu vaccine, following which additional production was voluntarily licensed by the patent holder.

1.3. Revisiting exclusions from patentability under the TRIPS Agreement

Discussions on flexibilities under the TRIPS Agreement sometimes ignore the significant flexibility WTO members retain over what they can exclude from patentability in the first place. Under Article 27(2) of the TRIPS Agreement, 'members may exclude from patentability inventions, the prevention within their territory of the commercial exploitation of which is necessary to protect *ordre public* or morality, including to protect human, animal or plant life or health or to avoid serious prejudice to the environment ...'.

The patentability of biotechnological inventions gave rise to discussions on the application of moral grounds for refusing to grant patents. Article 27(2) of TRIPS only authorizes members to exclude (from patentability) inventions where preventing *commercial exploitation* 'is necessary to protect *ordre publique* or morality'; Article 27(3)(a) further authorizes exclusions for medical, surgical and diagnostic methods for treating humans or animals. Many countries have adopted such exclusions. The Directive 98/44/EC of the European Parliament on the legal protection of biotechnological inventions says that 'inventions shall be considered unpatentable where their commercial exploitation would be contrary to ordre public or morality'.[50] The Directive's implementation in many EU countries was controversial due to the different positions of private and public sectors and non-governmental organizations. Outside the EU, many other countries either have laws with provisions on moral exclusions for certain biotechnology patents or exclude 'immoral' patents under a general morality exclusion authority, such as the Brazilian Industrial Property Law.[51] Some kinds of subject matter such as embryonic stem cells and gene sequences are especially controversial, raising ethical and moral concerns. Further studies are needed to assess the current and potential scope of the morality criterion in various countries.

Countries thus have significant flexibility in the interpretation of these provisions and on what they choose to exclude from patent protection. In addition to flexibilities in the interpretations of '*ordre public* or morality', the term 'invention' is not defined specifically in the TRIPS Agreement and Article 27(1) of the Agreement requires countries to authorize patents only for inventions that are 'capable of industrial application'. Most countries explicitly or by interpretation exclude from

[49] 28 U.S.C. § 1498(a).

[50] Council Directive 98/44/EC of 6 July 1998 on the legal protection of biotechnological inventions, Article 6(1), OJ No. L 213, p. 18 (1998).

[51] Article 18 of Brazil Industrial Property Law, No. 9,279, of 14 May 1996, available at: http://www.sice.oas.org/int_prop/nat_leg/Brazil/ENG/L9279eA.asp#grant (accessed 12 March 2010).

the definition of an invention newly discovered scientific principles and naturally occurring materials.[52] A number of developing countries have sought to limit what constitutes a patentable invention by legislation or judicial interpretation. By way of example, the Common Industrial Property Regime of the Andean Community countries provides that the following shall not be considered as inventions: 'Any living thing, either complete or partial, as found in nature, natural biological processes, and biological material, as existing in nature, or able to be separated, including the genome, or germplasm of any living thing' (CIPR 2002, p. 115).

In contrast to the provision under the Andean Community mentioned earlier, genes and gene fragments may be covered within the scope of patentable subject matter in some other jurisdictions, including the US. Article 27(3)(b) of the TRIPS Agreement provides that members 'may' exclude from patentability 'plants and animals other than micro-organisms, and essentially biological processes for the production of plants or animals other than non-biological and microbiological processes', but falls short of making it mandatory for WTO member states to exclude such plants, animals and processes from patentability. The future will likely see increasing debates in developed and developing countries over the scope and ethics of IPRs in regard to natural materials or medical and agricultural discoveries and inventions involving genes, gene fragments and genetically modified organisms (GMOs). Apart from ethical questions relating to the 'patenting of life and life-forms', there are debates as to whether such patents affect the advancement of research in the biomedical field, for example through restrictions on third-party use of research tools protected by patents. As highlighted in a report by Cornish, Llewelyn and Adcock (2003) entitled *Intellectual Property Rights (IPRs) and Genetics: A Study into the Impact and Management of Intellectual Property Rights within the Healthcare Sector:*

> Genetic research into diagnosis and therapies for humans now grow out of our new knowledge of the structure of the human genome and that necessarily conditions the work which can effectively be undertaken. It is therefore a field in which the existing rules governing the validity and scope of patents need to be applied with a real awareness of the new conditions for research and commercial exploitation in this field. The scope of what is patentable in pharmacology has, as we have sought to suggest, expanded very considerably. It has to be asked at what points there should be some retraction for the biotechnology industry and those who make use of the results of its research. (Ibid., p. 23)

One of the issues highlighted by Cornish et al. for further scrutiny is the concern that 'the simple identification of genes and partial fragments does not disclose any requisite industrial application and are therefore discoveries rather than inventions' (ibid., p. 30). For this reason, the European Biotechnology Directive requires identification of such an application to support patenting of genetic

[52] For example, European Patent Convention Article 52(2)(a) excludes from being considered an invention 'discoveries, scientific theories, and mathematical methods'. See Convention on the Grant of European Patents (Munich, 5 October 1973), 1065 U.N.T.S. 199, 13 I.L.M. 271 (1974) (*entered into force* 7 October 1977), *as last revised* 29 November 2000 (*entered into force as revised* 13 December 2007) [hereinafter 'European Patent Convention'], available at: http://www.epo.org/patents/law/legal-texts/epc.html (accessed 12 March 2010).

materials.[53] The authors also note that the enforcement of patent rights over genes which are used, for example, in diagnostic tests may require further scrutiny in terms of their impacts on costs for administration of such tests on patients, and on who has access to test results for future research (Cornish et al. 2003, p. 30). Concerning exclusions from patentability under the TRIPS Agreement, in the field of biotechnology the Brazilian Industrial Property Law does not consider as patentable living beings, in whole or in part, except transgenic microorganisms meeting the three patentability requirements – novelty, inventive activity and industrial application[54] – and which are not mere discoveries.[55]

1.4. Exceptions to exclusive patent rights

Article 30 of the TRIPS Agreement states that WTO members may provide limited exceptions to the exclusive rights conferred by a patent, provided that 'such exceptions do not unreasonably conflict with normal exploitation of the patent and do not unreasonably prejudice the legitimate interests of the patent owner, taking into account the legitimate interests of third parties'.

There is significant debate over the scope of these exceptions, for example, in terms of the extent to which WTO members can provide for research exemptions including experimental use of an invention subject to a patent. The scope of such exemptions varies significantly with jurisdictions. Comparing the scope of research exemptions under European and US law, Holzapfel and Sarnoff (2008) highlight the uncertainties that remain in both contexts. They note that in the US, the Supreme Court has adopted a broad construction of the regulatory approval exception to patent law infringement (under 35 U.S.C. § 271(e)(1)) for experiments conducted at early stages of the pharmaceutical development process (ibid., 2008). While this was the decision in the case of *Merck KGaA v. Integra LifeSciences I Ltd.*,[56] Holzapfel and Sarnoff (2008) qualify that the Supreme Court in that case refused to determine whether that exception applies to patented 'research tools'; a more recent appellate case, *Proveris Scientific Corp. v. Innovasystems, Inc.*,[57] limited application of the exception to patented inventions that are themselves potentially subject to regulatory approvals and thus could qualify for term extension provisions.

According to Holzapfel and Sarnoff (2008), the European experimental and regulatory approval exceptions may be subject to fewer interpretive uncertainties, particularly in light of decisions such as the UK *Monsanto* and German *Klinische Versuche (Clinical Trials)* cases.[58] However, they note that the nature and scope

[53] Council Directive 98/44/EC of 6 July 1998 on the legal protection of biotechnolical inventions, Article 5(3), OJ No. L 213, p. 18 (1998). See Case C-428/08 *Monsanto Technology LLC v. Cefetra BV* [2010].

[54] Brazil Industrial Property Law, Law No. 9,279 of 14 May 1996, available at: http://www.sice.oas.org/int_prop/nat_leg/Brazil/ENG/L9279eI.asp (accessed 12 March 2010). Article 8 provides that: 'To be patentable an invention must meet the requirements of novelty, inventive activity and industrial application' (ibid.).

[55] Ibid., Article 18.

[56] *Merck KGaA v. Integra LifeSciences I Ltd.*, 545 U.S. 193 (2005).

[57] *Proveris Scientific Corp. v. Innovasystems, Inc.*, 536 F.3d 1256 (Fed. Cir. 2008).

[58] *Monsanto Co. v. Stauffer Chemical Co.* [1985] R.P.C. 515 (High Ct. of Justice – Patents Court); *Klinische Versuche (Clinical Trials) I*, BGHZ 130, [1997] R.P.C. 623 (BGH); *Klinische Versuche (Clinical Trials)*

of the European exceptions may vary significantly among jurisdictions based on national legislative decisions to limit or extend patent protection – for example, the experimental use exception recently adopted in Belgian law[59] expressly applies to patented research tools. The authors assert that 'determining the proper scope and application of experimental use and regulatory approval exceptions remains a pressing concern in the United States as well as in Europe' (ibid., p. 127). These exceptions assure that patent laws intended to provide incentives for technological innovation do not unduly restrict scientific research, innovative medical product development and generic product competition.

A full discussion on research exemptions is beyond the scope of this chapter. In relation to biotechnological patents, Cornish et al. (2003) highlight that one major ambiguity about the experimental use exception concerns how far clinical tests can be regarded as 'experimental use' covered by a research exemption to patent liability, since treatment and the continuing search for further genetic knowledge often go hand in hand (Cornish et al. 2003, pp. 24–25). They note that as research on genetic diagnosis and therapy grows in volume and effectiveness the question of clinical testing, in particular resolving whether clinical trials fall within an 'experimental use' exception, will become an urgent issue (ibid., p. 32). While their discussion relates mainly to European law, it is highly relevant to other jurisdictions in resolving these difficult questions.

Other exceptions to the TRIPS requirements for exclusive patent rights also may be adopted. Little jurisprudence exists on the application of Article 30, or its correlate for exclusive copyrights in Article 13. However, it is clear that in determining whether national exceptions will conform to Article 30, contentious issues will arise in regard to the normative evaluation of such issues as 'normal exploitation', 'unreasonably prejudice', and the 'legitimate interests' of patent holders and the public (Holzapfel & Sarnoff 2008, p. 178).

1.5. Price controls, competition regulation and parallel imports restrictions

Additional concerns regarding affordable access to medicines pertain to the nature of the rights granted by patents, and how those rights relate to markets and to prices for patented products. There are significant policy questions for individual countries as to the extent to which the grant of patent rights should be subject to price and competition regulations. Given that a patent may convey monopoly economic power in the relevant product market for a pharmaceutical, it may also convey the

II, BGHZ 135, 217, [1998] RPC 423 (BGH). According to Holzapfel and Sarnoff (2008, p. 198): 'Europe's experimental use exception as stipulated in Article 27 (b) CPC 1989 and corresponding national provisions exclude from patent infringement acts of use that are carried out for experimental purposes relating to the subject-matter of the used invention. In this context, an experiment is defined as any systematic procedure aimed at discovering something unknown or testing a hypothesis. The motivation for gathering such information is irrelevant, as is whether or not the research has commercial application. Thus, e.g., pharmaceutical business interests may pursue clinical trials to assess effectiveness and a doctor may seek to identify a new drug indication, as long as the nature and scale of the acts of use reflect the purpose of obtaining new information. Similarly, the exception applies without differentiation between basic and applied research or between academic and commercial researchers.'

59 Belgium Patent Law, Art. 28(1)(b) (1997).

ability to price medicines at supra-competitive rates, creating a dominant position for the patent holder in the relevant product market. The TRIPS Agreement simply does not address the relationship between the legal right to exclude and the ability of the government to regulate the prices of patented products. Many countries set the prices of patented medicines directly through government regulation or negotiate significantly lower prices through uses of formularies. Similarly, most competition laws impliedly or expressly apply to patent holders, and some countries have provisions in their competition laws that treat excessive price-setting among other practices as potential abuses of dominant position. Some jurisdictions also consider the use of patents to block all competition in a particular market under the essential facilities doctrine to give rise to such remedies as requiring competitors to be supplied with access on reasonable and non-discriminatory terms.

Article 31(k) of the TRIPS Agreement recognizes the relationship between IP and competition laws, providing that compensation of patent holders is not required when compulsory licences are issued to remedy anti-competitive practices. But there are no minimum international standards in the TRIPS Agreement or elsewhere on the substance of what competition laws must require or may permit. Article 40 of the TRIPS Agreement specifically recognizes national authority for members to adopt prohibitions on licensing practices that are thought to constitute an abuse of IPRs and to have adverse effects on competition.

Significantly, IP in general and patents in particular are normally understood to grant only rights to exclude competition.[60] Exclusive rights do not themselves authorize the sale or use of products or services (including medicines whose marketing requires prior regulatory approval). Nor do they provide any legal authority in regard to prices that may permissibly be charged for such products or services. However, countries differ significantly in their views regarding the extent to which IPRs may grant immunity from competition requirements (e.g. by authorizing exclusionary conduct that would otherwise violate competition laws), or the extent to which IP rights holders may leverage those rights in regard to additional markets or downstream users.[61]

Extensive regulaton of price or extensive compulsory licensing of patented technologies to remedy broadly defined anti-competitive behaviours could theoretically be challenged either on the grounds that doing so conflicts with expectations regarding mandatory Article 28 exclusive rights (beyond what is authorized under Article 30 exceptions authority) or denies the benefit of such rights, potentially rising to the level of a 'non-violation' complaint (although there is currently a moratorium in effect on such complaints in regard to TRIPS Agreement obligations). However, such challenges are unlikely to succeed without further development of consensus regarding the nature of the relationship of IP rights to price and competition policies. The relationship of patent rights to prices and competition concerns

[60] *Bloomer v. McQuewan*, 55 U.S. 539, 549 (1852).

[61] For example, in the US, see *In re Independent Serv. Orgs. Antitrust Litigation*, 203 F.3d 1322 (Fed. Cir. 2002); *Mallinkrodt, Inc. v. Medipart, Inc.*, 976 F.2d 700 (Fed. Cir. 1992). In the European Union, see Case T-201/04 *Microsoft v. Comm'n* [2007] E.C.R. II-1; European Commission Decision of 24 March 2004 relating to a proceeding under Article 82 of the EC Treaty (Case COMP/C-3/37.792 *Microsoft*), COM (2004) 900 Final (21 April 2004). See generally Lemley 2007, pp. 1–8.

remains the subject of substantial dispute in some countries, and is likely to be the focus of significant attention in the near future.

A closer watch should be kept on an inquiry into competition in the pharmaceuticals sector launched in 2008 by the European Commission.[62] There are indications that competition in European pharmaceutical markets may not be working well. Fewer new drugs are being brought to market, and the entry of generic pharmaceuticals seems to be delayed. The inquiry set out to investigate whether: 'agreements between pharmaceutical companies, such as settlements in patent disputes, may infringe the EC Treaty's prohibition on restrictive business practices (Article 81)'; 'companies may have created artificial barriers to entry, whether through the misuse of patent rights, vexatious litigation or other means'; and if 'such practices may infringe the EC Treaty's ban on abuses of dominant market positions (Article 82)'.[63] The final report was published in July 2009 (see European Commission 2009a). In the Executive Summary of the Pharmaceutical Sector Inquiry Report, the European Commision (2009b, pp. 26–27) observes: 'The sector inquiry confirms that generic entry does not always take place as early as it potentially could under the current relevant legal framework. It shows that company practices are amongst the causes and suggests that a variety of other conditions might play also an important role. The sector inquiry also confirms a decline of novel medicines reaching the market and points to certain company practices that might, amongst other factors, contribute to this phenomenon.' The Commission will address the issues identified in the course of the sector inquiry 'by applying increased scrutiny under EC competition law to the sector and by bringing [enforcement actions in] specific cases, where appropriate' (ibid., p. 27). To reduce the risk that 'settlements are concluded at the expense of consumers', the Commission will also 'consider further focused monitoring of settlements that limit generic entry and include a value transfer from an originator company to a generic company' (ibid.). In January 2010, a new initiative was launched by the Commission. Patent settlements between originator and generic pharmaceutical companies will be monitored. The goal is to investigate 'patent settlements where an originator company pays off a generic competitor in return for delayed market entry of a generic drug' (see European Commission 2010).

[62] European Commission Decision of 15 January 2008 initiating an inquiry into the pharmaceutical sector pursuant to Article 17 of Council Regulation (EC) No. 1/2003 (Case COMP/D2/39/.514), available at: http://ec.europa.eu/competition/sectors/pharmaceuticals/inquiry/decision_en.pdf (accessed 1 February 2009).

[63] EUROPA – Press Releases, 'Antitrust: Commission Launches Sector Inquiry into Pharmaceuticals with Unannounced Inspections', Reference No. IP/08/49 (16 January 2008), available at: http://europa.eu/rapid/pressReleasesAction.do?reference=IP/08/49&format=HTML&aged=0&language=EN&guiLanguage=en (accessed 17 March 2010). For results of the preliminary research, see EUROPA – Press Releases, 'Antitrust: Preliminary Report on Pharmaceutical Sector Inquiry Highlights Cost of Pharma Companies' Delaying Tactics', Reference No. IP/08/1829 (28 November 2008), available at: http://europa.eu/rapid/pressReleasesAction.do?reference=IP/08/1829&format=HTML&aged=0&language=EN&guiLanguage=en (accessed 17 March 2010); for a press release regarding the Commission's final findings, see EUROPA – Press Releases, 'Antitrust: Shortcomings in Pharmaceutical Sector Require Further Action', Reference No. IP/09/1098 (8 July 2009), available at: http://europa.eu/rapid/pressReleasesAction.do?reference=IP/09/1098&format=HTML&aged=0&language=EN&guiLanguage=en (accessed 17 March 2010).

Another area that is likely to be one of increasing scrutiny and contention in terms of the distribution of pharmaceuticals around the world is that of parallel imports of pharmaceuticals. Essentially, the question is whether national laws allow IP right holders to invoke their IP rights to prevent the importation and marketing of a product which they have placed on the market in another country. In legal terms, the question is whether the relevant IP rights have been 'exhausted' through first sale in another country. Article 6 of the TRIPS agreement on the 'exhaustion' of IPRs essentially leaves it up to individual countries to decide appropriate parallel imports regimes, provided the principles of 'national treatment' and 'most-favoured-nation treatment' under the WTO agreements are observed. The Doha Declaration, in sub-paragraph 5(d), clarifies that 'the effect of the provisions in the TRIPS Agreement relevant to the exhaustion of [IPRs] is to leave each Member free to establish its own regime [on this front] without challenge', subject to the latter WTO principles. On the issue of parallel imports, the CIPR Report (2002) notes that:

> [D]eveloping countries should not eliminate potential sources of low cost imports from other developing or developed countries. In order to be an effective pro-competitive measure in a scenario of full compliance with TRIPS, parallel imports should be allowed whenever the patentee's rights have been exhausted in the foreign country. Since TRIPS allows countries to design their own exhaustion of rights regimes (a point restated at Doha), developing countries should aim to facilitate parallel imports in their legislation. (Ibid., p. 41)

The issue of exhaustion of rights is closely related to the earlier discussion over the scope and nature of the grant of exclusive rights within domestic markets. Countries may differ regarding whether to regulate price and market conduct of rights holders who may otherwise seek to enforce their exclusive rights on downstream purchasers after a first sale (or by limiting the grant of rights that can be transferred with protected property, through restrictive licensing terms). The legal rules in this regard may not be clear, and also may not be absolute but rather default principles that can be adjusted by contract (as suggested within the US context).[64] Similar concerns may apply to parallel imports for goods sold in one country, where the sales are conditioned on restrictions on export or other international limitations on rights. Questions also arise in regard to whether an importing country will recognize another country's law regarding the domestic exhaustion effect of sales of products that are subsequently imported, or whether exhaustion applies to products sold in jurisdictions where no IPRs attach (e.g. because a company did not seek patent rights in that jurisdiction or because the rules of that jurisdiction prohibited the grant of patent rights).

So far, discussions on parallel importing have tended to focus on the possibility of price differentiation between developed countries and developing countries or LDCs, perhaps out of a pragmatic approach towards resolving issues of access to

[64] For example, in a recent case the US Supreme Court reaffirmed that an unconditional first sale of a product embodying a patent exhausts the patent rights, but suggested that exhaustion may be avoided in some circumstances by clear contractual provisions limiting the scope of rights granted (at least to manufacturing licensees who would then lack authority to transfer those rights to purchasers by sale). See *Quanta Computer Inc. v. LG Elecs., Inc.*, 553 U.S. 617 (2008).

essential medicines in the latter countries. The CIPR Report suggests that price differentiation of pharmaceuticals between different markets, for example, between a developing country and a developed one, will depend on developed countries being able to maintain and strengthen their legislative regimes to prevent imports of low-priced pharmaceutical products originating from developing countries where these drugs are first sold by the rights owner (ibid., p. 41).[65] Without such measures to prevent parallel imports, it is said that incentives of the rights owners to sell the drugs at a lower price in the developing country than in the developed country market may be removed, especially if the latter is a dominant one for the pharmaceutical company (ibid.). However, this area is ringed with controversies as the public interest might require further scrutiny even within developed countries of the reasons for high pharmaceutical prices, especially given that underprivileged classes who need access to low-priced drugs exist in both developed and developing countries. Both within developed and developing countries, the ability of rights holders to segment their markets and to enforce restrictions will remain an important issue.

1.6. Appropriate technology transfer

There may be increasing focus in the future on provisions within the TRIPS Agreement relating to technological transfer from developed to developing countries. Article 66(2) of the Agreement provides that: 'Developed country Members shall provide incentives to enterprises and institutions in their territories for the purpose of promoting and encouraging technology transfer to least-developed country Members in order to enable them to create a sound and viable technological base'. According to Article 67: 'In order to facilitate the implementation of this Agreement, developed country Members shall provide, on request and on mutually agreed terms and conditions, technical and financial cooperation in favour of developing and least-developed country Members'.

Effective implementation of Articles 66(2) and 67 of the TRIPS Agreement to improve North–South and South–South technological collaboration – both public and private, which can ultimately assist developing countries in updating their innovation systems and expanding their innovation base – will require an international commitment. Various options for such collaboration might be explored, including innovative contracting mechanisms for technology transfer, as well as expanded technical and financial cooperation to promote local pharmaceutical production and stimulate the development of new health products (Morin 2005; Correa 2006). A good example of a South–South technology transfer process is the first factory in Mozambique for producing ARV drugs. The factory is funded by the Brazilian government which is also providing know-how and training to local staff.

Some argue that Articles 66(2) and 67 of the TRIPS Agreement oblige industrialized country signatories to assist developing countries in IP management capacity building (Koepsel 2004, p. 167). It is suggested that strengthening IPR management capacity and related legal infrastructure in developing countries will stimulate

[65] The CIPR Report suggests that, to secure the segmentation of markets, it would also be desirable for developing countries 'to act to prevent exports to developed countries of drugs that are part of a donation or differential pricing scheme', noting that 'it is especially important to avoid product diversion from those patients for whom the medicine is intended' (CIPR 2002, p. 41).

technology transfer and domestic innovation, enhance the ability of developing countries to attract foreign direct investment, foster greater integration into the global economy and ultimately improve standards of living (Homere & Colum 2004, p. 277).

There is a tendency, however, for many industrialized countries to emphasize enforcement of the IPRs of their companies as a primary goal, even when ostensibly invoking Article 67, and this trend requires further scrutiny (Reichman 2000). Indeed, it has been noted that IP technical assistance programs from these developed countries may promote standards of IP protection and enforcement higher than those required by the TRIPS Agreement (see Sagar 2006). The mixed effects of IP enforcement on human welfare in developing countries is explored further in Chapters 1 and 7 of this book.

Studying the impact of the TRIPS Agreement on access to medicines in developing countries, Abbott and Reichman (2007a) have made several recommendations in a study commissioned by the EU to promote R&D directed towards people in need in developing and developed countries and at promoting access to medicines. Among other things, the recommendations in the study encourage the EU and its member states to support transfer of technology to LDCs and local production of pharmaceuticals in all developing countries, especially LDCs, in keeping with the objectives of Article 66(2) (ibid., p. 55). They also discourage the EU from pursuing higher intellectual property standards affecting pharmaceuticals in multilateral, bilateral and regional forums (ibid.). In a published article drawing on the commissioned study, the authors (2007b, pp. 984–985) add that: 'The evidence suggests that the wealthy OECD nations are little inclined to promote the development of world-class pharmaceutical producers in poor countries, which might eventually compete with the existing originators. The rhetoric of "transfer of technology" does not extend to the reality of investment in plant and equipment, upgrading systems for compliance with OECD GMP quality standards, or to the licensing of important pharmaceutical compounds ... We strongly encourage a more proactive role for OECD transfer of technology to the developing country pharmaceutical sector. At the very least, OECD governments should not stand in the way of South-South cooperation'.

1.7. Proliferation of regional and bilateral trade agreements

Free trade agreements (FTAs) are being negotiated and increasingly established at the regional and bilateral levels, and there is currently an effort to negotiate a multilateral Anti-Counterfeiting Trade Agreement outside of the confines of the WTO or WIPO. These trade agreements often introduce new commitments for protection and enforcement beyond the minimum standards established in TRIPS, i.e. so-called TRIPS-plus provisions.[66] The implementation of FTAs demands that partners conform to new legislation and standards (Abbott 2006). Several bilateral FTAs

66 For example, in May 2004, the US signed the Central American Free Trade Agreement (CAFTA) with Costa Rica, El Salvador, Guatemala, Honduras and Nicaragua (the Dominican Republic was later added in August 2004). CAFTA requires both data exclusivity for five years and patent extensions to offset delays in the granting of a patent. See Westerhaus and Castro (2006), who note that TRIPS-plus measures have been included in similar US bilateral trade agreements with Singapore, Chile,

contain TRIPS-plus provisions limiting the grounds on which compulsory licences can be issued, whereas TRIPS does not restrict conditions for their use (see Khor 2007).[67] The coexistence of TRIPS and FTA standards has significant consequences for public health systems in both developing and developed countries, and produces further imbalances in IP regimes at the individual country level. Commentators (Morin 2005, pp. 37–53; Correa 2006) have identified the following as the most common TRIPS-plus provisions of relevance to health policies:

(1) stronger protection for regulatory data;
(2) extension of patent terms;[68]
(3) limitations to the exceptions of patent rights;
(4) linkage between drug registration and patent protection;
(5) establishment of conditions for use of compulsory or voluntary licensing;
(6) limitation of international exhaustion; and
(7) restrictions on patent revocation.

These TRIPS-plus FTA provisions may be on the way to becoming more widespread, as more and more countries become bound by FTAs which include some of them (particularly developing countries that lack the political or economic power to reject their inclusion in FTA negotiations). The diffusion of these provisions will likely create a less friendly environment for developing countries facing public health problems. In addition, recent FTAs (e.g. US–Australia and US–South Korea) have involved requirements of transparency for drug formulary registrations that affect price and other actions to limit government price regulation. It remains to be seen whether counter-pressures increasingly exerted by civil society against such provisions, and changes in the political composition of the US and EU, may limit TRIPS-plus developments in the future.

1.8. IP management and licensing for public-funded research

The management of IP stemming from public-funded research is an area of increasing significance for both developed and developing countries. Brazil is an example of a country that has an innovative law which gives universities the right to independently manage IP created with government funding. Other prominent examples include the US Bayh-Dole Act, which has been the source of much controversy. As explained by McManis and Noh in a conference paper,[69] the Bayh-Dole Act effected a major change in US policy with respect to the ownership of IPRs in federally funded research, and was designed to promote technology transfer by allowing

Peru, Columbia and Morocco. The full texts for these agreements are available at: http://www.ustr.gov/trade-agreements/free-trade-agreements (accessed 15 March 2010).

67 See Article 4, §20, of the FTA between the US and Jordan, available at: http://www.jordanusfta.com/free_trade_agreement_text_en.asp (accessed 3 February 2009); see also Article 16.7, § 6, of the FTA between the US and Singapore, available at: http://www.ustr.gov/Trade_Agreements/Bilateral/Singapore_FTA/Section_Index.html (accessed 3 February 2009). See Loy 2004; Khor 2007.

68 For example, the US – Chile Free Trade Agreement provides that: 'With respect to pharmaceutical products that are subject to a patent, each Party shall: (a) make available an extension of the patent term to compensate the patent owner for unreasonable curtailment of the patent term as a result of the marketing approval process' (Article 17.10(2)).

69 McManis, C.R., & Noh, S. 2006, 'The Impact of the Bayh-Dole Act on Genetic Research and Development: Evaluating the Arguments and Empirical Evidence to Date', p. 2, paper presented at the conference

universities, small businesses and other research institutions to retain ownership of the patent rights resulting from federally funded research, subject to an obligation on the part of universities and other non-profit institutions to share royalties with the actual inventor. According to the paper, prior to the Bayh-Dole Act, patent rights were in principle retained by the federal funding agencies themselves, though actual patent policies of federal funding agencies varied considerably, with some agencies allowing universities to patent publicly funded research discoveries in certain circumstances. McManis and Noh note the ongoing debate over the Act:

> Proponents of the Bayh-Dole Act argue that the Act was necessary because prior to 1980 many inventions resulting from federally-funded scientific research were not being commercialized, and that the Act has provided an effective framework for federal technology transfer, producing tremendous economic benefits not just for universities and private industry, but for the U.S. economy as a whole. Critics of the Bayh-Dole Act, on the other hand, question the theoretical and empirical assumptions on which the Bayh-Dole Act is based, and go on to argue that the use of patents in such areas as basic biological research may frustrate basic norms of 'open science' in the research community, and that the failure to distinguish between downstream inventions that lead directly to commercial products and fundamental research discoveries that broadly enable further scientific investigation may hinder rather than accelerate biomedical research, creating the risk of both 'blocking' patents on foundational discoveries or indispensable research tools and 'patent thickets,' or a 'tragedy of the anti-commons,' where basic research discoveries necessary for subsequent downstream development are owned by a large number of entities, thus impeding downstream development.[70] (Ibid., pp. 2–3)

Although the Bayh-Dole Act governs the patenting of federally funded research in all fields of technology, university patenting and licensing pursuant to the Act have thus far overwhelmingly involved the life sciences (ibid.). Other countries are implementing or considering approaches to deal with IPRs from publicly financed research. South Africa, for example, considered recommendations in this direction, based on studies comparing provisions of the Bayh-Dole Act with other national legislation such as in Denmark.[71] On 22 December 2008, it passed its Intellectual Property Rights from Publicly Financed Research and Development Act, following public consultations and significant revisions to the draft bill.[72] The proposed 'Indian Bayh-Dole Act' – the Protection and Utilisation of Public Funded Intellectual Property Bill of 2008 being considered by the Indian Parliament – has been controversial and is under revision at the time of this writing.[73]

on 'Commercializing Innovation', Washington University School of Law, 4–5 November 2005, available on the website of the Center for Research on Innovation & Entrepreneurship at: http://law.wustl.edu/CRIE/publications/mcmaniscommercializinginnovationpaper.pdf (accessed 19 October 2009).

70 See further Eisenberg 1987; Heller 1998; Rai 2003; Rai & Eisenberg 2003; National Research Council 2005.

71 An example is the study conducted by the Republic of South Africa's Department of Science and Technology 2006, 'Framework for Intellectual Property Rights from Publicly Financed Research', available at: http://docs.google.com/Doc?id=dc39jv73_0cshk9pcb (accessed 17 March 2010).

72 The text of the Intellectual Property Rights from Publicly Financed Research and Development Act, No. 51 of 2008, is available at: http://www.pmg.org.za/files/gazettes/090409propertyrightsregs.pdf (accessed 15 March 2010).

73 For a critique of the bill, see Kochupillai 2010.

How countries choose to legislate in the future on IPRs over public-funded research will have a significant bearing on research and development, including in the area of medicine. At the same time, changes in university licensing policies may make a difference in terms of retaining rights to conduct further research or to license inventions specifically with developing country needs in mind.[74] Some universities are exploring licensing practices that seek to make new innovation, including in biotechnology, readily available for 'humanitarian access' (see further Brewster, Chapman & Hansen 2005).

2. Strategies and public-private initiatives for research into new medicines and vaccines

Pharmaceutical innovation is not sufficiently dealing with diseases of primary concern to developing countries. Many chronic diseases and conditions typical of developed countries such as coronary disease and high blood pressure, attract significantly more private investment by pharmaceutical companies in developed countries (along with research investment into so-called lifestyle drugs). An important area of ongoing and future concern for developing countries and LDCs and their constituents is the development of drugs addressing diseases that are prevalent in these countries but less prevalent, or of decreasing incidence, in the developed world. These include 'neglected diseases' such as malaria, schistosomiasis and Chagas disease, as well as emergent and resurgent diseases such as HIV/AIDS and tuberculosis. These diseases present challenges for health surveillance systems and for government policy more generally. Local research agendas and purchasing arrangements must respond to the 'neglected diseases problem' and to shifting trends in disease incidence.

Several developments at the WHO deserve emphasis in relation to IP and health, especially for neglected and resurgent diseases. Significantly, in May 2003, the fifty-sixth WHA formed a time-limited body entitled the Commission on Intellectual Property Rights, Innovation and Public Health (CIPIH) to analyse the role of IPRs in promoting research and innovation in public health, especially for diseases that disproportionately affect LDCs. Various studies ranging from the prevalence of diseases worldwide to the global IP landscape and alternative models of innovation were reviewed. These reviews formed the basis of the Commission's final report in 2006, entitled *Public Health, Innovation and Intellectual Property Rights* [hereinafter 'CIPIH Report'],[75] which was presented to the Executive Board of the 116th session of the WHA.[76] Some key findings and recommendations of the CIPIH Report are described in Box 2.2. In 2008, the sixty-first WHA adopted the 'Global Strategy and Plan of Action on Public Health, Innovation and Intellectual Property' (Resolution

[74] California Institute of Technology et al. 2007, 'In the Public Interest: Nine Points to Consider in Licensing University Technology', White Paper [hereinafter 'Nine-Point Report'], available at: http://news-service.stanford.edu/news/2007/march7/gifs/whitepaper.pdf (accessed 18 October 2008).

[75] Commission on Intellectual Property Rights, Innovation and Public Health (CIPIH) 2006, *Public Health, Innovation and Intellectual Property Rights* [hereinafter 'CIPIH Report'].

[76] World Health Assembly (WHA) Resolution WHA56.27 (28 May 2003), available at: http://apps.who.int/gb/archive/pdf_files/WHA56/ea56r27.pdf (accessed 17 March 2010).

BOX. 2.2. Initiatives at the World Health Organization relating to intellectual property and public health[77]

The CIPIH was a time-limited body created in May 2003 by the fifty-sixth World Health Assembly (WHA). The CIPIH's task was to analyse the role of IPRs in promoting research and innovation in public health, especially for diseases that disproportionately affect LDCs. According to the 2006 CIPIH Report, poor countries face a 'double' burden of disease: they are the victims of both communicable diseases (like HIV/AIDS and tuberculosis) and non-communicable diseases (like diabetes and cancer) (ibid., p. 15). The report also states that 'diseases of poverty (i.e. communicable, maternal, perinatal, and nutrition-related diseases) contribute to over 50% of the burden of disease in low income developing countries' and that the burden of disease in developing countries is 'nearly ten times higher than [the] burden in developed countries' (ibid.). The establishment and work of the CIPIH was intended as a step towards increasing access to medicines and alleviating the burden of disease in the world.

The 2006 CIPIH Report focused on Type III diseases – diseases that are overwhelmingly or exclusively incident in developing countries, such as African sleeping sickness (trypanosomiasis) and African river blindness (onchocerciasis). Type III diseases are often termed 'very neglected diseases'. In contrast to the situation with diseases such as HIV/AIDS which affect both the developed and the developing world, it is very challenging to get pharmaceutical companies to invest in R&D for diseases that only represent a very small and low-income market. As stated in the report, companies are not willing to invest in pharmaceuticals for developing countries because 'they are inherently unprofitable, or the relationship between investment and risk, in relation to potential profit, is unattractive to the private sector' (CIPIH 2006, p. 30). Consequently, pharmaceutical companies are doing much less than is expected to develop new drugs. The CIPIH report notes that 'while R&D spending by pharmaceutical companies based in the United States doubled between 1995 and 2002, the number of new molecular entities approved by the United States Food and Drug Administration (FDA) has not risen between the first half of the 1990s and the first half of this decade' (ibid., p. 65). According to the report, the majority of pharmaceutical companies' R&D resources are being directed towards minor improvements of existing drugs that simply aim to increase profits, instead of significant therapeutic advances that could potentially eradicate diseases (ibid., p. 30).

The CIPIH Report found that the existing IP model, as currently implemented, was not achieving the desired goals of promoting the development of products for treatment and prevention of diseases, specifically for developing countries (ibid., pp. 23–24). Based on this conclusion, the CIPIH Report considered a wide range of proposed alternative innovation models which might better address the current lack of incentives for pharmaceutical R&D that meets the needs of developing countries. Some alternative IP and innovation schemes that the CIPIH reviewed included: orphan drug schemes which offer limited additional market exclusivity to promote the development of drugs for Type II and III diseases;[78] tax credits for clinical trials; prize funds and other reward systems; guaranteed market commitments; modalities for transferring IPRs to developing countries; and open source approaches (see ibid., pp. 102–107). A common thread amongst the various alternative proposals was the CIPIH's

(*continued*)

[77] This section was contributed by Claudia Trezza and Claire Comfort.

[78] Type II diseases are diseases that 'are incident in both rich and poor countries, but with a majority of cases in poor countries – Type II diseases are often termed neglected diseases'.

Box 2.2 (*continued*)

recognition of a need for more public-private partnerships, with long-term and sustainable funding mechanisms guaranteed by the WHO, as well as a need for increased efforts to strengthen clinical trials and regulatory infrastructure in developing countries (ibid., p. 173).

The report's sixty final recommendations are directed towards governments, international agencies and pharmaceutical companies (see ibid., pp. 196–210). Recommendations for developed countries include increasing funding for research and advanced purchase mechanisms. It is also recommended that developed countries refrain from seeking bilateral agreements with developing countries that undermine the spirit of the Doha Declaration and the goal of increasing access to medicines and improving public health (see ibid., pp. 197–204). Recommendations for developing countries include ensuring that the infrastructure for market approval and delivery of medicines to populations is put in place. Developing countries are also encouraged to use the compulsory licence flexibilities available within the framework of the TRIPS Agreement (see ibid., pp. 204–206). The report recommends that the WHO and other international agencies develop patent pools and secure sustainable financing schemes to ensure that access and delivery of medicines increases in the developing world (see ibid., pp. 197–210). The report further draws attention to the special responsibility of pharmaceutical companies to increase access to medicines in poor countries, given that they work in and profit from public health needs. To that end, it recommends coming up with differential pricing policies between developed country markets and developing country markets (see ibid., p. 205).

In May 2006, WHO Member States adopted a proposal to establish an Intergovernmental Working Group on Public Health, Innovation and Intellectual Property (IGWG).[79] The IGWG's task was to prepare a global strategy and plan of action based on the recommendations of the CIPIH Report. On 24 May 2008, following a week-long review of the eighteen months' work and final recommendations of the IGWG, the sixty-first WHA adopted the 'Global Strategy and Plan of Action on Public Health, Innovation and Intellectual Property' (Resolution WHA61.21). The global strategy reaffirms TRIPS flexibilities while aiming to 'promote new thinking on innovation and access to medicines' (ibid., Annex, para. 13). Among other elements, the Plan of Action sets out to encourage R&D in 'traditional medicine' in developing countries, promote 'upstream research and product development in developing countries', and includes a paragraph on competition policy against the abuse of IP rights (ibid., Appendix, paras. 1.3, 2.2, 6.3). A proposal with progress indicators for the Plan of Action was presented and approved at the sixty-second WHA in May 2009 (see WHO 2009). In terms of regional developments, the Pan American Health Organization (PAHO) is now organizing discussions on implementing the global strategy and action plan in the countries of the Americas.

[79] See WHA Resolution WHA59.24 (27 May 2006), available at: http://apps.who.int/gb/ebwha/pdf_files/WHA59/A59_R24-en.pdf (accessed 17 March 2010).

WHA 61.21) aimed at the removal of IP obstacles to R&D of new drugs and vaccines for public health (see New 2008). The global strategy recognizes that the price of medicines can impede access to treatment and recalls the flexibilities contained in many international IP agreements.[80] Although these flexibilities were inserted in the text of instruments such as the TRIPS Agreement to facilitate access to medicines by

[80] See WHA Resolution WHA61.21, Annex, paras. 11–12 (24 May 2008), available at: http://apps.who.int/gb/ebwha/pdf_files/A61/A61_R21-en.pdf (accessed 17 March 2010).

developing countries, the global strategy points out that barriers to the use of such flexibilities may exist (ibid., Annex, para. 12). The global strategy also incorporates a human rights approach by invoking and quoting Article 27 of the Universal Declaration of Human Rights (ibid., para. 10).[81]

Beyond the WHO, several international organizations and UN initiatives also deal with the intersection between IPRs and public health, including initiatives to facilitate research and access to medicines and vaccines. This includes, for example, the related work of the United Nations Development Programme (UNDP), WTO, WIPO, UNICEF, United Nations Conference on Trade and Development (UNCTAD) and the Joint United Nations Programme on HIV/AIDS (UNAIDS). While these multiple initiatives highlight the many dimensions and challenges posed for IP and public health, further information exchange and programme coordination is needed amongst these organizations. Section 3 of this chapter highlights two major scenario-planning processes undertaken recently by two organizations with implications for IP and health. Such planning processes can help bring together parallel initiatives by different organizations in search of coordinated and effective solutions in the public interest.

A variety of actors from the public, non-profit and private sectors have meanwhile come together to collaborate on new models of innovation for drugs and vaccines relevant to public health. In relation to the development of drugs for neglected diseases such as malaria and tuberculosis, product development partnerships (PDPs) present, for example, a significant opportunity for new and innovative collaborative research projects. Such partnerships have already started to yield results (Morel et al. 2005, pp. 401–404). As clarified by the Centre for Management of Intellectual Property in Health Research and Development (MIHR) in its 2006 publication, *Academic Licensing to Global Health Product Development Partnerships* ('MIHR Report'), these PDPs receive R&D support, both financial and in-kind, from a variety of sources both public and private, and focus on acquiring, developing and managing a portfolio of candidate products (MIHR 2006, p. 5).[82] According to the MIHR report, PDPs follow a non-profit business model, including a clearly articulated business plan based on market analyses, a portfolio management approach, and an access and advocacy strategy; their priorities are based on health inequities, social demand and considerations including the maturity of the science (ibid.).[83] Recent examples of partnerships include those for the development of a new

[81] See Universal Declaration of Human Rights (Paris, 10 December 1948), G.A. Res. 217A (III), UN Doc. A/810 (1948) [hereinafter 'UDHR'], Article 27, available at: http://www.un.org/en/documents/udhr (accessed 29 March 2010). The UDHR provides that 'everyone has the right freely to participate in the cultural life of the community, to enjoy the arts and to share in scientific advancement and its benefits' and that 'everyone has the right to the protection of the moral and material interests resulting from any scientific, literary or artistic production of which he is the author' (Art. 27).

[82] Such PDPs have been funded, for example, by the Bill & Melinda Gates Foundation's Global Health Program and the Rockefeller Foundation, as well as by national governments and international organizations.

[83] The MIHR Report further states that PDPs are critical licensing and drug development partners for university technology managers as they strive to promote global health equity and formulate university-generated R&D and technology transfer alliances (2006, p. 5).

antimalarial drug by the Drugs for Neglected Diseases Initiative (DNDI) and Sanofi-Avents, and of OneWorld Health's new leishmaniasis drug.[84] The more general term 'public-private partnerships' (PPPs) has been used to describe some of the initiatives in this vein.

Some interesting examples of alternative, collaborative models for R&D into medicines and vaccines – though by no means an exhaustive summary – are provided in Appendix B. These include public-private partnerships and non-profit pharmaceutical companies, medical R&D treaty and prize funds, advanced market commitments, patent pools and open source options.

3. Future scenarios relating to intellectual property and health[85]

Two main publications have been identified in the Public Interest Intellectual Property Advisors (PIIPA) literature survey as containing components directly related to IP and health. One of these is the European Patent Office (EPO) 2007 report entitled *Scenarios for the Future: How Might IP Regimes Evolve by 2025? What Global Legitimacy Might Such Regimes Have?* ('EPO Report').[86] The other is the UNAIDS report on *AIDS in Africa: Three Scenarios to 2025* ('UNAIDS Report').[87] The former is discussed in detail in Chapter 9 of this study. This section focuses on the 'IP and health' components of the EPO and UNAIDS scenario plans. Some of the major themes and trends introduced in Section 1 of this chapter are addressed in the scenario plans.

3.1. The IP and health component of the EPO scenarios

The EPO Report suggests a range of changes and outcomes for IP and health by the year 2025. According to the report: 'Scenarios are challenging, relevant and plausible stories about the future, used as tools to generate policy dialogue. They do not attempt to predict the future, but set out the landscape of a wider environment that encourages reflection on how the future might unfold' (EPO 2006, p. 13). While 'health' is one of the few sectors singled out by the report for direct comparison between scenarios,[88] it is given extended discussion only in one of the scenarios ('Trees of Knowledge'). Nevertheless, the EPO scenarios provide thought-provoking ideas and insights into some of the key technological and social driving forces for the future of IP and health. The following is a synthesis of the main elements relating to IP and health in the four EPO scenarios:

(1) **Scenario 1: Market Rules**
Under the **'Market Rules'** scenario, stricter IP rules, enforced by bilateral agreements often surpassing TRIPS and the increasing high-level

[84] It has been said that PDPs are most effective when partnerships are formed early in the drug development process. For further discussions, see Callan and Gillespie 2007, pp. 164–165.

[85] This section, synthesizing and analysing scenario plans relating to IP and health, was contributed by Tzen Wong.

[86] European Patent Office 2007, *Scenarios for the Future: How Might IP Regimes Evolve by 2025? What Global Legitimacy Might Such Regimes Have?*, EPO, Munich [hereinafter 'EPO Report'], available at: http://documents.epo.org/projects/babylon/eponet.nsf/0/63a726d28b589b5bc12572db00597683/$file/epo_scenarios_bookmarked.pdf (accessed 26 February 2010).

[87] UNAIDS 2005, *AIDS in Africa: Three Scenarios to 2025*, UNAIDS, Geneva [hereinafter 'UNAIDS Report'].

[88] See Table 'Comparing health across the scenarios' (ibid., p.105).

harmonization of IP rights worldwide, are said to leave fewer 'white spots' (i.e. areas not covered by patent protection) on the 'patent map' by 2025. IPRs are furthermore strengthened using supplementary protection and data exclusivity. There is increasing emphasis under this scenario on preventive diagnostics and pharmacogenomics, leading to what is described as a 'highly individualized' medicine, i.e., the use of medicines tailored to individual needs (ibid., p. 105). Health is said to have become a private commodity, with individual responsibility for health as the 'ground rule' (ibid.). There is philanthropic funding of rare and neglected diseases under this scenario. As health becomes more of a private commodity, the split widens between privatized and publicly funded health care. For drug companies, marketing becomes a pre-eminent concern (ibid.).

(2) **Scenario 2: Whose Game**
Under the **'Whose Game'** scenario (which foresees a development of the technological hegemony of Asian powers like China and India), the global gap between medical 'haves' and 'have-nots' widens (ibid.). New power blocs emerge in this scenario along the lines of geographic regions, shared histories, cultural habits and beliefs. Intellectual property is used differently in different regions, and remains a strong competitive tool in some of them. Some role reversal from the current world order is witnessed in this scenario, with new economies leading in innovation and older Western economies following and engaging in 'copying' of the latest technology (ibid.).[89] The fierce competition between the rising and existing powers permeates to the health sector. In the new powers, a mostly state-governed health insurance system tries to secure basic needs, while the traditional health care systems in the Western world are said to be increasingly unable to cope with rising costs. Ironically, it is the governments and health insurers in the Western world who are said to be unable to 'afford to pay the rights to expensive patented medicines' under this scenario (ibid.).

(3) **Scenario 3: Trees of Knowledge**
The two scenarios above assumed some continuation of patent rights over pharmaceuticals. In contrast, under the third **'Trees of Knowledge'** scenario, affordable access to health becomes a 'social clarion call' leading to the abolition of patents in the pharmaceutical sector by 2025. This scenario witnesses the emergence of alternative funding models for drug research, relying on so-called 'push' and 'pull' mechanisms (ibid.).[90] Social activism operates as a dominant driver in this scenario, and funding from governments as well as non-profit organizations figures prominently in shaping innovation in the health sector. Public-private partnerships, prize funds, advance payment schemes and outright government grants are mentioned as

[89] It is said that Western pharmaceutical industries have mostly turned into 'copy-cat' producers of drugs and treatments developed by the new, emerging powers (ibid., p. 105).

[90] In the context of pharmaceutical research, 'push' mechanisms generally refer to supply measures involving governments and other funding agencies or industry in actively encouraging certain R&D directions; 'pull' mechanisms refer to the dynamics of market demand, which creates incentives for R&D in certain health-related innovations including pharmaceutical products.

examples of modalities for innovation. Rare diseases or lifestyle-related conditions are not given 'first priority' in this scenario (ibid., p. 80). At the same time, human genes, stem cells and other parts of the human body become excluded from patentability under some jurisdictions, with research based on 'ethically sensitive' technologies (such as germ-line modification) moving almost entirely to less prescriptive jurisdictions (i.e. where the laws are less strict) (ibid., pp. 10, 80).

Dynamics in IP and health are discussed in greater detail under the 'Trees of Knowledge' scenario than under the other scenarios. Under this scenario, a disastrous flu pandemic (said to leave 20 million people dead) catalyses drastic changes in attitudes towards IP. During the initial flu outbreak, it is said that 'companies refused to lower the prices of existing vaccines and refused to allow generic manufacturers into the market' and 'complicated overlapping IP rights on different mutant variants of the flu virus severely hampered research into vaccines and therapeutics targeted to the precise strain of the virus' (ibid., p. 80). The delay of vaccine developments by several months 'severely damaged people's trust in the patent system',[91] with pharmaceutical companies also criticized for having prioritized 'lifestyle' drugs and 'me-too' drugs in their R&D (ibid.). Demonstrations eventually lead governments to grant compulsory licences for patented products in the interest of public health, while broadening research and clinical trials exemptions. In parallel, patent grant numbers are limited to ensure that 'only the most inventive' ideas receive monopoly protection (ibid.). As the pharmaceutical and health industry shifts its focus to less sensitive areas (where the perceived risks of not recouping its investments are smaller), gaps become filled by government-funded research, prize funds and PPPs. Under this scenario, many governments eventually replace the current patent system 'with a government regulated system' that allows companies performing clinical trials on drugs (said to be the really costly area of R&D) to 'sell their results to other companies' (ibid.). The price for such transactions is fixed in relation to the estimated public health benefit.

(4) **Scenario 4: Blue Skies**

Under the final **'Blue Skies'** scenario, pharmaceutical companies still rely on patents, 'albeit with restrictions that ensure research exemptions and access for poorer nations' (ibid., p. 105). Underlying this scenario are 'technofix' solutions to problems in health, with a 'globally positive attitude to technology' leading to flourishing health-care R&D (ibid.). Areas such as genetic diagnostics are mentioned in this scenario, and companies operating in these areas are said to have adopted 'a system of licensing, patent pools and clearing houses to ensure optimal use of available technologies' (ibid.). Under this scenario, ethical objections to biotechnology have given way to 'utilitarian' cost-benefit appraisal – stem-cell treatments, advanced

[91] Governments are blamed under this scenario for 'allowing a patent system that reinforced this "immoral" behaviour of the pharma industry, and for not having established alternative public research programmes' (ibid., p. 80).

prosthetics and embryo screening are accepted, and the first attempts at genetic enhancement are supported by large parts of society (ibid.). It is said that 'epidemiological, pharmaceutical and genetic research is helped by huge interconnected databases bringing genomic, clinical, familial and social data together on a worldwide scale' (ibid.). The most major breakthroughs come, however, from information and communication technologies (ICTs) that enable new forms of disease prevention by combining 'sophisticated diagnostics, advice and the control of human behaviour using technology' (ibid.). This scenario assumes that targeted patent restrictions will help ensure research exemptions and access to medicines for developing countries.

3.2. The UNAIDS scenario planning on AIDS in Africa as it relates to IP

In the large-scale scenario planning on 'AIDS in Africa' spearheaded by UNAIDS, IP is seen as only one component in the complex rubric of socio-economic and cultural factors shaping health-related research, development and delivery on the African continent. The UNAIDS Report contains three scenarios, each of which describes a different, plausible way in which the HIV/AIDS epidemic could play out across the whole of the African continent between now and 2025. As clarified in the report, these scenarios are 'rigorously constructed accounts of the future that use the power of storytelling as a means of going beyond the assumptions and understandings of any one interest group, in order to create a shared basis for dialogue and action about critical and difficult issues' (UNAIDS 2005, p. 12).

(1) Scenario 1: 'Tough Choices: Africa Takes a Stand'

The first scenario, '**Tough Choices**', suggests little likelihood that the attitudes of the rest of the world will change drastically to produce solutions for the HIV/AIDS situation in Africa. This scenario argues that much depends on African countries nurturing their domestic resources, including cultural strengths, to find their own way forward in the efforts to overcome the HIV/AIDS epidemic. The scenario emphasizes that, while there are enormous odds to overcome, there is much that countries in Africa can do on their own and collectively. It suggests that, with leadership and community mobilization, effective HIV/AIDS responses are possible without huge outlays of resources on stand-alone programming. This scenario ends with declining HIV incidence as over two decades of long-term investments in social, economic, and human capital begin to pay dividends (ibid., p. 178).

In relation to IP, the scenario contains a story where the unity shown by African and other G20 governments in the world trade rounds finally pays off and these governments succeed in extending the period for compliance with the provisions in the TRIPS Agreement relating to pharmaceutical products – from 2016 (as agreed under the Doha Declaration for LDCs) to 2026. Without the pressure of compliance deadlines, the countries are 'freed up to pursue pragmatic solutions' (ibid., p. 84). According to this scenario: 'The countries seized on the opportunities provided by the TRIPS Agreement and Doha Declaration and pursued whatever mix suited them best: importing from developing country generic manufacturers; locally manufactured products; or importing under voluntary or compulsory licenses' (ibid., p. 85). A number of publicly regulated low-cost manufacturing sites are established in East and West Africa (initially as subsidiaries of Brazilian, Indian, South African and other manufacturers). Leading a vigorous international debate on ways to make newly patented drugs available to developing countries, African governments soon make it clear that they are not interested in bilateral trade agreements favouring the interests of patent holders or restricting governments' capacity to produce medicines as cheaply as possible (ibid.). According to this scenario, the new generation of bilateral trade agreements and multilateral agreements maintain 'a balance between, on the one hand, the aspirations and safeguards of the Doha Declaration, and on the other hand, realizing the investment potentials of intellectual property' (ibid.).

(2) Scenario 2: 'Traps and Legacies: The Whirlpool'

An underlying message in the second scenario, **'Traps and Legacies'**, is that: 'It will be difficult to make a difference to the AIDS epidemic if HIV is viewed in isolation from its root social, economic and political context; or if it is seen only as a medical problem or an issue of individual behavioural change, addressed via programmes that only consider the symptoms' (ibid., p. 179). Under this scenario, the HIV/AIDS epidemic does catalyse people and institutions into some response, but they cannot make sufficient headway in the face of depleted capacity. In this less optimistic scenario, the continent is gripped in a 'downward spiral of disunity, denial and stigma, contested knowledge, wasted resources, and competing sources of power and authority' (ibid.). The capacity of systems, people and institutions to respond to the crises of AIDS and underdevelopment is 'systematically diminished' (ibid.). By 2015, the cost of financial obligations established by new patent regimes is 'many times higher than the value of any tariff concessions given by developed countries under the world trade agreements' (ibid., pp. 120–121).

According to this scenario, the agreement under the Doha Declaration to extend the grace period for LDCs' compliance with the TRIPS provisions relating to pharmaceutical products is not extended beyond 2016. As a result, the ambitious efforts of some countries to take over from India as centres for manufacture of generic drugs come under legal challenge (ibid., p. 120). Problems of counterfeit or adulterated drugs plague small-scale manufacture of drugs in this scenario. While there are efforts by research-based industries and generics manufacturers in countries as diverse as Brazil, Canada, India and South Africa to transfer technology to – and develop manufacturing capacity in – Africa, continuing polarization of the global IP debate means that these efforts are 'not well supported across the continent' (ibid., p. 121). Under this scenario, developing countries would remain the net importers of technology, with the related IP protection for technology continuing to expand and become globalized (ibid.).

(3) Scenario 3: 'Times of Transition: Africa Overcomes'

More optimistic and far-reaching than the first two scenarios, the third scenario, **'Times of Transition'**, describes a series of transitions in the way in which Africa and the rest of the world approach health, development, trade, security and international relations towards equitable outcomes. In relation to IP and health, the following transition is recounted:[92]

> As the new millennium unfolded, there was increasing consensus on the need to overcome the emotive opposition between access to life-saving medicines and the global extension of intellectual property protection. The spirit of social justice and collective global responsibility resulted in landmark arrangements to regulate the supply of medicines. African countries could keep access to low cost drugs! Over the next decade there was growing international interest in new models of medicine development that maximized poor people's access, while supporting the innovation required to produce new medicines. (Ibid., pp. 160–161)

This scenario highlights the success of 'groundbreaking' campaigns – the DNDI and the Medicines for Malaria Venture (MMV) are given as examples – where civil society and public research institutes join forces with private research companies and governments to address the lack of R&D for medicines for some of the world's neglected diseases. Innovative public-private collaborations begin to tap Africa's research potential more effectively; this happens in many areas, including biodiversity, benefit-sharing agreements harnessing traditional knowledge and global drug and vaccine development partnerships (ibid.). The development of an HIV/AIDS vaccine is hailed as one of the greatest successes of the new international regime under this scenario. This is said to be spurred by PPPs in vaccine R&D, with collaborative initiatives extending into the manufacture of vaccines in burgeoning industrial facilities situated across Africa. Following the year 2020, an international treaty-based framework is established to provide the legal and financial infrastructure necessary to support the development and manufacture of affordable essential medicines. Many of the compounds of potential use in treating the diseases that most affect the poorest countries are taken forward as 'open source' projects which enable countries and individuals to offset costs and pool capabilities (ibid., p. 161).[93] Free online access initiatives for academic journals, including medical journals, become increasingly widespread (ibid.).[94]

3.3. Some thoughts on the scenarios

It is impressive how the UNAIDS Report charts the many socio-economic and cultural influences shaping the future of the HIV/AIDS crisis on the African continent. This multidimensional approach is not forgotten in any of the scenarios described in the report. This presents an interesting contrast to some scenarios under the EPO planning exercise, in particular the 'Blue Skies' scenario which highlights the promise of a 'techno-fix' approach to problems of inequities, including in the health sector. Indeed, the UNAIDS Report emphasizes, rather, that technology is but one component in the challenge to overcome Africa's HIV/AIDS situation. It qualifies that the development and uptake of new technologies is shaped

[92] The past tense is used by the storytellers in these scenarios, as if looking back from the future on past events. This is a narrative device often used in scenario planning.

[93] See Appendix B on some current open source initiatives relating to medicine. On the relevance of 'open source' in other fields, see Chapter 3 (Box 3.3) and Chapter 7.

[94] Online access initiatives for journals are further explored in Chapter 7 of this book.

by different influences, and that 'successful development does not guarantee their effective deployment' (ibid., p. 54). Under the 'Traps and Legacies' scenario in the UNAIDS Report, the uptake of biomedical technology is described as increasingly inhibited by: limited access, frequent drug stock-outs, failure to address underlying beliefs, competition or ineffective integration with traditional healers, insufficient attention to the diversity of local languages and deteriorating education (ibid., pp. 54–56).

There is also acknowledgement in the UNAIDS Report of parallel systems of knowledge shaping the future of health in Africa. In the 'Times of Transition' scenario, it is noted that 'there is increasing integration between parallel systems and capacities, with greater inclusion of biomedical knowledge in traditional health systems and vice versa' (ibid., p. 56). The need to combine new technology with traditional know-how is emphasized in the report as part of the solution to the HIV/AIDS crisis on the continent, especially in building local capacity in R&D. An example of ongoing research involving traditional know-how of local communities in the Pacific region is the project for development of a new AIDS and cancer drug, Prostratin, derived from indigenous uses of the mamala tree in Samoa. The University of California, Berkeley (UC Berkeley) has an agreement with the government of Samoa for conducting this research project with the collaboration of local communities (IEGBIIP 2008, p. 31; see also Chapter 4, Box 4.5).

Traditional medicinal knowledge (TMK) is an important area in health care and research. Recognizing that up to 80% of the world's population depends on traditional medicine for its primary health needs,[95] the WHO adopted a *WHO Traditional Medicine Strategy 2002–2005* which includes among its main objectives the integration of 'relevant aspects of traditional medicine within national health care systems by framing national traditional medicine policies and implementing programmes' (see further Chapter 4 and Appendix C).[96] The overlap between IP and traditional knowledge, including TMK, is addressed in Chapter 4 of this study and is not repeated here.

Many of the alternative innovation models for R&D of vaccines and medicines (such as PPPs and prize funds) described in both the EPO 'Trees of Knowledge' scenario and the UNAIDS 'Times of Transition' scenario are already witnessed in collaborative efforts to address HIV/AIDS (see Appendix B). The UNAIDS Report furthermore emphasizes the importance of changes in mindset, alongside questions of resources and structural reforms, as central to finding viable solutions to the current vicious cycle in the HIV/AIDS crisis. In the 'Times of Transition' scenario, for example, a 'socially responsible' mindset permeates to different stakeholders, including corporate players. As observed in the scenario:

> Over this period, more companies were becoming more widely engaged in development. Those who ran the big companies moved from following a model of corporate philanthropy or social responsibility to a wider understanding of their role

[95] WHO, International Union for Conservation of Nature (IUCN) and World Wide Fund for Nature (WWF) 1993, *Guidelines for Conservation of Medicinal Plants*, IUCN, Gland, Switzerland.

[96] See WHO 2002, *WHO Traditional Medicine Strategy 2002–2005*, Doc. WHO/EDMTRM/2002.1, p. 5, available at: http://whqlibdoc.who.int/hq/2002/WHO_EDM_TRM_2002.1.pdf (accessed 26 November 2008).

> as agents of social change. By 2019, most multinationals had developed a 'foreign policy', which went beyond public relations to something far more extensive – far-reaching partnerships in a range of activities that helped build communities and even national governance capacities. (UNAIDS 2005, p. 161)

This part of the story may seem far-fetched given that the current socio-political reality more closely approximates the 'Market Rules' scenario in the EPO Report (which emphasizes a strengthening of patent protection and increasing harmonization of laws around the world, paralleled by increasing prioritization of 'marketing' by drug companies and R&D trends towards 'individualized' diagnostics and health care in rich countries). The UNAIDS story reflects, however, the growing public demand for greater scrutiny in areas such as corporate governance and corporate social responsibility in light of the extensive outreach of multinational corporations on the global map.

4. Conclusion

As discussed in this chapter, the overlap between IP and medicine is complex, going beyond issues of access to medicines to the impact of IP on medical research and exchange of related knowledge. As emphasized in the UNAIDS Report, IP is only one aspect of the many socio-economic and cultural factors affecting access to medicines and health care in both developed and developing countries. Developing countries (especially LDCs) still lag significantly behind in terms of benefits from recent progress in medical research, including biomedical research. Improved North–South and South–South cooperation, better education and appropriate technical cooperation could lead to more convergence between developed and developing contexts in standards of health protection. Scrutiny is needed, however, on how trade and IP regimes are shaping that future.

There is a tendency for many developing countries and LDCs to engage in policy-making and legislative activities relating to IP without full consideration of baseline information and alternative visions in the public interest. The health-related scenario plans explored in this chapter provide only a glimpse of many alternative possibilities, and further scenario planning targeting the particular needs of developing countries would be useful. Within countries, linkages among IP policy, innovation and industrial policy need to be formulated with public health objectives in mind. The interaction among IP laws, price regulation and competition laws, particularly to promote affordable access and pro-competitive environments in relation to new drugs and generic production of relevance to developing countries, also needs to be further explored. The capacity building of developing country stakeholders, especially marginalized stakeholders, towards their informed decision-making and engagement in policies to address the overlap between IP and public health is important. Such capacity building is dependent on country and local contexts, so that a case-by-case analysis is needed. It has been said that there is no 'one size fits all' solution. As some of the future scenarios discussed in this chapter suggest, thinking beyond the 'IP box' is important in addressing access to health and medicines, and exploring new models of innovation to meet the demands of global health equity.

REFERENCES

Abbott, F.M. 2005, 'The WTO Medicines Decision: World Pharmaceutical Trade and the Protection of Public Health', *American Journal of International Law*, vol. 99, no. 2, pp. 317–358.

Abbott, F.M. 2006, *Intellectual Property Provisions of Bilateral and Regional Trade Agreements in Light of US Federal Law*, International Centre for Trade and Sustainable Development (ICTSD), available at: http://www.unctad.org/en/docs/iteipc20064_en.pdf (accessed 19 October 2008).

Abbott, F.M. & Reichman, J.H. 2007a, *Access to Essential Medicines: Lessons Learned since the Doha Declaration on the Trips Agreement and Public Health and Policy Options for the European Union*, study prepared for the European Parliament's Committee on International Trade and commissioned by the Directorate-General for External Policies of the Union, Specifications, No. EXPO/B/INTA/2007/14.

Abbott, F.M. & Reichman, J.H. 2007b, 'The Doha Round's Public Health Legacy: Strategies for the Production and Diffusion of Patented Medicines under the Amended TRIPS Provisions', *Journal of International Economic Law*, vol. 10, no. 4, pp. 921–987, available at: http://papers.ssrn.com/sol3/papers.cfm?abstract_id=1025593 (accessed 19 November 2009).

Anderson, R.D. & Wager, H. 2006, 'Human Rights, Development, and the WTO: The Cases of Intellectual Property and Competition Policy', *Journal of International Economic Law*, vol. 9, no. 3, pp. 707–747.

Angell, M. 2004, *The Truth About the Drug Companies: How They Deceive Us and What to Do About It*, Random House, New York.

Anyangu-Amu, S. 2009, 'Anti-Counterfeit Law "Violates Right to Life and Health"', *Inter Press Service*, 21 December 2009, available at: http://ipsnews.net/news.asp?idnews=49764 (accessed 14 April 2010).

Barbosa, D.B., Chon, M. & Von Hase, A.M. 2007, 'Slouching Towards Development in International Intellectual Property', *Michigan State Law Review*, vol. 2007, no. 1, pp. 114–123.

Barton, J. 2003, 'Non-Obviousness', *IDEA: The Journal of Law and Technology*, vol. 43, pp. 475–476.

Brewster, A., Chapman, A. & Hansen, S. 2005, 'Facilitating Humanitarian Access to Pharmaceutical and Agricultural Innovation', *Innovation Strategy Today*, vol. 1, pp. 203–216.

California Institute of Technology, Cornell University, Harvard University, Massachusetts Institute of Technology, Stanford University, University of California, University of Illinois (Chicago and Urbana-Champaign), University of Washington, Wisconsin Alumni Research Foundation, Yale University and Association of American Medical Colleges (AAMC) 2007, *In the Public Interest: Nine Points to Consider in Licensing University Technology* ('Nine-Point Report'), available at: http://news-service.stanford.edu/news/2007/march7/gifs/whitepaper.pdf (accessed 3 June 2009).

Callan, B. & Gillespie, I. 2007, 'The Path to New Medicines', *Nature*, vol. 449, pp. 164–165.

Chapman, A. 2002, 'The Human Rights Implications of Intellectual Property Protection', *Journal of International Economic Law*, vol. 5, no. 4, pp. 861–882.

Chien, C. 2007, 'HIV/AIDS Drugs for Sub-Saharan Africa: How Do Brand and Generic Supply Compare?', vol. 2, no. 3, *PLoS ONE*, available at: http://www.plosone.org/article/info:doi%2F10.1371%2Fjournal.pone.0000278 (accessed 21 December 2008).

Cohen, W., Nelson, R. & Walsh, J. 2000, 'Protecting Their Intellectual Assets: Appropriability Conditions and Why U.S. Manufacturing Firms Patent (or Not)', *National Bureau of Economics Research Working Paper No. 7552*, available at: http://www.nber.org/papers/w7552 (accessed 19 October 2008).

Commission on Intellectual Property Rights (CIPR) 2002, *Integrating Intellectual Property Rights and Development Policy*, CIPR, London, available at: http://www.iprcommission.org/papers/pdfs/final_report/CIPRfullfinal.pdf (accessed 19 October 2008).

Commission on Intellectual Property Rights, Innovation and Public Health (CIPIH) 2006, *Public Health, Innovation and Intellectual Property Rights*, WHO, Geneva, available at: http://whqlibdoc.who.int/publications/2006/a88438_eng.pdf (accessed 21 December 2008).

Commission on Macroeconomics and Health 2001, *Macroeconomics and Health: Investing in Health for Economic Development*, WHO, Geneva, available at: http://whqlibdoc.who.int/publications/2001/924154550x.pdf (accessed 8 June 2009).

Committee on Economic, Social and Cultural Rights (CESCR) 2000, *General Comment No. 14: The right to the highest attainable standard of health* (art. 12), UN Doc.E/C.12/2000/4 (11 August 2000), available at: http://www.unhchr.ch/tbs/doc.nsf/0/40d009901358b0e2c1256915005090be?Opendocument (accessed 15 March 2010).

Committee on the Rights of the Child 2003, *General Comment No. 3: HIV/AIDS and the rights of the child*, UN Doc. CRC/GC/2003/3 (17 March 2003), available at: http://www.unhchr.ch/tbs/doc.nsf/(symbol)/CRC.GC.2003.3.En?OpenDocument (accessed 3 February 2010).

Committee on the Rights of the Child 2003, *General Comment No. 4: Adolescent health and development in the context of the Convention on the Rights of the Child*, UN Doc. CRC/GC/2003/4 (1 July 2003), available at: http://www.unhchr.ch/tbs/doc.nsf/(symbol)/CRC.GC.2003.4.En?OpenDocument (accessed 3 February 2010).

Commonwealth Secretariat 2007, *The Problem of Counterfeit Medicines in the Commonwealth*, Geneva, available at: http://www.thecommonwealth.org/Shared_ASP_Files/UploadedFiles/5B935D92-C69C-46C8-BCAE-84830D726DAB_HMM_G__07_INF3-Problemofcounterfeitmedicines.pdf (accessed 20 June 2009).

Cornish, W.R., Llewelyn, M. & Adcock, M. 2003, *Intellectual Property Rights (IPRs) and Genetics: A Study into the Impact and Management of Intellectual Property Rights within the Healthcare Sector*, Public Health Genetics Unit, Cambridge.

Correa, C.M. 2006, 'Implications of Bilateral Free Trade Agreements on Access to Medicines', *Bulletin of the World Health Organization*, vol. 84, no. 5, pp. 399–404.

Correa, C.M. 2007, *Guidelines for the Examination of Pharmaceutical Patents: Developing a Public Health Perspective*, International Centre for Trade and Sustainable Development (ICTSD), World Health Organization (WHO), United Nations Conference on Trade and Development (UNCTAD), available at: http://www.iprsonline.org/resources/docs/Correa_Patentability%20Guidelines.pdf (accessed 19 October 2008).

Department of Essential Drugs and Other Medicines, 1999, *Counterfeit Drugs, Guidelines for the Development of Measures to Combat Counterfeit Medicines*, World Health Organization, Geneva, Switzerland, available at: http://whqlibdoc.who.int/hq/1999/WHO_EDM_QSM_99.1.pdf (accessed 21 December 2008).

Department of Science and Technology 2006, *Framework for Intellectual Property Rights from Publicly Financed Research*, Brummeria, South Africa.

Eisenberg, R.S. 1987, 'Proprietary Rights and the Norms of Science in Biotechnology Research', *Yale Law Journal*, vol. 97, no. 2, pp. 177–231.

European Commission 2009a, *European Commission Pharmaceutical Sector Inquiry Final Report*, July 2009, available at: http://ec.europa.eu/competition/sectors/pharmaceuticals/inquiry/staff_working_paper_part1.pdf; http://ec.europa.eu/competition/sectors/pharmaceuticals/inquiry/staff_working_paper_part2.pdf (accessed 1 March 2010).

European Commission 2009b, *Executive Summary of the Pharmaceutical Sector Inquiry*, available at: http://ec.europa.eu/competition/sectors/pharmaceuticals/inquiry/communication_en.pdf (accessed 8 March 2010).

European Commission 2010, 'Antitrust: Commission Launches Monitoring of Patent Settlements Concluded Between Pharmaceutical Companies', *European Commission Press Release*, 12 January 2010, available at: http://europa.eu/rapid/pressReleasesAction.do?reference=IP/10/12&format=HTML&aged=0&language=EN&guiLanguage=en (accessed 20 February 2010).

European Patent Office (EPO) 2007, *Scenarios for the Future: How Might IP Regimes Evolve by 2025? What Global Legitimacy Might Such Regimes Have?*, EPO, Wolfram Förster, available at: http://www.marcasepatentes.pt/files/collections/pt_PT/1/178/EPO%20Scenarios%20For%20The%20Future.pdf (accessed 3 June 2009).

Faunce, T.A. & Nasu, H. 2008, 'Three Proposals for Rewarding Novel Health Technologies Benefiting People Living in Poverty: A Comparative Analysis of Prize Funds, Health Impact Funds and a Cost-Effectiveness/Competitive Tender Treaty', *Public Health Ethics*, vol. 1, no. 2, pp. 146–153.

Fleshman, M. 2005, 'Global AIDS Treatment Drive Takes Off', *Africa Renewal, United Nations*, vol. 19, no. 1, pp. 8–11, available at: http://www.un.org/ecosocdev/geninfo/afrec/vol19no1/191aids.htm (accessed 14 April 2010).

Ford, N., Wilson, D., Chaves, G.C., Lotrowska, M. & Kijtiwatchakul, K. 2007, 'Sustaining Access to Antiretroviral Therapy in the Less-Developed World: Lessons from Brazil and Thailand', *AIDS*, vol. 21, no. 4, S21–S29.

Gerhardsen, T.I.S. 2007, 'Thailand Presents Report on Compulsory Licensing Experience', *Intellectual Property Watch*, 12 March 2007, available at: http://www.ip-watch.org/weblog/index.php?p=563 & res=1024 & print=0 (accessed 19 October 2008).

Gervais, D. 2008, *The TRIPS Agreement: Drafting History and Analysis*, 3rd Edition, Sweet and Maxwell, London.

Goldman, D.P., Jena, A.B., Philipson, T. & Sun, E. 2008, 'Drug Licenses: A New Model for Pharmaceutical Pricing', *Health Affairs*, vol. 27, no. 1, pp. 122–129.

Goozner, M. 2004, *The $800 Million Pill: The Truth Behind the Cost of New Drugs*, University of California Press, Berkeley, Los Angeles and London.

Hale, V.G., Woo, K. & Lipton, H.L. 2005, 'Oxymoron No More: The Potential of Nonprofit Drug Companies to Deliver on the Promise of Medicines for the Developing World', *Health Affairs*, vol. 24, no. 4, pp. 1057–1063.

Helfer, L.R. 2007, 'Toward a Human Rights Framework for Intellectual Property', *U.C. Davis Law Review*, vol. 40, no. 3, pp. 971–1020.

Heller, M.A. & Eisenberg, R.S. 1998, 'Can Patents Deter Innovation? The Anticommons in Biomedical Research', *Science*, vol. 280, no. 5364, pp. 698–701.

Hollis, A. 2007, 'Prize, Advanced Market Commitments, and Pharmaceuticals for Developing Countries', in *New International Centre for Trade and Sustainable Development (ICTSD) Series on New Opportunities Through Innovation Fostering R&D and Promoting Access to Medicines*, Bellagio, Italy, 22–26 October 2007, ICTSD.

Holzapfel, H. & Sarnoff, J.D. 2008, 'A Cross-Atlantic Dialog on Experimental Use and Research Tools', American University WCL Research Paper No. 2008–13, available at: http://ssrn.com/abstract=1005269 (accessed 19 October 2008).

Homere, J.R. 2004, 'Intellectual Property Rights Can Help Stimulate the Economic Development of Least Developed Countries', *Columbia Journal of Law and the Arts*, vol. 27, no. 2, pp. 277–299.

International Expert Group on Biotechnology, Innovation and Intellectual Property 2008, *Toward a New Era of Intellectual Property: From Confrontation to Negotiation*, Centre for Intellectual Property Policy, McGill University, Montreal, Canada, available at: http://www.theinnovationpartnership.org/data/ieg/documents/report/TIP_Report_E.pdf (accessed 3 June 2009).

International Federation of Pharmaceutical Manufacturers (IFPMA) 2004, *The Pharmaceutical Innovation Platform: Sustaining Better Health for Patients Worldwide*, IFPMA, Geneva.

International Federation of Pharmaceutical Manufacturers Association (IFPMA) 2004, *Counterfeit Drugs: A Global Health Risk*, IFPMA, Geneva.

Janodia, M.D., Pandey, J., Venkara Rao, J., Sreedhar, D., Ligade, V.S. & Udupa, N. 2008, 'Patents Regime in India: Issues, Challenges and Opportunities in Pharmaceutical Sector', *The Internet Journal of Third World Medicine*, vol. 7, no. 1, available at: http://www.ispub.com/ostia/index.php?xmlFilePath=journals/ijtwm/vol7n1/patents.xml (accessed 3 June 2009).

Joint United Nations Programme on HIV/AIDS (UNAIDS) 2005, *AIDS in Africa: Three Scenarios to 2025*, UNAIDS, Geneva.

Joshi, H.N. 2003, 'Analysis of the Indian Pharmaceutical Industry with Emphasis on Opportunities in 2005', *Pharmaceutical Technology*, pp. 74–94.

Khor, M. 2007, *Patent, Compulsory License and Access to Medicines: Some Recent Experiences*, Third World Network, available at: http://www.twnside.org.sg/title2/par/TRIPS.flexibilities.30jan07.with.cover.doc (accessed 3 June 2009).

Knowledge Ecology International (KEI) 2007, 'Collective Management of Intellectual Property: The Use of Patent Pools to Expand Access to Essential Medical Technologies', *IGWG Briefing Paper on Patent Pools*, 23 January 2007, available at: http://www.keionline.org/content/view/65/ (accessed 3 June 2009).

Kochupillai, M. 2010, 'The Protection and Utilisation of Public Funded Intellectual Property Bill, 2008: A Critique in the Light of India's Innovation Environment', *Journal of Intellectual Property Rights*, vol. 15, no. 1, pp. 19–34, available at: http://papers.ssrn.com/sol3/papers.cfm?abstract_id=1540166 (accessed 25 March 2010).

Koepsel, K.M. 2004, 'How Do Developed Countries Meet Their Obligations Under Article 67 of the TRIPS Agreement?', *IDEA*, vol. 44, no. 167.

Kremer, M. & Glennerster, R. 2004, *Strong Medicine: Creating Incentives for Pharmaceutical Research and Neglected Diseases*, Princeton University Press, Princeton NJ.

Kuanpoth, J. 2007, 'Patents and Access to Antiretroviral Medicines in Vietnam after World Trade Organization Accession', *Journal of World Intellectual Property*, vol. 10, no. 3–4, pp. 201–224.

Law, J. 2006, *Big Pharma: How the World's Biggest Drug Companies Control Illness*, Constable, London.

Lemley, M.A. 2007, 'A New Balance Between IP and Antitrust', *Southwestern Journal of Law and Trade in the Americas*, vol. 13, pp. 1–8.

Levin, R., Klevorick, A., Nelson, R., Winter, S., Gilbert, R. & Griliches Z. 1987, 'Appropriating the Returns from Industrial Research and Development', *Brookings Papers on Economic Activity*, no. 3, pp. 783–831.

Love, J. & Hubbard, T. 2007, 'The Big Idea: Prizes to Stimulate R&D for New Medicines', *Chicago-Kent Law Review*, vol. 82, no. 3, pp. 1519–1554, available at: http://lawreview.kentlaw.edu/articles/82-3/Love%20Author%20Approved%20Edits(H)(P).pdf (accessed 17 January 2009).

Loy, W.L. 2004, 'The IP Chapter in the US-Singapore Free Trade Agreement', *Singapore Academy of Law Journal*, vol. 16, pp. 42–75.

Mansfield, E., 1986, 'Patents and Innovation: An Empirical Study', *Management Sciences*, vol. 32, no. 173, pp. 174–175.

Marmot, M. 2005, 'Social Determinants of Health Inequalities', *Lancet*, vol. 365, no. 9464, pp. 1099–1104, available at: http://www.who.int/social_determinants/strategy/en/Marmot-Social%20determinants%20of%20health%20inqualities.pdf (accessed 19 October 2008).

Mathers, C.D. & Loncar, D. 2006, 'Updated Projections of Global Mortality and Burden of Disease 2002-2030: Data Sources, Methods and Results', *Evidence and Information for Policy Working Paper*, World Health Organization, available at: http://www.who.int/healthinfo/statistics/bod_projections2030_paper.pdf (accessed 27 March 2010).

Maurer, S., Rai, A. & Sali, A. 2004, 'Finding Cures for Tropical Diseases: Is Open Source an Answer?', *PloS Medicine*, vol. 1, no. 3, pp. 183–186.

Management of Intellectual Property in Health Research and Development (MIHR) 2006, *Academic Licensing to Global Health Product Development Partnerships*, available at: http://www.tmgh.org/assets/MIHR-TMGH%20Sequel%20Booklet.pdf (accessed 19 October 2008).

McCarthy, D., Wolf, H. & Wu, Y. 2000, 'Malaria and Growth', *The World Bank Policy Research Working Paper No. 2303*, available at: http://papers.ssrn.com/sol3/papers.cfm?abstract_id=629153 (accessed 19 October 2008).

Moran, M. 2005, 'A Breakthrough in R&D for Neglected Diseases: New Ways to Get the Drugs We Need', *PLoS Medicine*, vol. 2, no. 9, available at: http://www.plosmedicine.org/article/info:doi/10.1371/journal.pmed.0020302 (accessed 3 June 2009).

Morel, C., Acharya, T., Broun, D., Dangi, A., Elias, C., Ganguly, N., Gardner, C., Gupta, R., Haycock, J., Heher, A., Hotez, P., Kettler, H., Keusch, G., Krattiger, A., Kreutz, F., Lall, S., Lee, K., Mahoney, R., Martinez-Palomo, A., Mashelkar, R., Matlin, S., Mzimba, M., Oehler, J., Ridley, F., Senanayake, P., Singera, P. & Yun, M. 2005, 'Health Innovation Networks to Help Developing Countries Address Neglected Diseases', *Science*, vol. 309, no. 5733, pp. 401–404.

Morin, J. 2005, 'Tripping up TRIPS Debates IP and Health in Bilateral Agreements', *International Journal for Intellectual Property Management*, vol. 1, no. 1–2, pp. 37–53.

National Research Council 2005, *Reaping the Benefits of Genomic and Proteomic Research: Intellectual Property Rights, Innovation, and Public Health*, National Academies Press, Washington, DC, available at: http://www.nap.edu/openbook.php?isbn=0309100674 (accessed 19 October 2008).

New, W. 2008, 'WHO Adopts "Most Important Document Since Doha" on IP and Public Health', *Intellectual Property Watch*, 29 May 2008, available at: http://www.ip-watch.org/2008/05/29/who-adopts-most-important-document-since-doha-on-ip-and-public-health/ (accessed 17 March 2010).

Ovett, D. 2006, 'Intellectual Property and Human Rights: Is the Distinction Clear Now? An Assessment of the Committee on Economic, Social and Cultural Rights' General Comment No. 17 (2005)', *3D Policy Brief*, Geneva.

Petersmann, E.U. 2000, 'The WTO Constitution and Human Rights', *Journal of International Economic Law*, vol. 3, no. 1, pp. 19–25.

Pogge, T.W. 2005, 'Human Rights and Global Health: A Research Program', *Methaphilosphy*, vol. 36, no. 1–2, pp. 182–209.

Rai, A.K. 1999, 'Regulating Scientific Research: Intellectual Property Rights and the Norms of Science', *Northwestern University Law Review*, vol. 94, no. 1, pp. 77–152.

Rai, A.K. & Eisenberg, R.S. 2003, 'Bayh-Dole Reform and the Progress of Biomedicine', *Law & Contemporary Problems*, vol. 66, no. 1–2, pp. 289–314.

Reichman, J.H. 2000, 'The TRIPS Agreement Comes of Age: Conflict or Cooperation with the Developing Countries', *Case Western Reserve Journal of International Law*, vol. 32, no. 3, pp. 441–470.

Roffe, P., Tansey, G. & Vivas-Eugui, W. (eds.) 2006, *Negotiating Health: Intellectual Property and Access to Medicines*, Earthscan, London and Sterling, VA.

Royal Pharmaceutical Society of Great Britain 2008, *Counterfeit Medicines Advice for Healthcare Professionals*, MHRA, available at: http://www.rpsgb.org/pdfs/counterfeitmedsguid.pdf (accessed 20 June 2009).

Sagar, R. 2006, Identifying Models of Best Practices in the Provision of Technical Assistance to Facilitate the Implementation of the TRIPS Agreement: Impacts of the IPR Rules on Sustainable Development, *IPDEV Work Programme 4 Report*, October 2006, Queen Mary University of London, available at: http://www.ecologic.de/download/projekte/1800–1849/1802/wp4_final_report.pdf (accessed 3 June 2009).

Scherer, F.M. & Watal, J. 2001, 'Post-TRIPS Options for Access to Patented Medicines in Developing Countries', *Commission on Macroeconomics and Health*, Working Paper Series, Paper No. WG4.

Sing, S. 2008, 'India Takes an Open Source Approach to Drug Discovery', *Cell*, vol. 133, pp. 201–203.

South Centre & Center for International Environmental Law (CIEL) 2009, 'Counterfeit Medical Products: Need for Caution Against Co-opting Public Health Concerns for IP Protection and Enforcement', *Intellectual Property Quarterly Update*, First Quarter 2000.

Strosberg, A.M., Barrio, K., Stinger, V.H., Tashker, J., Wilbur, J.C., Wilson, L. & Woo, K. 2007, *Chagas Disease: A Latin American Nemesis*, Institute for OneWorld Health.

Taylor, D. 2003, 'Fewer New Drugs from the Pharmaceutical Industry', *British Medical Journal*, vol. 326, no. 7386, pp. 408–409.

Thambisethy, S. 2008, 'Legal Transplants in Patent Law: Why Utility is the New Industrial Applicability', LSE Law, Society & Economy Working Paper No. 6.

US Food and Drug Administration (FDA) 2003, *Improving Innovation in Medical Technology: Beyond 2002*, FDA.

US FDA 2004, *Innovation or Stagnation: Challenge and Opportunity on the Critical Path to New Medical Products*, FDA.

US Government Accountability Office 2006, *New Drug Development: Science, Business, Regulatory, and Intellectual Property Issues Cited as Hampering Drug Development Efforts*, available at: http://www.gao.gov/new.items/d0749.pdf (accessed 19 October 2008).

United Nations Millennium Project 2005, *A Practical Plan to Achieve the Millennium Development Goals*, UN, New York, available at: http://www.unmillenniumproject.org/reports/fullreport.htm (accessed 19 October 2008).

Wang, S.S. 2008, 'Tricor Case may Illuminate Patent Limits', *The Wall Street Journal*, 2 June 2008.

Westerhuas, M. & Castro, A. 2006, 'How do Intellectual Property Law and International Trade Agreements Affect Access to Antiretroviral Therapy?' *PLoS Medicine*, vol. 3, no. 8, available at: http://www.plosmedicine.org/article/info%3Adoi%2F10.1371%2Fjournal.pmed.0030332 (accessed 1 June 2009).

World Health Assembly (WHA) 2008, *Global Strategy and Plan of Action on Public Health, Innovation and Intellectual Property*, WHA, Sixty-First Session, Resolution WHA61.21 (24 May 2008), available at: http://apps.who.int/gb/ebwha/pdf_files/A61/A61_R21-en.pdf (accessed 17 March 2010).

World Health Organization (WHO) 1999, *Counterfeit Drugs, Guidelines for the Development of Measures to Combat Counterfeit Medicines*, Department of Essential Drugs and Other Medicines, WHO, Geneva, available at: http://whqlibdoc.who.int/hq/1999/WHO_EDM_QSM_99.1.pdf (accessed 1 June 2009).

WHO 2002, *WHO Traditional Medicine Strategy 2002–2005*, Doc. WHO/EDMTRM/2002.1, available at: http://whqlibdoc.who.int/hq/2002/WHO_EDM_TRM_2002.1.pdf (accessed 26 November 2008).

WHO 2008, *Counterfeit Medical Products*, Report by the Secretariat, 124th Executive Board Session, Geneva, Doc. EB124/14 (18 December 2008), available at: http://apps.who.int/gb/ebwha/pdf_files/EB124/B124_14-en.pdf (accessed 20 June 2009).

WHO 2009, 'Public Health, Innovation and Intellectual Property: Global Strategy and Plan of Action: Proposed Progress Indicators', Report by the Secretariat, Doc. A62/16 Add.2 (7 May 2009), available at: http://apps.who.int/gb/e/e_wha62.html (accessed 28 February 2010).

WHO, International Union for Conservation of Nature (IUCN), and World Wide Fund for Nature (WWF) 1993, *Guidelines for Conservation of Medicinal Plants*, IUCN, Gland, Switzerland.

3

Food security and intellectual property rights: Finding the linkages

Hans Morten Haugen, Manuel Ruiz Muller and Savita Mullapudi Narasimhan[1]

Introduction

There is no easy way to identify the policy, economic and legal linkages between food security as a goal and intellectual property rights (IPRs) as an instrument to promote and enhance human creativity and overall social well-being. But connections do exist. Food security is part of the basic human right to food, broadly defined as timely access to sufficient and nutritious food.[2] It is inextricably linked to the right to health, discussed in an earlier chapter.[3] It is linked to intellectual property (IP) inasmuch as plant variety protection (PVP; also known as plant breeders' rights) and patents, as applied to genetic resources, biodiversity components and biotechnological processes, may be limiting the possibilities of cultivators to freely grow certain crops, and of people to consume resulting agricultural products.

Linkages may also be found in the overall social goals of distinct, long-established legal regimes including those protecting human rights – specifically in regard to the right to food – and IPRs. While pursuing different specific objectives, these regimes should, in theory, be complementary in advancing human welfare and development (Okediji 2007). From a strict legal perspective, IPRs should in no way undermine a very basic human right on which life – literally – depends. When applied not just to whole plants and animals but also to reproductive material including seeds, and to genetic resources in general, IPRs may affect the accessibility and availability of a large number of agricultural products. This is especially the case with IPRs such as patents which allow the rights holder to prevent third parties from commercial exploitation of the exclusive rights as defined in the patent claims.

[1] **Note by the co-authors:** In drawing out general trends for discussion, the authors acknowledge that there are country specificities which characterize different forms of agriculture and development. What is stated in one context may not be 100% valid in another context.

[2] See Article 25 of the Universal Declaration of Human Rights (Paris, 10 December 1948), G.A. Res. 217A (III), (1948), UN Doc. A/810 (1948), available at: http://daccess-dds-ny.un.org/doc/RESOLUTION/GEN/NR0/043/88/IMG/NR004388.pdf?OpenElement (accessed 3 February 2010).

[3] The right to health is embodied in the 1946 Constitution of the World Health Organization (WHO) (New York, 22 July 1946), 14 U.N.T.S. 185, 62 Stat. 2679 (*entered into force* 7 April 1948). For information on human rights treaties pertaining to the right of health, see Chapter 2. See also UN Office of the High Commissioner for Human Rights (OHCHR) and WHO, *Fact Sheet No. 31: The Right to Health* (June 2008), available at: http://www.ohchr.org/Documents/Publications/Factsheet31.pdf (accessed 18 March 2010).

Food security is also inextricably linked to poverty, as it is mostly poor people who suffer from limited access to appropriate food sources. Curiously, a considerable portion of the world's poor are farmers, which again raises issues associated with seeds and their protection through IP, including the consequences of restrictions on the use of seeds for these farmers. This is one of the themes explored in this chapter.

Intellectual property protection of technologies including biotechnology may also signify that countries and their communities (especially those of technologically disadvantaged nations) are unable to enhance their agricultural processes through appropriate application of these technologies. Private and public research sectors may meanwhile be affected by legal restrictions on the use of certain technologies, thus reducing options for agricultural development. This is even more serious in a context where, increasingly, the relationship between appropriate food intake and health has become apparent in both developed and developing countries (see example in Box 3.1).[4]

This chapter seeks to identify some of the connections and linkages between food security and IP, particularly in terms of how the right to food as a human right may become affected through policy and legal restrictions and limitations imposed by the very nature of IP. Section 1 undertakes an overview of some of the legal and conceptual foundations for the right to food. It looks at some of the key international instruments recognizing the right to food and food security. Section 2 presents and reflects upon some of the trends in technological innovation as it relates to agriculture, highlighting both social and environmental impacts. Section 3 analyses the impacts of patents and PVP, addressing also the flexibilities inherent in the TRIPS Agreement for countries to customize their PVP to local needs.[5] Section 4 highlights some concerns regarding enclosure of the commons in relation to seeds and biodiversity components under the 1992 Convention on Biological Diversity (CBD),[6] before moving on to discuss the implications of the International Treaty on Plant Genetic Resources for Food and Agriculture of 2001 (ITPGRFA).[7] This is followed by Section 5 which explores options for developing countries to ensure better use of genetic resources and strategies for research and development (R&D) more targeted towards local needs.

[4] Tansey (2008, pp. 7–8) discusses the changing global food system and challenges for national food policies in terms of 'ensuring a sustainable, secure, safe, sufficient and nutritious (in other words healthy), equitable and culturally appropriate diet for all'.

[5] Agreement on Trade-Related Aspects of Intellectual Property Rights (Marrakesh, 15 April 1994), Marrakesh Agreement Establishing the World Trade Organization, Annex 1C, 1869 U.N.T.S. 299, 33 I.L.M. 1197 (1994) (*entered into force* 1 January 1995) [hereinafter 'TRIPS Agreement'], available at: http://www.wto.org/english/tratop_e/trips_e/t_agm0_e.htm (accessed 3 February 2010).

[6] Convention on Biological Diversity (Rio de Janeiro, 5 June 1992), 1760 U.N.T.S. 79, 31 I.L.M. 818 (1992) (*entered into force* 29 December 1993) [hereinafter 'CBD'], available at: http://www.cbd.int/doc/legal/cbd-un-en.pdf (accessed 3 February 2010).

[7] Food and Agriculture Organization (FAO) International Treaty on Plant Genetic Resources for Food and Agriculture (Rome, 3 November 2001), FAO Conference Res.3/2001, S. Treaty Doc. No. 110-19 (*entered into force* 29 June 2004) [hereinafter 'ITPGRFA'], available at: http://www.planttreaty.org/texts_en.htm (accessed 16 March 2010).

BOX 3.1. Promoting healthy, culturally appropriate diets through local knowledge and biodiversity

Hattie Wells and Gary Martin[8]

In its General Comment No. 12 on '*The right to adequate food?*', the Committee on Economic, Social and Cultural Rights (CESCR) recognizes that the 'core content of the right to adequate food' implies, among other things, 'the availability of food in a quantity and quality sufficient to satisfy the dietary needs of individuals, free from adverse substances, and acceptable within a given culture' (CESCR 1999, para. 8). The Committee furthermore clarifies that the '*cultural and consumer acceptability*' of food implies 'the need also to take into account, as far as possible, perceived non nutrient-based values attached to food and food consumption and informed consumer concerns regarding the nature of accessible food supplies' (ibid., para. 11; see further Rajotte 2008, p. 163).

Many people around the world are experiencing a nutritional transition as traditional foods are progressively replaced by less healthy modern diets. Sedentary lifestyles, an increase in the consumption of refined carbohydrates and fats, and a decrease in dietary diversity are contributing to the prevalence of lifestyle diseases such as cancer, diabetes, heart disease and obesity. Doctors and nutritionists advocate a return to traditional food-ways, which are characterized by diets high in fibre, fruits, vegetables, spices and wild foods. Ironically, many of the cultural groups who developed these traditional culinary practices are adopting Westernized diets. In some cases, because of a genetic predisposition to obesity and diabetes, they are bearing the brunt of the nutritional transition.

Among the ethnic groups affected by this global trend are Southern Africa's oldest inhabitants, the San. They live mostly in the arid zones of Botswana, Namibia, South Africa, Angola and Zambia. Once numbering several million, their present population is estimated to be 100,000.

Buffering nutritional transitions in San communities

Accessing a reliable and nutritious food supply is a major concern for the San, who were formerly nomadic. Unable to sustain their traditional hunting-foraging subsistence due to dispossession and marginalization, they have become impoverished and largely reliant on food aid and welfare for their survival. They are eating more processed foods, in part because their access to nutritious wild foods is threatened by deforestation, overgrazing and competition for limited natural resources.

The effects of poverty and displacement have reduced the variety of food types available. Families often lack the income to supplement this loss. This leads to vitamin and mineral deficiencies, which can have a significant impact on people who have special dietary needs, especially children, and pregnant and lactating mothers.

Despite the lifestyle changes experienced over the last century, many San maintain an intimate knowledge of desert ecology and the natural resources on which they still depend. This knowledge is threatened by acculturation, formal schooling (which does not integrate local knowledge) and limited access to edible wild plants. The loss of this plant lore leads to greater dependency on fewer food types, most of which are provided by government food aid, thereby further diminishing the San potential for maintaining or re-establishing self-reliance.

(*continued*)

[8] Global Diversity Foundation, Southern Africa.

Box 3.1 *(continued)*

Projects which assist communities like the San of Southern Africa to maintain their biological and cultural diversity pay dividends in health, nutrition and the transmission of ecological knowledge. For example, in response to a request from San families living in the Omaheke region of Namibia, the Global Diversity Foundation is working with local organizations and communities through the Kalahari Garden Project to develop 60 household gardens as well as a local primary school garden. The horticultural plots are intended to enhance the diets of approximately 800 people and to promote agricultural, nutritional and ecological education within the community. They will also encourage the exchange of knowledge on edible and medicinal plants that were formerly a part of the San's traditional diet and reinforce the value of these plants among the younger generation.

1. The right to food: A conceptual and legal background

The tragedy of hunger in many parts of the world is incomprehensible alongside the affluence and overconsumption in other parts.[9] The Food and Agriculture Organization of the United Nations (FAO) estimated in June 2009 that 1.02 billion persons were hungry, an increase of more than 150 million people in just two years.[10] Increasing food prices represent a crucial part of the explanation, and the poorest, landless and female-headed households are the hardest hit (FAO 2008, pp. 1, 22–27).

Poverty is still the main explanation for hunger. Significantly, 70% of the world's hungry are involved in agriculture themselves, either as smallholders or as landless labourers. These simple truths show that something is clearly wrong in how agriculture and the food system are organized, both worldwide and nationally. To ensure food security and reduce poverty levels, urgent changes and responses are needed from governments, the research community including the international agricultural research centres, the private sector, the international financial community, international cooperation agencies, the retail business and society at large.

In 1996, the Heads of State and Government present at the World Food Summit defined food security as a situation that 'exists when all people, at all times, have physical, social and economic access to sufficient, safe and nutritious food that meets their dietary needs and food preferences for an active and healthy life'.[11]

[9] Tansey (2008, p. 3) suggests that: 'What is clear is that there are serious flaws in a food system that globally leaves more than 850 million people undernourished and over 1 billion overweight (300 million of these obese)'. He adds that: 'Some 2 billion people also suffer from vitamin and micronutrient shortages. Undernutrition in pregnant women and young babies can have irreversible effects for life, while obese people's lives are threatened by diet-related non-communicable diseases such as diabetes and heart attacks'.

[10] See World Food Program, '1.02 Billion People Hungry', available at: http://www.wfp.org/news/news-release/102-billion-people-hungry (accessed 18 March 2010). For further details on specific figures and facts regarding world food and hunger, see the International Food Policy Research Institute (IFPRI) website, available at: http://www.ifpri.org/ (accessed 18 March 2010).

[11] UN Food and Agriculture Organization (FAO), Rome Declaration on World Food Security and World Food Summit Plan of Action (Rome, 13 November 1996), UN Doc. WFS 96/3 (1996), para. 1, available at: http://www.fao.org/docrep/003/w3613e/w3613e00.HTM (accessed 2 April 2010).

Three elements are important in this definition: first, its emphasis on physical, social and economic access to food; second, its emphasis on the quality of the food; third, the emphasis that the intake of food must enable everyone to live an active and healthy life, not merely surviving.

Even more noteworthy is the first introductory paragraph of the Rome Declaration on World Food Security, which recognizes 'the right of everyone to have access to safe and nutritious food, consistent with the right to adequate food and the fundamental right of everyone to be free from hunger' (ibid., para. 1). The leaders also committed themselves to 'reducing the number of undernourished people to half their present level no later than 2015' (ibid., para. 2). In contrast, the term used to quantify hunger levels in the 2000 UN Millennium Declaration is 'proportion' (para. 19(1)).[12] The Millennium Declaration resolves 'to halve, by the year 2015, ... the *proportion* of [the world's] people who suffer from hunger' (ibid., emphasis added). Hence, the 1996 Summit was considerably more ambitious than the 2000 Summit, as the former is committed to a real halving from the 800 million hungry persons in 1996 to 400 million, while the latter is committed to a reduction to approximately 500 million, based on demographic trends towards 2015.

While the concept of 'food security' might still be more frequently used among decision makers, it is more relevant to analyse the relationship between IPRs and food by applying the right to food. As both human rights and IPRs are widely recognized legal regimes, any comparison between them should be done from their respective objectives and means for achieving these objectives, formulated in legal terms. Compliance with the legal obligations that States assume by ratifying international treaties and adopting legislation in the realm of human rights and IPRs is sought through the implementation of both global and national strategies.

States are responsible for ensuring an appropriate balancing between these rights. In this context of balancing between rights, it is relevant to quote in full a paragraph from the UK Commission on Intellectual Property Rights (CIPR):

> We therefore consider that an IP right is best viewed as one of the means by which nations and societies can help to promote the fulfilment of human economic and social rights. In particular, there are no circumstances in which the most fundamental human rights should be subordinated to the requirements of IP protection. IP rights are granted by states for limited times (at least in the case of patents and copyrights) whereas human rights are inalienable and universal.[13] (CIPR 2002, p. 6)

A similar emphasis on the relationship between IPRs and economic, social and cultural rights is expressed by the United Nations Committee on Economic, Social and Cultural Rights (CESCR) in its General Comment No. 17 (2005, para. 35).[14] The

12 United Nations Millennium Declaration (8 September 2000), G.A. Res. 55/2, UN Doc. A/RES/55/2 (2000) [hereinafter 'UN Millennium Declaration'], para. 19(1), available at: http://www.un.org/millennium/ (accessed 22 June 2009).

13 The significance of this Commission being comprised of highly recognized IP law scholars and attorneys cannot be underestimated. For details of the Commission's work, see the Commission for Intellectual Property Rights website, available at: http://www.iprcommission.org (accessed 18 March 2010).

14 Committee on Economic, Social and Cultural Rights (CESCR) 2005, General Comment No. 17: *The right of everyone to benefit from the protection of the moral and material interests resulting*

General Comments are not legally binding, but are frequently referred to in resolutions adopted by intergovernmental bodies, and in national strategies. A more precise understanding of human rights, in particular the right to food, is, however, needed before moving towards the linkages between IPRs and food.

The right to food in an international instrument was first formally recognized in the 1948 Universal Declaration of Human Rights.[15] At the time, it was expressed as: 'Everyone has the right to a standard of living adequate for the health and well-being of himself and of his family, including food, clothing, housing and medical care and necessary social services, and the right to security in the event of unemployment, sickness, disability, widowhood, old age or other lack of livelihood in circumstances beyond his control'.

The right to food is also explicitly recognized in the International Covenant on Economic, Social and Cultural Rights of 1966 (ICESCR).[16] The Covenant establishes that: 'The State parties to the present Covenant recognize the right of everyone to an adequate standard of living for himself and his family, including adequate food, clothing and housing. . . . ' Furthermore, it also recognizes 'the fundamental right of everyone to be free from hunger . . . '. The right to be free from hunger is actually the only human right recognized in either of the two Covenants from 1966 which is explicitly termed 'fundamental'.[17]

Moreover, unlike other human rights, the recognition of the right to be free from hunger is followed by a relatively specified list of objectives and measures. Article 11.2(a) of the ICESCR reads: 'The States Parties . . . shall take, individually and through international co-operation, the measures . . . which are needed: (a) To improve methods of production, conservation and distribution of food by making full use of technical and scientific knowledge, by disseminating knowledge of the principles of nutrition and by developing or reforming agrarian systems in such a way as to achieve the most efficient development and utilization of natural resources'.

This listing of measures cannot be considered to be exhaustive (Alston 1984, p. 34; Craven 1995, p. 316). This is also confirmed by Article 2(1) of the Covenant – which is the Covenant's 'general obligations' provision – using the phrase 'all appropriate means'.

When paragraph 11.2(a) of the Covenant was formulated, technology was seen as a panacea, and the awareness of power asymmetries inherent in technology was

from any scientific, literary or artistic production of which he or she is the author (art. 15, para. 1 (c)), UN Doc. E/C.12/GC/17 (12 January 2006) [hereinafter 'General Comment No. 17'], available at: http://www.unhchr.ch/tbs/doc.nsf/7cec89369c43a6dfc1256a2a0027ba2a/03902145edbbe797c125711500584ea8/$FILE/G0640060.pdf (accessed 3 February 2010).

15 Universal Declaration of Human Rights (Paris, 10 December 1948), G.A. Res. 217A (III), (1948), UN Doc. A/810 (1948), available at: http://daccess-dds-ny.un.org/doc/RESOLUTION/GEN/NR0/043/88/IMG/NR004388.pdf?OpenElement (accessed 3 February 2010).

16 International Covenant on Economic, Social and Cultural Rights (New York, 16 December 1966) 993 U.N.T.S. 3, 6 I.L.M. 360 (1967), G.A. Res. 2200A (XXI), UN Doc. A/6316 (1966) (*entered into force* 3 January 1976) [hereinafter 'ICESCR'], available at: http://www2.ohchr.org/english/law/cescr.htm (accessed 3 February 2010).

17 See ICESCR; see also International Covenant on Civil and Political Rights (New York, 16 December 1966) 999 U.N.T.S. 171 and 1057 U.N.T.S. 407, 6 I.L.M. 368 (1967), G.A. Res. 2200A (XXI), UN Doc. A/6316 (1966) (*entered into force* 23 March 1976), available at: http://www2.ohchr.org/english/law/ccpr.htm (accessed 3 February 2010).

not as clearly understood as today. Moreover, the awareness of environmental constraints was not as strong as it is presently. The emphasis on 'production, conservation and distribution of food' is, however, still both valid and relevant. If these three objectives are understood as closely interlinked, any strategy which impedes food distribution should be avoided (Haugen 2007b, pp. 142–146, 412–417). Moreover, an effective distribution strategy also implies that food-producing resources, such as seeds, should be made adequately available for farmers. The State should 'facilitate the production process so that the production of food is shared more equally…' (ibid., p. 145).

We will now analyse the implementation of the human right to food in more detail. The Committee on Economic, Social and Cultural Rights has identified two 'obligations of immediate effect' in its General Comment No. 3 (CESCR 1991, paras. 1 and 2):[18]

- The obligation to take measures or steps, both on a national and an international level (Article 2(1) of the Covenant).
- The obligation to guarantee that these rights will be exercised without discrimination of any kind (Article 2(2) of the Covenant).

The progressive realization of economic, social and cultural human rights does not imply that there ought to be any delay in the taking of appropriate measures for ensuring this realization. Many States have limited resources, however, and might have to give priority to compliance with other international treaties to which they are parties, and which might have more robust sanctions mechanisms for non-compliance.[19]

As discussed earlier, access to food is considered a crucial element in defining food security. This is further elaborated in General Comment No. 12, in which both *accessibility* and *availability* of food is emphasized as 'core content' of the right to food (CESCR 1999, para. 8).[20] The content of these two terms are elaborated upon in paragraphs 12 and 13, with the former emphasizing physical distribution of food and the latter emphasizing physical and economic accessibility. Notably, there are

[18] Committee on Economic, Social and Cultural Rights (CESCR) 1991, *General Comment No. 3: The nature of states parties obligations*, UN Doc. E/1991/23 (14 December 1990) [hereinafter 'General Comment No. 3'], available at: http://www.unhchr.ch/tbs/doc.nsf/0/94bdbaf59b43a424c12563ed0052b664?Opendocument (accessed 3 February 2010).

[19] The TRIPS Agreement specifies the use of the Dispute Settlement Understanding in Article 64. Note in this context the extension of the transition period under TRIPS Article 66.1 for the least-developed WTO member states from 1 January 2006 to 1 July 2013; see World Trade Organization (WTO), Decision of the Council for TRIPS of 29 November 2005, Extension of the Transition Period under Article 66.1 for Least-Developed Country Members, Doc. IP/C/40 (30 November 2005), available at:http://docsonline.wto.org/GEN_highLightParent.asp?qu=&doc=D:/DDFDOCUMENTS/T/IP/C/40.DOC.HTM (accessed 19 March 2010). The Decision also states in paragraph 6 that 'This Decision is without prejudice to […] the right of least-developed country Members to seek further extensions of the period provided for in paragraph 1 of Article 66 of the Agreement'. Observe, however, that paragraph 5 of the same decision says: 'Least-developed country Members will ensure that any changes in their laws, regulations and practice made during the additional transitional period do not result in a lesser degree of consistency with the provisions of the TRIPS Agreement' (ibid.).

[20] Committee on Economic, Social and Cultural Rights (CESCR) 1999, *General Comment No. 12: The right to adequate food*, UN Doc. E/C.12/1999/5 (12 May 1999) [hereinafter 'General Comment No. 12'], available at: http://www.unhchr.ch/tbs/doc.nsf/0/3d02758c707031d58025677f003b73b9 (accessed 3 February 2010). See further Chapter 1 on the nature of such General Comments and the extent of their legal authority.

also paragraphs within General Comment No. 12 which clarify that the available food must be culturally acceptable (paras. 8, 11; see Box. 3.1). On the face of it, the right to food conflicts with IPRs. The former emphasizes accessibility and affordability. The latter emphasizes the possibility of the right holder to restrict access to those products containing protected biological material over which the right holder exercises exclusive rights. If this were the whole story, the conclusion would be easy to make. As stated by economist Joan Robinson, however, if new technology has restrictions on its dissemination, the end result will be more technology to disseminate, because the private sector has increased stimulus to invest in new research (Robinson 1971). The costs of developing a new product to the stage of commercialization are considerable. It is, however, not always possible to monitor the actual research costs through the financial reports by the corporations themselves. Hence, the numbers presented by the corporations should be treated with caution.

The balance between controlled access and free access is at the core of the IP system. There are strong voices saying that the balance has shifted too much towards protection, effectively undermining the dissemination of new, applicable knowledge (see International Expert Group on Biotechnology, Innovation and Intellectual Property [IEGBIIP] 2008). The General Comment No. 17 (CESCR 2005) provides an interpretation of Article 15, paragraph 1 (c) of the International Covenant on Economic, Social and Cultural Rights. Even if there are problematic paragraphs in General Comment No. 17 (Haugen 2007a, p. 60; Helfer 2007, p. 994), paragraph 35 establishes a general requirement to ensure an appropriate balance between human rights, by stating: 'States parties should therefore ensure that their legal or other regimes for the protection of the moral and material interests resulting from one's scientific, literary or artistic productions constitute no impediment to their ability to comply with their core obligations in relation to the rights to food, health and education, as well as to take part in cultural life and to enjoy the benefits of scientific progress and its applications, or any other right enshrined in the Covenant'.

The General Comment No. 12 on the right to adequate food, however, does not say anything explicit about IPRs. A relevant paragraph reads: 'As part of their obligations to protect people's resource base for food, States parties should take appropriate steps to ensure that activities of the private business sector and civil society are in conformity with the right to food' (CESCR 1999, para. 27; see also paras. 25–26). Moreover, the emphasis on distribution of food-producing resources, which was said earlier to be crucial, is not explicitly acknowledged in General Comment No. 12. There are, however, paragraphs in General Comment No. 12 that address restricted access to food (ibid., paras. 15, 20), which implicitly might encompass concerns relating to IPRs (Haugen 2007b, pp. 377–393).

Another important document relevant to the implementation of the right to adequate food is the 'Voluntary Guidelines to Support the Progressive Realization of the Right to Adequate Food in the Context of National Food Security' ('Voluntary Guidelines'; FAO 2004b). Under the heading 'Access to resources and assets', the following is emphasized: access to research results enhancing food security, within the framework of intellectual property rights (Guideline 8.5), ensure the conservation and sustainable use of genetic resources for food and agriculture (Guideline 8.12) and promote more appropriate technologies to enable more efficient food production (Guideline 8.14). Guideline 2 is on 'Economic development policies' and emphasizes appropriate and affordable technologies (Guideline 2.6). Therefore, the Voluntary Guidelines do not give specific advice on how to reconcile the right to food and IPRs, as they only state that the policies should be 'within the framework of relevant international agreements ... ' (Guideline 8.5).

The strong support for the human right to adequate food can be discerned from the number of States voting for the annual resolutions in the General Assembly. For example, the adoption of the resolution on the right to adequate food in 2008 occurred by 184 votes to one, with no abstentions.[21] The report on which the latter resolution was based did address IP in a separate section (UN 2008, paras. 24–28; see also UN 2003, para. 29). Paragraph 28 of the 2008 report reads: 'Clearly, the privatization of genetic resources for agriculture resulting from the extension of intellectual property rights to plant varieties, plants or seeds may put this balance [between private and social interests] in jeopardy'. The report then outlines a process involving consultations with relevant international governmental organizations, concluding: 'Concrete recommendations will follow these consultations'. The 2008 resolution on the right to food highlights that implementation of the TRIPS Agreement should be supportive of food security (para. 25). The 2009 report promotes agricultural innovation and recommends detailed approaches for ensuring that IPRs are compatible with the human right to adequate food (UN 2009).

The issue will therefore continue to be on the UN agenda. To enrich these processes, three approaches might be relevant. First, an appropriate understanding of human rights realization is gained by elaborating on the human rights principles. Simply stated, these provide the guidance for public conduct relating to the implementation of the strategies for ensuring realization of human rights. The following human rights principles are recognized: human dignity, non-discrimination, transparency, accountability, participation, empowerment and the rule of law (FAO 2007, p. 2). These seven principles – if properly observed – would ensure a quality of public policy, based on an adequate involvement of all interested parties and based on international conventions and national law. There is a presumption that the efforts by the involved actors would both strengthen the implementation process itself and also make these actors more able to contribute in subsequent processes and decisions. It is hence reasonable to state that public policy would improve if the seven human rights principles were adequately observed.

Second, there is room for exploring how different provisions within human rights instruments must be balanced and reconciled with one another. It is an established principle of human rights that the enjoyment of one human right shall not negatively affect the enjoyment of other human rights (Haugen 2005a, p. 453). While not attempting to build a hierarchy among different human rights, a distinction must be made between rights linked directly to the human person and rights which contribute to the realization of other human rights (ibid., p. 452). Authors' rights as

[21] United Nations General Assembly, Resolution on the Right to Food (18 December 2008), G.A. Res. 63/187, UN Doc. A/RES/63/187 (2009), available at: http://daccess-dds-ny.un.org/doc/UNDOC/GEN/N08/482/01/PDF/N0848201.pdf?OpenElement (accessed 2 April 2010).

recognized in Article 15(l)(c) of the Covenant belong to the latter category (ibid.). It is essential that social human rights, such as the right to food or health, are not impeded as a result of the enjoyment of authors' rights. The rights which are related to the protection of the human person per se must be considered more important than the rights which are related to the moral and material interests of that person (ibid., p. 454). At the same time, it has to be qualified that any restriction of the author's rights should be made only after careful consideration of other principles, including the basic principle of non-discrimination, as well as the principles of participation, transparency and accountability (ibid.).

Third, specifically applied to the right to food, we have seen earlier that a policy objective should be that the production of food is shared more equally. In this context, it is relevant to recall one of the phrases introduced in the first UN report on the right to adequate food. In this report, UN Special Rapporteur Asbjørn Eide emphasized the 'command over food' as crucial for ensuring the realization of the right to food (Eide 1987, p. 27). However, this does not imply that one should seek to keep one's food and food-producing resources for oneself, not sharing it with others. Being involved in local networks or cooperatives for the purpose of saving, exchanging and developing new seeds will be of great importance. What it does mean is that one should not be made dependent on the provision of food-producing resources in an asymmetrical relationship, where the provider could set the prices and the conditions, as they consider appropriate. In Section 3, we assess in more detail what choices the farmers actually have. Before this discussion, there is a need to have a better understanding of recent developments in agricultural research.

2. Trends in agricultural innovation and technology: The impact on farming communities in developing countries

In most developing nations, farmers select, save and use shared seeds that form the basis for consecutive harvests, while developing new methodologies to create better quality harvests. This practice of informal exchange of knowledge and farm-saved seeds is atypical in the industrial farming model that is spreading from the industrialized world to other countries. Industrial farming companies rely on exclusive, monopolistic rights granted for the development of seeds and plant varieties, through modern forms of biotechnology and plant breeding. Business models in industrial crop improvement usually depend on patents and PVP, purportedly to provide incentives to innovate.

Meanwhile, in most developing nations innovation in agriculture has advanced through evolving customary practices based mainly on the sharing of knowledge and seeds. In many parts of the world, where small farming is linked to ancestral culture and traditions,[22] local innovation systems exist which continually evolve and adapt to new ecological conditions. Whether through participatory plant breeding initiatives or through the formal recognition of 'conservationist farmers' (as in Peru), there are many examples of dynamic intellectual outputs by small farming communities, which are far detached from IPR incentives or other compensation

[22] For example, in the Andes of Peru, Colombia, Ecuador and Bolivia; in the Himalayas in Nepal and Tibet; in many parts of India; and on the African plains.

mechanisms. Rather, culture and social recognition offer the strongest incentives in this regard (Vernooy 2003; In Situ Conservation Project – Peru; Smale 2006). A farming community that finds a new way to keep plants safe from rodents is no less innovative than an employee of a company that invents a new strain of rice in a company lab. But not all parties stand to benefit from the exclusive monopoly protection granted by patents for an invention (Kuyek 2002). In fact, IPRs in various forms, such as patents and PVP regimes that favour industrial breeders are largely irrelevant to, and might diminish, the work and the ingenuity of farming communities whose practices are essential for maintenance of biodiversity and ensuring food security for a broad population.

The extension of IPRs – specifically patents – towards rewarding innovation in the area of living organisms was only developed in the 1970s and the 'real' repercussions have yet to be fully understood. The push to extend patents has not only come from commercial interests in biology but also from developments in information science and the ability to digitally encode and manipulate all kinds of information (Tansey 2008; Biber-Klemm & Cottier 2006). Additionally, legal systems that established breeders' rights (systems favouring industrial breeders) largely reflected the economic and regulatory structures and circumstances of agriculture prevailing in developed countries (with patent systems pushed by US farming industries and plant variety laws promoted in Europe) around the second half of the twentieth century (Dutfield 2003).

Considering the short history of the use of IPRs in agriculture, even in developed countries, there is still much that we do not know about their long-term impacts over biodiversity, food security and public health. While a few studies have explored some potential implications (see e.g. CIPR 2002; FAO 2003; ICTSD/UNCTAD 2003; Cullet 2004; Srinivasan 2004; Louwaars et al. 2005; UPOV 2005; Tansey & Rajotte (eds.) 2008), more research is needed. One important question from a human development viewpoint in relation to IPRs is whether the latter create incentives for agricultural research and technology transfer which support a diversity of farming models and are relevant to the situation of poor farmers, who need to improve their harvests but cannot afford huge investments. The industrial farming model prevalent in many developed countries has steadily been transposed to developing countries and LDCs. Emphasizing the important linkages among food security, diversity of farming models and biodiversity, Tansey (2008, p. 3) observes that:

> Serious doubts have been raised about the long-term viability of the industrial farming model that is spreading from the industrialized world to other countries. Yet the long-term viability of farming is central to ensuring food security for everyone on this planet... Many now call for more ecologically sustainable approaches to farming built around biodiversity and ecology. Yet others, sure of humankind's inventive capacity or responding to their industry's interests, promote further intensification and industrial approaches to farming as the way forward. Thus the future direction of farming is highly contested. (Citations omitted)

The social and environmental impacts of intensive agriculture need to be further evaluated. While these impacts are interconnected, some social concerns are highlighted here, whereas environmental dimensions are further explored in Box 3.2. There are those who argue that the introduction of transgenic crops can have a

BOX 3.2. Intellectual property and the environment: Some issues and debates relating to agriculture

A clean environment is integral to all aspects of human development (see UNDP 2007) and is a precious public good. There is little consensus on how the environment is affected by the exercise of IPRs. While the present discussion focuses on patent protection of transgenic plants, the relationship between IP and the environment can be approached from many angles. Climate change, for example, will likely accentuate many existing issues and tensions relating to IPRs, food security and the environment. Whether access to new clean energy technology is facilitated or impeded by IPRs is another important topic (see Chapter 9), now on the agenda of the WIPO Committee on Development and Intellectual Property (see WIPO 2007, pp. 153–157, in particular, recommendations 22 and 25–31). The Intergovernmental Panel on Climate Change has also regularly addressed how IP and climate change relate in terms of the positive and negative externalities connected with the protection of clean-energy technologies and innovations.[23]

A distinction must be made between 'old' and 'new' biotechnology (Haugen 2007b, pp. 19–27). Since the early Neolithic revolution, there have been efforts to improve the qualities and yields of plants. Plant breeding has resulted in plants with substantially higher yields. From the 1970s, modern biotechnology was introduced by the means of transgenic technology, allowing for the alteration of the genetic structure of the plant through the insertion of DNA from other species. Some seek to identify the positive aspects of genetic technology in terms of reduced use of pesticides. This reduction is said to result from the use of seeds which have a Bt gene inserted (bacillus thuringiensis – a bacterium producing proteins which are toxic to many insects). It is further claimed that the reduced spraying of pesticides will lead to reduced pollution. While there has been some evidence of reduced use of pesticides when using seeds with Bt genes inserted (Frisvold & Tronstad 1999; Ishmael et al. 2002), recent reports suggest that pesticide use might actually increase, as plants are increasingly tolerant or resistant to herbicides (Friends of the Earth International 2008). There are also other concerns, such as the dominance of transgenic plants over other plants, which will be analysed later.

It is more common for so-called life science companies to provide packages which include both strong pesticides and seeds resistant to the provided pesticide, rather than to only offer seeds. Sometimes, highly restrictive technology use agreements are employed by the business, the terms of which may be strictly enforced against farmers alleged to violate them. In some cases, the products have been found not to be degradable (Agence France Presse 2007).

Other serious environmental concerns include the risk that transgenic plants are spreading onto farmers' fields and into the wild. Two cases have gained international attention. First, in the *Schmeiser* case, the Supreme Court of Canada held that farmer Percy Schmeiser had infringed Monsanto's patent on genes and plant cells found in canola growing in Mr. Schmeiser's fields.[24] The trial judge had dismissed the suggestion that the crop was the product of seed blown or inadvertently carried onto the appellants' land.[25] The majority

[23] Examples include technologies which serve to reduce emissions and/or to make industrial systems more efficient by reducing energy inputs.

[24] *Monsanto Canada Inc. v. Schmeiser*, [2004] 1 S.C.R. 902, 2004 SCC 34, available at: http://csc.lexum.umontreal.ca/en/2004/2004scc34/2004scc34.pdf (accessed 1 February 2009).

[25] See *Monsanto Canada Inc. v. Schmeiser* [2001], 2001 FCT 256, paras. 116–119. While the trial judge explored the possibility that 'some Roundup ready seed was carried to Mr. Schmeiser's field without his knowledge', he was convinced that this could not explain the concentration or extent of Roundup Ready canola ultimately found in Mr. Schmeiser's crop (ibid., para. 118). The majority in the Supreme Court did not challenge this part of the trial judge's analysis. See *Monsanto Canada Inc. v. Schmeiser*, [2004] 1 S.C.R. 902, 2004 SCC 34, paras. 66–68.

in the Supreme Court held that the farmer's conduct in saving and planting the seed, and in harvesting and selling the plants, constituted an infringing 'use' of the patented genes and plant cells.[26] Some issues raised by the decision include the extent of the farmers' privilege, their 'classic' property rights in seeds, and the effects of genetic contamination or gene flows over legitimate farming practices (see Phillips 2007, pp. 49–64; de Beer 2005). A Canadian report points toward the risks of herbicide-resistance becoming a 'weed problem' (Royal Society of Canada 2000, p. 129).

Second, there are published studies on the alleged spread of transgenic maize in the Mexican state of Oaxaca (see Quist & Chapela 2001, 2002; Piñeyro-Nelson et al. 2008), although another study in the same Mexican state found that 'transgenic maize seeds were absent or extremely rare in the sampled fields' (Ortiz-García et al. 2005, p. 1; see GMO Safety 2005).

Debates over GM crops and the long-term viability of the industrial farming model – where a majority of crops are now controlled by a few corporations – will no doubt be further heated by considerations of climate change. The UNDP *Human Development Report 2007/08* observes that 'climate shocks . . . wipe out crops, reduce opportunities for employment, push up food prices and destroy property, confronting people with stark choices' (UNDP 2007, p. 83). Further research is needed to address the specific linkages between IP, food security and climate change (see discussion in Chapter 9). On the one hand, there is increasing recognition of the role of small, diverse indigenous and local farmers in biodiversity preservation and climate change adaptation (IIED 2008), and the need for a diversity of farming models to ensure food security. On the other hand, there are those who argue that the answer is in more GM crops incentivized by IP – in this case crops genetically modified to withstand climate change effects.

[26] *Monsanto Canada Inc. v. Schmeiser*, [2004] 1 S.C.R. 902, 2004 SCC 34, paras. 69–97.

negative impact on the poor, particularly in developing countries (Lipton 2001, p. 842; Paarlberg 2001, pp. 13–14; Shoemaker 2001, p. 50). The asymmetrical power relationships that exist in most developing countries imply that while many richer farmers might benefit, this is often at the expense of the poor. Moreover, there are also findings that the social benefits of the Green Revolution are not as positive as originally envisaged, even if an overall increase in productivity is documented (Evenson 2003). The Green Revolution, unlike the present 'gene revolution', was initiated by benevolent foundations, governments and international agricultural research centres, not private corporations. As with the Green Revolution, it seems reasonable to suggest that the positive effect of the introduction of new 'gene' technology in agriculture will be limited unless the underlying social structures are addressed. For example, a farmer who pays more for seed expects, in exchange for her or his additional money, to enjoy an increased reliance on very good harvests. If the harvests fail or are otherwise insufficient to justify the additional outlay, this will have particularly serious effects for those who have taken out loans to buy seeds and expects to have their costs reimbursed through substantial harvest increases.

The impacts of IPR on farmers' rights and practices have been well documented.[27] It is essential that developing countries, whose agricultural structures

[27] One of the best-known cases is that of Canadian farmer Percy Schmeiser and Monsanto Canada Inc. See *Monsanto Canada Inc. v. Schmeiser*, [2004] 1 S.C.R. 902, 2004 SCC 34, para. 66, available at: http://csc.

vary from those prevailing in the developed countries, tread carefully before providing for IPRs in plant varieties, plants and other organisms. While the TRIPS Agreement does oblige countries to specifically provide some form of protection for plant varieties and patents for microorganisms, the objective of establishing a patent or other system directed at agricultural innovation must go beyond merely fulfiling a country's obligation under a multilateral trade agreement. The objective must be to establish a legal regime that includes and supports the interests of all affected groups including farmers, consumers, indigenous communities and local industries, as the obligations that countries sign into should be of benefit to all. The extension of IPRs in their current form (private, exclusive monopolistic rights for a certain period) to agriculture-related innovations is likely to cause a shift in the balance of power over food and to have effects over food security and livelihoods in developing nations, as is already becoming apparent in developed nations. Furthermore, it has been repeatedly noted that IP regimes need to be constructed based on specific social, economic and technological development indicators of countries and not based on general approaches or approximations (CIPR 2002; ICTSD/UNCTAD 2003).

One of the key trends in the food system has been a growing concentration of economic power in sectors involving farm input suppliers (agrochemical, energy or equipment companies), traders, retailers and caterers (Tansey 2008, p. 8). This means that 'fewer and fewer firms control more and more of the market' (ibid.). Tansey suggests that 'changing intellectual property rules have been important in fuelling this trend' (ibid.).[28] According to Falcon and Fowler (2002, pp. 204–206):

> [T]he plant genetics industry is now heavily concentrated in a half-dozen major firms that hold substantial numbers of key patents on germplasm. They also have IP coverage of the related enabling technologies.... [T]he control of patents and seed distribution networks exercised by these companies has substantially increased the barriers to entry for new firms in the field of germplasm development.

According to a study by the United Nations Conference on Trade and Development (UNCTAD 2006), the need to consolidate patent portfolios and thus ensure freedom to operate appears, on the one hand, to have created incentives for the extensive mergers and acquisitions that have occurred between agricultural biotechnology and seed businesses, and for other cooperative responses short of full integration (such as cross-licensing). On the other hand, because of the breadth of protection accorded to the patent holder (the seed or biotechnology company), concentration in agricultural biotechnology is giving the largest corporations unprecedented power vis-à-vis growers and other stakeholders (ibid.). The study also states that the privatization and patenting of agricultural innovation (gene traits, transformation technologies and seed germplasm) have supplanted the traditional agricultural understanding on seeds and farmers' rights, such as the right to save and replant seeds harvested from the former crop. In some jurisdictions, the privatization and patenting of agricultural innovation has resulted in a drastic erosion

lexum.umontreal.ca/en/2004/2004scc34/2004scc34.pdf (accessed 1 February 2009). See the discussion in Box 3.2. See Phillips 2007, pp. 49–64.

28 The story of the agricultural input industry is discussed in Tansey 2008, p. 9.

of these traditional farmers' rights, and the assertion of proprietary lines on seed technologies and genetic contents has changed farmers from 'seed owners' to mere 'licensees' of a patented product. Is it becoming an exception for farmers to freely reuse seeds (as traditionally asserted by small farmers in particular)? There are general allegations that farmers in some developed countries have ever-decreasing practical options other than to choose protected seeds. They then come into a relationship where they are dependent on the corporate providers of seed.

At the same time, statements to the effect that farmers have 'no option but protected seeds' need to be qualified. An important consideration is the diminished role of public sector R&D in agriculture. In many countries, the government has reduced its role in the provision of seeds and left it to the private sector to provide the seeds. This will often be achieved at the price and the conditions that the private sector demands.[29] Private firms are continuously looking for tools to help create a more secure market position, reduce risks and gain maximum benefits; one of the tools is the use and spread of IP laws into new potential markets so as to help them consolidate global positions. Global structures, including the international IP and trade frameworks, reinforce these trends in privatization. The TRIPS Agreement is only one such means towards achieving this goal. Bilateral and regional trade agreements with TRIPS-plus provisions that dilute flexibilities available under TRIPS, and investment treaties with IP provisions, are now being used as a carrot towards increased foreign direct investment (FDI) and technology transfer to the signatories.

3. Intellectual property rights in agriculture

Agricultural innovations may be protected by two different types of IPRs – by grant of a patent and/or by grant of a plant variety right through a *sui generis* law (also known as PVP). Specifically in the case of plant varieties, the TRIPS Agreement allows member countries the option of granting protection via patents or a *sui generis* form of protection or both. The option of a '*sui generis*' system is a TRIPS flexibility. Other flexibilities include permitting the use of a compulsory licence in a number of circumstances. These so-called flexibilities have been considerably diluted in bilateral trade agreements, with potential adverse effects over farmers' rights and food security.

3.1. Patents

Under Article 27.3(b) of the TRIPS Agreement, members may exclude plants and animals from patentability, but must grant patents on microorganisms and processes for non-biologically or microbiologically developing plants and animals. In addition to this, members must grant some form of protection towards plant varieties by either patents or a *sui generis* system or a combination of the two. The TRIPS Agreement allows for the exclusion from patentability of 'plants and animals' in general. Consequently, WTO members may exclude plants as such (including transgenic plants), plant varieties (including hybrids), as well as plant cells, seeds,

[29] Some findings indicate that the private sector is more efficient than the public sector in actually delivering the products resulting from research (Dalrymple & Srivastava 1994, p. 204; Louwaars et al. 2005).

and other plant materials. They may also exclude animals (including transgenic animals) and animal breeds.

The standards of protection set by the TRIPS Agreement operate on a minimum standards principle, and all member countries must provide for the provisions in their national regimes within certain time periods. It has been argued that the minimum standards laid down by the TRIPS Agreement are highly substantive and do not apply to the socio-economic or cultural status and structures of most developing countries (see UNDP 2001, pp. 102–109).

Countries may meanwhile adopt higher standards than those provided for in the TRIPS Agreement. Indeed, there has been a trend for national political authorities to extend the scope of the IP system, so that more inventions are eligible for patent protection, while reducing their public research efforts. In the US and Europe, this has taken place in the following ways. First, the US and Europe have been limiting the list of non-patentable products. For example, decisions to grant patents on animals were first taken in the US in the late 1980s and Europe in the early 1990s, with a European appeal regarding a patent for a transgenic mouse (oncomouse) going on until 2004.[30] A similar oncomouse application was rejected in Canada in 2002.[31] Another example is that double protection – both patent and PVP for the same plant– was first granted by the EPO in 1999.[32] Before this decision, PVP and patent protection could not both be granted on the same plant.[33] Second, these countries allow patent protection to be extended to all plants where the patented material is found. Third, the European patent system has been lowering the threshold for inventiveness, so that naturally occurring substances are patentable.[34]

30 See US Patent No. 4,736,866 (filed 22 June 1984) (issued 12 April 1988); European Patent No. 0169672 (filed June 1985) (issued 13 May 1992); European Patent Office (EPO) Boards of Appeal, *In re Transgenic Animals/ Harvard*, Case No. T 315/03 - 3.3.8 [6 July 2004], OJ EPO 1/2006, pp. 15-82, available at http://archive.epo.org/epo/pubs/oj006/01_06/01_0156.pdf (accessed 1 February 2010).

31 *Harvard College v. Canada (Commissioner of Patents)*, [2002] 4 S.C.R. 45, available at http://csc.lexum.umontreal.ca/en/2002/2002scc76/2002scc76.pdf (accessed 1 February 2009).

32 See European Patent Office (EPO) Enlarged Board of Appeal, *In re Transgenic Plant/ Novartis II*, Case No. G 1/98 [20 December 1999], OJ EPO 3/2000, pp. 111–41, available at http://archive.epo.org/epo/pubs/oj000/3_00/3_1110.pdf (accessed 15 February 2009).

33 During the appeal, the EU Biotechnology Directive /98/44/EC was adopted, reading in Article 4: '1. The following shall not be patentable: (a) plant and animal varieties; (b) essentially biological processes for the production of plants or animals. 2. Inventions which concern plants or animals shall be patentable if the technical feasibility of the invention is not confined to a particular plant or animal variety'. Directive 98/44/EC of the European Parliament and of the Council of 6 July 1998 on the legal protection of biotechnological inventions, OJ L 213 (1998). The EPO's decision in *Transgenic Plant/ Novartis II* (OJ EPO 6/1995, p. 115) stated that 'in all cases where a concept of genetic engineering applicable to more than one variety was the invention, the resulting products should be patentable, even if they were plant varieties'.

34 European Patent Office (EPO) Examining and Oppositions Division, *In re Howard Florey Institute* [8 December 1994], OJ EPO 6/1995, pp. 388-407, available at http://archive.epo.org/epo/pubs/oj1995/p373_460.pdf; see also European Patent No. 1069819 (filed April 1999) (issued July 2002); European Patent Office (EPO) Boards of Appeal, *Broccoli/ Plant Bioscience*, Case No. T 83/05 - 3.3.04 [22 May 2007], OJ EPO 12/2007, pp. 644–69, available at http://www.european-patent-office.org/epo/pubs/oj007/12_07/12_6447.pdf. The EPO decision in *Howard Florey Institute* (OJ EPO 6/1995, p. 396) reads: '... if a substance found in nature has first to be isolated from its surroundings and a process for obtaining it is developed, that process is patentable. Moreover, if this substance can be properly characterised by its structure and it is new in the absolute sense of having no previously *recognised* existence, then the substance *per se* may be patentable' (emphasis added).

Inventiveness is one of three basic requirements of patent protection, the other two being novelty and industrial applicability.

While most developed nations (specifically the US) provide for patents for all innovations relating to agriculture and the food sector, including plants and animals, developing countries have been increasingly pressured in bilateral trade agreements to sign away the flexibilities made available under TRIPS. The impact of FTAs on TRIPS flexibilities are discussed in a 2008 document published by UNDP entitled *Towards a Balanced 'Sui Generis' Plant Variety Regime: Guidelines to Establish a National PVP Law and an Understanding of TRIPS-Plus Aspects of Plant Rights* ('UNDP Guidelines').[35] The document provides examples of FTAs said to contain provisions either requiring patents on plants, accession to UPOV, the implementation of IPRs with the highest international standards, or a combination of these requirements (see UNDP 2008, p. 25). According to the document: 'Along with extended patent life TRIPS-plus agreements generally include longer protection periods for [agrochemical and pharmaceutical test] data of the protected innovation' (ibid., p. 26). It is suggested that this 'data exclusivity' creates a 'monopoly over the data and test trials that led to the successful innovation' and potentially 'excludes other researchers from creating generic versions, for example, generics of agricultural pesticides' (ibid.). Without generic competition agricultural input costs are likely to remain high, and this is said to leave 'little choice for impoverished farmers to lift themselves from subsistence levels' (ibid.). The UNDP Guidelines add that FTAs 'could further reduce or eliminate tariffs on certain imported technologies and facilitate an influx of monopolistically priced seeds and other farming inputs' (ibid.).[36]

The UNDP Guidelines suggest, moreover, that some requirements in investment treaties could reduce manoeuvring room for countries to make use of flexibilities granted under the TRIPS Agreement (ibid., p. 27). Noting arguments that TRIPS-plus regulations in bilateral investment treaties or investment chapters might increase FDI and technology transfer to the signatories, the UNDP Guidelines state that: 'In some ways, this investment could be targeted to developing plant and [traditional medicinal knowledge]-related industries, which could encourage the growth of small and medium enterprises (SMEs) and gain market access for small-scale producers' (ibid.).[37] The UNDP Guidelines suggest, however, some likelihood that the investment treaties do not translate into affordable technology transfer for developing countries (see also CIPR 2002, pp. 23–24). Adding that the reliance of developing

[35] This document was prepared as part of the work programme of the UNDP Bureau for Development Policy, Poverty Group. It was published as a working document on which comments were solicited (see UNDP 2008, p. i).

[36] Citing Smith, S. R. 2007, 'Intellectual Property in Free Trade Agreements', paper presented at UNDP RCC/UNDP Malaysia/Third World Network workshop, Doha and Beyond: Incorporating Human Development into Trade Negotiations, Penang, 17–18 December 2007. See further Correa, C., 'Human Development Implications of IPR Protection and TRIPS-plus provisions in Asia-Pacific', paper presented at the same conference.

[37] The UNDP Guidelines note that, for such schemes to be viable, 'the rights of the knowledge holders would need to be clearly defined; for instance, if investment and R&D goes towards developing medicinal properties of a plant, the original purveyors of this knowledge would need to have opportunities to fully participate in the R&D and gain from the potential derived benefits (e.g. in the form of IPRs)' (ibid., p. 27).

countries on importing the monopoly-priced technologies 'could further prevent the building of capacity for innovation and new technologies', the UNDP Guidelines observe:

> Foreign direct investment does not rely solely on high levels of IP protection; rather concomitant macroeconomic conditions and human capital are said to be determinants for driving FDI... There are clear human development implications for countries that continually pay out large sums to, often foreign, patent holders; these payments... could detract from state revenue that is crucial for providing essential services. A cut in essential services may have distinct gendered consequences; user fees may increase. As gender norms shape how women and men access these services, increased fees or limited availability of health, water, sanitation [etc.] services would contribute to a drop in women as consumers. (UNDP 2008, p. 27; citations omitted)

The threat of lawsuits may also curtail farming practices and local or traditional innovation. The case of *Monsanto Co. v. McFarling*[38] illustrates how (under US law) a farmer that saves a seed with patented genetic sequence faces patent infringement (the case was also about contract breach). In a North–South FTA, this has critical implications for impoverished farmers who cannot afford the legal expenses or compensation to companies (Spellman 2008). The sustainable benefits of patented agricultural technologies such as seeds, fertilizers, and pesticides have been questioned. While there are arguments that these technologies are more resilient with a faster and more abundant crop yield, some researchers assert that traditional and indigenous seeds are more sustainable (Kwa 2008). Meanwhile, most farmers in the developing South are subsistence farmers; paying for patented seeds at each harvest and not being able to communally share them could compound poverty in certain contexts. Price hikes on the latest, most resilient strains could result in the reallocation of farmers' expenses (potentially cutting into household expenditure) in order to finance agricultural livelihoods. It could also mean price hikes for consumers of a specific food variety – simply put, this could further jeopardize food security in parts of the Global South. Cuts in household expenditure also have gendered effects, often with the women of the households bearing the brunt.

3.2. Plant variety protection

The TRIPS Agreement allows member countries to develop a *'sui generis'* form of protection for plant varieties. *Sui generis* literally means of its own kind, which indicates that countries have the flexibility to put in place a protection regime appropriate to its local context and needs. The phrase 'effective *sui generis* system' of Article 27.3(b) TRIPS, which is the only reference to PVP in TRIPS, implies that the rights shall be enforceable by administrative and/or juridical procedures (UNDP 2008, p. 5). Hence, PVP legislation can be tailored to the specific needs of the respective countries. The UNDP Guidelines observe that:

[38] *Monsanto Co. v. McFarling*, 363 F.3d 1336, 1343 (Fed. Cir. 2004).

> Most countries have implemented Article 27.3 (b) by enacting some form of plant variety protection (PVP) law. While most countries are members of UPOV 1978 or 1991, very few countries have attempted to establish balanced national laws that are customized and take into account interests of various stakeholders such as Indigenous Peoples, farmers and environmentalists.[39] (Ibid., p. 6)

The International Union for the Protection of New Varieties of Plants (UPOV) is an independent intergovernmental organization with legal personality which administers the Convention for the Protection of New Varieties of Plants ('UPOV Convention').[40] Pursuant to an agreement concluded between WIPO and UPOV, WIPO provides administrative services to UPOV (UNDP 2008; see also Dutfield & Suthersanen 2008, p. 186). The UNDP Guidelines note that 'there has been a significant culmination of analysis and literature indicating that UPOV may not serve as the best available option for countries where a significant proportion of the population depends on an informal seed supply system of agriculture for their daily needs and sustenance' (UNDP 2008, p. 10). It adds that:

> As more developing nations become parties to UPOV, the flexibility of having considerable room to develop an independent and customized 'sui generis' system awarded by TRIPS is undermined and UPOV may become a norm. In the Uruguay Round negotiations, there were suggestions by the GATT Secretariat that UPOV may be accepted as the framework for PVP which suggests that industrialized nations may push for UPOV to be recognized as the only sui generis system by WTO in the context of review of Article 27.3(b). Though this review has been inconclusive thus far, its eventual outcome may well depend on the existence of different sui generis systems already in place. A large number of developing countries if signatories to UPOV may make it a de facto minimum standard having possible wide range impacts over farmers, women, food security and rural livelihoods in developing countries. (Ibid., pp. 9–10)

Notably, three states – India, Malaysia and Thailand – have adopted their own specific legislation (ibid., p. 6). None of these has had their plant variety legislation challenged before the Trade Policy Review Body (see WTO 2007a, 2007b, 2006b and 2003, respectively). This Body oversees the overall trade policies, including compatibility with TRIPS, of the various WTO member states. India, Malaysia and Thailand are not members of UPOV. For those states that currently approach UPOV, the only version of the UPOV convention that is available is UPOV 1991, which is the most 'patent-like' of the various versions of the UPOV Convention.

Space does not allow a detailed assessment of the various elements of UPOV 1991 or the respective legislations (see UNDP 2008, pp. 7–9; see also Chapter 4). It must be stressed, however, that WTO member states can comply with the WTO requirements on PVP without having to comply with the more detailed requirements of the UPOV Convention. The UNDP Guidelines provide some key considerations and

[39] As of 15 January 2009, thirty-nine developing countries (including emerging economies; based on IMF criteria) are members of UPOV: twenty-one are parties to the UPOV 1991 Act, while others had ratified the earlier UPOV 1978 Act.

[40] International Convention for the Protection of New Varieties of Plants (Paris, 2 December 1961), 815 U.N.T.S. 89 (*entered into force* 10 August 1968), *as revised at* Geneva, 10 November 1972, 23 October 1978 and 19 March 1991 [hereinafter 'UPOV Convention'], available at: http://www.upov.int/en/publications/conventions/index.html (accessed 24 February 2010).

parameters for designing alternative *sui generis* systems, while noting how the flexibilities and 'policy space' under the TRIPS Agreement for WTO member countries to design *sui generis* laws according to local needs are being curtailed by FTAs:

> The TRIPS Agreement provides the flexibility to member countries to design *sui generis* laws for protecting plant varieties . . . This policy space is threatened by . . . bilateral and regional trade agreements that are negotiated outside the WTO. These free trade agreements (FTAs), typically between the US, EU, Japan and developing countries often include provisions that go beyond TRIPS (TRIPS-plus). Increasingly, countries are being pressured to adopt patent laws or UPOV 1991 . . . diluting the flexibility under TRIPS which provides an alternative for countries to develop a tailored protection system for plant variety rights. The TRIPS-plus provisions . . . have particular implications for human development and policy space to protect plant varieties in developing countries. (Ibid., p. 24; citations omitted)

Guidance in the process of establishing a TRIPS-compatible legislation scheme can furthermore be sought through the Indian, Malaysian or Thai legislation. Moreover, several guidelines and options exist to assist states in the process of identifying an appropriate balance between breeders' rights and farmers' rights.[41] This includes the possibility to redefine the criteria for protection (novelty, distinctness, uniformity and stability). It is notable that in the Malaysian Protection of New Plant Varieties Act 2004[42] the term 'identifiable' replaces the two latter requirements for those varieties that are 'bred, or discovered and developed by a farmer, local community or indigenous people . . . ' (section 14(2)).

A plant variety law should also include an appropriate understanding of the term 'essentially derived varieties' (EDV). This term is applied in Article 14(5) of UPOV 1991. Dutfield and Suthersanen (2008, p. 189) note that:

> One difference between UPOV 1978 and UPOV 1991 is that the latter extends rights to varieties which are essentially derived from the protected variety. So the breeder of PVP-protected variety A has the right to demand that the breeder of variety B secure his or her authorization to commercialize B if it was essentially derived from A. The main idea here is that breeders should not be able to acquire protection too easily for minor modifications of extant varieties produced perhaps through cosmetic breeding or genetic engineering, or free-ride without doing any breeding of their own, problems that the increased application of biotechnology in this field appeared likely to exacerbate. Beyond resolving these particular issues, but related to them, the provision was also intended to ensure that patent rights and PVP rights operate in a harmonious fashion in jurisdictions where plants and their parts, seeds and genes are patentable and access to these could be blocked by patent holders. Such a practice would undermine one of the main justifications for PVP protection, which is that breeders should be able to secure returns on their investments but without preventing competitors from being able freely to access breeding material.

[41] Some reference may be made to Leskien and Flitner 1997, and the 2001 publication by Crucible Group II on *Seeding Solutions* (Volumes 1 and 2). Volume 1 deals with 'policy options for genetic resources', while Volume 2 addresses 'options for national laws governing control over genetic resources and biological innovations'.

[42] Malaysia Protection of New Plant Varieties Act 2004, available at: http://www.wipo.int/clea/en/text_pdf.jsp?lang=EN&id=3143 (accessed 12 April 2010).

The 2008 UNDP Guidelines suggest that 'EDVs are somewhat controversial because there is little consensus over the genetic conformity threshold required for the identification of EDVs from initial varieties of crops' (UNDP 2008, p. 8).[43] Legislators need to be aware of the scope of the term EDV in the process of drafting their legislation, even if they do not seek UPOV membership and compliance with UPOV 1991 (ibid.). Moreover, states should consider whether their plant variety legislation should only apply to certain plant varieties, to ensure that only plant varieties with the ability to reproduce are covered. There is a basis for such restrictions in Article 2(2) of UPOV 1978:

> Each member State of the Union may limit the application of this Convention within a genus or species to varieties with a particular manner of reproduction or multiplication, or a certain end-use.

The authors encourage that the limitation in Article 2(2) of UPOV 1978 be included in any 'effective *sui generis* system' of PVP, in one form or another. This could provide an exclusion from protection for those varieties which do not reproduce. The present authors are not aware of any legislation which has included this provision explicitly. However, the Thailand Plant Varieties Protection Act of 1999[44] reads in section 13 (extract):

> No registration under this Act shall be made of a new plant variety having a severely adverse impact, directly or indirectly, on environment, health or public welfare.

Finally, the term *sui generis* has also been understood to allow for IP systems beyond PVP (see van Overwalle 2008, p. 83). This possibility might apply to various forms of traditional IPRs. Yet, the term 'effective' preceding the term *'sui generis'* must be understood not as allowing for just any system of PVP in order to comply with TRIPS Article 27.3(b) but as requiring a system which specifies the rights and obligations of plant breeders, and enables them to enforce their rights by administrative and/or juridical procedures. The authors would on the same basis caution against accepting ratification of UPOV 1991 as a provision in any bilateral trade negotiation, and suggest that a more tailor-made legislation should be enacted instead to serve the interests of both the breeding sector and the overall agricultural sector, including the situation of female farmers, in developing countries.

4. Enclosure of the commons and some reactions

The overall global trend seems to be for genetic resources, critically important to supporting food security and the realization of the right to food, increasingly to become subject to private and sovereign rights as part of a general global movement towards strengthening IP and re-affirming state control over natural resources.

[43] The UNDP Guidelines note suggestions by some NGOs in India that the parent genetic material contributed by rural and tribal peoples should be included in the definition of 'initial variety' within the EDV provisions in the country's PVP law (ibid., p. 8).

[44] Plant Varieties Protection Act, B.E. 2542 (1999) (Thailand), available at: http://www.biothai.org/cgi-bin/content/pvp/show.pl?0001 (accessed 12 April 2010).

Some commentators caution that the extended scope of IPRs applied to biological resources may have undesirable social and environmental consequences. As Brush (1996, p. 18) put it: 'Privatization of biological resources could result in greater poverty and exploitation without achieving conservation or equity'.

Meanwhile, sovereign claims over genetic resources as effected through access and benefit-sharing (ABS) regulatory regimes are also undermining the biological commons. Roa-Rodríguez and van Dooren (2008, p. 188) note that: 'By the late 1990s, access and use of plant genetic resources for food and agriculture had been limited by both sovereignty and IP claims'. This section first examines some relevant developments under the Convention on Biological Diversity (CBD), before moving on to discuss the FAO International Treaty for Plant Genetic Resources for Food and Agriculture (ITPGRFA) as a possible countervailing influence on the enclosure trends.

4.1. The Convention on Biological Diversity

In the specific context of genetic resources, the CBD has dramatically changed the policy and legal framework under which biological materials can be accessed and used. Developing countries now have the expressly recognized right of regulating by whom, and under what conditions, these resources can be used and how benefits will be shared (between users and providers). As a result, countries have since 1993 embarked on a series of processes which have resulted in ABS and traditional knowledge (TK) protection laws being passed (Carrizosa et al. 2004). The latter topics are discussed in detail in Chapter 4 of this book. To an extent, developing countries are given a tool with which to balance an inherent imbalance of power with industrial and developed countries that have been historically in the position to technologically transform these resources and seek relevant IP protection. In this sense, there is certainly a tension between biodiversity-endowed countries and those supporting stronger IP mechanisms. It should be noted, however, that in most cases, implementation of these ABS policies and laws has been problematic.[45] The ongoing negotiations of an International Regime on Access to Genetic Resources and Benefit Sharing (as part of the CBD implementation process; see Cabrera 2006) is a reflection of continued efforts by biodiversity-endowed countries to control how genetic resources are accessed and utilized – including through the use of IP.

There is meanwhile some evidence of the challenges scientists around the world are facing in terms of timely access to genetic resources for non-commercial research purposes (Grajal 1999; Mansur & Cavalcanti 1999). Scientists in both developing and developed countries are experiencing these challenges, as most research in biodiversity, throughout the world, involves collaborative action and activities

[45] Complex administrative procedures, complex definitions of 'genetic resources' as subject matter, unclear scope and coverage, among other factors, have made ABS legislation very difficult to implement in practice, at least in a few countries such as Bolivia, Brazil, Costa Rica, Panama and Peru. For further discussion of the high transaction costs in access regulations, see Walloe Tvedt and Young 2007. As access to genetic resources becomes more problematic and limited, inappropriate incentives may also be created which, in cases, lead to illegal access to and use of these resources.

between a wide range of institutions and organizations from developing and developed countries alike. Collaborative efforts to undertake research in the areas of food and health (including in the improvement of native seeds and plants, generation of biodiversity-derived medicinal products for local consumption, development of nutritional supplements for poverty stricken areas, etc.) could be negatively affected by both restrictive access regimes and strong IP legislation. Ultimately, national research agendas will be the most affected.

Within this context, small communities and farmers constantly come up with innovative and creative ways to confront and address problems, whether because of cultural factors which guide their conservation and survival strategies (including food security and health needs) or in response to geographical isolation. While in many countries IP concerns are still far removed from indigenous communities' reality and social contexts, their voices are increasingly being heard in opposition to potentially disruptive and culturally insensitive IP regimes. In some countries, such as Peru, Ecuador and Bolivia, small farming communities have started to express their concerns regarding recent changes in IP legislation which seek to allow for patenting of genes and isolated biological components. Furthermore, there has been express opposition by local communities to obligations under FTAs, especially with the US, for UPOV-type regimes.[46]

4.2. The FAO International Treaty for Plant Genetic Resources for Food and Agriculture (ITPGRFA)

A possible exception to the enclosure of the biological commons discussed so far is the establishment of ITPGRFA (see Cullet 2004, p. 265). This treaty provides a mechanism for access to plant genetic resources for food and agriculture and the sharing of benefits resulting from such access for sixty-four important crops and forage species as listed in Annex 1 of the Treaty (see Gerstetter et al. 2007, p. 263). It is notable, however, that the Multilateral System only covers the crops listed in Annex 1 to the extent that they are 'under the management and control of the Contracting Parties and in the public domain' (Article 11.2). It is further suggested in Article 11.2 of the Treaty that the 'Contracting Parties invite all other holders of the plant genetic resources for food and agriculture listed in Annex I' to include these in the system 'with a view to achieving the fullest possible coverage of the Multilateral System'. In other words, the Treaty does not cover plant genetic resources for food and agriculture held by private owners, even though private holders are to be encouraged to include them in the system (see Gerstetter et al. 2007, pp. 263, 279).

[46] See declarations by indigenous communities opposing FTAs with the US (especially in Peru and the Andean Region). Some of these may be seen at the website of Red Muqui (Muqui Network for the Promotion of Sustainable Development), http://www.muqui.org. Another interesting network is Red Peruana por una Globalización con Equidad/Peruvian Network for Globalization with Equity (RedGE). This network (for citizens' vigilance of rights in FTAs) publishes and disseminates information and articles regarding the social, cultural and economic impacts of FTAs, especially on marginalized sectors and indigenous peoples. See the RedGE website, available at: http://www.redge.org.pe/ (accessed 15 March 2010).

Importantly, Article 9 of the ITPGRFA recognizes the responsibilities of national governments to promote and protect 'Farmers' Rights'. Article 9 of the ITPGRFA has been described as the 'first legally binding recognition of farmers' rights in public international law' (ibid., p. 263). This Article recognizes the 'enormous contribution that the local and indigenous communities and farmers of all regions of the world, particularly those in the centres of origin and crop diversity, have made and will continue to make for the conservation and development of plant genetic resources which constitute the basis of food and agriculture production throughout the world'. The rights under Article 9 include rights to the protection of TK relevant to plant genetic resources for food and agriculture; to equitably participate in sharing benefits arising from the utilization of such resources; as well as to participate in decision making at the national level on matters related to their conservation and sustainable use. Gerstetter et al. suggest, however, that the significance of the article 'should not be over-estimated' since 'the responsibility for realizing farmers' rights is, under article 9.2, assigned to national governments, which are given broad discretion if and how they want to promote and protect farmers' rights' (ibid.).

According to Article 13.3 of the ITPGRFA, the 'benefits arising from the use of plant genetic resources for food and agriculture that are shared under the Multilateral System should flow primarily . . . to farmers in all countries, especially in developing countries, and countries with economies in transition, who conserve and sustainably utilize plant genetic resources for food and agriculture'.

Meanwhile, the Standard Material Transfer Agreements (SMTAs) used under the ITPGRFA multilateral system for ex situ collections have come under significant scrutiny (Gerstetter et al. 2007; Chiarolla 2008; Roa-Rodríguez & van Dooren 2008).[47] Roa-Rodríguez and van Dooren (2008, p. 191) note two main areas of controversy in relation to SMTAs, namely, 'the voluntary and compulsory schemes proposed for monetary benefits to be paid to the Multilateral System, and the possibility of recipients making IP claims over materials derived from those acquired from the Multilateral System'. They highlight the possibility that materials provided through the Multilateral System 'might find their way into patents in countries that allow the patenting of isolated and unmodified genetic sequences' (ibid.). While Article 12.3(d) of the ITPGRFA provides that 'recipients shall not claim any intellectual property or other rights that limit the facilitated access to the plant genetic resources for food and agriculture, or their genetic parts or components, in the form received from the Multilateral System', other commentators have noted the significant ambiguities retained by this paragraph. Gerstetter et al. (2007, p. 264) suggest that 'in particular, the terms "genetic parts or components" and "in the form received" remain undefined and open to interpretation'.

In relation to the benefit-sharing requirement under Article 13.2(d) of the ITPGRFA,[48] Rajotte (2008, p. 153) suggests that: '[A] recipient that sells a PGRFA [plant genetic resources for food and agriculture] product incorporating material

[47] The SMTAs do not cover in situ collections which are still governed by national legislation (Article 12.3(h) of the ITPGRFA).

[48] Article 13.2(d) of the ITPGRFA requires that 'a recipient who commercializes a product that is a plant genetic resource for food and agriculture and that incorporates material accessed from the Multilateral

from the multilateral system *must* pay monetary benefits from commercialization under the following circumstances: either he/she owns a patent on the product and – as is normally the case – there is no exemption in the patent law of the relevant jurisdiction that would freely allow others to use it for further research and breeding, or if access to using the new PGRFA product for research or breeding is blocked through technological means and/or by restrictive contractual provisions' (original emphasis). Rajotte (2008, p. 153) furthermore notes that:

> PGRFA products protected under UPOV Convention-compliant laws (or more flexible *sui generis* models) which include research and breeding exemptions would not trigger the benefit-sharing mechanism. This reflects the political nature of the balance that was struck during negotiations – (i.e. what kind of protection would trigger mandatory benefit sharing and what would not; the dissatisfaction of companies that depend on patents) – and to a large degree the bargaining power (or savvy) of the players at that point in history. Definitions in international forums about where the public domain starts and stops will be a key point to watch in the future.

5. The challenges ahead for developing countries: Ensuring better use of genetic resources and more targeted research and development

As discussed in earlier sections, enclosure of previously free resources appears to be a recurring tendency, in terms of both the increasing privatization of genetic resources and the assertion of sovereign rights over resources under international frameworks including the CBD (and restrictive access laws as a result). While the ITPGRFA perhaps represents a counter-trend in its endeavour 'to maintain a level of openness for crops listed in its Annex 1 which are covered by the Multilateral System' (Cullet 2004, p. 265), commentators suggest it is still too soon to say whether the protected 'commons' within the ITPGRFA will deliver the desired benefits and help to increase R&D (Roa-Rodríguez & van Dooren 2008).[49] To reclaim 'common heritage' in the 'plant genetic resources regime complex', some commentators have meanwhile suggested exploring open source solutions to R&D in agriculture (see Aoki & Luvai 2007; Box 3.3).

Meanwhile, Maskus and Reichman (2005) raise very pertinent issues on international IP standard setting and implementation. Pointing to the wording of the preamble and Article 8(1) of the TRIPS Agreement, they note that: '[T]he implementation of international IP standards is necessarily limited by criteria of reasonableness. These standards, as implemented, must not become disguised barriers to the exercise of those other police and welfare powers that are normally reserved to states' (ibid., pp. 32–33). Moreover, they hold that 'states cannot be presumed

System, shall pay to [a financial mechanism to be established] an equitable share of the benefits arising from the commercialization of that product, except whenever such a product is available without restriction to others for further research and breeding, in which case the recipient who commercializes shall be encouraged to make such payment'.

49 There are some indications from the ITPGRFA Secretariat that the Standard Material Transfer Agreement and Multilateral System are starting to fulfil their goal of allowing for an unrestricted and open flow of plant genetic resources for food and agriculture (pers. comm. Shakeel Bhatthi, ITPGRFA Secretariat).

BOX 3.3. An 'open source' model for plant genetic resources?

Aoki and Luvai (2007, pp. 61–64) suggest that lessons could be drawn for the future of plant genetic resources (PGRs) from the open source movement for software. In their opinion, the concepts of plant breeders' rights and patented seeds are analogous to copyrighted software, and some groups advocating farmers' rights have the potential to evolve into what the open source software movement has become – a commons-based peer production network that facilitates the sharing of information (ibid., p. 63). Based on the 'General Public License' (GPL) developed by Richard Stallman,[50] the GPL open source model was driven by programmers' need to share source code (ibid., p. 60). The licence is 'viral' in the sense that a person downloading a program under the licence cannot make proprietary claims over any modifications made to the program, and shares the program with others under the same terms.[51]

Aoki and Luvai note that there is yet to be a robust equivalent to the GPL for software in the PGRs arena (ibid.). Noting that a web of expanding proprietary rights have spawned over the past two decades to cover not only PCRs but also related breeding tools and technologies, they suggest that an adaptation of the GPL from the software context into the PGR context may be useful (ibid.).[52] Based on the idea of farmers as user-innovators, such an open source PGR model might not only be applied to the development of plant varieties via selective breeding, genomics, and genetic manipulation of PGRs, but might also be extended to the development of related machinery, technology, and the sharing of agricultural information and know-how (ibid., pp. 63–64). Aoki and Luvai suggest that new plant varieties and plant breeding research tools and technologies created using this participatory process could then be made available to farmers and plant breeders using a GPL-styled licence with the same 'viral' effect – any subsequent modifications must be openly accessible under the GPL terms (ibid.). Those receiving the plant materials and related technologies would be bound by a contractual promise not to impose downstream restrictions on the rights of others to experiment, innovate, share or exchange the PGRs (ibid., p. 64).[53]

Source: Aoki and Luvai 2007

[50] For the terms under the GPL, see http://www.opensource.org/licences/gpl-license.php (accessed 10 December 2009).

[51] As Aoki and Luvai explain: 'The key thing about the GPL is that it contractually keeps you from claiming copyright – it can be viewed as a "private" alternative to "public" copyright law as it pertains to software. This is paradoxical; by using "private" contractual terms, the GPL keeps GNU/Linux "public", or freely available. One of Richard Stallman's mottos is "Free Software, Not Free Beer," which means that you may purchase a copy of open source software for cash, but you are "free" to copy and modify that software, subject only to the GPL' (ibid. p. 62).

[52] To illustrate parallels between the movements to ensure free access to software source code and PGRs respectively, Aoki and Luvai compare the manifesto of the GNU (http://www.gnu.org/gnu/manifesto.html) with the version of farmers' rights advocated by the Philippines-based Magsasaka at Siyentipiko Para sa Pag-unlad ng Agrikultura (MASIPAG), an organization bringing together farmers, scientists, and NGOs to engage in agricultural research (ibid., p. 63). See the MASIPAG (Farmer – Scientist Partnership for Development, Incorporated) website, available at: http://www.masipag.org/cms/ (accessed 13 April 2010).

[53] They venture that the material transfer agreements (MTA) that recipients of PGRs must currently sign in order to receive seeds from seed banks might conceivably be re-tooled to contain GPL-like terms (ibid., p. 64).

to have surrendered sovereign police and welfare powers in the course of intellectual property standard setting . . . ' (ibid., p. 31). In relation to the present discussion, this must be understood to imply that the full obligations of a State must be taken into account when IP legislation is to be adopted or enforced. A WTO member state ought to make sure that the flexibilities provided for in the TRIPS Agreement are fully considered and appropriately reflected. Pressures to have higher IP protection standards than those required in the TRIPS Agreement – for example, in FTAs or investment treaties – should be resisted, and it should be possible to have a review of certain paragraphs in the TRIPS Agreement in order to better reconcile the Agreement to other treaties.[54] At this point, flexibilities in national IP *and* ABS policies may be required to:

- facilitate research and the development of national and community-based seed banks – these may be extremely critical for biodiversity-rich countries and centres of origin and diversification of crops, as a means to support local farmers and communities in a context of growing climate change problems;
- stimulate collective participatory breeding – this may become a good alternative to bridge TK and local farmers needs with the scientific potential of national and international institutions; collaborative research could be explored, for example, with research institutions;
- protect and promote the TK of indigenous communities – there is a sufficient basis in different human rights provisions in favour of a position that traditional communities and indigenous peoples who nurture and improve plants should enjoy human rights protection over their production (Haugen 2005b, pp. 676–677; Pires de Carvalho 2005, p. 242, arguing that plant breeders are included in the category 'authors and inventors'); it remains to be seen whether certain forms of IP protection are appropriate and desired by these breeders;
- implement Farmers' Rights (as recognized in the FAO International Treaty), and ensure appropriate breeders' and farmers' exemptions – this may serve to support a continued availability of seeds and breeding materials for small farmers and developing country breeders in particular;
- explore open source or cross-licensing structures that may create a defined technology commons, as well as public-welfare-oriented licensing and pricing strategies, such as waiver of rights for certain users, humanitarian licensing, humanitarian and tiered pricing (see WIPO 2009, para. 288, pp. 79–80); and
- design inclusive development strategies (at the national and local levels) which effectively account for small farmers and poor farmers in particular – this calls for participatory planning processes which analyse future scenarios and assess national and local potential for contribution and involvement in these scenarios.

The examples of Brazil, China and India are quite illustrative of how public policies which provide appropriate incentives for research in biodiversity-related fields have resulted in the development of very strong national research capacities, including in biotechnology. These countries have been reluctant to modify their national IP policies and laws to a TRIPS-plus standard and, therefore, maintain appropriate flexibilities to protect certain types of innovation. At the same time, these countries have invested heavily in training and building the scientific capacities of their human resources, with a focus on both basic *and* applied research. Finally, they have undertaken careful planning strategies based on an analysis of national and local needs, and an assessment of global markets.

[54] For concrete proposals, see the 'disclosure requirement' proposal by Norway in 2006 (WTO 2006a) and by several States in 2008 (WTO 2008).

Looking ahead, Tansey (2008) describes various 'alternative futures' relating to food systems and IP. These are addressed in the literature review of future scenarios in Chapter 9 of this book. The alternatives include, for example, a 'future which is more monocultural, industrial, corporate-dominated and dependent on IP' (ibid., p. 215). A contrasting scenario is described, with an ecologically integrated approach which builds on the 'millennia of experimental empirical work by farmers in diverse environments that have led to a huge range of agricultural biodiversity' (ibid.; see also the International Assessment of Agricultural Knowledge, Science and Technology for Development 2008). Open systems of exchange and skilled farming are promoted in this scenario where 'the local goes first' in a local to global hierarchy (ibid.). Tansey goes on to discuss a 'technologically triumphalist' scenario where food is synthesized and extreme genetic engineering, synthetic biology, and nanotechnology take centre stage. In this future scenario, the differences blur between biological and other systems and everything is treated as a 'resource, able to be owned and patentable' (ibid.). Also mentioned is a scenario of 'collapse, be it economic, physical or a descent into violent conflict over resources or beliefs' (ibid.). Tansey notes that: 'The one vision of the future that is not being facilitated and encouraged by the way IP rules are developing and affecting the direction of R&D is the ecological approach; yet that is probably the one with the best chance of working in the long term' (ibid.; see Chapter 9).

Meanwhile, relevant international developments in various forums will have significant impacts on the future of IP and food security. The WIPO Development Agenda, for example, presents an opportunity for countries to reassess IP policies as part of broader development strategies (see Chapter 9 for discussion). The shape of the international regime for access and benefit-sharing to be elaborated by 2010 under the CBD framework will have significant impacts on many areas discussed here (see further Chapter 4). There are also components of the UN Millennium Project which deal directly with IPRs and food security, including efforts to interweave traditional and modern knowledge systems in agriculture (see Box 3.4).

BOX 3.4. Combining traditional and modern knowledge in agriculture

The traditional role of farmers as user-innovators of agricultural knowledge and technology is particularly relevant to ensuring food security for present and future generations. Strategies for enhancing food security in developing countries have to involve farmers in an appropriate manner, premised on the obvious fact that farmers are also plant breeders and local experts. At the same time, these strategies should seek to facilitate a process towards exchange of new and traditional knowledge. Concurrent efforts must be made with regard to storing and transport infrastructure, markets, land tenure, water accessibility, disease prevention and other areas. The basis for all this is that new knowledge must be made available to poor farmers – without their own knowledge being disregarded.

Two reports from the United Nations Millennium Project deserve mention here. One pertains to 'Innovation' (UN Millennium Project 2005a) and the other addresses 'Halving Hunger' (UN Millennium Project 2005b). The two Millennium Project reports are mutually reinforcing, with the Halving Hunger report emphasizing technology for increased food production in developing countries (ibid., p. 65). According to this report, the CGIAR agricultural research centres (also known as 'Future Harvest Centers') must be able to play a more active role if this increased food production is to take place without too heavy dependency on corporations (ibid., p. 95). The Halving Hunger report generally recommends biotechnology (ibid., pp. 116–18).

In contrast, the Innovation report addresses the convergence between modern and traditional knowledge, which will demand 'significant investment in coordination and management' (UN Millennium Project 2005a, p. 43). This seems to be an appropriate strategy, provided that the strategy is fully participatory. Asbjørn Eide, who has played a crucial role in promoting the right to food for almost three decades, says that one should not 'advocate a status quo concerning traditional production systems, but... when seeking to promote more effective methods [one] must take traditional knowledge and experience as the starting point, and translate it into approaches where modern science and traditionally adapted principles are combined in order to maximize the prospects for adequate food consumption, nutritionally balanced, and in respect of ecological constraints' (Eide 1987, p. 35). A similar approach is promoted by the International Assessment of Agricultural Knowledge, Science and Technology (IAASTD 2008).

6. Conclusion

In this chapter, we addressed a number of key concerns relating to IP and food security. In Section 1, we emphasized the need for balance between IPRs and human rights in discussing the right to food. In Section 2, we discussed the interface between IPRs and recent agricultural trends, focusing on how the increasing reliance on the private sector for agricultural research impacts farming communities in developing countries and biodiversity more generally. We looked especially at the impacts of patents and plant variety rights in Section 3. Along with socioeconomic concerns, we touched on the potential environmental effects of allowing patents on transgenic technology. Section 4 outlined international frameworks governing access to plant genetic resources, and how they further impact on the commons. We then explored in Section 5 potential strategies for developing countries in ensuring better use of their genetic resources and targeting R&D efforts towards priorities including food security.

The crucial balancing between access and incentives, as well as an acknowledgement of the various alternative options that should exist parallel to IPRs, is recognized in a recent report to the WIPO Standing Committee on the Law of Patents (WIPO 2009, paras. 286–288). Such recognition ought to provide an opening for different approaches to IP legislation which take into account national circumstances, and not uniform, harmonized models based on the laws of developed countries.

REFERENCES

Agence France Presse 2007, 'Monsanto Fined in France for "False" Herbicide Ads', 26 January 2007, available at: http://www.organicconsumers.org/articles/article_4114.cfm (accessed 15 December 2009).

Alston, P. 1984, 'International Law and the Human Right to Food', in P. Alston & K. Tomasevski (eds.), *The Right to Food*, Martinus Nijhoff Publishers, Dordrecht, The Netherlands, pp. 9–68.

Antons, C. 2007, 'Sui Generis protection for Plant Varieties and Traditional Agricultural Knowledge: The Example of India', *European Intellectual Property Review*, vol. 29, no. 12, pp. 480–485.

Aoki, K. & Luvai, K. 2007, 'Reclaiming "Common Heritage" Treatment in the International Plant Genetic Resources Regime Complex', *Michigan State Law Review*, vol. 2007, pp. 35–70, available at: http://msulr.law.msu.edu/back_issues/2007/1/Aoki.pdf (accessed 2 May 2009).

Barton, J.H. 2006, 'Knowledge', *Expert Paper Series Six: Knowledge*, Secretariat of the International Task Force on Global Public Goods, Stockholm, pp. 1–20.

Biber-Klemm, S. & Cottier, T. (eds.) 2006, *Rights to Plant Genetic Resources and Traditional Knowledge: Basic Issues and Perspectives*, CAB International, Wallingford, UK.

Brush, S.B. 1996, *Valuing Local Knowledge: Indigenous People and Intellectual Property Rights Access to Genetic Resources and Traditional Knowledge: Lessons from South and Southeast Asia*, Island Press, Washington, DC.

Cabrera Medaglia, J. 2006, *The International Regime on Access to Genetic Resources and Benefit-Sharing: Progress, Elements and Recommendation*, International Union for Conservation of Nature (IUCN), Quito, Ecuador, available at: http://data.iucn.org/dbtw-wpd/edocs/2006-066-En.pdf (accessed 17 December 2009).

Carrizoza, S. Brush, S.B., Wright, B.D. & McGuire, P.E. (eds.) 2004, *Accessing Biodiversity and Sharing the Benefits. Lessons from Implementing the Convention on Biological Diversity*, IUCN, Gland, Switzerland and Cambridge, UK, available at: http://www.grcp.ucdavis.edu/publications/docABSPacRim/ABSPacRimwww.pdf (accessed 2 May 2009).

Commission on Intellectual Property Rights (CIPR) 2002, *Integrating Intellectual Property Rights and Development Policy*, CIPR, London, available at: http://www.iprcommission.org/papers/pdfs/final_report/CIPRfullfinal.pdf (accessed 1 February 2009).

Committee on Economic, Social and Cultural Rights (CESCR) 1991, *General Comment No. 3: The nature of states parties obligations*, UN Doc. E/1991/23 (14 December 1990), available at: http://www.unhchr.ch/tbs/doc.nsf/0/94bdbaf59b43a424c12563ed0052b664?Opendocument (accessed 3 February 2010).

CESCR 1999, *General Comment No. 12: The right to adequate food*, UN Doc. E/C.12/1999/5 (12 May 1999), available at: http://www.unhchr.ch/tbs/doc.nsf/0/3d02758c707031d58025677f003b73b9 (accessed 3 February 2010).

CESCR 2005, *General Comment No. 17: The right of everyone to benefit from the protection of the moral and material interests resulting from any scientific, literary or artistic production of which he or she is the author* (art. 15, para. 1 (c)), UN Doc. E/C.12/GC/17 (12 January 2006), available at: http://www.unhchr.ch/tbs/doc.nsf/7cec89369c43a6dfc1256a2a0027ba2a/03902145edbbe797c125711500584ea8/$FILE/G0640060.pdf (accessed 3 February 2010).

Craven, M. 1995, *The International Covenant on Economic, Social and Cultural Rights: A Perspective on Its Development*, Oxford University Press, New York.

Crucible Group II 2001, *Seeding Solutions*, vols. 1–2, International Development Research Centre (IDRC), International Plant Genetic Resources Institute (IPGRI) and Dag Hammarskjöld Foundation, Montreal, Rome and Uppsala, available at: http://www.idrc.ca/en/ev-9424-201-1-DO_TOPIC.html (accessed 15 December 2009).

Cullet, P. 2004, 'Intellectual Property Rights and Food Security in the South', *Journal of World Intellectual Property*, vol. 7, no. 3, pp. 261–286.

Dalrymple, D.G. & Srivastava J.P. 1994, 'Transfer of Plant Cultivars: Seeds, Sectors and Society', in J.R Anderson (ed.), *Agricultural Technology: Policy Issues for the International Community*, pp. 180–207, CAB International, Wallingford, UK.

de Beer, J. 2005, 'Reconciling Property Rights in Plants', *Journal of World Intellectual Property*, vol. 8, no. 1, pp. 5–31.

Dutfield, G. 2003, *Intellectual Property Rights and the Life Science Industries: A Twentieth Century History*, Ashgate, Aldershot, UK.

Dutfield, G. & Suthersanen, U. 2008, *Global Intellectual Property Law*, Edward Elgar, Cheltenham.

Eide, A. 1987, *Report on the Right to Adequate Food as a Human Right*, UN Doc. E/CN.4/Sub.2/1987/23 (published in Human Rights Study Series No. 1: *Right to Adequate Food as a Human Right*, United Nations Publications Sales No. E.89.XIV.2).

Evenson, R.E. 2003, 'Production Impacts of Crop Genetic Improvement', in R.E. Evenson & D. Gollin (eds.), *Crop Variety Improvement and Its Effect on Productivity: The Impact of International Agricultural Research*, Commonwealth Agricultural Bureaux International (CABI), Wallingford, UK.

Falcon, W.P. & Fowler, C. 2002, 'Carving up the Commons – Emergence of a New International Regime for Germplasm Development and Transfer', *Food Policy*, vol. 27, no. 3, pp. 197–222.

Food and Agriculture Organization of the United Nations (FAO) 1996, *Rome Declaration on World Food Security and World Food Summit Plan of Action*, FAO, Rome, available at: http://www.fao.org/docrep/003/w3613e/w3613e00.HTM (accessed 31 January 2009).

FAO 2003, *Report of the Panel of Eminent Experts on Ethics in Food and Agriculture*, second session, 18–20 March 2002, FAO, Rome, available at: http://www.fao.org/docrep/005/Y8265E/y8265e00.htm (accessed 9 February 2009).

FAO 2004a, *Report of the Thirtieth Session of the Committee on World Food Security (CFS)*, FAO, Rome, available at: http://www.fao.org/docrep/meeting/008/J3345e/j3345e01.htm (accessed 31 January 2009).

FAO 2004b, *Voluntary Guidelines to Support the Progressive Realization of the Right to Adequate Food in the Context of National Food Security*, 127th Session of the FAO Council, 22–27 November 2004, FAO, Rome, available at: http://www.fao.org/docrep/meeting/009/y9825e/y9825e00.htm (accessed 2 May 2009).

FAO 2007, 'Right to Food and Indigenous Peoples', Focus On Series, FAO, Rome, available at: http://www.fao.org/righttofood/wfd/pdf2007/focus_indigenous_eng.pdf (accessed 31 January 2009).

FAO 2008, *The State of Food Insecurity in the World 2008*, FAO, Rome, available at: http://www.fao.org/docrep/011/i0291e/i0291e00.htm (accessed 31 January 2009).

Fowler, C., Hawtin, G., Ortiz, R. Iwanaga, M. & Engels, J. 2004, 'The Question of Derivatives: Promoting Use and Ensuring Availability of Non-Proprietary Plant Genetic Resources', *Journal of World Intellectual Property*, vol. 7, no. 5, pp. 641–663.

Friends of the Earth International (FOEI) 2008, 'Who Benefits from GM Crops? The Rise in Pesticide Use', Agriculture and Food, FOEI, Amsterdam, available at: http://www.foei.org/en/publications/pdfs/gmcrops2008full.pdf/view (accessed 31 January 2009).

Frisvold, G. & Tronstad, R. 1999, Economics of Bt Cotton, *Department of Agricultural & Resource Economics, The University of Arizona*, USA, available at: http://ag.arizona.edu/arec/ext/btcotton/display.html (accessed 31 January 2009).

Gerstetter, C., Görlach, B., Neumann, K. & Schaffrin, D. 2007, 'The International Treaty on Plant Genetic Resources for Food and Agriculture within the Current Legal Regime

Complex on Plant Genetic Resources', *The Journal of World Intellectual Property*, vol. 10, no. 3–4, pp. 259–283.

GMO Safety 2005, '"GM Maize" Disappeared – Questions Still Remain', 15 August 2005, available at: http://www.gmo-safety.eu/en/archive/2005/329.docu.html (accessed 9 February 2010).

Grajal, A. 1999, 'Régimen Andino de Acceso a Recursos Genéticos Impone Restricciones a la Investigación de la Biodiversidad en los Países Andinos', *Interciencia*, January-February 1999, vol. 24, no. 1.

Haugen, H.M. 2005a, 'Intellectual Property – Rights or Privileges?' *Journal of World Intellectual Property*, vol. 8, no. 4, pp. 445–459.

Haugen, H.M. 2005b, 'Traditional Knowledge and Human Rights', *Journal of World Intellectual Property*, vol. 8, no. 5, pp. 663–677.

Haugen, H.M. 2007a, 'General Comment No. 17 on Authors' Rights', *Journal of World Intellectual Property*, vol. 10, no. 1, pp. 53–69.

Haugen, H.M. 2007b, *The Right to Food and the TRIPS Agreement – With a Particular Emphasis on Developing Countries' Measures for Food Production and Distribution*, Hotei Publishing, Leiden and Boston.

Helfer, L. 2005, 'Using Intellectual Property Rights to Preserve the Global Genetic Commons: The International Treaty on Plant Genetic Resources for Food and Agriculture', in K.E. Maskus & J.H. Reichman (eds.), *International Public Goods and Transfer of Technology Under a Globalized Intellectual Property Regime*, pp. 217–224, Cambridge University Press, Cambridge and New York.

Helfer, L. 2007, 'Toward a Human Rights Framework for Intellectual Property', *University of California, Davis Law Review*, vol. 40, no. 3, pp. 973–1020, available at: http://lawreview.law.ucdavis.edu/issues/Vol40/Issue3/DavisVol40No3_Helfer.pdf (accessed 31 January 2009).

International Assessment of Agricultural Knowledge, Science and Technology for Development (IAASTD) 2008, *Executive Summary of the Synthesis Report*, available at: http://www.agassessment.org/ (accessed 31 January 2009).

International Centre for Trade and Sustainable Development (ICTSD)/United Nations Conference on Trade and Development (UNCTAD) 2003, 'Intellectual Property Rights: Implications for Development', *Policy Discussion Paper*, ICTSD and UNCTAD, Geneva available at: http://www.iprsonline.org/unctadictsd/policyDpaper.htm (accessed 9 February 2009).

International Expert Group on Biotechnology, Innovation and Intellectual Property (IEGBIIP) 2008, *Towards a New Era of Intellectual Property: From Confrontation to Negotiation*, available at: http://www.theinnovationpartnership.org/data/ieg/documents/report/TIP_Report_E.pdf (accessed 27 December 2008).

International Institute for Environment and Development (IIED) 2008, *Protecting Community Rights over Traditional Knowledge: Implications of Customary Laws and Practices*, available at: http://www.cbd.int/abs/project.shtml?id=18967 (accessed 24 June 2009).

International Union for the Protection of New Varieties of Plants (UPOV) 2005, *UPOV Report on the Impact of Plant Variety Protection*, UPOV, Geneva.

Ishmael, Y., Bennett, R. & Morse, S. 2002, 'Benefits from Bt cotton Use by Smallholder Farmers in South Africa', *AgBioForum*, vol 5, no. 1, pp. 1–5, available at: http://www.agbioforum.org/v5n1/v5n1a01-morse.pdf (accessed 1 February 2009).

Kuyek, D. 2002, *Genetically Modified Crops in African Agriculture: Implications for Small Farmers*, GRAIN, Barcelona, available at: http://www.grain.org/briefings/?id=12 (accessed 15 December 2009).

Kwa, A. 2008, 'Uganda: "Privatization of Seeds Moving Apace"', *Inter Press Service*, 21 February 2008.

Leskien, D. & Flitner, M. 1997, 'Intellectual Property Rights and Plant Genetic Resources: Options for a sui generis system', *Issues in Genetic Resources*, No. 6, IPGRI, Rome.

Lipton, M. 2001, 'Reviving Global Poverty Reduction: What Role for Genetically Modified Plants?', *Journal of International Development*, vol. 13, no. 8, pp. 823–846.

Louwaars, N.P., Tripp, R., Eaton, D., Henson-Apollonio, V., Hu, R., Mendoza, M., Muhhuku, F., Pal, S. & Wekundah, J. 2005, *Impacts of Strengthened Intellectual Property Rights Regimes on the Plant Breeding Industry in Developing Countries*, The Centre for Genetic Resources, Wageningen, The Netherlands, available at: http://www.iprsonline.org/resources/docs/LouwaarsCGN_Plants_05.pdf (accessed 1 February 2009).

Mansur, A. y Cavalcanti, K. 1999, 'Xenofobia na Selva: Paranoia Envolvendo Biopiratаria Perjudica Pesquisas Científicas com Especies Brasileiras', VEJA, Edición 1611, año 32, no. 32–33, Agosto 1999, Brasil.

Maskus, K. & Reichman, J. 2005, 'The Globalization of Private Knowledge Goods and the Privatization of Global Public', in K. Maskus & J. Reichman (eds.), *International Public Goods and Transfer of Technology Under a Globalized Intellectual Property Regime*, Cambridge University Press, Cambridge and New York.

Okediji, R.L. 2007, 'Securing Intellectual Property Objectives: New Approaches to Human Rights Considerations', in M. Salomon, A. Tostensen & W. Vandenhole (eds.), *Casting the Net Wider: Human Rights, Development and New Duty Bearers*, Intersentia, Antwerp and Oxford.

Ortiz-Garcia, S, Ezcurra, E., Schoel, B., Acevedo, F., Soberon, J. & Snow, A.A. 2005, 'Absence of Detectable Transgenes in Local Landraces of Maize in Oaxaca, Mexico (2003-2004)', *PNAS*, vol. 102, no. 35, pp. 1–6, available at: http://www.gmo-safety.eu/pdf/aktuell/corn_mexico_05-08.pdf (accessed 25 March 2010).

Paarlberg, R.L. 2001, 'The Politics of Precaution: Genetically Modified Crops in Developing Countries', *International Food Policy Research Institute (IFPRI) Food Policy Statement*, no. 35, IFPRI, Washington DC, available at: http://www.ifpri.org/pubs/fps/fps35.pdf (accessed 1 February 2009).

Phillips, P. 2007, 'Farmers Privilege and Patented Seeds', in P. Phillips & C. Onwuekwe (eds.), *Accessing and Sharing the Benefits of the Genomics Revolution, Series: The International Library of Environmental, Agricultural and Food Ethics*, vol. 11, Springer, The Netherlands.

Piñeyro-Nelson, A., Van Heerwaarden, J., Perales, H.R., Serratos-Hernández, J.A., Rangel, A., Hufford, M.B., Gepts, P., Garay-Arroyo, A., Rivera-Bustamante, R. & Álvarez-Buylla, E.R. 2008, 'Transgenes in Mexican Maize: Molecular Evidence and Methodological Considerations for GMO Detection in Landrace Populations', *Molecular Ecology*, vol. 18, no. 4, pp. 750–761, available at: http://www3.interscience.wiley.com/journal/121577870/abstract (accessed 25 March 2010).

Pires de Carvalho, N. 2005, *The TRIPS Regime of Patent Rights* (2nd Edition), Kluwer Law International, The Hague.

Quist, D. & Chapela, I.H. 2001, 'Transgenic DNA Introgressed into Traditional Maize Landraces in Oaxaca, Mexico, *Nature*, vol. 414, pp. 541–543.

Quist, D. & Chapela, I.H. 2002, 'Communications Arising: Response to Criticism of "Transgenic DNA Introgressed into Traditional Maize Landraces in Oaxaca, Mexico"', *Nature*, vol. 416, pp. 602–603.

Rajotte, T. 2008, 'The Negotiations Web: Complex Connections', in G. Tansey & T. Rajotte (eds.), *The Future Control of Food. A Guide to International Negotiations and Rules on Intellectual Property, Biodiversity and Food Security*, Earthscan, London and Sterling, VA, available at: http://www.idrc.ca/en/ev-118094-201-1-DO_TOPIC.html (accessed 15 December 2009).

Roa-Rodríguez, C. & van Dooren, T. 2008, 'Shifting Common Spaces of Plant Genetic Resources in the International Regulation of Property', *The Journal of World Intellectual Property*, vol. 11, no. 3, p. 176–202, available at: http://regnet.anu.edu.au/program/publications/PDFs/2008_CRoa_ShiftingCommonSpaces.pdf (accessed 2 May 2009).

Robinson, J. 1971, *The Accumulation of Capital* (3rd Edition), Palgrave MacMillan, London.

Royal Society of Canada 2000, *Elements of Precaution: Recommendations for the Regulation of Food Biotechnology in Canada*, available at: http://www.rsc.ca//files/publications/expert_panels/foodbiotechnology/GMreportEN.pdf (accessed 1 February 2009).

Ruiz, M. 2006, *The Protection of Traditional Knowledge: Policy and Legal Advances in Latin America*, German Federal Agency for Development (BMZ), IUCN and Sociedad Peruana de Derecho Ambient (SPDA).

Shoemaker, R. (ed.) 2001, 'Economic Issues in Agricultural Biotechnology', *Economic Research Service (ERS) Agriculture Information Bulletin*, no. 762, Resource Economics Division, US Department of Agriculture, Washington DC.

Smale, M. (ed.) 2006, *Valuing Crop Biodiversity. On Farm Genetic Resources and Economic Change*, CABI Publishing, Oxfordshire, Cambridge.

Spellman, D. 2008, 'Monsanto Co. Suing Jasper Famer', *The Joplin Globe*, 18 February 2008.

Srinivasan, C.S. 2004, 'Concentration in Ownership of Plant Variety Rights: Some Implications for Developing Countries', *Food Policy*, vol. 28, no. 5–6, pp. 519–546.

Tansey, G. 2008, 'Food, Farming and Global Rules', in G. Tansey & T. Rajotte (eds.), *The Future Control of Food. A Guide to International Negotiations and Rules on Intellectual Property, Biodiversity and Food Security*, Earthscan, London and Sterling, VA, available at: http://www.idrc.ca/en/ev-118094-201-1-DO_TOPIC.html (accessed 15 December 2009).

United Nations (UN) 2003, 'Report of the Special Rapporteur on the Right to Food', (prepared by J. Ziegler) presented to the UN General Assembly, fifty-eighth session, Provisional Agenda Item 119(b), UN Doc. A/58/330, available at: http://www.righttofood.org/new/PDF/A58330.pdf (accessed 1 February 2009).

UN 2008, 'Interim Report of the Special Rapporteur on the Right to Food', (prepared by O. De Schutter) presented to the UN General Assembly, sixty-third session, Agenda Item 64(b), UN Doc. A/63/278, available at: http://www2.ohchr.org/english/issues/food/docs/A.63.278_en.pdf (accessed 1 February 2009).

UN 2009, 'Interim Report of the Special Rapporteur on the Right to Food', (prepared by O. De Schutter) presented to the UN General Assembly, sixty-fourth session,

Provisional Agenda Item 71(b), UN Doc. A/64/170, available at: http://daccess-dds-ny.un.org/doc/UNDOC/GEN/N09/424/73/PDF/N0942473.pdf?OpenElement (accessed 5 April 2010).

United Nations Conference on Trade and Development (UNCTAD) 2006, *Tracking the Trend Towards Market Concentration: The Case of the Agricultural Input Industry*, UNCTAD, Geneva, available at: http://www.unctad.org/en/docs/ditccom200516_en.pdf (accessed 9 February 2009).

United Nations Development Programme (UNDP) 2001, *Human Development Report 2001: Making New Technologies Work for Human Development*, UNDP, available at: http://hdr.undp.org/en/media/completenew1.pdf (accessed 2 January 2009).

UNDP 2007, *Human Development Report 2007/2008: Fighting Climate Change: Human Solidarity in a Divided World*, UNDP, available at: http://hdr.undp.org/en/media/HDR_20072008_EN_Complete.pdf (accessed 2 January 2009).

UNDP 2008, *Towards a Balanced 'Sui Generis' Plant Variety Regime: Guidelines to Establish a National PVP Law and an Understanding of TRIPS-plus Aspects of Plant Rights*, authored by S. Mullapudi Narasimhan, UNDP, New York, available at: http: content.undp.org/go/cms-service/download/asset/?asset_id=1943122 (accessed 15 December 2009).

United Nations Millennium Project 2005a, *Innovation: Applying Knowledge in Development*, Task Force on Science, Technology, and Innovation, UNDP, London, available at: http://www.unmillenniumproject.org/documents/Science-complete.pdf (accessed 1 February 2009).

United Nations Millennium Project 2005b, *Halving Hunger: It Can be Done*, Task Force on Hunger, UNDP, London, available at: http://www.unmillenniumproject.org/documents/Hunger-lowres-complete.pdf (accessed 1 February 2009).

van Overwalle, G. 2008, 'Biotechnology and Patents: Global Standards, European Approaches and National Accents', in D. Wüger & T. Cottier (eds.), *Genetic Engineering and the World Trade System*, pp. 77–108, Cambridge University Press, Cambridge.

Vernooy, R. 2003, 'Bridging the Gap between Scientists and Farmers in China', *Seeds that Give: Participatory Plant Breeding*, International Development Research Centre (IDRC), Ottawa, available at: http://www.idrc.ca/uploads/user-S/10558775210Seeds_5_China.pdf (accessed 2 May 2009).

Walloe Twedt, M. & Young, T. 2007, *Beyond Access: Exploring Implementation of the Fair and Equitable Sharing Commitment in the CBD*, IUCN, Gland, Switzerland.

World Intellectual Property Organization (WIPO) 2007, *General Report of the Forty-Third Series of Meetings*, Assemblies of the Member States of WIPO, 24 September to 3 October 2007, Geneva, Doc. A/43/16, available at http://www.wipo.int/edocs/mdocs/govbody/en/a_43/a_43_16-main1.pdf (accessed 15 March 2010).

WIPO 2009, *Report on the International Patent System*, (prepared by the Secretariat) Standing Committee on the Law of Patents, Doc. SCP/12/3 REV.2, WIPO, Geneva, available at: http://www.wipo.int/meetings/en/doc_details.jsp?doc_id=116324 (accessed 15 January 2010).

World Trade Organization (WTO) 2003, *Trade Policy Review, Thailand – Minutes of Meeting*, available at: http://www.wto.org/english/tratop_e/tpr_e/tp223_e.htm (accessed 2 May 2009).

WTO 2006a, *Amending the TRIPS Agreement to Introduce an Obligation to Disclose the Origin of Genetic Resources and Traditional Knowledge in Patent Applications*, available at: http://www.grain.org/rights/tripsreview.cfm?id=129 (accessed 1 February 2009).

WTO 2006b, *Trade Policy Review, Malaysia – Minutes of Meeting*, Doc. WT/TPR/M/156, available at: http://www.wto.org/english/tratop_e/tpr_e/tp257_e.htm (accessed 2 May 2009).

WTO 2007a, *Trade Policy Review, India – Minutes of Meeting*, Doc. WT/TPR/M/182, available at: http://www.wto.org/english/tratop_e/tpr_e/tp283_e.htm (accessed 2 May 2009).

WTO 2007b, *Trade Policy Review, Thailand – Minutes of Meeting*, Doc. WT/TPR/M/191, available at: http://www.wto.org/english/tratop_e/tpr_e/tp291_e.htm (accessed 2 May 2009).

WTO 2008, *Draft Modalities for TRIPS Related Issues*, available at: http://trade.ec.europa.eu/doclib/docs/2008/september/tradoc_140562.pdf (accessed 1 February 2009).

4

Trends and scenarios in the legal protection of traditional knowledge

Charles McManis and Yolanda Terán[1]

Introduction

This chapter discusses the currently much debated issue of traditional knowledge (TK) protection. Opinions differ widely, not only as to *how* TK should be protected, but even as to *whether* TK should be protected at all. It is commonly accepted that intellectual property rights (IPRs) in their current form are ill-suited for this category of knowledge. But does it follow that TK should be placed or left in the public domain for anybody to use as they wish? For many indigenous peoples, traditional communities and developing country governments, this seems neither fair nor reasonable. In response, they have insisted that this issue be discussed at the highest level in such forums as the World Intellectual Property Organization (WIPO), the World Trade Organization (WTO) and the Convention on Biological Diversity (CBD) Conference of the Parties (COP), and also be addressed at the national and regional levels. Proposals have included reforms to current IP regimes in order to prevent misappropriation of TK and the development of *sui generis* systems that vest rights in TK holders and TK-producing communities. However, considerable conceptual and political difficulties remain, and these remaining difficulties make it hard to predict the future of TK, as a legal and diplomatic issue.

The trends discussed in this chapter suggest at least three potentially overlapping scenarios for the future legal protection of TK: (1) continuing and/or increased reliance on existing means of legal protection for TK; (2) development of non-uniform, country- or region-specific means for protecting TK; and (3) development of internationally harmonized approaches to the protection of TK. While significant efforts are taking place towards the development of internationally harmonized approaches, it is not impossible to envisage a break-down of negotiations on the subject due to developed country manoeuvring, widening differences among the developing countries, or a realization among the developing countries that the economic stakes are not as high as they had been led to believe. However, a breakdown at the international level would not preclude breakthroughs at the national and regional levels. Scenario planning by indigenous and local communities might be one way of teasing out the issues and challenges, as well as options, in the protection of their TK.

[1] Substantive inputs have been received from Graham Dutfield, Michael Gollin, Claudia Fernandini, Manuel Ruiz, Joshua Sarnoff and Tzen Wong.

Section 1 of this chapter introduces some basic concepts in relation to TK and its legal protection. Section 2 emphasizes that the preservation and transmission of TK depends not only on legal reforms in this area, but also on many socio-economic and environmental factors. Thus, legal protection for TK needs to be approached within integrated solutions to protect the bio-cultural heritage of indigenous peoples and local communities. Section 3 discusses international legal instruments of relevance to TK protection, while Section 4 highlights trends in using IP regimes or *sui generis* systems to protect TK at the national, regional and international levels. Some ideas and considerations for scenario planning in this area are explored in the conclusion.

1. Fundamental concepts and distinctions in the legal protection of traditional knowledge

Traditional knowledge has been defined as 'a body of knowledge built by a group of people through generations living in close contact with nature' (Johnson 1992, pp. 3–4).[2] It typically includes 'a system of classification, a set of empirical observations about the local environment, and a system of self-management that governs resources use' (ibid., p. 4). Contrary to popular belief, TK is not static and unchanging, but rather develops and changes over time, albeit by means of traditional or customary practices (Balick 2007, p. 280).[3]

Whether TK is understood in the strict sense as encompassing only knowledge and ideas as such or in a broader sense as extending to expressions of knowledge and ideas as well (i.e. traditional cultural expressions, or TCEs), TK serves as a means of physical survival and of cultural identity, and thus must be understood holistically. Its practical, cultural and spiritual elements serve to integrate a community with its environment (Pires de Carvalho 2007). Likewise, while the WIPO Intergovernmental Committee on Genetic Resources, Traditional Knowledge and Traditional Cultural Expressions ('IGC') has developed two sets of draft provisions, one for TK as such and one for TCEs, the IGC nevertheless recognizes that 'for many communities these are closely related, even integral, aspects of respect for and protection of their cultural and intellectual heritage'.[4] Meanwhile, national legislation in this area tends, albeit with a few exceptions, to keep to a separation of TK in a strict sense and TCEs. Accordingly, this chapter focuses on the protection of the former, while Chapter 5 addresses the protection of TCEs.

In a 2001 report, the WIPO IGC Secretariat highlights two main IP-related concerns articulated by WIPO member states in the field of TK, namely, the availability of IP protection for TK holders (i.e. the need for affirmative legal protection) and

[2] Quoted in United Nations Environment Programme/ Convention on Biological Diversity (UNEP/CBD) Ad Hoc Open-Ended Working Group on Access and Benefit Sharing 2001, para. 21 [hereinafter 'UNEP/CBD Report 2001'].

[3] See further UNEP/CBD Report 2001, p. 5, where it is clarified that: 'In the context of knowledge, innovation is a feature of indigenous and local communities whereby tradition acts as a filter through which innovation occurs. In this context, it is traditional methods of research and application and not always particular pieces of knowledge that persist. Practices should therefore be seen as the manifestations of knowledge and innovation.'

[4] See WIPO 2006a, Introduction Section.

the acquisition by parties other than TK holders of intellectual property rights over TK-based creations and innovations (i.e. the need for defensive legal protection) (see WIPO 2001, para. 63). Both these aspects of protection for TK are discussed in this chapter. In exploring legal protection for TK, the WIPO IGC Secretariat recognizes that it may not be possible to develop a singular and exclusive definition of the term 'traditional knowledge', given the highly diverse and dynamic nature of TK (ibid., para. 65). Such a singular definition may not be necessary to delimit the scope of subject matter for which IP protection is sought (ibid.). National IP systems are said to function satisfactorily without iron-clad definitions, and neither of the two basic IP conventions administered by the WIPO – namely, the Paris Convention for the Protection of Industrial Property[5] and the Berne Convention for the Protection of Literary and Artistic Works[6] – contain exclusive definitions of what constitute 'inventions', 'industrial designs', or 'literary and artistic works', respectively.[7]

Indigenous peoples, the custodians of much of the TK over which these legal reforms are taking place, emphasize a holistic approach towards protecting their TK. While legal and economic discussions tend to compartmentalize resources as land, minerals or genetic resources, indigenous peoples view their TK as inseparable from all these elements. TK has ancestral and historical value for these peoples and cannot be 'isolated' from larger questions of their cultural identity and survival. TK is seen as for the collective benefit and well-being of communities, not to be 'cut in pieces' and treated merely as merchandise. As Degawan (2008) notes: 'Traditional knowledge is an inseparable part of indigenous culture, social structures, economy, livelihoods, beliefs, traditions, customs, customary law, health and their relationship to the local environment'. Integrated solutions are thus important in preserving the 'bio-cultural' heritage of these peoples and other local communities.

An important consideration for legal protection of TK is the interaction between IP laws and the customary laws of indigenous and local communities. The IGC Secretariat notes in its 2001 report that 'many traditional societies have developed highly sophisticated and effective customary intellectual property systems ... [that] have, until now, remained invisible from the point of view of the formal intellectual property system ... ' and that there is 'a need to further study the relationship between customary protection of traditional knowledge and the intellectual property system' (WIPO 2001, para. 68). A World Bank publication furthermore states that: 'The creation of ... a legal regime adequate for the protection of collective traditional knowledge has to be based on the concept of legal pluralism and the recognition of the legal diversity existing in traditional societies. To understand the

[5] Paris Convention for the Protection of Industrial Property (Paris, 20 March 1883), *as revised at* Stockholm, 14 July 1967, *and amended* 28 September 1979, 828 U.N.T.S. 303 (*entered into force* 7 July 1884) [hereinafter 'Paris Convention'], available at: http://www.wipo.int/export/sites/www/treaties/en/ip/paris/pdf/trtdocs_wo020.pdf (accessed 3 February 2010).

[6] Berne Convention for the Protection of Literary and Artistic Works (Berne, 9 September 1886), *as revised at* Paris, 24 July 1971, *and amended* 28 September 1979, 1161 U.N.T.S. 30 (The Act of Paris *entered into force* 15 December 1972) [hereinafter 'Berne Convention'], available at: http://www.wipo.int/treaties/en/ip/berne/trtdocs_wo001.html (accessed 3 February 2010).

[7] WIPO 2001, para. 65. The Secretariat suggests that the more important definitional and conceptual issues have to do with the substantive and procedural standards affecting the availability, acquisition, scope, maintenance and enforcement of IPRs (ibid.).

essential elements of such a regime, it is necessary to accept a plurality of legal systems, recognizing that our society is pluralistic and has parallel legal systems manifest in the customary laws of local communities' (see World Bank 2006, p. 2).[8]

2. Transmission and loss of traditional knowledge

As recognized in the 2005 United Nations Development Programme (UNDP) Practice Note on 'Traditional Knowledge, Access to Genetic Resources, and Benefit-Sharing', there are inherent linkages between TK protection, the maintenance of indigenous cultural identity, language, customary laws and rights over traditionally occupied lands (UNDP 2005, p. 7; Thomas 2001). In relation to the latter, a study for the Ad-Hoc Working Group on Article 8(j) of the Convention on Biological Diversity adds that the political will to address land claims is essential to the retention and use of TK (see United Nations Environment Programme [UNEP] & Secretariat of the CBD 2003, p. 52). Importantly, this *Composite Report on the Status and Trends Regarding the Knowledge, Innovations and Practices of Indigenous and Local Communities* (Regional Report for North America) recognizes that:

> ...it is the loss of opportunity to pursue the traditional practices that will result in the loss of the knowledge. Without opportunities to constantly review the traditional knowledge, innovation and practice, the indigenous way of knowing the earth will cease, except as a collection of data in reports such as this. Traditional indigenous knowledge is knowledge of a land. A pillar of the efforts to redress the decline in traditional knowledge, innovation and practice is to acknowledge the critical link between the land, the people, and the knowledge. (Ibid.)

Intellectual property protection is thus but one component in the complex social and environmental rubric influencing the future preservation of TK. As emphasized in the Composite Report, the state of TK 'remains under threat' and efforts to protect TK are 'as yet insufficient' (ibid.). Along with persistent challenges facing indigenous peoples in retaining or recovering their land rights, the loss of TK is closely connected to other socio-economic factors including poverty, unemployment, rural-urban migration and the homogenizing effects of globalization on culture (UNDP 2004, p. 11; see generally Wood, Stedman-Edwards & Mang 2000). Along with these factors, the transmission of TK is affected by declines or interruptions in the transmission of indigenous languages, which encode TK.[9] Particular groups

[8] See also Pant, R. 2006, 'Globalization and Intellectual Property Legislation in India: Protection of TK and Plant Variety Protection', paper presented at the XVth Congress of the Commission on Folk Law and Legal Pluralism, 28 June – 2 July 2006, Depok, Indonesia, available at: http://www.solutionexchange-un.net.in/environment/cr/res02010702.doc (accessed 15 November 2010). She notes that: '[I]ncorporation of customary laws and principles in the *sui generis* systems will only provide protection to TK and the bio-genetic resources, when these get sufficient respect and recognition in the formal legal, judicial and administrative processes. Not only is the space provided to customary laws at the higher judicial levels wanting, these have to be comprehended by the society at large' (ibid., p. 20).

[9] Pretty, J., Adams, B., Berkes, F., Ferreira de Athayde, S. et al. 2008, 'How do Biodiversity and Culture Intersect?', paper presented at the conference 'Sustaining Cultural and Biological Diversity In a Rapidly Changing World: Lessons for Global Policy', organized by American Museum of Natural History's Center for Biodiversity and Conservation, International Union for Conservation of Nature (IUCN) and Terralingua, 2–5 April 2008, pp. 3–6, available at: http://symposia.cbc.amnh.org/archives/biocultural/pdf-docs/intersect.doc (accessed 16 November 2008). They note that 'languages encode

within indigenous societies, for example, women and elders, play important roles in the transmission of language and TK.

The threat to TK can furthermore be seen within the larger phenomenon of biodiversity loss which includes bio-cultural loss – that is, the 'extinction of experience' (Maffi 2001; see also Maffi 1998) – as well as genetic resource loss.[10] Climate change has greatly exacerbated these concerns and poses one of the most pressing challenges to the physical and cultural survival of many peoples (see Box 4.1). In terms of integrated approaches towards rescuing bio-cultural diversity, there are projects such as those stemming from the agreement between the Association for Nature and Sustainable Development (ANDES) and the International Potato Center (CIP), under which traditional potato varieties are being repatriated to the Quechua Communities. This is an interesting trend towards the recuperation of agrobiodiversity and associated TK, going beyond current debates centering on IP by focusing on transmission of TK and dynamic experimentation in relation to factors such as food security and climate change.

3. Principal international agreements relevant to the legal protection of traditional knowledge

The international agreements relevant to the legal protection of TK range from those that are essentially aspirational in character to those that impose on parties concrete legal obligations backed by international enforcement mechanisms. In the former category are such agreements as the International Covenant on Economic, Social and Cultural Rights,[11] the International Labour Organization's Convention (No. 169) Concerning Indigenous and Tribal Peoples in Independent Countries[12] and the Convention on Biological Diversity (CBD).[13] Some aspects of the CBD, the first international agreement to make explicit reference to the protection of TK, are

knowledge bases in a way that is often non-translatable into other languages but nonetheless bridges its speakers to their landscape inextricably' (ibid., p. 6).

10 Pimm and Brooks (1997) discuss the impending 'sixth great extinction' – due to the impact of human activity on the natural world.

11 International Covenant on Economic, Social and Cultural Rights (New York, 16 December 1966), 993 U.N.T.S. 3, 6 I.L.M. 360 (1967), G.A. Res. 2200A (XXI), UN Doc. A/6316 (1966) (*entered into force* 3 January 1976) [hereinafter 'ICESCR'], available at http://www2.ohchr.org/english/law/cescr.pdf (accessed 3 February 2010); see Articles 15 and 27, discussed in Chapters 1 and 5.

12 International Labour Organization (ILO) Convention Concerning Indigenous and Tribal Peoples in Independent Countries (No. 169) (Geneva, 27 June 1989), 1650 U.N.T.S. 383, 28 I.L.M. 1382, 72 ILO Official Bull. 59 (1989) (*entered into force* 5 September 1991), available at: http://www.un-documents.net/c169.htm (accessed 22 February 2010). Article 2 of the Convention states that: 'Governments shall have the responsibility for developing, with the participation of the peoples concerned, co-ordinated and systematic action to protect the rights of these peoples and to guarantee respect for their integrity.' Article 5 of the Convention states that: 'In applying the provisions of this Convention: (a) The social, cultural, religious and spiritual values and practices of these peoples shall be recognised and protected, and due account shall be taken of the nature of the problems which face them both as groups and as individuals; (b) The integrity of the values, practices and institutions of these peoples shall be respected; (c) Policies aimed at mitigating the difficulties experienced by these peoples in facing new conditions of life and work shall be adopted, with the participation and co-operation of the peoples affected.'

13 Convention on Biological Diversity (Rio de Janeiro, 5 June 1992), 1760 U.N.T.S. 79, 31 I.L.M. 818 (1992) (*entered into force* 29 December 1993) [hereinafter 'CBD'], available at http://www.cbd.int/doc/legal/cbd-un-en.pdf (accessed 3 February 2010).

BOX 4.1. Traditional ecological knowledge and climate change

Climate change is affecting both urban and rural societies, with potentially irreversible consequences for our common future (UNDP 2007). Communities whose cultural ways and sustainable livelihoods are closely bound up with the environment already experience the effects of climate change in an immediate and far-reaching manner. The unprecedented impacts of climate change may jeopardize the very survival of some peoples, whether located in the Arctic, on small islands or in other highly vulnerable areas (International Union for Conservation of Nature [IUCN] 2008, p. 35). As Degawan (2008, p. 53) observes:

> [C]limate-induced changes are happening faster than anything previously observed . . . While climate change is indeed impacting on everyone, indigenous peoples are affected more adversely due to factors such as direct dependence on natural resources, poverty, marginalization, access to services, abilities to cope, and their geographical, social, cultural and political position. As with other communities, indigenous peoples are affected by food shortages, extended drought, floods and other physical, easily measured impacts.[14]

Some emphasize that TK systems can help indigenous and other local communities adapt to climate change, for example, through maintenance of agrobiodiversity that support local food systems (IIED 2008, p. 16). Traditional ecological knowledge in one region may also provide ideas and strategies to cope with new challenges in other regions of the world caused by sea-level rise, shifts of vegetation zones, changes in animal species diversity, range and distribution (IUCN 2008). At the same time, the 'speed with which the climate is changing is putting the abilities of indigenous communities to adapt to the test' (Degawan 2008, p. 53). Since indigenous peoples' TK and cultural practices are closely linked to their use of and dependency on natural resources and biological diversity, Degawan notes that 'the loss in terms of traditional knowledge and cultural practices' has yet to be thoroughly reviewed (ibid.).

Particular sectors within indigenous communities may be harder hit. As noted in a report on *Climate Change & Indigenous Women* by the Indigenous Peoples' International Centre for Policy Research and Education (TEBTEBBA): 'Indigenous women may lose their traditional ecological knowledge, practices and sustainable livelihoods with the destruction of their resources to climate change. The loss of traditional plants or medicinal plants due to droughts or floods means the reduced opportunities for the coming generations to learn and practice traditional health, biodiversity conservation and protection and food security knowledge among others' (TEBTEBBA n.d., p. 3). Legal solutions to protect TK must thus be coordinated with strategies to protect the environment in which indigenous peoples and local communities live. An IUCN report emphasizes that 'it is essential to further explore culturally appropriate ways to enhance the resilience of traditional and Indigenous Peoples' (2008, p. 59). Along with traditional ecological knowledge, customary principles of indigenous peoples also hold lessons and hope for the earth's future – the understanding of 'rights and responsibilities' of many indigenous communities extend not only between persons, but also to other species and the earth.

Source: Degawan 2008; International Institute for Environment and Development (IIED) 2008; TEBTEBBA (n.d.); IUCN 2008.

---

[14] As Degawan (2008, p. 53) notes, indigenous peoples 'face the direct adverse consequences of climate change on a daily basis'. They experience the 'drying-up of once fertile farmlands, the torrential floodwaters that inundate their soon-to-be harvested gardens, the dwindling water supply during summer, and the diminishing of the fruits of the land in general' (ibid.).

discussed in Box 4.2. Significantly, the UN General Assembly adopted on 17 September 2007 the UN Declaration on the Rights of Indigenous Peoples, which includes provisions relating to TK.[15] At the other end of the spectrum is the World Trade Organization (WTO) Agreement on Trade-Related Aspects of Intellectual Property Rights ('TRIPS Agreement').[16] This Agreement requires its members to adhere to specific minimum standards for the protection and enforcement of IPRs, and establishes an international dispute settlement process to resolve disputes among members and to authorize the imposition of sanctions on members who fail to carry out their obligations under the Agreement.[17] Falling between these two extremes is the Food and Agriculture Organization (FAO) International Treaty for Plant Genetic Resources for Food and Agriculture (ITPGRFA),[18] which creates a formal 'Multilateral System' – that is, a system of 'common-pool goods' – in thirty-six genera of crops and twenty-nine genera of forages, guaranteeing both 'facilitated' (i.e. free or low-cost) access to these genetic resources and a system for equitable sharing of the benefits derived from any commercialized products that incorporate materials from the Multilateral System.[19]

An important TRIPS-related development with respect to the protection of TK was the 2001 Doha Ministerial Declaration of the WTO, which instructed the WTO's Council for TRIPS 'to examine, inter alia, the relationship between the TRIPS Agreement and the Convention on Biological Diversity, [and] the protection of traditional knowledge and folklore' (para. 19; see discussion in Section 4.3).[20] Of particular significance to the implementation of the CBD was the 2003 promulgation of the Bonn Guidelines on Access to Genetic Resources and Fair and Equitable Sharing of the Benefits Arising out of their Utilization ('Bonn Guidelines').[21] These Guidelines are designed to assist parties, governments and other stakeholders in developing an overall access and benefit-sharing (ABS) strategy and in identifying the

[15] See International Workgroup for Indigenous Affairs 2007, 'Declaration on the Rights of Indigenous Peoples', available at: http://www.iwgia.org/sw248.asp (accessed 21 November 2008).

[16] Agreement on Trade-Related Aspects of Intellectual Property Rights (Marrakesh, 15 April 1994), Marrakesh Agreement Establishing the World Trade Organization, Annex 1C, 1869 U.N.T.S. 299, 33 I.L.M. 1197 (1994) (*entered into force* 1 January 1995) [hereinafter 'TRIPS Agreement'], available at: http://www.wto.org/english/tratop_e/trips_e/t_agm0_e.htm (accessed 3 February 2010).

[17] See generally United Nations Conference on Trade and Development & International Centre for Trade and Sustainable Development (UNCTAD-ICTSD) 2005.

[18] Food and Agriculture Organization (FAO) International Treaty on Plant Genetic Resources for Food and Agriculture (Rome, 3 November 2001), FAO Conference Res. 3/2001, S. Treaty Doc. No. 110-19 (*entered into force* 29 June 2004) [hereinafter ''ITPGRFA'], available at: http://www.planttreaty.org/texts_en.htm (accessed 16 March 2010).

[19] Article 13.3 of the FAO ITPGRFA specifies that the benefits arising from the use of plant genetic resources for food and agriculture that are shared under the Multilateral System should flow primarily, directly and indirectly, to farmers in all countries, especially in developing countries, and countries with economies in transition, who conserve and sustainably use plant genetic resources for food and agriculture.

[20] See World Trade Organization (WTO), Ministerial Declaration (Doha, 14 November 2001), 41 I.L.M. 746 (2002), Doc. WT/MIN(01)/DEC/W/1 [hereinafter 'Doha Ministerial Declaration'], available at: http://www.wto.org/English/thewto_e/minist_e/min01_e/mindecl_e.htm (accessed 1 March 2010).

[21] See Conference of the Parties (COP) to the Convention on Biological Diversity (CBD), Decision VI/24/A: *Bonn Guidelines on Access to Genetic Resources and Fair and Equitable Sharing of the Benefits Arising out of their Utilization* (The Hague, 19 April 2002), UN Doc. UNEP/CBD/COP/6/20 (2002), pp. 262–278 [hereinafter 'Bonn Guidelines'], available at: http://www.cbd.int/decision/cop/?id=7198 (accessed 16 March 2010).

BOX 4.2. Prior informed consent, genetic resources and traditional knowledge[22]

According to Article 15 of the CBD, access to genetic resources is subject to the 'prior informed consent' (PIC) of the provider country, and the fair and equitable sharing of benefits. This Article affirms the sovereign rights of states over their natural resources, including genetic resources which until the CBD had been treated as part of an international commons. TK may be inextricably linked to the genetic resources accessed. The CBD recognizes the relevance of the 'knowledge, innovations and practices of indigenous and local communities' in conserving biological diversity. Article 8(j) of the CBD states that:

> Each party shall, as far as possible and as appropriate: . . .
>
> (j) Subject to its national legislation, respect, preserve and maintain knowledge, innovations and practices of indigenous and local communities embodying traditional lifestyles relevant for the conservation and sustainable use of biological diversity and promote their wider application with the approval and involvement of the holders of such knowledge, innovations and practices and encourage the equitable sharing of the benefits arising from the utilization of such knowledge, innovations and practices . . .

The text of the CBD essentially leaves it to sovereign states to pursue legal reforms and measures towards ensuring the 'approval and involvement' of TK holders in such cases. Article 8(j) does not indicate 'prior' approval of TK holders. In response to lobbying from indigenous peoples' organizations and their supporters, at the Fifth Meeting of the Conference of the Parties to the Convention on Biological Diversity in Nairobi in 2000, Decision V/16[23] was adopted. This Decision stated as a general principle that:

> Access to traditional knowledge, innovations and practices of indigenous and local communities should be subject to prior informed consent or prior informed approval from the holders of such knowledge, innovations and practices.

Detailed guidance to put PIC into practice is offered in the Bonn Guidelines on Access to Genetic Resources and the Fair and Equitable Sharing of the Benefits Arising out of their Utilization. These were adopted by the Conference of the Parties to the Convention on Biological Diversity at its sixth meeting in 2002.

Among other initiatives to develop voluntary codes of conduct to ensure that researchers rigorously apply the principle of PIC and establish equitable research relationships with indigenous peoples and local communities is the 'Code of Ethics' adopted in 2006 by the International Society of Ethnobiology (ISE) (Laird & Noejovich 2002).[24] Also, draft elements of a code of ethical conduct for respecting the cultural and intellectual heritage of indigenous and local communities relevant to the conservation and sustainable use of biological diversity are being elaborated as part of the programme of work relating to Article 8(j) of the CBD (COP9 Decision IX/13).

[22] Contributed by Graham Dutfield and Tzen Wong.

[23] Conference of the Parties (COP) to the CBD, Decision V/16: *Article 8(j) and related provisions* (Nairobi, 26 May 2000), UN Doc. UNEP/CBD/COP/5/23 (2000), pp. 139–146, available at: http://www.cbd.int/doc/decisions/COP-05-dec-en.pdf (accessed 26 March 2010).

[24] The ISE is also developing an internet-based 'ethics' toolkit with supporting material for implementation of the Code of Ethics. See the ISE website, available at: http://www.ethnobiology.net/ (accessed 23 April 2010).

Normative work relating to a principle of free, prior and informed consent (FPIC) beyond the CBD context is evolving in international law, particularly in relation to indigenous peoples' rights (Tamang 2005). Mackay (2004) suggests that:

> In contemporary international law, Indigenous Peoples' have the right to participate in decision making and to give or withhold their consent to activities affecting their lands, territories and resources or rights in general. Consent must be freely given, obtained prior to implementation of activities and founded upon an understanding of the full range of issues implicated by the activity or decision in question, hence the formulation, free, prior and informed consent.

The term 'free' in addition to 'prior' perhaps makes explicit what is implicit in the term 'consent'. Noting that the bargaining positions of stakeholders can be very different, the UNDP *Practice Note on Traditional Knowledge, Access to Genetic Resources and Benefit-Sharing* emphasizes that consent should be given without duress and that stakeholders including indigenous peoples and local communities should be educated as to their relevant rights and the circumstances of access to their TK and/or genetic resources embodying such TK (2005, p. 8). Thus, awareness and capacity-building measures are required to inform TK holders of such elements as legal frameworks (including those governing IPRs), intended uses of the TK, and mechanisms for benefit-sharing (ibid.).

steps relevant to ABS. Some guidance on the elements and basic principles of a prior informed consent (PIC) system, in accordance with Article 15 of the CBD, are provided in the Guidelines (see Box 4.2). An International Regime on Access and Benefit-Sharing is also currently being negotiated at the CBD and is discussed later in Section 4.3.

In September 2007, the UN General Assembly adopted the UN Declaration on the Rights of Indigenous Peoples, following twenty years of negotiations involving indigenous peoples and national governments.[25] The Declaration was adopted with an overwhelming majority of 143 votes in favour, only 4 negative votes cast (Canada, Australia, New Zealand and US) and 11 abstentions.[26] While the UN Human Rights Council had endorsed the Declaration on the Rights of Indigenous Peoples in 2006, the process for its formal adoption by the UN General Assembly had come to a halt in November 2006, when the UN General Assembly's Third Committee adopted a non-action resolution, apparently at the behest of a number of African states.[27] But this turned out to be a temporary hitch. As further considered in Chapter 5 of this book, the future of indigenous rights, including the protection of their TK, depends a great deal on the political will of governments to recognize these important rights,

[25] United Nations Declaration on the Rights of Indigenous Peoples (13 September 2007), 46 I.L.M. 1013 (2007), G.A. Res. 61/295, UN Doc. A/RES/61/295 (2007), available at: http://www.un.org/esa/socdev/unpfii/documents/DRIPS_en.pdf (accessed 24 March 2010).

[26] See the International Work Group for Indigenous Affairs (IWGIA) website, available at: http://www.iwgia.org/sw18043.asp (accessed 26 March 2010). Australia has recently changed its position and endorsed the Declaration. See Statement on the United Nations Declaration on the Rights of Indigenous Peoples, Parliament House, Canberra, 3 April 2009, available at: http://www.jennymacklin.fahcsia.gov.au/internet/jennymacklin.nsf/content/un_declaration_03apr09.htm (accessed 8 March 2010).

[27] Ibid. See International Workgroup for Indigenous Affairs 2006, 'Africa Proposes No Action on Adoption of the Declaration', available at: http://iwgia.synkron.com/graphics/SynkronLibrary/Documents/Noticeboard/News/International/AfricaproposesnoactionDD.htm (accessed 21 November 2008).

connected ultimately to historically rooted questions of indigenous peoples' self-determination.

A provision of particular significance to the IP protection of TK from the UN Declaration on the Rights of Indigenous Peoples is Article 31(1) which states that:

> Indigenous peoples have the right to maintain, control, protect and develop their cultural heritage, traditional knowledge and traditional cultural expressions, as well as the manifestations of their sciences, technologies and cultures, including human and genetic resources, seeds, medicines, knowledge of the properties of fauna and flora, oral traditions, literatures, designs, sports and traditional games and visual and performing arts. They also have the right to maintain, control, protect and develop their intellectual property over such cultural heritage, traditional knowledge, and traditional cultural expressions.

Article 31(2) provides that 'States shall take effective measures to recognize and protect the exercise of these rights', in conjunction with indigenous peoples. These rights are rather broad and could be better defined. Consequently, there are many possible ways to interpret and uphold them in national laws and policies. With respect to IP and the TRIPS Agreement, one can anticipate considerable debate on the question of whether certain provisions of TRIPS, or ways that these provisions tend to be implemented, would impinge on the full enjoyment of these indigenous peoples' rights. The TRIPS Agreement takes legal precedence over the non-binding Declaration. Nonetheless, some countries may still choose to give priority to the Declaration irrespective of what the international law of treaties indicates. Significantly, Bolivia has adopted provisions reflecting the UN Declaration on the Rights of Indigenous Peoples in its national law.[28]

The UN Declaration on the Rights of Indigenous Peoples makes explicit reference, furthermore, to the right of indigenous peoples to their 'traditional medicines' and to maintain their health practices, including 'the conservation of their vital medicinal plants, animals and minerals' (Article 24). The value of traditional medicinal knowledge (TMK) in meeting the primary health needs of populations around the world is highlighted in Chapter 2 of this book on medicine. Appendix C discusses relevant strategies and resolutions of the World Health Organization (WHO) to facilitate integration of traditional medicine into national health care systems, promote the IPRs of traditional practioners and encourage the development of national *sui generis* protection for TMK. An example of a national *sui generis* law designed and enacted for the protection of traditional medicine is the Act on Protection and Promotion of Traditional Thai Medicinal Intelligence (1999 [BE 2542]) (see Appendix C).

4. Trends in the legal protection of traditional knowledge

This section looks at current options and trends in the legal protection of TK. It first evaluates the relevance of existing forms of IP for the protection of TK,

[28] National Law 3760, passed in November 2007.

including both affirmative and defensive means for protecting TK. It then explores special ABS legislation relating to TK and associated genetic resources under national and regional laws. This is followed by a discussion of internationally harmonized approaches which are being developed for the protection of TK.

4.1. Existing means for extending IP protection to traditional knowledge

The TRIPS Agreement establishes minimum standards of affirmative legal protection for seven categories of intellectual property,[29] of which six are at least theoretically relevant to the protection of TK and TCEs (McManis 2004, pp. 434–447). Two of these categories (i.e. copyright and related rights; industrial design protection) have some relevance for the protection of TCEs; two categories (i.e. patents and undisclosed information) are primarily relevant to the protection of TK; and two categories (i.e. trademarks and geographical indications) are relevant to the protection of both TK and TCEs. The TRIPS Agreement also recognizes (but does not specify explicit minimum standards for) an additional form of IP protection for plant varieties (Article 27.3(b)), which is relevant to the protection of traditional agricultural knowledge (TAK). This chapter focuses on the categories of IPRs relevant to the protection of TK, while Chapter 5 focuses on the categories relevant to protection of TCEs.

An important supplementary (and independent) means of protecting both TK and TCEs is through the mechanism of contracts, although there are limitations to this mechanism. As noted in a UNDP Practice Note: 'A major drawback to private contracts between holders and users of TK could be the significant disparities in the bargaining power, resources, access to legal advice and negotiating skills between the indigenous community and its counterpart. Capacity building of TK holders is particularly important to level those differences' (UNDP 2005, p. 33).

4.1.1. Affirmative means for the protection of traditional knowledge

Traditional knowledge that is not widely known or readily accessible to humanity generally may be protected as undisclosed information (see McManis 2004, pp. 436–438). This protection is not limited to those who are engaged in a trade or business, but extends to any natural person or legal entity possessed of information that is valuable because it is not generally known (ibid.). Due to the widespread publicity given to national and regional efforts to ensure an equitable sharing of benefits arising out of the use of genetic resources (see Section 4.2) over the past fifteen years, both academic researchers and representatives from the private sector are becoming increasingly sensitive to the need to recognize the contributions of TK holders, to obtain their PIC to utilize their TK, and to engage in some form of equitable benefit-sharing.

In theory, at least, TK may also be protected under patent law. One of the grounds on which critics tend to dismiss the relevance of patent law for TK protection is that patent protection is limited to protection of individual inventors whose inventions

[29] See generally UNCTAD-ICTSD 2005.

meet the exacting standards of novelty, utility (or 'industrial application') and non-obviousness (or 'inventive step'). It should be noted that novelty in patent law means little more than that the claimed invention is not disclosed in the 'prior art' (ibid., p. 443). What counts as prior art and how novelty and non-obviousness are defined in various patent systems around the world is highly variable. In some regimes, patent protection has been granted for elements of TK, or innovations based on TK. In cases where the patents have been sought by third parties without the prior consent and involvement of TK holders, there has been considerable controversy over alleged 'misappropriation' of TK. Some examples, including the case of the *hoodia* plant, are discussed in Box 4.3.

Traditional knowledge that does not meet existing patent standards may in some cases be protected through the mechanism of contracts, including contracts assigning patent ownership (or a portion thereof) to the TK holder, if the TK in question provides the starting point for the development of a patentable invention. Some limitations of contracts have been discussed earlier.

Plant variety protection (PVP) is an alternative means for protecting TAK as embodied in plant varieties. It dispenses with any non-obviousness requirement, and generally requires only that new plant varieties be distinct, uniform and stable (DUS) (see McManis 2002, p. 64). It is important to note that the novelty and DUS standards may discriminate against some traditional landraces, although PVP may offer significant protection for innovative TAK holders. At the same time, PVP systems generally contain some sort of farmers' privilege as well as breeders' exemptions which explicitly permit protected varieties to be used to develop other new varieties, as long as the latter are not 'essentially derived' from the protected variety.[30] According to the International Seed Federation (ISF), this breeders' exemption 'is essential for continued progress from plant breeding'.[31] Some PVP systems also permit farmers to save and replant seeds of a protected variety, either at no cost or at a discount (see McManis 1998).

As discussed in Chapter 3, some countries are bound by the International Convention for the Protection of New Varieties of Plants as administered by UPOV (International Union for the Protection of New Varieties of Plants) for protection of plant varieties. The obligations of countries under the Convention vary significantly depending on whether they are signatory to the original 1961 Convention, the revised 1972 Act, the 1978 Act or the 1991 Act (see Chapter 3). Under the 1991 Act, countries have the option to restrict the breeders' right in relation to any variety to permit farmers to use for propagating purposes, on their

[30] The restriction in relation to 'essentially derived varieties' was introduced in the 1991 Act of the International Convention for the Protection of New Varieties of Plants as administered by UPOV for protection of plant varieties, and applies to countries bound by the said Act of the Convention. See International Convention for the Protection of New Varieties of Plants (Paris, 2 December 1961), 815 U.N.T.S. 89 (*entered into force* 10 August 1968), *as revised at* Geneva, 10 November 1972, 23 October 1978 and 19 March 1991 [hereinafter 'UPOV Convention'], available at: http://www.upov.int/en/publications/conventions/index.html (accessed 24 February 2010). See Jördens 2002, p. 19.

[31] International Seed Trade Federation/International Association of Plant Breeders (FIS/ASSINSEL) 1999.

BOX 4.3. Third-party patenting of innovations based on traditional knowledge: *Hoodia* and other case studies

There has been significant public scrutiny and controversy over the patenting of TK-based innovation by third parties without prior consent and involvement of TK custodians. Oft-cited case studies include the *neem, turmeric, quinoa, ayahuasca, maca* and *hoodia* patents.[32] In some cases, the TK involved is treated within national laws as part of the public domain, though this may not reflect the views of the TK custodians. In relation to patent law, questions are frequently raised as to whether there is sufficient novelty and 'inventive step' for patents on TK-related innovation to be granted and validly sustained (see Section 4.1). While a patent that has been granted can be invalidated through subsequent third party challenge, this will often involve substantial litigation costs.

In Thailand, several patents relating to the medicinal herb *kwao krua* (Pueraria mirifica)[33] have been challenged in the Thai courts on the ground that the grant of patents did not comply with the patentability requirements of novelty and inventive step (Robinson & Kuanpoth 2009, pp. 383–384). An earlier patent issued in May 1999 (Thai Patent No. 8912) claiming a chemical derivative of a plant product as part of a composition has not been challenged, though there are questions as to whether the so-called invention could be considered already to be in the public domain 'through documentation and public use' (ibid., p. 386). There are claims by some healers that the TK on *kwao krua* has origins in the Isan (Northeast) region of Thailand where the plant is most prevalent (ibid.). At the same time, the herb is endemic to the Southeast Asian region, and has been used by traditional healers in various indigenous communities in the region. The herb can be found, for example, in Thailand, Burma and Laos (ibid.). Kuanpoth and Robinson suggest that 'the debatable origin of *kwao krua* and of its therapeutic applications raises important questions about whose consent should be sought from in such a case and how fair and equitable benefits could be provided to custodians of the plant and associated traditional knowledge' (ibid.). Observing that not all the communities may be geographically locatable in the case of *kwao krua*, they suggest that a possible solution could be to provide benefits to traditional healers' networks which conserve the herb, if profits were created from the commercialization of patented *kwao krua* derivatives (ibid.). Cases such as *kwao krua* spurred legal reforms relating to TK in Thailand, including the enactment of the Act on Protection and Promotion of Traditional Thai Medicinal Intelligence (1999 [BE 2542]; see discussion in Appendix C).

The number of patents related to the *neem* tree (Azadirachta indica) has drawn significant attention (see Dutfield 2000, p. 66). Many of these appear to use public domain TK as a starting point, and a few have been the subject of particular controversy, especially in India, where many of the TK holders are found (ibid., p. 66). There have been patent challenges, for example, to a European Patent Office (EPO) patent for fungicidal effects of *neem* oil

(continued)

[32] See CIPR 2002, pp. 76–78, for some case studies. See also Dutfield 2000, pp. 65–67. Patent litigation has also been initiated through PIIPA's pro bono network on behalf of the Peruvian Working Group on Maca, to challenge the validity of a number of US patents involving maca root, a traditional medicine of the Inca. See Upano, A. 2004, 'D.C. Team Gets to the Root of the Problem', *Legal Times*, 12 January 2004, vol. XXVII, no. 2, available at: http://www.piipa.org/Upano1-12-04.pdf (accessed 26 March 2010).

[33] This includes Thai Patents Numbers 046779, 048605 and 052443 claiming extracts of Pueraria mirifica (white *kwao krua*), Butea superba (red *kwao krua*) and/or Mucuna collettii (black *kwao krua*). In addition, the claimed invention under Thai Patent No. 052443 was also the subject of a patent invention in the US filed under US Patent No. 6,673,377. See discussion in Kuanpoth and Robinson 2009.

Box 4.3 (*continued*)

(Patent No. 43627 B1), and a US patent for a storage stable azadirachtin formulation (Patent No. 5124349) (ibid.). Following the challenge to the former patent, the EPO invalidated it on the basis of lack of novelty.

In the case of *hoodia* (hoodia gordonii), the active ingredient was patented by the South African government's Council for Scientific and Industrial Research (CSIR) and licensed for further development to the British company Phytopharm (which in turn sold additional licences to Pfizer, a US drug company, and later to the food multinational Unilever). The San peoples of Southern Africa have known and used the appetite and thirst suppressant qualities of the succulent plant *hoodia* for hundreds of years (Laird & Wynberg 2008, p. 83). While the CSIR patent was obtained without prior consultation with the San people, following considerable media outcry the patent owner (CSIR) entered into a benefit-sharing agreement with the San community in South Africa in 2003, which gave the San a share (6%) of royalties from successful exploitation of products. The San would also receive 8% of the milestone income received by CSIR from Phytopharm when certain performance targets were reached during the product development phase (ibid., p. 89).

One approach to commercializing the *hoodia* is based on a patented *hoodia* extract under development as a functional 'weight loss' food for the mass market (ibid., p. 84). Here the situation has become uncertain since Unilever recently withdrew from the arrangement. The other approach is the commercialization of *hoodia* as a raw, ground up material through incorporation into herbal supplements (ibid., pp. 83–84). For the latter, a second benefit-sharing agreement was signed separately between the San and the South African Hoodia Growers in early February 2006 to ensure the San receive some benefits from products being commercialized outside of the CSIR agreement. The income derived from these contracts is to be paid into a fund to support the San communities.[34] Separately from these deals, *hoodia* products are on sale in health food shops and on the Internet. The San do not benefit at all from this, and these products tend in any case to be highly adulterated with insufficient content to produce much if any of the desired effect.

Laird and Wynberg suggest that the *hoodia* case demonstrates the value of having an integrated system to protect and promote TK (ibid., p. 98). While perhaps atypical in potentially bringing some financial benefits to TK holders under the agreements described earlier, the *hoodia* case also demonstrates many of the complexities on the ground for ABS laws and arrangements. These include: putting PIC into practice; identifying and valuating TK inputs into the patented innovations; the cross-border distribution of certain TK,which raises questions of uneven protection for TK holders inhabiting different countries; intra-community equity in terms of how benefits from arrangements involving third parties are shared within a community, as well as concepts of benefit-sharing with future generations. As Laird and Wynberg observe: 'If significant monies are eventually received by the San there will be extremely difficult issues to deal with in terms of determining who benefits and how benefits are spread across geographical boundaries and within communities . . . The due compensation of other communities such as the Nama, Damara and Topnaar will also require careful consideration. Overwhelmingly, there will be a need for continued legal, administrative and technical support to enable beneficiaries to claim what is rightfully theirs, and to do so in a manner that consciously and cautiously brings tangible and effective benefits to the original holders of *Hoodia* knowledge' (ibid., p. 98).

[34] See Berne Declaration website, 'The *Hoodia* Case – A Side Event at the COP in Curitiba', 29 March 2006, available at: http://www.bernedeclaration.ch/en/p25011028.html (accessed 26 March 2010).

While Laird and Wynberg emphasize the need to minimize any 'negative social and economic impacts and conflicts that could arise with the introduction of large sums of money into impoverished communities' (ibid.), financial benefits in most cases of ABS would hardly reach the potential magnitude of the *hoodia* case.[35] Expectations or concerns in other communities in relation to other TK have to be realistic. There are concerns, moreover, that local communities and rural producers may suffer when opportunities for commercialization of local products are cut off (ibid., p. 128) or alternatively when unauthorized commercial activity is allowed to take place. Without further international frameworks governing ABS, stark differences may meanwhile develop in relation to benefits that different custodian communities might derive from the same TK.[36] Sound and sustainable development policies which take into account human development needs are meanwhile required to ensure fair intracommunity benefit-sharing. Non-monetary benefits to the community need to be explored alongside monetary ones (Gupta 2004).

Source: Dutfield 2000; Laird & Wynberg 2008; Robinson & Kuanpoth 2009.

[35] While Laird and Wynberg (2008, p. 93) cite sources to give an idea of the high stakes potentially involved in the 'functional food' sector, earlier expectations of windfall benefits from *hoodia* might have been optimistic: turning *hoodia* into a functional food product is not a straightforward process, whether technically or commercially.

[36] For the most detailed converage of the *hoodia* case and its wider implications, see Wynberg, Schroeder and Chennells 2009.

own holdings, the product of harvest from protected varieties planted on those holdings. This privilege must, however, be exercised 'within reasonable limits and subject to the safeguarding of the legitimate interests of the breeders'.[37] Unlike the 1978 Act, the 1991 version of the farmers' privilege does not authorize farmers to sell or exchange seeds with other farmers for propagating purposes. As noted in a 2004 FAO report, commentators have criticized this limitation as inconsistent with the practices of farmers in many developing nations, where seeds are freely and unconditionally exchanged for purposes of crop and variety rotation (Helfer 2004, p. 25).

Finally, trademarks, certification marks and geographical indications can be used to protect the identity of TK holders against the likelihood of confusion in the marketplace or the dilution of famous identifying symbols (McManis 2004, pp. 441–442). These marks and indications also offer interesting means for protecting TCEs against certain forms of unauthorized commercial use, and are discussed in detail in Chapter 5.

4.1.2. Defensive protection of traditional knowledge

Defensive protection refers to the safeguarding against illegitimate third-party assertion of IPRs over TK. A principal means by which TK holders can prevent the assertion of IPRs by others is by making relevant disqualifying information available to patent and trademark examiners, either directly or through the development of publicly available and searchable databases (Pires de Carvalho 2007, pp. 247–248). A 2004 report by the United National University Institute of Advanced Studies (UNU-IAS) on the 'Role of Registers and Databases in the Protection of Traditional

[37] Art. 15(2) of the 1991 Act of the UPOV Convention, available at: http://www.upov.int/en/publications/conventions/1991/act1991.htm (accessed 30 November 2008).

Knowledge: A Comparative Analysis' notes, however, that 'one of the principle contradictions in the notion of defensive protection is that in order to prevent others from misappropriating TK, Indigenous Peoples may be required to place their TK in the public domain, where it can be more freely used by all' (see UNU-IAS 2004, p. 38). The paper recommends that:

> As a basic guiding principle there is a need to ensure that all reasonable efforts are made to obtain prior informed consent from the relevant Indigenous Peoples as a condition for placing information on a database, whether that TK is in the public domain or not. Explicit institutional policies need to be developed by museums, botanical gardens, universities, companies and all entities working with biological materials and related to TK. (Ibid., p. 39)

Unfair competition laws may, in some cases, provide protection from misappropriation of TK. Defensive measures also include requirements in national legislation for the disclosure of origin of genetic resources and associated TK used in research and development (R&D) of inventions for which patents are sought. Some national laws have already been adapted to include a requirement for disclosure of origin. Some countries that have made the requirement a formal condition of patentability include Brazil, Colombia, Peru, Costa Rica, Egypt, Switzerland and India (see Pires de Carvalho 2007, pp. 249–251; Hoare and Tarasofsky 2007). As of 1 October 2009, China's patent law required disclosure of the origin of any genetic resources used in an invention for which patent protection is sought in China (see Gollin & Barry 2009). Some other countries in the process of developing laws on 'disclosure of origin' are New Zealand and Turkey (ibid.). Disclosure requirements do not always extend to the TK associated with genetic resources. While some members of the European Union (e.g. Belgium, Denmark and Sweden) have incorporated disclosure requirements in their national laws, Hoare and Tarasofsky (2007, p. 154) observe that existing EU member state legislation applies only to genetic resources and does not refer to 'the use of TK in an invention'. In contrast, Switzerland's recently revised patent law obliges the patent applicant to give information regarding the source of a genetic resource and TK in the patent application.[38] Hoare and Tarasofsky point out that the disclosure requirements introduced in South and Central American countries also tend to cover both genetic resources and TK (ibid., p. 155). Pires de Carvalho (2007, pp. 249–251) suggests, furthermore, that the member states of the Andean Community, Brazil and Costa Rica have extended the requirement to other areas of industrial property law beyond patents, such as plant breeders' rights and, where it applies, utility model protection (see also Ruiz 2004; Correa 2005). Comparing approaches in different countries, Gollin and Barry (2009) observe the wide variance in 'the disclosure requirements in national laws, and penalties for failure to comply':

> At the lenient end of the spectrum is Sweden, whose law states that patent applicants should, but are not required to, provide information on the geographical origin of the material, but that failure to comply will not affect the examination

[38] See the Swiss Federal Institute of Intellectual Property website, 'Patent Law Reform – Biotechnological Inventions', available at: https://www.ige.ch/en/legal-info/legal-areas/patents/biotechnological-inventions.html (accessed 20 April 2010).

of applications or the validity of an issued patent. At the strict end of the spectrum, India requires disclosure of the source and geographical origin of biological material used in the invention, and provides that it is a criminal act, punishable by imprisonment, to apply for IP rights in any country for an invention based on a biological resource originating in India without prior approval from India's National Biodiversity Authority. More commonly, however, national laws require disclosure of the source or origin of the materials, and failure to comply may result in invalidity or unenforceability of the patent at issue (see e.g. South Africa).

The ongoing debates on the TRIPS compatibility of national requirements that make 'disclosure of origin' mandatory, and over the potential inclusion of disclosure requirements in an international regime on access to genetic resources and benefit-sharing, are addressed in Section 4.3. Meanwhile, Hoare and Tarasofsky (2007, p. 156) suggest that national disclosure requirements have had limited impact thus far, 'in part because they have not been in place very long'. Another reason for the limited observed impact is that these requirements usually refer to national patent applications only and thus do not affect patents filed, for example, through the European Patent Office (EPO) or under the Patent Cooperation Treaty (PCT) (ibid., pp. 153, 156).[39]

4.1.3. Limitations in existing forms of IP for protecting traditional knowledge

The principal limitations on the foregoing approaches to providing affirmative and/or defensive protection for TK are: (1) fragmentation of protection and a failure to address the protection of TK holistically (Pires de Carvalho 2007, pp. 259–261); (2) the high transaction costs that are often entailed in securing these forms of protection (Van Overwalle 2007, pp. 355, 360–361);[40] (3) the unavailability of competent and affordable legal counsel to represent the interests of TK holders in securing such protection (ibid.);[41] and (4) the complications generated by the fact that TK is often shared widely among communities, making it difficult, if not impossible, to identify (or even define) true or legitimate owners or to obtain PIC from the same.[42] While various types of capacity building can to some extent overcome the first three limitations, the fourth constitutes an inherent limitation in the use of IP tools such as patents and copyright as the primary or sole means of protecting TK. On the latter point, the UNDP Human Development Report 2004 on 'Cultural Liberty in Today's

[39] Patent Cooperation Treaty (Washington,19 June 1970), 1160 U.N.T.S. 231, 9 I.L.M. 978 (1970), 28 U.S.T. 7645 (*entered into force* 24 January 1978), *as amended* 3 October 2001 (*entered into force as amended* 1 April 2002), available at: http://www.wipo.int/pct/en/texts/articles/atoc.htm (accessed 3 February 2010).

[40] One means of lowering the cost of IP protection would be to adopt a lower fee structure for indigenous communities and other TK holders, somewhat analogous to the discounted fees that the United States Patent and Trademark Office (USPTO) charges individual inventors, small businesses, and non-profit educational institutions. United States patent law also allows for provisional patent applications, which effectively extends the period in which claims must be filed, and allows patent applications to remain confidential if the applicant waives the right to file in jurisdictions other than the US.

[41] This limitation, and to a certain extent the previous two limitations as well, can be ameliorated by appropriate legal capacity building, as represented by the activities of PIIPA. See Gollin 2007 and McManis 2007, who, respectively, discuss an existing network of pro bono IP lawyers and an existing IP legal clinic that have the capacity to provide IP legal services to TK holders.

[42] A partial response to this problem would be to relax any existing requirements that IP applicants be individuals or legal entities, and permit contractual associations of individuals to file for protection.

Diverse World' emphasizes that: 'If current intellectual property standards cannot accommodate commonly known traditional knowledge or its attributes of group ownership, the rules will need to be revised' (UNDP 2004, p. 11).

4.2. National and regional traditional knowledge protection models

The CBD's affirmation of the 'sovereign right' of states to exploit their own genetic resources pursuant to their own environmental policies has stimulated a variety of national and regional measures for regulating access to genetic resources and promoting benefit-sharing (see generally Barber et al. 2002). These measures may promote, tolerate or discourage the practice of 'bioprospecting' (ibid.).[43] If a country (or region) wishes to encourage bioprospecting, it would do well to follow the example of Costa Rica, and put in place a system that is: (1) relatively simple and attractive to the private sector and research institutions; and (2) adds value to its stock of genetic resources, which involves investing in building scientific capacity (ibid.).[44] One of the important objectives of the Costa Rican Biodiversity Law is to 'provide compensation for the knowledge, practices and innovations of Indigenous Peoples and local communities in the conservation and sustainable ecological use of the components of biodiversity'.[45] Other examples of how this approach can be used to provide affirmative legal protection for TK are to be found among the International Cooperative Biodiversity Group (ICBG) projects sponsored by the US National Institutes of Health (see Rosenthal 1999, p. 5; Soejarto et al. 2007; McManis 2003, pp. 547, 553–554, 565–576), although some difficulties have been experienced in their practical application (Heineke & Wolff 2004, p. 28).[46]

More and more national and regional legislative frameworks are being established to guard against misappropriation of genetic resources and associated TK, and to implement the principle of PIC. A WIPO document notes that almost all national *sui generis* laws for TK protection apply the principle of PIC to TK (see WIPO 2006b, p. 18 of Annex). For example, the African Model Law,[47] the Brazilian Provisional Measure,[48] the *sui generis* TK provisions under the Costa Rican

[43] An outright prohibition against access to genetic resources, however, would appear to violate the CBD requirement that members facilitate access to genetic resources.

[44] As a practical matter, such a system will largely rely on private contracting, with minimal state regulation and intervention.

[45] Article 10.6, Costa Rican Law No. 7788 of 1998 on Biodiversity ('Costa Rican Biodiversity Law'), available at: http://www.wipo.int/clea/en/text_pdf.jsp?lang=ES&id=896 (accessed 30 November 2008).

[46] Referring to the contractual solutions for ABS under the ICBG program, Heineke and Wolff (2004, p. 28) observe that: 'The actual outcome of negotiations in the form of a contractual agreement always depends on the bargaining power of the different actors involved. Indigenous and local communties often lack the knowledge of possible benefits or the legal capacity to negotiate a fair contract'.

[47] African Model Legislation for the Protection of the Rights of Local Communities, Farmers and Breeders, and for the Regulation of Access to Biological Resources of 2000 ('African Model Law'), available at: http://www.grain.org/brl_files/oau-model-law-en.pdf (accessed 30 November 2008).

[48] Brazilian Provisional Measure No. 2186–16 of 2001 Regulating Access to the Genetic Heritage, Protection of and Access to Associated Traditional Knowledge ('Brazilian Provisional Measure'). See Articles 16(9) and 16(4) on PIC generally, as well as Articles 21 and 24 on mutually agreed terms, available at: http://www.grain.org/brl/?docid=850&lawid=1768 (accessed 30 November 2008).

Biodiversity Law,[49] the Indian Biodiversity Act,[50] the Peruvian *sui generis* law,[51] the Indigenous Peoples' Rights Act of the Philippines,[52] and the *sui generis* law of Portugal[53] make access and acquisition to TK subject to PIC.[54] Some elements of the Peruvian *sui generis* law are described in Box 4.4 alongside the Andean Community regional framework for the protection of TK.

As national and regional systems give increasing weight to protecting against 'biopiracy' and safeguarding interests and values such as PIC,[55] there may be a 'race to the bottom', with bioprospecting activities shifting to those countries with the least restrictive legislation.[56] Regional agreements may ameliorate the latter problem, but only if coherent regional benefit-sharing arrangements are included, and if such agreements are widely adopted throughout the various regions of the world. It is the need for protection of TK beyond national and regional jurisdictions which has led increasingly to discussions of international frameworks for the protection of TK. This is discussed in Section 4.3.

A joint paper published by the Southern Africa Development Community (SADC), International Union for the Conservation of Nature (IUCN) and United Nations Development Programme (UNDP) has called for the development of a SADC sub-regional legislative and policy framework on ABS in line with the socio-economic realities of the region.[57] In this paper, Chishakwe and Young (2003, p. 15) highlight the need to develop standards promoting the interests of source countries especially, and to explore a regional or multi-regional 'collective' approach under which source countries could band together to increase their bargaining power 'in the face of the lack of credible information from genetic resource users on the value, markets, and mechanisms relevant to ABS'. Some have, indeed, argued that nothing short of a 'biodiversity cartel' will effectively combat biodiversity loss and promote equitable benefit-sharing (see e.g. Vogel 2007, p. 115).

49 See Article 63 (1)–(3).

50 Indian Biological Diversity Act of 2002 ('Indian Biodiversity Act'), available at: http://www.grain.org/brl_files/india-biodiversityact-2002.pdf (accessed 30 November 2008). See section 3.1 of the Act; see also section 21 on mutually agreed terms and benefit-sharing.

51 Law No. 27,811 of 2002 Introducing a Protection Regime for the Collective Knowledge of Indigenous Peoples Derived from Biological Resources ('Peruvian Sui Generis Law'). See Article 6.

52 Indigenous Peoples Rights Act of 1997 ('Philippines Act'), available at: http://www.grain.org/brl/?docid=801&lawid=1508 (accessed 10 December 2008). See section 35.

53 Portuguese Decree Law No.118 of 2002 Establishing a Legal Regime of Registration, Conservation, Legal Custody and Transfer of Plant Endogenous Material ('Portuguese Sui Generis Law'). See Article 7(1).

54 These laws are discussed in WIPO 2006b, p. 18 of Annex.

55 Two examples are the Philippines Executive Order 247 on Access to Genetic Resources and Benefit Sharing and Decision 391 of the Andean Community.

56 Although Philippines Executive Order 247 (EO 247) represents the first comprehensive ABS regime, for the first four years of EO 247's operation, only fifteen applications were received – most of them were from local universities seeking academic research agreements and only one commercial research agreement was approved. Moreover, Bristol-Myers Squibb announced that it would not pursue natural products research in countries that impose requirements similar to those contained in EO 247. See Barber et al. 2002, pp. 408–409. While regional agreements, such as Decision 391 of the Andean Community, may deter competition among countries and promote regional benefit-sharing, Decision 391 itself does not establish specific mechanisms through which benefits may be shared among member states (ibid., p. 381).

57 For recent developments in the SADC, see Wynberg, Taylor and Laird 2007; Wynberg and Taylor 2009.

BOX 4.4. Regional and national *sui generis* systems for the protection of traditional knowledge: A look at the Andean Community and Peru

Brendan Tobin and Emily Taylor[58]

The Andean Community (CAN) is empowered to enact regionally binding legislation.[59] In 1996, CAN adopted Decision 391,[60] which requires proof of prior informed consent, benefit-sharing and disclosure of origin for grant of patents (Cervantes-Rodriguez, 2006). Decision 391 was shaped by the belief that the sharing of genetic resources would become a source of considerable wealth for the countries involved; that states should have strict control over the flow of genes in order to combat biopiracy; and that parties entering into ABS agreements should consider not only national but also regional interests in decision making. The result was legislation requiring strict and complex state-led processes to regulate the use and transfer of genetic resources (Ruiz 2003a). Decision 391 also provided common regional standards to protect the rights of traditional communities.

In 2000, CAN adopted Decision 486,[61] establishing a regional regime for IPRs which sets out clear obligations regarding ABS and TK. Decision 486 was the first regional instrument to include binding legal obligations to disclose the origin and demonstrate a legal right to use genetic resources and TK in patent applications. These obligations apply to any application for a patent if the product or process for which the application is filed was obtained or developed from genetic resources, derived products or TK originating in any one of the CAN member countries. Decision 486 establishes an important precedent by subordinating the right to a grant of a patent to compliance with relevant Andean, international and national laws relating to acquisition of genetic resources and TK. This creates a link between the grant of IPRs and the manner of access to genetic resources and TK. Although the decision does not specifically mention customary law, its requirement that PIC be obtained from indigenous, Afro-American and local communities may in effect make the grant of patents conditional upon compliance with relevant customary laws relating to access and use of TK. The Decision provides that competent national authorities may, *ex officio* or upon request of a party at any time, declare a patent null and void when the applicant failed to show valid PIC for use of TK (Ruiz 2006).[62]

In August 2002, Peru adopted a legal protection regime for the collective knowledge of indigenous peoples derived from biological resources.[63] This *sui generis* law recognizes the rights of indigenous peoples and communities to their collective knowledge (Article 1). The PIC of the relevant community is required for access to collective knowledge for the purposes of scientific, commercial and industrial application (Article 6). This PIC is to be obtained through the representative organizations of the indigenous peoples possessing the knowledge (Article 6). A written licensing agreement must be signed with the representative organization in question for commercial or industrial use of the collective knowledge, on terms that ensure due reward and guarantee an equitable distribution of the benefits derived

58 Extract from Tobin and Taylor 2009, pp. 28–32.

59 The Andean Community of Nations includes Bolivia,Colombia, Ecuador and Peru. The Bolivarian Republic of Venezuela, a member of CAN and its predecessor the Andean Pact, retired from the regional group in 2004.

60 CAN Decision 391, Régimen Común sobre Acceso a los Recursos Genéticos (Common Regime on Access to Genetic Resources), available at: http://www.comunidadandina.org/normativa/dec/d391.HTM (accessed 17 November 2009).

61 CAN Decision 486, Régimen Común sobre Propiedad Industrial (Common Regime on Industrial Property), available at: http://www.comunidadandina.org/normativa/dec/d486.HTM (accessed 17 November 2009).

62 On some potentials and limitations of CAN Decision 486, see Ruiz 2003b.

63 Peruvian Law 27811, Protection of Indigenous Peoples' Collective Knowledge Associated with Biological Resources 2002, available at: http://www.grain.org/brl/?docid=81&lawid=2041 (accessed 10 November 2009).

from such use (Article 7; see also Articles 26 and 27). Article 13 provides that collective knowledge is deemed to be in the public domain when it has been made accessible to persons other than the indigenous peoples by mass communication media such as publication or, when the properties, uses or characteristics of a biological resource are concerned, where it has become extensively known outside the confines of the indigenous peoples and communities. In cases where the collective knowledge has passed into the public domain within the previous twenty years, a percentage (not less than 10%) of the value, before tax, of the gross sales resulting from the marketing of the goods developed on the basis of that knowledge shall be set aside for the Fund for the Development of Indigenous Peoples provided for in the Act (Articles 37 et seq.).

In 2009, Peru entered into a Free Trade Agreement (FTA) with the US, and adopted Law 29316 to implement this FTA.[64] Some aspects of the FTA and Law 29316 are on their face inconsistent with Decision 486 of the Andean Community and the national *sui generis* TK law, and have raised concerns about their implementation. Several concerns have been raised: first, that isolated genes and germplasm are not in the list of subject-matter exclusions from patentability; second, that there is not provision for the annulment of patents granted using TK for which evidence of a licence or authorization has not been provided; and third, that indigenous peoples' and local communities' rights to control access to and use of TK in the public domain are not secured. Law 29316 specifically states that access to TK in the public domain does not require PIC. As Decision 486 is directly binding upon Peru, implementation of both the FTA and Law 29316 will need to be carried out in a manner which conforms with its provisions.

Source: Tobin & Taylor 2009, pp. 28–32; UNDP 2005, pp. 11–12.

[64] Peruvian Law 29316, Ley Que Modifica, Incorpora y Regula Diversas Disposiciones a fin de Implementar el Acuerdo de Promoción Comercial Suscrito Entre El Perú Y Los Estados Unidos De América (El Peruano, Lima, 14 January 2009).

It is important, at the same time, to ensure that ABS legislation is transparent and not excessively burdensome towards access for academic or scientific research in good faith.[65] There are areas of research involving genetic resources and associated TK which could yield significant breakthroughs for human development in areas including health and agriculture. What is important is that research on TK and associated genetic resources involve the consent and decision-making of custodians. The research communities are not always familiar, however, with national laws and mechanisms to obtain PIC, and in many cases these regulatory frameworks

[65] The line may not always be clear between research for academic and commercial purposes, for example, in cases where primary or applied research at academic institutions is funded in part by commercial entities. The effects of some ABS policies on scientific research are considered by Laird and Wynberg (2008). They note that: 'Researchers in both academia and industry express significant concern about the negative impact ABS is having upon basic science and upon traditions of trust and collaboration among scientists. Just as scientific and technological developments have dramatically improved our ability to study and use genetic and biochemical resources, the availability of organisms to research has diminished, including in countries with extremely threatened ecosystems where the future of these organisms is uncertain. Many felt that countries were shutting themselves behind an "iron curtain" and setting back their own capacity and development. Craig Venter, Director of the Venter Institute, remarked at a recent public lecture, "If Darwin were alive today, he would not have been able to have done his research"' (ibid., p. 128).

BOX 4.5. Collaborative research between traditional knowledge holders and research institutions: AIDS and cancer research based on the mamala tree

Some collaborative arrangements between indigenous peoples and external research institutions for R&D based on TK have emerged over recent years. One development is an agreement entered into in 2004 between the University of California, Berkeley, and the government of Samoa, for development of prostratin, a new AIDS and cancer drug derived from indigenous uses of the mamala tree. Scientists on the project are attempting to clone genes from the tree that naturally produces prostratin for insertion into bacteria to make microbial factories for the drug. This project involves collaborative research with indigenous peoples and reportedly provides for benefit-sharing with various villages in Samoa (International Expert Group on Biotechnology, Innovation and Intellectual Property [IEGBIIP] 2008, p. 31). It is said that PIC from the elders in the collaborating villages was obtained for the project (Sanders 2004). Under the agreement, the state of Samoa and UC Berkeley will hold equal shares in any commercial proceeds from the project (ibid.). It is said that Samoa's 50% share will be allocated to the government, to villages, and to the families of healers who first taught the ethnobotanist Dr. Paul Alan Cox how to use the plant (ibid.). The agreement also states that UC Berkeley and Samoa will negotiate the distribution of the drug in developing nations at a minimal profit if the scientists involved are successful in this process (ibid.). A similar technology is currently being explored to produce the anti-malarial drug artemisinin (ibid.). UC Berkeley is said to have committed itself to 'exert reasonable efforts in licensing such patents or copyrights for public benefit, keeping in mind UC Berkeley's and Samoa's mutual goals of providing low cost therapies for free, at cost, or with minimal profit in the developing world' (IEGBIIP 2008, p. 31). As with other projects involving the collaboration of TK holders, it also remains to be seen what benefits are eventually shared with the local community, and what mechanisms are in place to divide these benefits equitably within the community.

Source: Sanders 2004; IEGBIIP 2008, p. 31.

are yet to be put in place (see Laird & Wynberg 2008, pp. 126-128).[66] As discussed earlier, some guidance on the principle of PIC is provided in the Bonn Guidelines. Beyond these guidelines, voluntary codes of conduct have been put together to help researchers apply the principle of PIC and establish equitable research relationships with indigenous peoples and local communities (see Box 4.2). As Laird and Wynberg observe: 'Obtaining the prior informed consent of communities holding knowledge about biodiversity from the very outset of a project – and engaging them as active partners – is an absolutely fundamental principle of benefit sharing' (ibid., p. 97). There should also be mechanisms for the results of the research to be shared with the local communities. Box 4.5 provides an example of research into medical cures involving the active collaboration of TK holders.

It is beyond the scope of this chapter to survey all regional and national efforts at *sui generis* TK and ABS systems. An important precedent in devising regional legislative frameworks for the protection of TK is the case of the Andean

[66] Laird and Wynberg (2008, p. 126) note that although more than 75 Contracting Parties have been involved in ABS law and policy development, only 26 of the 188 Contracting Parties to the CBD have adopted ABS laws and procedures.

Community (see Box 4.4). Regional frameworks are also being considered or established in other regions and sub-regions.[67] Examples include the Draft Framework for an African Instrument on the Protection of Traditional Knowledge ('Draft ARIPO/OAPI Framework')[68] and the Draft Legal Instrument for SAARC (South Asian Association for Regional Cooperation) Countries on Protection of Traditional Knowledge ('Draft SAARC Instrument')[69] which seek to balance access to TK with protection for the custodians of TK. The Draft SAARC Instrument states that TK protection 'should be for the principal benefit of the holders of that knowledge', and specifies as particular beneficiaries 'the traditional and tribal communities and peoples that develop, maintain and identify culturally with TK and seek to pass it on between generations, as well as recognized individuals within these communities and peoples'.[70] At the same time, in identifying exceptions and limitations, the Draft Instrument provides, for example, that TK protection 'should not adversely affect (i) the continued availability of traditional knowledge for the customary practice, exchange, use and transmission of traditional knowledge by traditional knowledge holders; and (ii) the use of traditional medicine for household purposes, use in government hospitals, or for other non-commercial public health purposes'.[71]

In relation to TAK, there are national and regional legislative attempts to recognize the important role of farmers as custodians of genetic resources and sustainers of crop evolution (i.e. 'farmers' rights'), for example, by accomplishing benefit-sharing through a centralized funding mechanism imposing a licensing fee on commercialization of protected plant varieties that will be paid into a fund to promote traditional farming techniques (see Brush 2007, pp. 297, 309–311).[72]

4.3. Development of harmonized international approaches to the legal protection of traditional knowledge

Looking towards the future, suggestions for developing a harmonized international approach to the legal protection of TK have taken three main forms. First, there are a

[67] For developments in the Asia-Pacific region, see Antons 2009.

[68] African Regional Industrial Property Organization (ARIPO) and Organisation Africaine de la Propriété Intellectuelle (OAPI), Draft Framework for an African Instrument on the Protection of Traditional Knowledge (1998) [hereinafter 'Draft ARIPO/OAPI Framework']; *incorporated in* ARIPO Regional Legal Instrument on the Protection of Traditional Knowledge and Expressions of Folklore (Maputo, 24 November 2006); OAPI Legal Instrument on 'The Protection of Traditional Knowledge and Folklore' (Niamey, 27 July 2007).

[69] South Asian Association for Regional Cooperation (SAARC), Draft Legal Instrument for SAARC Countries on Protection of Traditional Knowledge (approved by the SAARC Summit in 2006) [hereinafter 'Draft SAARC Instrument'], available at: http://www.sdc.gov.in/Downloads/TKDL/Reportmain.htm#point24 (accessed 21 April 2010).

[70] Article 8 of the Draft SAARC Instrument.

[71] Article 7 *ter* of the Draft SAARC Instrument.

[72] Taxing certified crop varieties in this manner is likely to offer meagre financial resources, for two reasons. First, even in industrialized countries, PVP certificates have relatively low or negligible economic value, depending on the scope of the statutory privilege of farmers to save and replant seeds of protected varieties. Second, modern breeding programmes are increasingly dependent on the use of 'elite' breeding lines that are several generations removed from farmers' varieties, thus making it difficult to estimate the contribution that a single landrace or collection makes to the value of a modern variety. One possible solution to this problem is the system of benefit-sharing envisioned in the ITPGRFA.

variety of suggestions for modifying international patent and/or plant variety standards to require, as a condition of acquiring or enforcing patents or PVP rights, that the applicant or rights holder disclose the origin of any genetic resources and/or TK relied upon in developing the relevant invention or plant variety and provide evidence of PIC of the relevant source countries, communities and/or individuals (Sarnoff & Correa 2006; see also McManis 2004, pp. 37, 469–474; Pires de Carvalho 2007, pp. 249–257). Second, there are a variety of more ambitious suggestions for creating an entirely new, *sui generis* regime of IP protection for TK. Third, there is the recent emergence of a hybrid form of facilitated access to plant genetic resources for food and agriculture, proprietary protection for improved plant varieties (including at least some landraces embodying TAK), and mandatory benefit-sharing, as adopted in the FAO International Treaty for Plant Genetic Resources for Food and Agriculture (ITPGRFA).

At the Seventh Session of the Conference of the Parties (COP7) to the CBD, the COP mandated the Working Group on Access and Benefit-Sharing (ABS Working Group), with the collaboration of the Working Group on Article 8(j), 'to elaborate and negotiate an international regime on access to genetic resources and benefit-sharing with the aim of adopting an instrument [or] instruments to effectively implement the provisions in Article 15 and Article 8(j) of the Convention and the three objectives of the Convention' (COP 7 Decision VII/19, Part D, para. 1).[73] In doing so, the ABS Working Group seeks to ensure 'the participation of indigenous and local communities, non-Governmental organizations, industry and scientific and academic institutions, as well as interGovernmental organizations' (ibid.). This mandate was renewed at the Eighth Session of the Conference of the Parties (COP 8), where a deadline was set to finalize the work of the ABS working group before the Tenth Session (COP 10) in 2010.[74]

At the Ninth Session (COP 9) in May 2008, the COP consolidated its work on a range of issues including those of relevance to IP, especially TK protection and the interplay between regulation of genetic resources and the patent system (see COP 9 Decision IX/12).[75] A comprehensive work program was set for the following two years, with the goals of adopting an ABS regime (referring both to genetic resources and TK) by 2010 and carrying out further work on TK questions concerning Article 8(j) and other related articles of the CBD. Along with many elements of the regime discussed through successive meetings of the COP, some components further highlighted at COP 9 in relation to access to genetic resources/associated TK include non-discrimination of access rules; international access standards (that do not require harmonization of domestic access legislation) to support compliance across jurisdictions; internationally developed model domestic legislation;

[73] Conference of the Parties (COP) to the CBD, Decision VII/19: *Access and benefit-sharing as related to genetic resources (Article 15)* (Kuala Lumpur, 20 February 2004), UN Doc. UNEP/CBD/COP/DEC/VII/19, available at: http://www.cbd.int/decision/cop/?id=7756 (accessed 21 April 2010).

[74] See Conference of the Parties (COP) to the CBD, Decision VIII/4: *Access and benefit-sharing* (Curitiba, 31 March 2006), UN Doc. UNEP/CBD/COP/DEC/VIII/4, available at: http://www.cbd.int/decision/cop/?id=11016 (accessed 21 April 2010).

[75] See Conference of the Parties (COP) to the CBD, Decision IX/12: *Access and benefit-sharing* (Bonn, 30 May 2008), UN Doc. UNEP/CBD/COP/DEC/IX/12, available at: http://www.cbd.int/decision/cop/?id=11655 (accessed 21 April 2010).

minimization of administration and transaction costs; and simplified access rules for non-commercial research (COP 9 Decision IX/12).

Discussions in relation to the proposed international ABS regime have focused largely on potential requirements that inventions claiming or using genetic resources and associated TK disclose the source of such resources and knowledge in their patent applications and provide evidence of PIC (see also Section 4.1.2). It has been argued by some that requiring disclosure of origin and evidence of PIC as a condition for *acquiring* patent protection is inconsistent with the TRIPS Agreement and would thus require a revision of TRIPS (see Pires de Carvalho 2000; 2007, pp. 251–255). A study commissioned by PIIPA suggests, on the other hand, that most forms of the disclosure of origin requirement, as conditions on patent acquisition, are not inconsistent with the TRIPS Agreement.[76] Notwithstanding the recent success in revising the TRIPS compulsory licensing requirements, however, it seems highly unlikely that the industrialized world will agree to such a condition for acquiring patent rights, for two reasons. First, such a requirement could be perceived as imposing on patent offices a crushing burden to evaluate the sufficiency of disclosures on potentially large numbers of patent applications with respect to matters about which patent offices have no particular expertise, as the expertise of patent examiners extends only to the assessment of technology, not to assessment of the sufficiency of disclosure of origin and evidence of PIC (McManis 2004, p. 471). Second, the cost of such a requirement might outweigh any economic benefits generated as a majority of issued patents ultimately turn out to be worthless (ibid.). In a study prepared for UNCTAD, Sarnoff and Corea (2006) identify, on the other hand, ways of implementing a disclosure obligation without imposing a 'crushing burden' on patent offices.

A more nuanced version of the disclosure of origin and PIC requirement may be to make it a condition for the *enforcement* of an otherwise valid patent or PVP certificate, by analogy to the well-established (in jurisdictions such as the US) equitable patent defence of unclean hands. While the appropriate disclosures could be required as a part of the application process, the sufficiency of those disclosures would be evaluated by courts, not patent offices. The rights holder of an otherwise valid patent or certificate would seek to enforce it through infringement proceedings only if the patent or certificate has sufficient value. The de facto penalty for inadequate initial disclosure of origin and/or PIC would be that, as a condition for enforcing an otherwise valid and clearly valuable IP right, the right holder would first be required to retroactively negotiate a benefit-sharing agreement with any relevant source country, communities and/or individuals from whom PIC originally should have been obtained (McManis 2004, pp. 471–472). The primary limitation on this form of TK protection is that it assumes the ability to define and identify

[76] See Sarnoff, J. 2004, Memorandum on 'Compatibility With Existing International Intellectual Property Agreements of Requirements for Patent Applicants to Disclose Origins of Genetic Resources and Traditional Knowledge and Evidence of Legal Access and Benefit Sharing', Washington College of Law, available at: http://www.piipa.org/DOO_Memo.doc (accessed 10 December 2008). PIIPA commissioned this legal report from the IP clinic at American University's Washington College of Law, based on an issue framed with the Peruvian Working Group. The report concludes that it is consistent with international treaties if a national patent law requires patent applicants to file proof that biological materials were obtained with a suitable ABS agreement. The report is available to the public to assist other developing countries in bilateral and multilateral trade negotiations.

those TK or genetic-resource holders from whom PIC must be obtained. As pointed out earlier, a resort to customary rules has been necessary in many practical cases to resolve complex issues over the identification of legitimate owners of TK and their representatives. This is one of the most problematic issues to overcome in any future scenario on protecting TK. Furthermore, challenging an issued patent usually requires significant mobilization and expenses in litigation, an option that is beyond the means of most TK custodians.[77]

Beyond the discussions on an ABS regime, one of the issues that has been increasingly raised is whether there should furthermore be an international treaty addressing the *sui generis* protection of TK. Pires de Carvalho (2007, pp. 264–268) suggests, for instance, that such a treaty could contain minimum, mandatory standards relating to the acquisition and enforcement of rights while leaving countries free to define, at the national level, the scope of protection and the identification of the owners (i.e. the attribution of rights). He adds that such a treaty could draw from the flexible notion of 'same treatment' adopted in the Paris Convention for the Protection of Industrial Property, to ensure reciprocity (ibid., pp. 264–265).[78]

In a paper prepared for the Commonwealth Secretariat, Drahos emphasizes that any treaty on TK would have to accommodate the diversity of TK and different national standards of protection, and that the key to any successful treaty at the international level is 'harmonious and cooperative relationships between indigenous groups and national governments'.[79] He suggests that, at this stage of the evolution of protection for TK, a treaty should not attempt to set substantive international norms of protection which might discourage the development of national approaches and norm-creation on TK. He argues, rather, that an international treaty should offer the treaty members a means of cooperating and coordinating with respect to the enforcement of TK.

The history of efforts to develop *sui generis* forms of IP protection, including the recent regional experience of the EU with respect to database protection, suggests some obstacles ahead. First, intense political lobbying on the part of a narrow class of interested stakeholders may result in a product reflecting the relative political clout of the various stakeholders rather than what is actually in the public interest, and is also more likely to generate conflict than consensus among competing stakeholders (McManis 2004, pp. 474–475). Second, in cobbling together hybrid IP systems, it may be difficult to calibrate the cost of acquiring protection with the

[77] Pro bono assistance may be available in some cases (see Upano 2004), but is not available in all cases.

[78] Article 2 of the Paris Convention for the Protection of Industrial Property provides that: 'Nationals of any country of the Union shall, as regards the protection of industrial property, enjoy in all the other countries of the Union the advantages that their respective laws now grant, or may hereafter grant, to nationals; all without prejudice to the rights specially provided for by this Convention. Consequently, they shall have the *same* protection as the latter, and the *same* legal remedy against any infringement of their rights . . . ' (emphasis added).

[79] Drahos, P. 2004, 'Towards an International Framework for the Protection of Traditional Group Knowledge and Practice', paper prepared for the Commonwealth Secretariat and presented at the UNCTAD-Commonwealth Secretariat Workshop on 'Elements of National Sui Generis Systems for the Preservation, Protection and Promotion of Traditional Knowledge, Innovations and Practices and Options for an International Framework', Geneva, 4–6 February 2004, available at http://r0.unctad.org/trade_env/test1/meetings/tk2/drahos.draft.doc (accessed 11 December 2008).

resulting value of the rights bestowed (ibid., pp. 475–476).[80] Third, *sui generis* IP protection, like other forms of IP protection, assumes the ability to define and identify TK owners.

The lack of consensus so far on whether there should be a TK treaty, and on the potential nature and coverage of such a treaty, has led the IGC at WIPO to focus meanwhile on drafting policy objectives and core principles, as encapsulated in the WIPO Revised Draft Provisions for the Protection of Traditional Knowledge.[81] These draft provisions may be developed further, and it remains to be seen whether they are eventually adopted as part of a treaty.

A third international approach to TK protection is embodied in the ITPGRFA, which envisions a hybrid system, ensuring 'facilitated access' to (i.e. no IP protection on) plant genetic resources in the precise form received into the Multilateral System, but also ensuring the development of both public and proprietary improved plant varieties based on plant genetic resources from the Multilateral System, and mandatory benefit-sharing with respect to commercially developed plant varieties (Brush 2003). These benefits are to be deposited into an appropriate mechanism, such as a Trust Account, which the Governing Body can utilize to implement the ITPGRFA.[82] Such funds could be used not only to compensate identifiable TAK holders but also to subsidize traditional farming practices that contribute genetic resources to the Multilateral System, thus ameliorating the problem of defining and identifying specific TAK holders (Guerin-McManus, Nnadozie & Laird 2002, pp. 333–359). According to Article 13.3 of the ITPGRFA, the benefits arising from the use of plant genetic resources for food and agriculture shared under the Multilateral System should flow, primarily, to farmers in all countries (especially developing countries and countries with economies in transition) who conserve and sustainably utilize plant genetic resources for food and agriculture. Importantly, Article 9 of the ITPGRFA recognizes the responsibilities of national governments to promote and protect farmers' rights. These include rights to the protection of TK relevant to plant genetic resources for food and agriculture; to equitably participate in sharing benefits arising from the utilization of such resources; as well as to participate in decision-making at the national level on matters related to their conservation and sustainable use (Article 9).

[80] Either the cost is too high and the rights turn out to be worthless, as is the case with the US plant variety protection, or the cost is too low in light of the private benefits bestowed, and the public winds up paying a subsidy to rights holders without any corresponding increase in innovation. The latter is arguably the case with respect to the EU's new *sui generis* form of protection for databases. See generally, Commission of the European Communities 2005, DG Internal Market and Services Working Paper: First evaluation of Directive 96/9/EC on the legal protection of databases (12 December 2005), available at: http://ec.europa.eu/dgs/internal_market/evaluation/evaluationdatabasesdirective.pdf (accessed 11 December 2008). See McManis 2002, pp. 71–72.

[81] These revised draft provisions are under discussion at the WIPO Intergovernmental Committee on Genetic Resources, Traditional Knowledge and Traditional Cultural Expressions (IGC). See WIPO 2006a (document contains both the Revised Provisions for the Protection of TCEs/ Expressions of Folklore and the Revised Provisions for Protection of TK, along with commentary on the provisions), available at: http://www.wipo.int/export/sites/www/tk/en/consultations/draft_provisions/pdf/draft-provisions-booklet.pdf (accessed 15 February 2010). The drafts have not been adopted or endorsed by the IGC and may be developed further. For the latest status of this aspect of WIPO's work, see http://www.wipo.int/tk/en (accessed 10 March 2010).

[82] See Articles 13.2(d)(ii) and 19.3(f) of the ITPGRFA.

5. Conclusion

The trends discussed in this chapter suggest at least three potentially overlapping scenarios for the future legal protection of TK: (1) continuing and/or increased reliance on existing means of legal protection for TK (McManis 2004); (2) development of non-uniform, country-specific (or region-specific) means for protecting TK (Barber, Glowka & La Vina 2002); and (3) development of internationally harmonized approaches to the protection of TK (Pires de Carvalho 2007). While there have been significant discussions and efforts towards harmonized approaches at the international level, the progress has been slow and it is not impossible to envisage a scenario where negotiations on the subject break down. The latter might be brought about by a variety of factors, such as developed country manoeuvring or widening differences among developing countries. There might also be a realization among developing countries that the economic stakes are not so high as they had been led to believe. This would not preclude breakthroughs at national and regional levels; it just suggests that multilateral solutions may never be achieved. The development of new disciplines and technologies such as bioinformatics, genomics, proteomics and synthetic biology may meanwhile dilute some of the attention on the use of TK for pharmaceutical R&D, by facilitating the alternative use of information tools to create and model new products. At the same time, the establishment of an international regime on access to genetic resources and benefit-sharing within the CBD framework, if successful at COP 10, might perhaps have a catalytic effect on negotiations towards multilateral frameworks targeting the protection of TK.

Scenario planning by indigenous and local communities might be one way of teasing out the issues and challenges, as well as options, in the protection of their TK. Our literature review found that little scenario planning has been conducted so far in this area, whether at the local or international level. Box 4.6 summarizes some of the driving forces and uncertainties which may combine with other factors to shape the legal protection of TK in the future. Along with the trends identified in this chapter, such considerations might be helpful towards any scenario planning carried out on this theme.

Among other issues discussed in the chapter, a major consideration for the future would be in clarifying the role of customary laws of indigenous peoples in informing and shaping the legal protection of TK. Few national *sui generis* systems currently make explicit reference to the customary laws of indigenous peoples. In this regard, a working group of indigenous experts on the TK of the Andean Community have notably elaborated a proposal for the *sui generis* protection of TK from the indigenous perspective, taking into account the customary laws and cultural practices of the indigenous peoples of the member countries of the Andean Community.[83] This proposal could present an interesting reference for other reforms at the national, regional and international levels (Ruiz 2006, pp. 175–176).

[83] Grupo de Trabajo de Expertos Indígenas sobre Conocimientos Tradicionales de la Comunidad Andina de Naciones 2004, *Elementos para la Protección Sui Generis de los Conocimientos Tradicionales Colectivos e Integrales desde la Perspectiva Indígena*, Documentos Informativos, Comunidad Andina, SG/di 724, available at: http: www.comunidadandina.org (accessed 26 March 2010).

BOX 4.6. Some uncertainties and driving forces for the future protection of traditional knowledge[84]

The future protection of TK is shaped by a number of uncertainties including:

(1) The choice of forum for resolving issues relating to TK and genetic resources, and whether there will be some concerted effort to coordinate the discussions and work at the different forums which have pursued quite separate agendas;[85]
(2) Potential strategic alliances amongst developing countries;[86]
(3) Indigenous peoples' access to decision-making processes whether at the national or international levels, and related capacity-building;
(4) Whether developing country governments will maintain a sustained interest in TK protection once market access is gained in other areas under the multilateral framework or through FTAs;[87]
(5) The extent to which international instruments and individual governments will go in recognizing the land rights, self-determination and customary law of indigenous peoples;
(6) The effects of new technology on future research demands for genetic resources and TK;
(7) Whether IP is increasingly seen as a problem in TK protection or part of the solution; and
(8) Whether protection of TK is approached piecemeal, or seen as part of integrated approaches towards the protection and transmission of indigenous bio-cultural heritage.

Given these and other uncertainties, scenario planning offers a way to grapple with several alternatives, including an international *sui generis* regime for the protection of TK. Would such a regime harmonize national laws in this area, or might it provide a system where different instruments play different roles?[88] As the protection of the TK of indigenous peoples is increasingly addressed within the framework of human rights, the interraction between IP and human rights regimes are likely to take on further importance.

[84] These considerations have been suggested by Graham Dutfield, Michael Gollin, Manuel Ruiz and Tzen Wong.

[85] In a paper for the South Centre, Correa (2004) suggests that a cooperative initiative involving several international organizations may be needed to develop international rules for the protection and promotion of TK.

[86] Dutfield (2006, p. 33) explores the possibility of strategic groups of developing countries agreeing on harmonized standards and then applying the reciprocity principle under WTO to extend this to nationals of other members.

[87] See Rodríguez Cervantes and GRAIN 2006.

[88] In a policy brief for the Science and Development Network, Ruiz (2004) emphasizes that it is the way in which tools, instruments and laws (including modified IPRs) are 'interrelated' in a 'synergistic manner' that will ensure that indigenous peoples' interests are safeguarded in the legal protection of their TK. Some opening for this might perhaps be provided by the WIPO Development Agenda (see Chapter 9).

Indeed, while there are many initiatives and discussions on the protection of TK at various levels, a pivotal component that is often missing is the indigenous peoples' full participation as their own representatives, describing their own vision of the future protection of TK and the directions this should take. As recently pointed out in a paper by the Call of the Earth (2007): 'While IP debates relevant to TK, cultural expressions and human genetic resources are all about Indigenous Peoples and directly affect their cultural integrity and livelihoods, Indigenous Peoples have only limited participatory rights in the international policy making fora where decisions are made'.[89] Referring to the 'Way Forward', this paper emphasizes that 'full and effective participation of Indigenous Peoples in all policy making processes that affect them is a necessary pre-cursor to appropriate policy making' and that 'in a number of different fora Indigenous Peoples have called for participatory arrangements that reflect their status as rights holders' (ibid.).

The effective participation of indigenous peoples and local communities in policymaking regarding the protection of TK requires significant capacity building, including training on these legal issues, access to planning resources,[90] the use of languages accessible to these peoples and communities in national and international forums addressing related reforms, access to decision-making in such forums, and the direct involvement of these peoples and communities in research on these issues. The results of relevant research have to be devolved to the indigenous and local communities in a comprehensible way and format. Importantly, integrated solutions are needed for the protection of TK, going beyond the legal measures discussed in this chapter. As Laird and Wynberg (2008, p. 98) point out, there is 'an urgent need to introduce new forms of protection for traditional knowledge that not only give communities rights over their knowledge but also enable the wider preservation and promotion of such knowledge systems'.

REFERENCES

Antons, C. (ed.) 2009, *Traditional Knowledge, Traditional Cultural Expressions and Intellectual Property Law in the Asia-Pacific Region*, The Max Planck Series on Asian Intellectual Property Law, Kluwer Law International, The Netherlands.

Balick, M.J. 2007, 'Traditional Knowledge: Lessons from the Past, Lessons for the Future', in C.R. McManis (ed.), *Biodiversity and the Law: Intellectual Property, Biotechnology and Traditional Knowledge*, pp. 280–296, Earthscan Publications Ltd., London, available at: http://law.wustl.edu/centeris/Papers/Biodiversity/PDFWrdDoc/Balick.pdf (accessed 15 November 2008).

Barber, C.V., Glowka, L. & La Vina, A.G.M. 2002, 'Developing and Implementing National Measures for Genetic Resources Access and Benefit-Sharing', in S.A. Laird (ed.), *Biodiversity and Traditional Knowledge: Equitable Partnerships in Practice*, pp. 363–374, Earthscan Publications Ltd., London.

Brush, S.B. 1996, *Valuing Local Knowledge: Indigenous People and Intellectual Property Rights Access to Genetic Resources and Traditional Knowledge: Lessons from South and Southeast Asia*, Island Press, Washington, DC.

Brush, S.B. 2007, 'The Demise of Common Heritage and Protection of Traditional Agricultural Knowledge', in C.R. McManis (ed.), *Biodiversity & the Law: Intellectual Property, Biotechnology & Traditional Knowledge*, pp. 297–311, Earthscan Publications

[89] See also the United Nations Economic and Social Council 2007, Report on the 'International Expert Group Meeting on the Convention on Biological Diversity's International Regime on Access and Benefit-Sharing and Indigenous Peoples' Human Rights', available at: http://www.un.org/esa/socdev/unpfii/documents/workshop_CBDABS_finalreport_en.doc (accessed 11 December 2008). The report emphasizes the need to further enhance indigenous peoples' rights to participate in CBD meetings. The Economic and Social Council endorsed this expert group at the recommendation of the Permanent Forum on Indigenous Issues.

[90] One practical option would be to establish a database with the contact information of indigenous peoples' representatives who are dealing with critical issues relating to TK and ABS.

Ltd., London, available at: http://law.wustl.edu/centeris/Papers/Biodiversity/PDFWrdDoc/StLouis1.pdf (accessed 11 December 2008).

Call of the Earth 2007, 'The Participation of Indigenous Peoples in International Intellectual Property Policy Making', in *Call of the Earth Issues in Intellectual Property Policy 6*, available at: http://www.earthcall.org/en/issues/background.html (accessed 24 June 2009).

Chishakwe, N. & Young, T.R. 2003, *Access to Genetic Resources, and Sharing the Benefits of their Use: International and Sub-regional Issues*, Southern Africa Development Committee (SADC), World Conservation Union (IUCN) and United Nations Development Programme (UNDP), available at: http://weavingaweb.org/absdocuments/eng_SADC.pdf (accessed 23 April 2010).

Commission on Intellectual Property Rights (CIPR) 2002, *Integrating Intellectual Property Rights and Development Policy*, CIPR, London, available at: http://www.iprcommission.org/papers/pdfs/final_report/CIPRfullfinal.pdf (accessed 19 October 2008).

Correa, C.M. 2002, *Protection and Promotion of Traditional Medicine – Implications for Public Health in Developing Countries*, South Centre, Switzerland, available at: http://apps.who.int/medicinedocs/en/d/Js4917e/ (accessed 24 June 2009).

Correa, C.M. 2004, 'Update on International Development Relating to the Intellectual Property Protection of Traditional Knowledge including Traditional Medicine', *Trade-Related Agenda, Development and Equity (T.R.A.D.E.) Working Papers 18*, South Centre, Switzerland.

Correa, C. 2005, 'Alcances jurídicos de las exigencies de divulgación de origen en el sistema de patentes y derechos de obtentor', Documento de Investigación, SPDA, Iniciativa para la Prevención de la Biopiratería, Año I, no. 2, Agosto 2005, available at: http://www.biopirateria.org/documentos/2-CarlosMCorrea.pdf (accessed 23 April 2010).

Degawan, M. 2008, 'Mitigating the Impacts of Climate Change: Solutions or Additional Threats', *Indigenous Affairs: Climate Change and Indigenous Peoples*, Issue 1–2/08, available at: http://www.iwgia.org/sw161.asp (accessed 13 November 2009).

Dutfield, G. 2000, *Intellectual Property Rights, Trade and Biodiversity: Seeds and Plant Varieties*, Earthscan Publications Ltd., London.

Dutfield, G. 2006, 'Protecting Traditional Knowledge: Pathways to the Future', *International Centre for Trade and Sustainable Development (ICTSD) Issue Paper No.16*, ICTSD, Geneva, available at: http://www.iprsonline.org/unctadictsd/docs/Graham%20final.pdf (accessed 25 January 2009).

European Region of International Lesbian and Gay Association 2007, *International Human Rights References to Sexual and Reproductive Health and Rights*, pp. 63–70, available at: http://www.ilga-europe.org/europe/publications/non_periodical/international_human_rights_references_to_sexual_and_reproductive_health_and_rights_regarding_lgbt_populations_and_hiv_aids_and_stis_december_2007 (accessed 16 November 2008).

Gollin, M.A. 2007, 'Answering the Call: Public Interest Intellectual Property Advisors (PIIPA)', in C.R. McManis (ed.), *Biodiversity & the Law: Intellectual Property, Biotechnology & Traditional Knowledge*, pp. 441–467, Earthscan Publications Ltd., London.

Gollin, M.A. & Barry, T.F. 2009, 'China's Disclosure of Origin Law to Enter into Force on October 1, 2009', *Venable LLP: News & Insights*, 22 September 2009, available at: http://www.venable.com/chinas-disclosure-of-origin-law-to-enter-into-force-on-october-1-2009-09-22-2009/ (accessed 22 April 2010).

Guerin-McManis, M. & Kim, D. 2002, 'Prior Informed Consent: Protocol and Form', in S.A. Laird (ed.), *Biodiversity and Traditional Knowledge: Equitable Partnerships in Practice, People and Plants Conservation Series*, pp. 223–240, Earthscan Publications Ltd., London.

Guerin-McManus, M., Nnadozie, K.C. & Laird, S.A. 2002, 'Sharing Financial Benefits: Trust Funds for Biodiversity Prospecting', in S.A. Laird (ed.), *Biodiversity and Traditional Knowledge: Equitable Partnerships in Practice*, People and Plants Conservation Series, pp. 333–362, Earthscan Publications Ltd., London.

Gupta, A.K. 2004, *The Role of Intellectual Property Rights in the Sharing of Benefits Arising from the Use of Biological Resources and Traditional Knowledge*, World Intellectual Property Organization (WIPO) & United Nations Environment Programme (UNEP), Geneva.

Heineke, C. & Wolff, F. 2004, 'Access to Genetic Resources and the Sharing of Benefits: Private Rights or Shared Use for Biodiversity Conservation?', *Environmental Law International Network Review*, February 2004, pp. 26–33, available at: http://www.agrobiodiversitaet.net/download/Corinna_Heineke_Fraenzi_Wolff.pdf (accessed 30 November 2008).

Helfer, L.R. 2004, 'Intellectual Property Rights in Plant Varieties: International Legal Regimes and Policy Options for National Governments', FAO Legislative Study 85, Rome.

Hoare, A.L. & Tarasofsky, R.G. 2007, 'Asking and Telling: Can "Disclosure of Origin" Requirements in Patent Applications Make a Difference?', *Journal of World Intellectual Property*, vol. 10, no. 2, pp. 149–169.

Indigenous Peoples International Centre for Policy Research and Education (TEBTEBBA), n.d., *Climate Change & Indigenous Women*, TEBTEBBA.

International Expert Group on Biotechnology, Innovation and Intellectual Property (IEGBIIP) 2008, *Towards a New Era of Intellectual Property: From Confrontation to Negotiation*, available at: http://www.theinnovationpartnership.org/data/ieg/documents/report/TIP_Report_E.pdf (accessed 27 December 2008).

International Institute for Environment and Development (IIED) 2008, *Protecting Community Rights over Traditional Knowledge: Implications of Customary Laws and Practices*, available at: http://www.cbd.int/abs/project.shtml?id=18967 (accessed 24 June 2009).

International Seed Trade Federation/ International Association of Plant Breeders (FIS/ASSINSEL) 1999, *Essential Derivation and Dependence: Practical Information*, available at: http://www.worldseed.org/positions.html (accessed 15 June 2007).

International Union for Conservation of Nature (IUCN) 2008, Indigenous and Traditional Peoples and Climate Change, Issues Paper (prepared by M. Macchi), March 2008, IUCN, Switzerland, available at: http://cmsdata.iucn.org/downloads/indigenous_peoples_climate_change.pdf (accessed 15 April 2010).

International Work Group for Indigenous Affairs (IWGIA) 2006, 'Africa Proposes No Action on Adoption of the Declaration', 9 November 2006, available at: http://iwgia.synkron.com/graphics/Synkron-Library/Documents/Noticeboard/News/International/AfricaproposesnoactionDD.htm (accessed 21 November 2008).

Jördens, R. 2002, 'Legal and Technological Developments leading to this Symposium: UPOV's Perspective', in World Intellectual Property Organization/International Union for the Protection of New Varieties of Plants (WIPO/UPOV) 2005, *Compilation of the 2002 & 2003 Joint Symposia Documents of the World Intellectual Property*

Organization (WIPO) and the International Union for the Protection of New Varieties of Plants (UPOV).

Kuanpoth, J. 2001, 'Legal Protection of Traditional Knowledge: The Case of Thai Traditional Medicine', ASEAN Workshop on the TRIPS Agreement & Traditional Medicine, WHO, Jakarta.

Laird, S.A. & Noejovich, F. 2002, 'Building Equitable Research Relationships with Indigenous Peoples and Local Communities: Prior Informed Consent and Research Agreements', in S.A. Laird (ed.), *Biodiversity and Traditional Knowledge: Equitable Partnerships in Practice*, pp. 179–220, Earthscan Publications Ltd., London.

Laird, S.A. & Wynberg, R. 2008, *Access and Benefit-Sharing in Practice: Trends in Partnerships Across Sectors*, Secretariat of the Convention on Biological Diversity, Technical Series No. 38, Montreal.

Mackay, F. 2004, *Indigenous Peoples' Right to Free, Prior and Informed Consent and the World Bank's Extractive Industries Review*, Forest Peoples' Programme, available at: http://www.forestpeoples.org/documents/prv_sector/eir/eir_ips_fpic_jun04_eng.pdf (accessed 16 April 2010).

Maffi, L. 1998, 'Linguistic and Biological Diversity: The Inextricable Link', *Terralingua Discussion Paper No. 3*, available at: http://www.terralingua.org/2/DiscPapers/DiscPaper3.html (accessed 24 June 2009).

Maffi, L. (ed.) 2001, *On Biocultural Diversity: Linking Language, Knowledge and the Environment*, Smithsonian Institution Press, Washington, DC.

McManis, C.R. 1998, 'The Interface between International Intellectual Property and Environmental Protection: Biodiversity and Biotechnology', *Washington University Law Quarterly*, vol. 76, no. 1, available at: http://lawreview.wustl.edu/inprint/76–1/761–18.html (accessed 30 November 2008).

McManis, C.R. 2002, 'Are There TRIPS-Compliant Measures for a Balanced Co-existence of Patents and Plant Breeders' Rights? Some Lessons from the United States of America', in World Intellectual Property Organization/International Union for the Protection of New Varieties of Plants (WIPO/UPOV) 2005, *Compilation of the 2002 & 2003 Joint Symposia Documents of the World Intellectual Property Organization (WIPO) and the International Union for the Protection of New Varieties of Plants (UPOV).*

McManis, C.R. 2003, 'Intellectual Property, Genetic Resources and Traditional Knowledge Protection: Thinking Globally, Acting Locally', *Faculty Working Papers Series No. 02–10–03*, Washington University in St. Louis School of Law.

McManis, C.R. 2004, 'Fitting Traditional Knowledge Protection and Biopiracy Claims into the Existing Intellectual Property and Unfair Competition Framework', in B. Ong (ed.), *Intellectual Property and Biological Resources*, Marshall Cavendish Academic, Singapore.

McManis, C.R. 2007, 'Answering the Call: The Intellectual Property and Business Formation Legal Clinic at Washington University', in C.R. McManis (ed.), *Biodiversity & the Law: Intellectual Property, Biotechnology & Traditional Knowledge*, pp. 468–474, Earthscan Publications Ltd., London.

Overwalle, V.G. 2007, 'Holder and User Perspectives in the Traditional Knowledge Debate: A European View', in C.R. McManis (ed.), *Biodiversity & the Law: Intellectual Property, Biotechnology & Traditional Knowledge*, pp. 355–372, Earthscan Publications Ltd., London.

Pimm, S.L. & Brooks, T.M. 1997, 'The Sixth Extinction: How Large, Where, and When?', in P.H. Raven & T. Williams (eds.), *Nature and Human Society: The Quest for a Sustainable*

World, pp. 46–62, available at: http://www.nap.edu/openbook.php?isbn=0309065550 (accessed 16 November 2008).

Pires de Carvalho, N.P. 2007, 'From the Shaman's Hut to the Patent Office: A Road Under Construction', in C.R. McManis (ed.), *Biodiversity & the Law: Intellectual Property, Biotechnology & Traditional Knowledge*, pp. 241–279, Earthscan Publications Ltd., London.

Rodríguez Cervantes, S. 2006, 'FTAs: Trading Away Traditional Knowledge', GRAIN, available at: http://www.grain.org/briefings/?id=196 (accessed 24 June 2009).

Rosenthal, J.P. 1999, 'Drug Discovery, Economic Development and Conservation: The International Cooperative Biodiversity Groups', *Pharmaceutical Biology*, vol. 37, no. 4, p. 5.

Ruiz, M. 2003a, *The International Treaty on Plant Genetic Resources and Decision 391 of the Andean Community of Nations: Peru, the Andean Region and the International Agricultural Research Centres*, Peruvian Society for Environmental Law (SPDA), Lima, Peru, available at: http://www.cipotato.org/library/pdfdocs/AN65154.pdf (accessed 15 April 2010).

Ruiz, M. 2003b, ¿Es Necesario Un Nuevo Marco Jurídico Para La Bioprospección En La Región Andina? Breve Revisión Crítica De La Decisión 391, SPDA, Lima.

Ruiz, M. 2004, 'National and Regional Laws to Protect Indigenous Knowledge Related to Genetic Resources', *Science and Development Network Policy Brief*, available at: http://www.scidev.net/en/policy-briefs/national-and-regional-laws-to-protect-ik-related-t.html (accessed 27 January 2009).

Ruiz, M. 2006, *The Protection of Traditional Knowledge: Policy and Legal Advances in Latin America*, International Union for Conservation of Nature (IUCN), BMZ, SPDA, Lima.

Sanders, R., 2004, 'Landmark Agreement between Samoa and UC Berkeley could help Search for AIDS Cure', 29 September 2004, UC Berkeley News, available at: http://berkeley.edu/news/media/releases/2004/09/29_samoa.shtml (accessed 23 April 2010).

Sarnoff, J.D. & Correa, C.M. 2006, *Analysis of Options for Implementing Disclosure of Origin Requirements*, United Nations Conference on Trade and Development (UNCTAD), New York and Geneva, available at: http://www.unctad.org/en/docs/ditcted200514_en.pdf (accessed 11 December 2008).

Soejarto et al. 2007, 'Bioprospecting Arrangments: Cooperation between the North and the South', in A. Krattiger, R.T. Mahoney, L. Nelson et al. 2007, *Intellectual Property Management in Health and Agricultural Innovation: A Handbook of Best Practices*, Management of Intellectual Property in Health Research and Development (MIHR), Oxford, UK, and Public Intellectual Property Resources for Agriculture (PIPRA), US.

South Centre 2002, *Protection and Promotion of Traditional Medicine – Implications for Public Health in Developing Countries*, South Centre, Geneva.

Tamang, P. 2005, 'An Overview of the Principle of Free, Prior and Informed Consent and Indigenous Peoples in International and Domestic Law and Practices', *Australian Indigenous Law Reporter*, Australasian Legal Information Institute, available at: http://www.austlii.edu.au/au/journals/AILR/2005/36.html (accessed 21 November 2008).

Thomas, V. (ed.) 2001, 'Traditional Occupations of Indigenous and Tribal Peoples: Emerging Trends', *Project to Promote International Labour Organization (ILO) Policy on Indigenous and Tribal Peoples*, International Labour Office, Geneva, available at:

http://www.ilo.org/public/english/standards/egalite/itpp/publication/1.htm (accessed 12 November 2008).

Tobin, B. & Taylor, E. 2009, *Across the Great Divide: A Case Study of Complementarity and Conflict between Customary Law and TK Protection Legislation in Peru*, Initiative for the Prevention of Biopiracy, Research Document, vol. IV, no. 11, May 2009, Peruvian Society for Environmental Law (SPDA), Lima.

United Nations Conference on Trade and Development – International Centre for Trade and Sustainable Development (UNCTAD-ICTSD) Capacity Building Project on Intellectual Property Rights (IPR) 2005, *A Resource Book on TRIPS and Development: An Authoritative and Practical Guide to the TRIPS Agreement*, available at: http://www.iprsonline.org/unctadictsd/ResourceBookIndex.htm (accessed 21 November 2008).

United Nations Development Programme (UNDP) 2004, *Human Development Report 2004: Cultural Liberty in Today's Diverse World*, available at: http://hdr.undp.org/en/media/hdr04_complete.pdf (accessed 16 November 2008).

UNDP 2005, *Practice Note on Traditional Knowledge, Access to Genetic Resources and Benefit-Sharing*, (authored by T. Wong, T. Hay-Edie, T. Akhtar & C. McNeill) UNDP, available at: http://www.energyandenvironment.undp.org/undp/index.cfm?module=Library&page=Document&DocumentID=6388 (accessed 12 November 2008).

UNDP 2007, *Human Development Report 2007/2008: Fighting Climate Change: Human Solidarity in a Divided World*, UNDP, available at: http://hdr.undp.org/en/media/HDR_20072008_EN_Complete.pdf (accessed 2 January 2009).

United Nations Environment Programme/ Convention on Biological Diversity (UNEP/CBD) Ad Hoc Open-Ended Working Group on Access and Benefit Sharing 2001, *Report on the Role of Intellectual Property Rights in the Implementation of Access and Benefit Sharing Arrangements*, available at: http://www.biodiv.org/doc/meetings/abs/abswg-01/official/abswg-01-04-en.pdf (accessed 15 November 2008).

UNEP & Secretariat of the CBD 2003, Composite Report on the Status and Trends regarding the Knowledge, Innovations and Practices of Indigenous and Local Communities' (Regional Report for North America), UN Doc. UNEP/CBD/WG8J/3/INF/8 (7 October 2003), available at: http://www.cbd.int/doc/?mtg=WG8J-03 (accessed 10 February 2010).

United Nations University – Institute of Advanced Studies (UNU-IAS) 2004, 'The Role of Registers and Databases in the Protection of Traditional Knowledge: A Comparative Analysis', p. 38, available at: http://www.ias.unu.edu/binaries/UNUIAS_TKRegistersReport.pdf (accessed 30 November 2008).

Upano, A. 2004, 'D.C. Team gets to the Root of the Problem', *Legal Times*, 12 January, vol. XXVII, no. 2, available at: http://www.piipa.org/Upano1–12–04.pdf (accessed 24 June 2009).

Vogel, J.H. 2007, 'From the 'Tragedy of the Commons to the Tragedy of the Commonplace: Analysis and Synthesis through the Lens of Economic Theory', in C.R. McManis (ed.), *Biodiversity & the Law: Intellectual Property, Biotechnology & Traditional Knowledge*, pp. 115–136, Earthscan Publications Ltd., London.

Wood, A., 2000, in Stedman-Edwards, P. & Mang, J. (eds.), *The Root Causes of Biodiversity Loss*, James & James/Earthscan, London.

World Bank 2006, Cultural Heritage and Collective Intellectual Property Rights, *Indigenous Knowledge Notes*, no. 95, p. 2, available at: http://siteresources.worldbank.org/INTINDKNOWLEDGE/Resources/iknt95.htm (accessed 16 November 2008).

World Health Organization (WHO), International Union for Conservation of Nature (IUCN) and World Wide Fund for Nature (WWF) 1993, *Guidelines for Conservation of Medicinal Plants*, IUCN, Gland, Switzerland.

WHO 2002, *WHO Traditional Medicine Strategy 2002–2005*, available at: http://whqlibdoc.who.int/hq/2002/WHO_EDM_TRM_2002.1.pdf (accessed 26 November 2008).

World Intellectual Property Organization (WIPO) 2001, *Matters Concerning Intellectual Property and Genetic Resources, Traditional Knowledge and Folklore – An Overview*, Inter-governmental Committee on Intellectual Property and Genetic Resources, Traditional Knowledge and Folklore, Doc. WIPO/GRTKF/IC/1/3, available at: http://www.wipo.int/edocs/mdocs/tk/en/wipo_grtkf_ic_1/wipo_grtkf_ic_1_3.pdf (accessed 15 November 2008).

WIPO 2006a, *Intellectual Property and Genetic Resources, Traditional Knowledge and Traditional Cultural Expressions/Folklore: Information Resources*, Doc. WIPO/GRTKF/INF/1, available at: http://www.wipo.int/tk/en/consultations/draft_provisions/draft_provisions.html (accessed 15 November 2008).

WIPO 2006b, *The Protection of Traditional Knowledge: Revised Outline of Policy Options and Legal Mechanisms*, Inter-governmental Committee on Intellectual Property and Genetic Resources, Traditional Knowledge and Folklore, Doc. WIPO/GRTKF/IC/9/INF/5, available at: http://www.wipo.int/edocs/mdocs/tk/en/wipo_grtkf_ic_9/wipo_grtkf_ic_9_inf_5.doc (accessed 30 November 2008).

Wynberg, R., Schroeder, D. & Chennells, R. (eds.) 2009, *Indigenous Peoples, Consent and Benefit Sharing: Lessons from the San-Hoodia Case*, Springer, Netherlands.

Wynberg, R., Taylor, M. & Laird, S. 2007, *Access and Benefit Sharing in South Africa: An Analysis of Legal Frameworks and Agreements*, Environmental Evaluation Unit, University of Cape Town, prepared for the Department of Environmental Affairs and Tourism on behalf of the Southern African Development Community Biodiversity Support Programme, Report No. 1/07/274.

Wynberg, R. & Taylor, M. 2009, 'Finding a Path through the ABS Maze: Challenges of Regulating Access and Ensuring Fair Benefit-Sharing in South Africa', in E.C. Kamau & G. Winter (eds.), *Genetic Resources, Traditional Knowledge and the Law: Solutions for Access and Benefit Sharing*, Earthscan Publications Ltd., London.

5

Traditional cultural expressions: Preservation and innovation

Tzen Wong and Claudia Fernandini[1]

Introduction

This chapter addresses challenges faced by indigenous peoples and local communities in the legal protection of their traditional cultural expressions (TCEs). It also highlights considerations for governments, public institutions and non-profit organizations in attempts to promote TCEs to support indigenous peoples and local communities in their cultural, economic and social development. While TCEs are embraced within the broad, holistic approach to traditional knowledge (TK) adopted in this book, there are legal issues and developments specific to the protection of TCEs which merit separate analysis from those elements of TK addressed in Chapter 4. This chapter first explores some relevant concepts towards understanding the overlap between intellectual property rights (IPRs) and the protection of TCEs. It poses questions relating to the commodification of TCEs by IPRs, and how this potentially transforms the social relations underpinning creative processes in indigenous communities. At the same time, it is recognized that the making and marketing of some forms of TCEs present potential sources of livelihoods to many indigenous communities currently marginalized in the socio-economic order. Given a global environment where TCEs are increasingly copied and commercially mass-produced by third parties, some options and limitations in relation to intellectual property (IP) protection of TCEs are discussed, along with *sui generis* protection. While the Latin term *sui generis* means 'unique' or 'of its own kind', it remains to be seen how far these hybrid solutions ultimately depart from typical concepts in IP law. Beyond legal measures, there are indigenous protocols and other standards governing third-party access to and use of TCEs, including those evolving within the context of the Internet. These are also explored briefly in this chapter.

1. Concepts and definitions

According to Article 1(a) of the *Revised Draft Provisions for the Protection of Traditional Cultural Expressions/Expressions of Folklore* being reviewed at WIPO ('WIPO Revised Provisions'),[2] 'traditional cultural expressions' or 'expressions of folklore' are 'any forms, whether tangible and intangible, in which traditional culture and

[1] The authors are grateful to Joshua Bell, Graham Dutfield, Haidy Geismar, Terence Hay-Edie, Honor Keeler, Uma Suthersanen and Molly Torsen for their invaluable comments.

[2] These draft provisions are under revision at the WIPO Intergovernmental Committee on Genetic Resources, Traditional Knowledge and Traditional Cultural Expressions (IGC). For the definitions and

knowledge are expressed, appear or are manifested', and comprise the following forms of expressions (or combinations thereof):

> (i) verbal expressions, such as: stories, epics, legends, poetry, riddles and other narratives; words, signs, names, and symbols;
> (ii) musical expressions, such as songs and instrumental music;
> (iii) expressions by action, such as dances, plays, ceremonies, rituals and other performances, whether or not reduced to a material form; and
> (iv) tangible expressions, such as productions of art, in particular, drawings, designs, paintings (including body-painting), carvings, sculptures, pottery, terracotta, mosaic, woodwork, metalware, jewelry, baskets, needlework, textiles, glassware, carpets, costumes; handicrafts; musical instruments; and architectural forms...

To be treated as subject matter for protection under the WIPO Revised Provisions, such forms of expression have to be 'characteristic of a community's cultural and social identity and cultural heritage' (Article 1(a)). They also have to fulfil other conditions, such as being 'maintained, used or developed by such community or by individuals having the right or responsibility to do so in accordance with the customary law and practices of that community' (Article 1(a)).

The United Nations Educational, Scientific and Cultural Organization (UNESCO) has been involved in the protection of tangible and intangible cultural heritage for many decades. The phrase 'expressions of folklore' is used in the UNESCO-WIPO Model Provisions for National Laws on the Protection of Expressions of Folklore Against Illicit Exploitation and Other Prejudicial Actions 1982 ('UNESCO-WIPO Model Provisions').[3] Section 2 of the Model Provisions provides that 'expressions of folklore' are understood as 'productions consisting of characteristic elements of the traditional artistic heritage developed and maintained by a community' in the country or 'by individuals reflecting the traditional artistic expectations of such a community'. Only 'artistic heritage' is covered by the Model Provisions.

While the term 'traditional cultural expressions' is used in this chapter instead of 'expressions of folklore', it is noted that WIPO uses these terms as 'interchangeable synonyms' (WIPO 2006, p. 3). At the same time, the term 'folklore' has been critiqued by some as 'reflecting a western attitude of folklore as something dead to be collected and preserved, rather than part of an evolving living tradition' (Shinya

provisions discussed in this chapter, see WIPO 2006, Intellectual Property and Genetic Resources, Traditional Knowledge and Traditional Cultural Expressions/Folklore, Doc. WIPO/GRTKF/INF/1 [hereinafter 'WIPO 2006'], available at: http://www.wipo.int/export/sites/www/tk/en/consultations/draft_provisions/pdf/draft-provisions-booklet.pdf (accessed 15 February 2010). The draft provisions have not been adopted or endorsed by the IGC and have undergone further revision since the writing of this chapter. For the latest status of this aspect of WIPO's work, see the WIPO website, 'Traditonal Knowledge, Genetic Resources, and Traditional Cultural Expressions//Folklore', available at: http://www.wipo.int/tk/en (accessed 24 March 2010).

[3] UNESCO-WIPO Model Provisions for National Laws on the Protection of Expressions of Folklore Against Illicit Exploitation and Other Prejudicial Actions 1982, reprinted in Copyright Bull. 62 (1982) [hereinafter 'UNESCO-WIPO Model Provisions'], available at: http://www.wipo.int/export/sites/www/tk/en/laws/pdf/unesco_wipo_1982.pdf (accessed 1 February 2010).

2004). Indeed, conceptual difficulties remain in relation to the various terminologies used in this field.[4]

The discussion in this chapter focuses mainly on traditional motifs, arts and crafts of indigenous peoples which form a part of their TCEs and address the impact on indigenous culture and livelihoods of mass reproduction of such TCEs within the global crafts industries. It is noted that TCEs extend well beyond these forms to include, for example, traditional music, dance and other rituals.[5] While it is impossible within the current discussion to address all those elements, some IP considerations for the performative aspects of these forms of TCEs are mentioned in this chapter as well as in Chapter 8. Further research and thinking is needed on each of these forms of TCEs.[6] It is also qualified that TCEs represent only a part of the cultural heritage of indigenous peoples, and there are many other aspects of cultural heritage protection which may or may not overlap with IP law.[7] Furthermore, there is no agreement on the meaning of 'protection' in relation to TCEs. Documents such as the UNESCO-WIPO Model Provisions and the WIPO Revised Provisions define protection differently (see Torsen 2008). To avoid confusion, this chapter restricts the use of the term to legal protection by instruments and provisions including IPRs, in contrast to possible broader meanings of protection in relation to preserving the integrity or 'authenticity' of TCEs. The latter concepts are also open to many interpretations (see Lindholm 2008).

There is no fixed definition of an indigenous people, and the definitions provided in international instruments vary in their language and scope (see Laird & Noejovich 2002, p. 180); the ILO Convention No. 169 provides some points of reference (see Articles 1(1) and 1(2)), although this remains a highly debated issue.[8] Apart from indigenous peoples living by customary practices, other non-indigenous local communities could be treated as custodians of TCEs under draft international provisions and some national laws. There is little international consensus as to which local communities the latter would comprise. This ambiguity has led

[4] See Oguamanam 2008, pp. 35–36, for an extended discussion of the 'terminological trap' and inherent conceptual difficulties in relation to the discourse surrounding 'traditional', 'indigenous' or 'local' knowledge.

[5] There has even been some discussion (e.g. in Peru) to include traditional recipes within the protection of cultural heritage.

[6] Some interesting studies have been conducted, for example, in relation to traditional music being increasingly rebranded as 'world music', and the effects of globalization and this 'world music' market on local music scenes (see Malm 2004a, 2004b).

[7] A distinction has to be made between IP laws which protect culture, and IP laws which co-exist with cultural laws. In many countries, heritage is protected through specific cultural heritage laws which can, as in the case of US, co-exist with IP laws. For example, architectural buildings of stature are well protected against mutilation and destruction both under US state cultural laws and federal copyright laws; indeed, moral right protection extends to buildings in the US (comment from Uma Suthersanen). For the various UNESCO instruments relevant to the protection of cultural heritage, see UNESCO – Culture, 'Normative Action', available at: http://portal.unesco.org/culture/en/ev.php-URL_ID=34328&URL_DO=DO_TOPIC&URL_SECTION=201.html (accessed 24 March 2010).

[8] See Laird and Noejovich (2002, p. 180) for differentiated definitions within international instruments, regional agreements and national laws. See International Labour Organisation (ILO) Convention Concerning Indigenous and Tribal Peoples in Independent Countries (No. 169) (Geneva, 27 June 1989), 1650 U.N.T.S. 383, 28 I.L.M. 1382, 72 ILO Official Bull. 59 (1989) (*entered into force* 5 September 1991) [hereinafter 'ILO Convention No. 169'], available at http://www.un-documents.net/c169.htm (accessed 22 February 2010).

WIPO to include in the Revised Provisions a rather broad and tentative definition of beneficiaries of TCEs protection as 'Indigenous Peoples and traditional and other cultural communities' in whom 'the custody, care and safeguarding of the traditional cultural expressions/expressions of folklore are entrusted in accordance with their customary law and practices' (Article 2(i)) and 'who maintain, use or develop the traditional cultural expressions/expressions of folklore as being characteristic of their cultural and social identity and cultural heritage' (Article 2(ii)). The WIPO Secretariat's commentary on the provisions suggests that the term 'cultural communities' is broad enough to 'include also the nationals of an entire country', apparently reflecting views from countries such as Egypt and Morocco that TCEs may be 'national folklore' and belong to all of the people of a particular country (WIPO 2006, p. 17). Such broad definitions of 'community' raise complex questions over the recognition of indigenous peoples and other local communities as culturally distinct groups within a nation state and have far-reaching implications, not least for the protection of their TCEs.[9]

It is also possible, of course, that more than one community might claim custodianship of the same or similar TCEs in a country. Furthermore, through geographical proximity, common history, migration or displacement of the TCE custodians to new territories, certain renditions of TCEs might well appear concurrently in different countries. All these raise complex, context-specific questions which cannot be adequately addressed within this chapter.[10] Transboundary TCEs seem to call especially for regional or international frameworks of protection, with mechanisms for distributing benefits to the various communities concerned (see the discussion on TK in Chapter 4).[11] Whether some of these cases would fall within the ambit of an international framework in future to protect TCEs remains to be seen, and present areas for further research.

2. Circulation and commodification of traditional cultural expressions

There is keen debate amongst indigenous communities, government officials, public negotiators and academic commentators alike over whether IPRs are appropriate for the preservation and legal protection of TCEs. These debates need to be understood in relation to the intrinsic nature of TCEs, and how TCEs carry with them

[9] Honor Keeler, a legal scholar and citizen of the Cherokee Nation in Oklahoma, observes that: 'This discussion is among the top reasons why indigenous peoples have trouble maintaining their distinct identities, cultures, and rights within the countries in which they live. This is especially important from a legal standpoint because ... governments [which] do not recognize their indigenous communities ... are unlikely to recognize [their] TCEs' (pers. comm. Honor Keeler, 10 December 2009). Any national laws or government decree classifying TCEs or other cultural material as national heritage would need to address potential claims of particular local communities to the TCEs involved. Antons (2010, pp. 107–112) explores some of the considerations in the 'distribution of rights and responsibilities' between national governments and communities in relation to TCE protection (ibid.).

[10] See, for example, the discussion in Antons 2010, pp. 113–116, on cross-border issues relating to the protection of TCEs in Southeast Asia.

[11] Discussing how transboundary TCEs can give rise to regional disputes, Antons adds that: 'As more national laws for TCE protection become enacted, dispute resolution mechanisms at the bilateral and regional levels will be important, especially to deal with those TCEs that have been widely spread across various borders' (ibid., p. 116).

'shared, symbolic meaning[s], which may represent for a community a link with the sacred... its history, or an attribute of its identity'.[12]

At the same time, the social or kinship relations underlying the creation of TCEs are continually challenged and re-defined by new contexts. Intellectual property protection of TCEs, along with the assumptions about ownership and property that come with it, poses one of the more recent challenges. This does not mean that traditional communities do not have concepts of ownership or property,[13] but rather that the ideas of property which underpin IP systems come from specific historical and largely Western contexts (Dutfield 2006, pp. 2, 8).

Leach (2005) argues that using IP as a 'register of ownership' may implicitly transform the social networks in a society which underpin its creative processes, thus undoing the very traditions and creative expressions that the laws are meant to protect. Drawing from anthropological fieldwork in the Madang region of Papua New Guinea, he suggests (2005, p. 37) that:

> Preservation of materials is one (important) thing, but it seems to me that of more basic importance is the preservation of the social conditions of creativity itself. Laws that take such property relations as their baseline inhibit the utilization of indigenously appropriate mechanisms for the control, distribution, and protection of indigenous resources. In other words, it is not just the material expressions (object outcomes of creative work), but the actual form of social relations, which must be considered in a discussion of protection or attribution.

It is important to nuance discussions such as the present one in terms of the historical and socio-economic realities of indigenous peoples around the world. Many indigenous peoples share histories of colonization and other impositions of political power which continue to the present day, and have common struggles in recovering or sustaining their land rights, cultural identity and customary practices. Indeed, the protection of TK and TCEs is seen by many indigenous peoples as 'central to their struggle for self-determination and control and management of their land and resources' (Aroha Te Pareake Mead 2005, p. 18; see also Burri-Nenova 2007, p. 208). Myers (2005, p. 54) observes that indigenous peoples 'see control over their

[12] International Commission of Jurists (ICJ) 2008, paper submitted to the Committee on Economic, Social and Cultural Rights (CESCR) for the 'Day of General Discussion on the right to take part in cultural life (article 15(1)(a) of the Covenant)', 9 May 2008, paras. 8–10, available at: http://www2.ohchr.org/english/bodies/cescr/docs/discussion/InternationalCommissionJurists.pdf (accessed 24 March 2010). Discussing historical sites, sacred buildings, rituals and ceremonies as 'collective goods' which serve as 'a token or as a medium for communal cultural practices', the ICJ paper suggests that: 'The collective character of these goods derives in the impossibility of their individual appropriation without losing [their] collective meaning. [Their] preservation... is of capital importance for the collective practices that inform cultural life and, therefore, their disregard often results in a shared sense of cultural offense' (ibid.). On how the protection of TCEs intersect with the protection of cultural rights as human rights, see Chapters 1 and 8.

[13] Leach (2005, p. 33) discusses, for example, customary rules governing a musical cult amongst people in the Madang region of Papua New Guinea: 'One aspect of Tambaran is a male musical cult with secret ritual paraphernalia. The tunes and designs used by this cult are associated with particular people, are owned by them, and handed down as heirlooms. That is, they have a named owner. Yet this ownership does not give the right of disposal. They are not "property", yet they are transacted. Spirit songs are being innovated all the time. There is a stock of ancestral songs for each residential group, but new spirits are coming into being today' (citations omitted).

own culture as a political issue, a remedy for historical loss, and a necessity for survival as a people, for survival as a culture' (see also Anaya 2004, p. 26; Chander & Sunder 2004).

At the same time, indigenous peoples' engagement with such issues as IPRs to protect their TCEs is differentiated among communities. Some indigenous communities may consider the concept and articulation of 'property rights' underlying Western IP systems as inapplicable to their TK, including their TCEs. Accordingly, any proposed legislation or other measures concerning TCEs should first undergo consultations with the indigenous peoples and local communities involved. The obligations under relevant international and regional instruments to obtain the free, prior and informed consent (FPIC) of indigenous and local communities for measures pertaining to TK (and genetic resources managed by them) are discussed in Chapter 4 and repetition is avoided here. It is worth highlighting, however, that the United Nations Declaration on the Rights of Indigenous Peoples (UNDRIP), adopted by the UN General Assembly in September 2007,[14] emphasizes that 'free, prior and informed consent' of indigenous peoples is to be obtained 'before adopting and implementing legislative and administrative measures that may affect them' (Art. 19). This and other provisions of the UNDRIP reinforce the right of indigenous peoples to 'determine and develop priorities and strategies for exercising their right to development' (Art. 23; see also Art. 34).

Depending on local contexts, some communities may see the protection of TCEs by certain forms of IPRs as consistent with their vision of human development and sustainable livelihoods, and as a possible legal redress for third-party copying of their TCEs for commercial purposes. It is important that the communities themselves have access to information (including information on the full-range of legal options) and decision-making to protect and promote their TCEs. Of particular significance to our present discussion, Article 31(1) of the UNDRIP makes explicit the right of indigenous peoples to 'maintain, control, protect and develop their intellectual property over [their] cultural heritage, traditional knowledge, and traditional cultural expressions' (see also Art. 31(2), discussed in Chapter 4). Article 11 further provides that indigenous peoples have the right not only to 'practise' but also to '*revitalize* their cultural traditions and customs' (emphasis added). This extends to the right to maintain, protect and develop the 'past, present and future manifestations of their cultures' (Article 11) and would include TCEs. The challenges in this area are accentuated by the fact that many indigenous communities remain socioeconomically marginalized in the countries in which they live (see United Nations 2009).

For some indigenous communities, or groups within the communities, marketing of objects based on TCEs may present an ongoing or potential source of income to help resolve problems of poverty. Importantly, Article 23(1) of the ILO

[14] United Nations Declaration on the Rights of Indigenous Peoples (13 September 2007), 46 I.L.M. 1013 (2007), G.A. Res. 61/295, UN Doc. A/RES/61/295 (2007) [hereinafter 'UNDRIP'], available at: http://www.un.org/esa/socdev/unpfii/documents/DRIPS_en.pdf (accessed 24 March 2010). While this instrument is non-binding, Wiessner (2009, p. 5) suggests that some of the rights stated therein already form part of customary international law. The provisions of the Declaration have also been absorbed directly into some national laws (see Chapter 1).

Convention No. 169 dealing with traditional occupations stipulates that 'handicrafts, rural and community-based industries ... shall be recognized as important factors in the maintenance of their cultures and in their economic self-reliance and development'.[15] Crafts, for example, often develop in a specific area or geographic concentration and may present one of the primary sources of income for the local community. Since craft making frequently involves self- and family employment, with the development of surrounding clusters, there may be a 'multiplier effect' on the number of persons benefiting from craft making in the community. As women are traditionally involved in craft making in many indigenous communities, such activities might present particular sources of income and autonomy to women. Strom notes, for example, that the sale of Maasai beadwork and other souvenirs based on TCEs present an important source of livelihood for indigenous Maasai women.[16]

Indigenous communities' understanding, attitudes and approaches towards IP protection of their TCEs may vary significantly even within the same region or country. Geismar (2005, p. 441) describes from anthropological field work in the North Ambrym region of Vanuatu how locals have been adapting copyright concepts towards protecting *kastom* carvings, drawing parallels with 'ritual injunctions concerning making and circulating' these traditional carvings. She notes how TCE custodians have actively pursued enforcement of their customary entitlements against third parties dealing with these artefacts allegedly without their consent (ibid., pp. 451–453). At the same time, she observes that indigenous women basket weavers from various regions of Vanuatu have yet to fully consider IP protection for their crafts. These baskets are woven from the leaves of pandanus trees and coloured using a combination of natural and synthetic dyes. Geismar notes that 'while their vibrant patterns are seen very much as local island resources, they circulate widely throughout Vanuatu and beyond ... ' (ibid., p. 33). She adds that:

> Despite the explicit linkage of innovative designs to individual women, there has been no move to restrict their movement (and thus control the potential capital to be raised by them) by galvanizing ideas about copyright. Patterns transmit themselves freely from woman to woman by the movement of baskets and therefore may be woven by any woman who sees them. (Ibid.)

This example also illustrates how the potential transformative effects of IPRs on TCEs need to be understood in relation to the systems of reciprocity that underpin both trade and gift exchange within and among traditional communities (Mauss 1950). Along with the historical relations of trade between indigenous and other communities, tourism and new information and communication technologies (ICTs) are contributing to the spread of some TCEs well beyond their area of origin. Studies on the effects of tourism on retention of ritual practices, for example,

15 Other provisions in the ILO Convention No. 169 of relevance to the protection of TK and TCEs are discussed in Chapter 4. On the international legal framework for the protection of bio-cultural heritage (including the case of TCEs), see the further resources at the PIIPA website, 'Intellectual Property and Human Development', available at: http://www.piipa.org/IP_and_Human_Development/.

16 Strom, S. 2008, 'Maasai Beadwork for Sale: Destruction of Culture or Perpetuation of Traditional Handicraft?', presentation at conference on 'Cultural Diversity and Mutuality', European Association of Social Anthropologists, Ljubljana, 26–29 August 2008.

would be relevant towards a better understanding of the impact of globalization on TCEs.[17] The research of Strom in relation to Maasai beadwork suggests that members of an indigenous community are moreover complex agents in their self-representation of cultural identity and integrity, including to tourists.[18]

Meanwhile, the commodification of TCEs of indigenous peoples by third parties other than their custodians is increasing at a scale which has prompted many indigenous communities around the world to seek urgent redress, including through legal measures. Dissemination of TCEs through digital technology and the Internet has exacerbated these concerns.[19] In some regions, including the Pacific, collective action and model laws are being pursued (see Section 6). Mindful that 'traditional knowledge and expressions of culture are the foundation of Pacific Island societies', the Secretariat of the Pacific Community has highlighted that:

> The heightened global competition for new products, processes and services brought about by the globalization of trade and advances in information technology has unfortunately triggered widespread appropriation of the cultural and social identity of Pacific Island peoples. In many Pacific Island countries and territories, handicrafts and souvenirs have been replicated and imported for sale to an unknowing tourism industry. Music and images are recorded for publication without the permission of traditional owners . . .[20]

Mass-produced copies of TCEs can dilute the cultural identity and other values associated with the latter. As TCEs become implicated in the global crafts market,[21] for example, newer techniques enabling increased volume of production and reduced production costs also result in lower-priced products by third parties. Faced with 'serial' copies of their TCEs, indigenous peoples are often unable to compete in terms of market access and price. Loss of traditional techniques may further occur through their efforts to accommodate lower market prices by altering techniques or materials used in craft making, or to cater to the aesthetic demands of the global crafts market. Along with addressing illegitimate mass copying by third

[17] For research within the Dogon context in Mali see, for example, Lane 1988; van Beek 2003; Schildkrout 2004; and Richards 2005.

[18] Strom, S. 2008, 'Maasai Beadwork for Sale: Destruction of Culture or Perpetuation of Traditional Handicraft?' (manuscript on file with author). See further Townsend-Gault 2004.

[19] Burri-Nenova (2007, p. 281) observes that '[w]ith the digitization of content and existence of the Internet as a tool for dissemination, the risk of misappropriation has increased dramatically now that any tourist can use his or her phone to photograph and record a TCE . . . '. She adds that 'exploiting the captured TCE commercially can be accomplished quickly [by third parties], thereby usurping the chance to use TCE as an asset of economic development' (ibid, pp. 281–282). TCEs disseminated by indigenous peoples or their authorized agents on the Internet may also be easily copied and used by third parties without permission in other contexts, including culturally inappropriate or offensive contexts.

[20] See Secretariat of the Pacific Community 2006, *Guidelines for Developing National Legislation for the Protection of Traditional Knowledge and Expressions of Culture Based on the Pacific Model Law 2002* [hereinafter 'Secretariat of the Pacific Community Guidelines'], p. vii, available at: http://www.wipo.int/export/sites/www/tk/en/laws/pdf/spc_guidelines_2002.pdf (accessed 10 March 2010).

[21] The global crafts market includes art pieces, textile articles, ceramic, bijouterie, baskets, among others. The US is the main receiving market for crafts. Five countries of the European Community are among the top ten markets receiving crafts, and China is the main crafts exporter. See Perú Ministerio de Comercio Exterior y Turismo (MINCETUR) 2004, *Plan Estratégico Nacional Exportador 2003–2013: Plan Operativo Exportador del Sector Artesanía*, May 2004. Further reports may be found on the MINCETUR website, available at: http://www.mincetur.gob.pe/index_f.asp?cont=572294 (accessed 24 March 2010).

parties, one challenge for the preservation of TCEs is in finding ways to differentiate authentic embodiments of TCEs from copies by third parties. For indigenous communities who do rely on making and marketing arts and crafts as a source of livelihood, a further challenge lies in identifying ways to support the price of these creations (among mass-produced copies) and cultivate a discerning eye in the purchaser for the provenance of the TCEs, including their cultural origins. These efforts are comparable to the 'fair trade' movement, although the latter has so far dealt mainly with agricultural products (DeCarlo 2007).

Towards understanding the overlap of IPRs with the protection of TCEs, it is helpful to bear in mind the variety of rights that make up the IP matrix (see Chapter 1), and their different histories and functions. In considering their relative relevance and implications for TCEs, it might be analytically useful to draw a distinction between IP regimes such as copyright and patents which typically emphasize individuals as 'authors' or 'inventors' of new works, and those which more readily accommodate concepts of incremental innovation by communities. As Zografos (2007, p. 178) notes: '[C]ertification marks and labels of authenticity are potentially unlimited in time and allow for collective use. They do not confer a monopoly right but limit the class of persons who can use a certain symbol'. She notes that such forms of IPRs can 'help protect consumers and indigenous communities from imitation products'. What this suggests at least is that distinct types of IPRs may operate differently in preserving or altering the social relations and creative processes in indigenous communities.

Equally challenging when setting out to 'preserve' social relations underpinning creative processes in a society is to reconcile these with other considerations from a human development perspective. Some TCEs may result, for example, from a highly hierarchical system of production, and 'narratives' of entitlement may in some cases serve to reinforce those hierarchies, with implications on gender roles and other concerns of social equality.[22] The *Human Development Report 2004: Cultural Liberty in Today's Diverse World*, published by the United Nations Development Programme (UNDP), invites reflection on the implications of 'inheritance laws that are biased against women, or decision-making procedures that are not participatory and democratic' on broader concepts of cultural liberty and human development (UNDP 2004, p. 89).

Discussions of IPRs and TCEs do not take place in a vacuum, but may furthermore be understood in relation to (the unravelling of) cultural assumptions surrounding European discourses of 'cultural property' and 'cultural heritage'. Leach suggests, for example, that there is a danger in current versions of cultural property regulations in 'obviating innovation among those with culture to protect'

[22] Geismar's account of the making of slit-drums in North Ambrym shows, for example, that the creation and rituals around such *kastom* carvings belong to the realm of village chiefs and other high-ranking men. She notes (2005a, p. 451) that these North Ambryn men 'both restrict the pool of producers and control the pool of consumers, whether dealers or tourists', and that concepts akin to copyright have long played a part in the 'simultaneous stringency and flexibility of local narratives about entitlement'. In another article, Geismar (2005b, pp. 33–42) contrasts this hierarchical treatment of entitlements to the practice of women basket weavers in Central Pentecost, who according to her, 'try to organize the concept of copyright amongst them in as equalitarian a manner as possible' in reproducing and transacting their *kastom* material (ibid., p. 41).

(2005, p. 41). He adds that: 'This in turn reinforces a stereotypical divide between traditional culture (valued as heritage, but barrier to innovation) and modern (no heritage value, but reliant on innovation)' (ibid.). Other commentators have questioned the stereotypical divides between the 'traditional' and 'modern' which amplify the isolation and 'otherness' of some societies (Boateng 2005; Oguamanam 2008). Boateng (2005, pp. 64–70) warns against drawing an artificial separation of the 'modern' and 'scientific' from what is termed as 'traditional' or 'folkloric', given that constant innovation exists in all realms. She notes that 'Ghanaian kente cloth, for example, has changed continually in its encounter with global markets', and that 'these changes go back to the era of mercantile capitalism during which colored silk yarns were introduced into the cloth-weaving economy from Europe' (ibid., p. 68). The latter apparently enabled 'weavers to extend their palette beyond the white of raw cotton and blue of indigo dyes'.[23] Strom has also noted the use of colours (and indeed materials) new to Maasai 'traditional' beadwork for some tourist 'souvenirs'.[24]

These raise complex questions relating to innovations based on TCEs. For example, can IP or *sui generis* laws be engaged to protect the interests of custodians of TCEs, while also encouraging innovations based on TCEs? Who can participate in these innovations, and to what extent? How far can an individual or a group innovate on TCEs without transforming the 'essential' or 'intrinsic' characteristics of the TCEs? Are there any countervailing concepts (e.g. equivalent to those of 'fair use or fair dealing' exceptions to copyright) which deal with public access to protected TCEs? While there are no straightforward answers to these questions in the evolving policies and laws around TCEs, the following sections seek to provide some background on the state of laws and reforms relevant to the topic. We begin by exploring how current IP regimes relate to the protection of TCEs. After identifying some unresolved areas, we look at contemplated reforms at the national, regional and international levels.

3. Limited protection of traditional cultural expressions through copyright, moral rights and design rights

Attempts to address the protection of TCEs through IP are not new. The issue of IP protection of folklore was already raised at the 1967 Stockholm revision of the Berne Convention.[25] While the insertion of an article into the Berne Convention to deal with 'the case of unpublished works where the identity of the author is unknown' (Article 15(4)) was intended to address the issue, doubts have persisted over the adequacy of copyright as a vehicle to protect TCEs.[26] Many TCEs are communally

[23] She adds that 'the distinctiveness of the resulting striking colored cloth translated into a source of prestige for local communities and centers of power rather than any sense that the purity of indigenous tradition had been diluted' (ibid., p. 68).

[24] Strom, S. 2008, 'Maasai Beadwork for Sale: Destruction of Culture or Perpetuation of Traditional Handicraft?' (manuscript on file with author).

[25] Berne Convention for the Protection of Literary and Artistic Works (Berne, 9 September 1886), *as revised at* Stockholm, 14 July 1967, 828 U.N.T.S. 222 (*entered into force* 29 January 1970).

[26] See Ficsor, M. 2005, 'The Protection of Traditional Cultural Expressions/Folklore', paper presented at the WIPO National Seminar on Copyright, Related Rights, and Collective Management,

created, for example, and do not fit easily within the notions of 'individual' authorship typically emphasized under national copyright laws (see Chapter 8).[27] There are also inherent difficulties in accommodating most TCEs within long-held copyright concepts such as originality, fixation, a fixed term of protection and 'fair dealing' or 'fair use' (Torsen 2008).[28] As such, communities guided by shared, customary practices tend to find limited solutions within copyright laws for the protection of their TCEs.

Under most national laws, TCEs which do not satisfy conditions for existing forms of IP protection would, by default, fall within the public domain. By way of example, indigenous art will frequently use traditional iconography, such as iconography found in archaeological sites and imbedded in the local culture. This iconography is considered to be part of the public domain in many countries and is usually not protected through copyright legislation.[29] Meanwhile, more and more 'souvenirs', jewellery and other crafts featuring traditional iconography are being mass-produced by third parties, often in countries other than the country of origin. Iconography is also copied or adapted for commercial use in designer and decoration trends. This tends to blur the cultural identity associated with some iconography and does not provide for re-distribution of profits towards the country of origin and especially towards the communities that practise and preserve some of these traditions.

Torsen (2008, p. 203) notes that copyright can be an option for TCE protection if the custodians grant permission to individual artists within the community to make new, 'original' art based on TCEs. There are some cases in Australia where the courts have stretched copyright protection to cover 'original' works based on TCEs. In the *Bulun Bulun* case, an image of the artist's painting 'Magpie Geese and Water Lilies at the Waterhole', based on the heritage of the Ganalbingu people to which he belonged, was reproduced by third parties on textile made in Indonesia and imported into Australia.[30] The artist, John Bulun Bulun, successfully brought

28 February–2 March 2005, Khartoum, Doc. WIPO/CR/KRT/05/8, available at: http://www.wipo.int/edocs/mdocs/arab/en/wipo_cr_krt_05/wipo_cr_krt_05_8.pdf (accessed 24 March 2010).

27 The communal nature of TCEs has been assumed in most discussions in relation to IPRs (see e.g. De Obaldia 2006) although creative processes in traditional communities may in fact have both individual and communal elements. Drawing on anthropological fieldwork conducted among the Nekgini speaking people on the Rai Coast of Papua New Guinea, Leach (2005, p. 31) qualifies that creativity in indigenous groups should not be 'imagined simplistically' as always the result of 'communal production, making cultural resources something resembling a tribal commons'. His research suggests, for example, that ownership of tunes and designs may be attached to particular persons in a community and handed down as heirlooms, even though this does not translate into private property concepts in the West (ibid., pp. 33–36). Drawing from examples in the Madang area of Papua New Guinea, he suggests that it is useful to think of ownership over TCEs, rather, in terms of 'multiple ownership' (ibid.).

28 See Torsen (2008) for an extended discussion on the relevance for TCEs of provisions under the Berne Convention for the Protection of Literary & Artistic Works (9 September 1886), *as revised at* Paris, 24 July 1971, *and amended* 28 September 1979, 1161 U.N.T.S. 30. See also UNDP 2005, pp. 12–14. Note that there is significant variation across national jurisdictions on the precise conditions for copyright subsistence; fixation, for example, is not required in all jurisdictions.

29 Note, however, that iconography and motifs including sacred motifs may be given some protection from offensive use in third party's trademarks under trademarks legislation in some jurisdictions. See Section 4.3 of this chapter; see further Frankel 2008.

30 *Bulun Bulun & Anor v. R & T Textiles Pty.* [1998] AILR 39, paras. 1–2 (von Doussa, J.) (Federal Court of Australia) ('Bulun Bulun' case).

an action for infringement by importation under the Australian copyright law. Recognizing the creation as an original work, the Federal Court of Australia held that copyright to the work resided with the artist John Bulun Bulun. One question was whether the community also had rights over the work. Among other arguments by the plaintiffs, the suggestion that the community might be considered joint-authors for the work failed before the court.[31] While the Federal Court of Australia found that there could be no 'communal title' to and group ownership of the copyright in the artistic work, whether under common law or the Copyright Act 1968, it nevertheless held that there was a fiduciary relationship between the artist and his clan which arose from the 'use with permission by Mr. Bulun Bulun of ritual knowledge of the Ganalbingu people, and the embodiment of that knowledge within the artistic work' in accordance with the law and customs of the Ganalbingu people.[32] It followed that equity law 'imposes on him [the artist] obligations as a fiduciary not to exploit the artistic work in a way that is contrary to the laws and custom of the Ganalbingu people, and, in the event of infringement by a third party, to take reasonable and appropriate action to restrain and remedy infringement of the copyright in the artistic work'.[33] The court did not find, however, that the Ganalbingu people had an equitable interest in the ownership of the copyright in the work, which rested with the artist himself. While the decision has been critiqued by commentators as failing to recognize the copyright of communities (Bowrey 2006; Anderson 2009), the court's reference to customary laws in determining the fiduciary relationship and duties of the artist to the community remains highly significant. The court found that the 'artist is required to act in relation to the artwork in the interests of the Ganalbingu people to preserve the integrity of their culture, and ritual knowledge'.[34]

While national copyright laws cannot typically accommodate communal claims to copyright over TCEs, there are some exceptions.[35] Geismar (2005, pp. 451–453) notes, for example, that copyright law has been adopted (though not as yet gazetted) in Vanuatu to cover communal TCEs.[36] There are also regional attempts to design *sui generis* protection for TCEs based, it would seem, on adaptation of copyright laws (see Section 6). To what extent these hybrid laws depart from provisions in the Berne Convention (1971 Paris Act, as amended in 1979) or from copyright principles more generally remains to be fully explored. While a re-definition of authorship (and 'joint-authorship') in copyright law to accommodate communal copyright ownership does not seem too far-fetched an idea, more fundamental challenges might be posed, for example, by attempts to protect TCEs perpetually through

31 Ibid., para. 91. This case is also discussed in Chapter 8 of this book, especially in relation to 'joint-authorship'.

32 Ibid., paras. 53, 76.

33 Ibid., para. 85.

34 Ibid., para. 78.

35 Countries such as Vanuatu, Indonesia, Tunisia, Sri Lanka, Bolivia, Panama, Chile, Kenya, Mali, Congo, Ghana and Togo have tried to provide protection of TCEs in the framework of their copyright laws, and some (Congo, Ghana and Sri Lanka) have made perpetual protection explicit in their laws (WIPO 1998).

36 See the provisions for protecting 'expressions of indigenous culture' under the Republic of Vanuatu Copyright and Related Rights Act No. 42 of 2000, full text available at: http://www.paclii.org/vu/legis/num_act/carra2000282 (accessed 1 March 2010).

copyright given the conventional approach to copyright as time-limited. Furthermore, Indigenous Declarations such as the Mataatua Declaration on Cultural and Intellectual Property Rights of Indigenous Peoples have called for 'retroactive coverage of historical as well as contemporary works', noting that these ideas do not fit neatly within existing copyright concepts.[37]

What about moral rights? Unlike copyright and neighbouring rights, moral rights comprise a bundle of rights which are non-pecuniary in nature (see discussion in Chapter 8). These include, for example, the author's right of paternity (i.e. the right to receive attribution for his work) and the right of integrity in the work, in terms of preventing distortion and/or destruction. The nature and boundaries of moral rights vary significantly with jurisdictions. They are perpetual and inalienable in some jurisdictions, and in this sense could potentially be interesting for the protection of TCEs where the custodians call for perpetual protection. However, as with copyright, moral rights attach to individual creators and do not typically apply to rights of communities, although specific legislation on 'indigenous communal moral rights'[38] has been considered in Australia (Torsen 2005, p. 7; see Anderson 2009b, pp. 209–217).

Some TCEs may be protectable by IPRs in relation to designs, depending on the national jurisdiction. However, a not uncommon qualification under design laws is that the design must fulfil the condition, among others, of 'novelty' (as in the case, e.g. of registered designs under the Community Designs Regulation in the European Community),[39] even though such conditions are usually less strict than the novelty requirements under patent law (Cornish & Llewelyn 2003, p. 544). Thus, while contemporary adaptations of traditional designs may in some cases be protectable by design law, truly old designs from TCEs may not be protectable (see WIPO 2003). It has furthermore been suggested that hand-woven textiles and handicrafts may not be protected in countries where there is a requirement that protected designs be capable of industrial replication (ibid., p. 46).

Thus, protection for TCEs in existing IP regimes such as copyright, moral rights and design rights under most national systems are likely to be more applicable to new renditions of TCEs. Where the IP laws in question specify standards of 'originality' or novelty, it is unlikely that pre-existing TCEs would pass the test. However,

[37] The Mataatua Declaration on Cultural and Intellectual Property Rights of Indigenous Peoples, First International Conference on the Cultural & Intellectual Property Rights of Indigenous Peoples, Whakatane, 12-18 June 1993, Aotearoa, New Zealand, available at: http://www.wipo.int/export/sites/www/tk/en/folklore/creative_heritage/docs/mataatua.pdf (accessed 3 December 2009). The Declaration recommended that states, national and international organizations 'note that existing protection mechanisms are insufficient for the protection of Indigenous Peoples Cultural and Intellectual Property Rights' (Article 2.3).

[38] The draft *Copyright Amendment (Indigenous Communal Moral Rights) Bill* 2003 has not been made readily available to the public and may perhaps be on the legislative 'back-burner' (pers. comm. Jane Anderson, 3 December 2009). See also New South Wales Government Aboriginal Education website, 'Indigenous Communal Moral Rights (ICMR)', available at: http://ab-ed.boardofstudies.nsw.edu.au/go/aboriginal-art/protecting-australian-indigenous-art/background-information/proposals-for-change/indigenous-communal-moral-rights-icmr (accessed 15 April 2010). See discussion of the Bill in Anderson 2009b, p. 211.

[39] Council Regulation (EC) 6/2002 of 12 December 2001 on community designs, OJ No. L 3 (2002); see also Commission Regulation (EC) 2245/2002 of 21 October 2002 implementing Council Regulation (EC) 6/2002 on community designs, OJ No. L 341 (2002).

von Lewinski (2007) points out that works made in the context of TCEs may in some cases be protected by copyright and neighbouring rights (e.g. rights relating to performers, sound-recording producers and broadcasters) even where the TCEs themselves do not meet existing thresholds for such protection. She notes that 'different kinds of recording of folklore may result in protection for the recordings rather than the folklore itself' (ibid., p. 213). In her words:

> A photographer who fixes folklore will receive copyright in the photographic work or a neighbouring right in a non-copyrightable photograph; the producer of a recording of folklore music or the producer of a film fixing folklore dances can be protected as a phonogram producer or a film producer respectively in relation to the phonograph or film (as opposed to the folklore as such). Also, researchers who collect expressions of folklore and arrange them in a certain order may be protected for such collections (i.e. not the folklore itself) if the general copyright conditions for collections are fulfilled. Performers of folklore may be protected in respect of their performances (not the folklore as such) and even have to be so under recent international law, namely article 2(a) of the WIPO Performances and Phonograms Treaty....(Ibid.)

According to von Lewinski, in most of these cases the indigenous communities would not in fact benefit from such protection, 'since they usually do not make fixations or collections of their own folklore' (ibid.).[40] However, she points out that performers of folklore will often stem from indigenous communities and therefore benefit from protection in their performances, so that 'the communities may be protected indirectly in respect of the folklore performed' (ibid.) As explored in Section 7 of this chapter, there are legal developments as well as soft-law measures seeking to address issues of indigenous peoples' consent for third-party access, use and recordings relating to their TCEs. Indigenous peoples and other custodians of TCEs are also increasingly at the helm of the recorder or camera (e.g. in participatory video) for their own performances or other rituals. Among other purposes, this might be for their inter-generational transmission of TCEs, language and other bio-cultural heritage.[41] Particular issues have been raised in relation to dissemination, whether by the custodians or third parties, of indigenous cultural expressions through media including the Internet (Deer 2009). This is discussed briefly in Section 7.

4. Labels denoting origin and other characteristics

Labelling devices such as trademarks, collective marks, certification marks and geographical indications may be relevant for denoting the origin, 'authenticity' or other characteristics associated with TCEs. In this sense, they may be helpful to indigenous communities trying to distinguish their renditions of TCEs from copies by

[40] This is changing, however, as indigenous communities themselves explore means to record some forms of their TCEs for purposes including preservation and transmission.

[41] On IP implications for such documentation, see WIPO's 'Creative Heritage Project' in relation to the development of 'IP Guidelines for Documenting, Recording and Digitizing Intangible Cultural Heritage', available at: http://www.wipo.int/tk/en/folklore/culturalheritage/index.html; see also Torsen 2008, pp. 213–214.

third parties. Historically, these forms of IP developed separately from patents and copyright, with objectives and functions distinct from the latter IPRs. While ideas of 'originality' or 'novelty' are part of the criteria for copyright and patents, respectively, labelling devices such as certification marks and geographical indications (GIs) can potentially be used by a community to reflect the traditional practices and concepts of 'authenticity' associated with their TCEs and other cultural heritage. As Zografos (2007, p. 178) notes, such labelling devices can 'reward the goodwill accumulated over time' and potentially provide for indefinite protection (this depends on any conditions, formalities or fees for renewal within a jurisdiction). At the same time, it should be qualified at the outset that these tools are primarily used within the context of trade, and like other forms of IPRs bring with them issues relating to the treatment of TCEs as products discussed in Section 2. The latter issues are not repeated here.

4.1. Trademarks, collective marks and certification marks

A trademark is basically a sign indicating trade origin of good and services (Bently 2008, p. 3). This distinctive sign can be owned (as a form of IP) by one or more individuals, one or more business organizations or any other legal entity (Das 2008). According to Article 15.1 of the TRIPs Agreement: 'Any sign, or any combination of signs, capable of distinguishing the goods or services of one undertaking from those of other undertakings, shall be capable of constituting a trademark'. . . . These marks operate as indicators of the trade source from which good or services come (or are in some other way connected) and may symbolize qualities associated by consumers with certain good or services (Cornish & Llewelyn 2003, p. 587). They can also serve to associate the reputation of a particular manufacturer or service provider with the good or service to which the trademark is attached. A WIPO-commissioned case study suggests that trademarks may be useful for indigenous peoples to protect their trade interests, though pointing out several shortfalls in this endeavour, such as the requirement to use the trademark (Janke 2003).

As far back as 1909, the trademark 'Harris Tweed' was introduced in the UK for tweed from the Outer Hebrides, Scotland, when competitors from the mainland set up industrial looms (Dutfield & Suthersanen 1998, pp. 193–194; Donkin 2001, p. 23).[42] This interesting example is discussed further in Box 5.1. Donkin (2001, p. 35) notes that:

> Governmental legislation can define standards of authenticity, thus protecting crafts products from competition from imitative industrial products. The identification of authenticity criteria for use in marketing has been successfully developed with regards to food products characteristic of a particular region and produced by a skilled and often manual process . . . However, despite notable exceptions such as Harris Tweed from the Outer Hebrides, such labelling is slower to be applied to crafts and is notable by its absence from British and European standards.

[42] The trademark testifies that the cloth concerned has been 'hand woven' by the islanders at their homes in the Outer Hebrides and made of pure virgin wool dyed and spun in the Hebrides (Donkin 2001, p. 23).

BOX 5.1. The story of the Harris Tweed trademark

Harris Tweed is a cloth made in the Scottish islands of Lewis, Harris, Uist and Barra, which together form a large part of an area known as the Outer Hebrides; it is handwoven and made from wool that is spun and dyed in the Outer Hebrides (Dutfield & Suthersanen 2008, pp. 193–194). While mechanization during the Industrial Revolution transformed production in other areas, the Outer Hebrides continued to make cloth entirely by hand, and it remained to a large extent a cottage industry (ibid.). From the mid-nineteenth century, this cloth became popular throughout the UK. At the time, the raw material, wool, was produced locally and part of it would have been used in its natural uncoloured state; the rest was dyed. In the nineteenth century vegetable dyes were used. The dyeing, spinning, and weaving of the wool into tweed followed traditional methods and 'was often accompanied by songs in Gaelic' (ibid.).[43] Around the beginning of the twentieth century, a degree of modernization took place and production increased in consequence. The Harris Tweed Association applied for a trademark to help the producers compete in a market in which industrial spinning mills able to mass-produce cloth were threatening to force out the small producers. The Harris Tweed mark, which was granted in 1909, comprises the words 'Harris Tweed' with an orb and a Maltese cross and has since become very well known. The official definition of Harris Tweed then was 'a tweed, hand-spun, hand-woven and dyed by the crofters and cottars in the Outer Hebrides'.

In 1934, the trademark definition was changed to the following: 'Harris Tweed means a tweed made from pure virgin wool produced in Scotland, spun, dyed and finished in Outer Hebrides and hand-woven by the islanders at their own homes in the Islands of Lewis, Harris, Uist, Barra and their several purtenances and all known as the Outer Hebrides'. This allows for increased production while ensuring that it was still at least to some extent a tradition-bound cottage industry. Production reached a peak of 7.6 million yards in 1966, but subsequently began to contract as Harris Tweed became less fashionable, and the British textiles industry, once the world's largest, was about to begin shrinking in the face of competition from lower cost producers overseas. To be more competitive, it was felt necessary to retrain weavers, introduce tougher standards and better meet new demands, including for softer, lighter cloth (ibid.). In 1993, the UK government came to the producers' aid by passing legislation, the Harris Tweed Act. The law set up the Harris Tweed Authority, a statutory body, in place of the Harris Tweed Association.

Source: Dutfield & Suthersanen 2008, pp. 193–194

[43] See Harris Tweed Authority website, available at: http://www.harristweed.org/ (accessed 24 March 2010).

Until recently, Labels of Authenticity have been used in Australia to identify works of Aboriginal origins. Janke (2003, p. 135) notes that these labels registered as trademarks under the country's laws were designed in response to the many imitation products that were flooding the indigenous arts market, and to assist consumers in identifying authentically produced indigenous art and cultural products. The 'Label of Authenticity' mark in Australia denotes that any work to which that label is attached is the authentic work of an Aboriginal or Torres Strait Islander. Notably, there has also been a registered 'Collaboration Mark' which denotes that any work to which this label is attached is the result of a collaboration in which an Aboriginal or Torres Strait Islander has a significant creative input, and is the subject of a fair agreement with the non-indigenous manufacturer.

Similarly, in New Zealand, the 'Toi Iho' Māori Made Mark is a registered trademark that has been used exclusively for artists of Māori descent, while two further marks have been used to acknowledge cross-cultural ventures between Māori and non-Māori – the 'Toi Iho' Mainly Māori Mark and the 'Toi Iho' Māori Co-production Mark. In the case of the 'Toi Iho' Labels of Authenticity, the Arts Council of New Zealand Toi Aotearoa (also known as 'Creative New Zealand') has elaborated detailed rules that govern usage of each of the 'Toi Iho' marks (see discussion in Chalk & Dunlop, p. 978). Under the New Zealand Trade Marks Act, the Commissioner of Trade Marks must approve regulations governing use of certification marks,[44] including 'Toi Iho' Labels of Authenticity.

While Chalk and Dunlop (2009, p. 978) suggest that the system for regulating and using the 'Toi Iho' Labels of Authenticity have resulted in the marks being more widespread in New Zealand compared to the parallel Labels of Authenticity in Australia, it is notable that the use of Labels of Authenticity in both countries is being discontinued at the time of writing.[45] This holds lessons for these and other jurisdictions in exploring and designing viable protection for TCEs. Anderson (2009b, p. 206) discusses how some inherent problems with the Labels of Authenticity in the Australian context 'ultimately contributed to their demise as an idea and a practical tool'. She observes, firstly, that 'in defining authenticity, it was difficult to escape historically informing categorisation and constructions of "Aboriginality" that remained as remnant markers in the art world' (ibid.).[46] Secondly, the nationwide 'pan-Aboriginal' label apparently 'left little room for an appreciation of indigenous individual, family, clan or community and/or cultural diversity within the Labels' (ibid., pp. 205–206). Thirdly, there was the practical problem of who was to certify, distribute, regulate and police the labels, along with issues for funding for such administration (ibid., p. 207). This topic is revisited later in the discussion on certification marks.

Collective marks are usually given to an association of traders to show that a member belongs to the association (Cornish & Llewelyn 2003, p. 864),[47] and to distinguish the goods or services of members of that association from those of others (Das 2008, p. 473). They thus serve to indicate trade origin although their definitions vary across national jurisdictions. They can be registered in the name of a collective entity, such as an association of producers, manufacturers, traders or service providers. While owned by the legal entity in question (typically an association or cooperative), a collective mark can be designed to be *used* by all members of the said association. In this sense, there can be 'communal' use of the mark. The association may often set its own standards, which its members must meet when using

44 Trade Marks Act 2002 (NZ), section 5.

45 On the recent situation in New Zealand, see *Creative New Zealand Statement on Disinvestment in 'Toi Iho'*, available at: http://www.toiiho.com/Home/tabid/227/Default.aspx (accessed 10 December 2009).

46 According to Anderson (2009, p. 206), 'this was most evident in the way many Aboriginal artists, often utilizing non-traditional styles and mediums, refused to be part of a national Aboriginal labelling system'.

47 Cornish and Llewelyn (2003, p. 864) note that collective marks are new to the UK register, though they are well known in other European countries. They point out that European Community trademarks may be collective.

the mark (ibid., p. 474). Collective marks need not indicate, however, anything about quality of the goods.

Certification marks convey the message that the relevant goods or services have been examined, tested or in some way certified by the registered proprietor of the mark as to characteristics such as origin, material, mode of manufacture of the goods or performance of the services, quality or precision (ibid., p. 473). They do not necessarily indicate trade origin, although in some cases they do. Certification marks can transmit information on natural and human conditions that accompany the production of the protected goods. Such considerations are assuming a growing importance in consumer decisions. For example, the public in many countries increasingly takes into account such ethical considerations as the absence of child labour and good practices in animal care in their purchasing decisions, along with environmental concerns including the sustainable use of resources and low-carbon footprints. A plethora of areas – for example, fair trade, workplace safety, conflict-free diamonds – may be the subject of certification as to standards of 'social responsibility' or 'sustainability' (see Chon 2009, pp. 116–117). These characteristics are not necessarily perceptible directly from the product, but can be certified with reference to prevailing standards or evolving good practices, as well as quality control systems.[48] The certification must come from a reliable source, on the other hand, and Chon (2009) highlights the need for competent authorities to monitor the growing number of certifiers in these areas.[49]

'Fair Trade' marks have been used mainly on agricultural products (DeCarlo 2007), although they have potential for the promotion of indigenous TCEs and TK-based products. The insistence on fair recompense to producers in different local contexts coincides, for example, with social calls for the rejection of sweatshop conditions of labour. This would be relevant in distinguishing crafts produced directly by TCE custodians from 'serial' imitations mass-produced by third parties under poor labour conditions.[50] 'Fair Trade' is but one form of certification. Marks certifying sustainable use of resources are also relevant to the promotion of TCEs.[51] Other certification marks can potentially be designed specially to draw attention to characteristics specific to TCEs. For example, certification may refer to the 'traditional' or 'artisanal' elements that have entered into the making of a craft. It could go further in conveying the message that a certain craft has been created by custodians of the TCEs, using traditional motifs, methods and materials. Concrete obligations could be clearly outlined and binding on those who obtain such 'TCE friendly'

48 See Crespi & Marette 2003; McCluskey & Loureiro 2003; Boizot et al. 2004; Berges et al. 2006.

49 As Chon (2009, p. 106) asserts within the context of the US: 'Several commentators have observed that virtually no overarching entity, whether public or private, is monitoring certification quality. Consumers may be removed from this process altogether, or at the very least, several steps from quality control'.

50 Chon notes, on the other hand, that 'developing countries and their stakeholders have complained about the anticompetitive effects of standards, even sustainability standards, especially in areas where they may have a comparative advantage, such as agriculture or labor costs' (2009, pp. 137–138).

51 By way of example, the important role of indigenous communities from the Amazon in conserving the rainforest can be validated and promoted, among other ways, through prices of their crafts based on sustainable use of natural resources.

certification. Consideration should also be given as to who would own the collective mark and the eventual cost of using the said mark.

The Labels of Authenticity discussed earlier in relation to Aboriginal and Māori art in Australia and New Zealand respectively are a form of certification marks registered as trademarks in those countries (Janke 2003, p. 135; Frankel 2008). The experience in those countries with using (and discontinuing) those marks perhaps provide lessons for other attempts at certification of TCEs. In relation to the protection of TCEs in Australia, for example, Anderson (2009b, p. 208) sees hope in a localized, community-based system of certification, particularly in light of difficulties associated with the nationwide Labels of Authenticity for works of Aboriginal origin (see discussion earlier). In her words:

> On reflection it is always easier to point to the shortcomings of the Labels. But the current localized success of community labelling perhaps points to a way forward. Cultural identity, respect and responsibility, the key elements that Wells[52] identified as what certain communities interpreted authenticity to be, can be delivered when each community is given certain tools to choose for themselves how artists within communities are to be represented to the market. For many artists within communities, it is the association with familial relationships as well as the community itself that is fundamental to identity, respect and responsibility. Shifting these to an amorphous category named 'Aboriginal' was never going to work where people have (to say the least) pride and responsibility to the familial networks, clan relations, the broader community and importantly the land. (Ibid.)

4.2. Geographical indications

Geographical indications present another, often discussed, form of IP of relevance to TCEs.[53] Article 22(1) of the TRIPS Agreement defines geographical indications as 'indications which identify a good as originating in the territory of a Member, or a region or locality in that territory, where a given quality, reputation or other characteristic of the good is essentially attributable to its geographical origin'.[54] Under Article 23 of the TRIPS Agreement, additional protection applies to spirits and wines, for which the EU, for example, has a strong export market. This is a point of contention at the World Trade Organization (WTO) where some member states are pushing for an extension of this special treatment to products beyond wine and spirits. There is currently an uneven protection for GIs around the world.[55]

[52] See Wells, K. 1993, 'Authenticity-Promotion and Protection of Aboriginal and Torres Strait Islander Art', Paper on Research and Development, presented as preliminary advice to the National Indigenous Arts Advocacy Association (NIAAA), 15 June 1995.

[53] Frequently GIs have Regulatory Councils that may require competing producer associations, public and private institutions to collaborate, including municipalities, technological centers, universities, chambers of commerce, cultural institutions, among others. Such associative qualities have strong social repercussions.

[54] The protection of GIs is not mandatory under the TRIPS Agreement, and can be addressed through trademarks or collective marks.

[55] The existence and regulation of GIs varies across jurisdictions. For a comparison of national laws in different regions, see the Organization for an International Geographical Indications Network (OriGIn) website, 'GI Protection in National Jurisdictions', available at: http://www.origin-gi.com/index.php?

One form of GIs is the 'appellation of origin'. Under the Lisbon Agreement, 'appellation of origin' means 'the geographical name of a country, region, or locality, which serves to designate a product originating therein, the quality and characteristics of which are due exclusively or essentially to the geographical environment, including natural and human factors' (Article 2.1).[56] Some examples of appellations of origin are 'Bordeaux' for wine and 'Lentilles Vertes Du Puy' for lentils.[57]

Like certification marks, GIs can convey natural and human elements associated with a product. While most GIs pertain to wines and spirits, food and agricultural products, examples of GIs in crafts include those used in France like Poterie de Vallauris for pottery and Toile de Chalet for cloth. Crafts such as Talavera ceramic and Bohemia crystal are covered also under the Lisbon Agreement.[58] In Peru, GI protection for ceramic has recently been obtained for Chulucanas. In Russia, GIs protect several 'old world' industries such as Gorodets painting, Rostov enamel and various toys (see Torsen 2005, p. 6). Certification marks often complement a GI but could be for products that do not meet strict GI criteria.

As von Lewinski (2007, p. 213) observes, along with trademarks, GIs may be a viable way of indirectly protecting expressions of folklore that are marketed. She suggests that 'these intellectual property rights may serve the authenticity needs of indigenous peoples by clearly designating the origin of the expressions of folklore and decreasing the market for "copycat" products' (ibid.). Parry (2008, p. 364) asserts, on the other hand, that any functions served by GIs can be better achieved by other legal means, including trademarks and the common law of 'passing off'.[59] In her opinion, GIs are limited by their explicit appeal to 'place' as a 'unique assemblage of inhabitants, environment and associated cultural (artisanal) methods of production' to provide a guarantee of the quality of the products produced in therein (ibid., p. 365).[60] She adds that: 'In order to achieve this handiwork, place must first be made to "sit still". It must be apprehended like a butterfly pinned to a board so that its constituents and their essential character may be examined and known with absolute certainty' (ibid.).

option=com_content&view=article&id=46%3Agi-protection-in-national-jurisdictions&catid=17%3Alegal-info&Itemid=43&lang=en (accessed 14 April 2010); see also the International Trademark Association (INTA) website, available at: http://www.inta.org/index.php?option=com_content&task=view&id=131&Itemid=145&getcontent=3 (accessed 25 March 2010).

56 Lisbon Agreement for the Protection of Appellations of Origin and Their International Registration (Lisbon, 31 October 1958), *as revised at* Stockholm, 14 July 1967, *and amended* 28 September 1979, 923 U.N.T.S. 205 (*entered into force with current regulations* 1 April 2002), available at: http://www.wipo.int/export/sites/www/lisbon/en/docs/lisbonagreement.pdf (accessed 3 February 2010).

57 See WIPO, 'Search Appellations of Origin (Lisbon Express)' database, available at http://www.wipo.int/ipdl/en/lisbon/search-struct.jsp (accessed 24 March 2010).

58 See the list on WIPO, 'Lisbon System for the International Registration of Appellations of Origin', available at: http://www.wipo.int/lisbon/en/ (accessed 24 March 2010).

59 In contrast, Gangjee (2008, p. 382) argues that GI law addresses challenges beyond the ambit of trademark law. Amongst other examples, he notes that trademark doctrine continues to view a geographical term either as a descriptive expression open to all or as an expression capable of individual appropriation through acquired distinctiveness, 'but is uncomfortable with a collective, geographical yet "brand"-like and distinctive usage'. See his discussion on pp. 396–397; see also Bently 2008, p. 30.

60 Parry (2008, p. 365) asserts that 'this reactionary claiming of a imaginary, unchanging identity (of both place and its constituents) necessarily denies the myriad ways in which both are every day remade through productive engagement with local and global communities' (citations omitted).

Gangjee (2008) offers a contrasting view. Examining the evolution of laws creating the Apellation d'Origine Contrôlée (AOC) regime for wine regulation in France – a history that has shaped much of the thinking and international legal architecture for the protection of GIs – he argues that the incorporation of traditional know-how ('*savoir faire*') and cultural heritage elements into concepts of '*terroir*' leads to a social construction of place which is not static (ibid., pp. 382, 396).[61] Gangjee furthermore notes that GIs are about recognizing traditional skills and innovations, 'while leaving the production practices to flow freely across national borders and boundaries' (ibid., p. 397). In other words, devices such as GIs, trademarks and certification or collective marks offer some degree of legal protection for originators of TCEs while leaving others free to access (and innovate on) methods of producing works based on TCEs, as long as they do not falsely claim authenticity of those reproductions or derivative works.

Meanwhile, the Organization for an International Geographical Indications Network (orIGIn), an association which is said to represent more than a million producers of traditional products from more than thirty countries, asserts that GIs are potential instruments for sustainable development in providing benefits for producers, consumers and local communities.[62] Zago and Pick (2002) suggest various economic justifications for GIs,[63] including protection to producers from unfair competition. Instruments like GIs have also been described as 'persuasive tools' to change consumer preferences over time (Yue, Marette & Beghin 2006). Like certification marks, they can arguably help to nurture over time a mindset and pattern of consumer social responsibility towards indigenous originators of arts and handicrafts.

India has passed legislation relating to GIs.[64] Interestingly, the Indian Act provides for protection of all 'homonymous' products (and not only wines and spirits) to a level of protection similar to Art 23 of the TRIPs Agreement (see Section 10 of the Act; Das 2008, p. 485). GIs have been applied for in relation to a variety of product types under the Indian Act. Apart from agricultural items (such as Darjeeling and Kangra Teas, respectively, and Mysore Betel vine) they have been issued to such art and handicraft items as Pochampalli Ikat, Kotpad Handloom fabric, Mysore Silk, Kullu shawls, Channapatna Toys and Dolls, Kasuti Embroidery, Orissa Ikat and Mysore Traditional Paintings (see tables in Das 2008, 2010). Some of these GIs overlap with indigenous peoples' TCEs. Whether similar GI protection might be explored in other developing countries remains to be seen. Dutfield and

61 '*Terroir*' is a key ingredient in differentiating between wines by reference to a distinct origin under the Apellation d'Origine Contrôlée (AOC) regime in France (Gangjee 2008, p. 383). Gangjee notes that at least three overlapping narratives have arisen, viewing '*terroir*' as (i) holistic and mystical, (ii) geographical and deterministic, and (iii) an evolving composite of nature and human factors (ibid.). While the first two narratives are built on an assumption of 'static place', 'the third begins to shake off its influence' (ibid.).

62 See the oriGIn website, 'Background Information', available at: www.origin-gi.com/index.php?option=com_content&view=article&id=32&Itemid=32&lang=en (accessed 24 March 2010).

63 Zago and Pick (2002) have developed an econometric formula which attempts to measure the effects on welfare of a GI declaration.

64 Geographical Indications of Goods (Registration & Protection) Act 1999 (*entered into force* 15 September 2003) [hereinafter 'Indian Act']. For a detailed and recent discussion of the Indian Act, see Das 2008.

Suthersanen (2008, p. 197) note that: 'At present the potential of geographical indications for developing countries is somewhat speculative because this type of intellectual property right has been used only in a few countries outside Europe. Moreover, many GIs have quite small markets, and a relatively small number are traded internationally'. In another study, Musungu (2008, pp. 13, 15) explores the potential benefits and challenges of GI protection for African countries, in relation to agricultural and cultural products (including handicrafts). It is observed in the study that legal means for the protection of GIs (whether through specific GI laws or through trademark regimes) are available in all but six African countries (ibid., pp. v, 8–11). Nevertheless, very few African GIs are registered either in the African country of origin or third countries (ibid., p. v). To help developing countries in Africa and elsewhere to determine appropriate strategies and legal reforms in relation to GIs, the study calls for 'interdisciplinary empirical research at country and producer levels including specific case studies on particular products' (ibid., p. 24; see also Zografos 2008).

4.3. Third-party use of indigenous insignia and motifs on products

Indigenous peoples and local communities in different parts of the world are increasingly grappling with third-party use of marks (in relation to products or services) which bear in part or in full their indigenous terms and motifs. They are often uncertain in such cases of their position in relation to free prior and informed consent (FPIC), the availability of legal remedies and other practical options. In some cases, the indigenous communities involved may indeed be oblivious to the use (and existing or potential registration) by third parties of trademarks bearing their traditional insignia and motifs. On this evolving topic, it may be observed that trademark laws and treaties do not typically contain specific prohibitions on registering indigenous names or symbols as trademarks, nor any mention of duties to obtain FPIC from indigenous groups for such use and to provide for benefit-sharing.[65] Some exceptions under domestic laws are explored later. In general, trademark rights are awarded on a first-to-use or first-to-register basis, depending on the country or regional system, without consideration of any 'cultural' entitlement rights. Nevertheless, to avoid the registration of indigenous names and symbols by non-indigenous applicants, some absolute refusal (and invalidation) grounds could be applicable under the trademark law procedure in a country. While such grounds would vary with national laws and circumstances of the case, refusal (or invalidation) of a trademark registration by third parties involving indigenous insignia might be based on the 'non-distinctiveness' of a mark, or on evidence that the use of the mark is misleading, deceitful, in bad faith, culturally offensive or scandalous.[66]

[65] The same discussion may be applicable to domain names incorporating indigenous names.

[66] See, for example, US Lanham Act, 15 U.S.C. § 1052(a); UK Trade Marks Act 1994, section 3(3); Trade Marks Act 1995 (Australia), section 42. The Lanham Act provides: 'No trademark by which the goods of the applicant may be distinguished from the goods of others shall be refused registration on the principal register on account of its nature unless it consists of or comprises immoral, deceptive or scandalous matter; or matter which may disparage or falsely suggest a connection with persons, living or dead, institutions, beliefs, or national symbols, or bring them into contempt or disrepute . . . '. Lanham Act, 15 U.S.C. § 1052(a).

An indigenous group may also invoke relative grounds for refusal of a trademark, such as better rights, passing off, unfair benefit and so forth.[67]

The 2002 New Zealand Trade Marks Act contains specific grounds for the refusal of trademarks incorporating Māori names and signs. Offensive use of Māori text and imagery in trademarks, for example, is prevented under the Act.[68] A Māori Trade Marks Advisory Committee has been established under Section 177 of the Act to advise the Commissioner of Trade Marks as to the likely offensiveness of trademarks containing Māori text and imagery to the Māori.[69] The Committee's function is to advise the Commissioner on whether 'the proposed use or registration of a trademark, that is, or appears to be, derivative of a Māori sign, including text and imagery, is, or is likely to be, offensive to Māori'.[70] As Frankel (2008, p. 22) notes, many trademark applications examined by the Committee have been withdrawn by the applicants from the registration process based on the Committee's advice.

Comparing the approaches to culturally offensive marks in different jurisdictions, Frankel (2008, p. 22) suggests that 'a greater level of objection' is available to the Māori in New Zealand than is available to indigenous peoples, for example, under the Lanham Act in the US. She cites the case of Native American petitioners who have been unsuccessful in challenging the registration under the Lanham Act for various marks containing the term 'Redskins' by the Washington Redskins Football Team.[71] This case does not deal directly with third-party use of indigenous insignia or motifs in trademarks, but rather with the use of the term 'Redskins'.[72]

Trademark legislation in some jurisdictions provides for avenues to prevent third-party registration and use of trademarks which are not necessarily culturally offensive. In 2001, the United States Patent and Trademark Office (USPTO) established a database containing the official insignia of all State and federally recognized

67 See, for example, US Lanham Act, 15 U.S.C. § 1052(d); UK Trade Marks Act 1994, section 5; Trade Marks Act 1995 (Australia), section 44.

68 Trade Marks Act 2002 (NZ), section 17(1)(c). Under the absolute grounds for not registering a trade mark in this section, it is provided that the Commissioner must not register any matter as a trade mark or part of a trade mark if the Commissioner considers that the registration or its use 'would be likely to offend a significant section of the community, including Māori' (Trade Marks Act 2002 (NZ), section 17(1)(c)). In 1997, the Māori Trade Mark Focus Group in New Zealand recommended the incorporation of provisions on prior informed consent for trademark registrations (see Māori Trade Mark Focus Group 1997).

69 For more background, see Māori Trade Marks Advisory Committee, 'Background Information', available at: http://www.med.govt.nz/templates/Page____1291.aspx (accessed 24 March 2010); see further Frankel 2008. The latter study compares the approaches of the domestic systems of the US and New Zealand with regard to culturally offensive trademarks and the grounds for opposition in the registration process.

70 Trade Marks Act 2002 (NZ), section 178.

71 See *Pro-Football, Inc. v. Harjo*, 565 F.3d 880 (D.C. Cir. 2009), *aff'g* 567 F. Supp. 2d 46 (D.D.C. 2008); *Pro-Football, Inc. v. Harjo*, 415 F.3d 44 (D.C. Cir. 2005).

72 The Trademark Trial and Appeal Board (TTAB) granted the petition in 1999, finding that the marks 'may be disparaging of Native Americans to a substantial composite of this group of people' and 'may bring Native Americans into contempt or disrepute' in violation of section 2(a) of the US Lanham Act (15 U.S.C. § 1052(a)). *Harjo v. Pro-Football*, Inc., 50 U.S.P.Q.2d 1705, 1748 (T.T.A.B. 1999). Unfortunately, the subsequent appeal decisions offered little guidance on the meaning of 'scandalous matter' or 'matter which may disparage' under section 2(a) of the Lanham Act, because these decisions focused instead on procedural issues. See *Pro-Football, Inc.*, 565 F.3d at 881–886 (where the Court of Appeals affirmed the district court's application of the defence of laches in *Pro-Football, Inc.*, 567 F. Supp. 2d at 62). A petition for hearing by the US Supreme Court was submitted in fall of 2009, but certiorari was denied. See Clayton 2010.

Native American tribes which cannot be registered as trademarks.[73] Section 9 of the Canadian Trade-marks Act forbids the registration of trademarks consisting of or similar to 'any badge, crest, emblem or mark, adopted and used by any public authority, in Canada as an official mark for wares and services'.[74] Some Canadian indigenous groups have used these provisions to register indigenous names or symbols as official marks, thereby forbidding their registration by others under the official marks provisions.[75]

There remains a lacuna in many jurisdictions in terms of specific laws to deal with third-party use of indigenous insignia, and this is an area where international and regional reforms will be useful. The extent to which general provisions in trademark law currently provide for remedies varies with jurisdictions. Public pressure and the fear of negative publicity can also play a strong role in encouraging businesses to be socially responsible to local communities in their use of marks.[76] If the indigenous communities object to the application of a trademark, for example, or request that a registration be voided, there is some likelihood that the trademark applicant or owner will withdraw their application or registration to avoid negative publicity. If substantiated (i.e. accompanied by some supporting evidence) such objections will usually be successful in court, although this varies with jurisdictions. Beyond the legal tools so far discussed, national laws and practices relating to unfair competition may be of additional assistance in dealing with false and misleading claims as to the authenticity and origins of products based on TCEs.[77] The common law tort of 'passing off' may also be relevant.[78]

5. Fixing or innovating?

There are several examples of national initiatives in Asia towards using labels (which may be trademarks or certification marks depending on the legal regime) to promote products of local food and craft industries based on the 'One Village One Product' (OVOP) concept which originated in Oita, Japan, in 1979.[79] Zografos (2007,

[73] See USPTO, 'Frequently Asked Questions About the Database of Native American Tribal Insignia', available at: http://www.uspto.gov/web/offices/tac/tribalfaq.htm. The database is used as an aid in the examination of applications for trademark registration. Section 2(a) of the Lanham Act, 15 U.S.C. § 1052(a), disallows the registration of various marks, including ones which falsely suggest a connection with particular institutions. If a mark that a party wishes to register as a trademark resembles an insignia of a Native American tribe, the USPTO might conclude that use of that mark would falsely suggest a connection with the tribe.

[74] Trade-marks Act (Canada), section 9(1)(n)(iii).

[75] The Snuneymuxw First Nation registered official marks for petroglyph rock carvings created by their ancestors. For a discussion on whether an entity qualifies as a public authority and what entities require such a test, see Spratley 2005.

[76] Corporate social responsibility (CSR) is discussed further in Section 8. See also Chapter 2.

[77] For example, under trade practices law in Australia, proceedings were brought against a company which misrepresented that some of its hand-painted Aboriginal-style souvenirs were 'authentic', 'certified authentic' and/or 'Australian Aboriginal Art', and it was held that these representations were likely to mislead consumers because the majority of the pool of artists who produced the souvenirs were not Aboriginal or of Aboriginal descent. See WIPO 2003, p. 49.

[78] On the law of passing off, see generally Cornish and Llewelyn 2003, pp. 593–628.

[79] See the Oita OVOP website, 'Oita OVOP International Exchange Promotion Committee', available at: http://www.ovop.jp/en/index.html (accessed 15 March 2010).

p. 173) notes that OVOP 'requires people to take up a product or industry distinctive to their region and cultivate it into a nationally and globally accepted one, which reflects pride in the local culture'. Such schemes now exist in many Southeast Asian countries including the 'Satu Kampung, Satu Produk' initiative in Malaysia, the 'One Barangay, One Product' project in the Philippines, the 'Back to Village' campaign in East Java, Indonesia, and the nationwide 'One Tambon, One Product' initiative in Thailand. Cambodia and Laos have started similar projects on a national scale (ibid., p. 175).[80] A presentation paper by the UNESCO Regional Bureau for Education in Asia and Pacific highlights the potential of the OVOP model for replication in other parts of the Asia-Pacific region.[81] It is notable that the 'OVOP' concept has also been applied in Africa through a project in Malawi.[82]

While the original OVOP movement focused on agriculturally based products, the Thai project is significant for TCE protection in that it focuses on the 'ability of the local communities to generate sustained income from effective commercialization of unique products and handicrafts made from locally available materials utilizing local wisdom and skills handed down from generation to generation'.[83] It is thus likely that promotion schemes based on the OVOP model will involve and impact TCEs to some extent. In such schemes, as with other endeavours to 'preserve' or 'promote' TCEs, complex questions may arise in relation to the extent to which innovations can take place while maintaining what are perceived as 'characteristics' typical of the TCEs in question. 'Authenticity' is, of course, a complex concept open to many interpretations and critiques, a full discussion of which is beyond the scope of this chapter (see e.g. Lindholm 2008). Drawing lessons from the French AOC system, Gangjee (2008, pp. 393–394) writes that:

> Authenticity is the accumulated result of collective historical experimentation. In this process, a number of actors including producers, consumers, local groups and political institutions come together to construct the heritage around a product. On occasion, tensions arise between this constructed tradition and the need for innovation, such as disputed decisions about raw materials or methods of production. Moreover, while events leading up the original product specification may have incorporated innovations along the way, why should one presume that at the time of 'fixing' they were the last word?

Innovations on TCEs by the custodians themselves are not uncommon, as seen in the discussions by Boateng (2005, pp. 64–70) in relation to Ghanaian kente

80 Apart from such initiatives, the protection of TCEs in Southeast Asia is said to be at its early stages even though the region possesses a rich and diversified range of TCEs (Zografos 2007, p. 2). On some recent developments in Indonesia, see Antons 2009.

81 See Shaeffer 2005, 'Creative Communities: A Strategy for the 21st Century-UNESCO and the promotion of cultural industries in the context of the Millennium Development Goals', paper presented at the Senior Expert Symposium on 'Asia-Pacific Creative Communities: A Strategy for the 21st Century', 22–26 February 2005, Jodhpur, India, p. 2, http://www.unescobkk.org/fileadmin/user_upload/culture/Cultural_Industries/presentations/Session_One_-_Sheldon_Shaeffer.pdf (accessed 24 March 2010).

82 See the Republic of Malawi – One Village One Product (OVOP) website, available at: http://www.ovop.org.mw (accessed 24 March 2010).

83 Zografos (2007, p. 176), citing the Thai Ministry of Foreign Affairs, One Tambon One Product Project (OTOP).

cloth, by Strom on the trading of Maasai beadwork,[84] and Sunder (2007) in relation to Mysore Silk in India. To what extent (and at what pace) can such innovation take place while still sustaining characteristics that may set the TCEs in question apart from other non-traditional cultural expressions for special legal protection? Arguably, such innovation ought to take place within a gradual evolution of local practices. In relation to the TCEs of indigenous peoples, these boundaries should respect and reflect what the custodians themselves find is consistent with their worldviews, customary laws and practices. These are complex questions, and the extent to which customary laws can be clearly identified and applied to such considerations vary with regions and historical contexts (see examples from different regions in IIED 2008).[85] Bowrey (2006, p. 72) moreover suggests that forms of 'custom' evolve and may appear in contemporary guises, for example, as indigenous cultural protocols (see Section 7).

Customary laws of indigenous communities are also likely to evolve in time in relation and response to the multiple dimensions of human development and aspiration (see UNDP 2004). Gender equality, education (including in native languages) and considerations of inter-generational equity that embrace the rights of children and youths are but a few areas where indigenous actors themselves are pushing for appropriate reforms in their own communities. Consistent with the capability approach discussed in Chapter 1, indigenous actors have to evolve, define and interpret their own customary laws to meet their human development needs, whereas the tendency is for third-party 'translation' of custom to fit within conventional Western legal concepts and frameworks (see Bowrey 2006; Okediji 2007).[86] Gibson (2005, p. 276) further adds that: 'An effective and relevant model of protection must not homogenise the Indigene nor historicise "tradition", but should provide a workable legal concept for the relationship between community and the individual, towards a model for community authority and capacity with respect to traditional knowledge'.

As emphasized in both the ILO Convention No. 169 (Article 8(2); see ILO 2009, p. 81) and the UNDRIP (Article 34), the development of traditional institutions and customs must also be consistent with international human rights standards. The UNESCO Universal Declaration on Cultural Diversity further qualifies that: 'No one may invoke cultural diversity to infringe upon human rights guaranteed by international law, nor to limit their scope' (Article 4; see Anaya 2004, pp. 25–26).[87]

[84] Strom, S. 2008, 'Maasai Beadwork for Sale: Destruction of Culture or Perpetuation of Traditional Handicraft?' (manuscript on file with author).

[85] There may also be disagreement within or among local communities in a region on what customary laws may exist and ought to prevail to govern a certain usage (see Antons 2009).

[86] For historical accounts of British colonial interpretations of indigenous 'customary' laws to suit colonial agendas, see Okediji 2007. Okediji (ibid., pp. 376–377) takes on a critical approach to customary laws in Africa, suggesting that the categorization of certain rules as 'customary' was historically part of a colonial device to emphasize the primacy of foreign-imposed laws.

[87] Article 4 of the United Nations Educational, Scientific and Cultural Organization (UNESCO), Universal Declaration on Cultural Diversity (2 November 2001), 41 I.L.M. 57 (2002), available at: http://unesdoc.unesco.org/images/0012/001271/127160m.pdf (accessed 24 March 2004). Anaya (2004, p. 26) observes the remaining question: 'By what process may it be legitimately determined that a particular cultural practice is illegitimate?' He adds that: 'Whatever the ultimate answer to this question, the internal decision-making dynamics that are themselves part of a cultural group identity should be the starting point' (ibid.).

The next section explores some *sui generis* laws and initiatives which, to different degrees, attempt to address the particular characteristics of TCEs in shaping legal protection for them. Some of the models being explored or implemented – whether internationally, regionally or nationally – include intended linkages to the customary laws and practices of indigenous peoples, although much remains to be achieved in integrating indigenous viewpoints on innovation and creativity into these frameworks, along with customary concepts of rights and responsibilities.

6. Some *sui generis* forms of protection for traditional cultural expressions

The elaboration of the UNESCO-WIPO Model Provisions was an early attempt at *sui generis* solutions for the protection of TCEs. As Mihaly Ficsor, the chairman of the UNESCO/WIPO Committee of Governmental Experts meeting which adopted the Model Provisions in June 1982, described in a presentation paper:

> The Model Provisions, *inter alia*, foresaw a *sui generis system* with a certain authorization procedure for any utilization made both with gainful intent and outside the traditional or customary context of folklore... Among the *acts against which adequate protection is required*, the Model Law indicated (i) use without authorization, (ii) violation of the obligation to indicate the source of folklore expressions, (iii) misleading the public by distributing counterfeit objects as folklore creations (a kind of 'passing off'), and the public use of distorted or mutilated folklore creations in a manner 'prejudicial to the cultural interests of the community concerned' (violation of a kind of collective 'moral right').[88] (Para. 7)

In December 1984, a WIPO/UNESCO group of experts considered a draft treaty for the international protection of expressions of folklore based on the Model Provisions. According to Ficsor, industrialized countries raised two realistic problems in rejecting the proposal, namely, the 'absence of any reliable source of identification of folklore creations in many countries; and the thorny question of "regional folklore", that is, folklore shared by more than one – or sometimes many – countries' (ibid., para. 8). The failure of agreement on an international instrument specifically dealing with folklore or TCEs meant that existing IP regimes have continued to govern this area for many countries, largely by default since these regimes were not originally designed for such purposes.

However, there are legislative initiatives at the national, regional and international levels to provide special protection for TCEs. While the term *sui generis* is often used to describe these initiatives, some frameworks may be essentially adaptations of existing IP concepts and regimes. The approach taken by member countries of the African Intellectual Property Organization (OAPI) through the Bangui Agreement of OAPI (as amended in 1999) ['Bangui Agreement'], for example, is to regard 'expressions of folklore' and their derivative works as works 'constituting

[88] Ficsor, M. 2005, 'The Protection of Traditional Cultural Expressions/Folklore', paper presented at the WIPO National Seminar on Copyright, Related Rights, and Collective Management, 28 February–2 March 2005, Khartoum, Doc. WIPO/CR/KRT/05/8, para. 7, available at: http://www.wipo.int/edocs/mdocs/arab/en/wipo_cr_krt_05/wipo_cr_krt_05_8.pdf (accessed 24 March 2010).

original creations of the mind in the literary, artistic and scientific fields' that can be protected by copyright law (Annex VII, Art. 5).[89] Significantly, the Agreement provides that such expressions need not be fixed on a material medium for copyright protection,[90] a contrast to conventional copyright law which usually requires that the protected expression be embodied in a tangible medium (although there are exceptions such as in Switzerland and some Latin American countries). Under the Bangui Agreement, copyright protection of 'expressions of folklore' is not perpetual but is subject to a copyright term of the author's life plus seventy years (Annex VII, Art. 22). However, the exploitation of such works after they fall into the public domain (upon expiration of the copyright term) is subject to payment of a relevant royalty to a national collective rights administration body, which according to the instrument shall be 'devoted to welfare and cultural purposes' (Annex VII, Art. 59(2)). This *domaine public payant* is an interesting concept which is revisited at the end of this section.

The Model Law for the Protection of Traditional Knowledge and Expressions of Culture (2002) ['Pacific Model Law'] adopted within the Pacific Regional Framework provides a basis or reference for potential reforms of national laws in the region.[91] This model law appears to provide far-reaching rights to custodians of TK or expressions of culture. The Pacific Model Law establishes 'traditional cultural rights' and 'moral rights' in TK or expressions of culture (see Clauses 6, 7 and 13). 'Traditional cultural rights' include rights to authorize and prevent third-party acts such as reproduction, publication, performance, and online distribution of TK and expressions of culture (Clause 7(2)).[92] These rights continue in force in perpetuity, are inalienable, and cannot be waived or transferred (Clauses 9, 10, 13(4)). Under this model law, traditional owners of TK and expressions of culture can be a group, clan or community, or individual 'in whom the custody or protection of the traditional knowledge or expression of culture are entrusted in accordance with the customary law and practices of that group, clan or community' (Clause 4), and these traditional owners are deemed as holders of the traditional cultural rights

[89] African Intellectual Property Organization (OAPI), Agreement Relating to the Creation of an African Intellectual Property Organization, Constituting a Revision of the Agreement Relating to the Creation of an African and Malagasy Office of Industrial Property (Bangui, 2 March 1977), *as amended* 24 February 1999 (revised agreement *entered into force* 28 February 2002), Annex VII, Article 5 [hereinafter 'Bangui Agreement'], available at: http://www.wipo.int/clea/en/text_html.jsp?lang=EN&id=3376 (accessed 26 February 2010).

[90] Ibid., Annex VII, Article 4(2). Performance of expressions of folklore is accorded the same protection as is accorded to other types of performance under the Bangui Agreement (see Annex VII, Art. 48).

[91] Secretariat of the Pacific Community, Regional Framework for the Protection of Traditional Knowledge and Expressions of Culture (2002), pp. 3–15, available at: http://www.forumsec.org/resources/uploads/attachments/documents/PacificModelLaw,Protectionof TKandExprssnsofCulture20021.pdf (accessed 26 February 2010); see also Secretariat of the Pacific Community 2006. According to the Secretariat: '[M]anifestations of intellectual creativity, traditional knowledge and expressions of culture deserve to be accorded the same legal protection that is provided to other forms of intellectual property. Robust measures need to be taken to guarantee the status of and economic support for the clans, groups or communities that are the creators, repository, custodians and trustees of traditional knowledge and expressions of culture' (ibid., p. vii).

[92] See also WIPO Intergovernmental Committee on Intellectual Property and Genetic Resources, Traditional Knowledge and Culture, *Comparative Summary of 'Sui Generis' TCEs Legislation*, Doc. WIPO/GRTKF/IC/5/INF/3 (28 April 2003), Annex, p. 9, available at: http://www.wipo.int/edocs/mdocs/tk/en/wipo_grtkf_ic_5/wipo_grtkf_ic_5_inf_3.pdf (accessed 1 March 2010).

protected by the Model Law (Clause 6). The reference to customary law and practices is particularly significant, and seems to echo some of the Australian Federal Court's openness to considering customary laws in approaching copyright of the TCE in the *Bulun Bulun* case, discussed earlier. In significant contrast to the latter Australian case, however, a 'group, clan or community' can be the holders of rights protected under the South Pacific Model Law.[93] Uses of cultural expressions require prior and informed consent from the traditional owners, for which application must be made through a 'Cultural Authority' or directly to traditional owners (Clauses 15 and 25). An authorized user agreement should contain terms and conditions including, among other things, sharing of financial and other benefits arising from use of the TK or expressions of culture (Clause 22). Customary use of TK or expressions of culture does not give rise to any criminal or civil liability under the Act (Clause 5).

The individual Pacific islands have apparently been slow to implement the 2002 Pacific Model Law. Commenting on the Model law, von Lewinski (2007, p. 230) suggests that 'although customary law has been taken into account to quite some extent, it seems that the Model Law is still too far away from rules with which local communities could feel comfortable'. It could be that the Model Law remains fairly rooted within conventional concepts of IP law, and ultimately approaches and interprets TCEs through an adaptation of these concepts. An interesting case study of national reforms in the Pacific to accommodate the protection of 'expressions of indigenous culture' within the IP rubric is the Republic of Vanuatu Copyright and Related Rights Act No. 42 of 2000 ('Vanuatu Copyright Act').[94]

Meanwhile, there have been national initiatives in other parts of the world to provide *sui generis* protection for TCEs.[95] An example from Latin America is Panama's Law on the Special Intellectual Property Regime Governing the Collective Rights of Indigenous Peoples for the Protection and Defense of their Cultural Identity and their Traditional Knowledge of 2000 (see Obaldia 2005; Torsen 2008).[96] Article 1 of the law states that its purpose 'is to protect the collective rights of intellectual property and traditional knowledge of the indigenous communities upon their creations... likewise, the cultural elements of their history, music, art and traditional artistic expressions, *capable of commercial use, through a special registration system, promotion, commercialization of their rights in order to stand out the value of the indigenous cultures and to apply social justice*' (emphasis added). Article 15 provides that the 'rights of use and commercialization of the art, crafts and other cultural expressions based on the tradition of the indigenous community, must be governed by the regulation of each indigenous communit[y], approved and registered

93 See Notes on Clauses, Clause 6.

94 See Part 7 of the Act, sections 41 and 42. This Act was passed by the Parliament of Vanuatu on 29 December 2000, but it still has not been gazetted (or put into force) as of the date of this writing. The full text is available at: http://www.paclii.org/vu/legis/num_act/carra2000282/ (accessed 1 March 2010). See discussion in Marahare 2004.

95 In some cases, this is part of a broader regime to protect biodiversity and associated TK (see Chapter 4).

96 For the full text of the law (translated into English), see the GRAIN website, 'Special Intellectual Property Regime: Panama', available at: http://www.grain.org/brl/?docid=461&lawid=2002 (accessed 26 February 2010).

in DIGERPI [General Office for the Registry of the Industrial Property of the Ministry of Commerce and Industry] or the National Copyright Office of the Ministry of Education, according to the case'.[97] As with other laws that may require registration of TCEs for protection, there are considerations as to whether the registration process is accessible and affordable to the indigenous and other local communities, and whether these communities forfeit protection where registration is not sought for a TCE (sometimes for lack of awareness of such laws and requirements) or where an application to register a TCE is not approved. The criteria for approval also need to be carefully considered. In the case of Panama, Torsen (2008, p. 210) furthermore notes that: 'If Panama's Law is meant to protect Indigenous art and knowledge, its focus on economic compensation for the commercialization of their cultural goods could undermine that goal' (see also Obaldia, p. 379).

A significant national *sui generis* instrument in Southeast Asia is the Philippines Act to Recognize, Protect and Promote the Rights of Indigenous Cultural Communities/Indigenous Peoples (No. 8371, of 28 July 1997). The Philippines Act confirms that these communities and peoples 'are entitled to the recognition of the full ownership and control and protection of their cultural and intellectual rights' and 'shall have the right to special measures to control, develop and protect their sciences, technologies and cultural manifestations...' (section 34). Among other elements, these cultural manifestations are said to include 'oral traditions, literature, designs, and visual and performing arts' (section 34; see also section 32 on 'Community Intellectual Rights').

A detailed discussion of national *sui generis* laws is beyond the scope of this chapter. Since some of the challenges faced by custodians of TCEs in relation to misappropriation by third parties extend beyond national borders, domestic *sui generis* laws remain inherently limited in that they are pertinent to national territories and cannot be enforced elsewhere unless systems of reciprocity are in place. They would also not resolve issues relating to transboundary TCEs. Significant local and national differences in approaches to TCE protection, or regional differences as illustrated by the examples described earlier, may meanwhile render it difficult for adoption of a harmonized *sui generis* protection scheme at the international level. In the latter respect, it is notable that the Revised Draft Provisions for the Protection of TCEs/Expressions of Folklore ('WIPO Revised Provisions') have not been endorsed by the WIPO Intergovernmental Committee on Intellectual Property and Genetic Resources, Traditional Knowledge and Folklore ('IGC') after years of review (see Antons 2009). This is so despite the fact that they incorporate some of the concerns raised by members in relation to earlier draft provisions. However, they 'will be developed further by the IGC under a renewed mandate for 2010 and 2011'.[98]

There is a visible attempt to incorporate customary laws of indigenous peoples into the definition of what is protectable subject matter under the WIPO Revised Provisions. Under Article 1, three conditions must apply for subject matter to fall within protection as TCE or folklore: (1) they must be 'products of creative

[97] On the registration of collective rights under the law, see Articles 7–9.

[98] See the WIPO website, 'Traditional Knowledge, Genetic Resources and Traditional Cultural Expressions', available at http://www.wipo.int/tk/en (accessed 24 March 2010). Since the time of the writing of this chapter, the IGC has initiated further revisions to these draft provisions.

intellectual activity', whether by the community or individuals; (2) the forms of expression must be 'characteristic of a community's cultural and social identity and cultural heritage'; and (3) it is necessary that these forms of expression are 'maintained, used or developed by' the community or by those individuals in the community with the 'right or responsibility to do so in accordance with the customary law and practices of that community'. The notable use of the term 'developed' in the latter sentence seems to allow room for innovation in relation to TCE which is consistent with customary laws and practices. In her commentary on the provisions, von Lewinski suggests (2007, p. 219) that this reflects the 'common feature of folklore as living heritage'. Meanwhile, the ownership of rights akin to copyright vests in the community rather than the individual. Indeed, even where individuals are deemed by customary laws and practices to be the producers of a TCE, the communities to which they belong are considered under the WIPO Revised Provisions to be the beneficiaries of any measures for the protection of the TCE (Article 2; see WIPO 2006, p. 18; von Lewinski 2007, p. 218).

Another feature of note in the WIPO Revised Provisions is the subjection of TCE protection to a trademark-like emphasis on 'current use'. Accordingly, once a community no longer uses the TCE, or no longer exists as a distinct entity, protection for the TCE would lapse.[99] Given the inextricable link between indigenous peoples' continuation of traditional practices and such issues as retention of their land rights, reforms on the protection of TK and TCEs to date (including the WIPO Revised Provisions) do not ultimately address the predicament of communities who are displaced from their ancestral surroundings and are no longer able to continue their traditional practices intimately bound to those surroundings. A further consideration, which is beyond detailed discussion in this chapter, pertains to the case of indigenous peoples who have been displaced, or who have migrated away from their ancestral lands but nevertheless continue to produce certain expressions based on traditional practices. Current TCE legislations, including *sui generis* laws, have not actively considered protection for such cases. This comes back, of course, to the ultimate question of what are the essential characteristics which render TCEs a special case for protection under IP and *sui generis* laws. Is linkage to ancestral lands, for example, an essential ingredient?

An area of controversy requiring further scrutiny is the proposal under the WIPO Revised Provisions that, while 'free, prior and informed consent' (FPIC) is needed for third-party use of TCEs of particular cultural or spiritual value to a community (Article 3(a)), prior notification or registration in a public register is required for this protection to apply (Articles 6, 7).[100] The scope of protection for TCEs thus registered or notified is far-reaching and includes among other things economic rights akin to

[99] See WIPO 2006, *Revised Provisions for the Protection of TCEs/ Expressions of Folklore*, p. 31, where it is explained that the discontinued use is 'analogous to abandonment of a trademark, or a trademark becoming generic'.

[100] For TCEs or expressions of folklore not registered or notified, their use would not be subject to prior authorization under the WIPO Revised Provisions. In such cases, the protection would focus rather on '*how* the TCEs were used', according to the WIPO commentary (ibid., p. 22; original emphasis). The commentary suggests applying concepts of moral rights, unfair competition principles, civil and criminal remedies, as well as the payment of an equitable remuneration or equitable benefit-sharing determined by a competent authority, 'akin perhaps to a compulsory license or equitable remuneration' approach found in some national *sui generis* laws (ibid.).

'classical exclusive rights in the field of copyright' as well as rights comparable to moral rights (von Lewinski 2007, p. 221). However, the application of this provision (particularly the consequences of non-registration) is unclear. It remains to be seen how a condition of prior notification or registration would tally with the international norms that are evolving around the principle of FPIC (see Tamang 2005; see also Laird and Noejovich 2002).

As with many existing national and regional *sui generis* laws, it could also be pointed out that the WIPO Revised Provisions remain very much within an 'IP' grid for approaching the protection of intangible creations. The complex nature of TCEs cannot be grasped without further integrating the viewpoints of the custodians and creators of TCEs in related reforms.

It is notable meanwhile that the WIPO Revised Provisions include exceptions where some cases of utilization outside the traditional or customary context will not be subject to TCEs protection if they fall within defined acts amounting to 'fair practice'.[101] This has important implications, for example, for fair access of the public to TCEs. As explored in Chapters 6, 7 and 8, there are considerations and exceptions under copyright law, for example, purporting to balance the exclusive rights of copyright owners with public access to protected works. The extent to which mechanisms to ensure such balance for fair public access will be built into national *sui generis* laws protecting TCEs remains to be seen, and is likely to be a source of further deliberation and debate, particularly where the rights established in relation to TCEs are far-reaching and perpetual.[102] Discussing the 1982 UNESCO-WIPO Model Provisions, the OAPI Bangui Agreement, and the Pacific Model Law, Belder (2007, p. 48) observes that:

> Interestingly, in each of these examples for a new law on proprietary rights to cultural expressions, there are exceptions that provide for the preservation of a public domain. All three have an exception for educational use and for use with a non-commercial intention. The first two [The UNESCO/WIPO Model Provisions and the OAPI Bangui Agreement] explicitly provide for the use of a cultural expression by an author/artist to create a new work, thus protecting the creativity and exchange of culture.

Belder further notes that all three model laws contain provisions for a *domaine public payant*, a system of fees for the use of traditional cultural expressions that are outside the scope of IPRs (ibid., p. 50). She questions how this approach relates to the idea of a public domain where access is free, adding that: 'A system of fees would suggest that in the process of refining property rights into a sui generis right on the

[101] See WIPO 2006, *Revised Provisions for the Protection of TCEs/ Expressions of Culture*, pp. 27–29. According to Article 5 of the WIPO Revised Provisions, this would include use by way of illustration for teaching and learning; non-commercial research or private study; criticism or review; reporting news or current events; use in the course of legal proceedings; the making of recordings and other reproductions of TCEs or expressions of folklore for purposes of their inclusion in an archive or inventory for non-commercial cultural heritage safeguarding purposes; and incidental uses.

[102] Belder (2007, p. 48) suggests that a new *sui generis* right for the protection of TCEs 'would have to balance the subjective rights of Indigenous Peoples or national states with the public interest in a public domain'. According to her, this right 'should provide for a legal regime of access and benefit-sharing that may draw on the basic scheme of intellectual property law, granting the right holder a bundle of rights, while at the same time providing restrictions for fair use in order to protect the public interest' (ibid.).

protection of cultural expressions, parts of the public domain have been shielded from access'.[103]

Belder acknowledges, however, that 'the public domain is a problematic venue for Indigenous Peoples' (ibid., p. 45). As with legal protection over other forms of TK, there are unresolved issues over the prevalent concepts of the public domain and calls by indigenous peoples for the protection of cultural heritage (see Chander & Sunder 2004; Dutfield 2006, pp. 8–9; Deer 2009). Some of the difficulties stem from prevalent definitions of the public domain as that which is not protected by private property. As discussed in Chapters 1 and 9 of this book, approaches which assume a dichotomy between private property rights and the public domain may not be able to accommodate other concepts of ownership or systems of knowledge creation. Leach (2005, p. 41) points out, for example, that 'property' is only one mode of approaching ownership and many indigenous peoples have other ways of organizing ownership beyond those implied by Western property. It has been said that indigenous communities have their own systems of rights, including exclusive rights to expressions of their cultures in some contexts (see Strathern 1999; Belder 2007, p. 46). Some indigenous groups have argued that while their cultural heritage is communally held and may not be subject to private property, this does not mean necessarily that it is in the public domain (UNDP 2005, pp. 13–14; see further Deer 2009). These debates are further discussed in relation to concepts of the public domain in Chapter 9. Is a re-visioning and redefinition of the 'public domain' (e.g. away from a dichotomy with IPRs) needed to accommodate different cultural views on creativity and property (see Chander & Sunder 2004; Suthersanen 2008)? Might this have transformative effects on how we view IP more generally?

7. Use of codes of ethics and protocols to supplement legal provisions

While legislative reforms to protect TCEs are being pursued and debated, there are those who emphasize the need for guidelines and protocols towards a more holistic approach in protecting indigenous culture.[104] Protocols could provide a non-legal and practical form of protection for TCEs and complement any *sui generis* legislative scheme that may be implemented in the future (Fiztgerald & Hedge 2007). Guidelines are also important in solving some of the difficult questions of public access to cultural material, for example, in relation to the cultural material of indigenous peoples held at museums, archives and libraries. A code of ethics has been produced by the International Council of Museums (ICOM) to help museums manage some of these and others issues.[105] Indigenous peoples are themselves

103 It also remains to be seen how any benefits from such *domaine public payant* will be channelled to the communities from which the TCEs have originated. At the same time, there are arguments that regulated access need not be incompatible with concepts of the 'commons' (Kneen 2004; see Chapter 9).

104 On the recent trend towards the development of bio-cultural protocols, see the website of Natural Justice, 'Bio-cultural Community Protocols', available at: http://naturaljustice.org.za/index.php?option=com_content&task=view&id=41&Itemid=72 (accessed 15 June 2010).

105 See International Council for Museums (ICOM), 'Code of Ethics for Museums' (2004), available at: http://www.wipo.int/tk/en/folklore/creative_heritage/codes/link0007.html (accessed 24 March 2010). There are also museum initiatives, such as the programme at the Smithsonian Institute entitled *Recovering Voices: A Learning Archive for Endangered Languages and Indigenous Knowledge*, which

raising questions of repatriation and other forms of control over such material.[106] Anderson argues that the indigenous 'subjects' of colonial projects are now also an indigenous 'public' needing access to and control over their cultural material held in cultural institutions worldwide, in making meaning of their past and future.[107]

Some relevant guidelines have been elaborated within an interesting project on 'Intellectual Property and Indigenous Knowledge: Access and Control of Cultural Material' at the Australian Institute of Aboriginal and Torres Strait Islander Studies (AIATSIS). The *Guidelines on the Legal Implications of Intellectual Property for Cultural Institutions* seek to raise the standard of institutional responsibility of cultural institutions in their relations with indigenous peoples, communities and cultural material. The *Framework for Protocols* addresses practical community needs and expectations around IP law, and control of knowledge between individuals, communities and external researchers.[108] There could be further linkages between the development of such protocols at domestic levels and the work conducted at the international level regarding the concept and application of FPIC (see Chapter 4; Laird & Noejovich 2002). The latter is crucial towards regulating access by research institutions, corporations and members of the public to TK of indigenous peoples, including their TCEs.

Indigenous protocols have been developed in some contexts to sensitize the public (including those working in particular sectors such as visual arts and film-making) to appropriate ways of approaching indigenous cultural material and working with indigenous communities. For example, the Australia Council for the Arts has produced and recently revised its protocol guides, covering different spheres of cultural endeavour, to help the Australian public better understand issues in accessing and using indigenous cultural material.[109] Close consultations with indigenous peoples are essential in processes to elaborate such protocols.[110]

There is, furthermore, scope for development of specific standards in relation to the social responsibilities of corporations and consumers towards indigenous originators of arts and crafts.[111] As seen earlier in Section 4, such standards have evolved

use museum collections to engage indigenous communities in issues surrounding knowledge and language loss.

106 Some related concerns, for example on the repatriation of ceremonial objects, are expressed in Article 12 of the UNDRIP.

107 Anderson, J. 2005, 'Access and Control of Indigenous Knowledge in Libraries and Archives: Ownership and Future Use', paper presented at a conference on 'Correcting Course: Rebalancing Copyright for Libraries in the National and International Arena', American Library Association and The MacArthur Foundation, Columbia University, New York, 5–7 May 2005.

108 See Australian Institute of Aboriginal and Torres Strait Islander Studies (AIATSIS) website, 'Completed Research Projects', available at: http://www.aiatsis.gov.au/research/past.html (accessed 15 April 2010); see further Bowrey 2006.

109 The five guides cover protocols for producing Indigenous Australian media arts, music, performing arts, visual arts and writing.

110 The Indigenous Protocols published by the Australia Council (second edition) were written by Indigenous intellectual property lawyers Terri Janke and Robynne Quiggin.

111 In the corporate sector, social responsibility or corporate citizenship is featuring more and more as a chapter in the year-end reports of leading companies. Initiatives such as the Global Compact of the United Nations encourage companies to 'formulate practical solutions for problems related to globalization, sustainable development and corporate civil responsibility within a context of multiple

alongside IP protection for certification marks and geographical indications relating to TCEs. Chon (2009, pp. 137–138) observes, at the same time that: 'Standards also raise issues of informed consent or choice of participation in forms of political economy – whether designated as "alternative trade", "fair trade", "corporate social responsibility" programs or mainstream trade'. She adds that: 'While it makes sense for standards to be set in part by the firms involved in the relevant industries, it is not equally sensible that they should be the only actors involved in enforcement through certification. Additionally, meaningful opportunity for consumer and producer involvement in the standards must be provided' (ibid., p. 138). In relation to our present discussion, it is important that indigenous and other local communities are directly involved in any attempts to set standards relating to the treatment and/or certification of their TCEs.[112] This ought to apply to standards setting not only by private firms but also by governmental and non-governmental organizations and other entities. In the context of Aboriginal art in Australia, Anderson (2009, p. 208) suggests that involving local communities in decision-making has made a difference in sustaining and regulating more recent certification schemes: '[L]ocally developed labels already have forms of regulation, and these conform to regulatory standards in operation within the communities themselves. Invigorating local decision-making capacity and determination around locally developed artistic practice should be a priority'.

Indeed, indigenous leaders have pointed out that indigenous peoples themselves have 'complex management systems [for TK including TCEs] founded on ethics and detailed sets of cultural protocols, anchored in the holistic nature of TK' (Deer 2009, p. 95). Part of indigenous customary laws, these principles and protocols relate, among other things, to the sharing, reproduction and use of TCEs (ibid., pp. 95, 98). Their application and evolution in new contexts, including those involving the onset of recent ICTs, is a matter of growing concern for indigenous peoples. Discussing the 'real-time global dissemination of digital content' enabled by the Internet, Deer points out that 'the unauthorized reproduction and digital dissemination of indigenous cultural expressions such as paintings, designs, artworks, songs and performances' may 'seriously disrupt' existing management systems for TK and TCEs, and are important matters for global Internet governance (ibid., pp. 94–95). An International Indigenous ICT Taskforce (IITF) with the involvement of indigenous leaders has been set up to look into the latter (ibid.).[113]

Fiztgerald and Hedge (2007) draw inspiration from modes of governance already visible on the Internet in considering how 'best practice' protocols could be developed to govern both 'pre-release' and 'post-release' of TCEs. They emphasize that

interests'. Such global initiatives and social trends may lead to more self-regulation and private initiatives by corporations. See the United Nations Global Compact website, available at: http://www.unglobalcompact.org/ (accessed 10 March 2010). At the same time, standards achieved through 'private ordering' can potentially replace or sidestep norm setting through public regulation, and thus need to be scrutinized. See Chon 2009.

112 This is important also in the case with agricultural and non-timber forest produce involving these communities.

113 For updates on the work of this taskforce, see the International Indigenous ICT Task Force (IITF) website, available at: http://iictf.blogspot.com/ (accessed 14 November 2009).

such protocols need to go digital – they should be generated specifically for the Internet context and complemented by campaigns to raise awareness of TCEs among access corporations, Internet users and communities. They argue, moreover, that terms of use for Internet services should expressly address TCEs: 'As a starting point, access corporations could, through their Terms and Conditions or Acceptable Use Policies explicitly mention and explain the notion of TCE and any applicable protocol to their customers, reserving themselves a contractual right to remove access to such material' (ibid., p. 21). Notice and take-down procedures could be considered (ibid., pp. 19–24). Principles and protocols relating to TCEs could also be woven into policies on 'user rated' tagging and flagging, so that users themselves could also implement a level of respect for TCE custodians through peer review and communication (ibid., p. 9). Additionally, the authors suggest that 'labelling' or 'badging' of TCEs could be explored:

> The notion of labelling intellectual property has been around for a long time; marks such as ™, © and ® are used everyday. More recently, labelling or badging has been used for licensing terms such as Creative Commons or Licensa licences. The labelling or badging of materials as 'TCE' would allow persons to realize that content they may be reproducing from other websites or hard copy is TCE and should be treated differently to other material. This would further enhance the spread of knowledge about TCE, what it is, and the importance of treating it respectfully. (Ibid., p. 22)

At the same time, challenges can be foreseen over how decisions are to be made on what material could be badged as TCE, as well as how to verify the accuracy or validity of such TCE badges (ibid.). It is also important that any selective 'badging' of TCEs does not obscure or excuse the fact that many other materials on the Internet might be considered to be TCEs. As with standards for the certification of TCEs discussed earlier, such procedures cannot be elaborated without the direct involvement of the indigenous peoples and the local community in question, and appropriate linkages to their customary practices.

8. Conclusion

Article 8 of the Universal Declaration on Cultural Diversity, adopted by UNESCO in November 2001, reminds us that particular attention must be paid to the 'specificity of cultural goods and services which, as vectors of identity, values and meaning, must not be treated as mere commodities and consumer goods'. The 2004 UNDP Human Development Report on *Cultural Liberty in Today's Diverse World* furthermore emphasizes that 'cultural goods convey ideas, symbols and lifestyles and are an intrinsic part of the identity of the community that produces them'. In approaching TCEs as 'vectors of cultural identity, values and meaning' to indigenous peoples and other custodians, it is also important to recognize that these expressions are constantly evolving and subject to re-definition with new contexts.[114] As Anderson

[114] It has been emphasized that cultural diversity exists across and within cultures. Sen (2005, p. 162) maintains that: 'Contrary to cultural stereotypes, the histories of different countries in the world have shown considerable variations over time as well as between different groups within the same country ... there

(2009, p. 11) suggests: 'The insistence on the "traditional" as the key marker of difference obscures contemporary indigenous practice and the reality that indigenous knowledge also undergoes transformation overtime in usage and circulation both within family or community contexts and/or between families, the communities and external parties'.

While sharing common aspirations and struggles in relation to the maintenance of cultural identity, indigenous language, land rights and self-determination, indigenous peoples around the world have nuanced experiences based on history, geographical and current socio-economic conditions. As discussed in Section 2, some communities may object to any commodification of their cultural heritage, and thus view the assertion of IPRs over their TCEs as implying such commodification. Other communities may depend on marketing of arts and crafts based on their TCEs for sustainable livelihoods, and may regard such practices as consistent with their worldviews. For those communities, there are some risks that come along with perceived opportunities. For example, contemporary bias in aesthetics by consumers (or the use of mass-produced materials) can significantly alter the traditional rendition of these cultural expressions. Some suggest, moreover, that the application of property concepts in IP to TCEs may end up transforming the social relations behind the mode(s) of creativity in indigenous cultures (Leach 2005). Following such arguments, IP ownership claims by individuals, for example, may transform the relations of exchange and reciprocity fundamental to the communal creation of TCEs (see further Anderson 2009b). A future scenario may be imaginable where increasing protection of TCEs through IP concepts and tools ultimately unravels the very characteristics that are said to set TCEs apart from other creative endeavours.[115]

Steering towards the middle ground, one could also envisage an alternative future scenario where certain forms of IPRs or *sui generis* protection might be designed or moulded to provide some measure of legal protection for custodians of TCEs (e.g. in relation to third-party commercial mass-production of their expressions) while also serving to reinforce some traditional practices and social relations. For this scenario to be plausible, TCE protection would arguably need to be situated within holistic approaches towards protecting the bio-cultural heritage of indigenous peoples and local communities, which take into account their customary principles and practices (IIED 2008, see Chapter 4). The future protection and promotion of TCEs is, after all, dependent on integrated solutions for the sustainable livelihoods and cultural survival of these peoples and communities. Increasing the social awareness, responsibility and accountability of other actors – whether private firms, governmental and non-governmental entities, consumers of cultural

is, typically, little note taken of substantial variations within each local culture – over time and even at a point of time'.

115 On the other hand, this line of critique might well be directed at IP more generally. To the extent that most (if not all) creative endeavours are to some extent dependent on social networks and incremental inputs (see Chapters 1 and 8), some might well argue that IP is by nature transformative of the social relations behind innovation. Are any creative endeavours really 'isolated' from the social fabric of the communities from which they spring?

products, and civil society more generally – to the communities and other local stakeholders involved would have a significant impact on such initiatives.

The Preamble of the 2005 Convention on the Protection and Promotion of the Diversity of Cultural Expressions furthermore recognizes the need 'to take measures to protect the diversity of cultural expressions, including their contents, especially in situations where the cultural expressions may be threatened by the possibility of extinction or serious impairment'.[116] While not a topic in this chapter, there is the largely unexplored question of whether there might be appropriate measures to 'recuperate' TCEs eroded by historical and socio-economic factors, including political domination, poverty, migration to urban areas, and loss of language or skill transmission. Might there perhaps be a role for IP in such attempts to safeguard cultural heritage? In *Llamas, Weaving, and Organic Chocolate*, Healy (2001, pp. 271–289) discusses traditional Jalq'a weavings from Bolivia which were lost to the villages of the Jalq'a people for some decades due to socio-economic and political factors, and how projects have taken off in recent years amongst women's cooperatives in the valley of Chuquisaca to revive those traditions, and to find viable means of supplementing family incomes in poverty-affected areas. Community-based certification schemes for such weavings are being explored, and other forms of IP protection might be relevant in such contexts.

The fact that TCEs are the product of social relations suggests that they are subject to evolution, and that these cultural endeavours do not exist in a vacuum from other considerations and aspirations in human development discussed in this book. Further research is needed to understand how the preservation and innovation of TCEs intersect with considerations such as gender equality, education (including inter-generational transmission of language and knowledge within the communities), sustainable livelihoods and cross-fertilization of ideas with other cultures.

REFERENCES

Anaya, J. 2004, 'International Human Rights and Indigenous Peoples: The Move Toward the Multicultural State', *Arizona Journal of International and Comparative Law*, vol. 21, no. 1, pp. 13–61, available at: http://www.law.arizona.edu/journals/ajicl/AJICL2004/Vol211/Anaya.pdf (accessed 18 November 2009).

Anderson, J. 2009a, 'Developments in Intellectual Property and Traditional Knowledge Protection', in U. Popova-Gosart (ed.), *Traditional Knowledge & Indigenous Peoples*, L'auravetl'an Information & Education Network of Indigenous Peoples (LIENIP) and World Intellectual Property Organization (WIPO), Geneva, pp. 58–63, available at: http://indigenouspeoplesissues.com/images/stories/TEK_IP_WIPO.pdf (accessed 6 March 2010).

Anderson, J. 2009b, *Law, Knowledge, Culture: The Production of Indigenous Knowledge in Intellectual Property Law*, Edward Elgar, Cheltenham, UK.

[116] UNESCO Convention on the Protection and Promotion of the Diversity of Cultural Expressions (Paris, 20 October 2005), 45 I.L.M. 269 (2006), UN Doc. CLT-2005/CONVENTION DIVERSITE-CULT REV (*entered into force* 18 March 2007), available at: http://unesdoc.unesco.org/images/0014/001429/142919e.pdf (accessed 3 February 2010). For a discussion on this and other UNESCO conventions of relevance to the protection of cultural diversity and intangible cultural heritage, see Chapter 8. See also further resources on the PIIPA website, 'Intellectual Property and Human Development', available at: http://www.piipa.org/IP_and_Human_Development/.

Anderson, J. & Torsen, M. (forthcoming), *Safeguarding Cultural Heritage and Protecting Traditional Cultural Expressions: The Management of Intellectual Property Issues and Options – A Compendium for Museums, Archives and Libraries*, World Intellectual Property Organization (WIPO), Geneva.

Antons, C. 2009, 'What Is "Traditional Cultural Expression"? – International Definitions and Their Application in Developing Asia', *The WIPO Journal: Analysis and Debate of Intellectual Property Issues*, no. 1, pp. 103–116, available at: http://www.wipo.int/about-wipo/en/pdf/wipo_journal.pdf (accessed 11 February 2010).

Barsh, R.L. 1999, 'Indigenous Knowledge and Biodiversity in Indigenous Peoples, Their Environments and Territories', in D.A. Posey (ed.), *Culture and Spiritual Values of Biodiversity*, Intermediate Technology Publication, London.

Belder, L. 2007, 'Cultural Expressions: From Common Source to Public Domain', in F. Macmillan (ed.), *New Directions in Copyright Law*, vol. 4, Edward Elgar, Cheltenham, UK, Northampton, MA.

Bently, L. 2008, 'The Making of Modern Trade Mark Law: The Construction of the Legal Concept of Trade Mark (1860–1880)', in L. Bently, J. Davis & J.C. Ginsburg (eds.), *Trade Marks and Brands: An Interdisciplinary Critique*, Cambridge University Press, New York, pp. 3–41.

Bergès-Sennou, F., Hassan, D., Monier-Dilhan, S. & Raynal, H. 2009, 'Consumer's Decision between Private Labels and National Brands in a Retailer's Store: A Mixed Multinomial Logit Application', *Revue Gestion 2000*, no. 3.

Boateng, B. 2005, 'Square Pegs in Round Holes? Cultural Production, Intellectual Property Frameworks, and Discourses of Power', in R.A. Ghosh (ed.), *CODE: Collaborative Ownership and the Digital Economy*, pp. 61–74, Massachusetts Institute of Technology Press, Cambridge, MA.

Boizot-Szantai, C., Lecocq, S. & Marette, S. 2005, 'Common Labels and Market Mechanisms', *Working Paper 05-WP 405*, Midwest Agribusiness Trade Research and Information Center, Iowa State University, available at: http://www.card.iastate.edu/publications/DBS/PDFFiles/05wp405.pdf (accessed 1 December 2009).

Bowrey, K. 2006, 'Alternative Intellectual Property? : Indigenous Protocols, Copyleft and New Juridifications of Customary Practice', *Macquarie Law Journal*, vol. 6, pp. 65–95.

Brownlie, I. 1998, *Principles of International Law*, 5th Edition, Clarendon Press, Oxford.

Chander, A. & Sunder, M. 2004, 'The Romance of the Public Domain', *California Law Review*, vol. 92, available at: http://ssrn.com/abstract=562301 (accessed 21 December 2008).

Chon, M. 2009, 'Marks of Rectitude', *Fordham Law Review*, vol. 77, pp. 101–141, available at: http://ssrn.com/abstract=1369922 (accessed 20 April 2010).

Clayton, C.M. 2010, 'Supreme Court Denies Certiorari in Trademark Challenge to Washington Redskins Name', *IP Law Alert*, 12 January 2010, available at: http://www.iplawalert.com/2010/01/articles/trademark/supreme-court-denies-certiorari-in-trademark-challenge-to-washington-redskins-name/ (accessed 24 March 2010).

Cornish, W.R. & Llewelyn, D. 2003, *Intellectual Property: Patents, Copyright, Trade Marks and Allied Rights*, 5th Edition, Sweet and Maxwell, London.

Crespi, J.M. & Marette, S. 2003, 'Some Economic Implications of Public Labeling', *Journal of Food Distribution Research*, vol. 32, no. 3, pp. 83-94, available at: http://ageconsearch.umn.edu/bitstream/27053/1/34030083.pdf (accessed 1 December 2009).

Das, K. 2008, 'Select Issues and Debates around Geographical Indications with Particular Reference to India', *Journal of World Trade*, vol. 42, no. 3, pp. 461–508.

Das, K. 2010, 'Prospects and Challenges of Geographical Indications in India', *Journal of World Intellectual Property*, vol. 13, no. 2, pp. 148–201.

DeCarlo, J. 2007, *Fair Trade: A Beginners' Guide*, Oneworld Publications, Oxford.

Deer, K. 2009, 'Indigenous ICT Taskforce', in U. Popova-Gosart (ed.), *Traditional Knowledge & Indigenous Peoples*, LIENIP and WIPO, Geneva, pp. 94–106, available at: http://indigenouspeoplesissues.com/images/stories/TEK_IP_WIPO.pdf (accessed 6 March 2010).

De Obaldia, I. 2006, 'Western Intellectual Property and Indigenous Cultures: The Case of the Panamanian Indigenous Intellectual Property Law', *Boston University International Law Journal*, vol. 23, pp. 337–394.

Donkin, L. 2001, *Crafts and Conservation: Synthesis Report for International Centre for the Study of Preservation and Restoration of Cultural Property (ICCROM)*, available at: http://www.iccrom.org/eng/02info_en/02_04pdfpubs_en/ICCROM_doc02_CraftsandConservation.pdf (accessed 25 January 2009).

Dutfield, G. 2001, 'TRIPS-Related Aspects of Traditional Knowledge', *Case Western Reserve Journal of International Law*, vol. 33, pp. 239–281.

Dutfield, G. 2006, *Protecting Traditional Knowledge: Pathways to the Future*, International Centre for Trade and Sustainable Development (ICTSD) Issue Paper No. 16.

Dutfield, G. & Suthersanen, U. 2008, *Global Intellectual Property Law*, Edward Elgar, Cheltenham, UK.

Farm Foundation 2003, *The Consumer Response to Food Labeling*, authored by J.J. McCluskey & M.L. Loureiro, available at: http://www.farmfoundation.net/topic.aspx?t=Food%20Labeling&a=138 (accessed 1 December 2009)

Fitzgerald, B.F. & Hedge, S. 2008, 'Traditional Cultural Expression and The Internet World', in C. Antons (ed.), *Traditional Knowledge, Traditional Cultural Expression and Intellectual Property in South East Asia*, Kluwer Law International, Alphen aan den Rijn, The Netherlands.

Frankel, S.R. 2008, 'Trademarks and Traditional Knowledge and Cultural Intellectual Property Rights' in G.B. Dinwoodie & M.D. Janis (eds.), *Trademark Law and Theory: A Handbook of Contemporary Research*, Edward Elgar, Cheltenham, UK.

Gangjee, D. 2008, '(Re)Locating Geographical Indications', in L. Bently, J. Davis & J.C. Ginsburg (eds.), *Trade Marks and Brands: An Interdisciplinary Critique*, Cambridge University Press, New York.

Geismar, H. 2005a, 'Copyright in Context: Carvings, Carvers, and Commodities in Vanuatu', *American Ethnologist*, vol. 32, no. 3, pp. 437–459.

Geismar, H. 2005b, 'Reproduction, Creativity, Restriction: Material Culture and Copyright in Vanuatu', *Journal of Social Archaeology*, vol. 5. no. 1, pp. 25–51.

Gibson, J. 2005, *Community Resources: Intellectual Property, International Trade and Protection of Traditional Knowledge*, Ashgate Publishing, Aldershot, UK, Burlington, VT.

Haugen, H.M. 2005, 'Traditional Knowledge and Human Rights', *Journal of World Intellectual Property*, vol. 8, no. 5, pp. 663–677.

Haugen, H.M. 2007, 'General Comment No. 17 on Authors' Rights', *The Journal of World Intellectual Property*, vol. 10, no. 1, pp. 53–69.

Healy, K. 2001, 'Recuperating a Wealth of Women's Weavings in the Valleys of Chuquisaca', in K. Healy, *Llamas, Weaving, and Organic Chocolate: Multicultural Grassroots Development in the Andes and Amazon of Bolivia*, University of Notre Dame Press, Notre Dame, IN.

International Institute for Environment and Development (IIED) 2008, *Protecting Community Rights over Traditional Knowledge: Implications of Customary Laws and Practices*, available at: http://www.cbd.int/abs/project.shtml?id=18967 (accessed 24 June 2009).

Janke, T. 2003, *Minding Culture: Case Studies on Intellectual Property and Traditional Cultural Expressions*, WIPO, Geneva, available at: http://www.wipo.int/tk/en/studies/cultural/minding-culture/studies/finalstudy.pdf (accessed 25 January 2009).

Kneen, B. 2004, 'Privatisation and the Public Domain', *The Ram's Horn*, vol. 220, available at: http://www.ramshorn.ca/archive2004/220.html (accessed 25 January 2009).

Kur, A. & Cocks, S. 2007, 'Nothing but a GI Thing: Geographical Indications under EU Law', *Fordham Intellectual Property, Media & Entertainment Law Journal*, vol. 17, no. 4, pp. 999–1016.

Laird, S.A. & Noejovich, F. 2002, 'Building Equitable Research Relationships with Indigenous Peoples and Local Communities: Prior Informed Consent and Research Agreements', in S.A. Laird (ed.), *Biodiversity and Traditional Knowledge: Equitable Partnerships in Practice*, People and Plants Conservation Series, Earthscan, London and Sterling, VA.

Lane, P. 1988, 'Tourism and Social Change among the Dogon', *African Arts*, vol. 21, no. 4.

Leach, J. 2005, 'Modes of Creativity and the Register of Ownership', in R.A. Ghosh (ed.), *CODE: Collaborative Ownership and the Digital Economy*, Massachusetts Institute of Technology Press, Cambridge, MA.

Lindholm, C. 2008, *Culture and Authenticity*, Wiley & Sons, New York.

Malm, K. 2004a, 'Copyright and the Protection of Intellectual Property in Traditional Music', *Music – Media – Multiculture Report*, no. 3, Royal Swedish Academy of Music, Stockholm.

Malm, K. 2004b, 'Intellectual Property Rights and Unfair Exploitation of Traditional Music and Other Traditional Knowledge in Africa', in S.M. Thorsén (ed.), *Sounds of Change – Social and Political Features of Music in Africa*, Swedish International Development Cooperation Agency (SIDA), Stockholm, pp. 120–134.

Māori Trade Mark Focus Group 1997, *Māori and Trade Marks: A Discussion Paper*, Ministry of Commerce, Wellington.

Marahare, D. 2004, 'Towards an Equitable Future in Vanuatu: The Legal Protection of Cultural Property', *Journal of South Pacific Law*, vol. 8, no. 2, available online at: http://www.paclii.org/journals/fJSPL/vol08no2/6.shtml (accessed 23 April 2010).

Mauss, M. 1950, 'Essai sur le Don', in *Sociologie et Anthropologie*, Presses Universitaires de France, Paris.

McCluskey, J.J. & Loureiro, M.L. 2003, 'Consumer Preferences and Willingness to Pay for Food Labeling: A Discussion of Empirical Studies', *Journal of Food Distribution Research*, vol. 34, no. 3.

Mead, A. 2005, 'Emerging Issues in Māori Traditional Knowledge – Can These be Addressed by United Nations Agencies?', *Technical Report for the International Workshop on Traditional Knowledge*, 21–23 September 2005, Panama City, Department of Economic and Social Affairs, United Nations, available at: http://www.un.org/esa/socdev/unpfii/documents/workshop_TK_mead.pdf (accessed 18 November 2009).

Ministerio de Comercio Exterior y Turismo (MINCETUR) 2004, *Plan Estratégico Nacional Exportador 2003–2013: Plan Operativo Exportador del Sector Artesanía*, Mayo de 2004, Perú.

Musungu, S.F. 2008, 'The Protection of Geographical Indications and the Doha Round: Strategic and Policy Considerations for Africa', *Quaker United Nations Office (QUNO) IP Issue Paper No. 8*, QUNO, Geneva.

Myers, F. 2005, 'Some Properties of Culture and Persons', in R.A. Ghosh (ed.), *CODE: Collaborative Ownership and the Digital Economy*, Massachusetts Institute of Technology Press, Cambridge, MA.

Oguamanam, C. 2008, 'Local Knowledge as Trapped Knowledge: Intellectual Property, Culture, Power and Politics', *Journal of World Intellectual Property*, vol. 11, no. 1, pp. 29–57.

Okediji, R.L. 2007, 'The Limits of Development Strategies at the Intersection of Intellectual Property and Human Rights', in D. Gervais (ed.), *Intellectual Property, Trade and Development: Strategies to Optimize Economic Development in a TRIPS-Plus Era*, Oxford University Press, pp. 355–384.

Parry, B. 2008, 'Geographical Indications: Not All Champagne and Roses', in L. Bently, J. Davis & J.C. Ginsburg (eds.), *Trade Marks and Brands: An Interdisciplinary Critique*, Cambridge University Press, New York.

Prott, L.V. 1998, 'Understanding One Another on Cultural Rights' in H. Niec (ed.), *Cultural Rights and Wrongs: A Collection of Essays in Commemoration of the 50th Anniversary of the University Declaration of Human Rights*, Institute of Art & Law, United Nations Educational, Scientific and Cultural Organization (UNESCO), pp. 161–175.

Richards, P. 2005, 'Masques Dogon in a Changing World', *African Arts*, vol. 38, no. 4.

Schildkrout, E. 2004, 'Drawing Tradition: Dogon Children's Art in the Age of Tourism', *African Arts*, vol. 37, no. 1.

Secretariat for the Pacific Community 2006, *Guidelines for Developing National Legislation for the Protection of Traditional Knowledge and Expressions of Culture based on the Pacific Model Law 2002*, available at: http://www.wipo.int/tk/en/laws/pdf/spc_guidelines.pdf (accessed 15 December 2009).

Sen, A.K. 2005, 'Human Rights and Capabilities', *Journal of Human Development*, vol. 6, no. 2, pp. 151–166.

Shinya 2004, '*Protecting Traditional Cultural Expressions Policy Issues and Considerations From a Copyright Perspective*', Canadian Heritage.

Strathern, M. 1996, 'Cutting the Network', *The Journal of the Royal Anthropological Institute*, vol. 2, no. 3, pp. 517–535.

Strathern, M. 1999, *Property Substance and Effect, Anthropological Essays on Persons and Things*, Athlone Press, London.

Strathern, M. 2005, 'Imagined Collectivities and Multiple Authorship', in R.A. Ghosh (ed.), *CODE: Collaborative Ownership and the Digital Economy*, Massachusetts Institute of Technology Press, Cambridge, MA.

Sunder, M. 2007, 'The Invention of Traditional Knowledge', *Law and Contemporary Problems*, vol. 70, no. 2, pp. 97–124.

Suthersanen, U. 2008, 'A2K and the WIPO Development Agenda: Time to List the "Public Domain"', UNCTAD-ICTSD Projects on IPRs and Sustainable Development, Policy Brief Number 1, December 2008, UNCTAD-ICTSD, Geneva.

Tamang, P. 2005, 'An Overview of the Principle of Free, Prior and Informed Consent and Indigenous Peoples in International and Domestic Law and Practices', *Australian Indigenous Law Reporter*, Australasian Legal Information Institute, available at: http://www.austlii.edu.au/au/journals/AILR/2005/36.html (accessed 21 November 2008).

Torsen, M. 2005, 'Anonymous, Untitled, Mixed Media: Mixing Intellectual Property Law with Other Legal Philosophies to Protect Traditional Cultural Expressions', *Centre for Advanced Study and Research on Intellectual Property (CASRIP) Newsletter – Spring/Summer*, vol. 12, no. 1, available at: http://www.law.washington.edu/Casrip/Newsletter/Vol12/newsv12i1Torsen.html (accessed 25 January 2009).

Torsen, M. 2008, 'Intellectual Property and Traditional Cultural Expressions: A Synopsis of Current Issues', *International Human Rights Review*, vol. 3, pp. 199–214.

Townsend-Gault, C. 2004, *Journal of Material Culture*, vol. 9, no. 2, pp. 183–202.

United Nations (UN) 2009, *State of the World's Indigenous Peoples*, Department of Economic and Social Affairs, ST/ESA/328, New York.

United Nations Development Programme (UNDP) 2004, *UNDP Human Development Report 2004: Cultural Liberty in Today's Diverse World*, UNDP, New York.

UNDP 2005, *Practice Note on Traditional Knowledge, Access to Genetic Resources and Benefit-Sharing*, (authored by T. Wong, T. Hay-Edie, T. Akhtar & C. McNeill) UNDP, available at: http://www.energyandenvironment.undp.org/undp/index.cfm?module=Library&page=Document&DocumentID=6388 (accessed 12 November 2008).

van Beek, W.E.A. 2003, 'African Tourist Encounters: Effects of Tourism on Two West African Societies', *Africa: Journal of the International African Institute*, vol. 73, no. 2.

von Lewinski, S. 2007, 'Adequate Protection of Folklore – A Work in Progress', in P. Torremans (ed.), *Copyright Law: A Handbook of Contemporary Research*, Edward Elgar Publishing, Cheltenham, UK, and Northampton, MA, pp. 207–231.

Wiessner, S. 2009, 'United Nations Declaration on the Rights of Indigenous Peoples', United Nations Audiovisual Library of International Law, available at: http://untreaty.un.org/cod/avl/pdf/ha/ga_61-295/ga_61-295_e.pdf (accessed 10 January 2010).

World Intellectual Property Organization (WIPO) 1998, *Intellectual Property in Asia and the Pacific*, January–June 1998, No. 56/57, WIPO Publication No. 435(E).

WIPO 2003, 'Traditional Cultural Expressions/Expressions of Folklore: Legal and Policy Options', (prepared by the Secretariat) Intergovernmental Committee on Intellectual Property and Genetic Resources, Traditional Knowledge and Folklore, WIPO, Doc. WIPO/GRTKF/IC/6/3.

WIPO 2006, *Intellectual Property and Genetic Resources, Traditional Knowledge and Traditional Cultural Expressions/Folklore: Information Resources*, WIPO, Doc. WIPO/GRTKF/INF/1, available at: http://www.wipo.int/tk/en/ (accessed 25 January 2009).

Yue, C., Marette, S. & Beghin, J.C. 2006, 'How to Promote Quality Perception in Wine Markets: Brand Advertising or Geographical Indication?', *Center for Agricultural and Rural Development Working Paper 06-wp426*, Center for Agricultural and Rural Development (CARD), Iowa State University, available at: http://www.econ.iastate.edu/research/webpapers/paper_12651.pdf (accessed 25 January 2009).

Zago, A. & Pick, D. 2002, 'The Welfare Effects of the Public Provision of Information: Labelling Typical Products in the European Union', *Istituto Nazionale di Economia Agraria Working Paper 24/02*, available at: http://www.inea.it/prin/risultati/wp24.pdf (accessed 25 January 2009).

Zografos, D. 2007, 'Legal Protection of Traditional Cultural Expressions in East and Southeast Asia: An Unexplored Territory?', *Australian Intellectual Property Journal*, vol. 18, no. 3, pp. 167–178.

Zografos, D. 2008, 'Geographical Indications and Socio-Economic Development', *IQsensato Working Paper 3*, IQsensato, Geneva.

6

Copyright and capability for education: An approach 'from below'

Margaret Chon[1]

> *You Don't Remember... but She's With You was a very emotional quilt for me to create. Making the quilt helped me deal with the loss of my mother when my younger son was still very small. She loved reading, loved to see children read and helped many children and adults to learn. I know she is watching as her grandchildren grow. I tell my son about her keen intellect, how proud she would be of his love of books and learning and, above all, that she is still with him.*[2] (Austin 2006)

> *Printed books require no mediating device to read and thus are immune to technological obsolescence. Paper is also extremely stable, compared with, say, hard drives or even CDs. In this way, the stability and fixity of a bound book is a blessing. It sits there unchanging, true to its original creation.* (Kelly 2006, p. 46)

Introduction

Global intellectual property regimes reflect a top-down approach to global intellectual property regulation, following from the interests and needs of intellectual property-rich states (Arewa 2006, pp. 79–80).[3] This approach fails to generate the full range of policy choices for both developed and developing countries to maximize global social welfare with respect to human development needs such as education. To address this bias, I propose an approach of intellectual property (hereinafter IP) 'from below', which links IP to distributive justice and human development. The term 'from below' also dovetails with the term 'Global South' that is increasingly being used to denote that subset of developing countries that are located primarily below the equator and also below the median in terms of development indicators,

[1] Very special thanks to Therese Norton (Class of 2010), as well as to Nancy Yamashiro (Class of 2009), Debbie Boe, Robert Chang (Class of 2007), Jennifer Dinning (Class of 2006) and to reference librarian Kerry Fitz-Gerald for their stellar research support. This chapter is a revised version of an article previously published as part of a March 2007 University of California, Davis Law Review symposium on intellectual property and social justice. It is dedicated to all my students – future, present and past.

[2] Lauren Austin, *That Black Girl Art – Art Quilts*, available at: http://www.thatblackgirlart.com/art_quilts.html (accessed 8 June 2009). One of my former law students, who is also a quilt artist, wrote this epigraph, illustrating the emotional, symbolic, and material power of literacy to the African-American community, which was historically denied the right to education.

[3] According to Arewa (2006, pp. 79–80): 'The TRIPs Agreement and other proposals on a global level largely tend to reflect a top-down approach. Unless they incorporate substantially more flexibility than current TRIPs standards, such approaches, by applying a fairly unitary and uniform standard across different local communities may have the ultimate effect of lessening local participation in questions of local knowledge. Further, by limiting the range of choices with respect to local knowledge, such approaches may in the end increase homogeneity within local knowledge systems'.

whether measured by Gross National Income[4] or the Human Development Index (see United Nations Development Programme [UNDP] 1990, p. 1; 1991, p. 2). This approach responds to the imbalance that observers in both the North and the South are identifying in both domestic and global IP policymaking settings.

In this chapter I first describe the approach from below and introduce 'development' as a key term of art in global IP. Employing a method from below, I then sketch the lack of access to basic educational materials in many developing countries, both descriptively and with respect to the copyright dimension. In the context of building capacity for education, the term 'development'– if taken seriously–should result in a mechanism for access by users to knowledge goods for education. For many countries, both developed and developing, books remain an appropriate and useful technology, especially for primary and secondary education. Just as the digitizing of books is allowing us to re-imagine our global digital informational universe, can access to hard copies for educational purposes be re-imagined? This chapter focuses primarily on Article 10(2) of the Berne Convention,[5] the so-called illustration for teaching exception, which endorses national exceptions to copyright for purposes of access to education.[6] Of course, copyright is only one of several factors affecting the provision of textbooks (Farrell & Heyneman 1988, pp. 33–39).[7] However, it is a significant one and deserves more scrutiny in this particular context.

1. Linking intellectual property to development

Approaching 'IP from below' highlights the needs of users in both developed and developing countries for knowledge goods that are accessible and affordable, particularly for purposes of basic human development. 'IP from below' promotes a bottom-up approach to innovation capacity building, especially for global sectors that are not technologically privileged. A top-down approach to capacity building in IP, by contrast, focuses on building capacity to comply with international IP's minimum standards, which in turn are thought to generate domestic innovative capacity through foreign direct investment, licensing and technology transfer (Gervais 2005, pp. 515–516).

[4] Currently, the World Bank uses 'gross national income (GNI) per capita' as the prime indicator of development. See the World Bank, 'Data & Statistics – Country Classification', available at: http://go.worldbank.org/K2CKM78CC0 (accessed 26 June 2009).

[5] Berne Convention for the Protection of Literary and Artistic Works (Berne, 9 September 1886), *as revised at* Paris 24 July 1971, *and amended* 28 September 1979, 1161 U.N.T.S. 30 (The Act of Paris *entered into force* 15 December 1972) [hereinafter Berne Convention], available at: http://www.wipo.int/treaties/en/ip/berne/trtdocs_wo001.html (accessed 3 February 2010). Article 10(2) ('Certain Free Uses of Works . . . Illustrations for Teaching') is discussed in Section 4.

[6] Textbook provision is problematic for reasons other than copyright. Nor will textbooks standing alone solve educational access problems. Textbooks involve many contentious issues regarding cultural content, the incorporation of indigenous languages and so on. And copyright is only one of several policy levers affecting access to education generally. As Greaney (1996, pp. 8–22) has pointed out, multiple factors pose barriers to access, including: inadequate health provisions, adverse home circumstances, gender inequities, other adverse school factors and inadequate school instruction.

[7] Farrell and Heyneman (1988, pp. 33–39) outline key issues, including readership size, who pays, politics of textbook content, as well as 'the advantages and disadvantages of copyright'.

'Development' is inherently ambiguous. Various foundational IP documents reference the key term 'development' without actually defining it. It is worth reiterating that the preamble to the 1994 Marrakesh Agreement establishing the WTO (Marrakesh Agreement) states:

> The *Parties* to this Agreement,
>
> Recogniz[e] that their relations in the field of trade and economic endeavour should be conducted with a view to raising standards of living, ensuring full employment and a large and steadily growing volume of real income and effective demand, and expanding the production of trade in goods and services, *while allowing for the optimal use of the world's resources in accordance with the objective of sustainable development, seeking both to protect and preserve the environment and to enhance the means for doing so in a manner consistent with their respective needs and concerns at different levels of development.*[8] (Emphasis added)

The Agreement on Trade-Related Aspects of Intellectual Property Rights ('TRIPS Agreement') also references development in its preamble, as well as in Articles 7 and 8.[9] Moreover, the World Intellectual Property Organization (WIPO) founding agreement with the United Nations (UN) includes language regarding the need to 'facilitat[e] the transfer of technology related to industrial property to the developing countries in order to accelerate *economic, social and cultural development*' (emphasis added).[10] Arguably, this reference to development incorporates universal access to primary education, which UN members have accepted as achievable by 2015 through the Millennium Development Goals (MDGs)[11] (Alston 2005, p. 774; see also Chapter 1 and Box 6.1). Similarly, Pamela Samuelson has inferred from the preamble of the WIPO Copyright Treaty (WCT)[12] an intent to preserve the traditional IP

8 Marrakesh Agreement Establishing the World Trade Organization (Marrakesh, 15 April 1994), 1867 U.N.T.S. 154, 33 I.L.M. 1144 (1994) (*entered into force* 1 January 1995) [hereinafter 'Marrakesh Agreement' or 'WTO Agreement'], available at: http://www.wto.org/english/docs_e/legal_e/04-wto.pdf (accessed 3 February 2010).

9 Agreement on Trade-Related Aspects of Intellectual Property Rights (Marrakesh, 15 April 1994), Marrakesh Agreement Establishing the World Trade Organization, Annex 1C, 1869 U.N.T.S. 299, 33 I.L.M. 1197 (1994) (*entered into force* 1 January 1995) [hereinafter 'TRIPS Agreement'], available at: http://www.wto.org/english/tratop_e/trips_e/t_agm0_e.htm (accessed 3 February 2010). The TRIPS Agreement incorporates Articles 1 through 21 of the Berne Convention through TRIPS Article 9 ('Relation to the Berne Convention').

10 Agreement between the United Nations and the World Intellectual Property Organization (*entered into effect* 17 December 1974), Article 1 [hereinafter 'UN-WIPO Agreement'], available at: http://www.wipo.int/treaties/en/agreement/index.html (accessed June 26 2009); see also paragraph 13(1) of the Convention Establishing the World Intellectual Property Organization (Stockholm, 14 July 1967), 828 U.N.T.S. 3, 21 U.S.T. 1749 (*entered into force* 26 April 1970), *as amended* 28 September 1979 (*entered into force as amended* 1 June 1984), available at: http://www.wipo.int/export/sites/www/treaties/en/convention/pdf/trtdocs_wo029.pdf (accessed 3 February 2010).

11 The Millenium Development Goals are found in the UN Millennium Declaration (8 September 2000), G.A. Res. 55/2, U.N. Doc. A/RES/55/2 (2000) [hereinafter 'UN Millennium Declaration'], available at: http://www.un.org/millennium/ (accessed 22 June 2009).

12 WIPO Copyright Treaty (Geneva, 30 December 1996), 36 I.L.M. 65 (*entered into force* 6 March 2002), available at: http://www.wipo.int/export/sites/www/treaties/en/ip/wct/pdf/trtdocs_wo033.pdf (accessed 3 February 2010).

BOX 6.1. Millennium Development Goals

The Millennium Development Goals (MDGs) are eight goals to be achieved by 2015 that respond to the world's main development challenges. The MDGs are drawn from the actions and targets contained in the Millennium Declaration[13] that was adopted by 189 nations and signed by 147 heads of state and governments during the UN Millennium Summit in September 2000. These goals are:

Goal 1: Eradicate extreme poverty and hunger
Goal 2: Achieve universal primary education
Goal 3: Promote gender equality and empower women
Goal 4: Reduce child mortality
Goal 5: Improve maternal health
Goal 6: Combat HIV/AIDS, malaria and other diseases
Goal 7: Ensure environmental sustainability
Goal 8: Develop a global partnership for development

The eight MDGs break down into twenty-one quantifiable and time-bound targets that are measured by sixty indicators. The MDGs synthesize, in a single package, many of the most important commitments made by states separately at the international conferences and summits of the 1990s. They recognize explicitly the interdependence between growth, poverty reduction and sustainable development. At the same time, the MDGs acknowledge that development rests on the foundations of democratic governance, the rule of law, respect for human rights and peace and security.[14]

[13] UN Millennium Declaration (8 September 2000), G.A. Res. 55/2, U.N. Doc. A/RES/55/2 (2000) [hereinafter 'UN Millennium Declaration'], available at: http://www.un.org/millennium/ (accessed 22 June 2009); see also UNDP 2003, Summary.

[14] This summary is drawn from UNDP, 'About the Millennium Development Goals', available at: http://www.undp.org/mdg/basics.shtml (accessed 18 June 2009); see further UNDP 2003.

balance within global digital copyright that was already present within the Berne Convention framework, for purposes of education.[15]

More generally, the Johannesburg Declaration[16] created 'a collective responsibility to advance and strengthen the interdependent and mutually reinforcing pillars of sustainable development – economic development, social development and environmental protection – at local, national, regional and global levels'.[17] In the most utopian sense, all states must cooperate to achieve certain basic levels of

[15] Samuelson (1997, p. 409) refers to language in the WCT preamble: 'Recognizing the need to maintain a balance between the interests of authors and the larger public interest, particularly education, research, and access to information, as reflected in the Berne Convention'. But see Dinwoodie, G. B., Remarks at Association of American Law Schools Mid-Year Conference (AALS) (16 June 2006), stating that allusion to balance in the WCT is a relatively new aspect of the international IP system (transcript on file with author).

[16] World Summit on Sustainable Development, Johannesburg Declaration on Sustainable Development (4 September 2002), UN Doc. A/CONF.199/20 (2002), available at: http://www.unctad.org/en/docs/aconf199d20&c1_en.pdf (accessed 12 March 2010).

[17] See Kates, Parris and Leiserowitz (2005, p. 12), citing the Johannesburg Declaration on Sustainable Development.

development: The global ethics premise underlying the MDGs is aimed at eliminating poverty through increased access to education, food and health care.[18]

How does 'IP from below' facilitate these human development goals?

2. Linking development to capabilities

Whether through economic treaties such as the WTO or through the UN MDGs, distributionally fair social welfare gains will take place only when norms are both in the interests of the less powerful and more powerful actors (Bell 1980, p. 518). Thus, 'IP from below' would highlight rather than footnote the perspectives of developing countries and, importantly, the non-elite users and consumers of knowledge goods within both developed and developing countries (Gerhart 2007, p. 158; Love 2007, p. 679).[19] This approach also overlaps with many prevailing critiques of IP maximalism.[20] National governments may not represent the public interest; an approach from below views social movements and non-governmental organizations as relevant legal actors (Rajagopal 2003, p. 233; Sell 2003, p. 173). 'IP from below' also explores the practices of everyday resistance, such as 'piracy'[21] or appropriation, rather than automatically demonizing them (Litman 2004, p. 1; see generally Coombe 1998). And it places high value on democratic participation and decision-making, although in the context of global IP most of the scholarly proposals thus far have focused on procedural rather than substantive reforms (Drahos & Braithwaite 2002, p. 189; Long 2002, pp. 260–268).

However, a key difference between an approach from below and other critiques of the current IP balance is its emphasis on global distributive justice outcomes. The perspectives and actions of the least empowered among us ought to be included in more than just a formal equality sense in shaping a normative legal agenda (Young 2002, p. 1). An approach from below explicitly shapes IP outcomes with respect to knowledge goods by specific groups, in this case, users in developing countries (see Chon & Ghosh 2000), for specific goals, which could include innovation, access and affordability. At least for purposes of this article, these goals also include basic human development as defined by the MDGs (see Chon 2006, p. 2836).

The global IP framework poses distributive justice choices with far different inputs for decision-making than on the domestic level. For developing countries,

[18] See United Nations Development Programme (UNDP) 2003, Summary.

[19] Gerhart (2007, p. 158) observes that: 'Under any reckoning of distributive justice, some wealthy consumers in poor countries ought to be treated the same as wealthy consumers in rich countries'. A corollary question might be asked: Do poor users in rich states have more in common with poor users in poor states than with the rich users in their own states?

[20] The public interest rationale in US copyright law has been articulated domestically in various, non-theoretically unified ways. It is sometimes cast as a critique of industry capture of the legislative process, which is supposed to represent the public interest (see Litman 1987; Samuelson 1997, pp. 430–431). Alternatively, it is a plea to preserve a robust public domain upon which other creative works can draw (see generally Boyle 2003). Those scholars who have chosen to engage economic theory on its own terms have critiqued some of the assumptions underlying the market efficiency approach to copyright (see Cohen 2000, pp. 1800–1801; Frischmann & Lemley 2006).

[21] The term 'piracy' has been widely applied to unauthorized copying. However, as several scholars have pointed out, the term already frames the question over where the proper line should be drawn between legitimate and illegitimate copying (see Halbert, Darch & Story 2006).

the impact of higher prices for global knowledge goods may be easier to discern than the relative impact for consumers in developed countries. Thus, policy choices will appear disproportionately to affect states with smaller markets, less international negotiating power, smaller budgets for public research, and poorer and less empowered consumers. But even in developed countries, which can more easily bear potential distributional burdens, the ongoing domestic debate on whether copyright law has over-privileged the author and submerged the user (Litman 1997, p. 245; see generally Cohen 2005) is one that goes squarely to the question of distribution. The globalization of IP sharpens distributive choices within all countries, especially in the context of digital networked technologies (Litman 2004, p. 7; see also Sunder 2006, p. 257). Within the global framework of TRIPS, the articulation of a possible user right was one of the earliest signs recognizing the proper distribution between producer and user claims to value in public goods (Dinwoodie & Dreyfuss 2006, pp. 220–21; Dreyfuss 2004, p. 27).

Restrictive IP laws narrow available options for deploying knowledge goods within a 'development as freedom' model. Little attention has been paid so far to this question of capacity building or development within a human capability model through IP (see Chapter 1). By human capability, I refer here primarily to the work of Amartya Sen (1999) and Martha Nussbaum (see generally Nussbaum 1995). According to the latter, there are 'certain basic functional capabilities at which societies should aim for their citizens, and which quality of life measurements should measure' (ibid., p. 82). This list includes:

> (1) Being able to live to the end of a human life of normal length; (2) Being able to have good health, including reproductive health; to be adequately nourished; (3) Being able to use the senses; being able to imagine, to think, and to reason – and to do these things in a 'truly human' way, a way informed and cultivated by an adequate education, including, but by no means limited to, literacy and basic mathematical and scientific training....[22] (Nussbaum 1997, p. 287)

This human capability or human development approach to capacity building comports with a bottom-up model rather than a top-down model of global IP. To flesh out an approach to 'IP from below', I focus here on the content of development as applied to copyrights and human capability for education. While at first blush, copyrights may seem to have less to do with public health and welfare than do patents, there is a very strong demonstrable link between education and public health measures such as fertility, infant and child mortality, and adult morbidity and mortality (Chon 2006, pp. 2896–2897; Rosenberg 2006, pp. 42–45). Moreover, arguably a right to education is embodied in various human rights documents,[23]

[22] This list appears to be slightly different from the version published earlier by Nussbaum (1995) and was apparently 'revised as a result of... visits to development projects in India' (Nussbaum 1997, p. 286).

[23] See Article 13 of the International Covenant on Economic, Social and Cultural Rights (New York, 16 December 1966), 993 U.N.T.S. 3, 6 I.L.M. 360 (1967), G.A. Res. 2200A (XXI), U.N. Doc. A/6316 (1966) (*entered into force* 3 January 1976) [hereinafter 'ICESCR'], available at http://www2.ohchr.org/english/law/pdf/cescr.pdf (accessed 3 February 2010). See also Article 29 of the Convention on the Rights of the Child (New York, 20 November 1989), 1577 U.N.T.S. 3, 28 I.L.M. 1456 (1989), G.A. Res. 44/25, U.N. Doc. A/44/49 (1989) (*entered into force* 2 September 1990) [hereinafter 'CRC'], available at: http://www2.ohchr.org/english/law/crc.htm (accessed 3 February 2010). See further

which form the legal basis for a human capability approach to the question of copyright on educational materials (3D 2005, p. 4).[24] As Okediji recently pointed out, '[E]ducation and basic scientific knowledge [are] . . . important component[s] in creating an environment in which domestic initiatives and development policies can take root. A well-informed, educated and skilled citizenry is indispensable to the development process' (2006, p. 5). To the extent that development is driven not only by economic growth but also by cultural and social change, education is foundational (Drache & Froese 2005, p. 28; cf. Cao 2004, p. 1078).[25]

In an earlier work, I posited the need for a substantive equality principle (Chon 2006) in global IP norm setting and interpretation. The focus in this chapter is on the application of that principle to educational exceptions to copyright. Within the international framework, Article 10(2) of the Berne Convention – the so-called illustrations for teaching provision – provides a potential policy space for signatory nations of either Berne or the TRIPS Agreement to mandate access to educational materials for development needs. It can extend the original linkage between trade and intellectual property even further to human development. By connecting the international IP regime complex[26] to other global regimes providing important

the Committee on Economic, Social and Cultural Rights (CESCR) 1999, *General Comment No. 13: The right to education* (art. 13), UN Doc. E/C.12/1999/10 (1999), UN Doc. E/C.12/1999/10 (8 December 1999) [hereinafter 'General Comment No. 13'], available at: http://www.unhchr.ch/tbs/doc.nsf/(Symbol)/ae1a0b126d068e868025683c003c8b3b?Opendocument (accessed 3 February 2010). While it should be noted that a right to education does not necessarily subsume a right to textbooks, the CESCR in General Comment No. 13 observes that: '[F]unctioning educational institutions and programmes have to be available in sufficient quantity within the jurisdiction of the State party. What they require to function depends upon numerous factors, including the developmental context within which they operate; for example, all institutions and programmes are likely to require buildings . . . trained teachers receiving domestically competitive salaries, *teaching materials*, and so on; while some will also require facilities such as a library, computer facilities and information technology' (para. 6(a); emphasis added).

24 The organization 3D (2005, p. 4) suggests that the right to education under Article 13 of the ICESCR and Article 29 of the CRC, as well as the UNESCO Convention Against Discrimination in Education, should be used as basis for expanding flexibilities under IP. See UNESCO Convention Against Discrimination in Education (Paris, 14 December 1960), 429 U.N.T.S. 93, available at: http://www.unesco.org/education/pdf/DISCRI_E.PDF (accessed 22 April 2010). The relationship of the human rights regime to the development regime, and the subsequent relationship of both to the global intellectual property regime, is complex and beyond the scope of this chapter. See generally Alston (2005, p. 755) describing the complex linkage of development and human rights. A couple of small observations are in order, however. As Helfer (2007, pp. 998–999) points out, regardless of the ultimate tilt of the human rights approach to intellectual property, existing ICESCR Committee documents provide that 'states have a duty to prevent unreasonably high costs for access to essential medicines, plant seeds or other means of food production, or for schoolbooks and learning materials, from undermining the rights of large segments of the population to health, food and education'. Second, according to Alston (2005, pp. 782–783), 'every single government in the world (except those of Somalia and the United States) has by virtue of ratification of the Convention on the Rights of the Child explicitly accepted that there is such a right [to education]'.

25 Drache and Froese (2005, p. 28) observe that: 'Developing skills for the information economy requires raising literacy rates with a greater investment in education – an area of primary importance for developing nations. As literacy levels rise, culture becomes more than entertainment; it becomes part of a strategy for social cohesion and inclusion. . . . Identity becomes a strategic resource to facilitate the active participation of both genders in the public life of southern societies.' Cao (2004, p. 1078) suggests that: 'Lest one too blithely disparages efforts to institute change through the educational system, it is important to note that scholars have long studied how "education constructs culture"' (footnote omitted).

26 For further discussion of the interplay between the IP regime complex and other international regimes, see generally Helfer 2007, Raustiala 2007 and Yu 2007.

public goods, such as education and communicable disease control, 'IP from below' begins to address the larger problem of fragmented global public goods policy-making.

Thus the key term 'development' in the TRIPS preamble and objectives,[27] implemented through related copyright treaties administered by WIPO such as the Berne Convention, should include the provision of basic education (Chon 2006, pp. 2893–2908; see generally Chon 2007). Accordingly, what would a truly development-sensitive copyright law and policy look like? It would reveal a human development focus on IP that has access to education as an outcome measure – resulting in a different normative tilt to existing doctrine.

3. Linking capabilities to educational access

The lack of adequate textbook[28] provision for basic education in developing countries is well documented (Commission on Intellectual Property Rights [CIPR] 2002, p. 103). As stated recently:

> [T]extbooks are a rare commodity in most developing countries. One book per student (in any subject) is the exception, not the rule,[29] and the rule in most classrooms is, unfortunately, severe scarcity or the total absence of textbooks.... For the majority of the world's students, access to basic tools for learning is so limited as to constitute a major crisis. (Sosale 1999, p. 1, quoting Askerud 1997, p. 16)

Although data on education for development are scarce and it is difficult to ascertain state expenditure on educational materials,[30] observers agree that expenditures for textbooks represent a relatively low proportion of total educational expenditures (1–10%).[31] Accurate information about the number and distribution of textbooks across developing countries is not collected on a regular basis. However, the UNESCO Basic Education Monitoring Report in 2000 suggests that 'textbooks are relatively available in [some countries such as] the People's Republic of China and Tunisia but supply remains a key problem in many low-income countries such as Guatemala, Madagascar, Pakistan, [Democratic Republic of the] Congo' (Heyneman 2006, p. 62).

27 The TRIPS Agreement, Article 8.

28 A textbook is defined as 'a book whose purpose is for "instructional use"... [as opposed to] materials whose authors did not intend the material for use in schools, for example, plays by Shakespeare' (Heyneman 2006, p. 36).

29 Data on textbook shortages are inconsistent because countries may report 'sufficient' textbooks that may mean one book per five students. Most estimates suggest that around 60% of developing countries lack sufficient textbooks. Although textbooks typically comprise less than 1% of the educational budget, few developing countries have a policy to provide and sustain the provision of textbooks (Oliveira 1996, pp. 80–82). The World Bank (2004, pp. 4–5) notes in the context of Uganda that, while the goal was one text for every three students, the actual ratio was 1:7 given an increase in enrollment.

30 The richest countries spend about $300 per student on books and the poorest spend less than $1 per student on books each year (MacPherson & Pearce 1990, p. 6). A study by Consumers International (2006, p. 2; p. 59, n.3) compared figures for public investment devoted to education in eleven countries based on the UNESCO Institute for Statistics Regional Reports for South and East Asia.

31 There is better data on spending on adult literacy programmes (see UNESCO 2006, Executive Summary). However, the Berne Convention Article 10(2) does not apply to teaching for these kinds of programmes. See Section 5 of this chapter.

On the other hand, evidence about the impact of textbook availability on basic learning is clear. As Heyneman, a major researcher in this area summarized:

> Analytic work sponsored by the World Bank in the 1970s contributed three lessons. The first was obvious, but often overlooked: that textbook availability was the single most consistent correlate of academic achievement in developing countries, thus justifying public investment in education reading materials. The second was the argument that textbook supply was analogous to that of other manufactured products in that quality, efficiency and price was a function of the private as opposed to public sources, hence justifying the Bank's priority for textbook supply as a legitimate investment.[32] The third was the evidence that textbook investments could significantly change the academic achievement of a nation's school children, and on occasion reach a level of effect unprecedented in the education sciences. (Ibid., p. 38, citations omitted)

The positive impact of textbooks on educational achievement seems to be much greater at the lowest levels of availability, such as increasing textbooks from one per class to one per student (ibid., p. 61; see also Farrell & Heyneman 1989, pp. 3–5). The obvious policy conclusion is that greater access to textbooks is desirable.

Access to textbooks for students varies greatly between developed and developing countries. Textbooks are typically distributed to students 'for free' in the United States, as part of the system of public education. Even in the US, which is one the most developed of the developed countries, textbooks can be out-of-date and in short supply.[33] In the vast majority of developing countries, however, the state does not provide textbooks; students must purchase them out-of-pocket (Heyneman 2006, p. 47).[34] The reasons for the lack of state provision include 'rises in enrollment, economic recession, civil conflict, and pressing economic priorities in public health' (ibid., p. 47). Additionally, structural adjustment policies have caused sacrifices across all public sector spending, especially education

[32] From 1962 to 1980, the World Bank treated textbooks as a 'recurrent' cost and not a legitimate Bank investment (Heyneman 2003, pp. 322, 323).

[33] Press Release, Association of American Publishers, 'NEA/AAP Survey Finds Nationwide Textbook Shortages, Teachers Don't Have Enough Books to Assign Homework', 8 October 2002; see also National Education Association 2002. Moreover, linguistic and cultural minorities even in resource-rich countries such as the US may not be provisioned with appropriate textbooks. Goldsmith et al. (2004, pp. 6–30) note that: 'Schools serving Alaska Natives, especially those in rural areas, have a greater challenge to meet than many schools. Most of the teaching materials and curricula were designed to connect with students whose lives are very different – children who live in cities and suburbs, with paved roads and public buses, whose first and only language is probably English'.

[34] Oliveira (1996, p. 82) observes that: 'Although textbooks seldom cost more than 1% of total education budgets, governments in developing countries rarely supply them regularly. . . . [Studies have] concluded that virtually no developing country has managed to establish a policy and the means to produce and provide textbooks on a sustainable basis. Relatively few countries have specific budget line items to acquire instructional materials. Even when they do, as is typical in Latin America, the funds are not adequately invested, which leads to erratic policies and irregular provision. Some countries attempt to provide textbooks using outside money from donors or lending institutions. In many cases, such projects are seen by donors as means to develop a textbook infrastructure. However, these projects are usually fragile and seldom lead to institutionalization'. One recent exception is Pakistan, which provided free textbooks up to grade 5 in an effort to combat child labour and illiteracy. See Bureau of International Labor Affairs, Department of Labor, 2005, 'Combating Exploitive Child Labor through Education in Pakistan', *Federal Register*, vol. 70, pp. 43182, 43184.

(see Farrell & Heyneman 1989, p. 2).[35] 'No nation chooses to have families cover school book costs on the basis of philosophy; rather it is a matter of exigency' (Heyneman 2006, p. 47).

The price of textbooks can be very high relative to per capita income for a number of reasons. In the case of state-owned or assisted publishing, these reasons include inefficient manufacturing methods, state monopolies and favouritism (Grahm & Pehrsson 2004, pp. 6–21; Heyneman 2006, p. 48). In the case of market-based textbook publishing, these reasons may include industry consolidation and lack of competition (Rens, Prabhala & Kawooya 2006, p. 12; Heyneman 2006, p. 56).[36] Higher prices may be caused by the failure of multinational publishers to engage in differential pricing, so that a student in a developing country may pay a relatively high price for a book as a percentage of per capita GDP compared to a student in a developed country (Consumers International 2006, pp. 41–42; Rachagan 2004, pp. 4–5).[37] Many developing countries, likewise, are 'dominated by the major international languages and this dominance places a further strain on limited publishing and other resources' (Altbach 1989, p. 93). It also makes these countries dependent on the nations which publish in the major international languages (ibid.). Moreover, the existence of minority languages within developing countries requires either de novo content creation or translation of existing materials that adds to the cost of textbook development.[38]

Reliance on trade books rather than textbooks does not solve the pricing or access issues (Oliveira 1996, pp. 85–88).[39] A literature-based approach to basic

35 Moreover, many countries charge fees to primary students to attend school (UNESCO 2006, p. 1). When the Ugandan President eliminated school fees in 1997, enrollment doubled (The World Bank 2004, p. ix).

36 Rens, Prabhala and Kawooya (2006, p. 12) note that: 'Among the main reasons for the excessive pricing of books in South Africa is a lack of competition in the market, evidenced in several ways across the spectrum of book publishing. In the Academic book publishing market (denoting textbooks and reference material primarily for tertiary education), the GPI report notes that three publishers (LexisNexis Butterworths, Pearson and Juta) have a combined market share of 62%. Academic book distribution is even more consolidated, with two firms – Van Schaik and Juta retail – holding close to a 100% market share. In the schoolbooks market (i.e. primary and secondary education), five publishers (Maskew Miller Longman, Macmillan, Nasou, Oxford University Press, and Juta) hold a combined market share of 71%'. Heyneman (2006, p. 56) further observes that: 'Eighty percent of the book sales in the US are controlled by five major conglomerates; the largest ten publishers were responsible for 75% of the annual revenue'.

37 According to Consumers International (2006, pp. 41–42), calculations show that asking an Indonesian student to pay $81.70 for a textbook would be equivalent to asking a US student to pay $3,170.97. One non-textbook example is Harry Potter, 'which [was] priced at 6.86% of per capita GDP in India but only 0.13% of per capital GDP in the UK'. Rachagan, S. 2004, 'Presentation at the Transatlantic Consumer Dialogue Workshop on Global Access to Essential Learning Tools', 5 April 2004, Summary, pp. 4–5. The CIPR final report made a very strong recommendation to publishers to 'review their pricing policies . . . to facilitate access to their products in developing countries' (CIPR 2002, p. 102).

38 But with 'recent implementation of second-language school instruction in China, Russia, Japan, and in many parts of Europe and Latin America, however, almost half of today's population of readers now read in English. This has extraordinary implications for the supply of school textbooks' (Heyneman 2006, p. 58).

39 The Berne Appendix addresses textbooks rather than trade books (the publishing industry uses the term 'trade books' to denote books intended for a general audience rather than for academic purposes). The Berne Appendix has a waiting period of five years for textbooks, but seven years for fictional works, as well as three years for science books – the rationale for a longer period for fictional works is that they are 'less necessary for the purposes of (developing) countries'(Ricketson & Ginsburg 2006, vol. 2, sec. 14.82, p. 943).

education is costly compared to a textbook-based approach. This is due to the lack of capacity and infrastructure to publish supplementary books (ibid., p. 86),[40] the expense of teacher training, and language difficulties including the challenge of multilingual nations (ibid., p. 87). However, the limited book supply is 'perhaps the biggest obstacle to literacy using [non-textbook] reading materials alone'.[41]

The combination of all these factors has led to severe access problems with respect to basic educational materials protected by copyright. The top-down way of understanding this problem is through the frequently invoked and succinct term 'piracy' with its heavy implication of blame and censure (Liu 2004, p. A43; Lloyd 2004, p. A41; Overland 2004, p. A40; see also Chapters 1 and 7). However, a 'from below' understanding is that this represents a failure in access to essential learning materials, combined with the necessary logic of an informal economy and with cultural factors (Rens et al. 2006, pp. 18, 25–30; Yu 2000, pp. 175–176; Yu 2001, pp. 56–57).

Considering the implications of reprography (i.e. photocopying) as an 'access tool' to educational materials in Africa, Rens et al. suggest that:

> Following from the earlier discussions of affordability and excessive pricing, and contrary to the mainstream market logic underlying the copyright system, a vast number of faculty and students in southern educational institutions cannot afford the material they need to read and study. At the institutional level, financial resource constraints deter libraries from adequately updating or expanding their collections. Whereas the use of electronic domain content is often discussed as a potential means to overcome rent collection problems in the copyright industry, in fact, poor infrastructure and low bandwidth, prohibitive subscription costs, legally endorsed technological constraints (such as TPMs) and the relative absence of open content licences combine to render digital content inaccessible or unfeasible. Photocopying, then, fills a crucial gap: it facilitates access in an environment where there are limited options to do so.... (2006, pp. 29–30)

Rens et al. qualify, at the same time, that photocopying of textbooks as a practice is neither limited to poor students alone, nor solely evident in southern countries (ibid.). They observe that existing studies focus excessively on the supply side of photocopying services rather than examining demand structures for copying of copyright protected material through reprography (ibid., pp. 27–34). They suggest that more attention needs to be placed on differentiating the socio-economic situation of actors, and understanding the 'workings of informal enterprises in educational settings and their contributions to the institutions in widening access to content' (ibid., pp. 29–30).

40 Oliveira (1996, p. 86) notes that: 'If developing a textbook publishing industry takes an estimated fifteen years, a more diversified one that could supply library and trade books would take considerably longer: print quantities are necessarily smaller, markets are reduced, language problems add to the complexity, and lack of distribution channels makes procurement and distribution complex.'

41 For all these reasons, Oliveira concludes that literature based instruction may be cheaper and less dependent on government publishing, but currently can only be effective as a supplement to textbooks, not a replacement for them (ibid., p. 87).

4. Linking educational access to copyright

Of course, the understanding that the dissemination of knowledge may take priority, in some instances, over the protection of knowledge is implicit in exceptions or limitations within national laws, such as the open-ended fair use provision of the US Copyright Act.[42] Other countries have enacted specific educational exceptions, summarized partially in Appendix D. Global IP law instruments, such as the illustration for teaching provision of Article 10(2) of the Berne Convention, may shape these various exceptions or limitations. As Okediji has pointed out:

> The absence of a set of minimum exceptions and/or limitations to copyright in the Berne Convention reflected the practice and understanding that the precise nature of such limitations and exceptions was to be left to the reserved powers of the State to protect the welfare interests of its citizens. Consequently, minimum rights were developed internationally through consensus, while specific exceptions and limitations remained the domain of the state.[43] (2006a, p. 5)

Yet this treaty structure does not seem to have trickled down into greater access by developing countries to textbooks and other knowledge inputs to education. Prevailing copyright practices and policies in the global book publishing industry have fostered inequality rather than addressed the glaring need to build domestic capacity in publishing or greater access to books published outside of a small national market (see Chakava 1995, pp. 20–24).[44] The net result is to promote unidirectional knowledge development and exchange in a manner that fails to benefit developing countries. As to the Berne Convention, several observers have recognized the glaring lack of transparency and functionality of the compulsory licensing provisions for educational use (Ricketson & Ginsburg 2006, vol. 2, sec. 14.106, p. 957; CIPR 2002, p. 104; Story 2003, p. 763; see generally Lazar 1971, p. 37).[45] These provisions were the result of a huge push by developing countries (arguably similar to the recent push in the WTO regarding TRIPS and public health) to

42 17 U.S.C. §§ 107, 110; see Appendix D.

43 Okediji (2006, p. 7) adds that: 'The Convention's silence with regard to exceptions and limitations can be understood simultaneously as an explicit expression of retained sovereignty (meaning that states reserved their right to regulate copyright as they deemed fit within their own borders constrained only by the obligations explicitly stated in the Convention) as well as the Convention's deference to such sovereignty. But in addition to states reserving their power over copyright matters more generally, there was some recognition in the context of the Convention itself that the international copyright rights being negotiated were inherently limited by the public interest'. See also Moncayo von Hase 1998, p. 134.

44 These include foreign (typically American or European) publishers' reluctance to grant reprint licences to domestic publishers even where there is local manufacturing capacity; harsh licensing terms with strict territorial restrictions, high licensing fees and demands for up-front payment of royalties; evidence that foreign publishers will publish the works of African authors without obtaining permission; the reluctance or outright refusal to grant translation rights to publishers in countries where native languages are not the lingua franca of Europe; and the lack of knowledge or implementation of the compulsory licensing provisions of the Berne Convention. See Chakava 1995, pp. 20–24.

45 As Ricketson and Ginsburg (2006, vol. 2, sec. 14.106, p. 957) observe: 'It is hard to point to any obvious benefits that have flowed directly to developing countries from the adoption of the Appendix. Indeed, [as of 2004] only a handful of developing countries have availed themselves of its provisions in the time since its adoption'. The CIPR Report (2002, p. 104) suggests that: 'Examining the evidence 30 years later, it is clear to us that the special provisions for developing countries that were added to the Berne Convention in 1971, as set out in the Appendix, have not been effective'.

shape copyright rules appropriate for the needs of developing countries, including more liberal translation rights, shorter duration of copyright, and use of works for broadcasting and educational purposes (Okediji 2005, p. 15; Okediji 2006a, p. 157). The compromise, the 1971 Appendix to the Paris Act Revision of the Berne Convention (also known as the Berne Appendix), contains provisions so complex and arcane that few developing countries have been able or willing to take advantage of them.[46] Thus, instead of building capacity, the Berne Convention poses structural impediments to the creation of local publishing industries and to the translation of textbooks from the world's dominant languages into minority languages (Basamalah 2000, pp. 544–545).[47]

Others scholars have noted the anti-competitive nature of the global publishing industry (Drahos & Braithwaite 2002, p. 78).[48] A pre-TRIPS analysis has also compared the copyright industries of the North to the OPEC cartel, with oligopolistic control over distribution and pricing and high barriers to entry resulting in sharp and systematic inequality of knowledge exchange (Altbach 1995, p. 5).[49] Often, trade sanctions or structural adjustment conditions exacerbate the problem. For example, no small part of Korea's success as one of the four 'Asian Tigers' is due to its government's deliberately weak copyright laws prior to the TRIPS Agreement (CIPR, 2002, p. 20).[50] Yet even before TRIPS, the US Trade Representative put pressure on Korea for what it perceived to be violations of copyright (Drahos & Braithwaite 2002, pp. 19–20).[51] TRIPS has exacerbated the net movement of global rents

[46] According to our count, only fifteen countries have filed declarations under Article 1 with respect to the facilities provided by Articles II and III (Notification numbers 79, 91, 109, 110, 232–40, 245 and 248). The Appendix exceeds the length of the original Berne Convention. Examples of its complexity include waiting periods from three to seven years to get a licence, after which the author can still terminate any time, and different provisions for translation and reproduction licences, which cover the same works.

[47] Under the Berne Appendix, translation licences are available if the language in general use is English, French or Spanish. Many African countries are English or French-speaking as a legacy of colonialism.

[48] As Drahos and Braithwaite (2002, p. 74) observe: 'For a long time copyright had been used by Western publishers to run cartels. Books were at their cheapest in the US where publishers from time to time faced antitrust actions and a more competitive domestic market than elsewhere in the world. London book publishers dominated the book markets of the [British] Empire and then the Commonwealth. After World War 2, New York and London publishers came to an agreement not to compete on each other's turf. Known as the British Publishers Traditional Market Agreement, it placed the book market of many developing countries under the influence of London publishers'.

[49] Altbach (1995, p. 5) comments that: 'There is a kind of OPEC of knowledge in which a few rich nations and a small number of multinational publishers have a great deal of control over how and where books are published, the prices of printed materials, and the nature of international exchange of knowledge'.

[50] The CIPR Report (2002, p. 20) notes that: 'Fourthly, the best examples in the recent history of development are the countries in East Asia which used weak forms of IP protection tailored to their particular circumstances at that stage of their development. Throughout the critical phase of rapid growth in Taiwan and Korea between 1960 and 1980, during which their economies were transformed, both countries emphasized the importance of imitation and reverse engineering as an important element in developing their indigenous technological and innovative capacity' (see also ibid., p. 22).

[51] Drahos and Braithwaite (2002, pp. 19–20) describe how USTR pressured the Korean government to prosecute 'highly respected Korean businessman who ran a publishing business called Tower Publications. Tower published textbooks for the South Korean market. This market had grown dramatically because South Korea had made the education and training of its population a priority. The presses at Tower reproduced tens of thousands of American textbooks, but American publishers and authors did not

towards developed countries. In addition to reducing flexibility in domestic regulatory strategies regarding global public goods, the benefits of TRIPS accrue overwhelmingly to publisher-rich countries such as the US and the UK (CIPR 2002, p. 97).[52]

Reasons for higher textbook prices may include the inability or unwillingness of Berne developing member countries to engage robustly in the compulsory licensing provisions of the Berne Appendix, as discussed previously. With narrow exceptions, the Berne Appendix does not allow a country issuing a licence to print books domestically to extend that licence to the publication of books outside the country with the purpose of importing them in.[53] Although permitted by Berne and TRIPS, parallel imports of cheaper editions of books from other countries may be banned by domestic law,[54] underutilized,[55] or foreclosed by TRIPS-plus agreements.[56]

Moreover, the conditions of education in many developing countries may not fall within the local exceptions for fair use or educational use. For example, under local South African copyright law, educational exceptions are limited to classroom use, and materials have to be used inside a classroom. Yet, in many rural schools, the teaching literally takes place outside and thus falls outside the exception.[57] A relatively recent phenomenon is the expansion of the reprographic collection society model to parts of the developing world that have questionable capacity to participate in the exchange of royalty fees between reproduction rights organizations and user groups (mostly educational institutions) (Copy/South Research Group 2006, p. 41).[58]

see any license fees or royalty payments.... The head of Tower Publications spent eight or so weeks in jail'.

52 According to the CIPR Report (2002, p. 97): 'From a global perspective, the direct rewards from copyright protection are largely directed to the publishing, entertainment and software industries in Europe and North America'.

53 Berne Convention Appendix Article IV(4). As Ricketson & Ginsburg (2006, vol. 2, sec. 14.95, p. 949) note: 'It follows from these territorial restrictions that a licensee will be excluded from having his translation or reproduction printed outside the territory of the country which has granted the license'.

54 See Rachagan, S. 2004, Presentation at the TransAtlantic Consumer Dialogue Workshop on Global Access to Essential Learning Tools, 5 April 2004, summary, p. 4. Rachagan notes that '[i]n Malaysia, for example, the prices of imported books are reviewed every three months', and yet books by Malaysian publishers are not allowed to be sold in Brunei and Indonesia (ibid.).

55 Ibid., pp. 4–5.

56 Abbott (2006, p. 14) cites the example of Morocco-US FTA, which prohibits parallel importation of copyrighted works, which is US-plus standard.

57 Caine, C. 2004, Presentation at the Transatlantic Consumer Dialogue Workshop on Global Access to Essential Learning Tools, 5 April 2004, summary, pp. 4–5.

58 Copy/South Research Group (2006, p. 41) note that there were thirty-three RROs in total globally in 2001, including in Kenya, Zimbabwe and South Africa; see also the testimony of J. Hofman summarized in G. Hinze, 'Blogging WIPO: Information Meeting on Educational Content and Copyright in the Digital Age', 21 November 2005, available at: http://www.eff.org/deeplinks/2005/11/blogging-wipo-information-meeting-educational-content-and-copyright-digital-age (accessed 22 April 2010). Hofman comments that: 'Where someone is using an online distribution in a way that impacts the sales, that person should be paying royalties. But where the use is in the normal course of education, it's a tax on learning and in a country where there are problems in education, this is an important problem' (ibid.).

Finally, most of the textbook publishing industry is concentrated in the developed countries (CIPR 2002, p. 97).[59] As Altbach puts it:

> The infrastructure for disseminating knowledge is basically controlled by the industrial nations. The prominent publishing firms are located in those nations, and they control the production and the distribution of books around the world. There is a large trade in the export of books from the industrial nations to developing countries.... Indeed, about half the sales of the British publishing industry are dependent on overseas trade, much of it to the developing world, and the French have a similar export market. The Americans, with only 10 percent of their publishing output exported, are more insular; but they too have had a growing interest in export sales – for political and cultural as much as for commercial reasons.[60] (1989, p. 93; citations omitted)

Thus, many developing countries represent markets that are composed asymmetrically of users rather than producers (Okediji 2006b, p. 241).[61] They also represent markets that, while perhaps altogether numerically large, are often individually neither profitable nor financially enticing to developed country producers. They are markets that are struggling to build domestic capacity and are not yet exporting globally.[62] One big exception is India (Alikhan 2000, p. 61).[63]

While publishers located in developed countries continue to engage in initiatives such as donation, differential pricing, publishing partnerships and the like (CIPR 2002, pp. 101–102),[64] there is consensus that much more needs to be done to ensure access to textbooks *and* to build local publishing capacity in developing countries.[65] As an expert in international textbook provision recently asked:

> The basic question is how to raise the supply and the quality of school textbooks most efficiently. Because the content and purpose is a public good, there is no obvious objection to state intervention. Whenever the public interest is at stake there is economic justification for state intervention. But what kind of intervention is called for? (Heyneman 2006, p. 48)

59 According to the CIPR Report (2002, p. 97), 'the US, UK, Germany, Spain, France and Italy between them produced nearly two thirds of global exports of books in 1998'.

60 See also Heyneman 2006, p. 68; Aoki 1998, pp. 24–26.

61 Okediji (2006b, p. 241) describes book-publishing industry in Africa as negligible and number of books in circulation and for sale in most African countries as 'abysmally low and unaffordable for the average African'.

62 See the testimony of O. Lawal-Solarin summarized in G. Hinze, 'Blogging WIPO: Information Meeting on Educational Content and Copyright in the Digital Age', 21 November 2005, available at: http://www.eff.org/deeplinks/2005/11/blogging-wipo-information-meeting-educational-content-and-copyright-digital-age (accessed 22 April 2010).

63 Alikhan (2000, p. 61) points out that in 1996, the contribution of cultural industry to India's GNP was 5.06%. He adds that: 'The private sector which has throughout had an important role, is present in most sectors of the economy, and generates around two-thirds of the country's GDP.... It has a sophisticated book publishing industry, which ranks amongst the top 10 in the world. The annual book title production was around 57,400 in 1997. The turnover was over US $455 million' (ibid.).

64 See also the testimony of S. Leong summarized in G. Hinze, 'Blogging WIPO: Information Meeting on Educational Content and Copyright in the Digital Age', 1 November 2005, available at: http://www.eff.org/deeplinks/2005/11/blogging-wipo-information-meeting-educational-content-and-copyright-digital-age (accessed 22 April 2010).

65 As the CIPR Report observed, 'our consultations with stakeholders and reading of the evidence suggests that the issues [of copyright access by developing countries] are most serious in relation to access to education materials where demand is not met by the local publishing industries or donor-financed programmes' (CIPR 2002, p. 100).

In the public goods jargon, static inefficiencies (or higher costs of goods) are generated as an inevitable residual of IP protection such as copyright. However, from a substantive equality perspective, the costs of copyright protection implicated here are several orders of magnitude greater, in both direct and indirect effects, than the costs for someone who is unable to access a Hollywood film for weekend leisure. As the CIPR report emphasized:

> [T]he evidence shows that weak levels of copyright enforcement have had a major impact on diffusion of knowledge and knowledge-based products... throughout the developing world. Indeed, it is arguably the case that many poor people in developing countries have only been able to access certain copyrighted works through using unauthorized copies available at a fraction of the price of the genuine original product. We are therefore concerned that an unintended impact of stronger protection and enforcement of international copyright rules as required, *inter alia*, by TRIPS will be simply to reduce access to knowledge products in developing countries, with damaging consequences for poor people. (CIPR 2002, p. 101)

5. Substantive equality: Copyright and capability for basic education

I have suggested that a substantive equality principle is needed in global IP norm-setting and norm-interpreting activities, to facilitate access to essential information goods (Chon 2006, p. 2886). This principle would be drawn from the key term 'development' in relevant international IP foundational documents (ibid., p. 2836; see Section 1). This principle would take the form of an extra 'thumb on the scale' of scepticism towards the enforcement of minimum rights expressed in multilateral or bilateral conventions as they pertain to certain types of development-sensitive categories (Chon 2007, pp. 479, 502). Conversely, this principle could express itself through a heightened embrace, as opposed to suspicion, of various exceptions and limitations expressed in these conventions (cf. Okediji 2006a, p. 8).[66] In either case, copyright norms would then be more responsive to the differently situated development concerns of various countries.

Others have already addressed the pressing need to reform the compulsory licensing provisions of Berne Appendix to provide access to educational materials for development (ibid., p. 29).[67] Not only have these provisions proved to be unworkable and unfair throughout their almost forty-year existence, but also they explicitly cover educational use, which under the US fair use doctrine is not a compensated use. Thus, users in developing countries, who are far less able to compensate copyright holders, are expected to provide equitable remuneration, whereas

[66] Okediji (2006a, p. 8) states that 'the exercise of sovereign discretion in policy spaces is deliberately curtailed by standards negotiated in international regimes... [and t]he integration of intellectual property with the free trade regime has meant that arguments in favor of limitations and exceptions to intellectual property rights are received with skepticism'.

[67] As Okediji observes: 'The Appendix must be reformed to reflect changing conditions in developing countries and also to facilitate a more expedient process for utilizing compulsory licensing to gain bulk access. Such reform should include at a minimum: 1) the elimination of the waiting period and the grace period; 2) the elimination of notification to the owner *prior* to issuing the license; 3) eliminating the economies of scale problem by allowing simultaneous application for the translation and reproduction licenses under the same conditions; 4) expanding the scope for which the license is issued to extend beyond teaching, education and research' (ibid., p. 29).

users in the US may rely on uncompensated educational use in certain situations.[68] From an 'IP from below' perspective, this global structure is distributionally unjust.

What are possible alternatives? Some may lie in the area of specific exceptions and limitations, enacted in domestic legislation of member states or through bilateral, regional, or even multilateral agreements. As stated by Okediji:

> [T]he recognized exceptions in the national legislation of each country were not rooted in a comprehensive philosophical perspective or policy with regard to copyright specifically, but instead tended to reflect broad themes within the socio-historical and political culture of the particular country. (2000, p. 99)

Most exceptions within the Berne Convention are left to national legislation (Ricketson & Ginsburg 2006, vol. 1, sec. 14.106, p. 789).[69] While not purporting to be complete, Appendix D demonstrates the variation among countries that have enacted specific educational exceptions. The wealthier, developed countries tend to have the most restrictive provisions (see also Goldstein 2001, p. 316; Newby 1999, pp. 1642–1645). The US is a notable exception to this rule; this is possibly because the US was a developing country itself when its courts were defining the parameters of the judge-made fair use doctrine. Moreover, the US acceded to the Berne Convention in 1988, well after its fair use doctrine was firmly established (see Leaffer 2001, p. 855; Okediji 2000, pp. 90–91).[70] However, even within the US, the scope of educational fair use is a contested policy space (see e.g. Bartow 1998, p. 150; Litman 1987, pp. 867–888).

From a distributive standpoint, fair use is a choice in favour of access to a knowledge good recognizing that socially beneficial uses may not always be better internalized by the rights holder. Leading commentators on fair use in the US view educational fair use as a special fair use case, not only because it is listed as one of the categories within section 107 but also because of its positive spillover effects on society as a whole. As Gordon (1982, p. 1630) stated, 'teaching and scholarship may yield significant "external benefits"; all of society benefits from having an educated citizenry and from advances in knowledge, ... [and thus] the market cannot be

[68] Because the problem in developing countries is the lack of domestic publishing capacity, most do not have domestic compulsory licensing provisions. According to Ricketson & Ginsburg, '... of those countries that have made the necessary declarations, very few actually seem to have implemented such licensing schemes in their domestic laws' (2006, vol. 2, sec. 14.106, p. 957). Among developed countries, the Netherlands, Poland and Switzerland subject textbook authors to remunerating authors of original work used in textbooks with a type of compulsory licence (Geller 2002, vol. 2, secs. 8[2][f] NETH-73, 8[2][e] POL-51, 8[2][a][i] SWI-69).

[69] Ricketson and Ginsburg (2006, vol. 1, sec.13.44, p. 789) observe that: '[A]t the 1885 Conference, ... it proved impossible to retain agreement on the form of a uniform international regulation of these kinds of "borrowings". The Consequence was that the 1885 draft, which ultimately became the Berne Act, reserved these matters to national legislation and bilateral agreements'. See further Goldstein 2001, p. 26; Ricketson & Ginsburg 2006, vol. 1, sec. 13.45, p. 791; Ginsburg 2000, p. 287. Ginsburg (2000, p. 287) observes that: 'Regarding exceptions to copyright, a strong case may also be made for application of each country's laws on its own territory. While international instruments impose a general framework, they preserve some national autonomy regarding the content (and, outside the EU, the form) of copyright exceptions. Thus, the flexible (perhaps unpredictable) US fair use exception may co-exist with a more rigid continental-style closed list of specific exemptions and limitations'.

[70] Leaffer (2001, p. 855) doubts the viability of the US fair use doctrine; Okediji (2000, pp. 90, 91) surmises that the US fair use provision possibly flunks the three-step test of TRIPS Article 13. But see Samuelson (1999 pp. 100–103), claiming that existing exceptions and limitations reflecting cultural values, such as the fair use exception, may have been grandfathered into TRIPS and therefore do not violate Article 13.

relied upon as a mechanism for facilitating socially desirable transactions' (see also Goldstein 2003, pp. 137–138).[71] From a non-economic lens, Fisher links fair use to a vision of 'the good society, … [which] would incorporate more than "schooling"' but also a variety of institutions designed to enhance people's knowledge of public affairs (1988, pp. 1751, 1754, 1770–1771).[72]

The so-called illustration for teaching provision of Berne, Article 10(2), states:

> It shall be a matter for legislation in the countries of the Union, and for special agreements existing or to be concluded between them, to permit the utilization, to the extent justified by the purpose, of literary or artistic works by way of illustration in publications, broadcasts or sound or visual recordings *for teaching, provided such utilization is compatible with fair practice.*[73] (Emphasis added)

From its inception, the term 'teaching' in Article 10(2) covered primary to tertiary levels of teaching (Ricketson & Ginsberg 2006, p. 789).[74] This broad coverage was affirmed at the 1967 Stockholm Revision Conference (ibid., p. 792). In developing countries, a substantive equality principle would suggest the fullest expansion of this Berne-endorsed exception whenever possible. Among countries that have not yet enacted educational exceptions (or that even have curtailed the optimal policy space for educational exceptions to copyright provided by Article 10(2)) (see Okediji 2006a, pp. 30–31; Consumers International 2006, p. xi),[75] these choices may reflect the lack of domestic institutional capacity to design appropriate policies (Okediji 2006b, p. 241) as much as deliberate social policy. Where the former is the case, the domestic enactment of the broadest possible exception, including an illustration for teaching purpose, can begin to create access to works for educational purposes that may counterbalance the lack of bulk access (ibid., p. 230)[76] to textbooks through the Berne Appendix.

[71] Goldstein (2003, pp. 137–138) describes the social benefit of educational use where 'people other than the immediate user will benefit from the use, and if the value of these benefits is aggregated the sum may well exceed the value of alternative uses to the copyright owner'.

[72] Fisher (1988, pp. 1751, 1754, 1770–1771) advocates 'preferential treatment in the fair use calculus to activities that facilitate education – either by enhancing access to information and argument on matters of public importance or by increasing the ability of teachers to design and deliver to students the packages of materials they deem most effective. The more a particular use would advance that end, the more of a boost it should get'.

[73] The exact meaning of 'fair practice' is unclear. Ricketson & Ginsburg (2006, vol. 1, sec. 13.41, p. 786) document that the programme for the 1967 Stockholm Revision Conference includes a statement that 'the use in question can only be accepted after an objective appreciation'.

[74] Ricketson and Ginsburg (2006, vol. 1, sec. 13.44, p. 789) suggest that: 'The words "by way of illustration" impose some limitation, but would not exclude the uses of the whole of a work in appropriate circumstances. For example, in the case of an artistic work or short literary work it might be argued that it is necessary to reproduce the whole work if it is to be properly utilized for teaching purposes' (ibid., p. 791). At least one delegate to the Stockholm Conference took the position that the term 'borrowings' in an earlier translation of the French 'emprunts' indicated 'the use of an entire work might be allowable within article 10(2), under some circumstances' (ibid., p. 792).

[75] A study of eleven developing countries in Asia shows that these exceptions are not fully maximized (Consumers International 2006, p. xi).

[76] Okediji (2006b, p. 230) notes that: 'Bulk access … is … critical to developing countries where education is a top development priority. For such countries, the freedom to quote from copyrighted material … is secondary to the need for affordable access to educational texts, scientific journals and other learning materials. Ironically, however, issues regarding bulk access have not featured prominently in the welfare critique or in demands for reform of the international intellectual property system'. Okediji (2006a, p. 3) further defines bulk access as 'access to sufficient copies of copyrighted works at affordable prices'; see also Okediji 2005, p. 148, defining access in four ways: uncompensated creative access, negotiated access, mandatory compensated access and bulk compensated access.

A 2003 WIPO study reiterated that utilization for teaching is a matter to be determined by national legislation (WIPO 2003, p. 14). Moreover,

> Unlike earlier versions of this Article, no quantitative limitations are contained . . . , apart from the general qualification that the utilization of works should only be 'to the extent justified by the purpose, . . . by way of illustration . . . for teaching, provided that such utilization is compatible with fair practice.' These references to purpose and fair practice are similar to those in Article 10(1), and make the provision more open-ended, implying no necessary quantitative limitations. The words 'by way of illustration' impose some limitation, but would not exclude the use of the whole of a work in appropriate circumstances, for example, in the case of an artistic work or short literary work. (Ibid.)

In tandem, developing countries might enact international exhaustion rules that would facilitate parallel importation of educational materials that pass muster under the provisions of the US fair use doctrine, the Canadian fair dealing doctrine (Tawfik 2005, pp. 2–7),[77] or other countries' educational exceptions.[78] This 'reverse parallel educational use' would be both Berne and TRIPS-compliant. These various strategies could provide an important point of access to educational materials from developed countries without the onerous licensing and equitable remuneration requirements of the Berne Appendix.[79] A substantive equality principle points strongly in the direction of these creative types of norm-setting.

Digital technology has tremendous potential to leverage information for development. The recent appearance of the $100 hand-cranked laptop, run on open-source software,[80] lends itself to a myriad of possibilities for non-textbook-based distance education. The WIPO Copyright Treaty (WCT) does not foreclose the enactment of further domestic exceptions and limitations to digital rights sounding in copyright.[81] There is currently an effort in WIPO, spearheaded by Chile, to

77 Tawfik (2005, pp. 2–7) describes the Supreme Court of Canada's enunciation of fair dealing as user right in CCH Canadian Ltd v. Law Society of Upper Canada, 2004 SCC 13.

78 Article 6 of the TRIPS Agreement refrains from setting rules of exhaustion and/or parallel importation. A recent study of eleven developing countries in Asia shows that this flexibility is greatly underutilized (Consumers International 2006, pp. ix–xi).

79 Interestingly, savvy consumers in developed countries such as the US are exploring parallel importation to maximize access to educational content. See Lewin 2003, p. A1.

80 Crowley (2005, p. 79) emphasizes that computers can be low cost if they use non-proprietary software. But see the testimony of O. Lawal-Solarin summarized in G. Hinze, 'Blogging WIPO: Information Meeting on Educational Content and Copyright in the Digital Age', 21 November 2005, available at: http://www.eff.org/deeplinks/2005/11/blogging-wipo-information-meeting-educational-content-and-copyright-digital-age (accessed 22 April 2010); Lawal-Solarin expresses doubt about the relevance of laptops: 'If you produce books that are cheap enough, it would provide six books per child for the same period. We're not allowing Africa to . . . produce culturally relevant books' (ibid.).

81 See Agreed Statements Concerning the WIPO Copyright Treaty (Geneva, 20 December 1996), Statement Concerning Article 10, Doc. CRNR/DC/97 [hereinafter 'Agreed Statements'], available at: http://www.wipo.int/treaties/en/ip/wct/statements.html (accessed 22 April 2010). According to the Agreed Statements: 'It is understood that the provisions of Article 10 permit Contracting Parties to carry forward and appropriately extend into the digital environment limitations and exceptions in their national laws which have been considered acceptable under the Berne Convention. Similarly, these provisions should be understood to permit Contracting Parties to devise new exceptions and limitations that are appropriate in the digital network environment. It is also understood that Article 10(2) [which is the WCT three-step test] neither reduces nor extends the scope of applicability of the limitations and exceptions permitted by the Berne Convention' (Statement Concerning Article 10). Ricketson and Ginsburg

study international minimum exceptions and limitations for educational and other uses in this context.[82]

Simultaneously, however, there are strong efforts by the copyright content industries in developed countries to expand digital rights (Dinwoodie 2004, pp. 173, 174; Correa 2002, p. 11). Furthermore, WCT signatories are enacting technological protection measures required by Article 11, such as the arguably draconian US Digital Millennium Copyright Act (DMCA).[83] These multilateral efforts have generated bilateral offspring (Hinze 2003, p. 5).[84] For developing countries, any additional ratcheting up of protections in the digital environment 'arguably constitute a dead weight loss on already fragile economies' (Okediji 2006b, p. 243) and should be viewed sceptically under a substantive equality paradigm.

Instead, the essential public goods nature of information should be viewed as a potential development asset. An 'IP from below' approach views the potential for diffusion and dissemination of digital knowledge at almost zero marginal cost (once infrastructure is established) quite differently. These characteristics should be used to nurture and expand the basic literacy and educational capacity that are prerequisites to the creation of a functioning future copyright content market. Especially where the danger to copyright interests associated with mass distribution via digital networks is reduced (e.g. because the work is culturally specific or is in a language that is not widely read), networked digital technology can and should be linked to diffusion models of information access.[85]

Countries should enact digital-specific educational exceptions where these are relevant and appropriate to their educational development policies. Arguably, these exceptions may even exceed the scope of Berne Article 10(2) (Agreed Statements 1996, p. 114).[86] Open course content initiatives in the tertiary textbook arena

(2006, vol. 1, sec. 4.23, p. 151) suggest that the purpose of the agreed statements 'is to provide guidance in the interpretation of particular treaty provisions'. Furthermore, '[a]greements of this kind are therefore not part of the "preparatory work" of the treaty, which may only be used as supplementary means of interpretation pursuant to article 32 . . . but will form part of the context of the treaty for the primary task of interpretation under article 31(1)' (ibid., p. 191).

82 See Proposal by Chile, Provisional Committee on Proposals Related to a WIPO Development Agenda, First Session, Geneva, 20–24 February 2006, Doc. PCDA/1/2, p. 5; WIPO 2005, Proposal by Chile on the Analysis of Exceptions and Limitations, 22 November 2005 (SCCR/13/5); WIPO 2005, Proposal by Chile on the Subject 'Exceptions and Limitations to Copyright and Related Rights', 2 November 2004 (SCCR/12/3).

83 17 U.S.C. § 1201.

84 These include the bilateral free trade agreements concluded between the US and Jordan (Article 4(13)), Singapore (Article 16.4(7)) and Chile (Article 17.7(5)). Hinze, G. 2003, Electronic Frontier Foundation, Technological Protections Issues Paper, 19 November 2003, p. 5 (on file with author).

85 Okediji (2005, pp. 182–186) proposes other mechanisms to increase access to copyrighted digital information works, including developing an international fair use doctrine, increasing the accountability of international property institutions and decreasing the pressure to participate in new developments, linking a moratorium on global intellectual property law-making to structural revisions of Article 20 of the Berne Convention, developing a proportional approach to access (limiting access to digital works in exchange for an increase in access to print works) and developing doctrines such as copyright misuse to address violations of copyright's underlying public policy. The substantive equality principle complements each of these proposals.

86 According to the Agreed Statements: 'Similarly, these provisions should be understood to permit Contracting Parties to devise new exceptions and limitations that are appropriate in the digital network environment' (Statement Concerning Article 10; see also ibid., p. 114). In this regard, developing countries should not follow the model of developed countries such as the US, which has understandably

indicate that market-based mechanisms for distribution are only one possible means for providing access to textbooks. Intergovernmental organizations[87] and prestigious educational institutions[88] are now providing content without charge. Private-public partnerships for library digitization projects (Vaidyanathan 2007, p. 1222) are proliferating.[89] These and other new digital initiatives have enormous potential to expand the informational universes of educational institutions (see Reed 2006, p. C09).

Are there possible roadblocks to such educational exceptions posed by the so-called three-step tests? Berne Article 9(2)[90] and its analogue in Article 13 of the TRIPS Agreement[91] set parameters for exceptions to rights under the respective treaties. Under a substantive equality principle, the interpretation of these norms should be generously construed in favour of development. The most generous interpretation, and one that is consistent with the drafting history of the Berne Convention, is that the 'operation of the [educational exception] provisions within their specific sphere is unaffected by the more general provision in Article 9(2), and that the uses allowed under them are therefore excluded from its scope' (WIPO 2003, p. 21).[92] Another view is that Article 10(2)'s requirement of 'fair practice' is 'essentially a question for national tribunals to determine in each particular instance', but is also possibly measured by the three-step test of Article 9(2) (Ricketson & Ginsburg 2006, vol. 1, p. 786). A substantive equality principle should lead a norm-interpreting body, such as a national court or WTO dispute settlement panel, to defer to the legislative intent regarding the 'fair practice' nature of the educational exception. A WTO dispute settlement panel should similarly construe Berne Article 9(2) (which affects the reproduction right only) and TRIPS Article 13 (which applies to exceptions to all rights) to allow the broadest possible exceptions to promote access to educational materials for purposes of development. Thus, domestic educational

tried to rein in the losses associated with digital reproduction of its music and film industries, by enacting domestic legislation that impede rather than promote access. See 17 U.S.C. § 1201; see also Digital Media Project 2006, pt. 3, sec. 7.4. In the education context, the TEACH Act is an example of an unnecessarily restrictive domestic legislation regarding access to copyrighted content for teaching purposes. See Gasaway 2001, pp. 223–224; see also Crews 2000, p. 17.

87 UNESCO Virtual University, 'Open Educational Resources: Open Content for Higher Education', available at: http://www.unesco.org/iiep/virtualuniversity/forums.php (accessed 3 July 2009).

88 Massachusetts Institute of Technology 2001, 'MIT to Make Nearly All Course Materials Available Free on the World Wide Web', 4 April 2001, available at: http://web.mit.edu/newsoffice/2001/ocw.html (accessed 3 July 2009); see also Rens et al. 2006, p. 21.

89 See 'The Literacy Project', available at: http://www.google.com/literacy/ (accessed 3 July 2009); see Carnegie Mellon University Libraries, 'Frequently Asked Questions About the Million Book Project', available at: http://www.library.cmu.edu/Libraries/MBP_FAQ.html (accessed 3 July 2009). The Carnegie-Mellon University's Million Book Project is a project where books are being scanned to supplement libraries in developing countries such as China and India.

90 According to Article 9(2) of the Berne Convention: 'Possible exceptions... (2) It shall be a matter for legislation in the countries of the Union to permit the reproduction of such works in certain special cases, provided that such reproduction does not conflict with a normal exploitation of the work and does not unreasonably prejudice the legitimate interests of the author'.

91 According to Article 13 of the TRIPS Agreement: 'Limitations and Exceptions... Members shall confine limitations or exceptions to exclusive rights to certain special cases which do not conflict with a normal exploitation of the work and do not unreasonably prejudice the legitimate interests of the right holder'.

92 See also Chapter 7.

exceptions enacted in developing countries pursuant to Article 10(2) would be consistent with the three-step test, in light of TRIPS Articles 7 and 8, which refer to development.[93]

To the extent that there is any conflict between an educational exception and TRIPS Article 13, an educational exception would comport with the first step ('certain special cases') under one WTO panel ruling if it is 'clearly defined and... narrow in its scope and reach'.[94] However, even if it is not clear, a norm interpreter should inquire into the public policy purpose of the exception. An analysis of a particular educational exception should push beyond the question of simply whether the exception is clearly defined.[95] Under a substantive equality principle, a decision maker should explicitly consider and defer to a developing country's stated policy of promoting education for development. This interpretive approach would contrast, again, with a differently weighted application of the three-step test towards exceptions of developed countries and/or disputes between them over the scope of such exceptions.[96]

Especially where schools are short on books, libraries have an important role in expanding educational access to copyrighted works through domestic exceptions and limitations (Gasaway 2000, pp. 121, 127).[97] While there is some uncertainty in developed countries over whether library exceptions pass the three-step

[93] Moncayo von Hase (1998, p. 136) observes that: '[I]t is... very important for developing countries to be able to shape the exceptions to the exclusive rights... in pursuance of any of the objectives set forth in Articles 7 and 8 of the Agreement. In such context, a delicate situation would arise if one member would question the scope and extent of an exception to the exclusive right of IPR holders... before a WTO panel. Unless the panel confines itself to determine whether such a measure or exception has the effect of abolishing the very existence of the exclusive rights of the right holder or not, such a dispute should not lead to the replacement of the member's legitimate policy views based on the public objectives acknowledged by Article 7 and 8 of TRIPs...'. See also Max Planck Institute for Intellectual Property, Competition and Tax Law ('Max Planck') 2009. Max Planck (2009) issued a declaration stating that 'the Three-Step Test should be interpreted so as to ensure a proper and balanced application of the limitations and exceptions' in copyright law.

[94] See WTO 2000, Panel Report on *United States – Section 110(5) of the US Copyright Act*, Doc. WT/DS160/R, adopted 27 July 2000 [hereinafter 'Panel Report']. The panel decision (paras. 6.111, 6.112, 6.266) strikes down 17 U.S.C. sec. 110(5); cf. Ginsburg (2001, p. 5) notes that the Panel agrees with the US position that Article 13 does not expand any exceptions.

[95] As stated in the Panel Report: '[W]e believe that the term 'certain special cases' should not lightly be equated with 'special purpose.'... However, public policy purposes stated by law-makers when enacting a limitation or exception may be useful from a factual perspective for making inferences about the scope of a[n]... exception...' (ibid., paras. 6.111, 6.112).

[96] For a more in-depth analysis of the second and third steps covered by the Section 110(5) panel, see generally Chon 2007. Generally, a deferential approach to development-sensitive copyright norm-interpretation should occur in the analysis of the second and third steps: whether the educational exception 'conflict[s] with a normal exploitation of the work' and whether it 'unreasonably prejudice[s] the legitimate interests of the right holder' (The TRIPS Agreement, Article 13). Indeed, the Section 110(5) panel itself acknowledged that 'it should not be forgotten that *domestic laws already contained a series of exceptions in favour of various public and cultural interests* and that it would be vain to suppose that countries would be ready at this stage to abolish these exceptions to any appreciable extent' (Panel Report, para. 6.181, quoting Swedish/BIRPI study).

[97] See also the testimony of T. Hackett summarized in G. Hinze, 'Blogging WIPO: Information Meeting on Educational Content and Copyright in the Digital Age', 21 November 2005, available at: http://www.eff.org/deeplinks/2005/11/blogging-wipo-information-meeting-educational-content-and-copyright-digital-age (accessed 22 April 2010).

tests of Berne/TRIPS (see Ricketson 2002, pp. 81–83; cf. Tawfik 2005, pp. 7, 14), a dispute settlement panel should apply the substantive equality principle to such domestic library exceptions enacted pursuant to Article 10(2) in developing countries. If there is evidence that they are linked with the development objectives of promoting access to basic education, then there should be more deference with respect to their legitimacy.

The main focus of the analysis here is the potential enactment of domestic legislation to maximize the policy space allowed by Article 10(2) of the Berne Convention. Since its beginning, Article 10(2) has had the imprimatur of consensus by Berne Convention members: Educational exceptions consistent with fair practice are acceptable, whether enacted domestically or through other special agreements. The exact parameters of this exception for purposes of development are still not explored fully as of this writing. The reasons for this *terra incognito* include the history of colonialism, associated lack of independent institutional capacity, a reform focus on the Berne Appendix, the current crisis over access to essential medicines, internal lobbying pressures, and the continuing external bilateral pressures to ratchet rights upwards (and perhaps to keep exceptions and limitations such as this somewhat elusive and mysterious).[98] Pragmatically, however, it would not require much in terms of technical assistance or capacity building to draft and implement model exceptions for educational fair practice. Coupled with a substantive equality principle in norm interpretation, these legal initiatives should easily be Berne and TRIPS-compliant. To further leverage human development, or capability for education, within global IP regimes, it is imperative to produce more information such as that partially summarized in Appendix D. Some of this data on exceptions and limitations to copyright for educational use is emerging, both regionally (see e.g. APEC 2008) and globally (see e.g. WIPO 2008, 2009a–f). More collaboration between national ministries of education and national IP agencies (or ministries) is also critical to fashioning educational exceptions consistent with Berne Article 10's broad parameters for 'illustration', as well as broad digital educational exceptions (such as exceptions to the broadcasting, communication and/or making available rights in the WCT), mirroring analogue exceptions already in existence. Some regional sectors have held discussions already along these lines.[99] The WIPO Committee on Development and Intellectual Property (CDIP) should address a multilateral translation exception to digital rights, to address this particular omission of the Berne Appendix. In the realm of 'soft' law, WIPO also could encourage use of 'open' rather than 'closed' standards for new digital content creation (such as Creative Commons), as well as create best practices for exceptions and limitations in the context of open educational resources (Center for Social Media 2009). Finally, the WTO and WIPO could coordinate stakeholders around specific amendments to

[98] See Barbosa, D. B. & Nunes Barbosa, A. B., 'School Material Reproductions in the Brazilian Legal System', available at: http://www.denisbarbosa.addr.com/summum.doc (accessed 3 July 2009). The authors describe narrow educational exceptions in the Brazil Copyright Code.

[99] See Rabajoli, G. & Báez, M. 2009, 'Uso tecnologías y producción contenidos educativos digitales en el Plan CEIBAL', presented at the First Regional Dialogue of Educators on the Implications of Copyright, Montevideo, Uruguay, 2–3 March 2009.

TRIPS to focus on specific human capabilities aspects of IP,[100] including minimum exceptions and limitations for education (Rens 2009).

Taken together, these proposed interventions would not completely supplant the need for a revision of the Berne Appendix, nor would they solve the tremendous need for other re-structuring efforts of the global IP regime. Nonetheless, they would go some way in remedying the indifference of the current structure to development concerns.

6. Conclusion

'IP from below' accounts for users who lack access to educational materials and pays attention to local context for capacity building. From a human development perspective, enhancing capability for education within a human development framework should take priority over guarding excess rent to creators generated from the regulatory intervention of the state in the form of a patent or copyright. Alternative business and innovation models can exist and indeed thrive in a world without copyright (Varian 2005, pp. 134–136; see also Love & Hubbard 2005, pp. 207, 212–217), but in any event, there is no revenue at all if the market itself is not first developed through widespread literacy and education.[101] A theory of 'IP from below' asks us to imagine the creative regulatory possibilities for ethical, humane and just uses of knowledge goods – so as to lessen rather than widen the gap between the IP haves and the IP have nots.

REFERENCES

3D 2005, *In-Depth Study Session on Intellectual Property and Human Rights: Report of a Study Session Aimed at How Human Rights Rules and Mechanisms Can Be Used to Support More Equitable and Development-Oriented Intellectual Property Regimes*, September 2005.

Abbott, F. M. 2006, *Intellectual Property Provisions of Bilateral and Regional Trade Agreements in Light of US Federal Law*, Issue Paper No. 12, UNCTAD-ICTSD, Geneva, Switzerland.

Alikhan, S. 2000, *Socio-Economic Benefits of Intellectual Property Protection in Developing Countries*, WIPO, Geneva, Switzerland.

Alston, P. 2005, 'Ships Passing in the Night: The Current State of the Human Rights and Development Debate Seen Through the Lens of the Millennium Development Goals', *Human Rights Quarterly*, vol. 27, no. 3, pp. 755–829.

[100] Kur, A. 2006, 'Agreement on Trade-Related Aspects of Intellectual Property Rights: Synopsis of Original Version and Proposals for Amendment', presented at the International Association for the Advancement of Teaching and Research in Intellectual Property (ATRIP) Congress, Parma, Italy, 4–6 September 2006, available at: http://www.atrip.org/upload/files/activities/Parma2006/Kur%20synopsis.pdf (accessed 15 February 2010); see also 'TRIPS Amendments (work in progress) – Background and Explanations', available at: http://www.atrip.org/upload/files/activities/Parma2006/Kur%20AMENDMENT.pdf (accessed 15 February 2010).

[101] As the famous economist John Maynard Keynes once observed of neoclassical economic theory, in the long run we are all dead. But, at least in the meantime, we can leverage IP to ensure that current populations are not dead prematurely from things that are preventable with technologies that currently exist and that could be used to promote indigenous innovation capacity.

Altbach, P.G. 1989, 'Copyright in the Developing World', in J.P. Farrell & S.P. Heyneman (eds.), *Textbooks in the Developing World: Economic and Educational Choices*, The World Bank, Washington, DC.

Altbach, P.G. 1995, 'The Subtle Inequalities of Copyright', in P.G. Altbach, *Copyright and Development Inequality in the Information Age*, Bellagio Publishing Network, Chestnut Hill, MA.

Aoki, K. 1998, 'Neocolonialism, Anticommons Property, and Biopiracy in the (Not-So-Brave) New World Order of International Intellectual Property Protection', *Indiana Journal of Global Legal Studies*, vol. 6, no. 1, pp. 11–58.

Aoki, K. 2007, 'Distributive and Syncretic Motives in Intellectual Property Law (with Special Reference to Coercion, Agency and Development)', *UC Davis Law Review*, vol. 40, no. 3, pp. 717–801, available at: http://lawreview.law.ucdavis.edu/issues/Vol40/Issue3/DavisVol40No3_Aoki.pdf (accessed 24 March 2010).

Arewa, O.B. 2006, 'Piracy, Biopiracy and Borrowing: Culture, Cultural Heritage and the Globalization of Intellectual Property', *Case Research Paper Series in Legal Studies, Working Paper No. 04-19*, available at: http://ssrn.com/abstract=596921 (accessed 10 July 2009).

Asia-Pacific Economic Cooperation (APEC) 2008, 'APEC-IPEG Survey on Copyright Limitations and Exceptions: Preliminary Report on Copyright Exceptions and Limitations' (submitted by the Ministry of Education – Chile), Intellectual Property Experts Group (IPEG) of the APEC, Singapore.

Askerud, P. 1997, *A Guide to Sustainable Book Provision*, UNESCO, Paris.

Association of American Publishers (AAP) 2002, 'NEA/AAP Survey Finds Nationwide Textbook Shortages, Teachers Don't Have Enough Books to Assign Homework', *US Newswire*, 8 October 2002.

Bartow, A. 1998, 'Educational Fair Use in Copyright: Reclaiming the Right to Photocopy Freely', *University of Pittsburgh Law Review*, vol. 60, no. 1, pp. 149–230.

Basalamah, S. 2000, 'Compulsory Licensing for Translation: An Instrument of Development?', *IDEA*, vol. 40, no. 4, pp. 503–548.

Bell, D. 1980, 'Brown v. Board and the Interest Convergence Dilemma', *Harvard Law Review*, vol. 93, no. 3, pp. 518–533.

Bently, L. 2008, 'United Kingdom', in P.E. Geller (ed.), *International Copyright Law and Practice*, vol. 2, sec. 3(2)(a), p. UK-49, Lexis Nexis, Newark, NJ.

Boyle, J. 2003, 'The Second Enclosure Movement and the Construction of the Public Domain', *Law & Contemporary Problems (Special Issue)*, vol. 66, no. 1, pp. 33–74, available at: http://www.law.duke.edu/pd/papers/boyle.pdf (accessed 1 April 2010).

Cao, L. 2004, 'The Ethnic Question in Law and Development', *Michigan Law Review*, vol. 102, no. 6, pp. 1044–1103.

Center for Social Media 2009, 'Code of Best Practices for Fair Use in OpenCourseWare', American University School of Communication, Washington, DC, available at: http://www.centerforsocialmedia.org/resources/publications/code_of_best_practices_in_fair_use_for_opencourseware1/ (accessed 13 February 2010).

Chakava, H.M. 1995, 'International Copyright and Africa: The Unequal Exchange', in P.G. Altbach (ed.), *Copyright and Development: Inequality in the Information Age*, Bellagio Publishing Network, Chestnut Hill, MA.

Chon, M. 2006, 'Intellectual Property and the Development Divide', *Cardozo Law Review*, vol. 27, no. 6, pp. 2821–2912, available at: http://site297.mysite4now.com/clrwebsite/Joomla1.5/content/27-6/CHON.WEBSITE.pdf (accessed 1 April 2010).

Chon, M. 2007, 'Substantive Equality in International Intellectual Property Norm-Setting', in D. Gervais (ed.), *Intellectual Property, Trade and Development*, Oxford University Press, New York.

Chon, M. & Ghosh, S. 2000, 'Joint Comment on WIPO Draft Report: Intellectual Property Needs and Expectations of Traditional Knowledge Holders', available at: http://www.wipo.int/tk/en/tk/ffm/ffm-report-comments/msg00008.html (accessed 10 July 2009).

Cohen, J. 2000, 'Copyright and the Perfect Curve', *Vanderbilt Law Review*, vol. 53, no. 6, pp. 1799–1819.

Cohen, J. 2005, 'The Place of the User in Copyright Law', *Fordham Law Review*, vol. 74, no. 2, pp. 347–374.

Commission on Intellectual Property Rights (CIPR) 2002, *Integrating Intellectual Property Rights and Development Policy*, CIPR, London, available at: http://www.iprcommission.org/papers/pdfs/final_report/CIPRfullfinal.pdf (accessed 19 October 2008).

Committee on Economic, Social and Cultural Rights (CESCR) 1999, *General Comment No. 13: The right to education* (art. 13), UN Doc. E/C.12/1999/10 (8 December 1999), available at: http://www.unhchr.ch/tbs/doc.nsf/(Symbol)/ae1a0b126d068e868025683c003c8b3b?Opendocument (accessed 3 February 2010).

Consumers International 2006, *Copyright and Access to Knowledge: Policy Recommendations on Flexibilities in Copyright Laws*, Consumers International Asia Pacific Office, Kuala Lumpur.

Coombe, R.J. 1998, *The Cultural Life of Intellectual Properties: Authorship, Appropriation and the Law*, Duke University Press, Durham, NC.

Copy/South Research Group 2006, in A. Story, C. Darch & D. Halbert (eds.), *The Copy South Dossier.*

Correa, C. 2002, 'Fair Use in the Digital Era, International Review of Industrial Property and Copyright Law', *International Review of Industrial Property and Copyright Law*, vol. 33, no. 5, pp. 570–585, available at: http://webworld.unesco.org/infoethics2000/documents/paper_correa.rtf (accessed 3 July 2009).

Cossman, B. 2000, 'Turning the Gaze Back on Itself: Comparative Law, Feminist Legal Studies, and the Postcolonial Project,' in A.K. Wing (ed.), *Global Critical Race Feminism: An International Reader*, New York University Press, New York.

Crews, K.D. 2000, 'Distance Education and Copyright Law: The Limits and Meaning of Copyright Policy', *Journal of College and University Law*, vol. 27, no. 1, pp. 15–51.

Crews, K.D. 2005, *Copyright Law for Librarians and Educators: Creative Strategies and Practical Solutions*, 2nd Edition, American Library Association, Chicago.

Crowley, M. 2005, 'The Laptop That Will Save the World', *New York Times Magazine*, 11 December 2005, p. 79.

Digital Media Project 2006, 'The Digital Learning Challenge: Obstacles to Educational Uses of Copyrighted Material in the Digital Age: A Foundational White Paper', available at: http://cyber.law.harvard.edu/media/files/copyrightandeducation.html (accessed 3 July 2009).

Dinwoodie, G.B. 2004, 'Private Ordering and the Creation of International Copyright Norms: The Role of Public Structuring', *Journal of Institutional and Theoretical Economics*, vol. 160, no. 1, pp. 161–180, available at: http://ssrn.com/abstract=604161 (accessed 3 July 2009).

Dinwoodie, G.B. & Dreyfuss, R.C. 2006, 'Patenting Science: Protecting the Domain of Accessible Knowledge', in L. Guibalt & P.B. Hugenholtz (eds.), *The Future of the Public Domain: Identifying the Commons in Information Law*, pp. 191–222, Kluwer

Law International BV, The Netherlands, available at: http://works.bepress.com/cgi/viewcontent.cgi?article=1026&context=graeme_dinwoodie (accessed 10 July 2009).

Doi, T. 2008, 'Japan', in P.E. Geller (ed.), *International Copyright Law and Practice*, vol. 2, sec. 8(1)(b), p. JAP-45, Lexis Nexis, Newark, NJ.

Drache, D. & Froese, M.D. 2005, 'The Global Cultural Commons after Cancun: Identity, Diversity and Citizenship', *Comparative Research in Law & Political Economics Research Paper No.* 2, available at: http://www.ssrn.com/abstract=829987 (accessed 10 July 2009).

Drahos, P. & Braithwaite, J. 2002, *Information Feudalism: Who Owns the Knowledge Economy*, Earthscan, London.

Dreyfuss, R.C. 2004, 'TRIPS-Round II: Should Users Strike Back?', *University of Chicago Law Review*, vol. 71, no. 1, pp. 21–35.

Emery, M.A. 2008, 'Argentina', in P.E. Geller (ed.), *International Copyright Law and Practice*, vol. 1, sec. 1(2), p. ARG-8, Lexis Nexis, Newark, NJ.

Farrell, J.P. & Heyneman, S.P. 1988, 'Textbooks in Developing Countries: Economic and Pedagogical Choices', in P.G. Altbach & G.P. Kelly (eds.), *Textbooks in the Third World: Policy, Content and Context*, Garland Publishing, New York.

Farrell, J.P. & Heyneman, S.P. 1989, 'Introduction', in J.P. Farrell & S.P. Heyneman (eds.), *The World Bank, Textbooks in the Developing World: Economic and Educational Choices*, The World Bank, Washington, DC.

Fisher, W.A. 1988, 'Reconstructing the Fair Use Doctrine', *Harvard Law Review*, vol. 101, no. 8, pp. 1661–1795.

Frischmann, B. & Lemley, M. 2006, 'Spillovers', *Columbia Law Review*, vol. 107, no. 1, pp. 257–301, available at: http://ssrn.com/abstract=898881 (accessed 10 July 2009).

Gasaway, L.N. 2000, 'Values Conflict in the Digital Environment: Librarians Versus Copyright Holders, *Columbia-VLA Journal of Law and the Arts*, vol. 24, no. 1, pp. 115–161.

Gasaway, L.N. 2001, 'Distance Learning and Copyright: An Update', *Journal of the Copyright Society of the USA*, vol. 49, no. 1, pp. 195–224.

Geller, P.E. (ed.) 2002, *International Copyright Law and Practice*, vol. 2, Mathew Bender/Lexis Nexis, Newark, NJ.

Gerhart, P.M. 2007, 'The Tragedy of TRIPS', *Michigan State Law Review*, vol. 2007, no. 1, pp. 143–184.

Gervais, D.J. 2005, 'Intellectual Property, Trade and Development: The State of Play', *Fordham Law Review*, vol. 74, no. 2, pp. 505–536.

Ghosh, C.S. 2005, 'Modeling Globalization from the Bottom Up: A Review Essay of John Braithwaite and Peter Drahos, Global Business Regulation', *Law and Society Review*, vol. 39, no. 4, pp. 965–979.

Ginsburg, J.C. 2000, 'International Copyright: From a Bundle of National Copyright Laws to a Supranational Code?', *Journal of the Copyright Society of the USA*, vol. 47, no. 1, pp. 265–290.

Ginsburg, J.C. 2001, 'Toward Supranational Copyright Law? The WTO Panel Decision and the "Three-Step Test" for Copyright Exceptions', *Revue Internationale du Droit d'Auteur*, vol. 187, no. 1, p. 3.

Goldsmith, S., Angvik, J., Howe, L., Hill, A. & Leask, L. 2004, *Status of Alaska Natives Report 2004*, University of Alaska Anchorage, Institute of Social and Economic Research, Alaska Federation of Natives, Anchorage, AK.

Goldstein, P. 2001, *International Copyright: Principles, Law, and Practice*, Oxford University Press, New York.

Goldstein, P. 2003, 'Fair Use in a Changing World', *Journal of the Copyright Society of the USA*, vol. 50, no. 1, pp. 133–148.

Gordon, W. 1982, 'Fair Use as Market Failure: A Structural and Economic Analysis of the Betamax Case and its Predecessors', *Columbia Law Review*, vol. 82, no. 8, pp. 1600–1657.

Grahm, L. & Pehrsson, K. (in collaboration with L.T.D. Minzi) 2004, *Textbooks for all PPP – The First Step on a Long Journey: Evaluation of the Pilot Project for Publishing in Tanzania*, Swedish International Development Cooperation Agency (SIDA), Department for Democracy and Social Development, Stockholm, Sweden.

Greaney, V. 1996, 'Reading in Developing Countries: Problems and Issues', in V. Greaney (ed.), *The World Bank, Promoting Reading in Developing Countries*, International Reading Association, Newark, DE.

Halbert, D., Darch, C. & Story, A. 2006, 'Education and Development on the High Seas of Copyright Infringement', Copy South and OpenDemocracy.net, available at: http://www.opendemocracy.net/arts-commons/icommons_3664.jsp (accessed 10 July 2009).

Helfer, L.R. 2007, 'Toward a Human Rights Framework for Intellectual Property Law', *UC Davis Law Review*, vol. 40, no. 3, pp. 971–1020.

Heyneman, S.P. 2003, 'The History and Problems in the Making of Education Policy at the World Bank', *International Journal of Educational Development*, vol. 23, no. 3, pp. 315–337.

Heyneman, S.P. 2006, 'The Role of Textbooks in a Modern System of Education Towards High Quality Education for All', in C. Braslavsky (ed.), *Textbooks and Quality Learning for All: Some Lessons Learned From International Experiences.* Geneva: UNESCO/International Bureau of Education available at: http://www.vanderbilt.edu/peabody/heyneman/PUBLICATIONS/roleoftextbooks.3.07.pdf (accessed 10 July 2009).

Hong, X. 2008, 'China', in P. E. Geller (ed.), *International Copyright Law and Practice*, vol. 1, sec. 2(4)(b), p. CHI-21, Lexis Nexis, Newark, NJ.

Hugenholtz, P.B. & Okediji, R.L. 2008, *Conceiving an International Instrument on Exceptions and Limitations to Copyright*, available at: http://www.ivir.nl/publicaties/hugenholtz/finalreport2008.pdf (accessed 18 January 2009).

Iglesias, E.M. & Valdes, F. 2000, 'Expanding Directions, Exploding Parameters: Culture and Nation in Latcrit Coalitional Imagination', *Michigan Journal of Race & Law*, vol. 5, no. 3, pp. 787–816.

Kates, R.W., Parris, T.M. & Leiserowitz, A.A. 2005, 'What Is Sustainable Development?' *Environment: Science and Policy for Sustainable Development*, vol. 47, no. 3, pp. 8–21, available at: http://www.hks.harvard.edu/sustsci/ists/docs/whatisSD_env_kates_0504.pdf (accessed 18 June 2009).

Kelly, K. 2006, 'Scan This Book!', *New York Times Magazine*, 14 May 2006, p. 43.

Lazar, A.H. 1971, 'Developing Countries and Authors' Rights in International Copyright', *Copyright Law Symposium*, vol. 19, pp. 1–42.

Leaffer, M. 2001, 'The Uncertain Future of Fair Use in a Global Information Marketplace', *Ohio State Law Journal*, vol. 62, no. 2, pp. 849–867.

Lewin, T. 2003, 'Students Find $100 Textbooks Costs $50, Purchased Overseas', *New York Times*, 21 October 2003.

Lindsey, D. 2001, 'Amy and Goliath', *Salon*, 1 May 2001, available at: http://dir.salon.com/news/feature/2001/05/01/aids/index.html (accessed 10 July 2009).

Lin-Liu, J. 2004, 'Textbook Pirates Find a Huge Market in China', *Chronicle of Higher Education*, 2 April 2004, p. A43.

Litman, J.D. 1987, 'Copyright, Compromise and Legislative History', *Cornell Law Review*, vol. 72, no. 5, pp. 857–904.

Litman, J. 1997, 'Copyright Noncompliance (Or Why We Can't "Just Say Yes" to Licensing)', *New York University Journal of International Law & Politics*, vol. 29, no. 1, pp. 237–254.

Litman, J. 2004, 'Sharing and Stealing', *Hastings Communications and Entertainment Law Journal*, vol. 27, no. 1, pp. 1–50.

Lloyd, M. 2004, 'Staggering Losses in Latin America: Public Indifference Allows Piracy to Flourish Throughout the Region, *Chronicle of Higher Education*, 2 April 2004, p. A41.

Long, D.E. 2002, '"Democratizing" Globalization: Practicing the Policies of Cultural Inclusion', *Cardozo Journal of International & Comparative Law*, vol. 10, no. 1, pp. 217–270.

Love, J. 2005, 'Risks and Opportunities for Access to Knowledge', in S. Bervegillo (ed.), *Vision or Hallucination?: Briefing Papers Towards the World Summit on the Information Society*, Third World Institute, Uruguay, available at: http://www.choike.org/nuevo_eng/informes/3592.html (accessed 10 July 2009).

Love, J. 2007, 'Measures to Enhance Access to Medical Technologies, and New Methods of Stimulating Medical R&D', *UC Davis Law Review*, vol. 40, no. 3, pp. 679–716.

Love, J. & Hubbard, T. 2005, 'Paying for Public Goods', in R.A. Ghosh (ed.), *Code: Collaborative Ownership and the Digital Economy*, The MIT Press, Cambridge, MA, p. 207.

Lucas, A. & Kamina, P. 2008, 'France', in P.E. Geller (ed.), *International Copyright Law and Practice*, vol. 1, sec. 1(4), p. FRA-16, Lexis Nexis, Newark, NJ.

MacPherson, J. & Pearce, D. 1990, *Publishing Educational Material in Developing Countries: A Guide to Policy and Practice*, Harold Macmillan Trust and Canadian Organization for Development, London.

Matsuda, M. 1987, 'Looking to the Bottom: Critical Legal Studies and Reparations', *Harvard Civil Rights-Civil Liberties Law Review*, vol. 22, no. 2, pp. 323–399.

Max Planck Institute for Intellectual Property, Competition and Tax Law 2009, *Declaration on a Balanced Interpretation of the 'Three-Step Test' in Copyright*, available at: http://www.ip.mpg.de/ww/en/pub/news/declaration_on_the_three_step_.cfm (accessed 31 July 2009).

Moncayo von Hase, A. 1998, 'The Application and Interpretation of the Agreement on Trade-Related Aspects of Intellectual Property Rights', in C.M. Correa & A.A. Yusuf (eds.), *Intellectual Property and International Trade: The TRIPS Agreement*, Kluwer Law International, London.

National Education Association 2002, *Instructional Materials Survey: Report of Findings*, Washington, DC.

Newby, T. 1999, 'What's Fair Here is Not Fair Everywhere: Does the American Fair Use Doctrine Violate International Copyright Law?', *Stanford Law Review*, vol. 51, no. 6, pp. 1633–1664.

Nussbaum, M.C. 1995, 'Human Capabilities, Female Human Beings,' in M.C. Nussbaum & J. Glover (eds.), *Women, Culture and Development: A Study of Human Capabilities*, Oxford University Press, New York.

Nussbaum, M.C. 1997, 'Capabilities and Human Rights', *Fordham Law Review*, vol. 66, no. 2, pp. 273–300.

Okediji, R.L. 2000, 'Toward an International Fair Use Doctrine', *Columbia Journal of Transnational Law*, vol. 39, no. 1, pp. 75–176.

Okediji, R.L. 2005, 'Sustainable Access to Copyrighted Digital Information Works in Developing Countries', in K.E. Maskus & J.H. Reichman (eds.), *International Public Goods and Transfer of Technology Under a Globalized Intellectual Property Regime*, Cambridge University Press, New York.

Okediji, R.L. 2006a, 'The International Copyright System: Limitations, Exceptions and Public Interest', Issue Paper No. 15, UNCTAD-ICTSD, available at: http://www.unctad.org/en/docs/iteipc200610_en.pdf (accessed 10 July 2009).

Okediji, R.L. 2006b, 'Africa and the Global Intellectual Property System: Beyond the Agency Model', *African Yearbook of International Law, 2004*, vol. 12, pp. 207–251.

Oliveira, J. 1996, 'Textbooks in Developing Countries', in V. Greaney (ed.), *The World Bank, Promoting Reading in Developing Countries*, International Reading Association, Newark, DE.

Osotimehin, B. 2005, 'The Other Half', *New York Times*, 19 August 2005.

Overland, M. 2004, 'Publishers Battle Pirates with Little Success in India', *Chronicle of Higher Education*, 2 April 2004, p. A40.

Oxfam 2002, *Generic Competition, Price and Access to Medicines: The Case of Antiretrovirals in Uganda*, available at: http://www.oxfam.org.uk/what_we_do/issues/health/downloads/bp26_generic.pdf (accessed 10 July 2009).

Pereira dos Santos, M.J. 2008, 'Brazil' in P.E. Geller (ed.), *International Copyright Law and Practice*, vol. 1, sec. 5(4), p. BRA-41, Lexis Nexis, Newark, NJ.

Rajagopal, B. 2003, *International Law From Below: Development, Social Movements, and Third World Resistance*, Cambridge University Press, New York.

Ramaiah, S. 2008, 'India', in P.E. Geller (ed.), *International Copyright Law and Practice*, vol. 2, sec. 9(1), p. IND-61, Lexis Nexis, Newark, NJ.

Raustiala, K. 2007, 'Density & Conflict in International Intellectual Property Law', *UC Davis Law Review*, vol. 40, no. 3, pp. 1021–1038.

Reed, F. 2006, 'Digital School Books Feasible?', *Washington Times*, 15 September 2006.

Rens, A. 2009, 'Implementing WIPO's Development Agenda: Treaty Provisions on Minimum Exceptions and Limitations for Education', in J. de Beer (ed.) *Implementing the World Intellectual Property's Development Agenda*, pp. 158–169, Wilfrid Laurier University Press, Ottawa, Canada.

Rens, A., Prabhala, A. & Kawooya, D. 2006, *Intellectual Property, Education and Access to Knowledge in Southern Africa*, UNCTAD – ICTSD, available at: http://www.iprsonline.org/unctadictsd/docs/06%2005%2031%20tralac%20amended-pdf.pdf (accessed 10 July 2009).

Ricketson, S. 2002, *The Three-Step Test, Deemed Quantities, Libraries and Closed Exceptions*, Centre for Copyright Studies Ltd., Strawberry Hills, Australia.

Ricketson, S. & Ginsburg, J. 2006, *International Copyright and Neighboring Rights: The Berne Convention and Beyond*, Oxford University Press, New York.

Rosenberg, T. 2006, 'When a Pill Is Not Enough', *New York Times Magazine*, 6 August 2006.

Samuelson, P. 1997, 'The US Digital Agenda at WIPO', *Virginia Journal of International Law*, vol. 37, no. 2, pp. 369–440.

Samuelson, P. 1999, 'Implications of the Agreement on Trade Related Aspects of Intellectual Property Rights for Cultural Dimensions of National Copyright Laws', *Journal of Cultural Economics*, vol. 23, no. 1, pp. 95–107.

Sell, S.K. 2003, *Private Power, Public Law: The Globalization of Intellectual Property Rights*, Cambridge University Press, New York.

Sen, A. 1999, *Development as Freedom*, Random House, New York.

Sosale, S. 1999, 'Introduction', in S. Sosale (ed.), *Educational Publishing in Global Perspective: Capacity Building and Trends*, The World Bank, Washington, DC.

Story, A. 2003, 'Burn Berne: Why the Leading International Copyright Convention Must Be Repealed', *Houston Law Review*, vol. 40, no. 3, pp. 763–802.

Sunder, M. 2006, 'IP^3', *Stanford Law Review*, vol. 59, no. 2, pp. 257–332.

Tawfik, M.J. 2005, 'International Copyright Law and "Fair Dealing" as a "User Right"', *Copyright Bulletin*, April–June 2005, UNESCO, Paris, available at: http://portal.unesco.org/culture/en/ev.php-URL_ID=5359&URL_DO=DO_TOPIC&URL_SECTION=201.html (accessed 15 April 2010).

United Nations Development Programme (UNDP) 1990, *Human Development Report 1990: Concept and Measurement of Human Development*, UNDP, available at: http://hdr.undp.org/en/reports/global/hdr1990/ (accessed 11 March 2010).

UNDP 1991, *Human Development Report 1991:Financing Human Development*, UNDP, available at: http://hdr.undp.org/en/reports/global/hdr1991/chapters/ (accessed 11 March 2010).

UNDP 2003, *Human Development Report 2003: The Millennium Development Goals: A Compact Amongst Nations to End Human Poverty*, UNDP, available at: http://hdr.undp.org/en/media/hdr03_complete.pdf (accessed 11 March 2010).

UNESCO 2006, *Education for All Global Monitoring Report 2006 Executive Summary*, available at: http://unesdoc.unesco.org/images/0014/001416/141639e.pdf (accessed 31 July 2009).

Vaidyanathan, S. 2007, 'The Googlization of Everything and the Future of Copyright', *UC Davis Law Review*, vol. 40, no. 3, pp. 1207–1232.

Varian, H.R. 2005, 'Copying and Copyright', *Journal of Economic Perspectives*, vol. 19, no. 2, pp. 121–138.

Volpp, L. 2001, 'Feminism Versus Multiculturalism', *Columbia Law Review*, vol. 101, no. 5, pp. 1181–1218.

The World Bank 1999, *World Development Report: Knowledge for Development*, Washington, DC.

The World Bank 2004, *Project Performance Assessment Report: Uganda*, Washington, DC.

World Intellectual Property Organization (WIPO) 2003, 'WIPO Study on Limitations and Exceptions of Copyright and Related Rights in the Digital Environment', (prepared by S. Ricketson) Standing Committee on Copyright and Related Rights (SCCR), WIPO, Geneva, Doc. SCCR/9/7, available at: http://www.wipo.int/edocs/mdocs/copyright/en/sccr_9/sccr_9_7.pdf (accessed 11 March 2010).

WIPO 2008, 'Study on Copyright Limitations and Exceptions for Libraries and Archives', (prepared by K. Crews) SCCR, WIPO, Geneva, Doc. SCCR/17/2, available at: http://www.wipo.int/edocs/mdocs/copyright/en/sccr_17/sccr_17_2.pdf (accessed 11 March 2010).

WIPO 2009a, 'Conclusions on Limitations and Exceptions', SCCR, WIPO, Geneva, Doc. SCCR/19/Conclusions, available at: http://www.wipo.int/edocs/mdocs/copyright/en/sccr_19/sccr_19_conclusions.pdf (accessed 11 March 2010).

WIPO 2009b, 'Study on Limitations and Exceptions for Copyright and Related Rights for Teaching in Africa', (prepared by J. Fometeu) SCCR, WIPO, Geneva, Doc. SCCR/19/5, available at: http://www.wipo.int/edocs/mdocs/copyright/en/sccr_19/sccr_19_5.pdf (accessed 11 March 2010).

WIPO 2009c, 'Study on the Limitations and Exceptions to Copyright and Related Rights for the Purposes of Educational and Research Activities in Latin America and the Caribbean', (prepared by J.C. Monroy Rodriguez) SCCR, WIPO, Geneva, Doc. SCCR/19/4, available at: http://www.wipo.int/edocs/mdocs/copyright/en/sccr_19/sccr_19_4.pdf (accessed 11 March 2010).

WIPO 2009d, 'Study on Limitations and Exceptions for Copyright for Educational Purposes in the Arab Countries', (prepared by V. Nabhan) SCCR, WIPO, Geneva, Doc. SCCR/19/6, available at: http://www.wipo.int/edocs/mdocs/copyright/en/sccr_19/sccr_19_6.pdf (accessed 11 March 2010).

WIPO 2009e, 'WIPO Study on the Copyright Exceptions for the Benefit of Educational Activities for Asia and Australia', (prepared by D. Seng), SCCR, WIPO, Doc. SCCR/19/7, Geneva, available at: http://www.wipo.int/edocs/mdocs/copyright/en/sccr_19/sccr_19_7.pdf (accessed 11 March 2010).

WIPO 2009f, 'Study on Copyright Limitations and Exceptions for Educational Activities in North America, Europe, Caucasus, Central Asia and Israel', (prepared by R. Xalabarder) SCCR, WIPO, Geneva, Doc. SCCR/19/8, available at: http://www.wipo.int/edocs/mdocs/copyright/en/sccr_19/sccr_19_8.pdf (accessed 11 March 2010).

Yamamoto, E.K. 1999, *Interracial Justice: Conflict and Reconciliation in Post-Civil Rights America*, New York University Press, New York.

Young, I.M. 2002, 'Status Inequality and Social Groups', *Issues in Legal Scholarship*, The Origins and Fate of Antisubordination Theory', art. 9, available at: http://www.bepress.com/ils/iss2/art9 (accessed 31 July 2009).

Yu, P.K. 2000, 'From Pirates to Partners: Protecting Intellectual Property in China in the Twenty-First Century, *American University Law Review*, vol. 50, no. 1, pp. 131–244.

Yu, P.K. 2001, 'Piracy, Prejudice, and Perspectives: An Attempt to Use Shakespeare to Reconfigure the US-China Intellectual Property Debate', *Boston University International Law Journal*, vol. 19, no. 1, pp. 1–88.

Yu, P.K. 2007, 'Reconceptualizing Intellectual Property Interests in a Human Rights Framework', *UC Davis Law Review*, vol. 40, no. 3, pp. 1039–1150.

7

Knowledge and education: Pro-access implications of new technologies

Dalindyebo Shabalala[1]

Introduction

The framework of 'Knowledge and Education' is broad, and overlaps with various areas of intellectual property (IP). Copyright is the dominant legal and policy regime governing this domain. As discussed in other chapters of the book, access to knowledge and education is also circumscribed by such concerns as the expanding scope of patents and its impact on basic research and research tools, public access to patent disclosure information, protection of traditional knowledge, general systems of access and distribution of information, and particular access issues for disabled persons. While Chapter 6 has extensively discussed the implications of copyright law and exceptions on access to textbooks in developing countries, this chapter focuses on implications of new technologies – especially information and communication technologies (ICTs) – on access to information products. In discussing some recent legislative trends, it looks at pro-access strategies by developing countries and civil society organizations (CSOs) relating to knowledge and education.

According to utilitarian theory, copyright is an incentive system which encourages the creation and dissemination of ideas and information products as widely as possible, by giving a creator/author an exclusive right, for a limited (but long) period, to control reproduction by third parties of the form in which the idea is expressed. That grant is meant to be balanced by limitations and exceptions, especially the right of reproduction and distribution for educational purposes. In particular it is important to remember that while copyright is ostensibly an incentive system for authors or creators, it has in practice been a system that primarily benefits intermediaries such as publishers and distributors. Changes in the nature of copyright subject matter, from analogue to digital, have presented significant opportunities for greater access as well as greater restrictions. One of the most significant developments in this arena is the impact of technology on the behaviour of creators, producers or distributors and end-users. The response to such developments significantly drives the scenario planning of actors in this field.

As discussed in Chapter 1, a distinction has to be made between the access to mere information and the accumulation of knowledge. True 'access to knowledge' requires the nurturing of human capabilities and appropriate contexts for the transformation of information into knowledge. Movements towards access to knowledge

[1] Invaluable inputs were received from Rosemary Wolson, Margaret Chon, Gwen Hinze, Graham Dutfield and Tzen Wong.

(A2K) ultimately need to go beyond discussions on access to information goods and related copyright issues, to consider many areas of human development. Among other things, they need to take on board how access to education by stakeholders is circumscribed by inequalities relating to gender, social classes, ethnic groups and geographical areas.

A number of provisions in international human rights instruments govern access to information and education. These include, for example, the right to education which embraces the right to access educational materials;[2] the right to seek, receive and impart information as part of the right to freedom of expression;[3] and the right to the enjoyment of the benefits of scientific progress and its applications (see Ovett 2006a, p. 7). The latter is enshrined in Article 15(1)(b) of the International Covenant on Economic, Social and Cultural Rights (ICESCR), and is the subject of significant scrutiny (Chapman 2002). Of further relevance is the 'right to take part in cultural life' reflected in Article 15(1)(a) of the ICESCR.[4] The Committee on Economic, Social and Cultural Rights (CESCR) recently published General Comment No. 21 on Article 15(1)(a) in an effort towards clarifying the nature of this right (see discussion in Chapter 8).[5]

1. Technology, education and copyright

One of the most significant drivers of better educational outcomes in developing countries is access to textbooks and other instructional materials (Askerud 1997, p. 3). As highlighted in Chapter 6, the price of textbooks can be exceptionally high relative to per capita income in developing countries. The latter chapter discusses distributive structures and aspects of copyright law which impede access to textbooks in developing countries, while focusing on exceptions and/or limitations for illustrative teaching. It argues convincingly that such exceptions and/or limitations should be construed as broadly as possible to enhance capabilities for education. This chapter does not repeat the main arguments in Chapter 6, but focuses on pro-access opportunities presented by new technologies, including digital technology, for educational sectors (at all levels), as well as libraries. These opportunities are especially significant in addressing major elements limiting access for developing countries including: cost of production of learning materials and knowledge products; high price of textbooks relative to per capita income; cost and capacity of distribution of learning materials and knowledge products; and maintenance and updating of learning materials and knowledge products. While not a panacea,

[2] See Article 13 of the International Covenant on Economic, Social and Cultural Rights 1966. See the interpretation in Committee on Economic, Social and Cultural Rights (CESCR) 1999, *General Comment No. 13: The right to education* (art. 13), UN Doc. E/C.12/1999/10 (1999), para 6(a). See also Article 28 of the Convention on the Rights of the Child 1989 (CRC).

[3] See Article 19 of the International Covenant on Civil and Political Rights 1966 (ICCPR). See the interpretation in Human Rights Committee (CCPR) 1983, *General Comment No. 10: Freedom of expression* (art. 19), reprinted in UN Doc. HRI/GEN/1/Rev.9, p. 181 (27 May 2008). See also Articles 13 and 17 of the CRC.

[4] See also Article 27 of the (non-binding) Universal Declaration of Human Rights 1948. Article 27(1) provides that: 'Everyone has the right freely to participate in the cultural life of the community, to enjoy the arts and to share in scientific advancement and its benefits'.

[5] Committee on Economic, Social and Cultural Rights (CESCR) 2009, *General Comment No. 21: Right of everyone to take part in cultural life* (art. 15, para. 1 (a)), UN Doc. E/C.12/GC/21 (21 December 2009).

the use of ICTs has the potential, along with the expansion of digital and Internet content, to reduce some of the problems of poverty and price such as insufficient storage and transport facilities and the absence of conservation practices for books (ibid., p. 4).

At the same time, we should not lose sight of the existing difficulties of access to ICTs in developing countries. Developing countries still lag significantly behind developed countries in this respect, and that gap may be growing (see United Nations Conference on Trade and Development [UNCTAD] 2004a, p. 96). Much of the growth in ICT access among developing countries is attributable to Brazil, China and India (see UNCTAD 2004b, p. 2). South–South gaps could become more pronounced, as some countries make the necessary investment and others fail to do so. Bandwidth, for example, still remains a serious constraint across much of Africa, although this concern may to some extent be allayed by the liberalization of telecommunications and the increasing dominance of cell phone networks.

Concerted public investment in ICT infrastructure is thus a necessary precondition for developing countries to take advantage of digital and Internet content for the education and library sectors.[6] Greater telecommunications deregulation is likely to lead to lower costs of Internet access in particular regions over the coming years. Asia is taking the lead in this regard, with Latin America following closely behind. New infrastructural projects, such as the East African Submarine Cable System (EASSy),[7] are creating the backbone for Internet to develop further in the Indian Ocean area, facilitating stronger and more direct connections between Africa and Asia. Telecommunications deregulation has also led to the explosion of mobile telephony, and now mobile Internet, in developing countries. While the digital divide between North and South may not disappear, absolute inability to access the Internet will become more rare. The nature and scope of access to content will therefore become increasingly important.

The practical structure of copyright has meanwhile favoured for-profit models of knowledge dissemination even in the field of education. The emphasis has been on ensuring the profits and return on investment of the intermediaries rather than on meeting the needs of authors or creators and end-users. This model has persisted despite significant doubts raised by some stakeholders on the necessity for strong profit-driven copyright standards to provide incentives for the production of educational and research materials. Many academics produce research, for example, not because of the profits that might be earned through royalties but because of the reputational value or potential social impact in being widely read and disseminated. This is discussed further in Box 7.1 where the implications of new digital technology on power relations between creators, producers and distributors of information products are explored.

Indeed, there is some consensus in the education arena that copyright holders ought to have less expectation of significant profits, notwithstanding the historical emphasis on for-profit production and distribution of knowledge goods. To fulfil and expand their role in advancing human development policy, educational

[6] See the example of South Africa in Adeya and Cogburn 2002, p. 22.

[7] See Waltner 2006.

BOX 7.1. Changing power structures: Creators, producers and distributors

Digital and Internet content has the potential to reshape the relationship between creators, commercial producers and distributors. Lowered production costs make creators less dependent on the capital traditionally provided by producers. In publishing, this means that those authors who are not primarily motivated by profits may have more leeway in disseminating their work for free or at lower costs to readers. Furthermore, as Landes and Posner (1989, p. 331) observe of non-pecuniary benefits to authors:

> Many authors derive substantial benefits from publication that are over and beyond any royalties. This is true not only in terms of prestige and other nonpecuniary income but also pecuniary income in such forms as a higher salary for a professor who publishes than for one who does not, or greater consulting income. Publishing is an effective method of self-advertisement and self-promotion. The norms against plagiarism (i.e. against copying without giving the author credit) reinforce the conferral of prestige by publishing; to the extent that those norms are effective, they ensure that the author will obtain recognition, if not always royalties, from the works he publishes.

At the same time, there remains a question of fair returns to compensate writers. While academic writers may be motivated to contribute some of their works without expectation of pecuniary return (e.g. academic authors are usually not compensated for journal articles, in contrast to receiving some royalties for textbooks), they may find it exploitative that publishers reap substantial returns from the distribution of their works. More importantly, the opportunity to publish with a mainstream publisher may come with the not uncommon condition of copyright assignment to the publisher. This copyright assignment may impose serious constraints on the author's ability to circulate (or authorize reproduction or translation of) the work, and to engage in transformation of the work for future publications. A lot depends on the contractual agreement between the author and the publisher, and the bargaining positions are often unequal (see Chapter 8).

The vast number of customers on the Internet has meanwhile expanded the size of the market for almost all knowledge products, eliminating the need to spend huge marketing costs for slices of the same domestic pie or limited space at traditional media outlets. The Internet allows more self-distribution by creators and cheaper production costs. This is increasingly evident in the academic publishing market as more and more academic and other writers are finding it expedient to self-distribute or to distribute through online outlets that provide free or low cost access. In particular, the options and incentives for educators to bypass traditional publishers are increased through digital and Internet production (and distribution). Several initiatives exist to increase such open access publishing, including, for example, the Public Library of Science (PLOS)[8] and the Social Science Research Network (SSRN).[9] While the latter database does not currently have a quality control or peer review system, open access need not entail the absence of either. There is much room for exploring open access repositories with a peer review mechanism for quality control, as the key present challenge in users' access to the vast material available on the Internet lies in separating useful and accurate material out from other information. There are also initiatives which combine traditional publishing and online dissemination.

(*continued*)

[8] See the Public Library of Science (PLOS) website, available at: http://www.plos.org (accessed 20 April 2010).

[9] See the Social Science Research Network (SSRN) 'eLibrary' website, available at: http://www.ssrn.com (accessed 20 April 2010).

Box 7.1 *(continued)*

Meanwhile, there is a real opportunity for artists to regain control of their materials and to have access to global markets and distribution channels (see Andersen, Kozul-Wright & Kozul-Wright 2000, p. 9).[10] Direct 'artist-to-consumer' transactions have become increasingly possible. Such a transition is furthered by the development of Creative Commons licences (distributed through the various national Creative Commons projects).[11] These projects leverage the increasing divergence among creators, producers and distributors in positive ways to increase access, and should be supported through appropriate policy measures at the national level.

[10] Andersen et al. (2000, p. 9) argue that developing country artists may be able to take advantage of new technologies more easily as new entrants.

[11] An example is Creative Commons South Africa, website available at: http://za.creativecommons.org/ (accessed 23 March 2010).

institutions and libraries must be empowered to communicate information to students and other users. An access to education policy must cover all educational uses of materials protected by copyright and related rights. A challenge for educators and others who provide the raw materials for education is how to expand the impact of existing tools and the use of new products, new distribution methods and new pedagogical systems to reach more users, including students. At the same time, it is important to view users not simply as passive recipients of information products, but rather as agents who actively search for relevant information and knowledge tools towards improving their capabilities. This is consistent with the capability approach in the human development paradigm described in Chapter 1 of this book. Under this approach, it is not mere access to information products that matters in human development, but what users are ultimately able to do in translating that access into improvements in their capabilities, including those capabilities related to education.

2. Pro-access implications of information technology on knowledge and education

This section details some pro-access trends in the knowledge and education arena, as catalysed by new information technologies. It looks at changes in production methods of information products, including educational materials (Section 2.1), developments in user access mechanisms (Section 2.2) and changes in modes of distribution (Section 2.3).

2.1. Changes in production methods of primary source materials and the introduction of new products

The next few years should see an explosion in open source production methods, particularly in developing countries. Open source production essentially relies on a distributed set of contributors all working on a project (to which the source code is freely available) and providing their input for free, on the condition that all such inputs and further uses of such inputs are licensed on the same basis of free use and free access. Open source methods rely on either copyright or patent rights to enforce a licensing structure that maintains the open nature of the software. There are several kinds of licences available to developers wishing to make software available to others under the free and open source software development models, the most common free software licence being the GNU 'General Public License' (GPL) for software (see also Chapter 3, Box 3.3).[12]

The most attractive features of free and open source content development approaches may be that they require little or no additional legislation or international agreements to implement. They operate as an alternative to copyright while using copyright to enforce their openness as can be seen in the GPL. In the coming years, we should witness trends such as: (1) greater use of free and open source software, (2) greater use and enforcement of free and open source licences and (3) the incentivization of open access approaches to production and dissemination of knowledge in the scientific and education arena through leveraging government funding (while disallowing the privatization and exclusive appropriation of materials produced with such funding).

Meanwhile, new types of products such as digital books and online curricular materials have emerged with significant impact on the availability of educational materials. Textbooks are a subset of the larger book publishing market which has undergone a significant shift in the way in which texts are produced. Almost all texts are now created on word processors on computers and e-mailed among authors, their colleagues and their publishers. Before a text is printed in paper form it now exists as an electronic document, formatted and ready to print. The e-mailing and Internet transmission or downloading of such texts addresses a major bottleneck of distribution to developing countries and, where access exists, can transform the costs of delivery and distribution of texts. A major project producing such texts on an open source model is Project Gutenberg.[13] It contains over 20,000 high-quality free electronic texts that are in the public domain in the United States (US), made available by a globally distributed set of volunteers.[14]

[12] In the software community, there is a developed distinction between open source software (meaning software licensed under a licence meeting the open source definition that may be sold (i.e. not free as in uncompensated)) and free software, meaning software licensed under the GPL that has the four freedoms. See Open Source Initiative, 'The Open Source Definition', available at: http://www.opensource.org/docs/definition.php (accessed 23 March 2010). For an explanation on the four freedoms, see GNU Operating System, 'The Free Software Definition', available at: http://www.gnu.org/philosophy/free-sw.html (accessed 23 March 2010).

[13] See the Project Gutenberg website, available at: www.gutenberg.org (accessed 18 January 2009).

[14] Project Gutenberg is organized into separate national projects because of differing national copyright terms – that is, works can be under copyright in one country even if they are in the public domain in their originating country. The main Project Gutenberg project makes available works that are in the public domain in the US and has a disclaimer about reading them outside of the US. Project Gutenberg Australia was threatened with litigation in 2004 for making available a work that was in the public domain under the then current Australian copyright law, but not under US copyright law. See Library-Law Blog, '*Gone With the Wind in the Public Doman? Will Peter Pan Never Grow Up?*', 8 November 2004, available at: http://blog.librarylaw.com/librarylaw/2004/11/emgone_with_the.html (accessed 23 March 2010).

Digitization of books is a difficult and costly process but a crucial one. The institutions best positioned to do such digitization, namely libraries, are constrained by copyright restrictions, while the copyright owners, usually publishers, often do not find it sufficiently in their interest to sell digital copies of their texts. In the meantime an opportunity for greater access and distribution is lost. Additional policy work on these issues is needed and is being conducted by organizations such as the American Library Association, the International Federation of Library Associations (IFLA) and Electronic Information for Libraries (eIFL). However, few organizations exist in developing countries to undertake such activities and the technology costs remain prohibitive. To increase the presence of such texts, initiatives will have to be pursued in developed countries for digitization and production of digital books. Commercial publishers are not able to fulfil this role adequately, and libraries should be supported in their pursuit of this goal. One caveat to note is the Google Books project, the largest digitization project ongoing at the moment, in collaboration with libraries and publishers. Although controversial, it has succeeded in pushing the publishing industry into the digital age, while ensuring that out-of-print works of authors are also given new life on the Web (Helft & Rich 2008; see discussion in Chapters 8 and 9).

We should also see the expansion of online curricular materials in terms of Open Courseware programmes, where educational institutions and their faculty members make their courses and teaching materials available for free over the Internet. An example of this is the 'Open Courseware' initiative at the Massachusetts Institute of Technology (MIT)[15] which provides a global commons from which educators can draw. These courses provide syllabi, teaching tools, transcripts and videos of lectures, some of them given by leading scholars in their field. Such resources are especially useful in the natural sciences where access to the most up-to-date concepts, methods and approaches has historically been difficult for educators and students living on the global periphery. These resources are available at both the secondary school and tertiary levels.

2.2. Changes in modes of accessing information: Digital content, new devices and new pedagogies

Students, teachers, librarians and other researchers are beginning to access a significant portion of the information they use from the Internet. This trend has become increasingly evident in educational institutions and libraries in industrialized countries, and is likely to spread to other contexts including developing countries. In fact, given new initiatives to increase access to ICTs, there are some suggestions that many developing country institutions may simply leapfrog past the hard-copy stage of information dissemination. Digitization is a contributing factor. For the moment, digitized information is dominated by commercially profitable works rather than by those for which publishers have few or no markets or those that are in the public domain. The challenge is to ensure that works that have fallen into the public

[15] See Massachusetts Institute of Technology, 'MIT Open Course Ware', available at: http://ocw.mit.edu/index.html (accessed 18 January 2009). The online courses range from Anthropology to Chemical Engineering and are available at both the undergraduate and graduate levels.

domain are digitized, as well as out-of-print and so called orphan works. Alongside initatives such as Google Books, new modes and incentives will have to be found to encourage the digitization of such works.

Another development is the advent of new devices that approximate the complexity and capacity of the general-purpose computer. This is accompanied by the spread of mobile phones and their expanding capacity to receive and send information in addition to voice data. What is becoming increasingly evident is that developing country markets are no longer simply dumping grounds for obsolete technologies but are becoming the primary growth markets for new devices with multiple functionalities. Consumers, many of whom are young people, are creating the demand for and experimenting with new and innovative uses of mobile devices for accessing and sharing information. It has to be qualified, however, that while this applies in many developed countries and developing ones such as India, China and Brazil, it is not necessarily the case in least developed countries (LDCs) and many countries, for example, in Africa.

We may also begin to see the expansion of distance learning, another area where the benefits of Internet and digital content are unmistakable, especially as it becomes possible to get larger amounts of content into smaller and smaller devices. However, cost per student remains a significant barrier to expanding access through such programmes (UNCTAD 2004b, p. 112). Quality assurance is a further issue which must be tackled in respect of distance education. Concerted distance education strategies at the national level are hard to find, although discussions in forums such as WIPO have focused on distance learning as the exemplar of why exceptions and limitations to copyright provisions at the international level need to be updated and made mandatory. There is discussion of placing an exception for distance learning explicitly in the text of any new IP-related treaties, including a potential Access to Knowledge (A2K) Treaty that would enshrine such exceptions and limitations in international law. In the norm-setting process at WIPO, significant progress has been made at placing such issues on the agenda.

The ability to seek out and identify relevant information on the Internet has been a crucial innovation. It also changes the pedagogical balance such that students are not passive recipients of information from teachers and institutions but are able to search more widely for information themselves. Access to ICTs affects the search capabilities of users, including students, in different regions and contexts. Developing country Internet users may have less access to alternative marketing information (e.g. through newspapers, magazines and television) than users in developed countries, and they may be more reliant on Internet search engines. Language options for web searching is a crucial consideration for human development. The language(s) used by a search engine often determine which populations are able to access materials relevant to their cultural contexts through the search engine. For example, the development of search engines in indigenous languages allows individuals to find websites already written in that language and thus increases usability. Indeed, being able to access and use materials in a person's or community's native language enhances individual and group capabilities, including those relating to education. The predominance of search engines and materials in the Internet in certain major languages, including English, implicitly shapes the scope of access to information (and the nature of that information) by communities around the world.

2.3. Changes in modes of distribution and their impact on conventional publishing

Digital and Internet technology facilitates the creation of perfect copies of knowledge products at a low cost and enables distribution without any destruction of the original. When the cost of producing, copying and disseminating any piece of information becomes so cheap as to approach zero, any person with access to a computer and the Internet can be a powerful distributor of information. The potential exists for any work (e.g., text, music, film) to be distributed worldwide, essentially instantaneously, without degradation and at an insignificant cost.[16] As a natural consequence, Internet delivery of texts and other learning materials has become increasingly the norm in developed countries. These modes of distribution may include for-profit venues, but there are also many non-profit or open access venues and methods.

2.3.1. Open access textbooks, electronic journals and online repositories

Open access textbooks have a strong impact on access to education. Several initiatives exist in this area, including the 'Free High School Science Texts' (FHSST) project that aims to provide free science and mathematics textbooks for use in secondary schooling in South Africa.[17] Other such initiatives include: BookPower,[18] California Open Source Textbook Project[19] and Textbook Revolution.[20] These initiatives should be supported and expanded, with better coordination encouraged between the projects and developing country governments.

Electronic journals, including open access journals, also have a far-reaching impact on access by readers to the latest research in many fields. The impact of electronic journals on the distribution of scholarship is explored in Box 7.2. Subscription fees for conventional academic journals can be phenomenally high in some specialized areas. Darnton (2008) notes that: '[C]ommercial publishers discovered that they could make a fortune by selling subscriptions to the journals. Once a university library subscribed, the students and professors came to expect an uninterrupted flow of issues. The price could be ratcheted up without causing cancellations, because the libraries paid for the subscriptions and the professors did not. Best of all, the professors provided free or nearly free labor'.[21]

Another significant factor for educators and scholars is the growth of open access scholarship repositories into which more and more scholars are placing

16 This, of course, presumes that the costs of accessing and using the Internet are on a par with telephone costs, or even cheaper.

17 See FHSST, 'Free High School Science Texts', available at: http://www.fhsst.org (accessed 20 April 2010).

18 See the BookPower website, available at: http://www.bookpower.org (accessed 20 April 2010).

19 See the California Open Source Textbook Project (COSTP) website, available at: http://www.opensourcetext.org/index.htm (accessed 20 April 2010).

20 See the Textbook Revolution website, available at: http://textbookrevolution.org/index.php/Main_Page (accessed 20 April 2010); see also Wikibooks, 'Help: About', available at: http://en.wikibooks.org/wiki/Wikibooks_portal (accessed 20 April 2010).

21 According to Darnton: 'The result stands out on the acquisitions budget of every research library: the *Journal of Comparative Neurology* now costs $25,910 for a year's subscription; *Tetrahedron* costs $17,969 (or $39,739, if bundled with related publications as a *Tetrahedron* package); the average price of a chemistry journal is $3,490 . . . owing to the skyrocketing cost of serials, libraries that used to spend 50 percent of their acquisitions budget on monographs now spend 25 percent or less' (ibid.).

BOX 7.2. Electronic journals and their impact on scholarly publications

Traditional journals provide a key service to scholars. They provide a peer-review process that evaluates and filters works while also enabling wide distribution of published works. In exchange for the rights to own and publish articles, the owners of journals provide the channels of distribution and the imprimatur of quality. The ability to distribute journals electronically has meant that the production and distribution costs of many journals have dropped by a significant factor. This also enables journal owners to deliver their journals to markets that were previously not worth the cost of servicing. The rise of free electronic journals provides an alternative mode of user access, while maintaining the crucial peer review and filtering mechanism.

Taking advantage of the 'freeing up' of distribution channels and the lowering of production costs, scholars in different subject areas are collaborating to produce free electronic journals that provide the advantage of peer review without the often high subscription costs (see Darnton 2008). In particular scientists and academics in science-related disciplines have taken the lead as they have experienced the increased costs of hard-copy journals more keenly as part of the general specialization and fragmentation of scientific work. This has, in turn, led to increased fragmentation of journals while major scientific work increasingly requires cross-disciplinary work. Physics scholars have led the way but have been followed by scholars in chemistry and biology-related disciplines. Some of these moves can be found in projects such as Science Commons,[22] BioMed Central[23] and the Public Library of Science.[24] These initiatives have been particularly aimed at addressing the certification/gate-keeping role of peer review. While major coordination and network costs remain, several methodologies have been found to be useful, including methods such as embedding a publication within educational institutions with professors as peer reviewers. All of these developments point to a more distributed process of certification that begins to approach the 'wiki' methodology where the value of a publication is determined by a combination of a larger number of examiners and constant examination and reflection on a document. To some extent, this distribution process may circumvent some of the 'gate-keeping' authority of established institutions and academic actors to determine who and what is published. However, the limits of the 'wiki' may need to be carefully analysed; improvements are needed to ensure that reviews and changes are not anonymous and that quality is better assured through citation formats which indicate the value of a source. Meanwhile, there is room for exploring and supporting more structures for peer review of open access journals. This would go some way in countering arguments that 'open access' does not necessarily ensure quality publications (see e.g. Elsevier 2004). While there are also arguments questioning the business viability of 'open access' models for publishing, Litman (2007, pp. 794–795) suggests that:

> Instead of asking whether open access journals can act like conventional scholarly journals without relying on the subscription revenues made possible by access restrictions, it's more useful to think about whether they can engender a less dysfunctional environment for scholarly publishing than the one we currently enjoy... universities

(*continued*)

[22] See the Science Commons website, available at: http://www.sciencecommons.org (accessed 20 April 2010).

[23] See BioMed Central: The Open Access Publisher, 'Welcome to BioMed Central', available at: http://www.biomedcentral.com (accessed 20 April 2010).

[24] See the Public Library of Science (PLOS) website, available at: http://www.plos.org (accessed 20 April 2010).

Box 7.2 *(continued)*

> and other research centers expend massive amounts of money to generate and support research, scholarship and scholarly publications. These expenditures vastly outweigh the modest operating budgets of even the most expensive scholarly journals . . . Where open access publishing can enhance the dissemination and impact of scholarly research, it seems like a good bargain for all concerned, for reasons that are primarily not financial . . . But making research more accessible, even if it generates no significant cost savings, seems likely to improve the quality of scholarly research across the board, and seems worth doing on these grounds alone.

Litman suggests that law journal publishing is one of the 'easiest cases for open access publishing' (ibid., p. 105).[25] She points out that: 'Nobody who participates in any way in the law journal article research, writing, selecting, editing, and publication process does so because of copyright incentives. Indeed, copyright is sufficiently irrelevant that legal scholars, the institutions that employ them, and the journals that publish their research tolerate considerable uncertainty about who owns the copyright to the works in question, without engaging in serious efforts to resolve it' (ibid.).

[25] She also notes that (at least in the US) the majority of law journals depend on unpaid students to undertake the selection and copy editing of articles (2007, p. 105).

their work. These repositories, while not necessarily peer-reviewed, frequently include papers published elsewhere in peer-reviewed journals. Works can be uploaded and downloaded fairly easily for free. This enables 'two-way traffic' by allowing scholars to place their works in such repositories, and to access the most up-to-date writings in their field. In this way the commons of scholarship can grow; such articles and writing can provide a free access basis on which developing country scholars and educators can build reading lists, based on Global South scholarship as well as scholarship from developed countries.

There may be some tensions, however, between publishing in a high-impact paper journal and making a work available via an open access repository. While the two are not always mutually exclusive, it is not automatically permissible for journal papers to be made available via open access. This might entail hard choices amongst authors on whether to place their works on online repositories. Some potential for reforms exists. For example, if authors (as some are doing) were to put pressure on journals to permit sharing on online repositories (and employing institutions were to put in place policies to encourage their academics to do so), this could be persuasive in getting this eventually recognized as a norm.[26] Meanwhile, there are 'meta'-sites such as the Directory of Open Access Journals[27] that

[26] This helpful insight is owed to Rosemary Wolson. Some publishers are also increasingly exploring modalities which enable contributors to publish through them in hard copy, while permitting the circulation of content (e.g. electronic drafts of articles) through online 'open access' repositories. The present book by the Public Interest Intellectual Property Advisors (PIIPA) is an example where such solutions towards ensuring some measure of 'open access' have been successfully explored with a mainstream publisher.

[27] See the Directory of Open Access Journals (DOAJ) database, available at: http://www.doaj.org (accessed 20 April 2010). Further electronic library websites can be accessed from the Electronic Information

provide a crucial service by collecting the widely dispersed resources available on the Internet and making them available in a single place. These are generally not-for-profit ventures that rely on external funding to remain sustainable.

2.3.2. Peer-to-peer (P2P) distribution networks

The growth of P2P networks will inevitably transform the distribution not only of music but also other forms of digital content. This is a powerful distribution mechanism that bypasses the traditional media channels and enables digital content to be immediately available to many users the moment someone places it on the network. These P2P networks are powerful tools for sharing information; P2P transfers now constitute almost half of all global Internet traffic (see Ghosh et al. 2006). The opportunity for developing countries (and by implication, for individuals and organizations within countries) is immense. While the advantages for the distribution of cultural commodities (e.g. books, CDs, DVDs) are clear, the advantages with respect to scientific research, health information, books, and other materials are even stronger. The ability to search many sub-networks for materials of particular concern to developing countries would be invaluable, especially for technology and knowledge transfer. The encouragement of the use of P2P networks for the distribution of such materials may be one of the most significant interventions states and organizations can make for creating access to knowledge.

3. Legislative developments and pro-access strategies

While ICTs present opportunities for better access by stakeholders to information products, including educational materials, there has been a trend towards a strengthening of IP protection around the world through the vehicles of treaty-making and free trade agreements (FTAs).

3.1. Legislative convergence on copyright subject matter

Along with the TRIPS Agreement, which sets minimum standards for copyright and other IP protection for a wide range of subject matter (see Chapter 1), many countries have signed up to the WIPO Copyright Treaty (WCT) and the WIPO Performances and Phonograms Treaty (WPPT).[28] Some implications of these treaties for access to information products are described in Box 7.3. These vehicles make way for legislative convergence in copyright protection between the North and the South, although some countries like the US have resisted similar harmonization in terms of copyright exceptions. Along with the increased copyright protection

for Libraries (EIFL) website, available at: http://www.eifl.net/cps/sections/home (accessed 18 January 2009).

[28] WIPO Performances and Phonograms Treaty (Geneva, 20 December 1996), 36 I.L.M. 76 (*entered into force* 20 May 2002) [hereinafter 'WPPT'], available at: http://www.wipo.int/export/sites/www/treaties/en/ip/wppt/pdf/trtdocs_wo034.pdf (accessed 3 February 2010). WIPO Copyright Treaty (Geneva, 30 December 1996), 36 I.L.M. 65 (*entered into force* 6 March 2002) [hereinafter 'WCT'], available at: http://www.wipo.int/export/sites/www/treaties/en/ip/wct/pdf/trtdocs_wo033.pdf (accessed 3 February 2010).

BOX 7.3. Expanding scope and term of copyright protection

The international copyright regime is less balanced than it has been at any point in the past. First, the range of rights granted to copyright owners has expanded. For instance, the 1994 TRIPS Agreement created a new right to control rental of copyrighted works and extended copyright to computer software. The 1996 WIPO Internet Treaties (WCT and WPPT) created a new right of 'making available', expanded the right of communication to the public and extended the right of reproduction into the storage of data in digital form.

Second, the length of copyright term has also expanded in recent years. Although the internationally harmonized term is 50 years after the life of the author, many countries have now adopted the higher term of life of the author plus 70 years (or in some cases up to 100 years), often as a result of recent bilateral trade agreements with the US and/or the European Community.

Third, while also creating new opportunities for the creation and dissemination of copyrighted works, new developments in ICTs have challenged the traditional balance embodied in the copyright system. The 1996 WIPO Internet Treaties required signatory countries to provide legal protection to technological protection measures (TPMs) – technologies that can be used by rights holders to control access to, and use of, digital copyrighted works. Private rights holders have been able to use legally enforced TPMs to control what level of access information users can have, and on what terms. As the US experience with the 1998 Digital Millennium Copyright Act[29] has suggested, overbroad TPM legal regimes can in cases override existing national copyright law exceptions and limitations. They can also hamper countries' ability to create new exceptions and limitations to meet their domestic needs.

Source: Hinze 2008.

[29] Digital Millennium Copyright Act (DMCA), Pub. L. No. 105-304, 112 Stat. 2860 (1998) (codified as amended in scattered sections of 17 U.S.C.).

embodied in these treaties, there are also tendencies on the part of rights holders to seek stronger protection for software and for new subject matter such as databases. For pedagogy delivered digitally, protecting databases and software may increase significantly the cost of access and use.

Developing countries are in the process of implementing the copyright elements of the TRIPS Agreement as well as the provisions of the WCT and WPPT. Furthermore, there is a push in bilateral FTAs to have developing countries ratify and implement these international treaties. The US increasingly has insisted on the latter as part of its trade policy, and we have seen significant attempts by the EU to push the same agenda. In particular, in its negotiations with the seventy-six-member group of African, Caribbean and Pacific countries, the EU has demanded that these countries comply with the substantive elements of the WCT and WPPT. If all these countries sign up to the latter agreements, this will leave a handful of Latin American countries as the main actors pushing at the international level for a better balance between copyright protection and public access to information products for development.

3.2. Copyright implementation and technical assistance

Since technical assistance to developing countries on the implementation of IP-related treaties comes mainly from developed country agencies (e.g. United States

Agency for International Development [USAID], US Patent and Trademark Office, European Patent Office, Japanese Patent Office) as well as from multilateral institutions (e.g. WIPO and WTO), much of the implementation has been modelled on the standards prevalent in developed countries. WIPO has been the primary vehicle through which the EU, Japan and the US have funnelled their technical assistance to developing countries. While ostensibly espousing a 'neutral' approach, such efforts tend to put in place the highest standards of IP protection beyond that strictly required under existing treaties. The nature, scope and independence of such technical assistance have been at the core of discussions on the Development Agenda at WIPO (see Chapter 9). In June 2007, the WIPO member states finally agreed on the Development Agenda to re-establish principles of neutrality and transparency and to establish a monitoring body.[30] This success has been the result of a coalition of developing countries and civil society actors.[31]

Many developing countries have not taken full advantage of the flexibilities enshrined in the TRIPS Agreement, the WCT and the WPPT. Nuanced implementation of these agreements according to developing country contexts and human development needs presents the next big challenge. Developing country coalitions and civil society organizations (CSOs) working on these issues have been developing strategies for monitoring and holding the WIPO secretariat and member states accountable for the standards set in the Development Agenda (see Chapter 9). Some organizations, for example, the International Centre for Trade and Sustainable Development (ICTSD), are identifying and evaluating the essential elements that would constitute a successful Agenda, in terms of technical assistance and other areas (Marchant & Musungu 2007).[32]

A spectrum of international CSOs and other institutions have sought in different ways to assist developing countries in building their capacity for nuanced policy-making and legislation relating to IP laws.[33] At the regional level the pro-access work of various organizations is significant as, for example, Enda Tiers Monde (Senegal), Trade Law Centre for Southern Africa (TRALAC, South Africa), African Trade Network (Ghana), Third World Network – Africa (Ghana), and Consumers International Asia Pacific. Pro-access groups in Europe, such as the Free Software Foundation Europe, have also made progress in initiating discussions on policy reforms with the European Commission, the European Parliament and the EU member states.

However, few organizations have placed themselves in a position to provide full technical assistance to developing countries at the national level. Technical expertise at the national level, which is sorely lacking, remains dependent on funds

[30] For further background on the Development Agenda and related proposals, see the WIPO website, 'Development Agenda for WIPO', available at: http://www.wipo.int/ip-development/en/agenda/ (accessed 23 March 2010). See also New 2009.

[31] This includes work at the South Centre, Knowledge Ecology International (KEI, formerly CPTech), CIEL, ICTSD, QUNO, Fundação Getulio Vargas Law School in Brazil, Electronic Frontier Foundation, Electronic Information for Libraries (eiFL) and the International Federation of Library Associations (IFLA), among other institutions.

[32] ICTSD has also been setting up Geneva-based and regional dialogues (e.g. workshops in the Pacific, West Africa and Southern Africa) on national implementations of the Development Agenda.

[33] Examples (non-exhaustive) include the Centre for International Environmental Law (CIEL), Oxfam International, Quaker United Nations Office (QUNO), Knowledge Ecology International (KEI), ICTSD, PIIPA and others.

from developed countries, with an increasing amount coming directly from the US Patent and Trademark Office, the US Copyright Office and the EU, as well as industries with vested interests. A balance on the other side is crucially needed with sufficient funds to counter the dominant influences and to build the capacity of developing country stakeholders. This requires the participation of organizations with significant national constituencies and networks, across several regions. Several organizations strive to carry out such work. Examples include eIFL in the library sector, ICTSD in TRIPS compliance and CIEL.[34] Strong conceptual backup in the development of model laws and 'model' implementation is needed. Such capacities tend to be divided among different organizations. For example, academic institutions such as the Yale Information Society Project (www.law.yale.edu/isp) are carrying out some of the conceptual work, along with Geneva-based organizations such as CIEL, ICTSD, and the South Centre among others. Such work requires significant support and coordination, including comprehensive approaches at the national or regional level to ensure coherence.

3.3. Increased copyright enforcement

The EU and the US have focused increasingly on pushing enforcement of copyright by extending techniques of infringement detection and copyright enforcement to authorities in developing countries. In addition, developed countries seek higher enforcement standards such as the criminalization of copyright infringement (see Box 7.4). The ongoing negotiation by developed countries (including the US, Canada, Japan and the EU) of an Anti-Counterfeiting Trade Agreement (ACTA), outside of WIPO, has also emerged as an area for further scrutiny (New 2009, p. 34; Stratton 2009, p. 23). These developments coincide with the increased capacity of rights holders to carry out private quasi-judicial enforcement through TPMs and digital rights management (DRM). Few public interest organizations have formal plans to address the enforcement issue, possibly because it has little political traction and is difficult to frame for advocacy. Increased enforcement of IP may, however, be one of the most important developments with respect to the impact it may have on fundamental rights and local livelihoods. As Rens, Prabhala and Kawooya (2006, p. 30) have noted, the informal economy in developing countries is a crucial component of earnings for the majority of people, including those who use and sell technically infringing services and products. Other actors who will be affected by increased enforcement and the criminalization of infringement will be students, researchers and journalists. This will in turn affect learning, research and freedom of expression in society.[35] Enforcement without due regard to societal impact and adjustment costs will severely damage the economies of developing countries. In addition, the push for enforcement may pressure developing countries to shift funds and personnel away from crucial welfare policies in health and other areas to spend on customs and border enforcement.

[34] See the eIFL homepage, available at: http://www.eifl.net (accessed 18 January 2009).

[35] Some discussion on the impact of enforcement on freedom of expression is included in Chapter 8 of this book; see further Heins and Beckles 2005.

BOX 7.4. Personal use, mass copying and criminal offences

Legislative tendencies in many countries have been towards toughening copyright laws and their enforcement, including a marked tendency to treat forms of copyright infringement increasingly as offences under criminal law (Munoz 2007). In some jurisdictions, criminal sanctions now apply not only to wilful infringement for commercial gain[36] or on a 'commercial scale',[37] but are also spilling towards cases of personal use of copyright-protected material.[38] While it is beyond the scope of this chapter to survey the expanding range of criminal sanctions for copyright in different jurisdictions (see Sugden 2009),[39] more scrutiny is needed of the increasing tendency to resolve civil disputes through criminal proceedings (see Tapper 2004; Laddie 1996). Noting how the criminal provisions in the UK Copyright Act are now 'being used in earnest', Sir Hugh Laddie (1996, pp. 14–15) observes: 'There is a great incentive to proceed in this way. The costs of the prosecuting copyright owner are usually paid out of central funds, even if the prosecution fails. . . . We have therefore reached the stage where taxpayers' money is being used to enforce private rights which many might think are more than adequately protected by civil remedies'.

Discussing criminal penalties under the US Digital Millennium Copyright Act of 1998 (DMCA) for wilful infringements other than for commercial purposes or financial gain (17 U.S.C. § 506(a)(1)(B)), Moohr (2003) suggests that the rationale for criminalizing what is effectively 'personal use' does not necessarily fit with the prevalent moral consensus in society nor accord with criminal law doctrines. She notes that: 'Criminal theory suggests it is appropriate to punish conduct that imposes a community harm or that breaches a moral standard . . . consensus that would condemn personal use is far from robust and the harm rationale provides only an equivocal basis for criminalization' (Ibid., p. 732).

Moohr draws a contrast between personal use and what she describes as the 'predatory practices of competitors or [] the self-enriching facilitation of copying by file sharing services' (ibid.). Other commentators have gone further in questioning whether there is moral consensus across societies, with different cultural attitudes towards IP, that commercial copying and handling of copyright-protected works without authorization should be treated as criminal offences (Bullard 2005; Rens et al. 2006; Munoz & Waitara 2007).[40] As seen in the ongoing and controversial negotiations of an Anti-Counterfeiting Trade Agreement (ACTA) by countries

(continued)

[36] For example, the US Digital Millennium Copyright Act of 1998 (DMCA) criminalizes 'willful infringement' for 'commercial advantage or private financial gain' (17 U.S.C. § 506(a)(1)(A)). Criminal penalties are not applicable to nonprofit libraries, archives, or educational institutions (17 U.S.C. § 1201(d)(3)).

[37] For a comparison of approaches to defining 'commercial scale' in different jurisdictions, see Sugden 2009.

[38] Under the US DMCA, criminal penalties extend to 'willful infringement' by the 'reproduction or distribution, including by electronic means, during any 180-day period, of 1 or more copies or phonorecords of 1 or more copyrighted works, which have a total retail value of more than $1,000' (17 U.S.C. § 506(a)(1)(B)). Moohr (2003, p. 13) suggests this includes the case of those 'who copy for personal use, who by definition do not act for commercial advantage . . . '. Loren (1999, pp. 862–864) provides hypothetical examples of how easily the threshold of US$1,000 may be reached in personal use. According to Sugden, the limits set in the US legislation 'mean that in the modern world of the internet, downloading individuals can breach these limits easily' (2009, p. 204; see also pp. 208–209).

[39] Some illumination may also be gained from the Federation Against Copyright Theft (FACT) website, available at: http://www.fact-uk.org.uk/ (accessed 23 March 2010), and the UK Intellectual Property Office homepage, available at: http://www.ipo.gov.uk/crime.htm (accessed 23 March 2010).

[40] Alford (1995) suggests there are cultural differences in perceptions of IP in his book entitled 'To Steal a Book is an Elegant Offence', which describes US-Sino discussions in the 1980s towards stronger IP protection and enforcement in China – although such differences may also be overstated (Shao 2007). For current IP-related laws in China, see the China IP Law Search Tool, available at: http://www.ipr2.org/ipsearch (accessed 23 March 2010). The gravity of some criminal sanctions in force in China is noticeable in an information document of the UK Intellectual Property Office, entitled 'China: An Enforcement Roadmap', available at http://www.ipo.gov.uk/chinaroadmap.pdf (accessed 25 February 2010).

Box 7.4 (*continued*)

including the US, the EU and Japan, there is little agreement on the threshold for treating copyright infringements as criminal.

Meanwhile, Sugden (2009, p. 203) observes that 'the harmonization of criminal infringement of intellectual property rights relating to counterfeiting and piracy activities in Europe has been a difficult process as not all countries recognize or accept the criminalization of copyright infringements'. Discussing recent EU debates and reforms towards limiting the use of criminal sanctions to cases of intentional infringements of IPRs on a 'commercial scale',[41] he notes the difficulties in providing a numerically precise definition of what constitutes a 'commercial scale' (ibid., p. 203). Comparing current approaches in different jurisdictions around the world, he adds that: 'These variations in the meaning of the words "commercial scale" demonstrate the difficulties of defining in the technological age the boundaries between legitimate and illegitimate uses of a copyright work' (ibid.).

[41] See text of the European Parliament A Series, Commission Report, sixth parliamentary term (2004–2009), no. 73 of 2007, available at: http://www.cr-international.com/2007_EU-Parliament_Report_on_Enforcement_Directive_27.3.pdf (accessed 23 March 2010). See discussion in Sugden 2009, p. 203.

In a South Center paper, Biadgleng and Munoz (2008, p. 27) discuss border measures and customs legislation dealing with IP enforcement, including the development of model legislation by the World Customs Organization (WCO). They warn that: 'One of the dangers of the increased focus on border control measures is the possibility that the powers given to customs authorities over intellectual property enforcement may be too broad if they have not been adequately trained to pass judgment on whether goods are actually counterfeit . . . '. Such border measures may create barriers to the flow of non-counterfeit products. Biadgleng and Munoz furthermore note that Interpol characterizes 'trademark counterfeiting and copyright piracy as serious intellectual property crimes' but does not provide a clear definition of the terms and what necessary elements must be present to constitute counterfeiting and piracy (ibid.). In their opinion: 'This is a serious concern for developing countries and consumers, given that the potential scope of the definition of counterfeit and piracy may be so wide as to include legitimate uses of works and cases where an individual may infringe an intellectual property right without knowing it'.

It is crucial that support is provided to developing countries for the development of strategies to combat enforcement approaches (e.g. through customs and border control) that ultimately serve external industries. Such strategies should explore win-win scenarios of enforcement which re-direct attention to the needs of domestic actors in developing countries (artists and creators especially) as well as enforcement against biopiracy and misappropriation of indigenous knowledge and cultural expressions (Kostecki 2006; see Chapters 4 and 5). While there are several organizations with the capacity to help develop strategies at the national level (a good example is Fundação Getulio Vargas Law School in Brazil), such approaches may be further pioneered by artists' associations and development aid donors, with potential partnering between academic institutions and other organizations.

The rising influence of collecting societies furthermore calls for scrutiny (see Chapter 9). Special attention will need to be paid to the structure of collecting societies to ensure that they are focused on domestic interests in a developing country rather than on foreign interests. What is needed is a counterbalance to the assistance provided to developing country collecting societies by foreign collecting societies, as well as the formulation of an international code of conduct for such groups to ensure that they do not unduly target educational institutions and libraries.

Further scrutiny is also needed on arrangements and guidelines encouraging self-enforcement by educational institutions and libraries of restrictions on reproducing and disseminating materials which may go beyond copyright law. For example, there are more and more contract-imposed limitations on institutions, including libraries, on the extent they can reproduce copyright-protected material. As noted by Heins and Beckles (2005), organizations representing owners of copyright and users of protected materials have also negotiated guidelines with specific limits on copying. Frequently used in education, these guidelines offer some security to teachers, and near-immunity from suit to the universities that follow them (ibid., p. 6). The authors note, however, how such guidelines are often ringed with arbitrary restrictions (e.g. numerical limits on the number of pages from a textbook, or words from a poem or story, that can be copied), and may ignore the flexibility provided by exceptions under copyright laws and conventions (ibid., pp. 6–7). Further attention is thus needed on the potentials and limitations of elaborating such guidelines in the field of education. In the US context, Jaszi warns in a publication by the Center for Social Media (2008, pp. 7–8) that:

> Today, some educators mistakenly believe that the issues covered in the fair use principles ... are not theirs to decide. They believe they must follow various kinds of 'expert' guidance offered by others. In fact, the opposite is true. The various negotiated agreements that have emerged since passage of the Copyright Act of 1976 have never had the force of law, and in fact, the guidelines bear little relationship to the actual doctrine of fair use ... many publications for educators reproduce the guidelines uncritically, presenting them as standards that must be adhered to in order to act lawfully. ...

Jaszi argues that this is an area in which educators 'can assert their own rights under fair use to make these decisions on their own, without approval' (ibid.). He adds that 'in rare cases where doing so would bring them into conflict with misguided institutional policies, they should assert their rights and seek to have those policies changed'. As an alternative reference and 'counterweight' to guidelines, he highlights a set of best practices for media literacy educators (ibid.).

3.4. More multilateral and national emphasis on copyright limitations and exceptions

While there has been successful international harmonization of rights holders' norms over the last twenty years, this has not been matched by a parallel harmonization of limitations and exceptions that serve the public interest (Hinze 2008). Within the international copyright framework, the so-called three-step test currently governs exceptions and limitations to copyright. This is discussed in Box 7.5 (see also Chapters 6 and 8).

In November 2004, the government of Chile (at the initiative of the Chilean Ministry of Education) asked WIPO to include the subject of exceptions and limitations to copyright and related rights (for the purposes of education, libraries and archives,

BOX 7.5. Exceptions and limitations within the international copyright framework

Gwen Hinze[42]

The Berne Convention contains various exceptions and permits signatories to set limitations on the scope of copyright protection. It contains a mandatory and uncompensated exception to copyright owners' exclusive rights, permitting quotation of copyrighted works in accordance with 'fair practice', in Article 10(1). It also gives signatory countries the discretion to create uncompensated exceptions and limitations, subject to certain conditions, for use of copyrighted works for illustration in publications, broadcasts and sound recordings for teaching purposes (Article 10(2)); news reporting on current events (Article 10bis(1) and (2)); compensated exceptions and limitations for rebroadcasting (Article 11bis(1)) and for recording musical works (Article 13); and a special compulsory licence regime for reproduction and translation of texts by developing countries, subject to strict conditions (the Berne Appendix). These exceptions are available to signatories of the TRIPS Agreement, which incorporates the Berne Convention.

While the Berne Convention recognizes an exception for 'teaching' purposes in Article 10(2), there is presently no recognition in the international copyright framework for exceptions to facilitate education (which includes both imparting knowledge by educators, and the ability of students to learn by accessing and interacting with information), nor specific exceptions for libraries and archives, or uses by persons with disabilities.

The Berne Convention also allows signatories to create additional uncompensated exceptions to rights holders' reproduction right if they meet the controversial 'three-step test' (Article 9(2)). Article 13 of the TRIPS Agreement adopted the same test for creation of exceptions to a broader set of rights, beyond the reproduction right. It provides that:

> Members shall confine limitations or exceptions to exclusive rights to certain special cases which do not conflict with a normal exploitation of the work and do not unreasonably prejudice the legitimate interests of the right holder.

To what exclusive rights Article 13 applies is still the subject of much debate. Legal commentators who take a maximalist approach claim that it applies to *all* exclusive rights of copyright owners, and conditions the creation of *any* new copyright exceptions and limitations on meeting that test (following the WTO Panel Decision in *United States – Section 110(5) of the U.S. Copyright Act*, concerning section 110(5) of the US copyright legislation). However, other legal commentators read it more narrowly, as applying only on top of existing Berne exceptions, when the test is compatible with the requirements of those in the Berne Convention. The history of the negotiation of the Stockholm Conference of the Berne Convention also supports the interpretation that the three-step test does not apply to those areas where discretion is given to Member States to create exceptions recognized in the Berne Convention, such as Articles 10(1) and 10(2). That view is also supported by the standard principles of interpretation in international law. As a result, there is a sound argument that countries can create exceptions for teaching purposes under Article 10(2) of the Berne Convention that do not have to be conditioned on a decision about satisfaction of the three-step test.

The three-step test was included in the 1996 WIPO Copyright Treaty (WCT Article 10) and WIPO Performances and Phonograms Treaty (WPPT Article 16) and governs the creation of exceptions and limitations to rights newly granted under those treaties. The WCT and WPPT formulation also applies to existing exceptions under the Berne Convention. Developing

[42] Extract from Hinze 2008.

countries expressed concern during the negotiations of the 1996 treaties about the impact of this provision on national sovereignty over national copyright law exceptions (which the Berne Convention had traditionally reserved to Member States) and the ability of countries to create new exceptions and limitations to facilitate domestic needs. As a result, the Agreed Statements Concerning the WIPO Copyright Treaty were adopted by Member States, to make clear that the intention was to preserve countries' existing copyright law exceptions and give countries the flexibility to introduce new copyright exceptions and limitations appropriate for the digital environment in order to meet domestic needs, such as distance education. The Agreed Statements also expressly shield Berne Convention exceptions from scrutiny under the TRIPS Agreement's three-step test, affirming that Article 10 of the WCT does not expand or reduce the scope of existing exceptions under the Berne Convention (see Chapter 6).

However, in practice, the uncertainty surrounding the interpretation of the three-step test, and the linkage between national IP regulation and trade law under the TRIPS Agreement, has resulted in the creation of relatively low levels of exceptions and limitations, particularly in developing countries' national copyright laws.

Source: Hinze 2008.

and disabled persons) on the agenda of the WIPO Standing Committee on Copyright and Related Rights (SCCR) and 'to strengthen international understanding of the need to have adequate limitations, learning from existing models and moving towards agreement on exceptions and limitations for public interest purposes, which, like minimum standards, were to be envisaged in all legislation for the benefit of the international community' (WIPO 2004).[43] Along with other proposals for reforms, this has prompted significant emphasis at WIPO on exceptions and limitations to copyright.

In March 2008, the WIPO SCCR met in Geneva to discuss exceptions to, and limitations on, rights granted to copyright holders by international instruments, a topic which is of vital importance to developing countries. WIPO member countries universally supported keeping the topic of exceptions and limitations on the Committee's agenda. There has since been some progress in this area. Studies have been commissioned by WIPO, for example, on exceptions and limitations for libraries and archives (see Box 7.6), as well as for the benefit of educational activities, including distance education and transborder aspects.

Libraries and library associations are active in pushing for legal reforms (see Stratton 2009). For example, the Library of Alexandria has recently published a toolkit on 'Access to Knowledge' which highlights salient issues in copyright exceptions and limitations for libraries and archives (see Essalmawi 2009). IFLA, eIFL.net and the US Library Copyright Alliance (LCA) have also issued a joint *Statement of Principles on Copyright Exceptions and Limitations for Libraries and Archives* at the eighteenth session of the SCCR.[44] Stratton notes that 'this important

[43] This summary was drawn from Hinze 2008, p. 1.

[44] IFLA, 'Statement of Principles on Copyright Exceptions and Limitations for Libraries and Archives', available at: http://www.ifla.org/en/publications/statement-of-principles-on-copyright-exceptions-and-limitations-for-libraries-and-archi (accessed 15 December 2009). See discussion in Stratton 2009, pp. 23–26.

BOX 7.6. Copyright limitations and exceptions for libraries and archives: The WIPO 2008 study

The WIPO-commissioned 'Study on Copyright Limitations and Exceptions for Libraries and Archives' (WIPO 2008) provides an overview of statutory exceptions for libraries in 184 WIPO member states, including library exceptions to the prohibition against circumvention of technological protection measures.[45] The statutory provisions surveyed primarily address such issues as reproduction of copyrighted works for purposes such as private research and study, preservation and replacement of materials, and document supply and interlibrary lending. Prepared by Kenneth Crews, the study noted variations among national statutes in nearly all respects, from the scope of applicable libraries to the specific activities encompassed.

The study notes that many libraries are struggling with issues such as large-scale digitization of collections and automated harvesting and collecting of Internet-based resources (see WIPO 2008, pp. 28–31). It provides case studies suggesting that libraries may have challenges interpreting the library exceptions under a domestic law (e.g. under Canadian law) and are active in bringing about legislative reforms in countries where the law provides no statutory provisions specifically applicable to libraries. For example, reforms have been considered [and recently passed] in Chile with far-reaching effects (ibid., pp. 30–31).[46] In a more extreme case, the study notes that 'librarians in South Africa have reported several examples of services that have been seriously hindered because of the lack of a provision in the S.A. Copyright Act that would clearly permit the making of even a single copy of a work in a digital format' (ibid., p. 35).

The study also draws attention to the prohibition against circumvention of technological measures under Article 11 of the WCT (ibid., p. 23). Under this Article:

> Contracting parties shall provide adequate legal protection and effective legal remedies against the circumvention of effective technological measures that are used by authors in connection with the exercise of their rights under this Treaty or the Berne Convention and that restrict acts, in respect of their works, which are not authorized by the authors concerned or permitted by law.

The study suggests that the language from Article 11 'references acts that may be "permitted by law"'. According to the study: 'That language opens an opportunity for countries to create exceptions to the anti-circumvention provision. Those exceptions have the potential of providing some balance and defusing some of the controversy surrounding the new law' (ibid.). The study notes that, of the 184 WIPO member countries, seventy-nine have a statutory prohibition against circumvention of TPMs (ibid., p. 31). Of those countries, twenty-six have an exception to the bar on circumvention that is explicitly applicable to libraries. Every country that has an anti-circumvention exception for libraries also has an exception to the economic rights for the benefit of libraries. Twenty-one of the twenty-six countries are EU members. The non-EU countries are Australia, Croatia, Norway, Singapore and the US.

Source: WIPO 2008.

[45] WIPO 2008, Executive Summary, pp. 7–8.

[46] The library provisions considered in Chile encompass the following possibilities: 'preserving or replacing a work that is part of the library collection, in case of loss or deterioration; substituting a work for another library or file that has become lost, destroyed, or made unusable, as long as the work is not available on the market; adding a work to the library's collection, if the work has not been available on the market for the last five years; making a copy of a work for a user's private study; making a copy simultaneously available to multiple users present at the library; translating a work if it has been published for three years and a Spanish or Castilian translation is not made available by the rightsholder' (ibid., pp. 30–31). Chilean Law No. 20,435, which amends Intellectual Property Law No. 17,336 (1970) and includes these exceptions for libraries and archives, was published and took effect on 4 May 2010.

document . . . sets out the library community's position on the barriers to the delivery of library and information services for access to knowledge in the 21st century digital age' (ibid.).

As WIPO and its member states respond to new demands posed by the Development Agenda (see Chapter 9), other potential exceptions and limitations have been brought to the fore. This is evidenced, for example, by the November 2008 SCCR Information Session on a WIPO-commissioned study on exceptions for the visually impaired (WIPO 2007) and the treaty proposal for facilitating access to copyright-protected material by the blind, visually impaired and other reading-disabled persons (considered at the eighteenth session of the SCCR in May 2009). This treaty proposal was placed on the Development Agenda by the World Blind Union (WBU). The reception by WIPO member states to the proposal has been politically divided (Ress 2009, pp. 46–50).[47] Ress observes that: '[D]espite the emergence of new publishing and distribution technologies, enormous barriers in accessing copyrighted works confront persons who are blind or otherwise reading disabled . . . While some countries have limitations and exceptions in their copyright laws to allow authorized entities to make works accessible for persons with reading disabilities without prior permission of copyright owners, there is no legal certainty' (ibid., pp. 41–43). She notes that exceptions vary from country to country, and are often restrictive or focused only on a single older technology (e.g. raised paper Braille) (ibid.).

Further exploration of exceptions and limitations to copyright provisions, including digital exceptions, will be important in maintaining balanced access by the public to copyright-protected works. Various approaches proposed at the multilateral level towards elaborating or clarifying 'exceptions and limitations' relevant to education are mentioned in the following section. Some examples of national laws relating to exceptions and limitations for educational use are provided in Appendix D (see Chapter 6). Both developed and developing countries will continue to face the challenge of adapting their domestic copyright laws to: (1) implement existing exceptions for education and libraries under the multilateral framework or FTAs; and (2) formulate new exceptions that address educational and library uses of digital content.[48]

3.4.1. Towards internationally recognized mandatory minimum exceptions and limitations?

There seems to be growing consensus that a new multilateral means of creating mandatory minimum exceptions and limitations to international copyright law is required to foster education, libraries and archives, to facilitate uses by disabled

[47] As New (2009, p. 30) notes, the issue of access to material for the reading-impaired 'has become a key focal point for some A2K activists who believe the effort will be difficult to oppose because of the combination of human rights and market failure in providing equal access'. Some developing countries are concerned, at the same time, that a move first to a treaty for the visually impaired may jeopardize other limitations and exceptions they consider as ripe for inclusion within a package for reform at WIPO (ibid.). The African Group, for instance, views broad support for libraries and access for all types of readers as essential (ibid.; see also Ress 2009, p. 50).

[48] For an example, see IFLA 2002, 'Limitations and Exceptions to Copyright and Neighbouring Rights in the Digital Environment: An International Library Perspective', available at: http://www.ifla.org/III/clm/p1/ilp.htm (accessed 26 June 2009).

persons and to rebalance the international copyright regime to serve the needs of all the world's citizens. Hinze (2008) notes that there are various mechanisms for providing formal recognition of an international consensus on mandatory minimum exceptions and limitations. One would be a treaty or other 'hard' norm, which would provide clear guidance for developing countries and serve as a strong counterbalance to pressures from bilateral and regional negotiations outside of WIPO. This could take the form of a treaty on copyright exceptions and limitations, or be part of a broader Access to Knowledge Treaty.

Hugenholtz and Okediji observe (2008, p. 3) that 'despite over a century of international norm setting in the field of copyright, limitations and exceptions have largely remained "unregulated space"'. According to them, 'nothing in the international acquis would prevent parties to the Berne Union, the WCT or the WTO from entering into a special agreement listing in an exhaustive or enumerative manner those copyright limitations that are permitted within the confines of the three-step test' (ibid).

Hugenholtz and Okediji suggest that a global instrument on limitations and exceptions could also be cast in soft law (ibid., p. 5). It could be broached, for example, through adoption of a 'soft' norm, such as a Statement made by the WIPO Standing Committee on Copyright and Related Rights, adopted by the WIPO General Assembly, adoption of WIPO Guidelines, or a Joint Statement made by the WTO TRIPS Council and WIPO Standing Committee on Copyright and Related Rights (ibid.).

While Hugenholtz and Okediji venture that an instrument for exceptions and limitations should be primarily couched in copyright law, other frameworks beyond copyright need to be explored (ibid., p. 34). As Hugenholtz and Okediji note:

> The framework of human rights bears some promise for an instrument on limitations based, in particular, on core fundamental freedoms, such as freedom of speech and right to privacy. The framework of competition law may provide the context for international norms on compulsory licensing concerning, for instance, software interoperability. The framework of consumer law has obvious potential for protecting consumers against unfair terms in standard licensing agreements and might contain norms that make private copying freedoms 'click-wrap resistant'. (Ibid.)

These frameworks need to be further debated and evaluated by civil society, academics and governments, along with the potential for a multilateral instrument governing exceptions and limitations. As Hinze (2008) notes, the first step towards a multilateral instrument is increasing understanding in the international community of the need for a rebalancing instrument, and the economic and social value that it would bring for all stakeholders.

3.5. Consolidated strategies for access to knowledge

Pro-access responses to the opportunities presented by ICTs for civil society, governments and international organizations are manifold, and it is impossible to do justice to all of them within the scope of this chapter. Some broad-based initiatives include the movement for a new Access to Knowledge Treaty, pioneered by a number of developing countries and civil society organizations including Knowledge Ecology International.[49] The conceptual framing for this movement has largely been carried out at some academic institutions – including the Yale Law School Information Society Project which has been holding Access to Knowledge (A2K) Conferences, Harvard Law School's Berkman Center for Internet & Society, Fundação Getulio Vargas in Brazil and the United Nations University-MERIT in the Netherlands.

Few organizations have developed a full digital agenda and strategy to address the impact of technological developments on knowledge and education. Most organizations are responding in a piecemeal fashion, depending on which aspect of the copyright landscape they are engaged with. Scenario planning is rare in this field. An exception is a study by the Berkman Center for Internet & Society (2005a) which suggested several possible scenarios for developments in the online environment, mainly in the US context, ranging from no change in present balances to the dominance of alternative methods of production and remuneration (see Chapter 9). The international supplement to this work[50] elaborates on some of the trends identified in this chapter. While academically useful, the scenarios remain to be further fleshed out in order to provide guidance on where developments are leading. An important follow up to this work is a 2006 paper by the Berkman Center entitled 'The Digital Learning Challenge: Obstacles to Educational Uses of Copyrighted Material in the Digital Age'.[51] This paper focuses on developments in the US and points to the problems that copyright poses for the use of digital content.

At the international level, the work of many organizations in this field has coalesced around the UN-based Internet Governance Forum (IGF), which developed out of the World Summit on the Information Society programme's work.[52] This summit has proven a valuable organizing force for addressing many of the issues surrounding digital and Internet content and access to knowledge. However, one of the major groups missing from these discussions and activities are educational institutions at the secondary level, especially teachers' unions and associations. This is a major lacuna which could be remedied by support for the attendance and participation of secondary level institutions in forums such as the IGF, the Yale A2K conferences, and discussions with library associations.

Meanwhile, organizations whose involvement in IP issues has arisen out of their work on trade issues may not have concerted planning scenarios for IP, and these organizations are thus unlikely to have given full consideration to the effects of digital and Internet content on knowledge and education issues. As Roffe (2007) has noted, outside the access to medicines arena, regional and national institutions

[49] See the website of Knowledge Ecology International, available at: http://www.keionline.org (accessed 19 April 2010).

[50] See Berkman Center for Internet & Society and GartnerG2 2005b.

[51] See Berkman Center for Internet & Society 2006.

[52] See, for instance, the creation in 2007 of the Dynamic Coalition on Digital Education involving members of the Open Access and Educational Resources, Creative Commons and public interest digital copyright advocacy communities – Yale University, 'Proposal No. 23: Overcoming Obstacles to Effective Digital Education', available at: http://www.intgovforum.org/cms/workshops_08/showmelist.php?mem=78 (accessed 23 March 2010).

do not generally engage in any significant planning or action on IP. Some exceptions do exist, however, as exemplified by the IP-related planning activities that have been carried out by the regional limbs of some international nongovernmental organizations. One such example was the 'Access to Knowledge' project undertaken by Consumers International Asia Pacific and funded by the Open Society Institute. Ensuring sustained and continuing regional or national strategies and actions on these issues in developing countries remains a challenge.

4. Conclusion

Given the broad range of actors and issues to be addressed in relation to pro-access implications of new technologies for knowledge and education, a unitary strategy can be difficult to discern. However, the cross-pollination and discussions engendered at the Yale A2K Conferences and the IGF have shown many organizations that they share the same agenda, especially on digital and Internet content. Many are beginning to work together, especially at the multilateral level. Serious capacity weaknesses at the regional and national levels need to be addressed, and some basic conceptual gaps in areas such as copyright enforcement need to be filled. A lot of work remains to be done and better coordination among actors is needed.

REFERENCES

Adeya, N. & Cogburn, D.L. 2002, 'Prospects for the Digital Economy in South Africa: Technology, People, Policy and Strategies', *UNU-INTECH Discussion Paper No. 2,* United Nations University-Institute for New Technologies (UNU-INTECH), The Netherlands, available at: http://ideas.repec.org/p/dgr/unuint/200202.html (accessed 18 January 2009).

Alford, W.P. 1995, *To Steal a Book Is an Elegant Offense: Intellectual Property Law in Chinese Civilization,* Stanford University Press, Stanford, CA.

Andersen, B., Kozul-Wright, Z. & Kozul-Wright, R. 2000, 'Copyrights, Competition and Development: The Case of the Music Industry', *UNCTAD Discussion Paper No. 145,* United Nations Conference on Trade and Development (UNCTAD), Geneva, available at: http://www.unctad.org/en/docs/dp_145.en.pdf (accessed 18 January 2009).

Askerud, P. 1997, *Distribution of Educational Materials: Problems and Issues,* United Nations Educational, Scientific and Cultural Organization (UNESCO), Paris, available at: http://unesdoc.unesco.org/images/0010/001090/109092Eb.pdf (accessed 18 January 2009).

Berkman Center for Internet & Society 2006, *The Digital Learning Challenge: Obstacles to Educational Uses of Copyrighted Material in the Digital Age,* Harvard Law School, Cambridge, MA, available at: http://cyber.law.harvard.edu/media/files/copyrightandeducation.html (accessed 17 May 2009).

Berkman Center for Internet & Society & GartnerG2 2005a, *Copyright and Digital Media in a Post-Napster World: 2005 Update,* Harvard Law School, Cambridge, MA, available at: http://cyber.law.harvard.edu/media/wp2005 (accessed 17 May 2009).

Berkman Center for Internet & Society & GartnerG2 2005b, *Copyright and Digital Media in a Post-Napster World: International Supplement,* Harvard Law School, Cambridge,

MA, available at: http://cyber.law.harvard.edu/media/wpsupplement2005 (accessed 1 June 2009).

Biadgleng, E.T. & Munoz Tellez, V. 2008, 'The Changing Structure and Governance of Intellectual Property Enforcement', *South Centre Research Paper No. 15*, South Centre, Geneva, available at: http://ssrn.com/abstract=1210622 (accessed 24 January 2009).

Bullard, A. 2005, 'Reinvindicando a los Piratas. ¿Es La Propiedad Intelectual un Robo?', *Latin American and Caribbean Law and Economics Association (ALACDE) Annual Papers*, Paper 7, University of California, Berkeley, available at: http://repositories.cdlib.org/bple/alacde/7 (accessed 21 December 2008).

Center for Social Media 2008, *The Code of Best Practices in Fair Use for Media Literacy Education*, School of Communication American University, available at: http://www.centerforsocialmedia.org/files/pdf/Media_literacy_txt.pdf (accessed 17 May 2009).

Chapman, A.R. 2002, 'The Human Rights Implications of Intellectual Property Protection', *Journal of International Economic Law*, vol. 5, no. 4, pp. 861–882.

Crews, K.D. 2001, 'The Law of Fair Use and the Illusion of Fair-Use Guidelines', *The Ohio State Law Journal*, vol. 62, no. 2, pp. 602–700, available at: http://moritzlaw.osu.edu/lawjournal/issues/volume62/number2/crews.pdf (accessed 17 May 2009).

Darnton, R. 2009, 'Google and the Future of Books', *The New York Review of Books*, vol. 56, no. 2, available at: http://www.nybooks.com/articles/22281 (accessed 1 June 2009).

Drahos, P. 1999, 'Intellectual Property and Human Rights', *Intellectual Property Quarterly*, vol. 1999, no. 3, pp. 349–371.

Elsevier 2004, *Elsevier's Comments on Evolutions in Scientific, Technical and Medical Publishing and Reflections on Possible Implications of Open Access Journals for the UK*, available at: http://www.elsevier.com/authored_news/corporate/images/UKST1Elsevier_position_paper_on_stm_in_UK.pdf (accessed 24 January 2009).

Essalmawi, H. (ed.) 2009, *Bibliotheca Alexandria Access to Knowledge Toolkit II: The Access to Knowledge Movement – Opportunities, Challenges and the Road Ahead*, Bibliotheca Alexandria, Egypt, available at: http://www.bibalex.org/a2k/attachments/references/reffileu24bkg55ykqwgc55zysxzq45.pdf (accessed 15 November 2009).

Ghosh, R.A. et al. 2006, *Economic Impact of FLOSS on Innovation and Competitiveness of the EU ICT Sector*, United Nations University-Maastricht Economic and Social Research and Training Centre on Innovation and Technology (UNU-MERIT) Final Report, available at: http://ec.europa.eu/enterprise/ict/policy/doc/2006–11–20-flossimpact.pdf (accessed 18 January 2009).

Heins, M. & Beckles, T. 2005, *Will Fair Use Survive? Free Expression in the Age of Copyright Control*, Brennan Center for Justice, New York University School of Law, available at: http://www.fepproject.org/policyreports/WillFairUseSurvive.pdf (accessed 18 January 2009).

Helft, M. & Rich, M. 2008, 'Google Settles Suit Over Book Scanning', *The New York Times*, 28 October 2008.

Hinze, G. 2008, 'Making Knowledge Accessible Across Borders: The Case for Mandatory Minimum International Copyright Exceptions and Limitations for Education, Capacity Building and Development', *Electronic Frontier Foundation*, San Francisco, CA, available at: http://www.eff.org/files/eff-making-knowledge-accessible-whitepaper.pdf (accessed 18 January 2009).

Hugenholtz, P.B. & Okediji, R.L. 2008, *Conceiving an International Instrument on Exceptions and Limitations to Copyright*, Open Society Institute, available at: http://www.ivir.nl/publicaties/hugenholtz/finalreport2008.pdf (accessed 18 January 2009).

Kostecki, M. 2006, 'Intellectual Property and Economic Development: What Technical Assistance to Redress the Balance in Favour of Developing Nations?' *ICTSD Programme on Intellectual Property and Sustainable Development, Issue No. 12,* International Centre for Trade and Sustainable Development (ICTSD), Geneva, available at: http://ictsd.net/downloads/2008/08/kostecki-final.pdf (accessed 18 January 2009).

Laddie, H. 1996, 'Copyright: Over-strength, Over-regulated, Over-rated?', *European Intellectual Property Review,* vol. 18, no. 5, pp. 253–260.

Landes, W.M. & Posner, R.A. 1989, 'An Economic Analysis of Copyright Law", *The Journal of Legal Studies,* vol. 18, no. 2, pp. 325–363.

Litman, J. 2004, 'Sharing and Stealing', *Hastings Communications and Entertainment Law Journal,* vol. 27, no. 1, pp. 1–50, available at: http://ssrn.com/abstract=472141 (accessed 24 January 2009).

Litman, J. 2006, 'The Economics of Open-Access Law Publishing', *Lewis & Clark Law Review,* vol. 10, no. 4, pp. 779–795, available at: http://ssrn.com/abstract=912304 (accessed 24 January 2009).

Loren, L.P. 1999, 'Digitization, Commodification, Criminalization: The Evolution of Criminal Copyright Infringement and the Importance of the Willfulness Requirement', *Washington University Law Quarterly,* vol. 77, no. 3, pp. 835–900, available at: http://lawreview.wustl.edu/inprint/77–3/773–835.pdf (accessed 1 June 2009).

Marchant, R. & Musungu, S.F. 2007, 'Essential Elements of a World Intellectual Property Organization (WIPO) Development Agenda: What Would Constitute Success?', ICTSD Programme on Intellectual Property Rights and Sustainable Development, ICTSD, Geneva, available at: www.iprsonline.org/ictsd/docs/PCDA%20essential%20elements.pdf (accessed 18 January 2009).

Moohr, G.S. 2003, 'The Crime of Copyright Infringement: An Inquiry Based on Morality, Harm, and Criminal Theory', *Boston University Law Review,* vol. 83, no. 4, pp. 731–741, available at: www.law.uh.edu/faculty/gmoohr/Criminal.pdf (accessed 28 December 2008).

Munoz Tellez, V. & Waitara, C. 2007, 'A Development Analysis of the Proposed WIPO Treaty on the Protection of Broadcasting and Cablecasting Organizations', *Research Paper No. 9,* South Centre, Geneva, available at: http://www.southcentre.org/index.php?option=com_content&task=view&id=66 (accessed 14 May 2009).

New, W. 2009, 'Access to Influence in WIPO's Development Agenda', in H. Essalmawi (ed.), *Bibliotheca Alexandria Access to Knowledge Toolkit II: The Access to Knowledge Movement – Opportunities, Challenges and the Road Ahead,* Bibliotheca Alexandria, Egypt, pp. 28–36, available at: http://www.bibalex.org/a2k/attachments/references/reffileu24bkg55ykqwgc55zysxzq45.pdf (accessed 15 November 2009).

Okediji, R. 2004, 'Fostering Access to Education, Research and Dissemination of Knowledge through Copyright', *UNCTAD-ICTSD Dialogue on Moving the Pro-Development IP Agenda Forward,* UNCTAD – ICTSD, available at: http://www.iprsonline.org/unctadictsd/bellagio/docs/Okideiji_Bellagio4.pdf (accessed 18 January 2009).

Ovett, D. 2006a, 'Policy Brief on Intellectual Property, Development and Human Rights: How Human Rights Can Support Proposals for a World Intellectual Property Organization (WIPO) Development Agenda', *3D Policy Brief 2,* available at: http://www.3dthree.org/pdf_3D/3DPolBrief-WIPO-eng.pdf#search=%22%2BOvett%20%2B%22Policy%20Brief%20on (accessed 2 January 2009).

Ovett, D. 2006b, 'Intellectual Property and Human Rights: Is the Distinction Clear Now?: An Assessment of the Committee on Economic, Social and Cultural Rights' General Comment No. 17 (2005)', *3D Policy Brief 3*, available at: http://www.3dthree.org/pdf_3D/3D_GC17_IPHR.pdf (accessed 2 January 2009).

Rens, A., Prabhala, A. & Kawooya, D. 2006, 'Intellectual Property, Education and Access to Knowledge in Southern Africa', *ICTSD Regional Research Paper Southern and Eastern Africa*, ICTSD, Geneva, available at: http://www.iprsonline.org/unctadictsd/docs/06%2005%2031%20tralac%20amended-pdf.pdf (accessed 18 January 2009).

Ress, M. 2009, 'Limitations and Exceptions for Reading Disabled Persons: A New Paradigm at the WIPO Standing Committee on Copyright and Related Rights', in H. Essalmawi (ed.), *Bibliotheca Alexandria Access to Knowledge Toolkit II: The Access to Knowledge Movement – Opportunities, Challenges and the Road Ahead*, Bibliotheca Alexandria, Egypt, pp. 36–51, available at: http://www.bibalex.org/a2k/attachments/references/reffileu24bkg55ykqwgc55zysxzq45.pdf (accessed 15 November 2009).

Roffe, P. 2007, 'Intellectual Property, Bilateral Agreements and Sustainable Development: The Challenges of Implementation', *Intellectual Property, Bilateral Agreements and Sustainable Development Series 1*, The Center for International Environmental Law (CIEL), available at: http://www.ciel.org/Publications/FTA_ImplementationPub_Jan07.pdf (accessed 18 January 2009).

Shao, K. 2007, 'The Justice of Balance: Intellectual Property in China's History', doctoral thesis, School of Law, Queen Mary, University of London.

Stratton, B. 2009, 'A2K Quinquennium – Now We Are Five – The Library Perspective', in H. Essalmawi (ed.), *Bibliotheca Alexandria Access to Knowledge Toolkit II: The Access to Knowledge Movement – Opportunities, Challenges and the Road Ahead*, Bibliotheca Alexandria, Egypt, pp. 16–27, available at: http://www.bibalex.org/a2k/attachments/references/reffileu24bkg55ykqwgc55zysxzq45.pdf (accessed 15 November 2009).

Sugden, P. 2009, 'How Long Is a Piece of String? The Meaning of "Commercial Scale" in Copyright Piracy', *European Intellectual Property Review*, vol. 31, no. 4, pp. 202–212.

Tapper, C.B. 2004, 'Criminality and Copyright', in D. Vaver and L. Bentley (eds.), *Intellectual Property in the New Millennium: Essays in Honour of William R. Cornish*, Cambridge University Press, Cambridge.

United Nations Conference on Trade and Development (UNCTAD) 2004a, *Development and Globalization: Facts and Figures*, UNCTAD, New York and Geneva, available at: http://www.unctad.org/templates/webflyer.asp?docid=4848&intItemID=2364&lang=1 (accessed 18 January 2009).

UNCTAD 2004b, E-Commerce and Development Report, UNCTAD, New York and Geneva, available at: http://www.unctad.org/en/docs/ecdr2004_en.pdf (accessed 18 January 2009).

Waltner, C. 2006, *International Undersea Fiber Optic Cable Promises Much Needed Bandwidth to East Africa but Specter of Monopoly Pricing Threatens Project's Benefits*, Cisco Systems Inc., San Jose, CA, available at: http://newsroom.cisco.com/dlls/2006/ts_053106.html (accessed 18 January 2009).

World Intellectual Property Organization (WIPO) 2004, *Proposal by Chile on the Subject 'Exceptions and Limitations to Copyright and Related Rights'*, Standing Committee on Copyrights and Related Rights (SCCR), Doc. SCCR/13/2, WIPO, Geneva, available at: http://www.wipo.int/edocs/mdocs/copyright/en/sccr_17/sccr_17_2.pdf (accessed 17 May 2009).

WIPO 2007, *Study on Copyright Limitations and Exceptions for the Visually Impaired*, (prepared by J. Sullivan) SCCR, Doc. SCCR 15/7, WIPO, Geneva, available at: http://www.wipo.int/meetings/en/doc_details.jsp?doc_id=75696 (accessed 18 January 2009).

WIPO 2008, *Study on Copyright Limitations and Exceptions for Libraries and Archives*, (prepared by K. Crews) SCCR, Doc. SCCR/17/2, WIPO, Geneva, available at: http://www.wipo.int/edocs/mdocs/copyright/en/sccr_17/sccr_17_2.pdf (accessed 17 May 2009).

8

Cultural diversity and the arts: Contemporary challenges for copyright law

Tzen Wong, Molly Torsen and Claudia Fernandini[1]

> *The whole of human development is derivative. We stand on the shoulders of the scientists, artists and craftsmen who preceded us. We borrow and develop what they have done; not necessarily as parasites but simply as the next generation.* (Laddie 1996, p. 259)

> *Human development is a cultural process. As a biological species, humans are defined in terms of our cultural participation.* (Rogoff 2003, p. 3)

Introduction

This chapter examines the relationship between copyright protection and the encouragement of creative expression by individuals and communities. It begins by exploring concepts of culture and cultural diversity as promoted by international organizations including the United Nations Educational, Scientific and Cultural Organization (UNESCO). It poses the question as to whether copyright law, in its current formulations, adequately promotes a diversity of cultural expressions by persons and peoples of all backgrounds. It evaluates the conventional rhetoric that copyright incentivizes the arts by protecting the material and moral interests of creators. It does this by exploring trends in copyright protection and ownership, including corporate ownership, highlighting some notable differences in the experiences of creators in different sectors, world regions and local contexts. Does the copyright lacuna in some sectors and contexts suggest that other incentives and motivations might be at work in spurring creative activity? The example of contemporary art is discussed as a case study, to illustrate the ambiguities faced by creators in some sectors in relation to copyright protection for their works, along with their potential infringement of copyright over other works.

Since many creators are both copyright owners and active users of other persons' protected works, a simple dichotomy cannot be drawn between rights owners and end users. Indeed, the line between 'producer' and 'consumer' of cultural works is increasingly blurred, with digital technology and the Internet making it ever easier for users to 'cut and paste' and 'remix' existing works. What challenges do such phenomena pose for copyright law? The second part of the chapter looks

[1] The authors would like to thank Molly Beutz Land, Graham Dutfield, Michael Gollin and Uma Suthersanen for their invaluable comments on earlier drafts of this chapter. Special thanks also to Claire Comfort and Fred von Lohmann for their contribution of legal updates for sections of the chapter.

at 'public access' to cultural works under existing copyright frameworks. It investigates whether access is provided on terms that ultimately enhance the capabilities of individuals or communities for free, creative expression.

1. Some concepts and definitions

The term 'culture' holds different meanings for different persons and peoples. In UNESCO's seminal publication *Cultural Rights and Wrongs*, Stavenhagen (1998, pp. 4–5) suggests at least three different conceptions of culture: (1) culture as the 'process of artistic and scientific creation', (2) culture as the 'accumulated material heritage of humankind' and (3) culture as the 'sum total of the material and spiritual activities and products of a given social group which distinguishes it from similar groups'.[2] These nuances are helpful in understanding the intersection between intellectual property (IP) and cultural diversity. Discussed in Section 3, the concept of 'cultural diversity' celebrates the creative endeavours and cultural heritage of individuals and peoples of different backgrounds, recognizing both intrinsic and developmental value in maintaining such diversity. While it has been argued that copyright protection goes hand in hand with the promotion of cultural diversity (Desurmont 2006), existing assumptions in copyright law may reveal particular preconceptions towards culture, and end up protecting or promoting certain creative activities or sectors more than others. This theme is explored throughout this chapter.

While 'the arts' as a phrase is also open to different interpretations, it is commonly associated with creative expressions such as literature, painting, sculpture, music and dance. These overlap to some extent with the so-called cultural industries. According to the Convention on the Protection and Promotion of the Diversity of Cultural Expressions,[3] adopted by UNESCO in 2005, cultural industries produce and distribute cultural goods or services (Article 4(5)) which 'embody or convey cultural expressions, irrespective of the commercial value they may have' (Article 4(4)). The term 'cultural industries' is said to embrace publishing, music, cinema, audiovisual production, multimedia, visual arts, performing arts, architecture, crafts and design (although not all of these are, strictly speaking, industries).[4] While it is beyond the scope of this chapter to cover all these areas in detail, examples may be drawn from different sectors to illustrate particular copyright-related issues and potential areas for reform in the future. The case of 'IP and contemporary art',

[2] Connected to the third conception is the conception of culture as a 'system of values, and symbols as well as a set of practices that a specific cultural group reproduces over time and which provides individuals with the required signposts and meanings for behaviour and social relationships in everyday life' (see Stavenhagen 1998, pp. 4–5).

[3] UNESCO Convention on the Protection and Promotion of the Diversity of Cultural Expressions (Paris, 20 October 2005), 45 I.L.M. 269 (2006), UN Doc. CLT-2005/CONVENTION DIVERSITE-CULT REV (*entered into force* 18 March 2007), available at: http://unesdoc.unesco.org/images/0014/001429/142919e.pdf (accessed 3 February 2010).

[4] United Nations Educational, Scientific and Cultural Organization (UNESCO) Bureau of Public Information, 'Cultural Industries', available at: http://www.unesco.org/bpi/pdf/memobpi25_culturalindustries_en.pdf (accessed 12 February 2009).

including both visual and multimedia works since the 1950s, is dealt with at length in Appendix E.

Commentators have meanwhile cautioned against strict demarcations which somehow separate 'the arts' from the realm of human experience (Dewey 1934, p. 1). In this vein, the Indira Gandhi National Centre for the Arts (IGNCA) in India, for example, seeks to understand 'the arts' in their 'eco-cultural and socio-economic contexts'; it approaches the former as 'a wide spectrum, encompassing subjects from archaeology to dance and anthropology to the photographic art, enveloping them in a complementary and non-demarcated vision'.[5] This approach accords with the observation that 'the idea of culture has over the years evolved from a narrow elitist concept, which mainly referred to the fine arts and literature, to a broader concept presenting culture as a process, including components such as language, religion and education' (Donders 2007, p. 232). Such viewpoints emphasize that creative activities are not only the domain of those involved in the 'cultural industries', and that cultural development is equally about empowering individuals and communities towards their own creative endeavour and free expression (see Section 2). Consistent with the human development perspective highlighted in this book, this approach views the individual and collective actors within the public not merely as passive recipients of cultural goods produced by certain segments of society, but also as expressive and creative agents in their own right (see Sunder 2008).[6]

There is meanwhile no agreement in IP law around the world on appropriate definitions for 'art'. For example, within French jurisprudence from the 1930s, there seems no beginning and end to art – and hence anything can theoretically be art – whereas the German courts appear to frown on 'frivolous' art.[7] Artists and art theorists have themselves grappled with the changing meaning of 'art' and its function in society. Tracing Walther Benjamin's theory of art, Rochlitz (1996, p. 48) highlights a fundamental question of post-Kantian aesthetics: 'How do we define the criterion allowing us to state accurately that a work of art is successful, that it is "beautiful", which is not the same thing as simply saying we like it'? Through their works, many artists including Marcel Duchamp, John Latham and Ad Reinhardt have challenged prevalent notions of art and its role in the aesthetic experience. Adorno and Horkheimer (1944, pp. 120–167) emphasize that 'art' has to be further understood within the context of its increasing commodification by the cultural industries and the impact of new technologies of mass reproduction.[8]

[5] The Indira Gandhi National Centre for the Arts (IGNCA) was established in 1987 as an autonomous institution affiliated with the Department of Culture in India, and envisioned as a centre for research, academic pursuit and dissemination in the field of the arts. See the IGNCA website, available at: http://ignca.nic.in/ (accessed 12 February 2009).

[6] See also the evolving literature on the 'creative economy' (Howkins 2001; United Nations 2008).

[7] Comment received from Uma Suthersanen. One example of Germany's more circumscribed approach to what constitutes art is its treatment of photographs. Moving snapshots, the result of holding a camera and capturing what passes in front of it, does not give rise to authorial protection. A photograph must reflect personal expression or be a visual statement by a photographer. See Vogel 1998, p. 123.

[8] Adorno and Horkheimer (1944, pp. 120–167) note how the 'achievement of standardization and mass production' through the 'technology of the culture industry' removes the work of art from the realm of aesthetic experience.

It is not only new technology and artistic movements which challenge existing copyright concepts. Traditional cultural expressions (TCEs) pose many unanswered questions for copyright law and are clearly relevant in a discussion on cultural diversity and the arts. At the same time, the specific legal developments and issues relating to TCEs call for their treatment within a separate chapter (see Chapter 5) in this book, and repetition is avoided here. While distinctions are often made between the 'traditional' and the 'contemporary' realms, it has been suggested that the boundary between these may be more porous than it seems (Boateng 2005; Bowrey 2006; Oguamanam 2008). Constant innovations abound in these contexts, and some challenges faced by creators within the so-called traditional and contemporary realms may be similar. Analogies have been drawn between social networks in cyberspace communities and kinship relations within indigenous societies (Strathern 2005), and some writers have gleaned common issues and lessons for legal reform in relation to IP (Bowrey 2006; see Section 4.2).

2. Cultural rights and intellectual property rights

While this chapter focuses on the implications of copyright law for the arts, it is noted that other intellectual property rights (IPRs) do intersect with the cultural sector. Some examples include geographical indications, trademarks, collective marks, certification marks, trade secrets and design rights. Other areas of law including contracts and torts are also relevant to the topic.[9] Meanwhile, a number of international conventions circumscribe copyright, moral rights and related rights. These include the TRIPS Agreement of 1994, the Berne Convention for the protection of Literary and Artistic Works of 1886 (as amended 1979),[10] the Rome Convention for the Protection of Performers, Producers of Phonograms and Broadcasting Organizations of 1961 ('Rome Convention'),[11] and various other international conventions managed by WIPO and UNESCO. It is important to remember that provisions from such international agreements are absorbed and enforced within particular national systems and jurisdictions differently, and there is significant variation in the national protection of IPRs.

An area of law that is very dependent on jurisdiction concerns moral rights – a bundle of non-economic rights that authors and artists may receive in addition to the pecuniary benefits of copyright law. The two most prevalent rights in this bundle

[9] Tortious rights of relevance include the common law tort of 'passing off' (applicable in the UK, Australia, New Zealand, India, Ireland, Nigeria, Singapore, Malaysia and various other common law jurisdictions). There may also be overlap with other laws including media laws, obscenity laws, defamation laws and racial hatred laws, as well as specific legislation such as US trade dress law. Comment received from Uma Suthersanen.

[10] See Berne Convention for the Protection of Literary and Artistic Works (Berne, 9 September 1886), *as revised at* Paris, 24 July 1971, *and amended* 28 September 1979, 1161 U.N.T.S. 30 (The Act of Paris *entered into force* 15 December 1972), available at: http://www.wipo.int/treaties/en/ip/berne/trtdocs_wo001.html (accessed 3 February 2010).

[11] International Convention for the Protection of Performers, Producers of Phonograms and Broadcasting Organizations (Rome, 26 October 1961), 496 U.N.T.S. 43 (*entered into force* 18 May 1964) [hereinafter 'Rome Convention'], available at: http://www.wipo.int/export/sites/www/treaties/en/ip/rome/pdf/trtdocs_wo024.pdf (accessed 2 March 2010).

are the author's right of paternity, under which he has the right to receive attribution for his work; and the right of integrity in the work, against distortion and/or destruction. The Berne Convention requires that these two benefits be folded into national copyright legislation and allows leeway for jurisdictions to go beyond these minimums. France, a strong proponent of moral rights, for example, also adds the rights of disclosure (an author decides when and where to publish his work) and the right to withdraw (an artist can purchase unsold copies of her works and prevent additional printing of her work if she decides she no longer wants to be associated with the work).[12] Under the French system, moral rights are perpetual and in some sense inalienable (Cornish & Llewelyn 2003, p. 453), in contrast to copyright which typically has a fixed term and is subject to assignment in most (though not all) jurisdictions.

Cultural rights are protected by a number of international instruments and are an integral part of human rights (Donders 2007, p. 232). None of these instruments 'define cultural rights as such' (ibid., p. 234).[13] Prott (1998a, p. 165) observes that concepts of 'cultural rights' are still in evolution, and defy precise definition under international law.[14] While an exhaustive study of the potential range of cultural rights is beyond the scope of this chapter,[15] some aspects relevant to our discussion of copyright are highlighted here. To begin with, there is some acknowledgement in the relevant instruments that creators need to be recognized and compensated for their innovative efforts. Article 27(2) of the Universal Declaration of Human Rights of 1948 (UDHR)[16] states that: 'Everyone has the right to the protection of the moral and material interests resulting from any scientific, literary or artistic production of which he is the author'. This right is counterbalanced by the emphasis that 'everyone has the right freely to participate in the cultural life of the community, to enjoy the arts and to share in scientific advancement and its benefits' (Article 27(1)). While the UDHR is not a legally binding instrument, many of its provisions have attained the status of international customary law.

The rights expressed in Article 27 of the UDHR are explicitly recognized in Article 15 of the binding International Covenant on Economic, Social and Cultural Rights (ICESCR), adopted by UN General Assembly in 1966.[17] The ICESCR recognizes 'the right of everyone to take part in cultural life' (Article 15(1)(a)), 'to enjoy the benefits of scientific progress and its applications' (Article 15(1)(b)), and 'to benefit from the

[12] The Intellectual Property Code, Dernier texte modificateur Loi 2003–706 du 01/08/03 (JO 02/08/03), Articles L-121(1) – (4).

[13] Donders argues that 'different concepts of culture may lead to different approaches to cultural rights' (2007, pp. 234–235).

[14] Prott (1998a, p. 165) points out that certain international instruments seem to refer to 'culture' as the highest intellectual and artistic achievements of a group (which she calls 'Culture' with a capital C), while others approach culture in the anthropological sense, as shared skills, beliefs and traditions.

[15] For further discussion of the different types of rights potentially falling within 'cultural rights' under international instruments, see Prott 1998b, pp. 93–106; Donders 2007, pp. 232–236.

[16] Universal Declaration of Human Rights (Paris, 10 December 1948), G.A. Res. 217A (III), UN Doc. A/810 (1948), available at: http://www.un.org/en/documents/udhr/ (accessed 29 March 2010).

[17] International Covenant on Economic, Social and Cultural Rights (New York, 16 December 1966), 993 U.N.T.S. 3, 6 I.L.M. 360 (1967), G.A. Res. 2200A (XXI), UN Doc. A/6316 (1966) (*entered into force* 3 January 1976) [hereinafter 'ICESCR'], available at: http://www2.ohchr.org/english/law/pdf/cescr.pdf (accessed 3 February 2010).

protection of the moral and material interests resulting from any scientific, literary or artistic production of which he is the author' (Article 15(1)(c)). It is provided in Article 15(2) of the ICESCR that 'the steps to be taken by the States Parties to the present Covenant to achieve the full realization of this right shall include those necessary for the conservation, the development and the diffusion of science and culture'. The States also 'undertake to respect the freedom indispensable for scientific research and creative activity' (Article 15(3)).

It is significant that in its General Comment No. 17 relating to Article 15(1)(c) of the ICESCR, the Committee on Economic, Social and Cultural Rights (CESCR) distinguishes the right to moral and material interests of authors from IPRs, clarifying that IPRs are not to be equated 'with the human right recognized in article 15, paragraph 1 (c)' (CESCR 2005, para. 3). The Committee emphasizes that 'in contrast to human rights, intellectual property rights are generally of a temporary nature, and can be revoked, licensed or assigned to someone else' (ibid., para. 2). The Committee observes that: 'While under most intellectual property systems, intellectual property rights, often with the exception of moral rights, may be allocated, limited in time and scope, traded, amended and even forfeited, human rights are timeless expressions of fundamental entitlements of the human person' (ibid.). Of particular significance is the Committee's qualification that:

> Whereas the human right to benefit from the protection of the moral and material interests resulting from one's scientific, literary and artistic productions safeguards the personal link between authors and their creations and between peoples, communities, or other groups and their collective cultural heritage, as well as their basic material interests which are necessary to enable authors to enjoy an adequate standard of living, intellectual property regimes primarily protect business and corporate interests and investments. Moreover, the scope of protection of the moral and material interests of the author provided for by article 15, paragraph 1 (c), *does not necessarily coincide with what is referred to as intellectual property rights under national legislation or international agreements.*[18] (Ibid.; emphasis added)

It is furthermore emphasized in General Comment No. 17 that 'the right of authors to benefit from the protection of the moral and material interests resulting from their scientific, literary and artistic productions cannot be isolated from the other rights recognized in the [ICESCR]' (ibid., para. 35). According to the General Comment, States parties are 'obliged to strike an adequate balance between their obligations' under Article 15(1)(c) and the other provisions of the ICESCR, 'with a view to promoting and protecting the full range of rights guaranteed in the [instrument]' (ibid.). Of particular relevance is the qualification that 'in striking this balance, the private interests of authors should not be unduly favoured and the public interest in enjoying broad access to their productions should be given due consideration' (ibid.).

[18] See also paragraph 1. The Committee's General Comment No. 17 has been critiqued, for example, by Ovett (2006, p. 6) for 'repeatedly emphasizing IP protection as a way of implementing this part of Art 15'. She argues that such an emphasis is 'problematic, as it does not make explicit enough that there may be instances where IP protection is not appropriate and other *sui generis* systems should take over, or indicate when these instances might arise' (ibid.).

The recent General Comment No. 21 of the CESCR explores what is meant by the right of everyone to 'participate' or 'take part' in cultural life (see CESCR 2009). As the CESCR recognizes, 'the term "everyone" in the first line of article 15 may denote the individual or the collective; in other words, cultural rights may be exercised by a person (a) as an individual, (b) in association with others, or (c) within a community or group, as such' (ibid., para. 9). These clarifications have important implications, for example, for indigenous peoples' right to practise and revitalize their cultural traditions and customs. In its discussion of 'persons and communities requiring special attention' in implementing Article 15(1)(a),[19] the CESCR emphasizes that: 'States parties should take measures to guarantee that the exercise of the right to take part in cultural life takes due account of the values of cultural life, which may be strongly communal or which can only be expressed and enjoyed as a community by indigenous peoples' (ibid., para. 36). Legal developments in relation to indigenous peoples' TCEs are discussed in Chapter 5 of this book and are not repeated here. The idea that cultural rights can be enjoyed by individuals as well as 'the collective' also has implications for other communities in their cultural endeavours.

In General Comment No. 21, the CESCR suggests that '[t]here are, among others, three interrelated main components of the right to participate or take part in cultural life: (a) participation in, (b) access to, and (c) contribution to cultural life' (ibid., para. 15). In relation to 'participation', the CESCR suggests that: 'Everyone... has the right to seek and *develop cultural knowledge and expressions* and *to share them with others*, as well as *to act creatively and take part in creative activity*' (ibid., para. 15(a); emphasis added). Among other things, 'access' covers the right of everyone to 'follow a way of life associated with the use of cultural goods... and to benefit from the cultural heritage and the creation of other individuals and communities' (ibid., para. 15(b)). 'Contribution to cultural life' includes the right of everyone to be involved in creating the spiritual, material, intellectual and emotional expressions of the community (ibid., para. 15(c)). Can these ideas help us to broaden our understanding, for example, of public access to copyright-protected goods?

While the CESCR does not explicitly mention IPRs in General Comment No. 21, Beutz Land has suggested that the right to take part in cultural life ought to extend not only to the right of access to cultural goods but also to the right to share and transform cultural works.[20] This echoes Donder's observation (2007, p. 233) that: 'Culture is no longer seen as a consumer product, but as an expression of the identity of an individual or a community. Cultural rights should accordingly be considered as more than merely rights to enjoy a cultural product'. Revisited again in Section 5, these ideas can perhaps help us to rethink what public access to cultural works ought to entail. In particular, they may help us to calibrate exceptions and limitations to copyright in terms of enhancing the capability of individuals and communities to use or transform a copyright-protected work as an expressive tool.

[19] Along with indigenous peoples, other categories specially mentioned as warranting special protection include women, children (i.e. 'the bearers and transmitters of cultural values from generation to generation'), older persons, persons with disabilities, minorities, migrants and persons living in poverty (CESCR 2009, Section E, paras. 25–39).

[20] Beutz Land, M. 2008, presentation at the third 'Access to Knowledge' Conference (A2K3), Geneva, 8–10 September 2008. See further Beutz Land 2008 and 2009.

Meanwhile, 'cultural development' is now recognized as an important component of development alongside the socio-economic development of peoples. This is made explicit, for example, in Article 22 (1) of the African Charter on Human and Peoples' Rights (1981) which asserts that: 'All peoples shall have the right to their economic, social and cultural development with due regard to their freedom and identity and in the equal enjoyment of the common heritage of mankind'.[21] In a presentation paper called 'Creative Communities: a Strategy for the 21st Century' by the UNESCO Regional Bureau for Education in Asia and the Pacific, Shaeffer notes that 'culture is now widely perceived to be an inalienable part of sustainable development' and that 'this changed perception constitutes a veritable paradigm shift in which cultural diversity and cultural industries have become linked as key elements in new development strategies'.[22]

3. Emerging framework of protection for cultural diversity

As highlighted in the UNDP Human Development Report 2004 on 'Cultural Liberty in Today's Diverse World', the pressures of globalization and standardization have exacerbated historical threats and issues relating to the preservation of diverse cultural identities and endeavours (UNDP 2004, p. 10).[23] Concerns over the promotion of 'cultural diversity' not only have surfaced at local and national levels but also are increasingly reflected through multilateral frameworks.

There has been significant norm setting at international organizations, notably UNESCO, towards the protection and promotion of cultural diversity in recent years (see UNESCO 2004). The Universal Declaration on Cultural Diversity adopted by UNESCO in November 2001 states in its Article 7 that: 'Creation draws on the roots of cultural tradition, but flourishes in contact with other cultures. For this reason, heritage in all its forms must be preserved, enhanced and handed on to future generations as a record of human experience and aspirations, so as to foster creativity in all its diversity . . . '.[24] Article 6 of the Declaration elaborates that: 'Freedom of

[21] African Charter on Human and Peoples' Rights (Nairobi, 27 June 1981), 1520 U.N.T.S. 217, 21 I.L.M. 58 (1981) (*entered into force* 21 October 1986), available at: http://www1.umn.edu/humanrts/instree/z1afchar.htm (accessed 3 February 2010). See generally Prott 1998a and 1998b.

[22] See Shaeffer, S. 2005, 'Creative Communities: A Strategy for the 21st Century, UNESCO and the promotion of cultural industries in the context of the Millennium Development Goals', presentation at '*Asia-Pacific Creative Communities – A Strategy for the 21st Century*', Senior Expert Symposium, 22–26 February 2005, Jodhpur, India, pp. 1–2, available at: http://www.unescobkk.org/fileadmin/user_upload/culture/Cultural_Industries/presentations/Session_One_-_Sheldon_Shaeffer.pdf (accessed 15 February 2009). She notes that the cultural industries have gained growing importance as an economic factor over the last twenty years, a trend that is closely linked to the rise of the information society and the growing consumption of cultural goods and services.

[23] In discussing socially divisive debates on cultural identity and diversity, the report adds: 'Globalization adds yet another dimension, as ethnic groups, indigenous people and nation-states challenge international agreements on trade and investment on the ground that they diminish cultural diversity' (ibid., p. 27). It stresses that: 'Globalization can threaten national and local identities. The solution is not to retreat to conservatism and isolationist nationalism – it is to design multicultural policies to promote diversity and pluralism' (ibid., p. 10).

[24] United Nations Educational, Scientific and Cultural Organization (UNESCO), Universal Declaration on Cultural Diversity (2 November 2001), 41 I.L.M. 57 (2002), available at: http://unesdoc.unesco.org/images/0012/001271/127160m.pdf (accessed 24 March 2010).

expression, media pluralism, multilingualism, equal access to art and to scientific and technological knowledge, including in digital form, and the possibility for all cultures to have access to the means of expression and dissemination are the guarantees of cultural diversity'.

Notions of cultural diversity also underpin recent international instruments such as the UNESCO Convention on the Protection and Promotion of the Diversity of Cultural Expressions of 2005 and the UNESCO Convention for the Safeguarding of the Intangible Cultural Heritage of 2003.[25] The Preamble of the 2005 Convention affirms that 'cultural diversity is a defining characteristic of humanity'. It observes that 'cultural diversity creates a rich and varied world, which increases the range of choices and nurtures human capacities and values, and therefore is a mainspring for sustainable development for communities, peoples and nations'. It further notes that 'while the processes of globalization, which have been facilitated by the rapid development of information and communication technologies, afford unprecedented conditions for enhanced interaction between cultures, they also represent a challenge for cultural diversity, namely in view of risks of imbalances between rich and poor countries'. An example of such risks is provided in the 2004 UNDP Human Development Report, where it is suggested that 'Hollywood's powerful film industry, with access to enormous resources, can squeeze the Mexican film industry and other small competitors out of existence' (UNDP 2004, p. 90). Discussing the impact of globalization on cultural choice, the report emphasizes that 'asymmetries in flows of ideas and goods need to be addressed, so that some cultures do not dominate others because of their economic power' (ibid.).

The Preamble of the UNESCO Convention for the Safeguarding of the Intangible Cultural Heritage recognizes the 'importance of the intangible cultural heritage as a mainspring of cultural diversity and a guarantee of sustainable development . . . '. For the present discussion, it is notable that Article 3 in the Convention qualifies that nothing in the instrument would affect state obligations under existing IP-related instruments.[26] One presumption under the Convention would thus seem to be that cultural diversity and IP rights go hand in hand.[27] This idea seems to be reinforced

[25] UNESCO Convention for the Safeguarding of the Intangible Cultural Heritage (Paris, 17 October 2003) 2368 U.N.T.S. 3, U.N. Doc. MISC/2003/CLT/CH/14 (*entered into force* 20 April 2006), available at: http:/unesdoc.unesco.org/images/0013/001325/132540e.pdf (accessed 3 February 2010). The Convention states that the intangible cultural heritage is manifested 'in the following domains [among others]: oral traditions and expressions, including language as a vehicle of the intangible cultural heritage; performing arts; social practices, rituals and festive events; knowledge and practices concerning nature and the universe; and traditional craftsmanship' (Article 2(2)).

[26] Article 3 of the UNESCO Convention for the Safeguarding of the Intangible Cultural Heritage, on the 'Relationship to other international instruments', specifies that: 'Nothing in this Convention may be interpreted as: . . . (b) affecting the rights and obligations of States Parties deriving from any international instrument relating to intellectual property rights or to the use of biological and ecological resources to which they are parties'. See also Article 20(2) of the UNESCO Convention on the Protection and Promotion of the Diversity of Cultural Expressions which provides that: 'Nothing in this Convention shall be interpreted as modifying rights and obligations of the Parties under any other treaties to which they are parties'.

[27] Despite this qualification, there are aspects of UNESCO's work under this convention, such as the creation of inventories of intangible cultural heritage, which potentially raise some IP-related concerns, for example, in relation to documentation of TK and TCEs (see Chapter 4). For information on WIPO's work in relation to the development of 'IP Guidelines for Documenting, Recording and Digitizing Intangible

by the Preamble of the UNESCO Convention on the Protection and Promotion of the Diversity of Cultural Expressions (2005), which emphasizes 'the importance of intellectual property rights in sustaining those involved in cultural creativity' (para. 17). Highlighting the latter emphasis by the framers of the convention, Desurmont (2006) asserts that 'there is no justification for claiming that respect for authors' rights is a barrier to the pursuit of cultural diversity when it is obvious that there can be no cultural development without protecting creators'.[28]

Is there perhaps a need for better understanding of the relationship between cultural diversity and the protection of IPRs? At the regional level, the European Commission appears to be grappling with this relationship in its attempts to integrate 'cultural diversity' into its copyright policies. Presenting at a conference on the 'Future of Intellectual Property', a Commission representative suggested that cultural diversity implies a far wider spectrum of creative activity than currently incentivized by the copyright system.[29] He stressed the role of 'social policy' in supporting such activities as independent film-making which may earn little by way of royalties from copyright if commercially unsuccessful.[30]

The relationship between the protection of IPRs and the promotion of cultural diversity thus needs to be understood in relation to the types of creators and creations currently incentivized by the IP systems. In evaluating the effects of IPRs on cultural diversity, it is necessary to consider what other economic support (e.g. state subsidies and private grants) or non-pecuniary factors are at work to spur creative efforts. One might also consider whether IP systems accommodate different cultural attitudes to creativity and 'property'. The UNDP Human Development Report 2004 emphasizes that 'recognizing diversity means that different notions of property rights and the cultural significance of knowledge and art forms be accommodated within global regimes' (UNDP 2004, p. 11). The report adds that international action is needed to ensure this, and that the rules relating to IP will need to be revised if current standards cannot accommodate certain forms of knowledge and art (ibid.). In this case, the report is referring to the example of commonly known traditional knowledge (TK) and TCEs, and their attributes such as group ownership (ibid.). These elements are discussed in Chapters 4 and 5, which deal with TK and TCEs, respectively.

Are IP frameworks equally relevant in contemporary and traditional contexts, within both formal and informal sectors? The following sections consider the implications of copyright for cultural diversity, comparing the incentive theory of

Cultural Heritage', see the WIPO website, 'Creative Heritage Project: Strategic Management of IP Rights and Interests', available at: http://www.wipo.int/tk/en/folklore/culturalheritage/index.html (accessed 24 March 2010).

28 See Desurmont 2006, pp. 2–3, who writes of a 'fundamental neutrality' of authors' rights in relation to cultural diversity.

29 Presentation by Tilman Luder, Head of Unit, Copyright Unit, DG Internal Market, European Commission (Brussels), at the 15th Annual International Intellectual Property Law and Policy Conference, Fordham Law, April 2007.

30 The need to promote a spectrum of independent film-making activities has been emphasized in other regions. This is seen, for example, in the mission of the Asian Film Archive, which is 'to save, explore and share the art of Asian Cinema' in supporting not only renowned gems of the cinematic world but also local film communities in Asia. See Asian Film Archive, 'About Us', available at: www.asianfilmarchive.org/About (accessed 29 March 2010).

copyright with some emerging trends in the complex international environment in which IP laws must operate. Section 4 first contrasts notions of authorship under copyright with structures and realities of IP ownership in the cultural industries (see also Appendix E, which looks in detail at some challenges faced by contemporary artists in relation to copyright). This is followed by Section 5 which discusses access by the public to cultural goods, creative processes and free expression under the copyright regimes. As will be seen, cultural diversity embraces a freedom of culture, which is in turn closely linked in legal and policy terms to issues of freedom of expression.

4. Revisiting copyright as an economic incentive to create

Justifications for copyright, whether from 'natural rights' or utilitarian perspectives, have been explored in earlier chapters of this book. This section evaluates the often-emphasized idea of copyright as an economic incentive to creators in relation to current trends of copyright protection and ownership. This idea is central, for example, to utilitarian arguments for copyright in Anglo-American copyright systems (see Chapter 1). Examining the incentive function of copyright in terms of structures of copyright ownership, this section seeks to understand which are some of the main constituencies benefitting from copyright protection. It then explores whether some forms of creative activity are less covered by copyright protection than others (or not at all), so that the incentive function of copyright towards spurring creations might be seen as less operative, or even redundant, in those cases. While it is beyond the scope of one chapter to survey all creative sectors and world regions, some discernible patterns are highlighted here for further study.

4.1. Corporations and creators as copyright holders

Cornish and Llewelyn (2003, p. 371) observe that 'while industrial property tends to establish bi-polar linkages – between right-owner and user – copyright has, on the right-owner side, both creators and entrepreneurs'. Indeed, it is important to distinguish conceptually between creators and the industry that may represent the creators (e.g. the publisher and recording industries or the collecting societies). Some argue from a historical perspective that copyright regimes benefitted not only creators but also intermediaries and institutions from the start (Woodmansee 1984; Rose 1993).

Copyright assignment being commonplace today in the music industries, publishing and the arts, a question can be legitimately raised as to the extent to which economic benefits from copyright really go to creators in the cultural industries. A brand of critique of copyright protection has centred on the increasing control of the intermediaries (e.g. publishing houses, recording companies and film corporations) over copyright through the creators' assignment of these rights in their contractual relations with these entities. While in theory it is the creators who are protected by copyright, in reality many creators habitually assign away their copyright (or significant elements of that right) in contractual agreements with third parties.[31] Statutory provisions may also render an employer the initial owner of any copyright work produced by an employee in the course of the employment and in the absence of contrary agreement (Cornish & Llewelyn 2003, p. 471).[32] For example, while the contributors to a film production are numerous – as the endless credits that typically follow a film illustrate – through a web of contractual relationships copyright ownership in many cases (though not all) resides with the producer, often a film company.[33]

Gollin (2008, p. 39) suggests that: 'By establishing assignable property rights, subject to recordation, intellectual property laws allow people to buy, sell, lease, or trade intangible property, or use it as collateral for loans, just as they would do with real or tangible property'. Among other questions, this calls attention to the valuation of IP. It is not uncommon for writers, for example, to assign away their copyright in particular works for the opportunity to publish, along with a 'lump sum' payment which may bear little correspondence to the extent of profits made eventually by a publisher on a successful work.[34] Few creators have the ability to 'valuate' their copyright accurately, making projections well into the future. Should creators be locked into contractual arrangements without possibilities of revisiting and 're-evaluating' the initial 'bargain', for example, taking into account the actual profits made by third parties in commercializing the work over time?[35] Standard contracts used in a particular sector or company may need to be fine-tuned to reflect such long-term considerations. Some contracts may also prevent creators from dealing with their own works in certain ways.[36]

Contract is thus a fundamental issue shaping creators' rights and livelihoods. There are significant differences between jurisdictions in how freedom of contract interacts with copyright law. Guibault (2002, p. 230) notes, for example, that 'the American legal system does not generally regulate contractual relations dealing

[31] In relation to moral rights, some jurisdictions ascribe inalienable moral rights to authors (e.g. France); others allow authors to assign, transfer or forfeit all or part of their moral rights.

[32] See UK Copyright, Designs and Patent Act 1988, c.1, s.11(2).

[33] See Council Directive 93/98/EEC of 29 October 1993 harmonizing the term of protection of copyright and certain related rights, OJ No. L 290 (1993), *replaced by* Council Directive 2006/116/EC of 12 December 2006 on the term of protection of copyright and certain related rights (codified version), OJ No. L 372 (2006) [hereinafter 'Copyright Duration Directive']. While the EC Copyright Duration Directive (Articles 2(1) and 10(4)) now requires the principal director of a film (made from 1994 onwards) to be considered one of its authors, Cornish and Llewelyn argue (2003, p. 400) that the director's copyright 'may be of greater ideological than practical consequence'. The work might be one produced in the course of employment (making it the property of the employer), and 'even directors who are commissioned rather than employed must normally expect to assign copyright to their producers' (ibid.). If directors have an 'extraordinary reputation', they may contract to do this on royalty-sharing or other special terms (ibid.).

[34] Especially at an early point in their career, writers may have few other options for having their work published in terms of the traditional channels (pers. comm. Melissa Sones, writer, 10 December 2008).

[35] The laws in different jurisdictions vary on this issue. Cornish and Llewelyn (2003, p. 474) highlight that: 'Under s.90(2)(b) of the U.K. Copyright, Designs and Patent Act 1988, for example, it is possible to assign for a limited term within the copyright period, but things are changing under EC rules'.

[36] Towse (2007, p. 761) notes within the context of performers' rights in the UK that: 'Once economic rights have been assigned, the performer has little residual control over their exploitation (unless moral rights are infringed). When the record label decides to delete their works from the catalogue, performers can rarely do anything to stop them: the copyright may last 50 years but the shelf life of the recording is more likely to be 5 years or less'.

with the exploitation or the utilisation of copyrighted works'. In contrast, she emphasizes that:

> The regulation of contractual practices in the field of copyright is not unusual in continental Europe. In several countries, publisher's agreements and contracts signed for the production of sound and audiovisual works are subject to specific rules of form and content. Where specific legislation has not been enacted, courts are often called in to alleviate the imbalance that could result from the strict application of the principle of freedom of contract. (Ibid., pp. 214–215)

Likewise, von Lewinski (2008, pp. 59–61) highlights some notable differences between civil law 'authors' rights' systems and common law systems (such as in the UK and the US) where freedom of contract is said to prevail. Discussing statutory provisions in some authors' rights systems (e.g. Germany), she notes the existence of rules 'restricting the freedom of contract in order to strengthen the weaker party to a contract' (ibid., p. 59).[37] Indeed, Dietz (2006) points out that the German authors' rights system does not provide for 'assignment' of rights in the strict sense of the word. According to him: 'German doctrine does not incorporate any notion equivalent to the English "assignments" or the French *cession* of copyright; rather it formulates contractual transfers of copyright interests as "grants of rights of use"' (ibid., sec. 4(2), p. GER-55; original emphasis).

While common law systems are usually associated with freedom of contract, it is notable that the US has a statutory provision which gives the author an opportunity to reassess a transfer in copyright after a certain number of years. Section 203 of the Copyright Act of 1976 provides that, in the case of grants of copyright interests made on or after 1 January 1978, authors and their statutory successors enjoy the right to terminate the grant after thirty-five years from the grant's execution.[38] The right of termination can be exercised at any time during a five-year period from the latter date and is non-waivable.[39] The legislators determined that 'a provision of this sort is needed because of the unequal bargaining position of authors resulting in part from the impossibility of determining a work's value until it has been exploited'.[40] Meanwhile, it is significant that the 1976 Act exempts works for hire from the operation of the termination of transfer provisions. Goldstein (2002, p. 262) comments that 'in addition to circumventing the termination of transfer provisions, the work for hire rubric can obliterate the rights of contributors to collective works because it vests rights initially in the author's employer'.

Assignment of copyright has to be distinguished from licensing. It has been said that an assignment is in essence a transfer of ownership (however partial), while a licence is in essence permission to do what would otherwise be an infringement

[37] Von Lewinski notes, for example, that 'provisions may voluntarily limit the duration of assignment, so that the author has a second chance to seek better return for an assignment' (ibid., p. 59).

[38] 17 U.S.C. § 203(a).

[39] Ibid.

[40] H.R. Rep. No. 94-1476, at 124 (1976), reprinted in 1976 U.S.C.C.A.N. 5659, 5740. At the same time, Goldstein (2004, p. 262) ventures that 'these regulations may require authors to forgo a present economic benefit – the added value a publisher would be willing to pay to be free of the threat of termination – that may be worth much more to authors than some future, and possibly dubious, benefit arising from contract renegotiation 35 years hence'. See also Cornish 2002.

(Cornish & Llewelyn 2003, p. 475).[41] Under licensing, the owner of the copyright retains ownership of the IP but authorizes a third party to 'carry out certain acts covered by his economic rights, generally for a specific period of time and for a specific purpose' (ibid.). An example is where the author of a novel grants a licence to a publisher to make and distribute copies of the novel, or grants a licence to a film producer to make a film based on the novel.[42] In some cases, there might be a grant of rights by exclusive licence to the publisher (ibid.).

Meanwhile, large corporations and independent artists often have unequal bargaining positions and access to legal support in negotiating contracts relating to copyright (see also Section 5 in relation to rethinking copyright exceptions). Observing that the increasing corporate concentration in the cultural industries has significant impact on the bargaining positions of individual creators, Towse (2007, pp. 760–761) suggests that:

> [T]he economic organization of the cultural sector plays a more important role than does copyright law in the contracts between artists and firms in the cultural industries (Caves, 2000). The more powerful the firm is in the industry, the greater is its bargaining power and the relatively weaker the performer is when it comes to striking an individual bargain. Except in the rare case of the superstar, the business side has the upperhand.

Towse suggests that the market structure of the cultural industries is thus an important aspect of the economics of copyright (ibid.). The earnings and incentives to artists from copyright are said to be weakened by the prevalence of oligopolies in the cultural industries (Bettig, 1996; Towse 2007, pp. 760–761). Corporate concentration is a key feature, especially in the music and film industries. This market structure also has an effect on the diversity of works available to the public. In their seminal work *Big Sounds from Small Peoples: The Music Industry in Small Countries,* Wallis and Malm (1984) discuss how, using the strategy of vertical and horizontal integration, five major companies achieved unprecedented oligarchy in the world market for music records and cassettes in the 1970s and 1980s. They note that as industry concentration increases, the diversity of phonograms decreases with more emphasis being placed on a few best sellers in the popular music market. Of relevance to our discussion of cultural diversity, the authors trace the responses of the local music scene in a series of small countries on four continents (including Africa, Asia, Latin America/ Caribbean and Europe) to this global challenge in maintaining their individual identity and flavour.

Three decades later in a world now of digital-dominated media, six firms are said to account for close to 80% of the world market in the cultural industries, with a vast number of small independent firms from all over the world sharing the remainder of the market (Caribbean Community [CARICOM] 2006, p. 29). These smaller

[41] In some countries assignment of copyright is not legally possible and only licensing is allowed (WIPO 2005, p. 15).

[42] Ibid. Cornish and Llewelyn (2003, p. 474) note that the most lucrative works are often exploited in a number of ways: in the case of the popular novel, there are the volume rights, the serial rights (in newspapers and magazines), the translation rights, the film rights, the dramatization rights and the electronic rights.

firms generally face the problem of limited international market access and media exposure (ibid.). The study notes that the 'independents' are often taken over by large corporations or are required to establish production and distribution contracts with the large firms after they have a significant 'hit' (ibid.).

4.2. Uneven protection amongst regions and sectors

Creators in different world regions, sectors, and contexts experience significant differences in copyright protection and enforcement. In its watershed study *Integrating IPRs and Development Policy*, the Commission on Intellectual Property Rights (CIPR) notes unequal access to the benefits of copyright protection between creators in the first world and in developing countries (CIPR 2002, pp. 95–110). In a summary of the World Bank sponsored 'Africa Music Project', Penna, Thormann and Finger (2004, pp. 95–112) discuss, for example, the lack of infrastructure in the African region to support artists and their livelihoods, including a lack of effective collecting societies, organized interest groups, effective copyright enforcement and IP practitioners.[43] In a section on 'The Musician's Dream', the authors describe the aspirations of some African musicians to gain control over production processes in the future, and secure their IP. Some concerns discussed include the 'education of musicians as to their existing rights and methods of securing these rights', as well as 'reforms in regulations, institutions, and procedures for policing rights' (ibid., p. 99).

Creators from different sectors and within sectors also experience notable differences in copyright protection. Concerns of authors, composers, film-makers, performers and visual artists are obviously distinct, and interact in different ways with existing IP regimes. Although it is beyond the scope of this chapter to discuss all of these areas in detail, a brief mention might be made of performers' rights. While a composer may have copyright in an original tune, for example, the performers' rendition of the tune (which necessarily reproduces the work) does not give rise to a copyright in the performance even though it may involve significant creativity (see Towse 2007; Cornish & Llewelyn 2003, p. 521).[44] Towse (2007, p. 745) notes that performers only 'gradually acquired statutory protection of their economic and moral rights' in certain jurisdictions over the last century. Tracing the evolution of performers' rights, Weatherall (2006, pp. 174–175) observes that:

> The first stage in the road to performers' rights saw the enactment of laws against the obvious wrong of 'bootlegging' – that is, the practice of making and/or distributing, for commercial purposes, unauthorised sound or film recordings of live performances, either at the actual concert or 'off air' (for example, recorded from

[43] Penna et al. (2004, p. 101) note that: 'Rampant piracy combined with weak collection societies makes the collection of royalties problematic; hence, African artists and composers often sell their songs to a publisher or recording company for an upfront payment'.

[44] Cornish and Llewelyn (2003, p. 521) suggest that: 'Performers engage in activities which are more immediately artistic and creative than those of entrepreneurs who enjoy copyrights in sound recordings, films, broadcasts and cable-casts. The greatest and the most charismatic interpreters of drama, film scripts and music are deeply treasured... Yet, there has been considerable reluctance to give performers an equivalent property right, which has been largely sustained by objections from these very entrepreneurs.'

> live broadcasts). The UK outlawed this activity in 1925; a multilateral treaty followed in the form of the Rome Convention in 1961 . . . The *second* stage of the performers' journey is the recognition of copyright-like rights to control certain uses of *authorised* recordings of performances. Such rights have been an even longer time coming, at an international and a national level. (Original emphasis, some footnotes omitted)

The rights currently enjoyed by performers are 'not copyright in the legal sense' but so-called 'neighbouring rights' or 'related rights' (ibid.; see Chapter 1, Box 1.1).[45] These rights have been said to be 'analogous to copyright', although they are given for 'somewhat shorter periods' (Cornish & Llewelyn 2003, p. 8). The law is in much flux in this complex area, and Arnold (2008, p. 308) suggests a 'wider trend towards treating holders of related rights, and in particular performers, more equally with owners of authors' rights'. Nevertheless, protection of performers' rights still varies significantly with jurisdiction. Whether a country is a signatory to one or several of the international conventions governing this realm will affect the rights of performers in that country. For example, under the Rome Convention, performers (including 'actors, singers, musicians, dancers, and other persons who . . . perform literary or artistic works') are protected against certain types of acts they have not consented to, including the fixation of their live performance without consent and the broadcasting and communication to the public of their live performance.[46] Under the TRIPS Agreement, it is provided that performers 'shall have the possibility of preventing . . . the fixation of their unfixed performance [on a phonogram] and the reproduction of such fixation' without their authorization (Article 14(1)). Performers shall also have the possibility of preventing 'the broadcasting by wireless means and the communication to the public of their live performance' (Article 14(1)). These rights have been extended by the WIPO Performances and Phonograms Treaty (WPPT) which deals with, among other things, rights relating to storage and transmission of works/performances of phonograms in the digital environment (for detailed discussion see Towse 2007; Munoz Tellez & Waitara 2007, p. 22).[47]

45 As generally understood, 'there are three kinds of related rights: the rights of performing artists in their performances, the rights of producers of phonograms in their phonograms and the rights of broadcasting organizations in their radio and television programs' (WIPO 2004, p. 46, sec. 2.2.03). It is said that 'protection of those who assist intellectual creators to communicate their message and to disseminate their works to the public at large, is attempted by means of related rights' (ibid.).

46 Rome Convention, Article 3(a) (definition of 'performers'), Article 7 (setting 'minimum protection for performers'). Other prohibited acts include the reproduction of a fixation of a performance if the original fixation was made without the performers' consent or if the reproduction is made for purposes different from those for which they gave their consent (Article 7(1)). See also the WIPO website, 'Summary of the Rome Convention for the Protection of Performers, Producers of Phonograms and Broadcasting Organisations', available at: http://www.wipo.int/treaties/en/ip/rome/summary_rome.html (accessed 12 February 2009). Article 14 of the Rome Convention set a minimum term for the protection of performers' rights of twenty years from the end of the year in which the performance was made; the TRIPS Agreement (Art. 14.5) has extended this to fifty years.

47 WIPO Performances and Phonograms Treaty (Geneva, 20 December 1996), 36 I.L.M. 76 (*entered into force* 20 May 2002), available at: http://www.wipo.int/export/sites/www/treaties/en/ip/wppt/pdf/trtdocs_wo034.pdf (accessed 3 February 2010). For a summary and comparison of the different international conventions as well as examples of protection in particular jurisdictions, see Arnold 2008, pp. 308–352. Arnold sets out in a table which countries have acceded to each of the three instruments

Weatherall (2007, pp. 177) notes that: 'Due to the failure of the EU and US to agree on provisions relating to transfer of rights (and choice of law), the expansion of rights in the WPPT only applies to performances as they are fixed in sound recordings (phonograms). So far the international community has been unable to agree on a treaty relating to performances captured in audio-visual form'. This means different levels of protection for different kinds of performers depending on the medium of fixation. Noting that Australia has stuck strictly to the WPPT in not granting rights related to performances in audio-visual form in its recent reforms to its Copyright Act, Weatherall suggests that there are no obvious grounds for establishing separate regulatory regimes for audio and audio-visual material (ibid., citing Sherman & Bently 1995, p. 7).

Further studies would be useful in examining the pecuniary factors (e.g. public subsidies, returns from performances, royalties if applicable) as well as non-pecuniary ones in spurring and shaping creative expression in the performing arts (see further Morgan 2002; Towse 2007). These questions have come to the fore, for example, in recent public debates in Europe over the European Commission's proposals to amend the EU Copyright Directive to provide a longer term of protection for music performers and phonogram producers.[48] In discussing alternative models for incentivizing and compensating performers, it may also be interesting to consider the 'network' effects which copying by third parties may have in augmenting the popularity of particular performers (see Takeyama 1994; Watt 2004, pp. 164–165; cf. Arnold 2008, pp. 9–10).[49] Watt (2008, pp. 164–165) gives the oft-cited example of 'singer's fan clubs' where 'the more copying that occurs, the more popular and "trendy" the singer becomes, and so the greater is the willingness to pay for concert tickets and original pre-recorded formats'. Case studies on the Brazilian technobrega music movement and the Nigerian film industry, for example, may be relevant to this line of enquiry.[50]

Some areas of creative activities fall largely outside the scope of copyright protection. As seen in Chapter 5, there is a lacuna in copyright protection for the cultural expressions of communities guided by customary practices. Many existing TCEs often do not meet the current requirements of 'originality' and/or 'fixation' in many

discussed here and the dates of their accession. It would appear from that table that some countries, such as Bhutan, Laos, Libya and Samoa, among others, are not yet signatories to any of the relevant conventions pertaining to performers' rights (ibid., pp. 314–327).

48 In 2009, the European Parliament adopted a proposal by the European Commission extending the term of protection of the rights of music performers and phonogram producers from fifty years to seventy years from first publication (this does not apply to audiovisual works). See European Parliament legislative resolution on the proposal for a directive of the European Parliament and the Council amending Directive 2006/116/EC of the European Parliament and the Council on the term of protection of copyright and related rights, 23 April 2009, P6_TA9(2009)0282, available at: http://www.europarl.europa.eu/sides/getDoc.do?pubRef=-//EP//NONSGML+TA+P6-TA-2009-0282+0+DOC+PDF+V0//EN (accessed 3 March 2010). A European Commission proposal in 2008 to extend the term of protection from fifty years to ninety-five years from first publication was hotly debated (see Hilty et al. 2008) and did not pass the European Parliament.

49 See also the discussion on the 'piracy paradox' by Raustiala and Sprigman 2007. See Bullard 2005.

50 On Brazilian technobrega, see Mizukami & Lemos 2008; see also the 'Nollywood' and other case studies on 'network effects' at the PIIPA website, 'IP and Human Development', available at http://www.piipa.org/IP_and_Human_Development/.

jurisdictions. While new works based on TCEs might be deemed 'original' and subject to copyright, establishing communal claims to copyright ownership over such TCEs remains a challenge in many jurisdictions. In the *Bulun Bulun* case[51] (see facts and discussion in Chapter 5), the Federal Court of Australia found the work in question by an Aboriginal artist to be 'original' and subject to the artist's copyright. While the work was based on traditional motifs and concepts of the Aboriginal community to which the artist belonged, the court found it inconsistent with the Australian copyright statute, as well as common law, to accept 'communal ownership' by the Aboriginal community of the copyright over the innovative work.

There seems room for further exploration of 'joint-authorship' concepts in such instances. While 'joint-authors' may share the copyright in a work, the court in the *Bulun Bulun* case found there was no joint-authorship in the case. As cogently summarized by Bowrey (2006, pp. 78–79):

> The precedent for joint authorship says that to come under this definition the coauthors' contributions need be inseparable from each other. In *Bulun Bulun*, the court said that this means the contributions that count as authorship must relate to the physical condition of the material form of the work. Unless the community were actually all involved in the painting of the work, they have no copyright in it. Indigenous authority, community-based authority to paint particular imagery and circulate it more broadly, is not thus recognized as part of the necessary conditions of production of those works for copyright purposes. Oversight and authority over the production is treated as too ephemeral a contribution to be recognized in copyright...

While concern for legal integrity may limit a court's ability to find communal 'joint-authorship' in the case of TCEs, Bowrey notes that Australian courts have demonstrated 'no comparable incapacity in stretching the very same legal ideas to accommodate the collective authority and production of corporations'. Referring to Australian case law, she adds that:

> Managerial supervision of production from afar, and contributions as ephemeral as identifying a potential market for a new product has been valued as a substantial original contribution that gives rise to the subsistence of copyright. The 'directional' visions for an interactive computer game that was communicated to the game programmers, but only brought into visual reality by the eventual player was sufficient to produce authorship of a cinematographic film. So *why is it that all the concepts and categories that touch on the indigenous involve impossible demands, and all those that relate to reinvigorating the rights to accommodate mainstream culture and economy show up the law as flexible, malleable and constantly able to be legally renewed?* (Ibid., p. 79; original emphasis; footnotes excluded)

New media and technology tend to bring their own set of challenges to copyright law. For example, it was only after several years of legal uncertainty that the US Supreme Court decided in 1884 that a photograph reached the bar of originality

51 *Bulun Bulun and Milpurrurru v. R & T Textiles Pty. Ltd.* [1998] AILR 39 ('*Bulun Bulun*' case), (1998) 3 AILR 547, (1998) IPR 513, available at: http://www.austlii.edu.au/au/journals/AILR/1998/39.html (accessed 2 March 2010).

under US copyright law so as to comprise copyrightable subject matter.[52] Stokes (2003, p. 33) suggests that: 'Photography is a problem area for copyright law as in a sense every photograph is a copy of something, and unlike drawing or painting the actual recording of the image can require no skill or labour beyond the mere mechanical operation of a "point and shoot" camera'. There remain ambiguities as to the extent photographs are covered by copyright, and the level of protection varies significantly among different jurisdictions. Cornish (1999, p. 390) notes, for example, that 'the British have never scrupled to place every variety of photography within copyright however merely technical the procedure of pointing the camera at a subject and pressing the shutter may be in a particular instance'. In contrast, he observes that *droit d'auteur* (authors' rights) systems 'tend only to give copyright to "photographic works", that is, the results of careful and distinctive arrangement (scene setting, lighting, angle, etc.), involving an element of aesthetic judgment which is personal to the photographer (and/or to some "director", rather than the mere cameraman)' (ibid).

Other examples of confusion regarding the law's place in the domain of artistic subject matter abound. Internationally, the extent to which moral rights are applicable to a wide range of arts remains highly controversial (Adeney 2006; Pitrout 2006. The legitimacy of appropriation art – art which borrows from or 'quotes' other art without attribution – is the source of much contention,[53] with artists using appropriation in their work pointing out that they are 'neither protected nor supported by the copyright laws that are meant to protect all artists'.[54] The lack of precision in the realm of copyright exceptions (fair use / fair dealing) is also a source of frustration for artists, art publishers, and producers of artistic productions,[55] and a source of confusion to others who need to access such works (see Section 5.1).

Indeed, contemporary art occupies a new niche in the context of IP law, and is given detailed treatment in Appendix E to illustrate some of the basic concepts and current ambiguities surrounding copyright law.[56] As seen in the discussion there, many of the assumptions upon which international copyright treaties are based do not necessarily hold true for contemporary artists who are experimenting with new concepts as well as technology and other media to create works that do not fit neatly within the concept of 'art' that was used even fifty years ago. Indeed, they often set out to deconstruct prevalent notions such as those surrounding 'the artist', aesthetics, originality and, indeed, property.[57]

52 *Burrow-Giles Lithographic Co. v. Sarony*, 111 U.S. 53 (1884).

53 See 'Damian Loeb Sued for Appropriation', Artnet News, 15 August, 2000, available at: http://www.artnet.com/Magazine/news/artnetnews/artnetnews8-15-00.asp (accessed 12 February 2009).

54 See the website of the Appropriation Art Coalition (a coalition of art professionals in Canada), available at: http://www.appropriationart.ca/?page_id=13 (accessed 12 February 2009). The Coalition is calling for government support towards related legal reforms.

55 For a thorough look at some of the problems that arise under US fair use principles, see Heins and Beckles 2005. See also the Art Law Blog, entries on fair use, available at: http://theartlawblog.blogspot.com/2009_02_01_archive.html (accessed 3 March 2010).

56 Particular challenges in the case of TCEs are dealt with separately in Chapter 5.

57 The 'property' question is an interesting one as new forms of art emerge, including 'born-digital' content as well as 'land art'. James Turrell, for example, is both the author of an artistic work that comprises a volcano and the owner of the land mass that is the volcano. See Walravens 2005, p. 132.

5. Public access to cultural works: Nurturing capabilities for creative expression

In his foreword to a study *From Access to Participation: Cultural Policy and Civil Renewal*[58] published by the Institute for Public Policy Research in the UK, Rogers (2006, p. 4) notes that:

> Insofar as cultural policy has tried to increase and broaden popular engagement, it has made little distinction between increasing more passive forms of cultural engagement – that is, increasing the size and representativeness of 'audiences' – and promoting more active involvement. The tendency has been to homogenise both, in a drive to increase 'access'.

An approach to human development focusing on building human capabilities as a means and measure of welfare advancement has been described in Chapter 1, drawing especially from the work of Amartya Sen, Marta Nussbaum and other development thinkers.[59] Following this approach, it might be argued that what ultimately matters in public access to cultural works is whether the access is framed in a way which promotes the capabilities of individuals and communities. This approach sees members of the public not only as consumers of cultural works but also as potential or ongoing creators in their own right (see Sunder 2008).

In discussing capabilities essential to human welfare, Nussbaum (2000, p. 78) lists not only such basic elements as capabilities relating to 'health' and 'food security' but also other considerations quite invisible to utility-centred arguments for development. She emphasizes, for example, human capabilities relating to 'senses, imagination and thought' (ibid.). These relate to whether one is ultimately 'able to use imagination and thought in connection with experiencing and producing self-expressive works and events of one's own choice, religious, literary, musical, and so forth' (ibid.).

The capability (or bundle of capabilities) for creative expression is inextricable from other capabilities such as those relating to education and freedom of expression, discussed earlier in Chapters 6 and 7. A myriad of copyright-related provisions contour these capabilities, including what elements of a work are subject to copyright, the duration of protection, how much copying is permitted under the exceptions or defences to infringement, and how user rights or capabilities might

[58] See Keaney 2006. In the book, Keaney sets out to explore patterns of cultural participation in the UK, looking at the contribution that participation in arts and heritage activity makes to civic life. She suggests ways in which this contribution could be increased, focusing particularly on marginalized communities.

[59] This approach sees inherent limitations in models of evaluating human welfare based solely on ideas of 'utility' (i.e. happiness or desire fulfilment) or commodity access. While the economic incentive theory for copyright assumes that the public 'benefits' simply by the sheer expansion of works incentivised by copyright, a human development perspective would go further in examining the types of works incentivized by market dynamics and how they impact human capabilities (see Chapter 1). Looking at access to commodities alone also does not tell us enough about how individuals are able to function with (or without) those commodities (see Sen 1985, pp. 18–20). As Sen clarifies: 'Commodity command is a *means* to the end of well-being, but can scarcely be the end itself'. Citing Marx, he adds that to think otherwise is to fall into the trap of 'commodity fetishism – to regard goods as valuable in themselves and not for (and to the extent that) they help the person' (ibid.).

further be curtailed through licence provisions and technological measures.[60] Many of these elements have been discussed elsewhere in this book (see especially Chapters 1, 6 and 7) and repetition is avoided here. In the following section, we focus on how copyright exceptions and limitations, such as the fair use defence in the US, circumscribe the ability of individuals and communities to reproduce or transform a copyright-protected work for purposes including self-expression. While few would deny the 'transformative powers' of a cultural work, for example, a work of literature, on individuals and communities, how far can a reader or an audience in turn use or transform a work for self-expression without first seeking permission from the rights owner or incurring concerns of copyright infringement?

5.1. Copyright exceptions and free expression

Exceptions and defences to copyright liability are an integral part of the mechanism built into national copyright laws to ensure a degree of access by the public to copyright protected works. Within a context of long and expanding copyright terms,[61] the exceptions and limitations to copyright become even more important in determining the contours and nature of public access to cultural works (see Suthersanen 2008). Internationally, these exceptions are currently circumscribed by the so-called three-step test set out in Article 9(2) of the Berne Convention (Paris text 1971) and Article 13 of the TRIPS Agreement. Article 13 of the TRIPS Agreement reads:

> Members shall confine limitations and exceptions to exclusive rights to certain special cases which do not conflict with a normal exploitation of the work and do not unreasonably prejudice the legitimate interests of the right holder.

The three-step test has come under substantial scrutiny by many commentators and is treated in detail in Chapter 7 (see further Gervais 2005; Koelman 2006, p. 407). While the general discussion is not repeated here, it is noted that Berne Article 9(2) addresses only exceptions to the reproduction right, whereas TRIPS Article 13 permits exceptions to any of the owner's rights (see WIPO 2008, p. 21). Furthermore, it has been noted that:

> Berne states the three-step test as a proviso to the exceptions. TRIPS declares the test in mandatory terms, requiring how countries 'shall confine' their statutory provisions. Berne refers to the interests of 'authors'; TRIPS references the interests of 'right holders'. Most important, TRIPS is enforceable. A country seeking to avoid having to justify its statutes before a WTO panel will probably give high regard to the language of the three-step test. (Ibid.; footnotes omitted)

The interpretation of the three-step test under TRIPS Article 13 was the subject of a World Trade Organization (WTO) dispute concerning US copyright provisions

[60] Beutz Land notes that navigating through a web of IP ownership renders access to cultural works a complex process. Beutz Land, M. 2008, presentation at the A2K3 Conference, Geneva, 8–10 September 2008.

[61] See the discussion in Chapter 1. There is an arbitrary element to the length of copyright protection. Cornish and Llewelyn (2003) note that 'it is the cultural value attaching to authorship which provides such copious moral legitimacy for legal protection' and provides authors with 'a longer-lasting right than could possibly be needed by way of economic incentive' (ibid., p. 371).

which exempted a broad range of retail and restaurant establishments from liability for the public performance of musical works (under copyright) by means of communication of radio and television transmissions. Marking the first time an international adjudicative body has interpreted either Article 13 of the TRIPS Agreement, or Article 9(2) of the Berne Convention, the dispute resolution panel of the WTO in June 2000 held the US in contravention of its obligation under Article 13 of the TRIPS Agreement.[62] Ginsburg (2001) notes of the decision that:

> The § 110(5) controversy, it bears emphasis, concerned a pork barrel exemption purely for the benefit of certain business consumers of copyrighted works; it did not implicate any of the free speech or scholarship interests that underlie many other copyright exceptions. As a result, the Panel decision does not purport to offer guidance toward analyzing the 'legitimacy' of right holder interests *when they are confronted with the creative interests of other authors.* (Emphasis added)

It is the 'creative interests of other authors', closely intertwined with freedom of expression, which concern us here. Freedom of expression is a human right guaranteed under international and regional instruments. This right extends to the 'freedom to seek, receive and impart information and ideas of all kinds, regardless of frontiers, either orally, in writing or in print, in the form of art, or through any other media' of one's choice.[63] Guibault and Hugenholtz (2003, p. 6) suggest that the principle of protecting expressions, not ideas, inherently limits the possible impact of copyright protection on freedom of expression, because in theory anyone may publish or reproduce the ideas of another contained in copyrighted material provided the form in which they are expressed is not reproduced. Nevertheless, they qualify that:

> While the idea/expression dichotomy contributes substantially to the freedom of public debate and news reporting, there may be circumstances where it is important to be able to use not merely a person's idea, but also his or her form of expression in order to have effective reporting or criticism of her thoughts. For example, it may be important for a news reporter or a critic to capture the mood, the tone or the nuances of an address, which may not be possible without reproducing part of the speaker's form of expression. Historians, biographers, and scientists also need to be able to portray reality in a truthful manner in their own work, by relying on prior writings. (Ibid.)

There is significant variation in the exceptions and limitations to copyright under domestic laws. Going beyond exceptions for news reporting, criticism and teaching, some regimes provide exceptions for 'parody' and other transformative uses. Defining parody as a 'humorous exaggerated imitation of an author, literary work, style', Guibault and Hugenholtz suggest that parodies conflict with the rights owners' copyright in their work almost by definition (ibid., p. 6). In relation to the critical function served by parody, they observe that:

[62] See WTO 2000, Panel Report on *United States – Section 110(5) of the US Copyright Act*, Doc. WT/DS160/R, adopted 27 July 2000. The dispute resolution proceeding was initiated by the European Union at the behest of the Irish Music Rights Organisation. See Ficsor 2002, pp. 110–251, and Ginsburg 2001.

[63] Article 19(2) of the International Covenant on Civil and Political Rights 1966. See also Articles 13 and 17 of the Convention on the Rights of the Child 1989.

> Parodies are considered not only to have entertainment value, but also to serve a critical function, pointing out human imperfections and the ironies of our existence. Encouraging the production of parodies is thus one of society's values since they constitute an important artistic vehicle, through which creators and critics exercise their freedom of expression, guaranteed under article 10 [European Convention on Human Rights].[64] (Ibid., p. 9)

While not a copyright case, a high-profile South African case involving a parody of a trademark illustrates potentials for the assertion of IPRs to limit free expression. In *Laugh It Off Promotions CC v. South African Breweries*, the parodist used a trademark for beer in a display on T-shirts which some might consider an anti-apartheid message.[65] The plaintiffs held trademark rights over a logo with the words 'America's lusty, lively beer – Carling Beer, Black Label'. The Constitutional Court of South Africa decided there was no trademark infringement through the defendant's use (on T-shirts it sold) of a logo with the words 'Africa's lusty, lively exploitation since 1652: White Guilt, Black Labour, No regard given worldwide'. The Constitutional Court of South Africa found the use of the trademark to be non-infringing on the basis that there was no likelihood of economic detriment to the plaintiffs.[66] Moseneke J. came to the conclusion: '[T]he claim of infringement of the respondent's marks stands to be dismissed because no likelihood of economic prejudice has been established. Secondly, where no economic harm has been shown, the fairness of parody or satire or lampooning does not fall for consideration'.[67] Concurring with the decision, Sachs J. was nevertheless of the view that the appeal should be upheld on more substantial grounds.[68] He suggested that: 'In our consumerist society where branding occupies a prominent space in public culture ... there is a legitimate place for criticism of a particular trademark, or of the influence of branding in general or of the overzealous use of trademark law to stifle public debate'.[69] In his view, the expression of humour is not only permissible, but necessary for the health of democracy.[70] As he observed: 'Humour is one of the great solvents of democracy. It permits the ambiguities and contradictions of public life to be articulated in non-violent forms. It promotes diversity ... It is an elixir of constitutional health'.[71]

[64] See also the First Amendment to the US Constitution, which states that: 'Congress shall make no law ... abridging the freedom of speech, or of the press; or the right of the people peaceably to assemble, and to petition the Government for a redress of grievances.' US Const. amend. I.

[65] See *Laugh It Off Promotions CC v. South African Breweries Int'l (Finance) B.V. t/a Sabmark Int'l*, Constitutional Court of South Africa, Case No. CCT42/04, paras. 7–11 (2005).

[66] *Laugh It Off Promotions CC*, Case No. CCT 42/04, paras. 51–59, 66 (2005).

[67] *Laugh It Off Promotions CC*, Case No. CCT 42/04, para. 66 (2005). Judge Moseneke observes: '[I]t is important to keep in mind the purpose for which the marks have been appropriated. What is being sold is not another beer or other product under the guise or on the back of the registered marks. What is being sold is rather an abstract brand criticism' (ibid., para. 62).

[68] *Laugh It Off Promotions CC*, Case No. CCT 42/04, para. 74 (2005) (Sachs, J., concurring).

[69] *Laugh It Off Promotions CC*, Case No. CCT 42/04, para. 86. Judge Sachs also asks: 'Does the law have a sense of humour? This question is raised whenever the irresistible force of free expression, in the form of parody, meets the immovable object of property rights, in the form of trademark protection' (ibid., para. 70).

[70] See Constitutional Court of South Africa, 'Media Summary', available at: http://www.scribd.com/doc/17710567/Laugh-If-Off-Promotions-case-media-summary (accessed 29 March 2010).

[71] *Laugh It Off Promotions CC*, Case No. CCT 42/04, para. 109.

The Berne Convention makes no specific reference to parodies. Guibault and Hugenholtz (2003, p. 9) suggest, nevertheless, that the making of a reproduction for the purposes of parody would probably fall under Article 9(2) of the Convention, or under the right to quote in Article 10(1) of the Convention. It is notable that, under the Directive 2001/29/EC on the harmonization of certain aspects of copyright and related rights in the information society ('EC Information Society Directive'), members *may* provide copyright exceptions and limitations for 'the purposes of caricature, parody or pastiche' (article 5(3)(k)).[72] These terms are not defined in the EC Information Society Directive, and provisions for such exceptions within national laws vary significantly.[73] Under French law, for example, after a work has been disclosed the author may not prohibit the making of parodies, pastiches or caricatures which observe the rules of the genre.[74] In contrast, there is no parody exception to copyright under UK 'fair dealing' provisions.[75] Indeed, the UK Gowers Review recommends that an exception for the purpose of caricature, parody or pastiche be created in the UK, as allowed for under the EC Information Society Directive (Gowers 2006, recommendation 12, p. 68).[76] However, a recent consultation paper on *Taking Forward the Gowers Review of Intellectual Property*, issued by the UK Intellectual Property Office (IPO), indicates that there is no proposal to change the current approach to parody, caricature and pastiche in the UK (see IPO 2009, pp. 34, 46).

It is interesting to note, meanwhile, that a defence has been enacted by statutory amendment[77] to the Copyright Act (Cth) 1968 in Australia to cover not only parody but also satire.[78] McCutcheon (2008, p. 178) suggests that 'Australia appears to be the first country to expressly permit fair dealing of a copyright work for a satirical purpose, thus affording broader protection than other jurisdictions, in particular the US fair use defence'. She points to a number of cases in the US, where courts have

[72] Council Directive 2001/29/EC of 22 May 2001 on the harmonization of certain aspects of copyright and related rights in the information society, OJ No. L 167 (2001).

[73] A 2007 Commission/ Council follow-up document suggests that: 'Some national laws expressly provide for a parody exception (for example France, Belgium), or cover parodies under the umbrella of a transformative use (Nordic countries) or of a "free use" defence (Germany and Portugal for example). However, the scope of the German "free use" rule appears rather narrow'. See European Parliament Legislative Observatory website (Document COD/1997/0359: 30/11/2007), available at: http://www.europarl.europa.eu/oeil/resume.jsp?id=93762&noticeType=null&eventId=1035933&backToCaller=NO&language=en (accessed 24 April 2009).

[74] See Article L.122–5, 4° of the French Intellectual Property Code, English translation available at: http://www.wipo.int/clea/en/text_html.jsp?lang=en&id=1610#JD_AL122_1; Guibault and Hugenholtz (2003, p. 9) observe that: 'French legal literature traditionally teaches that parodies apply to musical works, pastiches to literary works and caricatures to drawings and artistic works. This classification is somewhat technical and has been the source of much confusion in the case law'.

[75] Specific exceptions or limitations to copyright for 'fair dealing' are listed in Chapter 3 of the UK Copyright, Designs and Patents Act 1988. Cornish and Llewelyn (2003, p. 442) note that: 'By relying wholly on specified statutory limitations, British copyright law differs both from United States law, where the concept of "fair use" has a scope that is both general and central, and authors' rights systems, which tend to have a general defence of private use deriving from what are now human rights criteria.'

[76] For some common definitions of these terms, see Intellectual Property Office (IPO) 2009, p. 94.

[77] Copyright Amendment Act (Cth) 2006.

[78] Neither parody nor satire is defined under the Australian Copyright Act (Cth) 1968, as amended by the Copyright Amendment Act (Cth) 2006.

sought to make a distinction between satire and parody.[79] For example, in *Sun Trust Bank v. Houghton Mifflin*, the Court of Appeal said that: 'Parody, which is directed toward a particular literary artistic work, is distinguishable from satire, which more broadly addresses the institutions and mores of a slice of society'.[80] In that case, the estate of Margaret Mitchell (author of *Gone with the Wind*) sought to enjoin publication of Alice Randall's *The Wind Done Gone*, where Mitchell's classic story is retold from a slave perspective. The Court of Appeal classified Randall's work as a parody of Mitchell's (even though, arguably, the work could be seen as directed at institutions and *more* than a slice of society). In the *Campbell* case, the court said that:

> It is not enough that the parody use the original in a humorous fashion, however creative that humour may be. The parody must target the original, and not just its general style, the genre of art to which it belongs, or society as a whole (although if it targets the original, it may target those features as well).[81]

The court added in the *Campbell* case that: 'Parody needs to mimic an original to make its point, and so has some claim to use the creation of its victim's (or collective victims') imagination, whereas satire can stand on its own two feet and so requires justification for the very act of borrowing'.[82] It is true that satiric works could be achieved without use of a copyright-protected work. Thus, many satires would not infringe copyright in the first place (see Guibault & Hugenholtz 2003, p. 9). It would seem ironic, nevertheless, that a work verging on 'satire' and serving the function of broader social commentary should not be able to avail the fair use defence when not targeting the copyright-protected work itself. In the case of *Roger v. Koons*,[83] the fair use defence was denied for a satirical critique of society, rather than a parody of the copied work (McCutcheon 2008, p. 170; see Appendix E).

It is still open to interpretation in US law whether 'satire' might fall within fair use.[84] Noting that 'parody and satire often blur', McCutcheon comments that 'ultimately it seems incongruous that so much rests on analysis and argument over a relatively elusive conception of what a parody or a satire is, when what the

[79] *Acuff-Rose Music Inc v. Campbell*, 510 U.S. 569 (1994). See also the Court of Appeals ruling in *Sun Trust Bank v. Houghton Mifflin*, 252 F.3d 1165 (11th Cir. 2001). But note the earlier case of *Berlin v. E.C. Publications, Inc.*, 329 F.2d 541 (2d. Cir. 1964) where it was held that 'parody and satire are deserving of substantial freedom – both as entertainment and as a form of social and literary criticism' (ibid., p. 545). In *Elsmere Music, Inc. v. National Broadcasting Co.*, 482 F. Supp. 741 (S.D.N.Y. 1980), the District Court held that: '... the issue to be resolved by a court is whether the use in question is a valid satire or parody, and not whether it is a parody of the copied song itself' (ibid., p. 746).

[80] *Sun Trust Bank v. Houghton Mifflin*, 252 F.3d 1165, 1268 (11th Cir. 2001).

[81] *Acuff-Rose Music Inc. v. Campbell*, 510 U.S. 569, 597 (1994).

[82] *Acuff-Rose Music Inc. v. Campbell*, 510 U.S. 569, 580 (1994).

[83] *Rogers v. Koons*, 960 F.2d 301 (2d Cir. 1992). The Court in *Roger v. Koons* stated: 'The problem in the instant case is that even given that "String of Puppies" [defendant Koon's photograph] is a satirical critique of our materialistic society, it is difficult to discern any parody of the photograph "Puppies" itself.' Ibid., p. 310.

[84] A footnote in *Campbell* provides that in certain circumstances: '... looser forms of parody may be found to be fair use, as may satire with lesser justification for the borrowing than would otherwise be required'. *Acuff-Rose Music Inc. v. Campbell*, 510 U.S. 569, 580 n.14 (1994).

stakeholders are really concerned about are the broader reasons why we isolate parody or satire as tolerable infringements' (ibid., p. 187). She adds that:

> It is not really the magic of something falling into a box marked 'parody' or 'satire' that justifies the exemption – rather it is the relatively benign effect on the copyright owner's interests of the fair dealing for that purpose. That being said, provided the dealing is fair, why do we confine protection to these two particular forms of transformative work, and not others? What does it matter what form the infringing work takes? What matters is its effects . . . The reasons why we accord protection to parodies and satires . . . apply equally to other forms of creative output. (Ibid.)

McCutcheon suggests that the Australian defence of fair dealing ought to apply to other arguably 'transformative' works, regardless of whether they fall within 'parody or satire' (ibid.). She highlights the examples of appropriation art; remixing, 'mash-ups' and sampling of music or other media – including, making an 'unofficial' music video by remixing existing video footage or 'recasting a novel from a different cultural or character's perspective' (ibid., pp. 187–188).[85]

Reforms to the law to allow for certain forms of 'transformative use' are being considered in other jurisdictions. In a 2008 Green Paper on 'Copyright in the Knowledge Economy', the Commission of the European Communities (EC Commission) considers whether there ought to be an exception to copyright for 'transformative, user-created content' in European Union (EU) law. It cites an Organisation for Economic Co-operation and Development (OECD) study (2007, p. 9) in defining user-created content as 'content made publicly available over the Internet, which reflects a certain amount of creative effort, and which is created outside of professional routines and practices'. The EC Commission (2008, p. 19) notes that:

> The Directive does not currently contain an exception which would allow the use of existing copyright protected content for creating new or derivative works. The obligation to clear rights before any transformative content can be made available can be perceived as a barrier to innovation in that it blocks new, potentially valuable works from being disseminated. However, before any exception for transformative works can be introduced, one would need to carefully determine the conditions under which a transformative use would be allowed, so as not to conflict with the economic interests of the rightsholders of the original work.

In the context of the UK, the Gowers Review has recommended that an exception be created for 'creative, transformative or derivative works, within the parameters of the Berne Three-Step Test' (see Gowers 2006, recommendation 11, p. 68). The Review referred to the treatment of transformative use within US copyright law, and the example of sampling in the *Hip Hop* music industry (ibid., p. 67). Transformative use alone is not, however, a defence to copyright infringement in US law, but one of the conditions required for a use to qualify for the fair use defence under Section

[85] On cultural adaptation for a novel, see the interesting discussion on Harry Potter in Kolkata (*'Harry Potter Kolkataye')* in Chander and Sunder (2007, p. 610). In the book written in Bengali by Uttam Ghosh, 'Harry gets onto his Nimbus 2000 broom and zooms across to Calcutta' at the invitation of a boy named Junto, and apparently meets famous fictional characters from Bengali literature (ibid., citing text from the book). The unofficial Harry Potter book was withdrawn following a 'cease and desist' letter to the book publisher referring to the 'pirate' work (ibid., p. 611).

107 of the U.S. Copyright Act (see the *Harry Potter Lexicon* case in Box 8.1; see also EC Commission 2008, p. 19).

BOX 8.1. Harry Potter and the 'fair use' wand

The intricate and somewhat unpredictable balancing act under US fair use is illustrated by the recent *Harry Potter Lexicon* case, before the US District Court for the Southern District of New York ('the Court').[86] The plaintiff in that case was J.K. Rowling, author and copyright owner of the phenomenally successful Harry Potter novels and of two companion books that expand on the events in the novels. Warner Brothers Entertainment, Rowling's co-plaintiff, owns the copyright in the film versions of the novels. The defendant, RDR Books, sought to publish *The Harry Potter Lexicon*, a 400-page A-to-Z encyclopaedia describing the events and details – characters, places, magic spells and imaginary games – featured in the Harry Potter novels, companion books and films (see Clayton 2008). Finding that the latter work infringed Rowling's copyright, the Court awarded injunctive relief as well as statutory damages.[87] Contemplating the statutory factors that must be considered when assessing fair use under Section 107 of the Copyright Act of 1976, the Court (Judge Patterson) stated that:

> The evaluation of these factors is an open-ended and context-sensitive inquiry, and the examples listed in the statute (i.e., criticism, comment, news reporting, and teaching) are illustrative rather than limiting. The four statutory factors may not be treated in isolation, one from another; instead they all must be explored, and the results weighed together, in light of the purposes of copyright. The ultimate test of fair use, therefore, is whether the copyright law's goal of promoting the Progress of Science and useful Arts would be better served by allowing the use than by preventing it.[88]

Citing the US Supreme Court's decision in *Campbell v. Acuff-Rose Music*, the Court observed that 'most critical to the inquiry under the first fair-use factor is "whether and to what extent the new work is transformative"'.[89] On the one hand, the Court found that the *purpose* of the *Lexicon*'s use of the Harry Potter series was transformative,[90] the best evidence of this transformative purpose being 'its demonstrated value as a reference source'.[91] On the other hand, the Court also found that:

> The transformative character of the Lexicon is diminished, however, because the Lexicon's use of the original Harry Potter works is not consistently transformative. The Lexicon's use lacks transformative character where the Lexicon entries fail to 'minimize the expressive value' of the original expression.[92]

While the commercial nature of a secondary work does not itself bar a finding of fair use, it was emphasized in the *Harry Potter Lexicon* case that 'courts will not find fair use when the

(*continued*)

86 *Warner Bros. Entertainment, Inc. & J. K. Rowling v. RDR Books*, 575 F. Supp. 2d 513 (S.D.N.Y. 2008).

87 *Warner Bros. Entertainment, Inc.*, 575 F. Supp. 2d at 554.

88 *Warner Bros. Entertainment, Inc.*, 575 F. Supp. 2d at 540 (internal quotations omitted).

89 Ibid. (quoting *Campbell*, 510 U.S. at 579).

90 Ibid. at 541.

91 Ibid. at 542. The Court added that: 'The Lexicon, however, does not purport to be a work of literary criticism or to constitute a fair use on that basis; and its lack of critical analysis, linguistic understanding, or clever humor is not determinative of whether or not its purpose is transformative. ' Ibid. at 543.

92 Ibid. at 544 (citing *Bill Graham Archives v. Dorling Kindersley Ltd.*, 448 F.3d 605, 611 (2d Cir. 2006).

Box 8.1 *(continued)*

secondary use "can fairly be characterized as a form of commercial exploitation", but "are more willing to find a secondary use fair when it produces a value that benefits the broader public interest"'.[93] This led to the finding in the *Harry Potter Lexicon* case that:

> Seeking to capitalize on a market niche does not necessarily make Defendant's use non-transformative, but to the extent that Defendant seeks to 'profit at least in part from the inherent entertainment value' of the original works, the commercial nature of the use weighs against a finding of fair use. To the extent that Defendant seeks to provide a useful reference guide to the Harry Potter novels that benefits the public, the use is fair, and its commercial nature only weighs slightly against a finding of fair use.[94]

On the facts, the Court found that this was a not a case of fair use while recognizing that the infringers had not acted in bad faith. Steps by RDR Books to appeal the decision were soon discontinued, and RDR Books published an edited version of the *Lexicon* in January 2009. The defendants claim that the edited version was written to conform to the Court's guidelines on what is fair use (Roberts 2009). The case has invited many commentaries, including those relating to non-commercial fan-generated content on the Internet. Steve Vander Ark, the creator of the popular fan website 'The Harry Potter Lexicon', was the same individual responsible for putting together the *Lexicon* book. While much of the material in the book is the same as the material made available online, the website was not challenged by the plaintiffs (see Clayton 2008). Rowling is even said to have praised the website as a source of information about the Harry Potter series prior to the appearance of the *Lexicon* book; however, she testified at trial that she was concerned that publication of a book version of the Lexicon website would diminish the market for the Harry Potter encyclopaedia that she planned to write (ibid.).

The *Harry Potter Lexicon* case provides a glimpse into the ambiguities connected with applying the 'open-ended' approach under US fair use doctrine, and the unpredictability of litigation outcomes. The Court used the 'open-ended' approach to conclude that the *Lexicon* was not a fair use because it borrowed too closely from Rowling's original works.[95] Yet, the Court also made it clear that there is nothing inherently wrong with publishing a fiction-related reference work.[96] At present, the revised (and presumably legal) *Lexicon* sits on the market as an emblem of the sometimes fine line between what is and what is not legal fair use.

---

[93] Ibid. at 545 (quoting *Blanch*, 467 F.3d at 253).

[94] Ibid. (quoting *Elvis Presley Enters. v. Passport Video*, 349 F.3d 622, 628 (9th Cir. 2003)).

[95] Ibid.

[96] See the Court's statement that 'reference works that share the Lexicon's purpose of aiding readers of literature generally should be encouraged rather than stifled'. Ibid. at 553.

Discussing transformation of copyright-protected works in the context of non-commercial, community-based practices such as fan-generated content, Tushnet argues (2008, pp. 109–110) that 'using a work as a building block for an argument, or an expression of the creator's imagination, should be understood as a transformative purpose, in contrast to consuming a work for its entertainment value' (see also Reese 2008, p. 118). She adds that:

> Unauthorized, unplanned creativity has immense value even at the most instrumental level: beginning with popular sources gives young creators a place to start, heightens their enthusiasm for writing, and provides them with an eager and helpful audience. The social value of hundreds of thousands of unauthorized *Harry*

> *Potter*-inspired stories rests not merely in the stories' critical potential in challenging the sexual, racial and political assumptions of the original, but also in the skills that fans learn while writing, editing, and discussing them. The benefits of other forms of fan-based creativity, including video editing and music production, are similar. The transformation here is mainly of the creators and the audiences, and it should be recognized as a legitimate type of transformation.[97] (Tushnet 2008, pp. 109–110, footnotes omitted)

Chander and Sunder (2007, p. 612) suggest, moreover, that the use of cultural icons to 're-imagine the world by reworking the most powerful elements of popular culture' is particularly important where the popular culture is 'widely discriminatory and non-inclusive'. Discussing feminist elements in Mary Sue fan fiction, as well as racial undertones in *Gone with the Wind*, they assert:

> Theorists, both traditional and postmodern, affirm the discursive nature of creativity: all creators borrow from earlier masters. Contemporary cultural theorists recognize as an important discursive tactic the reworking of a *discriminatory* narrative to retell history and empower oneself. Rewriting the popular narrative becomes an act of not only trying to change popular understandings, but also an act of *self*-empowerment.[98] (Ibid.)

Lessig (2007) furthermore points out that the 'cut and paste' or 'remix' possibilities offered by digital technology present forms of expression by which the contemporary public engage in acts of creativity and free speech. Fitzgerald and O'Brien (2007) note the legal boundaries in cases where images protected by copyright and trademarks are appropriated by groups in social commentary and political activism in a process known as 'culture jamming'.[99] As seen earlier in relation to 'parody' and copyright infringement, free expression and 'fair use' issues are often intertwined.

Meanwhile, confusion about the legal limits for fair use may itself have a chilling effect on creativity.[100] Some creators may 'play safe', for example, in the face of personal and legal uncertainties over fair use.[101] In their policy paper 'Will Fair Use Survive?' for the Brennan Center for Justice, Heins and Beckles (2005) found that the 'fair use' exception is underutilized by the US public given its unpredictability,

[97] It has been said that, in assessing 'transformativeness', the courts generally emphasize the 'transformativeness' of the defendant's purpose in using the underlying work, rather than 'any transformation (or lack thereof) by the defendant of the content of the underlying work' (Reese 2008, p. 118; see Tushnet 2008, p. 110).

[98] They quote Rosemary Coombe's powerful question: 'What meaning does dialogue have when we are bombarded with messages to which we cannot respond, signs and images whose significations cannot be challenged, and connotations we cannot contest?' (Coombe 1991, p. 1879).

[99] According to Fitzergerald and O'Brien, 'the term culture jamming refers to a form of social and political activism, a resistance movement to the hegemony of popular culture which utilizes the mass media to criticize and satirize those very institutions that control and dominate the mass media' (ibid., p. 173). An example is the use of billboard images resembling those for 'iPod' advertisements, with the words 'Iraq' and spotting images of persons carrying weaponry instead of audio devices. For an illustration, see 'Blood for Oil', available at: http://www.bloodforoil.org/iRaq-posters/ (accessed 15 February 2009).

[100] There is perhaps confusion to a lesser extent among the public over the 'fair dealing' exception under many common law systems (including the Commonwealth systems), where 'fair dealing' is circumscribed by an enumerated set of defences to copyright infringement. Judges may, however, have less discretion in deciding whether the circumstances of a case fall within 'fair dealing' (see Laddie 1996, pp. 258–259).

[101] Or 're-mixing' amid the uncertainties is accompanied by a sense of 'guilt' (personal interview with visual art students in New Jersey, preferring to be anonymous, working on re-mix and re-mash).

the high cost of defending it in court,[102] and the crushing liability that may result if 'one guesses wrong'.[103] Their study suggests that artists and scholars have significant interest in the 'fair use' exception, but find little clarity about its operation. This is especially the case in 'appropriation art', where the boundaries of what is fair use are blurred (see Appendix E). Highlighting the further 'chilling effects' of 'cease and desist' letters from corporate rights owners on free expression and independent media, as well as the problems of a 'clearance culture' in the arts,[104] the study emphasizes the need for community support and accessible legal assistance to help artists strengthen their knowledge in their dealings with publishers, distributors and other cultural gatekeepers.

6. Changing notions of authorship

Transformations have meanwhile been taking place in relation to how creators and creative activities are perceived. In the scholarship relating to IP, there is a shift of focus from the individual inventors, and so-called 'discrete' innovation, to 'participatory processes' which recognize the incremental nature of innovation (Ghosh & Soete 2006; Suthersanen 2008; see Chapter 1). While the potentials of the Internet to accelerate the speed and extent of such participation has called attention to the role of social networks in creative activities (Benkler 2006), the 'deconstruction' of authors and authorship has, of course, taken place over a much longer period.

Within literary and social commentaries, there has been a self-reflecting search for the meaning of 'What is an author?'.[105] Some theories in literary criticism view the created written work as constantly recontextualized and given new meanings by the reader. Indeed, in 'Death of the Author', Barthes (1967) suggests provocatively that:

> [a] text consists of multiple writings, issuing from several cultures and entering into dialogue with each other, into parody, into contestation; but there is one place where this multiplicity is collected, united, and this place is not the author... but the reader... the unity of a text is not in its origin, it is in its destination... to restore to writing its future, we must reverse its myth: the birth of the reader must be ransomed by the death of the Author. (Ibid.)

[102] The legal defence of the *Harry Potter Lexicon* case was apparently assumed on a pro bono basis. See Crace 2008.

[103] The study was part of the 'Free Expression Policy Project' which sought to examine, among other things, how IP enforcement circumscribes free expression among artists, scholars, and others who make critical contributions to culture and democratic discourse. It involved focus group discussions, telephone interviews, an online survey, and an analysis of more than 300 'cease and desist' and take-down letters.

[104] Heins and Beckles note that threatening 'cease and desist' letters cause many people to forego their fair use rights; additional hurdles to fair use come from the 'clearance culture' in many creative industries, which assumes that almost no quote can be used without permission from the owner (ibid., p. ii).

[105] In his seminal essay of the title, Foucault (1979) studies the discursive function of 'authorship' in maintaining existing power structures in society. He observes that: 'The author... is a certain functional principle by which in our culture, one limits, excludes, and chooses; in short, by which one impedes the free circulation, decomposition, and recomposition of fiction. In fact, if we are accustomed to presenting the author as a genius, as a perpetual surging of invention, it is because, in reality, we make him function in exactly the opposite fashion. One can say that the author is an ideological product, since we represent him as the opposite of his historically real function' (ibid., pp. 118-119). As Bently (1994, p. 973) observes: 'Foucault drew attention to the fact that the notion of the "author" is socially constructed' (see also Opderbeck 2008, p. 14).

Barthes adds that 'literature is that neuter, that composite... into which every subject escapes, the trap where all identity is lost, beginning with the very identity of the body that writes' (ibid.).[106] This contrasts with notions of authorship in mainstream IP theories, where the individual 'author' has been a central figure both in the 'natural rights' and 'economic incentive' arguments relating to copyright. Studying the early development of copyright law in Europe, some commentators have suggested that the notion of the individual 'author' was constructed with the rise of the book trade and the need to justify proprietary claims for the control of printed material (Rose 1992; Woodmansee 1984, 1993).[107]

Art theories have also dwelled critically on notions surrounding the 'artist' and 'originality'. For example, Adorno traces how the Western concept of the 'genius' artist or inventor was itself a historical product which 'came in vogue in the late eighteenth century' (1997 translation, p. 171).[108] He adds that 'prior to the age of genius the idea of originality bore no authority' (ibid.). He observes that 'in their works composers of the seventeenth and early eighteenth centuries made use of whole sections of their own earlier works and those of others'; 'painters and architects entrusted their designs to students for completion' (ibid.).[109] As seen in Appendix E in relation to contemporary art, some artists themselves have actively challenged notions of the 'artist' and of 'originality' in their own works. It has been said that 'with a critical eye to art-historical perspective' some contemporary artists 'actively mine fine art and popular culture for their subject matter, questioning originality and at times effacing or disrupting the presence of the artist's hand'.[110]

Legislators and law courts dealing with copyright have generally not kept up with such philosophical searching on authorship and originality. It has been said that 'when a judge interprets the copyright law, he or she is likely to be much more concerned with legal coherence and continuity – with the presentation of the law as a logical whole – than with literary theory' (see Bently 1994, p. 980). At the same time, copyright law is able to 'imply and invent authors' where there is no corresponding cultural or other 'reality', including in circumstances which may not fit within conceptions of authorship in Romantic literary theory (ibid., p. 981).[111] Indeed, Bently provocatively suggests that 'the author is a notion which only needs

[106] Some defend authorship (see Hirsch 1967, pp. 1–23) or the validity of the author as narrator (see Wood 2008, pp. 3–4). Bently (1994, p. 973) notes that 'the notion of authorship has come increasingly to dominate other discourses, such as film, where the idea of the film director as author ('auteurism') has taken a firm hold'.

[107] Bently (1994, pp. 977–978) suggests, on the other hand, that authorship concepts predate the genesis of copyright law, and that 'authorship also operated as a category within law prior to the literary property debate of 1760–1775 in England'. For an excellent commentary on the debate on authorship and the emergence of copyright law which is also sceptical about the 'Woodmansee-Rose thesis', see Long 2001, pp. 7–12.

[108] He says that: 'The concept of genius represents the attempt... to bestow the individual within the limited sphere of art with the immediate power of overarching authenticity' (1997 translation; p. 170).

[109] He qualifies that what such practice 'demonstrates is that originality had yet to become the object of critical reflection, by no means that there was no originality in artworks' (ibid., p. 172).

[110] Curator's note referring to the art of Sherrie Levine, Richard Prince and Sigmar Polke, at the exhibition on 'Pipe, Glass, Bottle of Rum: The Art of Appropriation', 30 July – 10 November 2008, the Museum of Modern Art, New York.

[111] For example, under the UK Copyright, Designs and Patents Act 1988, investments of capital and administrative organization are recognized as constituting authorship of films and sound recordings (Bently 1994, p. 981).

to be sustainable for an instance' in law, since 'copyright serves paradoxically to vest authors with property only to enable them to divest that property' (ibid.). He adds that:

> At the same time as the law can invent authors where romantic literary theory would deny them, law can deny authorship where literary theory might recognise it. Thus, copyright law denies authorship to the contributor of ideas and, in cases of collaborative works, frequently refuses to recognise contributors as authors in an attempt to simplify ownership. Because a single property owner means that assignments and licences of copyright are easier and cheaper to effect, copyright law prefers to minimize the number of authorial contributions it is prepared to acknowledge rather than reflect the 'realities' of collaborative authorship. (Ibid.)

This interpretation suggests limitations in copyright law especially in assimilating notions of collective or incremental creativity (see also Chapters 1 and 5). In reality, many participants in collaborative projects are probably quite invisible to the copyright compass. Increasing corporate ownership of IP, as discussed earlier, also challenges the romantic notions of the isolated 'author' or 'creator' as the prime beneficiaries of copyright protection. As will be seen in the following section, new technology is further altering conceptions of creators and creative processes.

7. Technology as a driving force for change

Halbert (1996) notes how electronic communication is providing new avenues for incremental, collective authorship which are undermining traditional concepts of 'authorship' under copyright law. She also discusses new challenges posed by 'machine authorship', and how boundaries are blurred as to whether computer programs can be said to create 'art'.[112] Other implications of new technology on copyright have already been explored in Chapters 6 and 7 of this book, particularly in terms of their effects in altering the power relations among creators, intermediaries and end users. As discussed in Chapter 7, new technology can bring production processes closer to the artists, for example, in the music industry, rendering them less dependent on producers with capital. This had been witnessed to some extent when music cassette technology was introduced decades ago. Wallis and Malm (1984, p. 270) studied, for example, how music cassette technology replacing phonograms in the 1970s and 1980s helped some musicians record their works cheaply and overcome certain production and distribution barriers.[113] In a similar vein, the World Bank 'Africa Music Project' has been focusing on how information technology could provide a solution to improving the livelihoods of African musicians in bypassing existing barriers in their access to recording technology and world markets

[112] See the chapter on 'The Future of Intellectual Property Law and Authorship' in the author's completed doctoral thesis at the Hawaii Research Center for Future Studies (manuscript on file with author). Discussing machine-created art in her thesis, Halbert provides the example of computer-generated fractals. Bently (2006, p. 981) suggests meanwhile that the UK Copyright, Designs and Patents Act 1988 'invents' authors for computer-generated works, where no human author exists.

[113] Noting how cassettes can be used by local musicians in the countries studied to record their own musical sounds, Wallis and Malm (1984, p. 270) state that: 'The very accessibility of music industry technology has brought about another common pattern of change, particularly noticeable in smaller cultures. It has provided the pre-requisite for a counter-reaction against the transnationalization of music'.

(Penna et al. 2004, pp. 96–97).[114] This technological euphoria may have to be qualified, of course, by what some perceive as a persistent digital divide not only between the North and the South but also within regions (Gomez 2005, p. 41).

Meanwhile, new technology has visibly multiplied the possibilities for reproduction and handling of cultural content by third parties other than the content providers in a variety of contexts, whether for personal use, 'peer-to-peer' (P2P) file-sharing, commercial ends, public service or other purposes. Reproduction of cultural material occurs at a greater speed and magnitude with digital technology. Digitization also provides unprecedented possibilities for the preservation of cultural and other works. With digitization come both opportunities for increased public access to cultural works and new legal grey areas (see Chapter 7, Box 7.5). While libraries, for example, play a crucial role in digitizing and making works more accessible to the public, domestic laws differ significantly and are often ambiguous regarding the limits for library digitization and other treatment of copyright-protected materials (see WIPO 2008).

The phenomenon of Google Books encapsulates the far-reaching consequences of digital technology and public-private arrangements, as well as the rising role of collecting societies in regulating public access to cultural works (see Chapter 9). Over recent years, Google has been digitizing millions of books, including many covered by copyright, from the collections of major research libraries, and making the texts searchable online; it has been said that of the 7 million books that Google reportedly had digitized by November 2008, 1 million are works in the public domain; 1 million are in copyright and in print; and 5 million are in copyright but out of print (Darnton 2008). A class action brought by authors and publishers in the US (claiming that digitizing constituted a violation of their copyrights) has resulted in a complex settlement (and recent resettlement) pending court review of validity (ibid., 2008; see the discussion in Chapter 9).[115] While awestruck that 'here is a proposal that could result in the world's largest library', Darnton observes of the Google case that 'we are allowing a question of public policy – the control of access to information – to be determined by private lawsuit'. In discussing public access to works covered by the US settlement, one should further note the different position of the US users to users outside the US (see Chapter 9).

As the Google case also illustrates, digital and Internet technology is adding new stakeholders to the copyright matrix. Suthersanen (2007, p. 134) suggests that: 'The latest stakeholders in the copyright game are not the large contents providers but

[114] According to Penna et al. (2004, pp. 96–97), the 'dream' of the Africa Music Project is one involving 'African musicians recording in African studies, with computerized equipment recording the song and making the created record available online to a paying audience around the world'. Following this idyllic vision, 'as a listener downloads or plays the song, his bank or credit card account is automatically debited, and the musician's account is automatically credited'. Some cultural economists suggest, however, that the scope for 'self-promotion' on the Internet is limited to artists who have already made a name for themselves (see Towse 2007, p. 760).

[115] Given that the litigation was structured as a class action, the settlement required the court's approval. In response to objections made by rights holders and the US Department of Justice, the parties negotiated an amended settlement agreement, which had been granted preliminary approval by the court at the time of this writing. See the discussion on both the original settlement and the amended settlement agreement in Band 2009; Samuelson (forthcoming). The terms of the resettlement are reflected in the discussion in this chapter.

merely large organizations who were peripheral to the Internet and digitization phenomena twenty years ago. They are online stakeholders such as corporations who own or manage digital search engines like Yahoo and Google, software and content producers like Microsoft, and online retailers like Amazon . . . '. She adds that:

> These new stakeholders will join the existing world of stakeholders such as librarians (our traditional guardians of access to knowledge and learning), the publishing industry, the film and recording industries and the broadcasting industry (which is currently pushing for a new international treaty on broadcasting) . . . And, of course, the authors.

Suthersanen argues that irrespective of the various theoretical justifications, the fundamental role of copyright law 'has always been to balance the competing interests of the main stakeholders that each new technology inevitably disrupts and then recalibrates' (ibid., pp. 133–134; see further Chapter 9). Indeed, just as high technology has yielded increased possibilities for production as well as mass copying of content, it is providing the controls to limit access to content. Restrictive digital rights management (DRM) schemes and technological restrictions such as encryption have notably been engaged by content providers to create barriers to users' access and control of digital content. Can such restrictive practices, pushed to an extreme, amount to a 'Technology Lock-Down' scenario, as discussed among the five scenarios on digital media in a paper by the Berkman Center for Internet & Society (see Chapter 9)?[116] Some suggest technological restrictions may extend to prevention of access otherwise allowed by the law within fair use or fair dealing exceptions.[117] As discussed in several chapters and not repeated here, these technological restrictions are increasingly given the force of law through international treaties and domestic provisions (see especially Chapter 7).

7.1. Movements supporting 'incremental' modes of creation

Hybrid licensing arrangements have evolved through movements such as Creative Commons and Copyleft, and are particularly visible within the context of the Internet. Creative Commons' goal is to 'build a layer of reasonable, flexible copyright in the face of increasingly restrictive default rules'.[118] It provides a licensing mechanism that functions within the ambit of copyright law. Whereas the standard language for a copyright notice is 'all rights reserved', Creative Commons licences offer the alternative of reserving just *some* rights. As such, an artist might make a digital copy of her painting and upload it to her personal website. If she uses, for example, an 'Attribution-No Derivative Works 3.0 United States License', she is allowing others to download her work and upload it to their own websites, whether for commercial or non-commercial purposes, so long as her work is not modified and she receives

[116] See Berkman Center for Internet & Society and Gartner 2005.

[117] See Hinze 2007. On some of the effects of DRMs on fair use as raised by the public interest group 'Public Knowledge' within the US, see the Public Knowledge website, 'Public Knowledge Federal Trade Commission DRM Townhall Comments', available at: http://www.publicknowledge.org/node/1996 (accessed 29 March 2010). See further Lessig 2004; Chowdhury 2008, p. 106.

[118] For the history of Creative Commons, see http://wiki.creativecommons.org/History (accessed 15 February 2009).

attribution as the artist. This is one of many licences that Creative Commons offers. The licences tend to ensure that the author or artist retains her right of attribution. Other factors, such as whether third parties can modify the work, whether the work can be used in a commercial environment and what jurisdiction the licence is to be used in are options that the potential licensor can choose.

Copyleft is a similar concept to Creative Commons except that its licences require that any work derived from any copyleft work also be copyleft-licensed. Described as 'viral', this kind of licence is perhaps best demonstrated by Creative Commons' ShareAlike licences, which allows others to distribute derivative works only under a licence identical to the licence that governs (the original) work. For example, if a photograph is licensed under the 'Non-Commercial and Share Alike Terms' and is posted to that photographer's website, a collage artist could use that photograph in her work so long as she offers her work to the public on the same terms as the photographer; that is, they may use and modify her collage. Another example is Artlibre's 'Free Art License', which operates similarly by authorizing the public to copy, distribute and freely transform the work of art while respecting the rights of the originator.[119]

Coates (2007, p. 94) notes that 'while there are only limited statistical evidence currently available about Creative Commons licence use, based on general observations and anecdotal evidence it is possible to see trends emerging in how and why individuals and institutions alike are choosing to make their copyright material available under the open content licensing system'.[120] According to her: 'Creative Commons provides a valuable resource for the modern "cut and paste" culture that has been neglected by traditional copyright law. The need for content management tools that are both easy to use and free, and material that can be legally utilized by private individuals for creative purposes without the need to obtain additional permissions, will only increase as user-generated content grows in importance and popularity' (ibid.).

The extent to which creators, including copyright owners, are likely to consent to 'remixing' and other 'transformations' by the public of their works will, however, vary with context and between sectors. To begin with, creators are unlikely to authorize or license reproductions or transformations which may be critical or derogatory of the work in question (see Chander & Sunder 2007, p. 621). There are also worries by some creators that 'remixing' or 'cut and paste' may strip away the context relevant to the creation of a work. The TCEs of indigenous peoples or other local communities are an example where the expressions are closely bound up with the cultural identity and spiritual beliefs of the creators, rendering third-party access to and use of such expressions a complex and debated topic (see Chapter 5).

In the case of documentary film-making, the Australian independent film-maker Richard Jones (2007, p. 105) observes, moreover, that film-making involves a whole chain of players/participants beyond the film-maker, whereas models such as The

[119] See Artlibre.org: Free Art License 1.3, available at: http://artlibre.org/licence/lal/en (accessed 29 March 2010).

[120] For further discussions on trends and visions relating to the Creative Commons movement, see Fitzgerald et al. (eds.) 2007.

Creative Commons model seem 'to be geared for a sole author, not for the complex network of creators that contribute their images, stories and creative work' to a film. He emphasizes that the 'context' in which a part of a film is reused or remixed affects not only the copyright and moral rights of the film-maker but also the interests of other participants in the film (ibid. p. 101). He gives the separate examples of indigenous communities featured in a film and that of prison inmates who have consented to participating in a film documentary. In his opinion, there is a risk of the Creative Commons movement stripping away the 'politics of context', and further thought is required to resolve issues including how the movement can better qualify the 'context of use' (ibid. pp. 103–105). Indeed, it remains to be seen how the Creative Commons and Copyleft movements will in future address jurisdictional issues over the 'moral rights' of creators in relation to their works. Creative Commons licences (with exceptions in some jurisdictions such as Canada) tend to leave moral rights untouched, and potential issues between copyright-related licences and moral rights retention may be foreseen in some jurisdictions.[121]

8. Some scenarios and reflections for the future

In her article 'Intellectual Property Law, Technology and Our Probable Future', Halbert (1996) discusses three future scenarios relating to copyright law, digital technology and changing patterns of creation. The first is a 'Business as Usual' scenario under which:

> The division between professionals who created for money and nonprofessionals who created for pleasure remained quite clearly drawn. The copyright law continued to be unreflective of the motivations behind creation and instead continued to rely upon the assertion that providing protection of expressions and providing the opportunity for making money facilitates creation.... (Ibid., p. 152)

In contrast, under a second 'Hackers and the Future' scenario:

> Authorship did not serve as a clear marker for the text in this world because ownership was so fleeting. Copies and appropriations appeared almost as fast as the 'original'. In such a world, authorship lost its meaning, because it became difficult to tell the duplicate from the original and most people gave up the notion of the romantic author completely. (Ibid., pp. 154–155)

In a third scenario called 'Sharing as Utopia', Halbert (1996, p. 156) suggests that competition would be tempered by an 'overriding aura of cooperation'. She notes that:

> This type of sharing was especially appropriate for intellectual property. Sharing ideas is different from sharing tangible goods, because ideas can reside in more than one mind simultaneously... Authorship in the sharer future was not a 'profession'. Everyone participated in the creation of art and 'texts'. Many people utilized their creative capacity by linking and developing already existing works. Because creation was premised on facilitating cultural development and not on

[121] See Creative Commons, 'Frequently Asked Questions', available at: http://wiki.creativecommons.org/Frequently_Asked_Questions (accessed 15 February 2009).

> monetary rewards, the possibilities opened up. It was recognized that 'originality' is always culturally dependent, and great ideas did not appear from nowhere as the romantics had believed. Rather, everything was connected in the sharer world, including creation. (Ibid., pp. 156–157)

Movements such as Creative Commons suggest a glimpse of the 'Sharing as Utopia' scenario discussed by Halbert (1996). Creative Commons falls short of 'undoing' the relevance of the IP regime as they promote a 'compromise' solution relying finally on a system of licensing IP-related rights. The pervasive reach of contractual relationships in shaping creative endeavours and arrangements for the dissemination and transformation of cultural works is also seen in the Copyleft movement.

As discussed earlier, contract is a fundamental consideration for future reforms relating to creators' rights and livelihoods in most jurisdictions.[122] Alongside questions of often unequal bargaining positions at the time of contract, few creators can foresee all uses of their work (and the value of their copyright) in the future. The attitudes of creators over the sharing of their works with members of the public, including other creators, may also change over time and with different contexts. In some cases, creators who assign away their copyright to a work by contract may find themselves powerless to effect such farther-reaching decisions in relation to their works. There is significant room for law reforms to better govern the interaction between copyright law and contract law. Indeed, contracts may currently provide for exclusive rights in controlling reproduction or distribution of a work well beyond stipulations under copyright statutes, and standard contractual terms require closer scrutiny.[123] As Guibault (2002, p. 111) notes:

> In principle, any use of copyrighted material carried out in compliance with the provisions of copyright law preserves the balance established by the legislator... To what extent are the parties to a copyright license obliged to respect the legislator's balance of interests? For years, rights owners and users have been negotiating licenses for the production and distribution of copyrighted works. On occasion, these contractual arrangements have purported to restrict the user's actions with respect to protected material, sometimes even beyond the bounds normally set by copyright law. More recently, the balance set by the copyright regime has come under greater strain than before in view of the increased use of standard form contracts that aim to regulate the end-users' permitted actions with respect to copyrighted material. Besides the provisions of copyright law, end-users of copyright material must often comply with contractual restrictions imposed by the rights owners.

Another key consideration for the future pertains to how evolving concepts of 'creation' and 'creators' may further strain some basic assumptions of 'authorship' under conventional copyright law. As discussed in this and other chapters, opportunities from digital technology and the Internet are blurring the lines between 'producer' and 'consumer' of cultural works, even though the observed phenomenon

[122] As discussed earlier, the laws in different countries treat this issue differently: German law insists, for example, that 'rights of natural authors' cannot be assigned or undermined by contract.

[123] The Association of Photographers in the United Kingdom, for example, actively provides guidance to its members to deal collectively with issues relating to contracts.

of incremental, participatory creative processes is not itself a new one – 'communal' concepts of creation behind the TCEs of indigenous peoples have long challenged assumptions of individual creators under conventional copyright law (see Chapter 5). Tracing some trends in contemporary art, Dufrenne (1979, p. 203) notes, moreover, how many contemporary artists are establishing a relationship with the 'public' which is more 'fraternal', rather than one emphasizing the divide between 'creators' and their 'audience':

> They offer the public (if it still wants it) the dignity of co-creator, for they have come to realize that the act of creation is not complete until a work is received, with the necessary perception, in a manifestation of sensibility. And sometimes, they go farther still. Just as certain musical compositions leave it to the interpreter to choose the order of the pieces, or allow him to improvise in accordance with his 'reflexes', so certain kinetic works look to the audience to 'perform' them. The creator then stands aside, delegating to other partners, delegating to his audience the task of pulling the strings. But he may also give way to other partners, when he works as part of a team, more democratically than formerly in the studies of the masters and in medieval corporations. (Ibid.)

Is the comment that 'all art is, to some degree, appropriation art' entirely spurious? To the extent that creative endeavours are seen as a result of social networks (see Chapter 1), this calls for a fresh look especially at the economic incentive theories for copyright which focus on individual creators, as well as a rethinking of the prevalent concepts of 'copying' and transformation of copyright protected works by users. There is room, for example, for the 'rights of users' under the IP system to be better articulated. Sun (2007) suggests that more attention should be paid towards rethinking the 'legal status' of users. Can one, for example, rethink the exceptions to copyright in terms of a user's right of access not only to cultural goods but also to cultural participation (see Sunder 2008; Beutz Land 2009)?

A number of commentators have explored the relevance of human rights in grounding reforms to IP law at the international and national levels (Afori 2004; Ovett 2006; Beutz Land 2009).[124] Discussing the possibility of an international instrument 'codifying user freedoms expressed not in the language of copyright, but in terms of fundamental (human) rights and freedoms proper', Hugenholtz and Okediji (2008, pp. 30–31) note that:

> The norms of such a freedoms-based international instrument – say, a 'Treaty on User Freedoms' – might include user freedoms reflecting the 'hard core' of fundamental rights and freedoms (notably freedom of expression and information and protection of privacy) as well as softer 'welfare rights', such as cultural freedoms, right to education, etc. A major advantage of such a human rights-based instrument would be that it could define user freedoms not as (negative) 'exceptions' to property rights, but in terms of positive 'rights' or freedoms.

Hugenholtz and Okediji point out that 'this approach would keep more or less intact a coherent framework of international IP law, while making intellectual property

[124] Afori (2004) explores how human rights might inform a rethinking of US copyright law, searching for 'natural rights' underpinnings in both copyright and human rights.

"subservient" to (the higher objectives of) human rights' (ibid.).[125] They add that: 'In doing so, the law of international copyright would immediately reflect the general public interest – as an overriding norm, not as an afterthought in the final part of a three-step test' (ibid., p. 30). Suggesting some limitations to the human rights approach, however, the authors call for an international instrument 'grounded in the law of copyright' to codify exceptions and limitations across the board (ibid., pp. 31–32; see Chapter 7).

Some commentaries look at pushing flexibilities within domestic copyright exceptions, rethinking underlying 'fair use' doctrines (Fisher 1988), or better calibrating the three-step test on the basis of notions of 'balance'.[126] Others have called for a more fundamental rethinking of copyright law. In a lecture in 1996 entitled 'Copyright: Over Strength, Over-Regulated, Over-Rated?', then UK High Court judge Sir Hugh Laddie (1996, p. 259) invited the audience to 'stand back and imagine that we were not building our copyright law on a foundation of accumulated rights, commercial interests and monetary expectations':

> Imagine that we have just a blank sheet of paper and are being invited to create a copyright law now from scratch for the new millennium and that the purpose is to give some reasonable measure of protection to those who write books or computer programmes or make films for television. Would we really choose to construct a monopoly which might last a century and a half? Would we really make it a crime to copy even quite small parts of the copyright work throughout those many decades? . . . I think not. But, if we are going to start with a fresh piece of paper, let us do a proper job and really start from first principles. . . . (Ibid.)

This gauntlet seems to be taken up by an interesting initiative underway called 'Copyright 2010'. This project seeks 'to rethink the basic principles of copyright law from scratch, putting the public interest first and taking into account the interests of both developed and developing countries'.[127] More radical are some of the future scenarios developed by Halbert (1996), as discussed earlier, where IPRs including copyright no longer play a role in cultural creation (see further Halbert 2001, discussed in Chapter 9).

Meanwhile, political and economic forces continue to drive the future alongside ideological shifts. Conventional justifications for copyright may be based on rewarding the individual creator's efforts, but rampant copyright assignment and a marked presence of corporate ownership of IP assets in major sectors of the cultural industries drive a lot of the agenda for copyright and other IP reforms at the national and international levels. Several chapters of this book have noted how continued trade pressures on developing countries from certain developed countries, at the behest of industrial lobbyists, have shaped the negotiation and impact

[125] Citing Drahos 1999.

[126] See the 'Declaration on a Balanced Interpretation of the Three-Step Test in Copyright Law' initiated by four well-known copyright scholars: C. Geiger, J. Griffiths, R. Hilty and U. Suthersanen, available at http://www.ip.mpg.de/ww/en/pub/news/declaration_on_the_three_step_.cfm (accessed 31 March 2010).

[127] John Howkins (pers. comm.). This initiative, which involves proponents of the Adelphi Charter (http://www.adelphicharter.org), the Queensland Technological University (www.law.qut.edu.au), and others, is expected to culminate in an international conference to coincide with the 300th anniversary of the world's first copyright law, the Statute of Queen Anne (1710). See Fitzgerald 2008.

of FTAs. Some of these agreements transplant US normative standards into other legal regimes without necessarily exporting the accompanying exceptions and limitations in US law that seek to provide a crucial balance between private and public interests.[128] Pressures on developing countries for copyright enforcement, and the increasing tendency in both developed and developing countries to 'criminalize' forms of copyright infringement, also have immediate consequences on human well-being and the informal sectors within societies. What unintended consequences might result from those measures lobbied for by the US, the EU and the transnational music, film and publishing industries, along with countermeasures advocated by oppositionists?[129] Is the adoption by developing countries of an 'Access to Knowledge' (A2K) treaty a plausible future scenario?

As highlighted in this chapter, there is significant scope for examining more closely the relationship between copyright (and IPRs in general) and cultural diversity. The emerging ideas of cultural diversity are complex, and may in some ways be seen as a reaction to some of the perceived 'homogenizing' influences of globalization (UNDP 2004; see Section 3). Lundberg, Malm and Ronström (2003) suggest, moreover, that the discourse of 'cultural diversity' itself needs to be approached within the dynamics of how globalization has also accentuated the appreciation of the 'local'.[130] In a contemporary context where globalization and new technologies bring both threats and opportunities for cultural endeavours at the local level, could one perhaps view 'the tensions between the global and local' as in themselves constituting a driving force for further human creativity? Studying 'transcultural' music, Wallis and Malm (1984, p. xiv) remind us that:

> [H]uman beings have incredible qualities of resilience which can be called on when things dear to their hearts are threatened. The threat of being flooded by a nationless transnational music culture leads to counter-actions in the form of local sub-cultures.[131]

Without undermining the importance for professional creators to be able to maintain their livelihoods, there is a need to open up the discussion to embrace different cultural interpretations and motivations for creative activities. Spiritual pursuits, for example, marked the artistic and architectural endeavours in both the East and the West for centuries, and these dimensions continue to shape the cultural expressions of many peoples. Individuals in both secular and non-secular contexts

[128] Hinze, G. 2007, 'Latest U.S. Free Trade Agreement Contains New Twist', Electronic Frontier Foundation: Deeplinks Blog, 1 June 2007, available at: http://www.eff.org/deeplinks/2007/06/latest-u-s-free-trade-agreement-contains-new-twist (accessed 15 February 2009). Indeed, the US 'fair use' doctrine operates in the American constitutional context of Article 1, Section 8 (i.e. the intellectual property clause) and the First Amendment (i.e. free speech) and has limited relevance abroad. See further Abbott 2006.

[129] Comment received from Graham Dutfield.

[130] In *Music, Media, Multiculture: Changing Musicscapes,* Lundberg et al. assert that: '[T]he amplification of local identities during recent decades, is in itself a global phenomenon. The ideas about local identity as something important and desirable are globalised, like so many of the forms that are used to shape such local identities' (ibid.).

[131] Lundberg et al. (2003, p. 410) note that: 'A clear example from our cases studies of the close interaction between the global and the local is how the rapid concentration of the music industry to a few global conglomerates has created a growing space for small local companies that exploit the areas and niches that are too small for the big companies'.

continue to express themselves through art and other creative pursuits.[132] Through its current focus on economic incentives for creative activities, copyright law misses out on (or implicitly plays down) the many dynamics and motivations which drive creative endeavours by individuals and communities. What reforms to copyright law are needed to accommodate such diverse values and how can we think beyond copyright?[133]

If copyright is indeed about validating and incentivizing creative endeavours, then a better understanding of its relation to other economic rewards (such as subsidies to artists) and non-monetary incentives is needed. In particular, there is a strong case for copyright protection to be coordinated with the broader policy goals of cultural development as part of human development. Can we imagine, for example, a future scenario where domestic copyright policies are situated more properly within the sphere of cultural policy and development? As Towse (2007, p. 759) suggests:

> [C]opyright policy must be thought of as part of cultural policy (as it already is in some countries and the trend is increasing); logically, therefore, the objectives of cultural policy – fostering creativity, cultural diversity, freedom of information and expression, broadening audiences for cultural events, etc. – should be used to judge whether a reform to copyright law is a welfare improvement or not.

9. Conclusion

In this paper, we explored the role and effectiveness of copyright in incentivizing cultural works. We looked at how copyright thresholds and ownership structures relate to the cultural right of creators to the protection of their 'moral and material interests'. We noted that commonplace copyright assignment by creators to corporations in several sectors presents a contractual phenomenon that ultimately shifts the long-term benefits and interim control over many copyright-protected works away from individual creators. The interaction between contract law and copyright law is an area requiring further scrutiny. In some cases, the profits eventually made by intermediaries may bear little proportion to any benefits provided to the creator under a contract of copyright assignment or licence – few creators have the ability to 'valuate' their copyright accurately by making projections well into the future.

In examining whether copyright can incentivize a diversity of cultural creations, we also looked at the uneven protection for creators in different regions and sectors. There are still some significant lacunae in copyright protection, for example, for individuals working in the contemporary or performing arts, and communities

[132] While there are arguments of the 'Romantic genius pursuing art for art's sake at all costs' (Towse 2007, p. 759), one might perhaps look at the creative endeavours of young children for both intrinsic and social factors shaping creativity. See the Smithsonian website, 'Invention at Play', a 'traveling exhibit that focuses on the similarities between the way children and adults play and the creative processes used by innovators in science and technology', available at: http://invention.smithsonian.org/CENTERPIECES/iap/resources.html (accessed 29 March 2010). This approach 'departs from traditional representations of inventors as extraordinary geniuses who are "not like us", to celebrate the creative skills and processes that are familiar and accessible to all people' (ibid.).

[133] Some potential principles for copyright reform are discussed, for example, in Geller 2008; see also Fitzgerald 2008.

evolving TCEs. That creative expressions continue to thrive in these sectors suggest that other incentives and modes of validation beyond those considered in the copyright paradigm are actively at work. Returning to the various definitions of 'culture' put forward at the beginning of this chapter, it could be said that copyright, in fact, intersects with only a limited segment of cultural life and creative processes. The lack of relevance of copyright to the promotion of TCEs, for example, is recognized in Chapter 5, where other forms of IPRs, *sui generis* laws and non-legal options are explored.

To answer the question whether a diversity of cultural works is currently being incentivized by the copyright system, we also need to look at how individuals and communities make use of copyright works to improve their capabilities. Indeed, as the case study on contemporary art in Appendix E suggests, the line between creators and users is by no means clear in relation to cultural works. All creators, professional or amateur, need adequate access to the raw materials for their creations, in many cases building on the works of others. With creators on both sides in the trade-off between private and public interests in copyright law, it is not easy to find the appropriate balance. Linking copyright law and exceptions to the promotion of capabilities, including those for free expression, may provide new perspectives for reform.

REFERENCES

Abbott, F. 2006, 'Intellectual Property Provisions of Bilateral and Regional Trade Agreements in Light of U.S. Federal Law', *UNCTAD – ICTSD Project on IPRs and Sustainable Development Issue Paper No. 12,* available at: http://www.unctad.org/en/docs/iteipc20064_en.pdf (accessed 15 February 2009).

Adeney, E. 2006, *The Moral Rights of Authors and Performers: An International and Comparative Analysis,* Oxford University Press, New York.

Adorno, T.W. & Horkheimer, M. 1944, 'Enlightenment as Mass Deception', in *Dialectic of Enlightenment,* English translation (1979), Verso, London.

Adorno, T.W. 1997, *Aesthetic Theory,* translation by R. Hullot-Kentor in *Theory and History of Literature,* vol. 88, University of Minnesota Press, Minneapolis, MN.

Afori, O.F. 2004, 'Human Rights and Copyright: The Introduction of Natural Law Considerations into American Copyright Law', *Fordham Intellectual Property, Media & Entertainment Law Journal,* vol. 14, no. 2, pp. 497–565, available at: http://law.fordham.edu/publications/articles/200flspub6402.pdf (accessed 31 January 2009).

Arnold, R. 2008, *Performers' Rights,* 4th Edition, Sweet & Maxwell, London.

Band, J. 2009, 'The Long and Winding Road to the Google Books Settlement', *The John Marshall Review of Intellectual Property Law,* vol. 9, no. 227, pp. 227–329, available at: http://www.jmripl.com/Publications/Vol9/Issue2/Band.pdf (accessed 6 March 2010).

Barthes, R. 1967, 'Death of the Author', *Aspen,* nos. 5–6, available at: http://www.ubu.com/aspen/aspen5and6/threeEssays.html#barthes (accessed 15 April 2010).

Benjamin, W. 1938, 'The Work of Art in the Age of Mechanical Reproduction', in *Illuminations,* English translation by H. Zohn (1999), Pimlico, London.

Benkler, Y. 2006, *The Wealth of Networks: How Social Production Transforms Markets and Freedom,* Yale University Press, New Haven and London, available at: http://www.benkler.org/Benkler_Wealth_Of_Networks.pdf (accessed 21 December 2008).

Bently, L. 1994, 'Copyright and the Death of the Author in Literature and Law', *Book Review, Modern Law Review*, vol. 57, no. 6, pp. 973–986.

Berkman Center for Internet & Society & Garner 2005, *Copyright and Digital Media in a Post-Napster World: 2005 Update*, Harvard Law School, Cambridge, MA, available at: http://cyber.law.harvard.edu/media/wpsupplement2005 (accessed 24 January 2009).

Bettig, R. 1996, *Copyrighting Culture: The Political Economy of Intellectual Property*, Westview Press, Boulder, CO.

Beutz Land, M. 2008, 'Intellectual Property Rights and the Right to Participate in Cultural Life', *White Paper Series 08/09*, no. 2, Institute for Information Law and Policy, available at: http://www.nyls.edu/user_files/1/3/4/30/58/Beutz_Cultural_Rights.pdf (accessed 31 January 2009).

Beutz Land, M. 2009, 'Protecting Rights Online', *Yale Journal of International Law*, vol. 34, no. 1, pp. 1–46, available at: http://papers.ssrn.com/sol3/papers.cfm?abstract_id=1295448 (accessed 31 January 2010).

Boateng, B. 2005, 'Square Pegs in Round Holes? Cultural Production, Intellectual Property Frameworks, and Discourses of Power', in R.A. Ghosh (ed.), *CODE: Collaborative Ownership and the Digital Economy*, pp. 61–74, Massachusetts Institute of Technology Press, Cambridge, MA.

Bowrey, K. 2006, 'Alternative Intellectual Property? : Indigenous Protocols, Copyleft and New Juridifications of Customary Practice', *Macquarie Law Journal*, vol. 6, pp. 65–95.

Brennan, D. J. & Christie, A.F. 2000, 'Spoken Words and Copyright Subsistence in Anglo-American Law', *Intellectual Property Quarterly*, Issue 4, pp. 309–349.

Bullard, A. 2005, 'Reinvindicando a los Piratas. ¿Es La Propiedad Intelectual un Robo?', *Latin American and Caribbean Law and Economics Association (ALACDE) Annual Papers*, Paper 7, University of California, Berkeley, available at: http://repositories.cdlib.org/bple/alacde/7 (accessed 21 December 2008).

Caribbean Regional Negotiating Machinery (CARICOM) 2006, *The Cultural Industries in CARICOM*, Jamaica.

Carpenter, M.M. 2004, 'Intellectual Property Law and Indigenous Peoples: Adapting Copyright Law to the Needs of a Global Community', *Yale Human Rights and Development Law Journal*, vol. 7, no. 51, pp. 51–78.

Caves, R.E. 2000, *Creative Industries: Contracts between Art and Commerce*, Harvard University Press, Cambridge, MA.

Chander, A. & Sunder, M. 2007, 'Everyone's a Superhero: A Cultural Theory of "Mary Sue" Fan Fiction as Fair Use', *California Law Review*, vol. 95, no. 2, pp. 597–626.

Chowdhury, A.R. 2008, 'The Future of Copyright in India', *Journal of Intellectual Property Law and Practice*, vol. 3, no. 2, pp. 102–114, available at: http://jiplp.oxfordjournals.org/cgi/content/abstract/3/2/102 (accessed 14 May 2009).

Coates, J. 2007, 'Creative Commons – The Next Generation: Creative Commons License Use Five Years On', *SCRIPT-ed – A Journal of Law, Technology and Society*, vol. 4, no. 1, available at: http://www.law.ed.ac.uk/ahrc/script-ed/vol4-1/coates.asp (accessed 31 January 2009).

Cohen, J.E. 2006, 'Copyright, Commodification and Culture: Locating the Public Domain', in L. Guibault & P.B. Hugenholtz (eds.), *The Future of the Public Domain*, pp. 121–166, Kluwer Law International, available at: http://ssrn.com/abstract=663652 (accessed 1 June 2009).

Commission of the European Communities (EC Commission) 2008, *Green Paper on Copyright in the Knowledge Economy*, Doc. COM(2008) 466/3, Brussels, available at: http://eurlex.europa.eu/LexUriServ/LexUriServ.do?uri=COM:2008:0466:FIN:EN:PDF (accessed 14 May 2009).

Commission on Intellectual Property Rights (CIPR) 2002, *Integrating Intellectual Property Rights and Development Policy*, CIPR, London, available at: http://www.iprcommission.org/papers/pdfs/final_report/CIPRfullfinal.pdf (accessed 31 January 2009).

Committee on Economic, Social and Cultural Rights (CESCR) 2005, *General Comment No. 17: The right of everyone to benefit from the protection of the moral and material interests resulting from any scientific, literary or artistic production of which he or she is the author* (art. 15, para. 1 (c)), UN Doc. E/C.12/GC/17 (12 January 2006), available at: http://www.unhchr.ch/tbs/doc.nsf/7cec89369c43a6dfc1256a2a0027ba2a/03902145edbbe797c125711500584ea8/$FILE/G0640060.pdf (accessed 3 February 2010).

Committee on Economic, Social and Cultural Rights (CESCR) 2009, *General Comment No. 21: Right of everyone to take part in cultural life* (art. 15, para. 1 (a)), UN Doc. E/C.12/GC/21 (2009), available at: http://www2.ohchr.org/english/bodies/cescr/comments.htm (accessed 15 January 2010).

Cornish, W.R. 1999, *Intellectual Property: Patents, Copyright, Trade Marks and Allied Rights*, 4th Edition, Sweet and Maxwell, London.

Cornish, W.R. 2002, 'The Author as Risk-Sharer', *Columbia Journal of Law and the Arts*, vol. 26, no. 1, pp. 1–16.

Cornish, W.R. & Llewelyn, D. 2003, *Intellectual Property: Patents, Copyright, Trade Marks and Allied Rights*, 5th Edition, Sweet and Maxwell, London.

Crace, J. 2008, 'Harry Potter: The Last Battle', *The Guardian*, 11 March 2008, available at: http://www.guardian.co.uk/books/2008/mar/11/harrypotter.law (accessed 12 May 2009).

Darnton, R. 2009, 'Google and the Future of Books', *The New York Review of Books*, vol. 56, no. 2, available at: http://www.nybooks.com/articles/22281 (accessed 1 June 2009).

Desurmont, T. 2006, 'Considerations on the Relationship between the Convention on the Protection and Promotion of the Diversity of Cultural Expressions and the Protection of Authors' Rights', *e-Copy Bulletin Doctrine and Opinions*, United Nations Educational, Scientific and Cultural Organization (UNESCO), available at: http://portal.unesco.org/culture/en/files/32555/11655864341desurmont_en.pdf/desurmont_en.pdf (accessed 31 January 2009).

Dewey, J. 1934, *Art as Experience*, Perigee Trade, New York.

Dietz, A. 2006, 'Germany', in P.E. Geller (ed.), *International Copyright Law and Practice*, vol. 2, sec. 4(2), p. GER-55, LexisNexis, Newark, NJ.

Donders, Y. 2007, 'The Legal Framework of the Right to Take Part in Cultural Life', in Y. Donders & V. Volodin (eds.), *Human Rights in Education, Science and Culture: Legal Developments and Challenges*, UNESCO and Ashgate Publishing, Paris.

Donders, Y. & Volodin, V. (eds.) 2007, *Human Rights in Education, Science and Culture: Legal Developments and Challenges*, UNESCO and Ashgate Publishing, Paris.

Drahos, P. 1999, 'Intellectual Property and Human Rights', *Intellectual Property Law Quarterly*, vol. 1999, no. 3, pp. 349–371.

Drahos, P. & Braithwaite, J. 2002, *Information Feudalism – Who Owns the Knowledge Economy?*, Earthscan Publications Ltd., London.

Dufrenne, M. 1979, *Main Trends in Aesthetics and the Sciences of Art*, Holmes & Meier Publishers, Inc., New York and London.

Dutfield, G. & Suthersanen, U. 2007, 'Innovation and development', in U. Suthersanen, G. Dutfield & K.B. Chow (eds.), *Innovation Without Patents: Harnessing the Creative Spirit in a Diverse World*, pp. 3–12, Edgar Elgar Press, Cheltenham, UK.

Ficsor, M. 2002, 'How Much of What? The "Three-Step Test" and Its Application in Two Recent WTO Dispute Settlement Cases', *Revue Internationale du Droit D'Auteur*, vol. 192, pp. 110–251.

Fisher, W. 1988, 'Reconstructing the Fair Use Doctrine', *Harvard Law Review*, vol. 101, no. 8, pp. 1659–1759.

Fisher, W. 2001, 'Theories of Intellectual Property', in S.R. Munzer (ed.), *New Essays in the Legal and Political Theory of Property*, Cambridge University Press, New York.

Fitzgerald, B.F. 2008, 'Copyright 2010: The Future of Copyright', *European Intellectual Property Review*, vol. 30, no. 2, pp. 43–49.

Fitzgerald, B.F., Coates, J.M. & Lewis, S.M. (eds.) 2007, *Open Content Licensing: Cultivating the Creative Commons*, Sydney University Press, Sydney, available at: http://eprints.qut.edu.au/archive/00006677/ (accessed 31 January 2009).

Fitzgerald, B. & O'Brien, D. 2007, 'Digital Sampling and Culture Jamming in a Remix World: What Does the Law Allow?', in B.F. Fitzgerald, J.M. Coates & S.M. Lewis. (eds.), *Open Content Licensing: Cultivating the Creative Commons*, pp. 156–187, Sydney University Press, Sydney.

Foucault, M. 1979, 'What Is an Author?' in *The Foucault Reader*, P. Rabinow (ed.) 1984, Pantheon Books, New York; English translation reprinted from *Textual Strategies: Perspectives in Post-Structuralist Criticism*, J.V. Harari (ed.), Cornell University, Ithaca, NY.

Geller, P.E. 2008, 'Beyond the Copyright Crisis: Principles for Change, *Journal of the Copyright Society of the USA*, vol. 55, no. 2-3, pp. 165–200, available at: http://ssrn.com/abstract=1114372 (accessed 1 December 2009).

Gervais, D.J. 2005, 'Towards a New Core International Copyright Norm: The Reverse Three-Step Test', *Marquette Intellectual Property Law Review*, vol. 9, no. 1, pp. 1–35.

Ghosh, R.A & Soete, L. 2006, 'Information and Intellectual Property: The Global Challenges', *United Nations University – Maastricht Economic and Social Research and Training Centre on Innovation and Technology (UNU-MERIT) Working Paper Series #2006–029*, available at: http://www.merit.unu.edu/publications/wppdf/2006/wp2006–029.pdf (accessed 27 December 2008).

Ginsburg, J.C. 2001, 'Toward Supranational Copyright Law? The WTO Panel Decision and the "Three-Step Test" for Copyright', *Revue Internationale du Droit d'Auteur*, vol. 187, pp. 2–65, available at: http://ssrn.com/abstract=253867 (accessed 16 May 2009).

Goldstein, P. 2004, 'Paternalism and Autonomy in Copyright Contracts', in D. Vaver & L. Bently (eds.), *Intellectual Property in the New Millennium: Essays in Honour of William R. Cornish*, Cambridge University Press, New York.

Gollin, M. 2008, *Driving Innovation: Intellectual Property Strategies for a Dynamic World*, Cambridge University Press, New York.

Gomez, G. 2005, 'Threats and Opportunities for Cultural Diversity: WSIS between WTO and UNESCO', Instituto del Tercer Mundo (ITeM), Montevideo, Uruguay, available at: http://wsispapers.choike.org//papers/eng/gustavo_wto_wsis_unesco.pdf (accessed 1 June 2009).

Gowers, A. 2006, Gowers Review of Intellectual Property 2006, HM Treasury, London, available at: http://www.hm-treasury.gov.uk/d/pbr06_gowers_report_755.pdf (accessed 14 May 2009).

Guibault, L. 2002, 'Copyright Limitations and Contracts. An Analysis of the Contractual Overridability of Limitations on Copyright', *Information Law Series*, vol. 9, Kluwer Law International, London, The Hague and Boston.

Guibault, L. & Hugenholtz, P.B. 2003, 'The Nature and Scope of Limitations and Exceptions to Copyright and Neighbouring Rights with regard to General Interest Missions for the Transmission of Knowledge: Prospects for their Adaptation to the Digital Environment', *Copyright Bulletin*, December 2003, UNESCO, Paris.

Halbert, D.J. 1996, 'Intellectual Property Law, Technology and Our Probable Future', *Technological Forecasting and Social Change*, vol. 52, no. 2/3, pp. 147–160.

Halbert, D.J. 2001, 'Intellectual Property in the Year 2025' *Journal of Futures Studies*, vol. 6, no. 1, pp. 25–60, Tamkang University – Graduate Institute of Futures Studies, Taipei.

Heins, M. & Beckles, T. 2005, *Will Fair Use Survive? Free Expression in the Age of Copyright Control*, Brennan Center for Justice at New York University School of Law, available at: http://www.fepproject.org/policyreports/WillFairUseSurvive.pdf (accessed 31 January 2009).

Hilty, R., Kur, A., Klass, N., Geiger, C., Peukert, A., Drexl, J. & Katzenberger, P. 2008, 'Comment by the Max Planck Institute on the Commission's Proposal for a Directive to Amend Directive 2006/116 EC of the European Parliament and Council Concerning the Term of Protection for Copyright and Related Rights', 10 September 2008, *Max Planck Institute for Intellectual Property, Competition & Tax Law Research Paper Series No. 08–01*, available at: http://ssrn.com/abstract=1288620 (accessed 16 May 2009).

Hinze, G. 2007, 'Latest U.S. Free Trade Agreement Contains New Twist', *Deeplink*, Electronic Frontier Foundation (EFF), available at: http://www.eff.org/deeplinks/2007/06/latest-u-s-free-trade-agreement-contains-new-twist (accessed 31 January 2009).

Hirsch, E.D. 1967, 'In Defense of the Author', in *Validity in Interpretation*, pp. 1–23, Yale University Press, New Haven, CT.

Hodin, J.P. 1951, 'Contemporary Art: Its Definition and Classification', *College Art Journal*, vol. 10, no. 4, pp. 337–354.

Howkins, J. 2001, *The Creative Economy: How People Make Money from Ideas*, Penguin, London.

Hugenholtz, P.B. & Okediji, R.L. 2008, *Conceiving an International Instrument on Exceptions and Limitations to Copyright*, available at: http://www.ivir.nl/publicaties/hugenholtz/finalreport2008.pdf (accessed 18 January 2009).

Intellectual Property Office (IPO) 2009, *Taking Forward the Gowers Review of Intellectual Property: Second Stage Consultations on Copyright Exceptions*, IPO, UK, available at: http://www.ipo.gov.uk/consult-gowers2.pdf (accessed 5 March 2010).

Jones, R. 2007, 'Creative Commons and the Creative Industries: Perspectives from the Creative Industries', in B.F. Fitzgerald, J.M. Coates & S.M. Lewis (eds.), *Open Content Licensing: Cultivating the Creative Commons*, Sydney University Press, Sydney.

Keaney, E. 2006, *From Access to Participation: Cultural Policy and Civil Renewal*, Institute for Public Policy Research, London.

Koelman, K.J. 2006, 'Fixing the Three-Step Test', *European Intellectual Property Review*, vol. 28, no. 8, pp. 407–412.

Laddie, H. 1996, 'Copyright: Over-Strength, Over-Regulated, Over-Rated?', *European Intellectual Property Review*, vol. 18, no. 5, pp. 253–260.

Landes, W.M. 1999, *The Arts and Humanities in Public Life: Copyright Protection and Appropriation Art*, University of Chicago Law School, available at: http://culturalpolicy.uchicago.edu/conf1999/landes.html (accessed 31 January 2009).

Lange, D. 1981, 'Recognizing the Public Domain', *Law & Contemporary Problems*, vol. 44, no. 4 pp. 147–177, available at: http://www.law.duke.edu/pd/papers/lange_background.pdf (accessed 1 June 2009).

Lange, D. 2003, 'Reimagining the Public Domain', *Law & Contemporary Problems*, vol. 66, no. 1/2, pp. 463–483, available at: http://www.law.duke.edu/journals/lcp/downloads/LCP66DWinterSpring2003P463.p df (accessed 1 June 2009).

Lessig, L. 2004, *Free Culture: How Big Media Uses Technology and the Law to Lock Down Culture and Control Creativity*, Penguin Press, New York.

Lessig, L. 2007, 'The Vision for the Creative Commons: What Are We and Where Are We Headed? Free Culture', in B.F. Fitzgerald, J.M. Coates & S.M. Lewis, *Open Content Licensing: Cultivating the Creative Common*, Sydney University Press, pp. 36–50, available at: http://eprints.qut.edu.au/6677/1/6677.pdf (accessed 31 January 2009).

Liang, L. 2004, *A Guide to Open Content Licence*, Piet Zwart Institute, Willem de Kooning Academey Hogeschool, Rotterdam, available at: http://pzwart.wdka.hro.nl/mdr/pubsfolder/opencontentpdf (accessed 31 January 2009).

Litman, J. 1990, 'The Public Domain', *Emory Law Journal*, vol. 39, no. 4, pp. 965–989.

Long, P. 2001, *Openness, Secrecy, Authorship: Technical Arts and the Culture of Knowledge from Antiquity to the Renaissance*, Johns Hopkins University Press, Baltimore.

Lufkin, M. 2005, 'Why Harvard Had to Sign 45 Contracts to Install a Work by Pierre Huyghe', *The Art Newspaper*, 6 January 2005, London and New York.

Lundberg, D., Malm, K. & Ronström, O. 2003, *Music, Media, Multiculture: Changing Musicscapes*, Svenskt Visarkiv, Stockholm, available at: http://www.visarkiv.se/mmmindex.htm (accessed 31 January 2010).

McCutcheon, J. 2008, 'The New Defence of Parody or Satire under Australian Copyright Law', *Intellectual Property Quarterly*, Issue 2, pp. 163–192.

Merges, R.P., Menell, P.S. & Lemley, M.A. 2003, *Intellectual Property in the New Technological Age*, 3rd Edition, Aspen Publishers, New York.

Mizukami, P.N. & Lemos, R. 2008, 'From Free Software to Free Culture: The Emergence of Open Business', in L. Shaver (ed.), *Access to Knowledge in Brazil: New Research on Intellectual Property, Innovation and Development*, Information Society Project, Yale Law School, New Haven, CT, available at http://www.law.yale.edu/documents/pdf/ISP/A2KBrazil_bkmk.pdf (accessed 10 May 2010).

Morgan, O. 2002, *International Protection of Performers' Rights*, Hart Publishing, Oxford.

Munoz Tellez, V. & Waitara, C. 2007, 'A Development Analysis of the Proposed WIPO Treaty on the Protection of Broadcasting and Cablecasting Organizations', *Research Paper No. 9*, South Center, Geneva, available at: http://www.southcentre.org/index.php?option=com_content&task=view&id=66 (accessed 14 May 2009).

Nussbaum, M.C. 2000, *Women and Human Development: The Capabilities Approach*, Cambridge University Press, Cambridge.

Oguamanam, C. 2008, 'Local Knowledge as Trapped Knowledge: Intellectual Property, Culture, Power and Politics', *The Journal of World Intellectual Property*, vol. 11, no. 1, pp. 29–57.

Opderbeck, D.W. 2008, 'Deconstructing Jefferson's Candle: Towards a Critical Realist Approach to Cultural Environmentalism and Information Policy', *Seton Hall Public Law Research Paper No. 1091024*, available at: http://ssrn.com/abstract=1091024 (accessed 26 February 2010).

Organisation for Economic Co-operation and Development (OECD) 2007, *Participative Web and User-Created Content*, OECD, available at: http://www.oecd.org/dataoecd/57/14/38393115.pdf (accessed 14 May 2009).

Ovett, D. 2006, 'Intellectual Property and Human Rights: Is the Distinction Clear Now?: An Assessment of the Committee on Economic, Social and Cultural Rights' General Comment No. 17 (2005)', *3D Policy Brief 3*, available at: http://www.3dthree.org/pdf_3D/3D_GC17_IPHR.pdf (accessed 31 January 2009).

Penna, F.J., Thormann, M. & Finger, J.M. 2004, 'The Africa Music Project', in J.M. Finger & P. Schuler (eds.), *Poor People's Knowledge: Promoting Intellectual Property in Developing Countries*, World Bank and Oxford University Press.

Pitrout, J. 2006, 'An Authors' Rights-based Copyright Law: The Fairness and Morality of French and American Law Compared', *Cardozo Arts and Entertainment*, vol. 24, no. 549, pp. 549–615.

Prott, L.V. 1998a, 'Understanding One Another on Cultural Rights', in H. Niec. (ed.), *Cultural Rights and Wrongs: A Collection of Essays in Commemoration of the 50th Anniversary of the University Declaration of Human Rights*, Institute of Art & Law, UNESCO, Paris.

Prott, L.V. 1998b, 'Cultural Rights as Peoples' Rights in International Law', in J. Crawford (ed.), *The Rights of Peoples*, pp. 93–106, Clarendon Press, Oxford.

Raustiala, K. & Sprigman, C. 2006, 'The Piracy Paradox: Innovation and Intellectual Property in Fashion Design', *Virginia Law Review*, vol. 92, no. 8, pp. 1687–1777, available at: http://ssrn.com/abstract=878401 (accessed 31 January 2009).

Reese, R.A. 2008, 'Transformativeness and the Derivative Work Right', *Columbia Journal of Law & the Arts*, vol. 31, pp. 467–494.

Rens, A., Prabhala, A. & Kawooya, D. 2006, 'Intellectual Property, Education and Access to Knowledge in Southern Africa', *ICTSD Regional Research Paper Southern and Eastern Africa*, International Centre for Trade and Sustainable Development (ICTSD), Geneva, available at: http://www.iprsonline.org/unctadictsd/docs/06%2005%2031%20tralac%20amended-pdf.pdf (accessed 18 January 2009).

Roberts, G. 2009, 'Rowling Powerless to Block "Potter Guide"', *The Independent*, 3 January 2009, available at: http://www.independent.co.uk/arts-entertainment/books/news/rowling-powerless-to-block-potter-guide-1222855.html (accessed 10 March 2010).

Rochlitz, R. 1996, *The Disenchantment of Art: The Philosophy of Walter Benjamin*, Guildford Press, New York and London.

Rogers, B. 2006, 'Foreword', in E. Keaney, *From Access to Participation: Cultural Policy and Civil Renewal*, Institute for Public Policy Research, London.

Rogoff, B. 2003, *The Cultural Nature of Human Development*, Oxford University Press, New York.

Rose, M. 1993, *Authors and Owners: The Invention of Copyright*, Harvard University Press, London and Cambridge, MA.

Samuelson, P. 2006, 'Enriching Discourse on Public Domains', *Duke Law Journal*, vol. 55, no. 4, pp. 783–834, available at: http://ssrn.com/abstract=925052 (accessed 26 February 2010).

Samuelson, P. (forthcoming), 'Google Book Search and the Future of Books in Cyberspace', *Minnesota Law Review*, available at: http://papers.ssrn.com/sol3/papers.cfm?abstract˙id=1535067 (accessed 6 March 2010).

Sen, A.K. 1985, *Commodities and Capabilities*, Elsevier Science Publishers, Oxford.

Sherman, B. & Bently, L. 1995, *Performers' Rights: Options for Reform – Consultants Report for the Interdepartmental Committee*, Department of Communications and the Arts, Canberra.

Stavenhagen, R. 1998, 'Cultural Rights: A Social Science Perspective', in H. Niec. (ed.), *Cultural Rights and Wrongs*, UNESCO, Paris.

Stokes, S. 2003, *Art and Copyright*, Hart Publishing, Oxford.

Strathern 2005, 'Imagined Collectivities and Multiple Authorship', in R.A. Ghosh. (ed.), *CODE: Collaborative Ownership and the Digital Economy*, MIT Press, Cambridge, MA.

Sun, H.C. 2007, 'Overcoming the Achilles Heel of Copyright Law', *Northwestern Journal of Technology and Intellectual Property*, vol. 5, no. 2, pp. 265–331, available at: http://ssrn.com/abstract=1021027 (accessed 1 June 2009).

Sunder, M. 2008, 'Intellectual Property and Development as Freedom', in N.W. Netanel (ed.), *The Development Agenda: Global Intellectual Property and Developing Countries*, Oxford University Press, New York.

Suthersanen, U. 2007, 'Copyright Law: A Stakeholder's Palimpsest', in F. Macmillan (ed.), *New Directions in Copyright Law*, vol. 5, Edward Elgar, Cheltenham, UK.

Suthersanen, U. 2008, 'A2K and the WIPO Development Agenda: Time to List the "Public Domain"', *UNCTAD-ICTSD Projects on IPRs and Sustainable Development*, Policy Brief No. 1, December 2008, UNCTAD-ICTSD.

Takeyama, L. 1994, 'The Welfare Implications of Unauthorized Reproduction of Intellectual Property in the Presence of Demand Network Externalities', *Journal of Industrial Economics*, vol. 42, no. 2, pp. 155–166.

Towse, R. 2007, 'The Singer or the Song? Developments in Performers' Rights from the Perspective of a Cultural Economist', *Review of Law and Economics*, vol. 3, no. 3, article 6, available at: http://www.bepress.com/rle/vol3/iss3/art6 (accessed 31 January 2009).

Tushnet, R. 2008, 'User-Generated Discontent: Transformation in Practice', *Columbia Journal of Law & the Arts*, vol. 31, pp. 497–516, available at: http://ssrn.com/abstract=1146461 (accessed 14 May 2009).

United Nations (UN) 2008, *Creative Economy Report – The Challenge of Assessing the Creative Economy: Towards Informed Policy-Making*, available at: http://www.unctad.org/en/docs/ditc20082cer_en.pdf (accessed 31 January 2009).

United Nations Development Programme (UNDP) 2004, *UNDP Human Development Report 2004: Cultural Liberty in Today's Diverse World*, UNDP, New York.

United Nations Educational, Scientific and Cultural Organization (UNESCO) 2004, *UNESCO and the Issue of Cultural Diversity: Review and Strategy 1946–2004*, UNESCO, available at: http://portal.unesco.org/culture/en/files/12900/10958784163DivCult-BilanStrategies-ENG-sept04.pdf/DivCult-BilanStrategies-ENG-sept04.pdf (accessed 31 January 2009).

United States Copyright Office 2006, *Report on Orphan Works*, available at: http://www.copyright.gov/orphan/orphan-report-full.pdf (accessed 16 May 2009).

Vander Ark, S. 2009, *The Lexicon: An Unauthorized Guide to Harry Potter Fiction and Related Materials*, RDR Books, Muskegon, MI.

Vogel, J. 1998, in G. Schricker (ed.), *Urheberrecht: Kommentar*, 2nd Edition, Beck, Munich.

Wade, A. 2003, 'Can You Own an Idea?', *The Guardian*, 6 May 2003, available at: http://www.guardian.co.uk/law/story/0,3605,949979,00.html (accessed 31 January 2009).

Wallis, R. & Malm, K. 1984, *Big Sounds from Small Peoples: The Music Industry in Small Countries*, Pendragon Press, New York and London.

Walravens, N. 2005, 'L'oeuvre d'Art en Droit d'Auteur, Forme et Originalité des Oeuvres d'Art Contemporaines', *Economica*, Institut d'Etudes Supérieures des Arts (IESA).

Watt, R. 2004, 'The Past and the Future of the Economics of Copyright', *Review of Economic Research on Copyright Issues*, vol. 1, no. 1, pp. 151–171, available at: http://ssrn.com/abstract=1143022 (accessed 12 May 2009).

Weatherall, K.G. 2006, '"Pretend-y Rights"': On the Insanely Complicated New Regime for Performers' Rights in Australia, and How Australian Performers Got Gypped', in F. Macmillan & K. Bowrey, *New Directions in Copyright Law*, vol. 3, pp. 171–197, Edward Elgar Press, Cheltenham, UK, available at: http://ssrn.com/abstract=809905 (accessed 14 May 2009).

Wood, J. 2008, *How Fiction Works*, Farrar, Straus and Giroux, New York.

Woodmansee, M. 1984, 'The Genius and the Copyright: Economic and Legal Conditions of the Emergence of the 'Author'', *Eighteenth Century Studies*, vol. 17, no. 4, pp. 425–448, available at: http://www.compilerpress.atfreeweb.com/Anno%20Woodmansee%20Genius%20&%20Copyright.htm (accessed 12 May 2009).

Woodmansee, M. 1993, *The Author, Art and the Market: Rereading the History of Aesthetics*, Columbia University Press, New York.

World Intellectual Property Organization (WIPO) 2004, *WIPO Intellectual Property Handbook: Policy, Law and Use*, WIPO Publication No. 489(E), WIPO, Geneva.

WIPO 2005, *Understanding Copyright*, WIPO Publication No. 909(E), WIPO, Geneva.

WIPO Standing Committee on Copyrights and Related Rights 2008, *Study on Copyright Limitations and Exceptions for Libraries and Archives* (prepared by K. Crews) SCCR, WIPO Geneva, Doc. SSCR/17/2, available at: http://www.wipo.int/edocs/mdocs/copyright/en/sccr_17/sccr_17_2.pdf (accessed 17 May 2009).

9

Scenario planning on the future of intellectual property: Literature review and implications for human development

Michael A. Gollin, Gwen Hinze and Tzen Wong[1]

Introduction

This chapter summarizes scenario planning relating to intellectual property (IP). Future scenarios are stories created to describe alternative future outcomes, each a plausible example of what might happen under particular assumptions (see Millennium Ecosystem Assessment 2005). Participants in scenario planning develop these stories of possible outcomes through a process of identifying the driving forces and uncertainties existing today (McNeely 2005, p. 62). The intention of scenarios is to consider a wide variety of possible futures rather than to focus on the accurate prediction of a single outcome (Evans et al. 2006, p. 6). Thus, future scenarios are not predictions, forecasts or projections. Projections need to be grounded in empirical evidence and accepted assumptions about trends.[2] Since IP comprises such a broad spectrum of legal rights, each subject to trends of uncertain duration and consistency, few credible projections relating to the future of IP exist. Given the complex driving forces and multiple stakeholders shaping IP and human development, scenario planning may present an interesting alterative tool for exploring the future.

Section 1 introduces scenario planning as a tool for planning processes pertaining to IP and development. Section 2 discusses the most ambitious scenario planning process so far in the IP arena, conducted by the European Patent Office on 'Intellectual Property in the Year 2025', along with other scenario work addressing IP globally. Sections 3 and 4 explore how scenario planning has been used to address particular themes on IP and human development, such as the future of the public domain and the implications of new technology. Other potential themes for scenario planning are suggested along the way. Section 5 describes the World Intellectual Property Organization (WIPO) Development Agenda and suggests how scenario planning might help the multiple stakeholders clarify future directions for this agenda.

1. Scenario planning and intellectual property

Any discussion of IP rights inevitably involves a tension between the interests of right holders in creative works who want to control access to their works, and other

[1] Invaluable text and comments have been received from Claire Comfort, Graham Dutfield, Hans Haugen Morten, Fred von Lohmann, Savita Mullapudi Narasimhan, Manuel Ruiz and Matt Spannagle towards sections of this chapter.

[2] Quite in contrast to future scenarios, projections have been defined as 'estimates of future conditions based on the study of recent ones' (McNeely 2005, p. 62).

people who want to gain access to these works, including those creating new innovations. The tension between exclusivity and access cannot be resolved without a fair and balanced system of IP laws to provide limited exclusivity and sufficient access consistent with the public interest (Gollin 2009). The requisite balance is dynamic and unstable and is tested and retested with each new technology, along with continued economic shifts and global development. Any new tool to help find that balance should be welcome. Scenario planning may be such a tool.

Scenario planning has its origins in military and corporate strategic planning (Evans et al. 2006, p. 11). However, it has increasingly been applied by international organizations and non-governmental organizations (NGOs) to help convey a longer-term vision in their strategic planning processes. In their publication *What If: The Art of Scenario Thinking for Nonprofits,* Scearce and Fulton (2004, p. 8) outline the scenario planning process and its potential:

> The scenario thinking process begins by identifying forces of change in the world, such as new technologies or the shifting role of government, that may have an impact on the people served by a nonprofit organization, as well as on the strategic direction of the nonprofit itself. These forces are combined in different ways to create a set of diverse stories about how the future could unfold. Once these futures have been created, the next step is to try to imagine what it would be like for an organization or community to live in each of these futures. The exercise may sound simple – and in many cases it is. But the results are often surprising and profound. In the process of adding detail and color to each future, new issues or strategic concerns rise to the surface, and old issues get reframed.

Our literature survey suggests that scenario planning is still at its nascent stages in IP-related areas, but it has great potential for encouraging forward-thinking and creative solutions to some of the complex debates about IP. Apart from a handful of notable exceptions which are discussed and analysed in this chapter, the scenario planning approach remains quite new to IP-related organizations and professionals. Although there are many published positions and recommendations about IP, there are few attempts to use future scenarios to inform these recommendations or to visualize their consequences. In the following sections, we highlight existing scenario plans produced by organizations and commentators in relation to IP, and address some gaps in the current literature. Along with other themes discussed, a scenario planning process could be helpful for clarifying future directions for the WIPO Development Agenda.[3]

2. Intellectual property in the year 2025

Our literature survey identified two future scenario plans relating explicitly to IP in the year 2025. These plans highlight geopolitical trends and ambitiously try to map the future role of IP within these larger, tectonic shifts. The first plan resulted from the European Patent Office (EPO)'s scenario planning process completed in April 2007, the most extensive and innovative process of its kind in the IP sector.

[3] Searce and Fulton (2004, p. 20) discuss a 'decision tree' for determining 'whether scenario thinking is an appropriate tool' for addressing a particular challenge.

The other scenario plan consists of alternative stories on IP in the year 2025, by Halbert (2001). While not the outcome of an institutional scenario planning process, the latter scenario plan nevertheless presents a useful comparison with the EPO scenario plan.

2.1. European Patent Office scenarios on the future of IP

The EPO scenario planning took three years and involved interviews with approximately 100 academics, patent office officials, activists and practitioners in the field. The EPO's goal was to listen to a cacophony of voices from all over the world in order to find ways to ensure that the IP system 'remains fit for its purpose in support of innovation, competitiveness and economic growth for the benefit of the citizens of Europe' (Introductory letter from EPO President Alain Pompidou). The EPO paid particular attention to transformative innovation in biotechnology, nanotechnology, robotics and the patent system. However, they also pursued interconnections between multiple areas of IP, including the intersection between IP and ethics and the proper balance between the rights of developed and developing countries.

A 124-page report was completed and presented in April 2007 by the EPO. The report is entitled *Scenarios for the Future: How Might IP Regimes Evolve by 2025? What Global Legitimacy Might Such Regimes Have?* ('EPO Report').[4] Based on the extensive interviews it conducted, the EPO decided to identify several plausible holistic long-range IP scenarios. These scenarios are complex stories about the potential consequences of the decisions countries and organizations are being asked to make today.[5] A simplistic scenario – a world without any IP laws at all – was not analysed in detail because it was seen as not plausible in view of the history of IP law and practice as it has evolved over the past several centuries. Some of the current pressures shaping the future of IP systems, as identified in the report, include new technologies, territorial expansion, increased desire to protect even minor innovations with IP rights, and fears about the risks of new technologies.

The EPO identified five particularly influential driving forces that may shape the future of IP. First, power relationships are in flux – due in part to globalization and cross-cutting alliances formed between and among multinational corporations, global networks of civil society, special interest organizations and international bodies and trade blocs – such that it is not clear who will have authority over the IP system in the future. Second, a global jungle of competition emerges among local communities and countries, companies and industry groups and market sectors

[4] EPO 2007, *Scenarios for the Future: How Might IP Regimes Evolve by 2025? What Global Legitimacy Might Such Regimes Have?*, EPO, Munich [hereinafter 'EPO Report']. See also EPO 2006.

[5] According to the EPO Report: 'Scenarios are challenging, relevant and plausible stories about the future, used as tools to generate policy dialogue. They do not attempt to predict the future, but set out the landscape of a wider environment…By taking a long-term view, it is possible to examine a range of possible realistic outcomes that might have to be faced and therefore make more informed decisions …Scenarios are concerned with the external driving forces over which an organisation or system has little or no control: the political, economic, societal, ethical, technological, environmental and historical pressures that could impact the system and the way it functions. The issues at stake and the most likely driving forces that might force change on the system are identified by a team of scenario builders as a collective brainstorming process' (ibid., p. 13).

and workforces, making it hard to predict which ones will survive and which will not. Third, a faster rate of change in technology and economics contrasts with slower changes in human psychology, culture and the environment. Fourth, interdependence creates massive systemic risks and poses a threat of regional, ethnic and cultural conflicts. Fifth, a paradox exists between the increasing use of IP rights to restrict innovation and the increased availability of knowledge around the world. The EPO refers to this fragmented but interconnected world with dramatic demographic shifts as a 'Kaleidoscope Society', one in which no trends dominate and accurate predictions are impossible. These five influential driving forces are said to affect both the legal systems and the practices organizations use to operate within them.

Based on its view of the present situation and the five driving forces, the EPO imagined four separate scenarios that could result from these driving forces. The assumptions in each scenario overlap. However, projecting the analysis in each case over a twenty-year period results in very different futures. The following is a summary of key points drawn from the EPO scenarios:[6]

(1) **Market Rules:** Here, business has its way. This is the most familiar scenario.[7] Projecting forward, new forms of technology are patentable, and more people seek patent protection. Corporations use patent portfolios to dominate particular technologies. Patents are traded as financial assets. Given the sheer volume of patent applications, a global patent treaty is finally implemented. Market forces dominate, with anti-competition laws as the principle tool for curbing abuse of the system and correcting problems such as boom-bust economic cycles. Successful business lobbying would signal a trend in this direction, where success would be defined by speed and efficiency.

(2) **Whose Game:** In this scenario, geopolitics dominates the IP agenda. Players in wealthy countries fail to maintain technical superiority with strong IP rights, and some developing countries catch up, while others migrate to a communal use paradigm. Differences among IP systems are increasingly used as weapons in trade wars between nations and trade blocs. Global enforcement becomes more difficult in an increasingly fragmented world. A trend in this direction would be signalled by assertiveness by new entrants (such as China, Brazil and India), and success would be defined in terms of a mindset of 'my society wins'.

The EPO Report discusses genetic resources and traditional knowledge (TK) in this scenario, observing that developing countries are asserting new forms of IP protection for these innovation assets (ibid., p. 55). Under the scenario, the expansion of IP rights under the TRIPS Agreement and more protective TRIPS-plus bilateral agreements has not satisfied the demand for technology transfer to developing countries for medicine and seeds, leading

[6] The synthesis and analysis of the EPO scenarios was contributed by Michael Gollin.

[7] But other scenarios are becoming increasingly plausible with more stakeholders ready to fight for their alternative approaches. 'This transition has happened so quickly that it has been hard for many inside the world of patents and intellectual property to recognise all the changes and adapt to the very different environment in which they now operate' (EPO 2007, p. 13).

to tensions about compulsory licensing of drugs and other controversial initiatives for 'catch-up' development (ibid., pp. 59–63). Drugs are meanwhile freely available under this scenario. Projecting forward in this scenario, weak economies in the developed countries and low investment in research lead many scientists to move to intermediate countries like China and India. This scientific emigration dramatically increases the levels of innovation in intermediate countries. This shift in innovation eventually leads to a bipolar world: a bloc of North America and Europe and an Asian-South American bloc. Africa is not highlighted in this scenario.

(3) **Trees of Knowledge:** Social groups are the dominant force in this scenario. Heightened criticism and distrust lead to an erosion of the IP system. In an increasingly kaleidoscopic society, fleeting alliances form around specific issues and crises, such as health, knowledge, food and entertainment. Popular movements and the media drive towards dominance an A2K (access to knowledge) approach, with reward for innovation being secondary. A rise in political impacts on the IP system would signal a move in this direction, where success is measured by broad social acceptance.

The tension between private property and public good is emphasized in this scenario. The open access movement is examined in more detail than in the first two scenarios, as an example of conflicting and overlapping licensing practices, technological innovation and copyright and patent law restrictions. Tensions among artists, studios and media consumers polarize to a point where the debate becomes dominated by civil society interest groups (such as anti-IP pirates and copy-left advocates of freedom) who do not support IP for media. This change pushes the entertainment industry to explore new models. Similar tensions exist among scientific researchers who are not only pushing for open access to scientific information (like genetic sequence data) but also operating in collaboration with industry (e.g. under the US Bayh-Dole Act) and therefore pursuing patent protection. Technology causes tension because of its environmental, economic, philosophical and religious implications, and IP becomes a topic in resulting debates, for example, over medicine and whether strong patent protection promotes innovation or, instead, simply creates inappropriate incentives for incremental inventions.

Projecting forward to 2025 in this scenario, a flood of trivial patents leads to patents becoming available only for mechanical and chemical inventions, not for genetics and software. An open access political movement results in a weaker copyright regime for books and digital media. However, this weaker and highly digitized copyright regime is potentially advantageous because it supports widespread dissemination and sharing of information. Politicized patent offices evolve to serve as knowledge agencies implementing various incentive programmes. A global pandemic results in a 'patents kill' movement, and leads to demands for limitations on patentability and the expansion of compulsory licensing. Prizes, grants and advance purchase commitments are used in an attempt to fill in gaps in private research. Likewise, a global blight in maize and soybeans leads to a public model for agricultural research, in contrast to a concentration of the global seed market among very few multinational corporations (a situation which could have resulted in reduced research). Secrecy and branding become the primary protectors of innovation, and some areas like biotechnology wither in importance. Politics comes to dominate research and innovation, rather than science and market forces.

(4) **Blue Skies:** In this scenario, technology is the main driver in a fragmented world. Incremental innovations are protected under a legal system that is essentially the same as the current one. However, with fast-moving technology, patents become less important. Meanwhile, special IP practices apply to integrative technologies in biotechnology, information technology and nanotechnology. Integrative technologies are crucial to overcoming challenges like disease and hunger. Novel licensing practices such as pooling and compulsory licensing prevent blockage and profiteering, and promote collaboration and diffusion of these critical technologies.

Looking ahead to 2025, a soft IP system (with access in exchange for mandatory payments) is applied to most technologies, including environmental technology addressing climate change and technologies in the telecommunications sector. Patent offices use technology to become more efficient, but are burdened by the need to administer complex licensing systems. An international IP court resolves some disputes. Soft patents work to foster collaboration in the pharmaceutical and other similar industries. Open source approaches become integrated into the international IP system. The Report predicts growing tension between the new and classic technology sectors, with success being measured in terms of technology diffusion and resilience.

The EPO Report concludes that dramatic change in the future of IP is likely, and that the results will resemble some hybrid of the aforementioned scenarios. The EPO Report furthermore invites readers to form workshops to develop their own scenarios (ibid., p. 111).

2.2. Analysis of EPO scenarios

In summary, the EPO's set of four challenging, relevant and plausible scenarios describes four possible future worlds. Each of the possible scenarios was defined in accordance with a strong driving force – the business market ('Market Rules'), geopolitics ('Whose Game'), civil society ('Trees of Knowledge') and technology ('Blue Skies') – that could come to dominate the future of IP and its role in our world.

The EPO Report is an excellent and inspiring example of creative thinking by a regional intergovernmental agency and the first large-scale effort applying scenario planning to the IP field. The success of the end product demonstrates the value of scenario planning in IP policy. However, the EPO Report has gaps that limit its usefulness for developing countries and future non-profit interventions. First, it operates at a level of abstraction which renders it difficult to apply towards concrete paths and strategic solutions for most organizations whose work overlaps with

IP. Future scenario planning on IP should focus instead on closely defined themes (such as, for example, those in this book) in order to yield practical results to which stakeholders can both relate and contribute. It might be more helpful in some cases to conduct scenario planning according to innovation sector instead of by societal driver/political influence groups. For example, scenario planning on the future of traditional knowledge (TK) protection would be more useful for informing policies and strategies in TK-related areas (see some TK-related considerations for scenario planning in Chapter 4, Box 4.6) than a general scenario planning study is. The EPO Report gives uneven amounts of attention to different sectors. Open source issues, science and entertainment were given much attention. In contrast, agriculture was only dealt with in a few places. Of the sectors of interest to developing countries and marginalized groups, only health was singled out for separate treatment (ibid., p. 100; these health-related scenarios have been analysed in Chapter 2). Areas such as TK and biodiversity were only treated nominally.

Second, because of its European focus, the EPO report only deals with emerging economies peripherally and all but ignores dynamics within the least developed countries. For example, while the 'Market Rules' scenario envisions active participation by China and Korea in future patenting, it is largely silent about the impact of Brazil and other developing countries. It is notable in the 'Whose Game' scenario that the continent of Africa is not highlighted in the new bipolar world envisaged. Therefore, there is a need for scenario planning that more prominently brings to the fore the voices and concerns of developing and least developed countries, especially those of marginalized stakeholders within national borders. Such a process could visualize future scenarios from a perspective not only of economic development but also of sustainable human development, and might be helpful in informing future initiatives, for example, as background for the WIPO Development Agenda.

Third, while the EPO Report recognizes the power of politically active NGOs to shape the IP regime, it does not sufficiently highlight the dynamics and capacity building required of these players and developing country stakeholders to act effectively in this respect. The crucial role of technical assistance and capacity building of stakeholders in IP-related decision-making and management is dealt with only tangentially in the EPO report. In reality, the ability of developing countries, non-profit organizations and marginalized stakeholders to participate in or modify the IP system depends heavily on ready access to information about the IP system and professional expertise by these parties. Marginalized stakeholders, who are in greatest need of technical assistance and capacity building to tap into the decision-making processes in an informed manner, are precisely those who currently lack access to such information and expertise. Such access, as facilitated by Public Interest Intellectual Property Advisors (PIIPA) and others, could help to promote a more balanced system than one in which inequalities in the bargaining positions of stakeholders are accentuated by differential levels of access to legal support.

Despite these shortcomings, the EPO report stands alone as a uniquely detailed and creative evaluation, based on extensive research and a wide range of viewpoints on the options facing society and their potentially fateful consequences. Future scenario planning projects relating to IP will benefit greatly from the pioneering effort reflected in the EPO report.

2.3. Other scenarios on IP in the year 2025

In an article predating the EPO scenarios, Halbert (2001) describes the following three possible scenarios for the future in relation to IP:

- The first scenario, 'Chinese and Indian Hegemony – the Rise of the East', describes the rise of Asia as a hegemonic force in IP and technology.
- The second scenario, 'When Corporations Rule the World – Globalization and Western Hegemony', envisions a future where multilateral corporations and their Western hosts retain power over IP.
- The third scenario, 'The Open Source Revolution and the Demise of Intellectual Property', elaborates on parallel systems of protection and sharing that do not rely on property ownership to protect creative work.

According to Halbert, the third scenario is a desirable one in that it describes collaborative projects and hybrid models which attempt to balance protection for innovators and creators with the public interest. In contrast to the two earlier scenarios, the third scenario envisions the decentralization of rights over new creations and an accentuation of the value of the public domain (ibid., p. 45). Under this scenario, parallel systems of protection for work conventionally understood as IP would evolve to acknowledge the importance of creative work and reward the creators, while avoiding IP ownership and the centralization of IP assets implied by the other two scenarios mentioned earlier. Open source software is discussed as an example of such parallel systems (ibid., pp. 45–47).[8] The author comments that:

> The idea that open source software is based on helps to provide an alternative way to think about creative work and collaboration. Open source software can serve as an excellent model for overcoming the problems inherent in traditional copyright law by creating a true public domain where information is free to use and everyone contributes what they have created... It has created an alternative framework to understand creative work in an era dominated by private ownership. (Ibid., p. 52)

Other examples of scenario thinking on IP are discussed in the following sections. The future of the public domain, for example, is a common theme in scenario plans and other literature relating to IP. This largely reflects growing concerns over the privatization of IP assets and a perceived 'second enclosure' of the commons, as discussed in various chapters of this study. At the same time, the discourse on the public domain has its own conceptual challenges, and the perspectives of different stakeholders are explored in Section 3. The challenges and opportunities posed by new technologies are then discussed in Section 4.

3. The future of the public domain: Scenario analysis

The 1994 TRIPS Agreement did much to rouse public awareness and debate over the relationship between intellectual property rights (IPRs) and the public interest, by

[8] Halbert (2001, p. 47) notes of this scenario: 'The Open Source movement and the free software movement [have become] strong examples of the capabilities of innovation despite a clear lack of proprietary ownership over the [source] code. For computer programmers this brought back the good old days of programming before copyright got in the way ...'.

inserting IPRs into the international trade agenda. Wallis (2006) notes, for example, that no consensus exists on the critical point at which protection of private interests ceases to be a gain and starts to become a loss for innovation and the public interest, let alone a methodology for computing it.

Changing social values are meanwhile reshaping the public's perception of IPRs. Much public as well as academic debate has focused on the need for balance between protecting private IPRs and cultivating a robust public domain (Litman 1990; Boyle 2008). The interested public is not a passive recipient in the equation, but is increasingly active in defining this balance. This is visible from such developments as the Creative Commons and Open Source movements, as well as the growth of civil society representation and engagement in IP-related issues.

In a paper called 'The Public Domain: Why WIPO Should Care', the International Federation of Library Associations and Institutions (IFLA), Library Copyright Alliance (LCA) and Electronic Information for Libraries (eIFL) observe that the public domain is 'under threat' from extending terms of copyright protection and the increasing use of technology protection measures (TPMs) which lock up content without time limit.[9] Given that the public domain is often defined as that which is not protected by IPRs, the future of the public domain is closely intertwined with the future of IP.[10] Some scenario work relating to IP at an organization promoting scenario planning ('scenariothinking.org') is worth a brief mention here. Although it is titled more broadly as scenario planning on the future of IP, it touches on issues pertaining to the future of the public domain:[11]

> **Scenario I:** Every fact becomes 'privately' owned, and everything on the web becomes IP by 2011.
>
> **Scenario 2:** Everything on the web is freely available, with no IP, and Creative Commons replacing rigid IP rules by 2011.
>
> **Scenario 3:** IP will be customized in each country and at every level by 2011, leaving it 'always up to the individual/ business to indicate what they want to share and what not'.

Future scenarios are intended to be creative though 'plausible' stories, reflecting combinations of alternative futures which take into account existing trends and important driving forces for change. It should be observed that the first scenario in the immediately aforementioned exercise does not account for the historical development and workings of IP regimes, where principles (albeit not foolproof) exist to limit the subject matter of IP. These include, for example, the

[9] IFLA, LCA, and eIFL, 2007, 'The Public Domain: Why WIPO Should Care', presented to the Provisional Committee on Proposals Related to a WIPO Development Agenda, Third Session, Geneva, 19 – 23 February 2007.

[10] There are in fact many definitions of the 'public domain' (see Suthersanen 2008), and some scholars have explored whether it is more appropriate to speak of 'public domains' in the plural (see Samuelson 2006; Waelde & MacQueen 2007; Boyle 2009).

[11] The scenarios can be found at the ScenarioThinking.org website, 'Future of Intellectual Property', available at: http://scenariothinking.org/wiki/index.php/Future_of_Intellectual_Property (accessed 20 March 2009).

requirement of 'originality' and the 'idea/expression' dichotomy for copyright protection, and principles of fair use/fair dealing. Trademarks must be distinctive as to the source of the goods or services, and trade secrets must remain secret. Requirements such as 'novelty', 'inventive step' or 'non-obviousness' exist to limit patentable subject matter even though there are debates over whether the thresholds are set optimally (see Chapter 2). It is true that the extension of IP protection in some jurisdictions to databases may in cases be arguably extending IP protection to 'facts'. But, it is not plausible that future developments would bring into existence a scenario where all facts are privately owned.

In the second scenario, the Creative Commons movement eventually takes over IP rules. This perhaps reflects a common misconception about the nature of Creative Commons. Creative Commons is ultimately a system of flexible licensing for copyrights. The system provides IP owners with a standardized set of licence agreements to facilitate the sharing of content with others. As with most licence agreements, Creative Commons licences allow the IP owner to retain ownership while permitting uses of the copyright-protected work in a manner consistent with the terms of the licence.[12] As noted by Coates (2007), taking inspiration from open source licences, the Creative Commons founders decided to create a 'free culture' by developing a set of licences that creators could use to make their creative material more freely usable without giving up their copyright. Creative Commons licences build on the 'all rights reserved' model of traditional copyright to create a voluntary 'some rights reserved' system.[13]

The third scenario – that all IP protection gets customized at the national and individual levels – echoes the 'Whose Game' scenario in the EPO Report and is opposite to trends witnessed historically towards the harmonization of protection for various types of IP through the multilateral framework (such as under the TRIPS Agreement, and earlier IP instruments including the Berne Convention, in place since 1886), as well as bilateral and regional free trade agreements and investment agreements. Some 'customization' may occur during the implementation and annual review of bilateral agreements; a CIEL paper outlines the opportunities for developing countries to 'claw back' policy space through diverse implementation options (Roffe 2007; see also Abbott 2006). Meanwhile, discussing the accession process for new members to the WTO, Abbott and Correa (2007) observe that accession negotiations have been used in certain cases to secure commitment to obligations in the field of IPRs that are more extensive than those established by the TRIPS Agreement.

Formulations of the public domain which emphasize the latter as the opposite of property may not be able to accommodate different worldviews about knowledge

[12] For more on Creative Commons licences, see Lessig 2004; Merges 2004; OECD 2008; see also Chapter 8 of this book.

[13] See Coates 2007, p. 73; Lessig 2004, p. 285. Coates (2007, p. 72) provides a description of the features of the six most commonly used or 'core' licences, and examines how and by whom the licences are being used. By identifying trends in how licence use has changed over time, Coates attempts to 'rebut arguments that Creative Commons is a movement of academics and hobbyists, and has no value for traditional organizations or working artists'. For further discussions on trends and visions relating to the Creative Commons movement, see Fitzgerald et al. 2007.

creation and ownership claims.[14] As Worsley (1997) points out in his work *Knowledges*, challenging conventional Western ways of thinking about science and culture, one need not approach knowledge in the singular but could instead think of coexisting knowledge systems around the world. The diversity of knowledge systems, and forms of innovation accompanying these different systems, has not been fully addressed in the current literature relating to IP and the public domain. For example, TK and customary practices of indigenous peoples contribute to an 'informal' knowledge economy increasingly brought into interaction with the formal knowledge economy through global trade and new information technologies. Chapters 4 and 5 in this book have already introduced key concepts of TK and evaluated the relevance of conventional IP regimes to the legal protection of TK, including traditional cultural expressions (TCEs).

By self-referentially defining the 'public domain' as that which is 'not IP-protected', for example, IP law treats many aspects of the TK of indigenous peoples by default as part of the public domain. This treatment works as if to deny any property interests, rights or duties that indigenous people may have in their knowledge. It thus remains to be seen how the 'public domain' discourse can be reconciled with a framework of promoting cultural diversity, generally, and protecting indigenous peoples' TK, in particular. As indicated in the UNDP Human Development Report 2004, many indigenous groups maintain that their rights over their TK are perpetual and do not dissolve simply because of a classification within the 'public domain'. For example, the *Saami* Council of Scandinavia challenges formulations of the 'public domain' that ignore obligations to the community where knowledge is publicly known (UNDP 2004, p. 93; UNDP 2005, pp. 13–14). While themes such as the future of the public domain have shown up significantly in the few scenario plans identified in our literature review, there has in fact been little scenario planning relating to the themes of interest, for example, to TK holders. Chapter 4 (Box 4.6) provides some examples of considerations and driving forces which might be relevant for future scenario planning relating to TK and IP.

Critics have furthermore pointed out that notions of 'public domain' are not necessarily in the 'public interest'. A project relating to 'Access to Knowledge/Creative Commons Movements' at the Australian Institute of Aboriginal and Torres Strait Islander Studies (AIATSIS) in Australia invites 'critical reflection upon the cultural agendas produced through networks of power and imaginary politics within the commons movement'; it asks 'what or where is the public interest in the production of an information commons and whether there is scope for recognizing that the public is not all of one kind?'[15] Dutfield (2006, pp. 8–9) moreover notes that: 'The public domain is being promoted in opposition to privatization as part of a debate about intellectual property rights, a discussion that does not easily accommodate

[14] For example, some may not view what is 'in the public domain' as necessarily 'devoid of any property interests' (comment from Graham Dutfield).

[15] The research emphasizes that 'the "common" ground upon which the access to knowledge movement (A2K) seeks to tread, that is, the notion of humanity sharing a commons, is actually a fault line of significant proportions that involves colonial and post-colonial conflict, politics, power, economics and histories of human relationships'. See the AIATSIS website, 'Completed Research Projects', available at: http://www.aiatsis.gov.au/research/past.html (accessed 15 April 2010).

the specific interests and claims of non-Western societies.'[16] Debates over the digitization of TK encapsulate the clash of ideological viewpoints relating to the public domain and TK. While there have been some initiatives to digitize and place indigenous cultural heritage on the Internet, these have been met with public controversy (Kawooya 2006; Britz & Lor 2004).

Are all stakeholders with potential IP claims – big and small, corporate and non-corporate – being swept under one umbrella in the process of safeguarding the public domain? In 'The Romance of the Public Domain', Chander and Sunder (2006, p. 1335) suggest that public domain advocates resist 'each and every new claim for property rights as an encroachment on the public domain'. They observe that this may '(1) legitimate the current distribution of intellectual property rights, (2) mask how current constructions of the public domain disadvantage and subordinate indigenous and other disempowered groups globally, and (3) impair efforts by disempowered groups to claim themselves as subjects of property . . . ' (ibid.).

Under the Convention on Biological Diversity of 1992, access to TK and associated genetic resources is framed in terms of the 'prior informed consent' (PIC) of TK custodians, with emphasis on arrangements for 'access and benefit-sharing' (ABS).[17] As discussed in earlier chapters of this book, the UN Declaration on the Rights of Indigenous Peoples, adopted by the UN General Assembly in September 2007, refers in its Article 31(1) to the rights of indigenous peoples to 'maintain, control, protect and develop their *intellectual property* over such cultural heritage, traditional knowledge, and traditional cultural expressions' (emphasis added). The struggles of indigenous peoples over control of intangible resources have been expressed as an extension of their historical struggles to retain tangible resources including land and minerals, along with their cultural and political identity as peoples (WIPO 2009). Discussing the interplay between identity politics and IP in the realm of TK, Sunder (2006) notes that: 'These new claims for intellectual property understand rights not just in the familiar terms of incentives-for-creation, but also as tools for both recognition and redistribution'. At the same time, some are concerned that the application of property concepts to TK and TCEs, in the course of 'protecting' such material from third-party exploitation, may transform the very social relations and processes underpinning the creation of such knowledge and expressions (Leach 2003).

These otherwise complex and nuanced relationships are lost to a binary analysis of IP ownership and public domain. The latter approach homogenizes the diverse stakeholders claiming some form of IP and simplifies the idea of the 'public domain'

[16] Dutfield (2006, pp. 8–9) writes that: 'Disclosed TK has from the distant past to the present been treated as belonging to nobody. Consequently, many indigenous peoples' representatives are concerned that the pro-public domain rhetoric, sympathetic as many of them are about the sentiments behind it, may inadvertently threaten their rights.'

[17] While 'prior informed consent' (PIC) is the term used under the Convention on Biological Diversity, the term 'free prior informed consent' (FPIC) is reflected in recent instruments referring to indigenous rights. See, for example, Indian Treaty Council 2008, 'Indigenous Peoples and the Right to Free, Prior and Informed Consent', available at: http://www.treatycouncil.org/PDFs/FPIC_ENG_110908WEB.pdf (accessed 28 April 2010); see also Article 32 of the UN Declaration on the Rights of Indigenous Peoples of 2007.

as somehow seamless and even. One challenge is in viewing the latter as a textured landscape, more bumpy for some than for others. Chander and Sunder (2004, p. 1331) observe that:

> [S]cholars obscure the distributional consequences of the commons. They presume a landscape where every person can reap the riches found in the commons. This is the romance of the commons – the belief that because a resource is open to all by force of law, it will indeed be equally exploited by all. But in practice, differing circumstances – including knowledge, wealth, power, access, and ability – render some better able than others to exploit a commons.

Gollin (2008, pp. 48–51) tries to 'map' the public domain according to the extent to which people can access particular information. This approach recognizes that increases in proprietary rights do not necessarily diminish the accessible public domain, which may have expanded due to the explosion of media and knowledge in recent years. Gollin argues that, from a practical perspective, the issue is not so much whether there are IP rights in particular information or innovations, but whether individuals and organizations in society have access to the latter on acceptable terms (ibid.).

It is interesting to note in the meantime that some *sui generis* laws have provided for 'economic' compensation to particular right-holders for access by third parties to material technically within the public domain (see Chapter 5). The legal underpinnings of such provisions need to be clarified. Noting that various model laws relating to TCEs contain provisions for a *domaine public payant*, a 'system of fees for the use of traditional cultural expressions that are outside the scope of intellectual property rights', Belder (2007, p. 50) queries how this relates to the 'concept of a public domain where access is free'. She adds that: 'A system of fees would suggest that in the process of refining property rights into a sui generis right on the protection of cultural expressions, parts of the public domain have been shielded from access' (ibid.).

Other commentators suggest that more focus could be placed on governing access to intangible material falling technically in the public domain. Kneen (2004) notes, for example, that a commons need not be 'free for all' simply because it is 'open to all'.[18] He points out that 'access may be denied to those who refuse to play by the rules governing use of the public space and "property"' (ibid.).[19]

Future scenario planning work may help to bring these parallel discussions into intersection, so that lessons can be shared. An underlying question is whether the public domain discourse can ultimately accommodate the concerns of different

[18] Page numbers not available on electronic newsletter.

[19] Kneen (2004) suggests that the public domain is often misconstrued as the commons: 'The term "commons" is wrongly used to describe what is considered as public... In reality, commons historically referred to property and space that was "owned" communally – by a group of fisher folk or a village, for example – and managed for the long-term good of the group, including succeeding generations. Access to the property and space – fields, fishing grounds, forests – was limited to the group "owning" and managing it. It was not open to exploitation by outsiders, though limited use of the space could be extended by the group to "outsiders"'. Contrast Kneen's theory with Hardin 1968, pp. 1243–1248.

stakeholders in debates relating to IP and human development. Can we, for example, 're-imagine' the public domain away from a dichotomy with IPRs, with potential spaces outside both exclusive IPRs and the public domain?[20] From a human development viewpoint, as discussed in Chapter 1, another important challenge is in clarifying which individuals and groups ultimately comprise the 'public' in these 'public domain' discussions. Indeed, Halbert (2003) explores the evolution of different conceptions of the 'public' and the need to further apprehend the 'plurality' of 'publics' in the multifaceted world in which IP operates. As Samuelson (2006, p. 783) explores in her essay entitled 'Enriching Discourse on Public Domains', is there in fact 'one public domain, or are there many'?

Like the public domain, the concept of piracy has generally been understood as a counterpoint or derivative of IP. However, Johns (2010) provides a detailed history from the time of Gutenberg to support his view that piracy of books, ideas and things, not only predated but, has continually reshaped IP law, doctrine, policy and practice. Many useful insights can be gained by reframing old concepts such as the public domain and piracy in a new light, and scenario planning can help use such insights to evaluate the impact of present decisions on future generations.

4. Challenges and opportunities from new technology

The UNDP Human Development Report 2001 notes that technological innovation 'can directly enhance human capabilities' (UNDP 2001, p. 28). It adds that: 'Many products – drought-tolerant plant varieties for farmers in uncertain climates, vaccines for infectious diseases, clean energy sources for cooking, Internet access for information and communications – directly improve people's health, nutrition, knowledge and living standards, and increase people's ability to participate more actively in the social, economic and political life of a community' (ibid.). At the same time, the report emphasizes that 'technological change, like all change, poses risks . . . the more novel and fundamental is the change, the less is known about its potential consequences and hidden costs' (ibid., p. 1).

As discussed in many chapters of this book, new technologies bring about a recalibration of stakes among different individuals, entities and communities, including their stakes in IP. In health, there is a question of whether IP incentivizes the kinds of inventions needed by persons with less purchasing power, including poor sectors in both developing and developed countries. This topic has been discussed extensively in Chapter 2, with future scenarios on IP and public health highlighted there, along with alternative models of innovation for research and development (R&D) into neglected or resurgent diseases. In agriculture, there are concerns that farming models based on intensive use of biotechnology, often patent protected, are crowding out traditional farming practices and landraces which might be more suited to local conditions (see Chapter 3). The following sub-sections first look at some literature on 'alternative futures' for IP and agricultural technology. We

[20] Lange (2003, p. 474) asserts that: 'Intellectual property can go on being intellectual property, reformed or otherwise. Meanwhile, the public domain certainly can and should be envisioned as a thing apart, and strengthened accordingly'.

then examine the implications of IPRs for climate change technology before moving on to a discussion of information and communication technologies (ICTs).

4.1. Alternative futures: Biotechnology and agricultural systems

Several scenarios outlined by Tansey (2008, pp. 214–216) address how current rules shape our future food systems, encouraging or discouraging 'different kinds of roles for small farmers, different approaches to biodiversity, and different approaches to the distribution of wealth and power' (ibid., p. 214). He first summarizes two conflicting visions of the future presented by Lang and Heasman (2004). One, the 'life sciences integrated paradigm', envisages a 'highly technological, highly controlled, broad application, wide adaptation approach to the future of food, with large production units and professionalized supply systems from inputs and seeds to final consumer' (Tansey 2008, p. 215). This future is 'more monocultural, industrial, corporate-dominated and dependent on IP' (ibid.). The life sciences paradigm leaves little future for smaller farmers. The displacement and migration of such farmers 'could cause major social and political upheaval in countries still with large farming populations' (ibid.). The second approach, the 'ecologically integrated paradigm', aims to preserve ecological diversity:

> This approach sees biodiversity and diversity in general as a strength and says humans must live within ecological realities and work with them rather then dominate and ignore them. It wants to build on the millennia of experimental empirical work by farmers in diverse environments that have led to a huge range of agricultural biodiversity and to promote connection between producers and consumers; favours the micro, small and medium-sized enterprises, rather than the transnational; and sees a local to global hierarchy, where the local goes first. It promotes organic, integrated pest management, low external inputs, more skilled, open systems of exchange, family-farm-based biodiverse farming, healthy diets, and keeping cooking and farming skills alive from farm to flat. (Ibid.)

Tansey notes other possibilities. One is collapse, 'be it economic, physical or a descent into violent conflict over resources or beliefs' (ibid.; see Diamond 2005). Another scenario involves extreme genetic engineering, synthetic biology, nanotechnology and the technological enhancement of human beings (see Tansey 2008, p. 215). Practices that support biodiversity may help avoid collapse, but a 'technologically triumphalist' vision that 'treats everything as a resource, able to be owned and patentable' may not (ibid.).

Tansey expresses concern that the current trend in IP rules is not facilitating and encouraging R&D toward the ecological approach, which he believes has the best chance of success over the long term (ibid., p. 216). He asserts that:

> Ultimately, there is a basic tension between IP and biodiversity that those in favour of global IP standards have failed or refused to discuss. IP owners do best (in terms of profit) if they have a global standard or product (Windows, Viagra, Roundup and so on) that is protected globally by high IP standards. Yet innovation in food and agriculture does best if it can draw on a rich biodiversity, a biodiversity that depends on fragile variables such as TK, local farming systems and free exchange

of materials. By building a property rights system that rewards standardization and homogeneity, we almost certainly risk affecting those variables that underpin our systems of biodiversity. (Ibid.)

The climate change dimension remains to be fully explored in scenario planning of IP. While Strauss (2008, p. 59) queries whether there is a 'global warming of patents' from the 'nearly exponential global growth in numbers of patent applications', legal literature is only beginning to tackle the real linkages between IP and climate change. As discussed in Chapter 3, climate change debates will further accentuate many existing issues and tensions relating to IPRs and food security while bringing up new challenges. Since food security depends on the conservation of agro-biodiversity (and animal genetic diversity) to which climate change poses real and increasing threats, IPR issues in relation to genetic resources and agriculture will become all the more pertinent. The requirements of climate change mitigation and adaptation will also further highlight questions of control and access to genetic information as scientific data, along with the implications of new technologies including genomics, bio-informatics and synthetic biology.

Scenario planning may be helpful to tease out some of the implications of climate change on IP and agriculture. Incremental improvements in agro-technology, incentivized by IPRs, such as drought resistant strains of maize, may enable monocultures to remain productive in regions with declining, but relatively predictable climates, such as North Africa and inland Australia.[21] However, until anthropogenic greenhouse gas emissions are dramatically reduced, greenhouse gas concentrations in the atmosphere will continue to rise, and continue to drive warming. Even under the most ambitious targets of the Copenhagen Accord,[22] climate stabilization is unlikely before 2100. Crops will not need just a single technological improvement; instead they will require frequent enhancement just to maintain the same level of productivity. Intellectual property rights may facilitate advancements among agribusinesses that can afford the R&D investment or royalties, but people in developing countries (who are generally much more reliant on agriculture) will be obliged to pay for the technologies, or risk food insecurity and the volatile politics that go with it. Free or conditional transfer of IP may alleviate this problem, but would leave recipients reliant on the ongoing goodwill of IP owners. An alternative scenario that could work to better serve the interests of those who do not own IP is, for example, to forego drought resistant maize and continue to grow some traditional maize with lower yields, while switching part of the land to other productive purposes such as growing wheat, timber or grazing. Approaches which require the abandonment of current farming practices will not be easily accepted by local communities. While probably less productive on an annual basis, this higher diversity

[21] This paragraph was contributed by Matt Spannagle, Environment and Energy Group, UNDP.

[22] Conference of the Parties (COP) to the UN Framework Convention on Climate Change (UNFCCC), Copenhagen Accord (Draft Decision –/CP.15) (18 December 2009), UN Doc. No. FCCC/CP/2009/L.7 (2009), available at: http://unfccc.int/resource/docs/2009/cop15/eng/l07.pdf (accessed 19 March 2010). For the latest updates on the Copenhagen Accord, see the UN Framework Convention on Climate Change (UNFCCC) website, available at: http://unfccc.int/2860.php (accessed 5 March 2010).

approach avoids the complete 'collapse' scenario discussed earlier, and is therefore likely to be a more stable system in the medium-term.

4.2. Climate change and clean energy technology

The role of IP in relation to the development and diffusion of clean energy technology is another area of uncertainty and increasing debate, particularly within the context of climate change. On the one hand, an article published by WIPO on the subject suggests that: 'The intellectual property (IP) rights system makes no distinction between environmentally friendly and other technologies. IP contributes to the development and diffusion of new technologies for combating climate change much as it does in any other innovative technology field . . . ' (WIPO 2008, p. 3). Derclaye (2008) holds the view, on the other hand, that IP laws could be interpreted or reformed to discourage environmentally unsound technologies:

> If a particular state has chosen to implement the *ordre public* and compulsory licensing provisions found in international treaties, courts if they wish can already use these provisions to prevent the protection of inventions and works emitting (too much) CO_2 . . . But international, regional, and national intellectual property laws could be honed further if governments wish to decrease levels of CO_2 even more. A specific public policy and morality provision prohibiting patenting inventions and copyrighting works generating above a certain level of CO_2 should be enacted, preferably internationally. Similarly, states should be forced to enact compulsory licenses, but the latter should only be used when the patent or copyright owners have a dominant position.

A different approach would be to make it easier to obtain patents on green technology. This is the intent of a recent programme in the US to accelerate patent prosecution for eligible green technology applications.[23] Meanwhile, the impact of IP rules on access to clean energy technology is a concern being raised by both developed and developing countries, notably within the context of the UN Framework Convention on Climate Change (UNFCCC).[24] Parties to the UNFCCC have, for example, debated on whether the current provisions within the TRIPS Agreement provide sufficient flexibilities to ensure a rapid and widespread transfer of clean energy technology (see ICTSD 2008, pp. 6–8). A European Parliament report includes a proposal to look into the feasibility of amending the TRIPS Agreement to allow for the compulsory licensing of 'environmentally necessary' technologies.[25] While a preliminary research paper by the late John Barton (2008) suggests that IP rules do not presently prevent developing country access to relevant technology in the solar, biofuels and wind energy sectors, these are areas necessitating further

[23] 'Pilot Program for Green Technologies Including Greenhouse Gas Reduction', 74 Fed. Reg. 64666 (7 December 2009).

[24] United Nations Framework Convention on Climate Change (New York, 9 May 1992), 1771 U.N.T.S. 107, 31 I.L.M. 849, UN Doc. A/AC.237/18 (Part II)/Add.1 (*entered into force* 21 March 1994) [hereinafter 'UNFCCC'], available at: http://unfccc.int/resource/docs/convkp/conveng.pdf (accessed 19 March 2010).

[25] European Parliament (EP) resolution of 29 November 2007 on trade and climate change (2007/2003(INI)), available at: http://www.europarl.europa.eu/sides/getDoc.do?Type=TA&Reference=P6-TA-2007-0576&language=EN (accessed 28 April 2010); see further WIPO 2008.

research. Transfer of technology has been one of the five main themes in the climate negotiations, facilitated by the Contact Group on Enhanced Action on Development and Transfer of Technology.[26]

Scenario planning may help to flag the different options for the future in this area. Some options that have been debated so far by stakeholders are: the full use of flexibilities contained in the TRIPS Agreements including compulsory licensing; steps to ensure sharing of publicly funded technologies and related know-how; the creation of a 'global technology pool for climate change' with potential access to technologies on low-cost or royalty-free terms; or the exclusion of certain technology from patents.[27] It has been argued, at the same time, that the exclusion of climate-friendly technology from patenting would remove the incentives for investors to put research dollars into areas such as solar technology, wind turbines and hybrid engines for vehicles. Other suggested alternatives are to reduce the protection period for patents on climate-friendly technologies (although this might currently raise issues with the non-discrimination of technological fields required by the TRIPS Agreement, Article 27), or to exempt LDCs, for example, from royalty payments.[28]

4.3. Information technology and the Internet

Meanwhile, new information technology has significantly altered the relationship between private rights and public interest (especially digital and Internet technology). The digital communications revolution is putting stronger tools directly into the hands of creators, consumers and civil society for expressing the changing social values on IP. New developments in information technology have brought rapid changes to modes of accessing as well as distributing knowledge products. As discussed in various chapters of this study, ICTs have enabled the collaborative production of global knowledge goods (an example is the Wikipedia online encyclopaedia) and provided new opportunities for peer production and distribution of information. They have democratized the creation and distribution of video content, by facilitating the rapid growth of user-generated content (which has now dwarfed, for example, the production of the Hollywood film industry). Ownership of the majority of global knowledge and cultural goods has been concentrated in several industry organizations. Now the creation and ownership of knowledge and cultural goods is becoming far more diffuse. IPRs may thus have a diminishing role in incentivizing the creation of these new technologies and user-generated content.

[26] Although the issue of IPRs as applying to this technology was not addressed in the Copenhagen Accord, the Declaration establishes a 'Technology Mechanism' (Copenhagen Accord, para. 11), consisting of a 'Technology Executive Committee' and a 'Climate Technology Centre and Network'. See UNFCCC Ad Hoc Working Group on Long-term Cooperative Change Under the Convention, 'Outcome of the Work of the Ad Hoc Working Group on Long-term Cooperative Action Under the Convention', UN Doc. FCCC/AWGLCA/2009/L.7/Rev.1 (16 December 2009), para. 43, available at: http://unfccc.int/resource/docs/2009/awglca8/eng/l07r01.pdf (accessed 28 April 2010). Update provided by Hans Haugen Morten.

[27] Comment from Savita Mullapudi Narasimhan.

[28] Comment from Matt Spannagle.

These trends are discussed in detail in Chapter 7 which addresses the implications of information and communication technologies (ICTs) on 'knowledge and education'. Focusing on copyright, the chapter discusses the impact of digitalization and the Internet on production, distribution and updating of learning materials and other knowledge products. Chapter 8 on contemporary challenges for copyright in promoting cultural diversity furthermore discusses the impact of new technology on creative processes and the relations among creators, intermediaries and end-users. While publishing houses, recording companies and other business intermediaries have until recently controlled the means of production as well as distribution channels for many knowledge and cultural goods, lowered production costs through digital technology now make creators less dependent on producers for production capital. The Internet greatly facilitates self-distribution by creators, for example, in the music industry where new ways of downloading and purchasing music (e.g. through iTunes and Napster), along with the growing number of Internet users, may have expanded the market for musical creations (but note Towse 2008 on some limitations).

At the same time, as discussed in Chapter 7, there is a trend towards the use of digital rights management (DRM) and licences to expand IP rights. IP rights holders have used legally enforced technological protection measures (TPMs) and end user licence agreements to expand their IP rights beyond those granted by copyright and patent law, and to impose post-sale use restrictions on a range of goods, including printer cartridges, software, music compact discs, books and model legislation codes.[29] This has overridden existing exceptions and limitations to copyright and patent laws that protect consumers and innovators, and impeded libraries from providing services. Because TPMs increasingly rely on devices to enforce technological restrictions, this may increase technological lock-down and exclusion of free and open source software technologies. As more and more information goods are covered by TPMs and licence agreements, this can restrict access to knowledge. Some scenario planning relating to IP has highlighted the potential impacts of restrictive DRM on access to knowledge and users' experience of digital media.

The Berkman Center for Internet & Society at Harvard Law School has published scenarios relating to information technology. These scenarios are featured in their joint white paper with GartnerG2 on 'Copyright and Digital Media in a Post-Napster World: 2005 Update'.[30] According to the white paper, digital technology and

[29] Electronic Frontier Foundation (EFF) report, *Unintended Consequences: Ten Years Under the DMCA*, October 2008, available at: http://www.eff.org/files/DMCAUnintended10.pdf (accessed 16 April 2010); EFF 'Briefing Paper on Technological Protection Measures' to WIPO Development Agenda meeting delegates, April 2005, available at: http://www.eff.org/files/filenode/dev_agenda/EFF_WIPO_briefing_041205.pdf (accessed 16 April 2010); *UMG Recordings, Inc. v. Augusto*, 558 F. Supp. 2d 1055 (C.D. Cal 2008) (order granting counter-defendant's motion for summary judgment as to counter-claim), available at: http://www.eff.org/files/filenode/umg_v_augusto/LA07CV03106SJO-O.pdf (accessed 16 April 2010); Electronic Frontier Foundation White Paper, 'Dangerous Terms: A User's Guide to EULAs', February 2005, available at: http://www.eff.org/wp/dangerous-terms-users-guide-eulas (accessed 16 April 2010).

[30] See Berkman Center for Internet & Society and GartnerG2 2005a. These scenarios seem to have evolved through the Center's analytical work on the white paper rather than through an extensive scenario-planning process. The white paper is available at: http://cyber.law.harvard.edu/media/wp2005 (accessed 15 April 2010).

the Internet are 'altering many industries and changing the way people use and enjoy electronic products, media and entertainment (ibid., p. 2). Although 'beneficial in many respects', this evolution also 'exacerbates the tensions among copyright holders (individual creators and corporate content providers), technology companies and consumers'(ibid.). The paper identifies the following five scenarios as possible outcomes of technological, business, legislative and legal developments.[31]

1. The **No-Change** scenario assumes that confusion remains about doctrines like fair use and first sale as the DMCA and copyright law continue to guide digital media distribution.
2. The **Speedbumps** scenario predicts that technological restrictions like encryption will create small barriers to users' access and control of digital content.
3. The **Technology Lockdown** scenario projects that restrictive Digital Rights Management (DRM) schemes will unilaterally determine users' experience of the content they purchase.
4. The **Alternative Compensation System** scenario imagines that users access digital content through a state-run system that taxes consumers according to use and rewards creators according to the popularity of their work.
5. The **Entertainment Co-op** scenario envisions that voluntary associations emerge within the existing copyright structure to allow distribution of digital content between subscribers and creators.

The increased use of DRM technologies to limit users' conduct poses notable constraints on the public's access to and use of digital media. DRM technologies also frequently limit legitimate exploitation of exceptions and limitations to copyright, such as in terms of 'fair use' in the US, and the operation of the doctrine of 'first sale'. These technologies impose privacy issues and may potentially be used by copyright holders and DRM standards creators to 'lock out' disfavoured digital media devices and software creators (ibid., pp. 47–48). The third scenario of 'Technological Lockdown' is thus one which would raise serious public interest concerns.

The fourth and fifth scenarios explore future strategies that might compensate copyright holders while also encouraging innovation. The 'Alternative Compensation System' scenario emphasizes state and private party mechanisms and imposes levies on consumers as a solution. In terms of ways forward under the Entertainment Co-op Scenario, the Electronic Frontier Foundation has published a white paper called 'Let the Music Play' where it envisages a voluntary collective licensing system for music downloads and peer-to-peer sharing. In exchange for consumers paying a reasonable regular amount, rights holders would agree to license downloading and sharing of music files on the Internet. A collective management organization or organizations would distribute payments to artists based on the

[31] Ibid., pp. 53–54. According to the Berkman Center, these scenarios will be analysed in a series of publications as potential models for distribution of digital content (ibid., p. 54). Another Berkman Center white paper deals with international legal and regulatory issues, but does not mention scenarios. See Berkman Center for Internet & Society and GartnerG2 2005b.

popularity of their music. This compensation and licensing system would avoid the current lawsuits and copyright enforcement problems visible on the Internet.[32]

Meanwhile, the presence and power of collecting societies has risen, corresponding with a noticeable international movement towards collective licensing arrangements. This will move copyright towards an opt-in or opt-out compensation regime, and increase the relative importance of the role played by collective management organizations in the administration and enforcement of copyright. This is a cross-sector phenomenon, but it is most visible presently in the music industry, where collective management organizations have moved towards blanket licensing in various contexts.

The recent Google Book Search lawsuit settlement proposes to create a similar regime for books to which it applies.[33] The settlement agreement, which still must be approved by the courts, creates an independent, non-profit Book Rights Registry to administer royalties collected by Google for access to the collection of over 10 million books that Google has already scanned in the US.[34] If approved, the settlement (and recent re-settlement) may radically expand access to books for US readers, depending on how many publishers choose to remove their works from the Google collection, particularly for public domain books. The settlement would particularly expand access to 'orphan works' – books which are in copyright but out-of-print and whose right holders are unknown or cannot be located – which may comprise as much as 50% of Google's scanned collection.[35] Subject to contrary instructions from rights holders, the Google Book Search settlement would authorize Google to allow US readers to view up to 20% of each book in a free preview mode, and to make the entire full-text available through public library terminals. Full-text access on a paid fee basis would be made available to US universities and other entities on a blanket basis as part of an institutional subscription, or to individuals on a title-by-title basis. Google will split the revenue it receives from providing access to digital copies with the Book Rights Registry, which would then disburse royalties to the appropriate rights holder.[36] It is anticipated that the Book Rights Registry, in the course of locating rights holders in order to pay royalties, will also negotiate

[32] Electronic Frontier Foundation, 'A Better Way Forward: Voluntary Collective Licensing of Music File Sharing', April 2008, available at: http://www.eff.org/wp/better-way-forward-voluntary-collective-licensing-music-file-sharing (accessed 28 April 2010). See also Digital Media Project, Entertainment Co-op Scenario, available at: http://cyber.law.harvard.edu/media/scenario5 (accessed 28 April 2010).

[33] See Google Book Search Litigation US Settlement Agreement, available at: http://books.google.com/googlebooks/agreement/ (accessed 28 April 2010). See also Settlement FAQ, available at: http://books.google.com/googlebooks/agreement/faq.html (accessed 28 April 2010).

[34] See Google Book Search Litigation US Settlement Agreement, ibid.; Fred von Lohmann, EFF Senior IP Attorney, 'Google Book Search Settlement: A Reader's Guide', EFF Blogpost, 31 October 2008, available at: http://www.eff.org/deeplinks/2008/10/google-books-settlement-readers-guide (accessed 16 April 2010); Jonathan Band, 'A Guide for the Perplexed: Libraries and the Google Library Project Settlement', American Library Association and Association of Research Libraries paper, available at: http://www.arl.org/bm%7Edoc/google-settlement-13nov08.pdf (accessed 16 April 2010).

[35] The books scanned by Google from US and European library collections include a number of works from non-American authors; some estimate as many as 3 million of the 7 million scanned books. See Peter Hirtle, 'Google Book Settlement, Orphan Works and Foreign Works', LibraryLaw Blog, 21 April 2009, available at: http://blog.librarylaw.com/librarylaw/2009/04/google-book-settlement-orphan-works-and-foreign-works.html (accessed 28 April 2010).

[36] Google will retain 37% and pay 63% to the Book Rights Registry.

with rights holders for the right to license digital book vendors other than Google. It therefore offers, over time, the possibility of a central rights clearance mechanism for most digital book access licences, at least within the US. Critics of the proposed settlement argue that the settlement effectively gives Google a monopoly over access to orphan works, and that the Book Rights Registry poses an antitrust threat because it is tasked with setting the prices for digital book access.[37]

Initiatives such as Google books will have an immense impact on future models for disseminating digitized works (including copyright-protected works). The current Google settlement applies to all US works, as well as works first published in the UK, Canada and Australia, unless rights holders have opted-out of the settlement prior to its approval. If the settlement agreement is approved, rights holders will still be entitled to 'remove' their works from the Google collection for a period of years. Thereafter, rights holders will still have the ability to block many uses, but they will not be able to demand complete removal of their work from the Google collection. Given that the Google Settlement is over a US class action, it will only cover US-based viewers – that is, US institutions and libraries, along with individuals attempting to view from within the US. Readers outside the US will continue to be able to see only books that are presumptively in the public domain in the US. However, it is possible that Google may seek to make agreements for copyrighted books on similar terms with authors and publishers in other countries in the future, and the US settlement agreement may form the model for such licensing agreements in some other jurisdictions.

Scenario planning approaches might help to evaluate the consequences of variations on the Google settlement. Scenario planning could address questions like: What are the plausible impacts of the settlement on particular communities? Would other approaches result in a more favourable outcome?

5. Scenario planning and the Development Agenda

Many of the themes discussed so far in this chapter and the rest of the book are being considered within the ongoing work at WIPO on the Development Agenda. In September 2007, WIPO member states adopted a series of recommendations to enhance the development dimension of the organization's activities.[38] The member states agreed to establish a Committee on Development and Intellectual Property to develop a work-programme for implementation of the adopted recommendations, as well as to monitor, assess, discuss and report on its implementation. The Development Agenda proposals are intended to require WIPO to take a broader approach to promoting creativity and innovation, instead of focusing solely on the creation of exclusive IPRs. As the adopted recommendations under this 'Development Agenda' are broadly worded, some scenario planning focusing on the overlap

[37] Critics also argue that the settlement effectively gives Google a monopoly right to deal with digital copies of orphan works since currently only Google possesses the scanned copies of orphan works and would have a first-to-market advantage. See Grimmelmann 2009.

[38] See the WIPO website, 'Development Agenda for WIPO', available at: http://www.wipo.int/ip-development/en/agenda (accessed 28 April 2010); see further Halbert 2007; de Beer (ed.) 2009; New 2009.

between IP and development may help to clarify alternative visions and options for mainstreaming human development concerns into WIPO's future agenda and activities.

This section first provides some background on the Development Agenda, before outlining the adopted proposals under the Agenda and some challenges in their implementation. Some ideas for scenario planning in this area are then explored. Such planning will need to be complemented by the collection and exchange of baseline information relating to IP and the public interest, as well as attention to the long-term capacity building of stakeholders.

5.1. Some background on the Development Agenda

In October 2004, Brazil and Argentina proposed that WIPO should establish a Development Agenda. Along with the thirteen developing countries in the Group of Friends of Development who joined them in pressing for this Agenda, Brazil and Argentina expressed concerns that WIPO has historically focused on creating exclusive rights for IP rights holders at the expense of other important public policies (see Musungu & Dutfield 2003, sec. 4.6).[39] A purpose of the Development Agenda would be to mainstream development concerns into WIPO's work. This would accord with the promotion of development being a key element of the UN's founding purpose as stated in the 1945 UN Charter[40] and with the UN's continuing commitment to development as embodied in the UN Millennium Development Goals (MDGs)[41] and with the work of other UN development agencies such as the United Nations Conference on Trade and Development (UNCTAD), United Nations Educational, Scientific and Cultural Organization (UNESCO) and UNDP. Although WIPO has been a specialist agency of the UN since 1974 and has an agreement with the World Trade Organization (WTO) to provide member states with technical assistance on TRIPS implementation, proponents contended that this commitment has not been evident in WIPO's work.

The proposal to establish a Development Agenda was also influenced by factors outside of WIPO. Since the adoption of the TRIPS Agreement in 1994 as part of the Uruguay Round of negotiations that established the WTO, many developing countries have argued that the heightened IP standards required by TRIPS have restricted or removed policy options available to them to address national development priorities (Drahos & Braithwaite 2003; Sell 2003; Gervais 2007). These restrictions are said to be exacerbated by bilateral trade agreements with the US and the European Union (EU) incorporating 'TRIPS-plus' provisions which further limit domestic policy-making (Musungu & Dutfield 2003; Vivas-Eugui 2003).

[39] See also UK Commission on Intellectual Property Rights (CIPR) 2002, chapter 8.

[40] Charter of the United Nations (San Francisco, 26 June 1945), 3 Bevans 1153, 59 Stat. 1031, T.S. No. 993 (*entered into force* 24 October 1945) [hereinafter 'UN Charter'], available at: http://www.un.org/en/documents/charter/ (accessed 3 February 2010). The 1945 UN Charter states that 'the United Nations shall promote: (a) higher standards of living, full employment, and conditions of economic and social progress and development' (ibid., Art. 55).

[41] See United Nations Millennium Declaration (8 September 2000), G.A. Res. 55/2, UN Doc. A/RES/55/2 (2000) [hereinafter 'UN Millennium Declaration'], available at: http://www.un.org/millennium/ (accessed 22 June 2009).

The three years of negotiations, including seven formal meetings, leading to the adoption of the forty-five Development Agenda proposals, were marked by various disagreements among countries, including disagreement over the meaning of the term 'development'. As noted by Barbosa, Chon and Moncayo von Hase (2008), many developed countries tended to view development in terms of economic growth. For instance, the US delegation submitted a proposal calling on WIPO to conduct baseline national surveys for economic growth to identify weaknesses in national IP regimes and studies to analyse the relationship between the rates of piracy of IP and technology transfer, foreign direct investment and economic growth.[42] By comparison, a significant number of developing countries at the negotiations conceptualized development in terms of capability expansion following a human development approach (Sen 2000; Fukada-Parr & Shiva Kumar 2005) and recognized that development determinants are country specific.[43] The divergence of views manifested in a series of supplementary proposals and counterproposals from the group of African countries, the group of Arab countries, Colombia, Chile, the Group of Friends of Development, Mexico, the US and the UK. This resulted in 111 (sometimes countervailing) proposals; from which the forty-five final proposals were adopted.

The Group of Friends' Development Agenda proposal and subsequent Elaboration on Issues Raised in the Development Agenda was endorsed by thousands of leading scholars, citizens and public-interest NGOs through the Geneva Declaration on the Future of WIPO 2004.[44] The Geneva Declaration summarized the public policy concerns raised by the expansion of the scope and duration of IP regimes in recent decades. It called on global policymakers at WIPO to consider alternative incentive regimes for the creation of global knowledge goods and to take account of the needs of all the world's citizens. It stated:

> Humanity stands at a crossroads – a fork in our moral code and a test of our ability to adapt and grow. Will we evaluate, learn and profit from the best of these new ideas and opportunities, or will we respond to the most unimaginative pleas to suppress all of this in favor of intellectually weak, ideologically rigid, and sometimes brutally unfair and inefficient policies? Much will depend upon the future direction of the World Intellectual Property Organization (WIPO), a global body setting standards that regulate the production, distribution and use of knowledge.

5.2. The new Development Agenda

The forty-five adopted proposals are grouped in six clusters, reflecting the broad scope of the agenda: Cluster A: Technical Assistance and Capacity Building; Cluster B: Norm-Setting, Flexibilities, Public Policy and the Public Domain; Cluster C:

[42] See Proposal submitted by the United States of America to the First Session of the Provisional Committee on Proposals Related to a WIPO Development Agenda, Doc. PCDA/1/4, 17 February 2006, available at: http://www.wipo.int/edocs/mdocs/mdocs/en/pcda_1/pcda_1_4.pdf (accessed 28 April 2010).

[43] See Proposal submitted by Chile to the First Session of the Provisional Committee on Proposals Related to a WIPO Development Agenda, Doc. PCDA/1/2, 9 January 2005, available at: http://www.wipo.int/edocs/mdocs/mdocs/en/pcda_1/pcda_1_2.pdf (accessed 28 April 2010).

[44] Consumer Project on Technology (CPTech) and Open Society Institute (OSI), 'Geneva Declaration on the Future of the WIPO', 29 September 2004, available at: http://www.cptech.org/ip/wipo/futureofwipodeclaration.pdf (accessed 19 March 2010).

Technology Transfer, Information and Communication Technology and Access to Knowledge; Cluster D: Assessments, Evaluation and Impact Studies; Cluster E: Institutional Matters including Mandate and Governance; and Cluster F: Other Issues (Enforcement of Intellectual Property Rights). Amongst other things, the proposals require WIPO to:

- provide technical assistance that is development-oriented, demand-driven and transparent, taking into account the priorities and special needs of developing – countries, especially LDCs (Proposal 1);
- consider the preservation of the public domain within WIPO's normative processes and deepen the analysis of the implications and benefits of a rich and accessible public domain (Proposal 16);
- promote norm-setting activities related to IP that support a robust public domain in WIPO's Member States, including the possibility of preparing guidelines which could assist interested Member States in identifying subject matters that have fallen into the public domain within their respective jurisdictions (Proposal 20);
- initiate discussions on how, within WIPO's mandate, to further facilitate access to knowledge and technology for developing countries and LDCs to foster creativity and innovation and to strengthen such existing activities within WIPO (Proposal 19);
- ensure that its norm-setting activities should be supportive of the development goals agreed within the UN system, including those contained in the Millennium Declaration. The WIPO Secretariat, without prejudice to the outcome of Member States' considerations, should address in its working documents for norm-setting activities, as appropriate and as directed by Member States, issues such as: a) safeguarding national implementation of intellectual property rules; b) links between IP and competition; c) IP-related transfer of technology; d) potential flexibilities, exceptions and limitations for Member States; and e) the possibility of additional special provisions for developing countries and LDCs (Proposal 22; WIPO 2007, Annex A).

These recommendations are far-reaching and cut across the full spectrum of WIPO's activities. However, their impact on WIPO's institutional culture and the development of future IP norms will depend on how they are implemented and the establishment of an effective evaluation process. The WIPO Secretariat has proposed several plans to implement the adopted proposals.[45] In 2009 it was decided that recommendations that deal with similar subject matter would be grouped together

[45] See Working Document for the Committee on Development and Intellectual Property, Thematic Projects, Doc. CDIP/3/4, 1 April 2009, available at: http://www.wipo.int/edocs/mdocs/mdocs/en/cdip_3/cdip_3_4.pdf (accessed 28 April 2010). See also Addendum, available at: http://www.wipo.int/edocs/mdocs/mdocs/en/cdip_3/cdip_3_4_add.doc (accessed 28 April 2010). The prior implementation plan developed by the Committee on Development and Intellectual Property (CDIP) sought to stagger implementation of the proposals. For nineteen of the forty-five proposals that the WIPO Secretariat determined could be implemented without any additional financial or human resources, the CDIP listed activities currently being undertaken by the WIPO Secretariat, which the CDIP considered implemented the proposals. For the remaining twenty-six proposals, the CDIP proposed new activities, subject to budgetary approval. See the Initial Working Document for the Committee on Development and Intellectual Property, Doc. CDIP/1/3, 3 March 2008, available at: http://www.wipo.int/edocs/mdocs/mdocs/en/cdip_1/cdip_1_3.pdf (accessed 28 April 2010).

and implemented by a set of 'thematic projects' beginning in January 2010. These will cover four themes: Intellectual Property and the Public Domain; Intellectual Property and Competition Policy; Intellectual Property, Information and Communication Technologies; and Developing Tools for Access to Patent Information.

Many proponents consider that the Development Agenda will be successful at achieving its intended purpose only if the proposals are implemented across all areas of WIPO's work, and particularly in the various Standing Committees where the majority of WIPO's norm setting occurs. Mechanisms are also being explored to evaluate whether implementation activities are spurring WIPO's development dimension and ensuring consistency of application across various parts of WIPO's operations (see Mara 2009).

5.3. Scenario planning as a potential process for building the Development Agenda

As scenario planning provides a mechanism for devising new perspectives and thinking outside of the parameters of what has gone before (Schoemaker 1995), it could provide useful information for creating a work plan to implement the Development Agenda. Scenario planning is guided by three key principles: first, enabling stakeholders to take a long-term view; second, outside-in thinking, to identify key external forces of change;[46] and third, creating a platform for multiple perspectives to cast new light on strategic challenges (Searce & Fulton 2004, pp. 10–14). A broad range of stakeholders and experts might be invited by WIPO or other facilitators to engage in scenario planning to generate ideas about implementing the Development Agenda proposals. While it is unclear whether institutional and political forces at WIPO would permit use of scenario planning in framing a Development Agenda implementation plan, such a process would provide several concrete benefits for developing a WIPO Development Agenda work plan.

First, scenario planning would allow the discussion to take place free, at least conceptually, from current institutional processes, with their budgetary and normative constraints. It would bring additional stakeholders, beyond governments, to the discussion, including not only civil society entities and academics but also voices from the creative sectors, libraries, educational institutions, local communities, industry, small enterprises and others.[47]

Second, it would provide a framework for considering alternative paradigms of development, including a human development approach emphasizing enhancement of human capabilities and freedoms (see Chapter 1 of this book; see also

[46] Searce and Fulton (2004, p. 12) observe that: 'Most individuals and organizations think from the inside – the things they can control – out to the world they would like to shape... Conversely, thinking from the outside-in begins with pondering external changes that might, over time, profoundly affect [an individual's or organization's] work – a seemingly irrelevant technological development that could prove advantageous for service delivery, for example, or a geopolitical shift that could introduce unforeseen social needs.'

[47] Non-governmental organizations currently have observer status at specific WIPO meetings. A large proportion of such organizations attending meetings represent trade associations or other commercial outfits (New 2009). Public Interest Intellectual Property Advisors (PIIPA) is an example of a non-profit organization with permanent observer status at WIPO.

Netanel 2008; de Beer 2009). While a human development approach does not dismiss considerations of economic growth and efficiency for development (UNDP 1996; de Beer 2009), it sees the latter as just one of many means instrumental towards improving human capabilities and well-being. As Chon (2007, p. 522) observes: 'The Development Agenda debate so far points to the constraints upon WIPO to reflect on its own changing identity and role vis-à-vis development. This is due in part to its historical "embeddedness" within a development as growth model, and in part to disagreement among member states about what development should mean'. These basic differences in viewing development, and the role of IP in development, are likely to result in divergent implementation proposals and evaluation criteria for the Development Agenda. Along with the human development approach, proponents have highlighted other related and important perspectives on development, including a human rights-based approach (see Ovett 2006; Fukuda-Parr 2009) and an approach to development with 'culture and identity'.[48]

Third, scenario planning could identify indicators of human development against which the design and implementation of a Development Agenda would be monitored and evaluated. Measuring the success of a Development Agenda in terms of improvements in human development in developing countries requires a starting point different from current attempts to measure the impact of IP through looking at income indicators, statistics relating to the strength of IP infrastructure in a country, the amount of 'technical assistance' rendered to create that infrastructure, the number of patents filed and granted or other ad-hoc collection of empirical information (see Chon 2006, p. 5; The International Expert Group on Biotechnology, Innovation and Intellectual Property [IEGBIP] 2008, p. 36).[49] There is scope, for example, for linking the evaluation of IP policies and enforcement to indicators of human development. The latter extend beyond income and growth indicators to include considerations such as access to medicine, improved nutrition, access to knowledge and education, protection of political and cultural freedoms and participation in cultural life. The measurements of human development are increasingly sophisticated and multidimensional, going beyond what is currently covered by the UNDP Human Development Index (Ranis, Steward & Samman 2006).[50]

[48] Note the special theme of 'Indigenous Peoples: Development with Culture and Identity' at the UN Permanent Forum on Indigenous Issues (UNPFII), Ninth Session, 19 – 30 April 2010. See UNPFII, 'UN Permanent Forum on Indigenous Issues', available at: http://www.un.org/esa/socdev/unpfii/ (accessed 16 April 2010).

[49] Such measurements can be circular in gauging the development impact of IP (see Chon 2006, p. 5).

[50] See also United Nations University – World Institute for Development Economics (UNU-WIDER) 2007. The existing work of UNDP in measuring human development through the 'Human Development Index' (HDI) offers some means to track certain aspects of human development empirically, for comparison over time and space. Ranis et al. (2006) qualify, however, that: 'Human development (HD) goes well beyond the Human Development Index (HDI), with which it is often equated. ... The HDI itself is clearly a reductionist measure, incorporating just a subset of possible human choices. In fact, the measure, which includes life expectancy, literacy, years of education, and a modified measure of income, is directed at the choices referred to as "most critical" in the first *Human Development Report* of the UNDP (1990)'. The UNDP HDI is reviewed periodically and now extends (beyond the original HDI) to such indices as – the Gender-related Development Index (GDI), the Gender Empowerment Measure (GEM), and the Human Poverty Index (HPI 1 and HPI 2). See Dhruv 2006. Other potential measures to reflect equality and empowerment are being explored in the (forthcoming) twentieth edition of the UNDP *Human Development Report*.

Fourth, while WIPO's mandate as a UN specialized agency extends to facilitating 'the transfer of technology related to industrial property to the developing countries in order to accelerate *economic, social and cultural development*',[51] its traditional focus has been on IP norm-setting and IP-related technical assistance. Creating scenarios for the WIPO Development Agenda could involve imagining WIPO as a different sort of organization, as a facilitator of dialogue between different communities of stakeholders affected by IP regulation (see Deere 2009, p. 43; Gold & Morin, p. 57). In relation to the information economy, for example, it might bring together citizens, educators, libraries and archives, technology innovators, free and open source software developers and users, collective management organizations, individual and corporate IP rights holders and communities with particular knowledge assets and claims. In terms of assisting ongoing work under the Development Agenda, such as the proposals and initiatives to 'map' the public domain (see Suthersanen 2008 for a detailed discussion), scenario planning might help to clarify the accessibility and relevance of the public domain to different stakeholders.

Fifth, scenario planning can enable diverse themes in human development to be addressed and connected in relation to IP. Thus far, the many intergovernmental committees of WIPO have tended to deal separately with particular sectors or areas of IP, while the Development Agenda is meant to cut across all aspects of WIPO's work. Apart from the many sectoral issues discussed in this and other studies, there are cross-cutting themes which could be brought out through scenario planning. For example, the impact of ICTs needs to be understood and linked for different areas of human development. An alternative innovation model that is developed in one sector can also have lessons for other sectors. For example, as discussed in chapters of this study, 'open source' – which began with computer programming – is an innovation model spreading to the medical field (Maurer, Rai & Sali 2004), education (see Chapters 6 and 7), the area of plant genetic resources (Aoki & Luvai 2007), biotechnology (Hope 2008), biodiversity and TK (Oldham 2009), and to clean energy innovations. A patent pool called the 'Eco-patent commons' for environmentally sustainable technology has been formed, based on an open source model (Srinivas 2008, p. 16). The tensions and potential cross-pollination between modern technologies and traditional innovation systems (e.g. between health-related biotechnology and traditional medicinal knowledge) are also visible in many sectors. Sustainable use of resources and climate change are further considerations which cut across all fields.

Meanwhile, one significant blind-spot in IP-related planning is the interaction between formal and informal economies in terms of access by marginalized sectors to educational and cultural works (Rens, Prabhala & Kawooya 2006; see Chapters 6–8). Scenario planning might serve to draw out some of these linkages, while highlighting that many marginalized communities around the world, in fact, have intangible assets and creative capacities which remain largely invisible to the formal

[51] Agreement between the United Nations and the World Intellectual Property Organization, (*entered into effect* 17 December 1974), Article 1 [hereinafter 'UN-WIPO Agreement'], available at: http://www.wipo.int/treaties/en/agreement/index.html (accessed 26 June 2009); see also para. 13(1) of the Convention Establishing the World Intellectual Property Organization (Stockholm, 14 July 1967), 828 U.N.T.S. 3, 21 U.S.T. 1749 (*entered into force* 26 April 1970), *as amended* 28 September 1979 (*amendments entered into force* 1 June 1984), available at: http://www.wipo.int/export/sites/www/treaties/en/convention/pdf/trtdocs_wo029.pdf (accessed 3 February 2010).

economy and IP compass (Finger & Schuler 2004). Apart from areas such as the protection of traditional knowledge and cultural expressions, where the IP of local custodians is increasingly recognized, IP-related policies and discussions in relation to the informal sectors tend to focus mainly on issues of 'piracy' and IP enforcement. A development agenda needs to seriously re-examine the 'piracy' rhetoric and focus further attention on the socio-economic impact of IP enforcement in developing countries and LDCs, including the far-reaching consequences of criminal sanctions on human development.[52]

As WIPO is only one of many forums where discussions affecting IP and different aspects of human development are being pursued, the success of a development agenda will depend significantly on cross-fertilization of ideas and coordination of actions with other forums, and with all sectors, both for profit and nonprofit. Gold & Morin (2009) explore avenues for building a network around WIPO – involving other inter-governmental organizations, academics, think-tanks and non-profit organizations – to implement the Development Agenda. Discussing the programmatic focus of other international organizations in advancing the MDGs, Netanel (2008, pp. 12–13) notes:

> [A]lmost all the UN agencies identified in the Development Agenda's call for intensified cooperation have taken positions at odds with IP maximalism. Both WHO and UNESCO have expressed concern that uniformly strong IP rights run counter to human rights, particularly with regard to access to essential medicines; UNCTAD has sharply criticized the erosion of least developed countries' flexibilities in setting IP policies, particularly under TRIPS-plus agreements, as erecting barriers to development; and UNIDO has placed a premium on promoting technology transfer to least developed countries. One would thus expect that WIPO's close cooperation with other UN agencies would reinforce the Development Agenda's fundamental reorientation of WIPO's goals and priorities. (Footnotes omitted)

International agencies and governments may support a weakening (or strengthening) of rights in pursuit of specific human development objectives. Furthermore, the earlier discussion clarifies that views on IP strength levels will also depend on the technological and creative sectors involved and the interests and agendas of the stakeholders in question. A consequence is that both governments and stakeholders will seek to engage in forum shopping for the international organization with views most in alignment with their interests, and will then seek to transfer 'gains' in one forum to the others. Thus, ongoing processes at the WTO and the Convention on Biological Diversity (CBD), among others, will also affect how the future of the Development Agenda at WIPO unfolds.

6. Conclusion

In the terms used by the EPO Scenarios Report, the current environment for global knowledge production and dissemination is very much a 'Kaleidoscope

[52] These concerns are not limited to developing countries and LDCs, as seen from the civil society debates over the ongoing negotiations of an Anti-Counterfeiting Trade Agreement by countries including the US, the EU, Japan and Switzerland. See Ermert, M. 2010, 'Scope of Anti-Counterfeiting Agreement Again a Big Issue in Round Nine', Intellectual Property Watch, 26 June 2010, available at: http://www.ip-watch.org/weblog/2010/06/26/scope-of-anti-counterfeiting-agreement-again-a-big-issue-in-round-nine/ (accessed 28 June 2010).

Society', characterized by interconnected but fragmented communities and ongoing dynamic shifts in geopolitical power, all of which makes accurate predictions about the future innovation environment and IP impossible. Scenario planning, on the other hand, presents a promising tool for addressing the challenges posed by the complex, often polemic, nature of IP-related issues, the large number of different stakeholders involved and the absence of one-dimensional solutions (Scearce & Fulton 2004). While reviewing the scenario plans produced by organizations on the future of IP, this chapter briefly explored other IP-related themes for which scenario planning might be further considered. Some of these themes might even be addressed globally. For example, the future role of IP for clean energy innovation and transfer is particularly well-suited for a global scenario planning approach. The implications of climate change on human development across sectors has been discussed extensively in multiple forums (see UNDP 2007). Along with other driving forces shaping the future of IP and human development, considerations of climate change are likely to come increasingly into focus. Several other important themes which might be explored through scenario planning at the regional, national or local levels include, for example, the future implications of IP for preserving bio-cultural heritage including TK, the relationship between IP and food security and the impact of IP enforcement on access to education and livelihoods in developing countries. Approaching the future through narrative forms such as 'stories' and pictures may be culturally more accessible than legal writing to many stakeholders, including local communities.

IP protection remains at a global crossroads, and it is difficult to predict where it will go.[53] Driving forces – including changes in ideologies, geopolitical factors, new technologies and constituencies with stakes in the creative economy – and civil society action will likely have an impact in reshaping IP-related institutions as well as the general landscape for IP and human development. A variety of approaches can be taken by governments and civil society, at various levels, in shaping the future of IP. The future scenarios reviewed in this chapter can be placed within the context of several basic alternatives. One possibility is a gradual expansion of IPRs as countries come into compliance with the TRIPS Agreement at different implementation deadlines (Gollin 2008, p. 57).[54] Many developing and developed countries have, however, not made full use of the delayed implementation provided under the TRIPS Agreement (see Musungu 2006; Roffe 2007), and some have signed up to TRIPS-plus agreements (see Abbott & Reichman 2007). A second alternative is a broad expansion of protection of all types of IP around the world. For example, the US extended its term of copyright in 1998 (see discussion in Chapter 1). Expansion of IPRs, including enforcement, has been a foreign policy goal of the US government and global industry in implementing TRIPS and other bilateral and multilateral agreements (Gollin 2008, p. 57; see Chapters 2, 3 and 7).[55]

[53] The following three paragraphs draw from, and expand on, future options discussed in Gollin 2008, pp. 57–58.

[54] On transition periods for developing countries and LDCs, see Chapter 2 (Box 2.1) of this book.

[55] In relation to the EU, Abbott and Reichman (2007, p. 965) suggest that:'The EU has nominally adopted a policy of not pursuing pharmaceutical-related TRIPS-plus commitments in its negotiations with developing countries, while nonetheless 'free riding' on the pharmaceuticals commitments obtained by the United States'. They qualify, at the same time, that, 'it is not really the case that the EU foregoes additional pharmaceutical-related commitments in its bilateral and regional negotiations' (ibid.).

A third alternative is a rollback or reduction of IP protection, already visible in certain areas (ibid.). Some developing countries are pushing to expand compulsory licensing for national health reasons, and there are segments of the research community who advocate broadly exempting scientific research from patent infringement. Some countries, notably those rich in biodiversity, are adding restrictions on patents by requiring the applicant to identify the source of any genetic material or TK used in the invention. There has also been some rollback in developed countries in relation to particular areas of IP. For example, a string of US Supreme Court patent decisions have made it harder to obtain and enforce patents over the past several years.[56]

A further challenge for the future is to find new ways in which IP can promote social goals consistent with the global population's human development needs, including its needs in health, food security, education, promotion of bio-cultural heritage and contemporary cultural expressions, clean-energy and sustainable use of resources. The chapters of this book identified sectoral trends and options for policy and legal reforms in each of these areas. They explored, among other things, practical steps to facilitate access by marginalized stakeholders (in both developed and developing countries) to IP-protected knowledge goods and innovations of relevance to human development. They also highlighted ways to support local knowledge systems and innovation models in developing countries and LDCs. We hope that these ideas will generate further discussion and collaboration by a spectrum of organizations, communities and individuals to promote human development. As explored in the last section of this chapter, the evolving Development Agenda at WIPO could provide a context for a wide range of stakeholders in identifying alternative future scenarios relating to IP and human development. Such a process could help to clarify the social functions of IP in terms of enhancing the capabilities of individuals and communities in all spheres of human development.

REFERENCES

Abbott, F.M. 2006, 'Intellectual Property Provisions of Bilateral and Regional Trade Agreements of the United States in Light of U.S. Federal Law', *United Nations Conference on Trade and Development-International Centre for Trade and Sustainable Development Issue Paper 12*, UNCTAD-ICTSD, Geneva, available at: http://ictsd.net/downloads/2008/06/frederick20abbott201220final.pdf (accessed 25 January 2009).

Abbott, F.M. & Correa, C.M. 2007, 'World Trade Organization Accession Agreements: Intellectual Property Issues', *Global Economic Issues Publication*, Quaker, United Nations Office, Geneva, available at: http://frederickabbott.com/uploads/Abbott___Correa_Accession_WTO-IP-English.pdf (accessed 27 January 2009).

Aoki, K. & Luvai, K. 2007, 'Reclaiming "Common Heritage" Treatment in the International Plant Genetic Resources Regime Complex', *Michigan State Law Review*, vol. 2007,

[56] See, for example, *KSR Int'l Co. v. Teleflex*, 550 U.S. 398 (2007), a case raising the nonobviousness requirement for obtaining a patent; *Microsoft Corp. v. AT&T Corp.*, 550 U.S. 437 (2007), a case in which the Supreme Court ruled that a US software patent does not protect against copies of the patented software being installed abroad; and *eBay Inc. v. MercExchange, LLC*, 547 U.S. 388 (2006), a case establishing a more difficult standard for obtaining a permanent injunction against the use of patented material after a finding that a patent is valid and infringed.

no. 1, pp. 35–70, available at: http://msulr.law.msu.edu/back_issues/2007/1/Aoki.pdf (accessed 2 May 2009).

Barton, J. 2008, 'Patenting and Access to Clean Energy Technologies in Developing Countries', *WIPO Magazine*, February 2008, available at: http://www.wipo.int/wipo_magazine/en/2008/01/article_0003.html (accessed 27 January 2009).

Belder, L. 2007, 'Cultural Expressions: From Common Source to Public Domain', in F. Macmillan (ed.), *New Directions in Copyright Law*, vol. 4, Edward Elgar, Cheltenham, UK, and Northampton, MA.

Berkman Center for Internet & Society & GarnerG2 2005a, *Copyright and Digital Media in a Post-Napster World: 2005 Update*, Harvard Law School, Cambridge, available at: http://cyber.law.harvard.edu/media/wpsupplement2005 (accessed 24 January 2009).

Berkman Center for Internet & Society & GartnerG2 2005b, *Copyright and Digital Media in a Post-Napster World: International Supplement*, Harvard Law School, Cambridge, available at: http://cyber.law.harvard.edu/media/wpsupplement2005 (accessed 1 June 2009).

Borges Barbosa, D., Chon, M. & Moncayo von Hase, A. 2008, 'Slouching Towards Development in International Intellectual Property', *Michigan State Law Review*, vol. 2007, no. 1, available at: http://ssrn.com/abstract=1081366 (accessed 1 August 2009).

Boyle, J. 2008, *The Public Domain: Enclosing the Commons of the Mind*, Yale University Press, New Haven and London, available at: http://www.thepublicdomain.org/download (accessed 30 November 2009).

Britz, J.J. & Lor, P.J. 2004, 'A Moral Reflection on the Digitization of Africa's Digital Heritage', *IFLA Journal*, vol. 30, no. 3, pp. 216–224.

Chander, A. & Sunder, M. 2004, 'The Romance of the Public Domain', *California Law Review*, vol. 92, no. 5, pp. 1331–1374, available at: http://ssrn.com/abstract=562301 (accessed 27 January 2009).

Chon, M. 2006, 'Intellectual Property and the Development Divide', *Cardozo Law Review*, vol. 27, no. 6, pp. 2821–2912.

Chon, M. 2007, 'Substantive Equality in International Intellectual Property Norm Setting and Interpretation', in D. Gervais (ed.), *Intellectual Property, Trade and Development: Strategies to Optimize Economic Development in a TRIPS-Plus Era*, Oxford University Press, Oxford and New York.

Coates, J. 2007, 'Creative Commons – The Next Generation: Creative Commons License Use Five Years On', *SCRIPTed*, vol. 4, no. 1, pp. 73–94, available at: http://www.law.ed.ac.uk/ahrc/script-ed/vol4–1/coates.asp (accessed 27 January 2009).

Commission on Intellectual Property Rights 2002 (CIPR), *Integrating Intellectual Property Rights and Development Policy*, CIPR, London, available at: http://www.iprcommission.org/papers/pdfs/final_report/CIPRfullfinal.pdf (accessed 19 October 2008).

Correa, C. 2008, 'Expanding Patent Rights in Pharmaceuticals: The Linkage between Patents and Drug Registration', in N.W. Netanel (ed.), *The Development Agenda: A Global Intellectual Property and Developing Countries*, Oxford University Press, New York.

de Beer, J. (ed.) 2009, *Implementing the WIPO Development Agenda*, Wilfrid Laurier University Press and International Development Research Centre (IDRC), Ottawa.

Deere, C. 2009, 'Reforming Governance to Advance the WIPO Development Agenda', in J. de Beer (ed.), *Implementing the WIPO Development Agenda*, Wilfrid Laurier University Press and International Research Development Centre, Ottawa.

Derclaye, E. 2008, 'Intellectual Property Rights and Global Warming', *Marquette Intellectual Property Review*, vol. 12, no. 2, pp. 265–297.

Derclaye, E. 2009, 'Should Patent Law Help Cool the Planet? An Inquiry from the Point of View of Environmental Law – Part I', *European Intellectual Property Review*, vol. 31, no. 4, pp. 168–184.

Dhruv, B.P. 2006, 'Does the International Intellectual Property Regime Impact or Influence Progress in Human Development?', Indian Law Society (ILS) Law College, Pune, India.

Diamond, J. 2005, *Collapse: How Societies Choose to Fail or Survive*, Allen Lane, London.

Drahos, P. & Braithwaite, J. 2003, *Information Feudalism: Who Owns the Knowledge Economy?*, Earthscan Publications Ltd., London.

Dutfield, G. 2006, 'Protecting Traditional Knowledge: Pathways to the Future', *International Centre for Trade and Sustainable Development (ICTSD) Issue Paper No. 16*, ICTSD, Geneva, available at: http://www.iprsonline.org/unctadictsd/docs/Graham%20final.pdf (accessed 25 January 2009).

Dutfield, G. 2009, *Intellectual Property Rights and the Life Science Industries: Past, Present and Future*, World Scientific Publishing, Singapore.

Electronic Frontier Foundation (EFF) 2004, 'A Better Way Forward: Voluntary Collective Licensing of Music File Sharing', *Let the Music Play White Paper*, EFF, San Francisco, available at: http://www.eff.org/files/collective_lic_wp.pdf (accessed 25 January 2009).

European Patent Office (EPO) 2007, *Scenarios for the Future: How Might IP Regimes Evolve by 2025? What Global Legitimacy Might Such Regimes Have?*, EPO, Munich.

Evans, K., Velarde, S.J., Prieto, R., Rao, S.N., Sertzen, S., Dávila, K., Cronkleton, P. & de Jong, W. 2006, *Field Guide to the Future: Four Ways for Communities to Think Ahead*, E. Bennett E. & M. Zurek (eds.), Center for International Forestry Research (CIFOR), ASB-Partnership for the Tropical Forest Margins and the World Agroforestry Centre, Nairobi, available at: http://www.asb.cgiar.org/ma/scenarios (accessed 4 June 2009).

Finger, J.M. & Schuler, P. (eds.) 2004, *Poor People's Knowledge: Promoting Intellectual Property in Developing Countries*, World Bank and Oxford University Press, Washington, DC.

Fukada-Parr, S. & Shiva Kumar, A.K. (eds.) 2005, *Readings in Human Development: Concepts, Measures and Policies for a Development Paradigm*, Oxford University Press, Oxford and New York.

Fukuda-Parr, S. 2009, 'Human Rights and Human Development', in K. Basu & R. Kanbur (eds.), *Arguments for a Better World: Essays in Honour of Amartya Sen*, vol. 2, Oxford University Press, New York.

Gervais, D. (ed.) 2007, *Intellectual Property, Trade and Development: Strategies to Optimize Economic Development in a TRIPS Plus Era*, Oxford University Press, Oxford and New York.

Gold, E.R. & Morin, J.F. 2009, 'From Agenda to Implementation: Working Outside the WIPO Box', in J. de Beer (ed.), *Implementing the WIPO Development Agenda*, Wilfrid Laurier University Press and International Research Development Centre, Ottawa.

Gollin, M. 2008, *Driving Innovation: Intellectual Property Strategies for a Dynamic World*, Cambridge University Press, Cambridge and New York.

Gollin, M. 2009, 'Intellectual Property Rights and Innovation', *eJournal USA, Roots of Innovation*, vol. 14, no. 11, pp. 31–35, available at: http://www.venable.com/files/Publication/d0a0d9de-f2dd-48dc-afa0-81f3469dc78e/Presentation/Publication

Attachment/77952a4c-2a83-4671-bd05-87d12fecc092/IPR_Innovation.pdf (accessed 20 January 2010).

Gould, D.M. & Gruben, W.C. 1996, 'The Role of Intellectual Property Rights in Economic Growth', *Journal of Development Economics*, vol. 48, no. 2, pp. 323–350.

Grimmelmann, J. 2009, 'How to Fix The Google Book Search Settlement', *Journal of Internet Law*, vol. 12, no. 10, pp. 11–20.

Halbert, D.J. 2001, 'Intellectual Property in the Year 2025', *Journal of Futures Studies*, vol. 6, no. 1, pp. 25–60, Tamkang University – Graduate Institute of Futures Studies, Taipei.

Halbert, D.J. 2003, 'Theorizing the Public Domain: Copyright and the Development of a Cultural Commons', in A. Sarat & P. Ewick (eds.), *Studies in Law, Politics, and Society*, vol. 29, pp. 3–36, Jai Press, New York.

Halbert, D.J. 2007, 'The World Intellectual Property Organization: Past, Present and Future', *Journal of the Copyright Society of the USA*, vol. 54, nos. 2–3, pp. 253–284.

Hope, J. 2008, *BioBazaar: The Open Source Revolution*, Harvard University Press, Cambridge, MA.

International Centre for Trade and Sustainable Development (ICTSD) 2007, 'WIPO Members Agree on Development Agenda', *Bridges Weekly Trade News Digest*, vol. 11, no. 22, available at: http://ictsd.net/i/news/bridgesweekly/6513/ (accessed 25 January 2009).

International Expert Group on Biotechnology, Innovation and Intellectual Property (IEG-BIIP) 2008, *Toward a New Era of Intellectual Property: From Confrontation to Negotiation*, Centre for Intellectual Property Policy, Montreal.

International Federation of Library Associations (IFLA), Library Copyright Alliance (LCA) and Electronic Information for Libraries (eIFL) 2007, 'The Public Domain: Why WIPO Should Care', in *Committee on Copyright and Other Legal Matters (CLM)*, Provisional Committee on Proposals Related to a WIPO Development Agenda Third Session, Geneva, 19–23 February, available at: http://www.ifla.org/III/clm/p1/CLM-pr08032007.htm (accessed 25 January 2009).

McNeely, J.A. 2005, 'Protected Areas in 2023: Scenarios for an Uncertain Future', *Conservation Practice at the Landscape Scale*, vol. 22, no. 1, pp. 61–74, available at: http://www.georgewright.org/221mcneely.pdf (accessed 15 February 2010).

Johns, A. 2009, *Piracy: The Intellectual Property Wars from Gutenberg to Gates*, University of Chicago Press, London.

Kawooya, D. 2006, 'Copyright, Indigenous Knowledge and Africa's University Libraries: The Case of Uganda', in World Library and Information Congress: 72nd IFLA General Conference and Council, Seoul, Korea, 20–24 August 2006, IFLA, available at: http://www.ifla.org/IV/ifla72/papers/116-Kawooya-en.pdf (accessed 1 August 2009).

Kneen, B. 2004, 'Privatisation and the Public Domain', *The Ram's Horn*, vol. 220, available at: http://www.ramshorn.ca/archive2004/220.html (accessed 25 January 2009).

Lang, T. & Heasman, M. 2004, *Food Wars: The Global Battle for Mouth, Minds and Markets*, Earthscan Publications Ltd., London.

Leach, J. 2005, 'Modes of Creativity and the Register of Ownership', in R.A. Ghosh (ed.), *CODE: Collaborative Ownership and the Digital Economy*, Massachusetts Institute of Technology Press, Cambridge, MA.

Litman, J. 1990, 'The Public Domain', *Emory Law Journal*, vol. 39, no. 4, pp. 965–989.

Mara, K. 2009, 'WIPO Development Committee Deepens Look at Technology Transfer, Coordination', *Intellectual Property Watch*, 19 November 2009, available at:

http://www.ip-watch.org/weblog/2009/11/19/wipo-development-committee-deepens-look-at-technology-transfer-coordination/ (accessed 22 January 2010).

Masser, A.L. 2009, 'Measurement Methodologies for Legal Empowerment of the Poor', *United Nationals Development Programme (UNDP) Oslo Governance Centre Discussion Paper 6*, available at: http://ssrn.com/abstract=1370406 (accessed 1 August 2009).

Maurer, S., Rai, A. & Sali, A. 2004, 'Finding Cures for Tropical Diseases: Is Open Source an Answer?', *PloS Medicine*, vol. 1, no. 3, pp. 183–186.

Millennium Ecosystem Assessment 2005, *Ecosystems and Human Well-being: Synthesis*, Island Press, Washington, DC, available at: http://www.millenniumassessment.org/en/synthesis.aspx (accessed 25 January 2009).

Musungu, S.F. 2006, 'A Conceptual Framework for Priority Identification and Delivery of IP Technical Assistance for LDCs During the Extended Transition Period Under the TRIPS Agreement', QUNO, Issue Paper No. 7.

Musungu, S.F. & Dutfield, G. 2003, *Multilateral Agreements and a TRIPS-Plus World: The World Intellectual Property Organization (WIPO)*, Quaker United Nations Office (QUNO), Geneva, and Quaker International Affairs Program (QIAP), Ottawa, available at: http://www.quno.org/geneva/pdf/economic/Issues/Multilateral-Agreements-in-TRIPS-plus-English.pdf (accessed 25 January 2009).

Netanel, N.W. 2008, 'Introduction: The WIPO Development Agenda and Its Development Policy Context', in N.W. Netanel (ed.), *The Development Agenda: Global Intellectual Property and Developing Countries*, Oxford University Press, New York, available at: http://ssrn.com/abstract=1310388 (accessed 28 April 2010).

Oldham, P.D. 2009, 'An Access and Benefit-Sharing Commons? The Role of Commons/Open Source Licenses in the International Regime on Access to Genetic Resources and Benefit Sharing', *Initiative for the Prevention of Biopiracy, Research Documents*, vol. 4, no. 11, available at: http://papers.ssrn.com/sol3/papers.cfm?abstract_id=1438027 (accessed 20 November 2009).

Organisation for Economic Cooperation and Development (OECD) 2004, *Patents and Innovation: Trends and Policy Challenges*, OECD, Paris, p. 26, available at: http://www.oecd.org/dataoecd/48/12/24508541.pdf (accessed 25 January 2009).

Ostergard, R.L. 2007, 'Economic Growth and Intellectual Property Rights Protection: A Reassessment of the Conventional Wisdom', in D. Gervais (ed.), *Intellectual Property, Trade, and Development*, Oxford University Press, New York.

Ranis, G., Steward, F. & Samman, E. 2006, 'Human Development: Beyond the Human Development Index', *Journal of Human Development*, vol. 7, no. 3, pp. 323–324.

Rens, A., Prabhala, A. & Kawooya, D. 2006, *Intellectual Property, Education and Access to Knowledge in Southern Africa*, UNCTAD – ICTSD, available at: http://www.iprsonline.org/unctadictsd/docs/06%2005%2031%20tralac%20amended-pdf.pdf (accessed 10 July 2009).

Rhoades, G. 2001, 'Whose Property Is It: Negotiating with the University', *Academe Online*, available at: http://www.aaup.org/AAUP/pubsres/academe/2001/SO/Feat/rhoa.htm (accessed 25 January 2009).

Roffe, P. 2007, 'Intellectual Property, Bilateral Agreements and Sustainable Development: The Challenges of Implementation', *Intellectual Property, Bilateral Agreements and Sustainable Development Series 1*, Center for International Environmental Law (CIEL), available at: http://www.ciel.org/Publications/FTA_ImplementationPub_Jan07.pdf (accessed 18 January 2009).

Ruiz, M. 2004, 'National and Regional Laws to Protect Indigenous Knowledge Related to Genetic Resources', *Science and Development Network Policy Brief*, available at: http://www.scidev.net/en/policy-briefs/national-and-regional-laws-to-protect-ik-related-t.html (accessed 27 January 2009).

Samuelson, P. 2006, 'Enriching Discourse on Public Domains', *Duke Law Journal*, vol. 55, no. 4, pp. 783–834, available at: http://ssrn.com/abstract=925052 (accessed 15 February 2010).

Scearce, D. & Fulton, D. 2004, *What If? The Art of Scenario Thinking for Non-Profits*, Global Business Network (GBN), San Francisco, available at: http://www.gbn.com/articles/pdfs/GBN_What%20If.pdf (accessed 25 January 2009).

Schoemaker, P.J.H. 1995, 'Scenario Planning: A Tool for Strategic Thinking', *Sloan Management Review*, vol. 36, no. 2, pp. 25–40.

Sell, S. 2003, *Private Power, Public Law: The Globalization of Intellectual Property Rights*, Cambridge University Press, Cambridge and New York.

Sen, A. 2000, *Development as Freedom*, Anchor Books, New York.

Srinivas, R.K. 2008, 'Sink or Swim: Eco-Patent Commons and Transfer of Environmentally Sustainable Technologies', *Bridges Trade BioRes*, vol. 2, no. 2, International Centre for Trade Sustainable Development (ICTSD).

Strandburg, K.J. 2009, 'Evolving Innovation Paradigms and the Global Intellectual Property Regime', *Connecticut Law Review*, vol. 41, no. 3, pp. 861–920, available at: http://ssrn.com/abstract=1229543 (accessed 1 August 2009).

Strauss, J. 2008, 'Is There a Global Warming of Patents', *Journal of World Intellectual Property*, vol. 11, no. 1, pp. 58–62.

Sunder, M. 2007, 'The Invention of Traditional Knowledge', in J. Boyle & L. Lessig (eds.), *Symposium, Cultural Environmentalism @10, Law & Contemporary Problems*, vol. 70, no. 2, pp. 97–124, available at: http://www.law.duke.edu/journals/lcp/lcptoc70spring2007 (accessed 27 January 2009).

Sunder, M. 2008, 'Intellectual Property and Development as Freedom', in N.W. Netanel (ed.), *The Development Agenda: Global Intellectual Property and Developing Countries*, Oxford University Press, New York.

Suthersanen, U. 2008, 'A2K and the WIPO Development Agenda: Time to List the "Public Domain"', *UNCTAD-ICTSD Project on IPRs and Sustainable Development, Policy Brief Number 1*, available at: http://ictsd.net/downloads/2009/02/uma_final2.pdf (accessed 15 June 2009).

Tussey, D.S. 2008, 'What if Employees Owned Their Copyrights?', *Michigan State Law Review*, vol. 2008, pp. 233–244, available at: http://ssrn.com/abstract=1223461 (accessed 1 August 2009).

United Nations Development Programme (UNDP) 1996, *UNDP Human Development Report 1996: Economic Growth and Human Development*, UNDP, New York, available at: http://hdr.undp.org/en/reports/global/hdr1996/ (accessed 25 January 2009).

UNDP 2004, *UNDP Human Development Report 2004: Cultural Liberty in Today's Diverse World*, UNDP, New York, available at: http://hdr.undp.org/en/reports/global/hdr2004/ (accessed 25 January 2009).

UNDP 2005, *Practice Note on Traditional Knowledge, Access to Genetic Resources and Benefit-Sharing*, (authored by T. Wong, T. Hay-Edie, T. Akhtar & C. McNeill) UNDP, available at: http://www.energyandenvironment.undp.org/undp/index.cfm?module=Library&page=Document&DocumentID=6388 (accessed 12 November 2008).

UNDP 2007, *UNDP Human Development Report 2007/2008: Fighting Climate Change: Human Solidarity in a Divided World*, UNDP, New York, available at: http://hdr.undp.org/en/media/HDR˙20072008˙EN˙Complete.pdf (accessed 25 January 2009).

United Nations University – World Institute for Development Economics (UNU-WIDER) 2007, *Measuring Human Well-Being: Key Findings and Policy Lessons*, UNU Press.

Vivas-Eugui, D. 2003, *Regional and Bilateral Agreements and a TRIPS-Plus World: The Free Trade Area of the Americas*, QUNO, Geneva, and QIAP, Ottawa, available at: http://www.quno.org/geneva/pdf/economic/Issues/FTAs-TRIPS-plus-English.pdf (accessed 25 January 2009).

Waelde, C. & MacQueen, H. (eds.) 2007, *Intellectual Property: The Many Faces of the Public Domain*, Edward Elgar Publishing, Cheltenham and Northampton, MA.

Wallis, B. 2006, 'The Politics and Ideology of Intellectual Property', *IPFrontline*, available at: http://www.ipfrontline.com/depts/article.asp?id=11817&deptid=6 (accessed 25 January 2009).

World Intellectual Property Organization (WIPO) 2003, *IP: A Power Tool for Economic Growth*, available at: http://www.wipo.int/edocs/prdocs/en/2003/wipo_pr_2003_337.html (accessed 27 January 2009).

WIPO 2005, *Overview of Policy Directions, Priority Areas and Projects in WIPO's Support of the Development Objectives of Developing Countries*, available at: http://www.wipo.int/edocs/mdocs/mdocs/en/pcipd_4/pcipd_4_2.pdf (accessed 27 January 2009).

WIPO 2007, *General Report of the Forty-Third Series of Meetings*, Assemblies of the Member States of WIPO, 24 September to 3 October 2007, Geneva, Doc. A/43/16, available at http://www.wipo.int/edocs/mdocs/govbody/en/a 43/a 43 16-main1.pdf (accessed 15 March 2010).

WIPO 2008, 'Climate Change – the Technology Challenge', *WIPO Magazine*, February 2008, available at: http://www.wipo.int/export/sites/www/wipo_magazine/en/pdf/2008/wipo_pub_121_2008_01.pdf (accessed 15 April 2010).

Worsley, P. 1997, *Knowledges: What Different Peoples Make of the World*, Profile Books, London.

APPENDIX A

Capability, opulence and utility[1]

David A. Clark

The conceptual foundations of the capability approach can be found in Sen's critiques of traditional welfare economics, which typically conflate well-being with either opulence (income, commodity command) or utility (happiness, desire fulfilment)...Like Adam Smith, Sen (1983) emphasizes that economic growth and the expansion of goods and services are necessary for human development. However, like Aristotle, he reiterates the familiar argument that '...wealth is evidently not the good we are seeking; for it is merely useful and for the sake of something else' (Sen 1990, p. 44). In judging the quality of life we should consider what people are able to achieve. Sen then observes that different people and societies typically *differ* in their capacity to convert income and commodities into valuable achievements. For example, a disabled person may require extra resources (wheelchairs, ramps, lifts and so on) to achieve the same things (moving around) as an able-bodied person...In comparing the well-being of different people, not enough information is provided by looking only at the commodities each can successfully command. Instead we must consider how well people are able to function with the goods and services at their disposal.

Sen also challenges the welfare or utility approach, which concentrates on happiness, pleasure and desire fulfilment...Following Rawls he recognizes that utility does not distinguish between different sources of pleasure and pain or different kinds of desires (Sen 1984, p. 308; Rawls 1971, pp. 30–31). In particular, utility fails to discriminate against offensive tastes...More fundamentally, Sen points out that there is more to life than achieving utility: 'Happiness or desire fulfilment represents only one aspect of human existence' (Sen 1984, p. 512). While it is important to take note of utility, there are many other things of intrinsic value (notably rights and positive freedoms) that are neglected by the welfare approach (Sen 1987, p. 8; 1992, p. 54; 1999, p. 62)...

These considerations lead to the conclusion that neither opulence (income, commodity command) nor utility (happiness, desire fulfilment) constitute or adequately represent human well-being and deprivation. Instead what is required is a more direct approach that focuses on human function(ing)s and the capability to achieve valuable function(ing)s...[For Sen,] '[a] functioning is an achievement of a person: what she or he manages to do or be. It reflects, as it were, a part of the "state" of that person' (Sen 1985a, p. 10). Achieving a functioning (e.g. being

[1] This is an extract from Clark 2006, pp. 32–35. The references cited in this Appendix are found in the reference list for Chapter 1 of this book.

adequately nourished) with a given bundle of commodities (e.g. bread or rice) depends on a range of personal and social factors (e.g. metabolic rates, body size, age, gender, activity levels, health, access to medical services, nutritional knowledge and education, climatic conditions, etc.). A functioning therefore refers to the *use* a person makes of the commodities at his or her command. [Capability, on the other hand,] reflects a person's *ability* to achieve a given functioning ('doing' or 'being') (Saith 2001, p. 8) ... For example, a person may have the ability to avoid hunger, but may choose to fast or go on hunger strike instead ... In practice Sen uses the term 'capability' in a broader sense ... to refer to 'the alternative combination of functionings the person can achieve, from which he or she can choose one collection' (Sen, 1993, p. 31; 1992, p. 40; 2005, p. 153) ... Sen argues that capability or freedom has intrinsic value and should be regarded as 'the primary informational base' (Sen 1993, pp. 38–39).

One of the chief strengths of Sen's framework is that it is flexible and exhibits a considerable degree of internal pluralism, which allows researchers to develop and apply it in many different ways (Alkire 2002, pp. 8–11, 28–30) ... Sen indicates that the capability approach can be used to assess individual advantage in a range of different spaces ... For example, the assessment of poverty might involve concentrating on a relatively small sub-set of basic capabilities. Evaluating well-being or human development on the other hand seems to require a much longer and more diverse list of capabilities (see e.g. Sen 1993, pp. 31–2, 40–42). The focus of the capability approach can be broadened further to include 'agency', which recognizes that individuals often have values and goals (such as preserving the environment, purchasing free trade products or opposing injustice, tyranny and oppression) that transcend and sometimes even conflict with personal well-being (see Sen 1985a, 1985b, 1992). The capability approach has also been adjusted to focus on inequality, social justice, living standards and rights and duties (among other things). Finally, Sen (1999, p. 77) recognizes that the capability approach is not sufficient for all evaluative purposes. By itself the capability approach does not provide a complete theory of justice or development (see Sen 1983; 1988; 1992, p. 77; 2005).

Source: Clark, D.A. 2006, 'Capability Approach', in D.A. Clark (ed.), *The Elgar Companion to Development Studies*, Edward Elgar, Cheltenham, UK, pp. 32–45.

APPENDIX B

Exploring alternative, collaborative models of innovation for medicines and vaccines[1]

There has been increasing debate over the appropriateness of the intellectual property (IP) system for the promotion of pharmaceutical innovation and access to medicines. Some have argued that the reason poor countries have difficulty accessing medicines is not related to the IP system, but due to deficient health infrastructures and precarious local sanitation systems in the developing world (International Federation of Pharmaceuticals Manufacturers & Associations [IFPMA] 2004, p. 49). Others have qualified that a differentiation in local infrastructures does not detract from the fact that global structures, including the international IP system, actively shape those local variants and inequities.[2] Among those who think that the IP system is flawed, whether in its design or implementation, there are increasing discussions about finding new and better models of innovation and medical progress. In a recent report by the International Expert Group on Biotechnology, Innovation and Intellectual Property entitled *Toward a New Era of Intellectual Property: From Confrontation to Negotiation* ('IEGBIIP Report 2008'), a distinction is made between so-called 'Old IP' and an evolving 'New IP' era. The former refers to the way the IP system has been interpreted traditionally, mainly using principles of competition and profit-making as the basis for innovation. The core finding of the report is:

> [P]olicy-makers and business leaders must give shape to a new era of intellectual property (IP) to stimulate innovation and broaden access to discoveries. The current system, 'Old IP', rests on the belief that if some IP is good, more must be better. But such thinking has proved counterproductive to industry, which in health fields has seen declining levels of innovation despite increasing stakes in IP. The era of Old IP has also proved counterproductive to the world's poor who await advances in health and agriculture long available to the global elite.

According to the IEGBIIP Report, the actors involved in research and development (R&D) need a shift in paradigm towards a 'New IP' model based on the concept of sharing knowledge rather than hoarding knowledge – a model where IP is viewed as a 'servant to ... values such as equity and fairness' (ibid., p. 14). This emphasis that IP should be evaluated as a means towards attaining social justice and improving human well-being, rather than simply as an end in itself, echoes the human development paradigm discussed in Chapter 1 of this book. The 'New

[1] Contributed by Claudia Trezza and Tzen Wong. See reference section for Chapter 2 for full references to this Appendix.

[2] Pogge T. 2008, 'Human Rights: The Second 60 Years', paper presented at the United Nations University (UNU) lecture series 'Emerging Thinking on Global Issues', New York, 11 December 2008.

IP' model also reflects cultural factors in the innovation process, along with collective processes as a route towards equitable reforms. Innovation is seen as a social and communal phenomenon, a product of actors collaborating rather than working in isolation. The IEGBIIP Report offers numerous examples of this collaborative approach, including many public-private partnerships (PPPs).[3] From the Public Interest Intellectual Property Advisors (PIIPA) literature review for this book, other examples of alternative, collaborative models for pharmaceutical innovation have been identified. Some models are briefly described here along with challenges or obstacles. Most of the models seek to direct funding to treatments for diseases where traditional market incentives have been insufficient, or explore different means of financing and rewarding research efforts.

1. Public-private partnerships (PPPs) and non-profit pharmaceutical companies

Some public-private partnerships (PPPs) have been created specifically to develop pharmaceutical products, while others focus on distribution. A multitude of PPPs, such as the International AIDS Vaccine Initiative (IAVI), the Medicines for Malaria Venture (MMV) and the TB Alliance, involve non-profit and corporate entities joining forces to tackle specific diseases – using a portfolio management approach and outsourcing the development of the product to an external body, usually a drug company. Another PPP model involves engaging non-profit pharmaceutical companies for the development of the product. This model is exemplified by OneWorld Health. The latter carries out R&D activities that are said to be led 'not by the large anticipated revenues of a product, rather by global health needs' (Hale, Woo & Lipton 2005). Yet, its organizational structure and efficiency models are said to be the same as those in the for-profit companies (ibid.). The company develops drugs based on chemical compounds donated by for-profit companies, in many cases because they promise little or no monetary return (ibid.). An example is the donation by Celera Genomics to OneWorld Health of a licence for the compound K-777 for the development of a treatment for Chagas disease, a life-threatening disease caused by parasites (Strosberg et al. 2007). OneWorld Health is currently working on the development of this treatment (see Chapter 2).

The challenges that a non-profit pharmaceutical company faces cannot be disregarded. Besides having to produce low-cost medicines at low production costs while ensuring high medical quality, a non-profit pharmaceutical company may have little room to decide where to invest in R&D and may be constrained by the donation decisions of external for-profit companies. Philanthropic and other financial backing for such companies is very important. As with other pharmaceutical companies, a non-profit pharmaceutical company faces the challenge of recouping the high costs of pharmaceutical development (particularly the costs of clinical trials after research has identified likely targets). Moreover, no matter how many

[3] The Human Genome Project is cited as an example that reflects the 'New IP' paradigm shift. The Project is an international collaboration of public research centres that sequenced the entire human genome and provided the information publicly.

products the non-profit company is able to produce, the challenge of having a reliable health care system on the ground that is capable of distributing the drugs to patients still remains.

There are initiatives where R&D involves compounds derived from plant genetic resources and associated traditional medicine knowledge (TMK). As noted in the IEGBIIP Report, Artemisinin is a traditional herbal remedy in Chinese medicine that has been proven as a treatment for malaria, particularly in combination with other drugs. A research team at the University of California, Berkeley (UC Berkeley), which is at the forefront of some PPP efforts, has developed a process to extract this compound. This work was done in conjunction with a small biotechnology company, Amyris Biotechnologies (IEGBIIP 2008, p. 31). Backed by a $42.6 million grant from the Bill & Melinda Gates Foundation, the Institute for OneWorld Health entered into a non-profit partnership with UC Berkeley and Amyris Biotechnologies. Under the arrangement, Amyris is committed to taking 'no profit from the sales of this product to the developing world' (ibid.). UC Berkeley is also involved in a project for development of a new AIDS and cancer drug, Prostatin, derived from indigenous uses of the mamala tree in Samoa (ibid.; see Chapter 4, Box 4.5). Such collaborative projects involve particular considerations relating to the important inputs of custodians of TMK, the need to obtain their free, prior and informed consent (FPIC), as well as regulations under the Convention on Biological Diversity on access and benefit-sharing for genetic resources and associated traditional knowledge (see Chapter 4, Box. 4.2).

2. Medical R&D treaty and prize funds

In February of 2005, a group of medical researchers, non-governmental organizations (NGOs), parliamentarians, government officials, and other stakeholders submitted a letter to the WHO asking that it evaluate a proposal for a new global treaty to support medical R&D.[4] The model of the so-called Medical Research and Development Treaty requires signatory countries to commit to spending a proportion of their gross domestic product (GDP) on medical R&D, more specifically on Qualified Medical Research and Development (QMRD), which includes basic biomedical research, development of pharmaceutical products, medical evaluations and the protection of traditional medical knowledge (ibid.). The treaty is based on the concept of R&D innovation as a shared responsibility (which seems to resonate with the 'New IP' model mentioned earlier). It is built on the model of the 'prize fund', under which a specific amount of money is awarded to the first firm that can meet a specified medical target (Faunce & Nasu 2008).

The logic behind prize funds is that the current system of financing R&D is flawed – prices of drugs are too high and the money is being invested on marketing campaigns for 'unimportant' pharmaceutical products rather than on products that are needed to save lives in the poorest countries of the world (Love & Hubbard 2007).

[4] See 'Letter to Ask World Health Organization to Evaluate New Treaty Framework for Medical Research and Development', delivered to WHO on 24 February 2005, available at: http://www.cptech.org/workingdrafts/rndsignonletter.html (accessed 30 April 2010).

Within this framework, governments need to create incentives to develop drugs for neglected diseases instead of simply for diseases that can yield high profits. As Love and Hubbard explain in their paper 'The Big Idea: Prizes to Stimulate R&D for New Medicines':

> Reforming the way we pay for R&D on new medicines involves a simple but powerful idea. Rather than give drug developers the exclusive rights to sell products, the government would award innovators money: large monetary 'prizes' tied to the actual impact of the invention on improvements in health care outcomes that successful products actually deliver. (Ibid., p. 2)

In their conclusion, Love and Hubbard explain how the use of a prize model can 'reward successful R&D projects, while permitting marginal cost pricing of products and avoiding the trap of overly bureaucratic and centralized decision-making' by separating the rewards for successful R&D investment from the sales of products (ibid., p. 35). Along with ensuring adequate funding for prizes, some challenges facing prize funds include clearly defining the medical target before the research has started and specifying the corresponding fair amount of funding the researcher would receive.

3. Advanced market commitments

Advanced market commitments (AMCs), also called 'advanced purchase commitments', are undertakings made by an international body to make a supplementary payment to any firm which is able to produce and sell a 'qualifying vaccine' at a fixed price. Under this framework, a vaccine is 'qualified' if it meets certain criteria of efficacy and safety that have been determined in advance. This model is explained in depth by Kremer and Glennerster (2004). Advanced market commitments are a refined version of prizes. Instead of granting prizes based on a specific technical target, AMCs grant awards when the pharmaceutical product is sold. In other words, AMCs reward commercial success, not just technical efficacy (Hollis 2007). In February 2007, a pilot AMC was launched to target pneumococcal disease, a major cause of pneumonia and meningitis. Various developed country governments[5] along with the Bill & Melinda Gates Foundation pledged $1.5 billion to provide incentives for the development of a new vaccine that promises to prevent up to an estimated 5.8 million childhood deaths by 2030.[6]

One difficulty with AMCs is in identifying the technical requirements of product eligibility (Hollis 2007). Since these have to be defined before research begins, it is not easy to capture all contingencies (ibid.). To tackle the limitations of AMCs, comprehensive advanced market commitments (CAMCs) have been proposed whereby a desired health effect is established and a payment is made to the patentee over a period of years for innovative drugs or vaccines based on a measured health effect. This means that an estimate has to be given on the effectiveness of the product to

[5] These include Italy, the UK, Canada, Russia and Norway.

[6] See GAVI Alliance, 'Advance Market Commitments', available at: http://www.gavialliance.org/vision/policies/in_financing/amcs/index.php (accessed 15 February 2009).

be developed (ibid.). Studying such schemes, Pogge (2005, pp. 182–209) and Hollis (2007) have proposed a model whereby the benefits reached through research and the appropriate award are measured in proportion to so-called 'quality-adjusted life years' (QALYs). According to Pogge, what is needed is a reward mechanism for pharmaceutical innovation based on global health impact, rather than on profits from sales, under which a condition for the reward is that companies make the products available to the global market at the lowest feasible costs. In fact, what Pogge has in mind is a 'Global Health Impact Fund', a 'generalized commitment, whereby any medicine that works gets rewarded on the basis of its global health impact'.[7] The company participating in this scheme would have to agree to sell the product at cost; the reward would be based on the product's quality (i.e. how much it helps the people who need it) and on the quantity sold and used (i.e. how many people who obtain the medicine actually take it according to the correct regime).[8] In other words, Pogge proposes a reward that is proportional to the health impact of the medicine. This scheme would be complementary to the current patent system and voluntary for the pharmaceutical company. However, the firm accepting payments under this format must freely license its patent rights (Hollis 2007).

4. Patent pools

Patent pools are being studied and piloted to fill the market gap for neglected diseases. They enhance innovation in areas of high therapeutic need by enabling patent holders to earn royalties from licensing and gain facilitated access to the inventions of others. The NGO Médecins Sans Frontières (MSF) has defined patent pools in the following way:[9]

> A patent pool s a mechanism whereby a number of patents held by different entities, such as companies, universities or research institutes, are made available to others for production or further development – for example of paediatric formulations or fixed-dose formulations. The patent holders receive royalties that are paid by those who use the patents. The pool manages the licences, the negotiations with patent holders and the receipt and payment of royalties.[10]

[7] Interview with T. Pogge, 'Episode 1: Thomas Pogge on Pharmaceutical Innovation', *Public Ethics Radio*, 22 August 2008, available at: http://publicethicsradio.org/2008/08/22/episode-1-thomas-pogge-on-pharmaceutical-innovation/ (accessed 30 April 2010).

[8] Ibid.

[9] Médecins Sans Frontières (MSF) 2008, 'MSF Welcomes UNITAID Patent Pool Endorsement', press release, 9 July 2008, Geneva, available at: http://www.msfaccess.org/media-room/press-releases/msf-welcomes-unitaid-patent-pool-endorsement/ (accessed 15 September 2009).

[10] According to another definition: 'A patent pool is a portfolio of assets consisting of the entire set of patents (and, if desired, know-how, dossiers and other intellectual assets) held by various actors (companies, universities, government institutions) related to a particular technology that are made available on a non-exclusive basis to a group of (in our case) manufacturers and distributors of medications. The pool is operated through the auspices of a licensing agency which holds licences to the patents (and other intellectual assets) for sub-license to manufacturers and distributors'. See the UNITAID website, 'Eighth Board Meeting', Geneva, 2–3 July 2008, available at: http://www.unitaid.eu/en/Eighth-Board-Meeting-Geneva-2-3-July-2008.html (accessed 15 December 2009).

The idea of using patent pools to address neglected diseases has been proposed in various contexts including the 2006 Commission on Intellectual Property Rights, Innovation and Public Health (CIPIH) Report:

> Patent pools of upstream technologies may be useful in some circumstances to promote innovation relevant to developing countries. WHO and WIPO should consider playing a bigger role in promoting such arrangements, particularly to address diseases that disproportionately affect developing countries. (Ibid., p. 53)

The WHO Intergovernmental Working Group of Public Health, Innovation and Intellectual Property (IGWG) included this proposal as an instrument to increase access to medicines in poor countries (Knowledge Ecology International [KEI] 2007). KEI and MSF have been among the most active non-profit organizations pushing this model forward. In 2006, MSF and Essential Inventions (now part of KEI) submitted a proposal to the international drug purchase facility, UNITAID, for creation of a patent pool for patented medical technologies to develop generic combinations of antiretroviral drugs relevant to the treatment of HIV/AIDS. In December 2009, UNITAID's Executive Board decided to establish a patent pool for AIDS medicines.[11] The pool, scheduled to start operating in mid-2010, aims to 'make newer medicines available in patient-adapted form, at lower prices, for low- and middle-income countries'.[12] UNITAID has undertaken to provide start-up funds for the patent pool.[13] It has had consultations with such companies as Gilead, Tibotec, Merck and Sequoia for their participation in the patent pool.

5. Open source medicine

Although open source licensing is most common in computer software engineering, where it has proved effective, a number of open source initiatives have started in the medical field in the last decade. Open source medicine is based on the idea that sharing medical information and international collaboration among scientists will advance medical research and ultimately help patients all over the world suffering from neglected diseases (see the vision described in Maurer, Rai & Sali 2004). India's Council of Scientific and Industrial Research, for example, is currently working on creating a medium to accelerate the development of new drugs for infectious diseases for the developing world. It is called Open Source Drug Discovery

[11] UNITAID Executive Board, Res. No. 5: Patent Pool Implementation Plan (15 December 2009), 11th session, UN Doc. UNITAID/EB211/2009/R5, available at: http://www.unitaid.eu/images/EB11/05%20_eb11%20res.5%20implementation%20of%20patent%20pool.pdf (accessed 16 March 2010); see also UNITAID Executive Board, Special Session on Patent Pool Res. No. 1: Patent Pool Implementation Plan (15 February 2010), 11th session, UN Doc. UNITAID/EB11/SSPP/2010/R1, available at: http://www.unitaid.eu/images/EB11/EB11_SSPP_Resolution1_signed.pdf (accessed 16 March 2010).

[12] See UNITAID 2009, 'UNITAID Executive Board Approves Breakthrough Plan to Make AIDS Treatment More Widely Available at Lower Cost', press release, 14 December 2009, Geneva, available at: http://www.unitaid.eu/en/20091215237/News/UNITAID-APPROVES-PATENT-POOL.html (accessed 30 April 2010).

[13] Ibid. According to UNITAID, 'The Patent Pool will allow generic companies to make lower cost versions of widely patented new medicines by creating a common space for patent holders to license their technology in exchange for royalties. This will spur competition and further bring down the price of vital new and effective medicines, giving hope to millions of patients' (ibid.).

(OSDD) and consists of an interactive open source platform listing current design challenges to developing drugs for the treatment of drug-resistant tuberculosis, malaria and HIV. The OSDD concept is to collaboratively aggregate the biological and genetic information available to scientists in order to use it to hasten the discovery of drugs. Scientists contributing research to the platform can receive monetary and non-monetary rewards through a system of credit accruement. According to the founders of OSDD, the need for better drugs to combat neglected diseases in the developing world will ultimately drive the platform and make this model effective.[14]

Another example of open source medicine is CAMBIA, a non-profit institution that aims to create new technologies for innovation in health, food security and natural resource management for the developing world by using different platforms, including its open access database called 'Patent Lens', which provides updated information on patents filed worldwide. More importantly, CAMBIA provides 'BiOS (Biological Open Source) agreements';[15] these are licencing agreements whereby the licensee cannot appropriate the technological improvements of the research product, but is required to share these improvements with others who agree to the same terms of the BiOS agreement. Licensees cannot prevent the dissemination of the technology or the advancement of the product by others who receive and refine the product under the same agreement. The end result is that 'the original developer of the technology benefits, and so does anyone that improves it, because improvements can be tested and implemented rapidly'.[16]

[14] Singh, S. 2008, 'India Takes an Open Source Approach to Drug Discovery', *Cell*, vol. 133, no. 2, pp. 201–203.

[15] See BiOS, 'What Characterises a BiOS-Compliant Agreement?', available at: http://www.bios.net/daisy/bios/mta/bios-mta-faqs.html (accessed 10 February 2010).

[16] See BiOS, 'Do Open Source Agreements Work?', available at: http://www.bios.net/daisy/bios/2533.html (accessed 15 January 2009).

APPENDIX C

Strategies and laws to promote traditional medicinal knowledge[1]

The value of traditional medicinal knowledge (TMK) in meeting the primary health needs of populations around the world is well documented. Recognizing the widespread use of traditional medicine in various regions including Asia, Latin America and Africa (e.g. up to 80% of the population in Africa depends on traditional medicine for its health care needs),[2] the World Health Organization (WHO) has pursued strategies and activities 'to facilitate integration of traditional medicine into the national health care system[s] by assisting Member States to develop their own national policies on traditional medicine'.[3] A 2003 resolution at the World Health Assembly urges WHO member states to:

> ...take measures to protect, preserve and to improve if necessary traditional medical knowledge and medicinal plant resources for sustainable development of traditional medicine, depending on the circumstances in each country; such measures may include, where appropriate, the intellectual property rights of traditional practitioners over traditional medicine formulas and texts, as provided for under national legislation consistent with international obligations, and the engagement of WIPO in development of national *sui generis* protection systems.[4]

A national *sui generis* law which deals specifically with the protection of traditional medicinal knowledge is the Act on Protection and Promotion of Traditional Thai Medicinal Intelligence (1999 [BE 2542]) [hereinafter 'Thai Act']. The Act distinguishes among different categories of 'traditional formulations': '*national formulae*' are formulations which are crucial for human health and are held by the State; '*private formulae*' can be freely used by the owner (third parties must obtain permission from the owner to use the formula); '*general formulae*' may be used freely by anybody and comprise traditional formulae that have been widely used or whose

[1] Invaluable comments have been received from Jakkrit Kuanpoth towards this case study. Full references for this Appendix are found in the reference list of Chapter 4.

[2] See World Health Organization (WHO) 2002, *WHO Traditional Medicine Strategy 2002–2005*, WHO, Doc. WHO/EDM/TRM/2002.1, p. 1, available at: http://whqlibdoc.who.int/hq/2002/WHO_EDM_TRM_2002.1.pdf (accessed 26 November 2008). See also WHO, International Union for Conservation of Nature (IUCN), and World Wide Fund for Nature (WWF) 1993, 'Guidelines for Conservation of Medicinal Plants', IUCN, Gland, Switzerland.

[3] See the WHO website, 'WHO Traditional Medicine Strategy', available at: http://www.who.int/medicines/publications/traditionalpolicy/en/index.html (accessed 20 April 2010).

[4] World Health Assembly (WHA) Resolution WHA56.31 (28 May 2003), para. 2(6), available at: http://whqlibdoc.who.int/wha/2003/WHA56_31.pdf (accessed 18 May 2010).

intellectual property protection have expired (see Kuanpoth 2001).[5] The Act stipulates that the Minister of Public Health has authority to decree a certain formula of traditional Thai medicine as a 'national formula' (section 17). To be eligible, the traditional formula must be of significant benefit or have special medical or public health value (section 17). After the announcement, the rights of such a formula belong to the State. The use of a national formula for R&D of drugs for commercial benefit is subject to permission from the authorities and the payment of fees (see section 19); criminal sanctions are provided for in the case of infringement (section 78; Kwanpoth 2001, pp. 6–7).

The request for the registration of a 'private formula' can be submitted by an inventor or developer of the formula, or an inheritor of the inventor or developer of such a formula (section 21). The Act grants the owner of the registered personal formula exclusive rights to use the formula for research and to sell and distribute any product developed or manufactured by using the formula (section 34). Some exceptions to the exclusive rights are provided for in section 34, for example, in the production of drugs for household use or by state hospitals. The rights over a registered personal formula remain in force throughout the life of the owner and subsist for a further period of fifty years from the date of the applicant's death (section 33). In its report on *Protection and Promotion of Traditional Medicine – Implications for Public Health in Developing Countries*, the South Centre (2002) suggests 'the Thai Act provides a model of a special regime for the "protection" and the "promotion" of TRM which does not prevent the traditional healers from continuing to produce preparations for individual use'. Along with some implementation issues, the report notes concerns over the long period of protection for traditional medicine registered as private formula. Commentators have also raised the need for frameworks and principles to govern access and benefit-sharing (ABS) with traditional communities who are custodians of relevant TK given the Thai Act does not address this explicitly (Robinson & Kuanpoth 2009).

Along with a Committee on Protection and Promotion of Thai Traditional Medicinal Intelligence, the Thai Act establishes the Fund on Traditional Thai Medicinal Intelligence. The income of the Fund would mainly come from state subsidies and the private sector. A number of Ministerial regulations to implement the Thai Act have been scrutinized by the Council of State and will have to be approved by the Cabinet before the provisions of the Act are fully implemented. Robinson & Kuanpoth (2009) suggest that the delay of the implementation of the regulations has left the traditional medicine law of Thailand ambiguous in many areas, including the issues of who has authority to grant access permits, the sharing of benefit among custodian communities, prior informed consent, the continuing traditional practices of traditional healers, and issues of competing or overlapping jurisdiction of different Ministerial departments over protected forest areas.

Meanwhile, there are interesting developments in the region in relation to the promotion of TMK, particularly within the context of the Association of Southeast Asian Nations (ASEAN). The delegates of the Conference on Traditional Medicine

[5] The Minister of Public Health has the power to notify a formula of traditional Thai drugs as 'general formula' (section 18).

in ASEAN Countries, held in Bangkok on 31 August–2 September 2009, adopted the Bangkok Declaration on Traditional Medicine in ASEAN. In the Declaration, the delegates acknowledge that traditional medicine is often the most widely available and affordable source of health care in ASEAN, and reiterated the WHO's specific objectives in its *Traditional Medicine Strategy for 2002–2005* to support countries to integrate traditional medicine with national health care systems. The Declaration also recognized that ASEAN Member States 'possess an abundance of untapped and newly discovered herbal and medicinal plants and other natural resources, as well as *indigenous traditional knowledge and practices* which have evolved from different ethnological, cultural, geographical, philosophical backgrounds, and the need to ensure sustainable management of biological diversity' (emphasis added). Among other things, the signatories to the Declaration undertook to 'to develop specific activities to enhance collaboration in Traditional Medicine by involving practitioners and providers, industries, non-profit and professional organisations, academia, communities as well as partner organisations as key partners' (para. 3).

The Bangkok Declaration will lead to an action plan, and will be integrated with other ASEAN initiatives.[6] This may present opportunities, for example, for exploring regional frameworks or measures to regulate ABS relating to TMK. Such frameworks could potentially address ABS relating not only to TMK within national borders, but also to transboundary TMK (see the example of medicinal uses of the *Kwao Krao* plant in Chapter 4, Box 4.3). These initiatives will also need to be coordinated with international work and norm setting relating to genetic resources and associated TK, notably under the Convention of Biological Diversity (CBD) of 1992. As discussed in Chapter 4 of this book, the United Nations Declaration on the Rights of Indigenous Peoples (UNDRIP) of 2007 furthermore refers to the right of indigenous peoples to their 'traditional medicines' and to maintain their health practices, including 'the conservation of their vital medicinal plants, animals and minerals' (Article 24; see also Article 31(1)). The principle of free, prior and informed consent (FPIC) of TK custodians and arrangements for benefit-sharing in relation to use of TK is discussed in Chapter 4, along with the ongoing work of the CBD Secretariat and the World Intellectual Property Organization (WIPO) in these areas.

Sources: Kuanpoth 2001; South Centre 2002; Robinson & Kuanpoth 2009

[6] See Association of Southeast Asian Nations (ASEAN) 2009, 'Conference on Traditional Medicine in ASEAN Countries', *ASEAN Bulletin*, 1 September 2009, available at: http://www.aseansec.org/Doc-Bangkok-Declaration-on-Traditional-Medicine.pdf (accessed 16 March 2010). See also Lee-Brago, P. 2010, 'ASEAN Agrees to Further Promote Integration of Traditional Medicine', *The Philippine Star*, 7 January 2010, available at: http://www.philstar.com/Article.aspx?articleId=538589&publicationSubCategoryId=75 (accessed 30 January 2010).

APPENDIX D

Educational use exceptions to copyright: A comparison among selected jurisdictions[1]

Argentina*

Specific statutory educational use exception

Allows the publication for teaching or scientific purposes up to 1000 words (Emery 2008, sec. 8(2)(b), p. ARG-50).

Brazil*

Specific statutory educational use exception

Exceptions limited to theatrical and musical performances in educational contexts and reproduction of class notes (Pereira dos Santos 2008, sec. 8(2), p. BRA-62).

China*

Specific statutory educational use exception

Permits the 'translation or the limited reproduction of a published work for use by teachers or scientific researchers in classroom teaching or scientific research, provided that the translation or reproduction is not released to the public at large'. Further, 'uses may neither interfere with the normal exploitation of the works used, nor unreasonably prejudice the legitimate interests of right-holders' (Hong 2008, sec. 8(2)(b), pp. CHI-65–66).

Non-voluntary licence

China permits 'non-voluntary licence allowing for the compilation and publication of textbooks' (Hong 2008, sec. 8(2)(e)(v), p. CHI-70).

[1] See reference section for Chapter 6 for full references to this Appendix.

Czech Republic*

Specific statutory educational use exception

Permits incorporation of small works in their entirety into works for teaching purposes, use of published works in a lecture for educational purposes, and use of quotes to a 'justified degree'.[2]

France

Specific statutory educational use exception

Permits 'the reproduction or communication of excerpts from works when such reproduction or communication is intended exclusively for purposes of illustration in research or teaching, provided that such use does not give rise to a commercial exploitation and that an equitable remuneration is paid, to be negotiated on a lump-sum basis' (Lucas & Kamina 2008, sec. 8(2)(a)(iii), p. FRA-120).

India*

Specific statutory educational use exception**

Includes the reproduction of a literary work 'by a teacher or pupil in the course of instruction or as part of the questions to be answered in an examination or in answers to such questions' (Ramaiah 2008, sec. 8(2)(b), p. IND-45). Further, the Act allows for making not more than three copies of a book for the use in a library if such book is not available for sale in India (ibid., p. IND-46).

Non-voluntary licence

Compulsory licence may be issued for literary, scientific, or artistic works 'in connection with systematic instructional activities at a price reasonably related to that normally charged in India for comparable works by the owner of the right . . . ' (ibid., p. IND-51).

Jamaica*

Specific statutory educational use exception**

Permits the reprographic copying of passages from published literary, dramatic or musical works by an educational establishment for purposes of instruction. However, may not use more than 5% of the work. Further, inclusion of a 'short passage' of a literary work in a collection intended for use in educational establishments

[2] Czech Republic – Copyright Act art. 31, 4 July 2000, no. 121, available at: http://www.wipo.int/clea/docs_new/pdf/en/cz/cz029en.pdf (accessed 30 July 2009).

permitted, but only if collection consists mainly of material in which no copyright subsists.[3]

Japan

Specific statutory educational use exception

Allows teachers and students to reproduce works, already made public, to the extent necessary for use in the course of education, but only if the use does not unreasonably injure the interests of the copyright owner (Doi 2008, sec. 8(2)(b)(i), p. JAP-56).

Non-voluntary licence

Works already made public 'may be reproduced to manufacture textbooks for use at elementary, secondary, or high schools' so long as author of work is notified and paid compensation in an amount fixed annually by the Commissioner of the Agency for Cultural Affairs (ibid., p. JAP-62).

Jordan*

Specific statutory educational use exception

Published works may, for educational purposes, be presented, used by way of illustration in publications, broadcasts or sound and audiovisual recordings for educational purposes, or quoted.[4]

Non-voluntary licence

Allows any Jordanian citizen, for school education purposes, to obtain a non-exclusive and non-transferable licence to translate into the Arabic language (ibid.).

Nigeria*

Specific statutory educational use exception**

Permits educational broadcasting and 'any use made of a work in an approved educational institution for the educational purposes of that institution . . . '. However, reproduction must be destroyed before the end of the prescribed period or, if there is no prescribed period, within twelve months of making the reproduction.[5]

[3] Jamaica – The Copyright Act, 9 January 1993, no. 4, available at: http://www.wipo.int/clea/docs_new/pdf/en/jm/jm001en.pdf (accessed 30 July 2009).

[4] Jordan – The Law Amending the Copyright Protection Law art. 4(A), 1999, no. 29, available at: http://www.wipo.int/clea/docs_new/pdf/en/jo/jo003en.pdf (accessed 30 July 2009).

[5] Nigeria – Copyright Act Second Schedule, (Consolidation Ch. 68), 1988 (1999), no. 47 (no. 42), available at: http://www.wipo.int/clea/docs_new/pdf/en/ng/ng001en.pdf (accessed 30 July 2009).

Non-voluntary licence

Permits compulsory licence for translations for 'purposes of teaching, scholarship or research' (ibid.).

United Kingdom

Specific statutory educational use exception**

'The Act sets out strictly limited exceptions relating to uses of works in "educational establishments"' (Bently 2008, sec. 8(2)(b)(iii), p. UK-117). Such uses include non-reprographic copying for instruction, copying for filmmaking courses, copying short passages in collections, preparing or giving examinations, playing or showing works and lending copies (ibid., pp. UK-117–118).

* indicates a developing country. For purposes of this table, we adopt the World Bank definition of 'developing country.' Thus, as used herein, the term developing country refers to a country having low-income or middle-income economy (based on 2005 gross national income [GNI] per capita, calculated using the World Bank Atlas method) available at: http://web.worldbank.org.

** In addition to a specific statutory exemption, general or limited fair use/fair dealing exemption also available.

United States of America

General exception

Permits the 'fair use' of a copyrighted work for purposes such as teaching, scholarship, or research, including reproduction of multiple copies for classroom use, based on a case-by-case balancing of four factors set forth in the statute: purpose of the use, nature of the work, amount of the work, and effect of the use (1976 Copyright Act, 17 U.S.C. § 107).

Specific statutory education use exception

Also permits certain displays and performances critical to teaching; however, distinguishes between displays and performances in face-to-face teaching and those in distance learning; face-to-face teaching exception allows performances and displays of all types of works in a live classroom setting or similar place at most governmental or accredited nonprofit educational institutions, while displays and performances in distance education are constrained under conditions set forth in the *Technology, Education and Copyright Harmonization (TEACH) Act of 2002*, codified at 17 U.S.C. § 110(2) (Crews 2005).

Includes many other statutory exceptions, such as the library copying exemption that can further academic development (17 U.S.C. § 108).

APPENDIX E

Copyright and contemporary art: A case study

Molly Torsen[1]

Copyright, the category of intellectual property (IP) most associated with the arts, is currently undergoing scrutiny from several sectors. Industry-oriented copyright owners, like music labels, are lobbying for more control of their songs. At the same time that digital rights management models are being reworked, the public is demanding greater access and less cost for copyrighted works. Authors and artists (who are not necessarily owners of their copyrighted work) are, ironically, not at the centre of this debate, although it is usually their creations over which these other parties are debating.

Indeed, the individual artist working in today's IP environment has a different set of concerns than does the agency that commodifies his or her work. The legal interests of creators and the legal interests of copyright holders can be very different, and many of the legal issues at stake (e.g. moral rights) are highly dependent upon the jurisdiction in which the artist is working. The following sections describe some of the situations where contemporary artists face challenging IP issues, including jurisdictional inconsistencies. For these purposes, 'contemporary art' comprises visual and multimedia creative expressions made after the Second World War.[2]

1. The threshold for copyright protection

As the beginning of this chapter explains, the terms 'culture' and 'the arts' can have different meanings, depending on their context. Certainly, in a legal sense, 'art' is an amorphous concept to which no court of law should assign a rigid definition. Indeed, 'courts are not authorized to judge the artistic merit of the work in deciding whether pictorial, graphic, and sculptural works ought to qualify for copyright protection other than to determine that the threshold of original expression has been attained' (Merges, Menell & Lemley 2003, p. 368). Similarly, within the context of the 'art world', there is very little attempt to define the contours of what constitutes a work of art.[3] Within different contexts, as has been explored earlier in Chapter 8 of this book, 'art' takes on different meanings.

[1] The references for this Appendix are found in the reference list for Chapter 8.

[2] The definition of 'contemporary art', as well as the definition of 'art', has been debated and discussed since at least the 1950s. See, for example, Hodin 1951.

[3] See, for example, Christie's – Fine Art Auction, 'Glossary', available at: http://www.christies.com/glossary/auction_glossary.asp (accessed 12 February 2009). Individual artistic movements or styles are

Copyright law requires that an artist contribute something 'original', something not already there. The meaning of originality, however, is sometimes unclear. The definition for 'originality' under copyright law varies with different legal systems and national regimes, and is not necessarily bound to the 'aesthetic' value of a work. By linking rewards to efforts put in by the creator (i.e. 'the sweat of the brow'), the common law system largely avoids an evaluation of the 'aesthetic' worth of a creation in determining originality.[4] Meanwhile, a society's definition and appreciation of the 'aesthetics' changes over time.[5]

In the realm of reproductions and restorations, it is not yet internationally settled whether the artist making the reproduction is entitled to a new copyright in the reproduced work. The controversial *Bridgeman* case[6] would seem to indicate, at least in the United States, that the purpose of a reproduction – to 'slavishly copy' – would a priori disqualify the new work from copyright protection. In this case, digital reproductions of two-dimensional artworks in the public domain were denied copyright protection because there was not seen to be any independent creation or distinguishable variation from the pre-existing works. The viability of an argument for originality remains unclear in other similar circumstances, such as the restorations of murals or buildings, in which a restorer arguably uses a great deal of judgment and creativity to make a new work *based on* but not *identical to* the original work.

2. The idea/expression dichotomy

Henry Lydiate, Emeritus Professor of Art and Law, University of the Arts, London, has said: 'No one knew anything of dadaism, Marcel Duchamp and conceptual art when the (UK) legislation was framed, and in contemporary art – where the idea is more important than the form – there is a lack of protection for ideas.'[7] It is central to many jurisdictions' copyright laws that it is the expression of an idea, rather than the idea itself, that receives copyright protection. For example, Amadeo Modigliani's elongated and stylized portraits are protected under copyright only as they are embodied as individual paintings; his style is not copyrightable and, as such, other artists are free to paint elongated and stylized portraits so long as they do not exactly copy Modigliani's work. Some contemporary artists are struggling with this distinction because they feel the root of their creation is not necessarily any particular manifestation of their idea; rather, it is the idea that they would like to claim as their own.

described (such as 'Futurism' and 'Rococo'), but no overarching definition for terms such as 'art' or 'contemporary art' or 'medieval art' is attempted.

4 Bently (1994, p. 81) notes examples of US and UK case law which suggest that 'there is no requirement that the work be of any artistic quality'. See further Ginsburg 1990. Ginsburg suggests that Anglo-American copyright law has historically protected not only works of creativity but also works of commercial value.

5 As pointed out by Prott (1998a, p. 164): 'What is not valued as high Culture in one age may be seen as a peak achievement in another period by the same society' (original capitalization by author).

6 *Bridgeman Art Library, Ltd. v. Corel Corp.*, 25 F. Supp. 2d 421 (S.D.N.Y. 1998).

7 Wade A., 'Can You Own an Idea?', *The Guardian*, 6 May 2003, quoting Henry Lydiate.

One example where this issue is highlighted is in the work of Christo and Jeanne-Claude, until Jeanne-Claude's passing in November 2009. They were an artistic duo who created installation art – art that uses a variety of media to modify the way people experience a given space. Some of the work they have done includes wrapping the Pont Neuf bridge in Paris, and creating a twenty-four-mile-long curtain in the Marin and Sonoma counties in California.[8] They have created a similar 'curtain' in New York City's Central Park. Under current US copyright law – and under most Western copyright laws – the idea/expression dichotomy, which reserves copyright protection for delineated expressions of ideas, would solely prevent an exact replica of any of these works.[9] If, however, another installation artist decided to wrap the Brooklyn Bridge in the same material Christo and Jeanne-Claude used to wrap the Pont Neuf, copyright law would not prevent it.

3. The fixation requirement

Many jurisdictions, with some notable exceptions,[10] require that a work be fixed in a tangible form of expression before copyright can inhere. As such, a sketch in the sand on a beach and an ink drawing on a human body will not achieve copyright status because the water will wash them away. While the requirement that a work be fixed has been debated and criticized (see Brennan & Christie 2000), it remains the international norm with the exception of some jurisdictions. This has presented at least a hypothetical problem for artists like Dan Harvey and Heather Ackroyd, two British artists who have been collaborating since 1990 and who use elements of living organisms in their work. Grass, for example, is incorporated into a work to communicate the artists' exploration of transience, alchemy and decay.[11] Harvey and Ackroyd have won numerous awards for their work but the extent to which their work is copyrightable is debatable, at best. At no given moment is their work 'fixed', given that the growing grass (amongst other organic materials they employ) is constantly changing their art. This legal 'rule' can also be showcased with regard to a choreographed dance. The dance itself is only protected under copyright when it is 'fixed', either as a video (or some other tangible audiovisual rendering) of the dance or as a write-up of its choreographic parts.

4. Copyright exceptions and appropriation art

Copyright exceptions – including 'fair dealing' and 'fair use' in common law jurisdictions – take on an important role in the realm of contemporary art, especially with regard to appropriation art. Appropriation art, another category of art that

[8] For photographs of selected examples of their work, see Christo and Jeanne-Claude, The Vogel Collection at the National Gallery of Art, available at: http://www.nga.gov/exhibitions/2002/christo/intro.shtm (accessed 12 February 2009).

[9] 17 U.S.C. § 102(b): 'In no case does copyright protection for an original work of authorship extend to any idea, procedure, process, system, method of operation, concept, principle, or discovery, regardless of the form in which it is described, explained, illustrated, or embodied in such work'.

[10] Exceptions include Switzerland and several Latin American jurisdictions.

[11] See Heather Ackroyd & Dan Harvey, Artsadmin UK, available at: http://www.artsadmin.co.uk/projects/artist.php?id=40 (accessed 12 February 2009).

is difficult to define with precision, generally addresses art that 'borrows common images from advertising, the mass media and elsewhere, places them in new contexts and, thereby, aims to change the way we think about these images' (Landes 1999). 'Appropriation (art) was developed ... in the readymades created by the French artist Marcel Duchamp from 1915. Most notorious of these was *Fountain*, a men's urinal signed, titled, and presented on a pedestal'.[12] However, an example like *Fountain* does not necessarily present the copyright problems that can crop up with other examples of appropriation art because the creator of the original urinal was probably not interested in copyrighting it for artistic reasons.

The same is not true with Jeff Koons' art. Jeff Koons is a contemporary artist with a background both as a commodity broker on Wall Street and as a senior representative for a modern art museum.[13] It has been said that 'with his stated artistic intention to "communicate with the masses", Koons draws from the visual language of advertising, marketing, and the entertainment industry'.[14] Amongst other forms of art, Koons has 'quoted' various types of contemporary pop culture, including a postcard photograph of a series of puppies seated on the laps of two people in the Midwest (Koons created a life-size sculpture of that image) and an advertisement for silk Gucci sandals (Koons created an oil painting very similar to the Gucci advertisement).

In the first scenario, the photographer of the original postcard sued Koons and won; the judge in that case[15] found that an artist's copy of a photograph could not be protected when there is no clear need to imitate that *specific* photograph for the sake of parody. Parody is a copyright exception in US law (see Chapter 8, Section 5.1) under which Koons argued his case. In the second (silk sandals) scenario, Koons won his case partly based on the judge's opinion that Koons' transformation of the original advertisement was substantial enough to differentiate between the two. Koons was, again, using the original artwork as visual fodder for his commentary on the consequences of popular media; yet, the outcomes of the cases were completely different. From an artistic or aesthetic perspective, the contours of fair use in these scenarios are difficult to understand and to predict.

5. Moral rights

The influence of natural rights arguments for the protection of creative works as an extension or expression of the creator's personality is particularly evident in moral rights protection. Fisher (2001, p. 174) observes: 'The French and German [authors' rights] regimes, for example, have been strongly shaped by the writings of Kant and Hegel. This influence is especially evident in the generous protection

[12] Patry, W., 'The Patry Copyright Blog', Appropriation Art and Copies, 20 October 2005. For an image of *Fountain*, see the San Francisco Museum of Modern Art, available at: http://www.sfmoma.org/msoma/artworks/1466.html (accessed 15 June 2007). This replica of *Fountain* is glazed ceramic with black paint, purchased through a gift of Phyllis Watts.

[13] Ottmann, K., Interview with Jeff Koons, *Journal of Contemporary Art*, October 1986.

[14] Jeff Koons, Guggenheim Collection, available at: http://www.guggenheimcollection.org/site/artist_work_md_P65.html (accessed 12 February 2009).

[15] *Rogers v. Koons*, 960 F.2d 301 (2d Cir. 1992).

those countries provide for "moral rights" – authors' and artists' rights to control the public disclosure of their works, to withdraw their works from public circulation, to receive appropriate credit for their creations, and above all to protect their works against mutilation or destruction.' While 'natural rights' arguments are often associated with civil law jurisdictions, they have had their influence as well on the evolution of common law copyright systems (see Afori 2004). The introduction of 'moral rights' to common law copyright systems through international harmonization means that arguments to protect the creator's 'personality' are also at work today in those systems (Guibault 2002, p. 8).

Often debated even in the context of orthodox artistic media, moral rights laws are receiving renewed interest in the realm of contemporary art and digital media. In the context of contemporary art, moral rights can pose very interesting problems. In the international arena, moral rights law has not been heavily litigated and there is therefore a paucity of case law to inform artists of their rights (Adeney 2006, p. 627). For example, an artist whose work is best viewed in person may have granted a museum the right to reproduce her art in a large-scale 'coffee table' book but she may take issue with her work being reproduced on the museum's website if the image looks distorted to her. Depending on the jurisdiction of the museum and the language in any given copyright release contract, the artist may be able to argue that her moral rights entitle her to prevent her artwork from being reproduced on the Internet.[16]

Certainly, moral rights and appropriation art can also grate at each other. The right to attribution is often surpassed in the context of appropriation art, especially if the original image is so well-known that its iconic stature is the appropriation artist's purpose for quoting it. Andy Warhol's *Marilyn Monroe* was a piece of appropriation art, inspired by Gene Korman's 1953 photograph of the actress. Today, Warhol's painting is much better known than the original photograph but, at the time, Warhol was making an artistic comment that certainly quoted Korman's work. The moral rights of Korman, as a photographer, did not make it to court; in the United States, moral rights are protected either through common law or through the very narrow Visual Artists Rights Act[17] which only took effect in 1990. Had Warhol worked in France, his work may have been suppressed or his work may have had to credit Korman in some way. These and other scenarios highlight some of the jurisdictional differences and overall uncertainties about moral rights in the modern era.

6. Multimedia works

Another dimension to the IP/contemporary art nexus is that of the multimedia work, where many of the aforementioned issues occur simultaneously. Multimedia

[16] See Johnston, L., 'Displaying Visual Art on the Internet', *ART+ Law*, June 2007, available at: http://www.artslaw.com.au/ArtLaw/Current/07DisplayingVisualArtOnTheInternet.asp (accessed 1 June 2007). Johnston notes that: 'For those reproducing visual art online it is important that they ensure the moral rights of the artist are kept intact. Respecting the creator's moral rights involves crediting the artist (right to attribution), not crediting the artwork to someone who is not the artist (right against false attribution) and not using the artists' work in a way which would damage their reputation (right of integrity)'.

[17] 17 U.S.C. § 106A.

works may also have an audio component. Videos and other multimedia art can elicit an entirely new set of IP issues because they are protected quite differently from purely visual works. 'Multimedia' is another term whose semantics are undefined in the realm of the arts. It can include a range of works, including basic audio-visual works (like videos) and interactive, multidisciplinary works and complex installations.

One example of a complex multimedia work is Pierre Huyghe's *Celebration Park*, which features 'objects, texts, architectural features and films, all orchestrated within [an] exhibition space to create a landscape of discovery'.[18] Indeed, visitors to Huyghe's work 'experience a number of surprising apparitions, such as a set of gigantic doors which dance through the gallery'.[19] The work includes puppet shows, natural history films and staged celebrations. It also includes a film showing an opera staged in Antarctica and New York City's Central Park. Clearly, *Celebration Park* is a multifaceted work with a long list of copyrightable features. For an installation work that Huyghe exhibited at Harvard University, the school had to sign forty-five different contracts to install and exhibit it.[20] While the scope of those contracts and the various rights at play are beyond the scope of this writing, it is representative of the sometimes difficult fit that copyright provides for artworks that can be broken down into several component copyrightable parts.

[18] Pierre Huyghe, Tate Modern, available at: http://www.tate.org.uk/modern/exhibitions/pierrehuyghe/ (accessed 12 February 2009).

[19] Ibid.

[20] Lufkin, M. 2005, 'Why Harvard Had to Sign 45 Contracts to Install a Work by Pierre Huyghe', *The Art Newspaper*, 6 January 2005.

Index

Note: Page number followed by *n* indicates footnotes.